Simpler Networks and Behavior

SIMPLER
AND

NETWORKS BEHAVIOR

Edited by John C. Fentress

Dalhousie University

SINAUER ASSOCIATES, INC • PUBLISHERS
Sunderland, Massachusetts

THE COVER

Photograph of the isolated nervous system of the marine mollusk *Pleurobranchaea californica*, which is the subject of research on the cellular basis of behavioral hierarchies ("choice") and associative learning (see Chapters 15 and 16). At the top of the photograph is the orange-pigmented brain, connected by nerves to the two pedal ganglia (left and right) and the buccal ganglion (bottom). In large specimens the brain may attain a width of nearly one centimeter, with individual nerve cell bodies of 500 μm diameter. (Courtesy of W. J. Davis, J. M. Pinneo and A. Donaldson, University of California at Santa Cruz)

SIMPLER NETWORKS AND BEHAVIOR

First Printing

Copyright © 1976 by Sinauer Associates, Inc.

Printed in U.S.A.

Library of Congress Catalog Card Number: 75-30150

ISBN: 0-87893-182-1

Contents

Preface

Integrated patterns of behavior are the raison d'être of nervous systems. As such, they provide a critical focus for research in the neurosciences. Historically, efforts to relate nervous system structure and operation in a precise way to behavior have been hampered in part by the complexity of the systems investigated. At the behavioral level this complexity is often cosmetically disposed of by acceptance of broadly and often vaguely defined functional units, and inferred causal mechanisms, such as "hunger," "thirst," "aggression," etc. All too commonly insufficient attention is paid to the detailed patterning of behavior, where each act is examined explicitly in the context of preceding, following, simultaneous and/or alternate modes of expression. In neurobiology the enormous complexities of structure and function frequently lead either to partial analyses of entire systems, or to an artificial segregation of the whole into incomplete, but not truly independent subsystems. It is particularly at the junction between neuroscience and behavior that the lack of sophistication in our insights becomes most disappointing.

A fundamental strategy in science is to seek simplified representations that capture the basic features of the particular universe under discussion. In this way one may gain a rigor of analysis which otherwise remains elusive. The theme of this book reflects such a strategy. *Simpler networks* of behavioral and neurobiological organization are examined together so that each can be comprehended with greater precision, and, most particularly, so that these apparently disparate levels of discourse can in the future be joined more satisfactorily.

The basic strategy, and indeed the title, for this book are drawn from the pioneering efforts of the late Donald M. Maynard. Don Maynard was a leader in the use of simpler neural networks as an analytical tool to understand the mechanisms of behavior. He was late in his appreciation of what the behavioral and neurobiological sciences have to offer *each other*. That is, he saw clearly the need for a *two-way* interaction between these disciplines in terms of networks of descriptive, causal and functional organization.

The emphasis upon *networks* is as fundamental as that upon manageable simplicity. Networks imply multiple patterns of convergence and divergence among individual components, rather than unrealistic linear causal chains. Such statements do not negate the potential value of other approaches to questions of nervous system organization and behavior. However, the simpler networks approach has proven itself many times in recent years. Yet, until the present book, no systematic assessment of the state of the art which critically evaluates behavioral and neurobiological pattern formation in both vertebrate and invertebrate species has been available. Our goal has been to attempt such a synthesis.

We have strived to achieve an appropriate

balance between diversity of perspectives and a thematic unity in presentation. The volume is accordingly organized into six major sections, each of which is prefaced by a brief editorial overview. Part I provides a set of introductory perspectives on simpler networks in behavior and neurobiology. Part II examines, in greater detail, problems of integration among component parts of various neurobehavioral control systems. Part III concerns the more permanent (phenotypic) substrates of transient neural and behavioral expression. Part IV focuses on problems of plasticity and experience. Part V emphasizes recent advances in the analysis of vertebrate brains and their relationship to systems studied in invertebrates. Part VI returns to the raison d'être of nervous systems, organism behavior.

The challenge of relating the neurobiological and behavioral sciences is one of conceptual as well as analytical proportions. For this reason, the first and last chapters of the book emphasize a relatively broad range of issues, while the intervening chapters are more narrowly focused. The Editor has not attempted to remove redundancies where different perspectives are involved, nor to censor important disagreements among individual contributors. These differences express the basic vitality of a rapidly growing field of inquiry.

The selection of chapters, their arrangement, the connecting essays, illustrations, collected bibliography, and indexes are all designed to provide readers of various backgrounds with material that will be maximally useful.

The Editor has benefited from many contributors to this venture. First, I wish to thank the individual authors, who worked diligently to make their chapters useful to students at all levels. Their joint efforts are viewed as a tribute to Don Maynard and a contribution to the educational enterprise which he valued. Second, I wish to thank Andrew Sinauer, the Publisher, who has aided in every phase of the preparation and publication of this book. He has been assisted by many others, of whom Joseph Vesely (Production Manager) and Barbara Zeiders (Copy Editor) deserve special mention. Third, I acknowledge with gratitude the support of the University of Oregon and Dalhousie University, my many colleagues and students at each of these institutions, and the National Institutes of Health and National Research Council of Canada. Fourth, I express my appreciation to Nancy Kinsman and Marie MacMillan for their able assistance at various stages in the preparation of this manuscript.

And a very special thanks to Edith Maynard, who, quietly and behind the scenes, served as an inspiration throughout.

John C. Fentress
Halifax
March 1976

Contributors

DAVID BENTLEY
Department of Zoology, University of California, Berkeley, California

THEODORE HOLMES BULLOCK
Neurobiology Unit, Scripps Institution of Oceanography *and* Department of Neurosciences, School of Medicine, University of California, San Diego, La Jolla, California

MELVIN J. COHEN
Department of Biology, Yale University, New Haven, Connecticut

WILLIAM J. DAVIS
The Thimann Laboratories, University of California, Santa Cruz, California

ROBERT W. DOTY, SR.
Center for Brain Research, University of Rochester Medical School, Rochester, New York

ROBERT C. EATON
Department of Neurosciences, School of Medicine, University of California, San Diego, La Jolla, California

JOHN S. EDWARDS
Department of Zoology, University of Washington, Seattle, Washington

EDWARD V. EVARTS
Laboratory of Neurophysiology, National Institute of Mental Health, U.S. Department of Health, Education and Welfare, Bethesda, Maryland

JOHN C. FENTRESS
Department of Psychology, Life Sciences Centre, Dalhousie University, Halifax, Nova Scotia, Canada

WALTER J. FREEMAN
Department of Physiology—Anatomy, University of California, Berkeley, California

ALAN GELPERIN
Department of Biology, Princeton University, Princeton, New Jersey

WALTER HEILIGENBERG
Scripps Institution of Oceanography, University of California, San Diego, La Jolla, California

GRAHAM HOYLE
Department of Biology, University of Oregon, Eugene, Oregon

KAZUO IKEDA
Department of Neurophysiology, City of Hope National Medical Center, Duarte, California

DONALD KENNEDY
Department of Biological Sciences, Stanford University, Stanford, California

CHARLES B. KIMMEL
Department of Biology, University of Oregon, Eugene, Oregon

RODOLFO LLINÁS
Division of Neurobiology, University of Iowa, Oakdale, Iowa

PETER MARLER
Rockefeller University, New York, New York

JOHN PALKA
Department of Zoology, University of Washington, Seattle, Washington

KEIR G. PEARSON
Department of Physiology, University of Alberta, Edmonton, Canada

ROBERT R. PROVINE
Department of Psychology, University of Maryland, Baltimore, Maryland

ALLEN SELVERSTON
Department of Biology, University of California, San Diego, La Jolla, California

JAMES W. TRUMAN
Department of Zoology, University of Washington, Seattle, Washington

KERRY WALTON
Division of Neurobiology, University of Iowa, Oakdale, Iowa

ROBERT J. WYMAN
Department of Biology, Yale University, New Haven, Connecticut

I

NETWORK
PERSPECTIVES

The four chapters in Part I provide basic perspectives on the *simpler networks* approach to patterned behavior and its neural control. Emphasis here, and throughout the book, is upon the foundations of animal behavior from two complementary perspectives. The first perspective is that of behavior as a dynamic *process* in which the task of the investigator is to determine the precise patterning of behavioral events over time. This is akin to examining the notes and pauses, and particularly the relationships between these elements, in the performance of a musical composition. How are the behavioral activities of an organism distributed with respect to one another over time, and how do we determine the underlying network of causal events? The second perspective concerns the more stable *phenotypic* structuring of an organism which sets the potentialities and constraints for any given behavioral performance; this is analogous to a musical score. In biological systems phenotypic structures are the resultant of inherited genetic material and the developmental context (including individual experiences) under which the genes, and their products, operate. How do we tease these genetic, maturational, and experiential factors apart, and how do we relate them precisely to the dynamic processes of behavioral and neural activity that we observe? As pointed out in Chapters One and Three, the latter question is particularly complex, both conceptually and analytically, and present answers do little more than set the stage for future research.

A musical performance also depends upon the instruments employed and their coordination. Neurons are the instruments of primary concern here, and as in woodwinds, brasses, and strings they come in many shapes and forms. This raises an additional point. Rules of music can be derived from rules of performance, but knowledge of precise orchestration demands an understanding of individual instruments and their operation. Psychologists and, to a large extent, ethologists have as a group (with notable exceptions) concentrated upon rules of performance, whereas neurobiologists have paid particular attention to the construction and properties of neuronal instruments. Obviously we need both approaches. To switch metaphors, dissection of a telegraph key will in itself not crack the Morse code, but it will tell us something about how the code is transmitted.

Analogies can be useful in establishing a frame of reference, but they can be misleading if carried too far. Biological systems have special properties and generate special questions. For example, animals must acquire nourishment to survive as individuals and reproduce to perpetuate the species; these are not questions of relevance when speaking of musical instruments or telegraph keys, even though basic physical principles as viewed in isolation may be indistinguishable. Different levels of inquiry generate different questions and different research strategies – a point that we should keep in mind as we seek meaningful linkages between behavioral phenomena at the organism level and intraorganismic biological components.

One strategy is to seek questions that appear equally relevant to each of the levels of analysis with which we are directly concerned. Is there any set of questions of primary importance to both behavior and neurobiology? The answer is clearly "yes," if we probe the relations between organism and environment. It is with this set of questions concerning organism—environment relationships that we find not only the most fundamental biological issues of adaptation and survival itself but also basic clues concerning the operation of mechanism. For example, to what extent are expressed patterns of behavior dependent upon events intrinsic to the organism as opposed to external environmental determinants, and to what extent do neural networks operate endogenously as opposed to being dependent upon events external to them? This set of questions in its most abstract and general form is fundamental to all natural science (e.g., Spencer Brown, 1969), and its particular relevance to the issue of neurobiology and behavior should become clear in the pages that follow. Indeed, it is one of the basic organizing themes of the entire volume.

Given the importance of general and operationally defined questions as organizers for inquiry, detailed answers are often limited to particular instances (e.g., Hinde, 1970). Here we are face with the biologist's (and psychologist's) dilemma of meaningful generalizations in the face of diversity. For example, do extrapolations from "simpler networks" provide useful insights to less simple biobehavioral systems? Views here diverge.

One approach that is fundamental to all science is to seek common *rules* of organization which transcend the *details* of organization in specific instances. Hoyle (Chapter Two) and Bullock (Chapter Four) demonstrate a particularly clear awareness of this problem. As a problem, this will recur frequently in this volume, and the reader should develop his or her own thoughts on the matter. A last analogy may be useful here. Apples and oranges are obviously distinct from one another. Yet there is something in common about two apples and two oranges that transcends these particular distinctions in form. At which of these levels are most meaningful generalizations likely to occur, and what is the relevance of these generalizations to the specific questions with which we are most concerned?

In Chapter One, Fentress provides a basically behavioral perspective to the simpler networks approach. He reviews briefly three basic strategies summarized by Donald Maynard in his article from which the title of the present volume was derived and emphasizes the fact that the issue of "system isolation" is a major criterion for research at both the behavioral and neurobiological level. Criteria for "simplicity" are also discussed. Fentress then takes the dual themes of *process* and *phenotype* as a framework for outlining basic problems common to neurobiology and behavior.

The question of *network* as explicitly applied to behavior is subsequently examined. Fentress stresses that signals may interact in several distinct ways with intervening processes and that rarely if ever is it useful to think in terms of simple linear causal chains. Converging and diverging patterns of interaction are the rule. He cites several behavioral examples that warn against simple generalizations from one system to another and which also indicate possible dangers of generalizing within a system as it operates in different contexts. From this he suggests several complementary stages in the analysis of behavioral networks and argues that these stages may apply at the neurobiological level as well. Fentress concludes by indicating some limitations of historically applied behavioral categories but argues that the search for general principles, if pursued judiciously, may provide insights of considerable importance.

In Chapter Two, the author's approach is based upon a combined framework of ethological and neurobiological perspectives, which he synthesizes under the heading of *neuroethology*. Hoyle argues for the search for general "rules" of neurobiological and behavioral organization, while recognizing that these general rules must account for the diversity of individual expressions we find in nature. His own stance emphasizes the control of behavior in invertebrates, particularly the larger insects (Chapter Two, Table I), as well as the importance of behavioral considerations in setting the goals for analysis. Hoyle is particularly strong in his arguments against the chain reflex view of behavior. The chain reflex view suggests direct causal interconnection between one act in a temporal sequence and the next, via sensory intermediaries. Like other contributors to this volume, Hoyle stresses the fine line between reflex activity and centrally mediated behavioral sequences, although he obviously prefers the latter as a general principle. He is, however, aware of the problems of simple generalization from one preparation to another.

One issue raised by Hoyle is the importance of seeking ultimate explanations in terms of individually identified neurons. He points out that neuron identification can proceed either at the level of individual cells or in terms of basic cell types. He clearly prefers the former. At the level of general principles, or "rules," Hoyle questions previous approaches and includes his own suggestions. The fact that any combination of specific suggestions concerning general principles is likely to need modification on the basis of future research is perhaps less important than that rules of general applicability are currently being sought in a sophisticated manner.

In Chapter Three, Cohen takes as a main focus the balance between stability and plasticity in neurobehavioral systems. He is careful to point out that the *relationship* between these two basic dimensions, in addition to our understanding of each as individual issues, is at a very primitive stage. Cohen is also concerned with the explicit comparison of invertebrate and vertebrate systems. Toward this end he presents data on neuronal responses of a "primitive" vertebrate (the lamprey) to denervation of sensory inputs, and compares these responses to those found in various other vertebrate and invertebrate preparations. Cohen starts his discussion by reviewing three important criteria for precise analysis of simpler networks and behavior: (1) there should be a relatively small number of definable elements; (2) these should be subject to direct analysis both at the level of individual units and at their interconnections; and (3) the total output of the system should be open to direct monitoring, both independent of and in conjunction with defined extrinsic influences. He also stresses the importance of working with individually defined elements (neurons).

The "classic" vertebrate neuron can be subdivided into three parts: (1) the soma or cell body, which integrates a variety of specific inputs, which contains the basic metabolic neuronal machinery, and which in the majority of cases initiates patterned activity that is in turn passed on to other cells in the network; (2) the axon, which for present purposes can be viewed as the major output relay from the cell body to other neurons; and (3) the dendrites, which collect afferent information from a variety of specific interconnections. Obviously the detailed formation and operation of dendrites, with their highly specialized processes, plays a particularly important role in vertebrate neurobehavioral integration. By comparing responses to axotomy (surgical removal of axons) of various vertebrate and invertebrate afferent and/or dendriform processes, important clues of both integrative function and phenotypic predispositions can be obtained.

Cohen points out that, as a class, invertebrate neurons are constructed so that the basic macromolecular machinery of the soma is relatively isolated from the electrochemical consequences of specifiable neuronal inputs, whereas vertebrate neurons as a whole are constructed such that intrasomatic macromolecular constituents are more directly subjected to electrochemical influences. This dichotomy between vertebrate and invertebrate neuronal systems needs further investigation, but Cohen's proposal suggests ways that general principles of neurobehavioral organization may be sought in the face of biological diversity. An additional point raised by Cohen's essay is that processes of integrative function may influence basic phenotypic substrates as well as responding to them. This is a particularly important issue which has to date received relatively little attention (e.g., Fentress, 1966, 1967b).

Chapter Four, by Bullock, addresses directly the question of finding general principles (or "rules") of neurobehavioral organization while dealing adequately with our growing understanding of the diversity of particular neuronal properties and mechanisms. Within this context Bullock presents in tabular form 46 distinct variables that underlie the operation of individual elements in neuronal circuits, and then discusses how these particular variables might be related to more general principles. He is particularly careful to point out dangers of premature generalization while not precluding the search for general principles as a basic, and in some respects, ultimate goal.

The question of "circuit breaking" forms the focus of Bullock's argument. He clearly recognizes that the details of any given circuit in its complete form (defined as "one complete act from receptors to effectors") are persistent goals at the neuronal level and that their relation to more general principles of behavioral organization are even more elusive. Intermediate between basic variables at the single-element level and behavior at the organism level are operational principles of specified neuronal networks. Bullock stresses the fact that at present only a few networks have been worked out to a satisfactory degree of detail. In particular, analyses of networks with feedback and systems that can be traced completely between receptors and effectors provide a major challenge for future research. Yet the rate of progress in this regard should not be underestimated, and Bullock shares with most other contributors to this volume the basic conviction that by examining in detail diverse expressions of neural integration and anatomical form a more firm foundation for meaningful generalizations will be achieved.

This goal, however, can only be approached effectively with what Bullock has called a "targeted effort" which seeks explicit links between different levels and forms of analysis, from component properties at the subcellular level through integrated patterns of behavior as expressed in intact organisms. It is hoped that the rest of this volume will help chart the course, a necessary prelude to completing it.

CHAPTER ONE

Behavioral Networks and the Simpler Systems Approach

JOHN C. FENTRESS

INTRODUCTION

Neurophysiologists commonly assume that the function of complex nervous systems can and should be understood in terms of the activity and interrelationships of their basic components, the neurons. Most nervous systems, however, contain so many neurons with such varied properties and complex connectivity networks that an analysis in terms of single-neuron activity is clearly beyond our current technical and conceptual skills (Maynard, 1972, p. 59).

With this introduction to his paper on "simpler networks" Maynard outlined the major challenge of relating in a precise way activity patterns in identified nervous system elements with integrated patterns of behavior in intact organisms. It has been estimated that the human brain contains approximately 10^{12} neurons with an average of approximately 10^3 direct synaptic connections per neuron. When one considers that (1) functional connections within the nervous system involve complex *networks* of converging, diverging, and feedback patterns of synaptic connection, (2) functional connections between any two elements can be very indirect (i.e., separated by a number of intervening steps), and (3) properties of individual elements can range widely and shift with time, the enormity of the task facing neuroscientists and behavioral scientists who wish to speak meaningfully to one another is apparent. Maynard suggested three approaches to the problem.

1) We may lower the goal of explanation of the total system in terms of single elements and instead seek to understand it in terms of the properties of empirically determined functional subcomponents, each of which in turn represents a complex system.

2) We may artificially isolate a few elements from the total system and examine them in detail with the hope that eventually such elements may be

recombined to give the total functional system. This is essentially the approach of the reflexologists and has merit insofar as the arbitrarily selected isolates can be combined linearly to reproduce the entire system. If significant properties of the system are unknowingly destroyed or ignored during the initial isolation, then results must be accordingly limited.

3) We may search out and utilize simpler neural systems which can be isolated as reasonably intact systems without disturbing their relevant biological activity, and which can be thoroughly analyzed by our current techniques (Maynard, 1972).

Maynard clearly preferred the third approach for his own research. The fact of this volume is testimonial to his skills, dedication, and leadership in a rapidly growing area of inquiry. He was, however, perhaps unique in his understanding of the critical importance of complementary research on rules of behavioral patterning at the organism level in diverse species. As indicated in Chapters Two, Five, and Nine of this volume, for example, selection pressures that eventually constrain the operational properties of neural systems act most directly at the level of interaction between an organism and its environment. It is adaptive systems of patterned behavior which are selected for, and to achieve a full understanding of nervous system operation we must determine rules that function at the behavioral level. Commonalities of operation at the behavioral level may be mediated by quite different mechanisms, such as in load compensation in vertebrate and invertebrate species (see Chapter Five), and quite distinct behavioral operations may result from similar, and even identical, mechanisms (see Chapter Two).

SYSTEM ISOLATION AND INTERACTION

A point of particular importance both for neurobiologists and behavioral scientists which was recognized by Maynard is that of "system isolation." Precisely where, for example, do we draw the boundary between one set of events and another, and, once we have defined a "system" for investigation, to what extent can its operational properties be attributed to events intrinsic to the system as opposed to events with which this system can at least potentially interact? We draw a conceptual boundary between organism and environment, but to what extent are observed patterns of behavioral activity generated by factors intrinsic as opposed to extrinsic to the organism? We segregate one dimension or class of behavior from another, but to what extent are these aspects of behavior truly independent in their expression and control? We speak of genetic and environmental contributions to the behavioral phenotype, but when, if ever, is it appropriate to speak about the behavior as genetically "preprogrammed"? The balance between factors intrinsic and extrinsic to a system, by whatever criteria the system is classified, is a fundamental analytical issue in all of natural science. Classifications by structure and function may give different results, as may classifications at the neurobiological and behavioral levels of analysis. To reconcile these classifications with each other we must first examine them in their diversity. We must seek rules of commonality that do justice to this diversity, or our generalizations will remain vague and even trite.

A great value of the simpler systems approach is that it permits direct convergence of techniques for the analysis of structure and function at complementary levels of complexity. The extrapolation to more complex systems, or systems in different species, must be made with great caution at the present time, however. The dangers are particularly apparent, as Maynard pointed out, when a "system" isolated for analysis turns out to be part of a more complex level of organization. Depending on the extent to which this isolated subsystem is intrinsically organized, our views of its operational properties may change radically when it is viewed within a broader context. Extrapolations between systems, particularly those which underlie different classes of behavior and/or occur in different species, demand direct empirical testing.

Maynard recognized that the concept of "simplicity" is a relative one, depending upon the criteria we employ for a given analysis and the precision with which that analysis is carried out. Invertebrate nervous systems may have relatively few neurons, but the variation and complexity of these individual neurons and their connection patterns is often not obviously less than that found in vertebrates (see Chapters Four and Nineteen). Furthermore, complexity is not necessarily reduced as one reduces one's level of analysis; for example, behavioral constancies may be observed in spite of variations in the operation of specific neural and neuromuscular subcomponents (e.g., Hoyle, 1964), and relations between behavioral acts may be more regular than the individual acts themselves (e.g., Fentress, 1972, 1976). When we recall that clarity and constancy of operation are selected primarily at the level of integrated behavioral output this need not surprise us, but it must be kept in mind in the construction of our explanations.

The issues I have raised thus far depend upon where and how we define a "system" for analysis, and how independent we consider that system to be from its surround. This is the question of *continuity versus discontinuity*, which is basic to all natural science (e.g., Bohm, 1969). A second issue of equal importance is *stability versus change* in biological systems. These two themes will form a major focus in the discussion which follows (see also Chapter Twenty-Three).

BEHAVIOR AS PATTERNED PROCESS AND PHENOTYPE

The term *behavior* in its most general and abstract sense refers to *process*, that is, change of state over time. Thus the physicist can speak about the behavior of subatomic particles and the developmental biologist can speak about the behavior of cells in a tissue culture; in each case the term refers to the idea of change, process, or dynamic pattern. The temporal framework is critical to our analyses. Thus we must ask how individual component activities distribute themselves with respect to one another over time. We can think here of an analogy to a musical composition, which is defined by the *relationship* between individual notes and pauses with respect to one another over time (see Chapter Five). It is partially for

this reason that the emphasis of temporally patterned output in neural circuits and behavior is of such fundamental importance (e.g., consider human speech).

On the other hand patterned behavior in living organisms also exhibits *stabilities* in organization which reflect the organisms' *phenotypic structure* (see Fentress, 1967a). These stabilities can be viewed as analogous to a musical score, from which any given performance is ultimately derived. The phenotypic structure that underlies behavior represents a subtle and incompletely understood interplay between genetic substrates and experience during the life of the individual. As pointed out in Chapter Three, one of the major challenges to both neurobiology and behavior is to relate the ephemeral expressions (performances) of behavior to mechanisms of structural stability (the score). I think that it is fair to state that we have only just begun to look critically at the relations between process and phenotypic structure in behavior, yet analyses of simpler networks are providing some important clues (see Part III of this volume).

The concept of *pattern* deserves special mention in the study of behavior. Pattern refers to the idea of components and their relationships; it is, for example, a defining feature of neural networks. Pattern in behavior, either at the organism or neuronal level, refers in most cases to temporally segregated component activities linked together over time by specifiable rules. Continuous functions may also be patterned, however, such as in sign waves produced by an electronic generator. Basically, we can define "pattern" as "rules of linkage between component dimensions." These rules of linkage can remain relatively constant even though the individual components vary, such as in the transposition of a musical composition to a new key. This immediately raises the question of what level of organization we should look to in order to determine *principles* or *rules* of organization (see Chapters Two, Four, and Twenty).

Finally, for biological systems the most fundamental perspective, at least for initial inquiry, is the relationship between events intrinsic and extrinsic to the organism. It is at this level, for example, that one finds the basic questions of adaptation and survival itself (e.g., Darwin, 1872). Subsequently, questions can be asked about the relations between control systems within the organism and relations between genetic and environmental factors that form the behavioral phenotype.

At this point we can break the study of behavior and its neuronal substrates into three major parts.

1. What are the relations between factors intrinsic and extrinsic to the organism viewed *in toto*?

2. What are the relations between one activity pattern (or control system) and another as expressed within the framework of temporal integration?

3. What are the relations between genetic substrates and individual experiences during ontogeny in the establishment of the phenotypic foundations of behavior and neural activity?

To gain a more adequate understanding we must also ask how each of these three questions relates to the other two. For example, are there rules of intrinsic and extrinsic organization that apply to the level of the organism and its environment as well as to the relations between one system and another within the context of behavioral integration, or between genetic and environmental substrates during development? To pursue these questions in a meaningful way we must reconsider the idea of control *networks* in behavior.

DESCRIPTION, CLASSIFICATION, AND ANALYSIS

Careful descriptions and classifications of behavior by explicit criteria are essential preludes to analysis. They often receive insufficient attention, however. Their importance was clearly recognized by Don Maynard, who developed a famous laboratory exercise based upon the single question: How does a cockroach walk? What initially appeared to many students to be a surprisingly simple injunction soon left them hopelessly short of time at the end of a 3-hour laboratory section. Ethologists today lead the behavioral sciences in their recognition of the necessity for detailed description to set the stage for subsequent analysis. Relatively exhaustive descriptions of the behavioral repertoire of dif-

ferent species, called *ethograms*, provide important raw material for subsequent determination of mechanism (a term which, after all, must be defined in terms of the precise phenomena it is used to explain).

Hinde (1970) has made the useful point that descriptions of behavior can be based either upon movement patterns or upon the functional end points that these movement patterns appear to serve. The two need not be coincident, and confusion between them can cloud rather than clarify basic issues. For example, terms such as aggressive behavior, sexual behavior, or even grooming are based upon actual or presumed consequences, and each of these categories may incorporate a variety of distinct movement patterns, some of which may be similar in different functional contexts (e.g., the biting movements of certain carnivores used in prey catching and copulation). Description of the temporal flow of movement itself is a major undertaking, as demonstrated by the abstraction of a "grooming" sequence in an infant mouse (Figure 1).

The situation is confounded further when descriptions either by movement or consequence are *assumed* to imply necessary and sufficient causal antecedents. This often happens when terms based upon functional consequences, such as "aggression," are presumed to indicate a unitary center or drive which is both indivisible and totally distinct from causal factors that contribute to other functional units of behavior. Neither ethology nor psychology is totally immune to this criticism. The problem is enhanced when supposedly descriptive terms carry excess interpretation. Thus the term "displacement activity" in the ethological literature does not refer only to diverse movement patterns that may appear to be out of context from a functional perspective but which, by the very nature of the label employed, are too easily presumed to be *explained*. In this case the model is a Descartian model of nervous "energy" which, being blocked from normal channels of expression, is "displaced" to apparently irrelevant motor activities. If a term is accepted too literally, such confusion between descriptive and interpretative labels may actually preclude rather than enhance

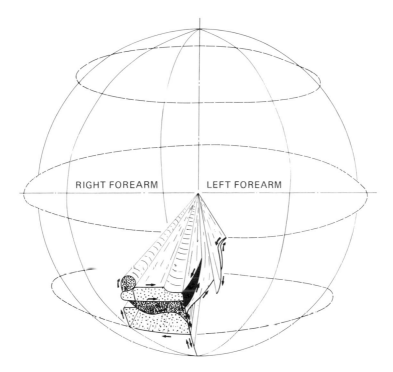

RIGHT FOREARM   LEFT FOREARM

FIGURE 1.   Three-dimensional representation of grooming movements in a 3-day-old mouse which emphasizes the temporal flow of movement through space as well as the relations between the two forelimbs. Through such descriptions it is possible to abstract principles of sequential organization which can clarify operational boundaries of nervous system output. A major task for the behavioral scientist is to find methods for abstracting initially exhaustive descriptions (here made through high-speed motion picture films in orthogonal perspective) in a manner that brings these operational principles into clear focus. (From Fentress and Golani, in preparation.)

subsequent analysis. This issue becomes particularly insidious when outdated models, such as simple energy models of neural integration, are employed (see Hinde, 1959).

It is important for the behavioral scientist interested in biological mechanism to be aware of these issues and potential sources of confusion. I can illustrate the ease of confusing descriptive and interpretative issues by recounting a lecture I heard from a cybernetically oriented behavioral scientist when I was a research student in animal behavior at Cambridge University. This individual placed two toy tractors dressed in white rat clothing in a maze at the front of the lecture room. We were asked to presume that these tractors were indeed white rats and to "describe" their behavior accordingly. Once the toy tractors were turned on, it became

distressingly easy to see one "chasing" the other, one as "subordinate" and "dull" (it kept getting stuck in corners), and so on. In reality the behavior of the two tractors was controlled by very simple operations: they would move forward in a straight line until they encountered an obstacle, then reverse for a short period with the front wheels spinning an indeterminant number of times, and subsequently proceed again in a forward direction. The ease with which surplus interpretative terminology surfaced in descriptions at this level indicates how very easily careless methods of "describing" the behavior of real organisms can confuse rather than clarify the very operational *principles* we wish to uncover and explain. A brief survey of behavioral journals, even most recent editions, will clarify that this remains a legitimate concern.

This is not to suggest that our descriptions

of behavior can be made in a totally unbiased manner, for in the process of looking for certain features we preclude awareness of others which may eventually turn out to be of fundamental importance. But at least we can be made aware of these difficulties. Hinde (1970) has pointed out that all descriptions involve a degree of abstraction (e.g., we cannot record *everything* in complete detail), and Beer (1973) has challenged the ethologist's premise of "immaculate perception" in the recording of behavioral data.

Whatever categories of behavior we establish, we shall do well to recognize that upon finer analysis, at least for most vertebrate species, they are unlikely to be either unitary or totally independent from one another in terms of mechanism. It is also not without importance to appreciate that our basic vocabulary places events within a static framework, while as behavioral scientists we must continually grapple with dynamic change. Further, our terms used in behavioral description may easily carry surplus meaning which, if not recognized, can preclude rather than clarify subsequent analysis. Finally, Spencer Brown's (1969) reminder that we "take the form of the distinction for the form" serves to make us aware that our descriptive and categorical labels are dependent upon the particular criteria we employ. This issue in itself is too easily passed over without sufficient awareness of its consequences (see Fentress, 1973b, 1976). These considerations become particularly important when we strive to forge meaningful connections between different levels of analysis, such as between behavior defined at the organism level and neurobiology. The very issue of how we define a functional unit is of major importance, whether our emphasis is upon neurons or behavior: the issue becomes more complex when we try to relate these analysis levels (see Chapters Two, Five, Seven, Twenty, and Twenty-One for further discussion).

BEHAVIORAL NETWORKS

The basic idea of a behavioral network is that a variety of inputs converge in their effect upon any given output that we choose to examine, and that each input has divergent effects upon a variety of separately classified outputs (Fentress, 1968a, 1968b, 1973b; Figure 2A and B). This is a fundamentally distinct mode of thought from simple, linear, causal chain models and appears more in accord with the empirical data (Hanson, 1959; Hinde, 1970; Maynard, 1972; Fentress, 1973b, 1976). To illustrate, a variety of distinct variables, such as genotype, home-pen rearing conditions, ongoing behavior, and physiological state, have been shown to converge in their effects upon fleeing, freezing, and grooming activities in rodents; and a given input, such as an overhead moving stimulus, can elicit a variety of different acts from one time period to another (Fentress, 1968a, 1968b).

A second basic and related point is that each input that we define interacts with a given intervening state in the production of output (Figure 2C). When considering neurobehavioral control systems three ranges of interaction can be discerned. (1) The input is *transferred* to output via intervening processes. This means that the patterning of the output can be accounted for entirely by the pattern of input. (2) The input is *transformed* by intervening processes in the production of the observed output. This is perhaps the most common situation. It implies that knowledge of the output depends both upon the details of the input and the current state of intervening processes. For example, rodents may either flee or freeze in response to a standardized input as a function of their ongoing behavior (Fentress, 1968a, 1968b). (3) The input may serve to *trigger* a given output whose details depend upon intervening mechanisms rather than the input per se. This is analogous to dropping a tone arm on different phonograph records. The output of the speaker is triggered by the presence of the tone arm but depends in detail upon the particular record being played. An even more extreme situation is where patterned output appears to be generated autonomously in the absence of any definable input. In the latter case mechanisms intrinsic to the control system are predominately important, and in that sense the system appears self-organized (Fentress, 1976).

Historically, our thinking about the neural control of behavior has moved from the idea of

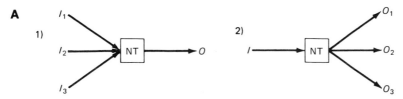

To define a behavioral or neural network by input—output operations it is necessary initially to ask two sets of questions. 1. What are the separate and combined influences of a diverse range of specified inputs (I) upon a given output (O)? 2. What is the range of outputs affected by a given input, and how are these outputs coordinated with respect to one another over time? Subsequently, these initially separate input and output analyses can be combined, although on logical grounds the networks they reveal may be distinct (see Fentress, 1973a). [NT is used here as shorthand notation for intrinsic, or intervening, processes, separated in (C) below.]

B 1) $I \xrightarrow{+} O$ 2) $I \xrightarrow{+} NT \xrightarrow{+} O$ 3) $I \xrightarrow{-} NT \xrightarrow{-} O$
                                        $(+)$ $(+)$

Initial input—output analyses at behavioral or neurobiological levels should be assumed to encompass a population of intervening mechanisms which have distinct properties even though they produce the same overall effect. For example, a case of behavioral excitation (1) may be mediated either through the excitation of an intervening mechanism which in turn activates behavior (2), or through the inhibition of an intervening mechanism which normally inhibits the behavioral output (3). In each of these cases the overall relations between input and output are indistinguishable. This illustrates the need for direct empirical investigation at several levels, whether one begins with neural networks or with organism behavior.

C 1) TRANSFER   2) TRANSFORM   3) TRIGGER   4) INTRINSIC

$I \xrightarrow{III} \boxed{NT} \xrightarrow{III} O$ $I \xrightarrow{III} \boxed{NT} \xrightarrow{II\ II} O$ $I \xrightarrow{I} \boxed{NT} \xrightarrow{II\ II} O$ $I \xrightarrow{\ } \boxed{NT} \xrightarrow{II\ II} O$

There are four logically distinct types of relationship between inputs and outputs in neurobehavioral control systems. In the first, patterns of input are *transferred* in detail to patterns of output, with the result that input characteristics are sufficient to account for output characteristics. In the second, and most safely assumed case, input characteristics are *transformed* by intervening states which themselves may change over time. Here one must monitor both the system's inputs and its concurrent state to predict the output. Third, the input may serve to *trigger* the output rather in the way that finger pressure triggers the firing of a rifle. Here the detailed pattern of input becomes unimportant as long as it contains essential characteristics for triggering. The details of output pattern are produced by intrinsic properties of the system. Fourth, a system may display *intrinsic* patterns of activity in the absence of any defined input. A fifth possibility could be added in which no output is observed in spite of intervening activity, but this becomes interesting only in comparison with one of the four previously outlined modes of operation. In each of the four cases diagrammed here it is necessary to ask how these isolated components fit "into" the total operational system.

FIGURE 2. Some common operations in the definition of behavior and neural networks.

signal "transfer" to "transform," "trigger," and "spontaneity." This places an important emphasis upon intrinsic control mechanisms that are completely at odds with earlier simple reflex or stimulus—response models. Many of the chapters in this volume reflect this change. Systems have become defined more tightly and independently; the question is whether the data fully justify this departure from previous thought.

CONTROL IN TERMS OF CONTEXTUAL AND COMPONENT ANALYSES

With regard to contextual and component analysis, two facts are critical. First, each dimension of behavior that we initially define, describe, and classify occurs in the context of other dimensions of behavior. Analysis of the broader contextual framework of a given behavioral expression can provide important clues as to underlying mechanism (e.g., Fentress, 1967a, 1968a, 1968b, 1972, 1973b). Second, each dimension of behavior that we initially define, describe, and classify is unlikely to be unitary at more refined levels of analysis. Thus we must seek component dimensions of these initial behavioral categories as well as their relationships to one another (e.g., Fentress, 1972; Fentress and Stilwell, 1973).

I shall attempt to illustrate these principles by examining the context of expression and components of grooming behavior in rodents. First, it is important to recognize that the term *grooming* is one of presumed function rather than description per se (see above). Second however, the motor patterns used in rodent grooming are relatively stereotyped and thus come close to traditional ethological models of "fixed action pattern." As we shall see, the label of fixed action pattern has limits as to its applicability when applied at a detailed level of analysis, but subsequent occurrences of grooming are sufficiently stereotyped to permit detailed analyses of sequential patterning, central programming, phenotypic substrates, and the like. Third, the grooming movements employed by rodents occur in definable contexts, which permits an evaluation of the interplay between variables that underlie diverse classes of behavior distinguishable by descriptive and functional criteria.

For the purpose of illustration it is useful to start with an examination of the context within which grooming occurs. For example, rodents frequently wash their faces during transitions between states of inactivity and locomotion or after periods of vigorous bouts of a variety of behavior, ranging from feeding to fighting to sexual behavior. With practice the observer can predict with considerable accuracy when a bout of grooming will and will not occur, which indicates that the transitions between broad classes of behavior follow systematic principles. This in turn indicates that there are definable rules of relationship between apparently heterogeneous classes of behavioral expression, and that these rules of relationship may help clarify mechanisms defined as intrinsic to any one given class of behavior (Fentress, 1968a, 1968b, 1972, 1973b). In particular, it appears that low-level activation of variables that normally underlie a variety of classes of behavior can facilitate the expression of grooming, whereas at higher levels of activation these various dimensions of behavior block grooming (see Chapter Twenty-Three). Figure 3 illustrates the predictable occurrence of grooming in voles following the presentation of a moving overhead stimulus as well as the relation of grooming to behavior patterns such as freezing and subsequent locomotion. Analyses of these contextual boundaries indicate that simple models of specific versus nonspecific processes of integration in vertebrate behavior may be misleading and that more realistic models may have to consider partial and shifting overlap among underlying processes of control.

Most important to the present discussion is that grooming is not a homogeneous category of behavioral expression but that it can be divided into operationally defined subcomponents which are sequentially articulated by definable, although not totally invariant, rules. It is possible, for example, to separate grooming into face and body components, each of which can also be subdivided from both descriptive and analytical perspectives. A major question concerns the sequential articulation of these grooming components, for careful analysis can reveal basic parameters of the central nervous system as a temporal machine. To illustrate, face grooming typically precedes grooming movements directed at either the belly or back *even when* mild peripheral disturbances are applied to the latter regions. This is indirect support for the idea of central bias in which certain sequential arrangements of movement patterning are favored over others.

The details of sequential articulation are relatively complex even for defined subcomponents of grooming, however. For example, face-grooming sequences in adult mice can be reliably divided into seven or eight basic

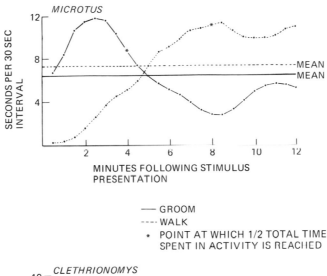

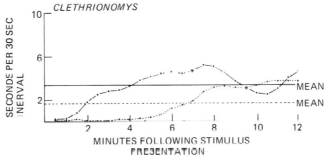

FIGURE 3. After presentation of an overhead stimulus, to which voles respond initially by fleeing and/or freezing, self-grooming behavior may increase over control levels with a peak at predictable time intervals (the details of which depend upon species, stimulus characteristics, ongoing behavioral state, etc.). Specific temporal relations between different classes of behavior, such as grooming and locomotion, can also be determined. Thus, by examining a given class of behavior in the broader spatiotemporal context in which it occurs, one can determine rules of linkage, which in turn help clarify the operational boundaries of underlying control processes. (From Fentress, 1968a.)

components which follow one another by statistically determined rules. One point that becomes clear immediately is that these movement components can be described with reference to one another most effectively if they are grouped hierarchically rather than merely subjected to unidimensional stochastic (sequential) analysis. This is because given elements participate in the formation of different clusters, rather like the different combinations of letters in different words, and these clusters are themselves arranged sequentially as are the words in different phrases of human language (Figure 4).

The "grammatical" analogy to sequentially patterned behavior in vertebrates has important implications in terms of possible hierarchical structure at the level of mechanism, although one must be careful in interpreting the implications of this term (see Chapters Two, Five, Ten, and Fifteen). The analogy to human grammar is limited, however, by the fact that duration of a given behavioral event can be an important indicator of its sequential location

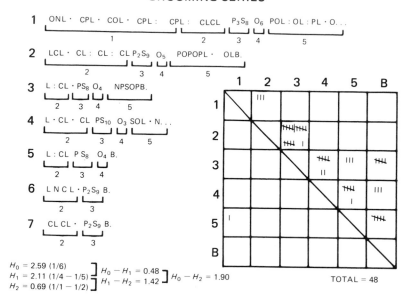

GROOMING SERIES

FIGURE 4. *Face-grooming sequences for DBA/2J mice were divided into seven basic components, as indicated by the individual letters in rows 1–7. (B represents body grooming, an eighth component in the total grooming sequence examined.) When sequential analyses are made for the six most common face-grooming components, predictability of events can be made on the assumption that each event is equally likely (H_0), from the actual probabilities of individual components (H_1). When the previous component is known (H_2) one can predict components with a probability of greater than 50 percent ($1/1 - 1/2$). It is also possible to find higher-order groupings (face grooming units 1–5 and body grooming) whose sequential relations are indicated in the matrix (the first unit in a pair is represented on the vertical axis). Note that individual components may be found in more than one unit, and, like words in a language, the units are defined in part by the sequential relations between components. (From Fentress and Stilwell, 1973.)*

defined in terms of other dimensions of behavioral expression. For example, we have found that the duration of licking movements is an important indicator as to whether movements defined as single strokes or overhands are most likely to follow (Fentress, 1972; Fentress and Stilwell, 1973). Here again, the analogy to a musical composition, which preserves an explicit time referent, appears more adequate.

Without going into great detail I wish to emphasize here that careful description of both the context and components of a given dimension of behavioral expression can provide invaluable clues with respect to mechanisms of control. All too frequently, behavioral dimensions are considered isolated from one another and unitary in their operation. They are also typically formulated within static framework, which may do injustice to the very dynamic features of behavioral organization that should define a major focus of our attention.

As I indicated above, it is necessary to deal directly with the *network* of causal factors that are operative, rather than simple unidirectional linear chains, to account fully for integrated patterns of behavior. It is the rule rather than the exception for vertebrate behavior that numerous inputs converge in their effect upon a given output and that each of these inputs has divergent, direct or indirect, influences upon a variety of outputs. Analyses must be focused upon the question of teasing out these interlocking networks in terms of explicit reference to qualitative, quantitative, and temporal parameters (see Fentress, 1973b, 1976, for more extensive discussion).

One simple but basic point to note is that *every* causal statement involves interaction between at least two variables, and it is at this point of interaction that many of the most fundamental issues of control arise. Fentress (1968a, 1968b) found, for example, that a given sensory input would produce qualitatively different behavioral responses in voles (e.g., freezing versus fleeing) as a function of the animal's ongoing behavioral state and that a variety of definable inputs combined in their influence upon several different classes of behavioral expression. Similarly, the details of muscular contraction depend upon the current state of the muscle as well as upon the particular activity pattern of motoneurons (see Chapter Five); the specific response of a neuron to a given volley of synaptic activity cannot be fully understood without determination of the cell's internal state at the moment of input from extrinsic sources (e.g., Eccles, 1964). This is a further reason why Maynard's emphasis on both element and network properties is of such fundamental importance. The lesson has frequently been lost, through emphasis on only a single side of the equation, but Maynard's extrapolation from his analyses of the lobster stomatogastric ganglion was decisive and clear: "it is necessary to know both the functional wiring diagram of the relevant elements *and* the essential properties of the component neurons; neither alone is sufficient" (Maynard, 1972, p. 169). I shall return to this in the final chapter of this volume, for, as the reader should recognize by that time, this balance between systems and mechanism thinking is critically important at both the behavioral and neurobiological levels of analysis.

ON THE RELATIONSHIP OF INTRINSIC AND EXTRINSIC FACTORS

The issues of control can be illustrated further, as well as simplified, by returning to the question of intrinsic versus extrinsic factors in behavior — for example, the linkage between organism and environment. I pointed out

previously that normal face—belly—back sequences of grooming in rodents can be produced by the application of mild irritants to either the belly or back. This central bias which normally operates can be obscured, however, when very strong peripheral irritants (such as ether) are applied to the belly or back. Under the latter circumstances grooming is focused immediately and directly upon the disturbed bodily region. This indicates a subtle interplay between central and peripheral mechanisms that deserves further documentation.

It is possible to remove sensory input to the face of mammals by sectioning sensory branches of the trigeminal nerve. We can ask what the consequences are of such a manipulation. As it turns out, the answer to this question depends upon the context under which grooming behavior is examined. When the animals are tested in their home cages under conditions of minimal disturbance, considerable modifications of grooming movements are observed. However, when these same animals are tested in novel environments, the performance of grooming is relatively unaffected. How do we account for these differences?

From a descriptive perspective it is possible to demonstrate that grooming in novel environments frequently occurs in a particularly rapid and stereotyped fashion. When this happens, the animals become less sensitive to modulations of peripheral input. In this sense we can say that the behavior becomes more centrally focused in terms of mechanisms of control. Two facts are clear from an examination of grooming in a variety of environmental contexts. The first is that neither intrinsic nor extrinsic variables alone are sufficient to explain the occurrence of grooming; that is, we must examine the interplay of each. Second, the relative balance between central and peripheral mechanisms may shift as a function of the particular context of behavioral expression. Neither either—or nor static models are likely to be sufficient with respect to more refined analysis. These principles probably apply to a variety of forms of behavioral expression in a variety of species, although specific details will have to be worked out for each.

The removal of extrinsic input, defined at

the organism level, is not in itself sufficient for evaluation of intrinsic mechanisms, or central programming. For example, a given movement generates feedback information from sensory receptors which inform the central nervous system of immediately preceding consequences. One important route by which such sensory feedback is received is via the proprioceptors of different muscle groups. This information channel can be removed in mammals by sectioning the dorsal roots of the spinal cord. To what extent does this operation modify grooming and other classes of behavioral expression?

Several facts have emerged from our investigations of this question. (1) Grooming is relatively unaffected in its overall probability and expression by dorsal root lesions. (2) Other classes of behavior, such as exploratory "patting" movements made by mice upon the sides of a novel cage, are totally obliterated, however. (3) Fine-level examination of grooming through the use of high-speed films does indicate some differences as a consequence of the lesions. For example, (a) long trajectory grooming movements may become both more variable and slower (Figure 5), whereas the more rapid movements appear unaffected at the level of resolution we employed, and (b) the sequential connection between individually defined movements shows greater stationarity — that is, less flexibility in rules of sequential pattern, following the lesion (Fentress, 1972, and unpublished observations). These experiments yield two lessons. First, the temporal organization of a relatively stereotyped movement sequence in mammals may be programmed centrally to a greater extent than previously suspected. Second, this central programming is not absolute, however, and the precise conclusions one draws depend upon the particular dimension of behavior being examined, the context within which it occurs, and the particular form that it takes under these different contexts (e.g., speed, amplitude, stereotypy).

One interesting possibility that deserves further investigation is that phasic patterns of proprioceptive input serve not only to reinforce and even "carve out" particular patterns of motor output but they also have more "tonic" functions of modulating the overall speed of

motor performance. This would be akin to speeding up a phonographic turntable with a series of discrete pushes, which would reduce the mean internote interval although the major details of patterning remain "intrinsic" to the particular record being played (see Chapter Five). Phasic proprioceptive input may also serve an important role in the correction for unexpected loads, particularly in slow movements, even if it is not a necessary pattern generator in the usual sense (see Chapter Five), and it may also help mold central pattern generators during ontogeny (see Chapter Twenty-Two). One lesson here is that we must look for a variety of functions as well as causal antecedents for any given subsystem rather than focus on a single dimension that seems most relevant upon initial inspection.

It is also necessary to recognize that removal of a sensory input is not the same as phasic modification of this input, and we have experiments currently underway in which momentary shifts in proprioceptive "load" are employed. The data here are preliminary but suggest that during particularly rapid, vigorous, and stereotyped movements the animal is much more insensitive to changes in afferent (sensory) information (see Fentress, 1973b, 1976; Chapter Five). This also indicates that rules of control for a given act when defined broadly may shift from one specific circumstance to another (see Fentress, 1967a).

We can summarize the major point of this section by noting that it is possible to consider three broad classes of factors that may underlie the sequential articulation of behavior (Figure 5). First, each act in the sequence may be elicited by specific extrinsic input. Tinbergen's classic study of courtship behavior in the three-spined stickleback, where each act is affected by changes in the animal's sensory world, is a particularly clear illustration of this type of control (Tinbergen, 1951). By this model one would postulate that the individual movements of a grooming sequence are elicited by response to specific sources of peripheral irritation. This sequencing could be accounted for by different thresholds for different responses (either at the sensory or motor level) and perhaps by inhibitory connections between the specific behavioral components. Second, each act might be viewed as part of a

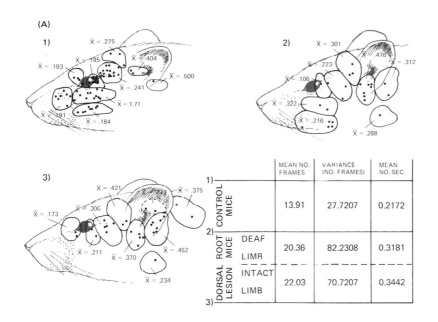

		MEAN NO. FRAMES	VARIANCE (NO. FRAMES)	MEAN NO. SEC.
1)	CONTROL MICE	13.91	27.7207	0.2172
2)	DORSAL ROOT LESION MICE — DEAF LIMB	20.36	82.2308	0.3181
3)	DORSAL ROOT LESION MICE — INTACT LIMB	22.03	70.7207	0.3442

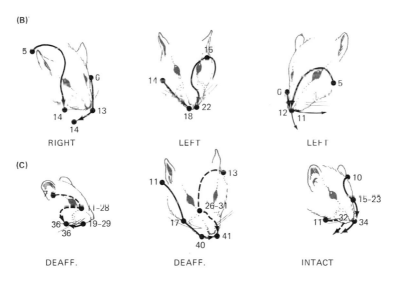

FIGURE 5. *In (A) the point of furthest limb excursion in long trajectory overhand strokes is indicated for C57 mice with unilateral dorsal root lesions. (1) Control mice; (2) deafferented limb; and (3) intact limb of unilaterally lesioned mice. As indicated in the table, overhand movements in lesioned mice tend to be slower and more variable. Mean duration (seconds) of strokes of different amplitudes are indicated by clusters on the mouse drawings. Typical overhand trajectories in control and experimental mice (both for the deafferented and intact limb) are shown in (B) and (C), respectively. The numbers refer to frames taken from film at 64 fps. Dots followed by a pair of numbers (e.g., 11−28) indicate where and for how long a particular stroke in experimental animals was "stuck" in a single position. Greater variability and reduced smoothness of strokes in the experimental animals are apparent. (From Fentress, 1972.)*

A

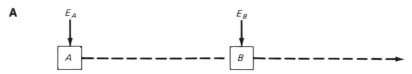

Here each act in the sequence is elicited by appropriate environmental inputs (E_A, E_B, etc). The sequential activation of behavioral components can thus be attributed to sequential processing of factors external to the organism.

B

In this case the performance of a given act in the sequence is dependent upon, and caused by, the performance of a previous act in the sequence (i.e., the performance of **A** elicits **B**, etc.). This is the chain reflex model of behavior, which can be tested initially by removing sequentially available signals from the external environment.

C

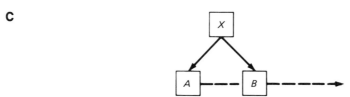

This represents centrally controlled sequencing of behavioral acts. An endogenous control "center" can be established by preventing the expression of acts in the total behavioral chain while removing potentially critical external cues.

FIGURE 6.   Three dimensions in the control of behavior sequences.

chain-reflex system, in which the *performance* of behavior A elicits behavior B, and so on. This is the traditional model of the Sherringtonian reflex school (e.g., Sherrington, 1906). Finally, there is the possibility that has only recently come into active consideration — a central program generator that produces the basic features of sequential organization even in the absence of exteroceptive and proprioceptive information. This model has received considerable support from both invertebrate and vertebrate preparations, as is clear from reading subsequent chapters in this volume. It was one of Don Maynard's major contributions to examine the source of this intrinsic pattern generation. He stressed, for example, that "it is important to know whether the patterned output observed originates in the ganglion or simply reflects and relays temporal patterns sent out from the CNS" (Maynard, 1972, p. 62). Our answers to these questions are still very incomplete, and there is some danger of "band wagoning" in light of the recent impressive evidence that central programs may be more fundamental than we previously

suspected. The precise analysis of mechanisms as well as the limitations of our current conceptual orientation are major challenges to future research. These three alternatives are summarized in Figure 6.

It is important to recall that the question of intrinsic/extrinsic control can be asked at several different levels. In particular, three complementary questions can be usefully applied at both the behavioral and neurobiological level of analysis. The first concerns the relation between intrinsic and extrinsic factors defined at the level of the organism. The question of rodent grooming in the absence of normal peripheral input is an illustration. Second, one can ask about the relations between factors defined as intrinsic to a given control system in integration and the broader context within which that system operates. It is at this level that Maynard was particularly concerned with the problem of system isolation. At the behavioral level this question can be most easily illustrated by asking the extent to which factors that underlie one class of behavior are independent in their operation from factors that underlie a different class of behavior. Just as each organism lives in the context ·of its extrinsic environment, so does each class of behavior that we can define occur in the context of other definable classes of behavior; and the extent to which these different classes of behavior are controlled by their own *separate* "intrinsic" factors is an issue of major importance (see Fentress, 1973b, 1976). Finally, we can ask questions of intrinsic/extrinsic control in the context of establishing the behavioral or neural phenotype. To what degree, for example, do genetic factors "predetermine" a given class of behavior or neural organization? Here the term "phenotype" reminds us in particular that both genetic ("intrinsic") and environmental ("extrinsic") factors must be taken into account: the question is whether their relative contributions can be segregated for any particular set of phenomena.

The last point deserves further comment, for our views have altered radically in recent years. To cite a single behavioral example, mice who have had their forelimbs painlessly amputated at birth do not have available to them the normal flow of sensory information which might be expected to contribute necessarily to the production of grooming sequences. Yet these animals show remarkably normal maturation of upper-arm grooming movements. This includes not only a peak in total grooming-type movements of the upper arms at days 18 to 21, as seen in normal mice, but also a precise coordination of forelimb, tongue, and eye movements at appropriate stages of the "grooming" sequence (Figure 7). This indicates, at least to me, that genetic ("endogenous") instructions are of more basic importance than I would have previously suspected; and, as will become clear from Part III of this volume, the importance of genetic factors in the formation of a variety of neurobehavioral control systems has gained increasing acceptance (Fentress, 1972, 1973a). Because of this, let me state two cautions. First, detailed analysis of high-speed films of mouse grooming reveals that some adjustments to the absence of the forelimbs from postnatal day 1 are made. For example, animals with amputated limbs tend to tuck their heads toward their bodies in an exaggerated manner (as if to reach the face with upper arms), and they also spend an abnormal amount of time licking other animals or environmental objects, as if to "make up for" normal sensory stimulation of the tongue by the forepaws. The question I pose to the reader is whether these alterations in behavior indicate a basic change in response as a consequence of removed extrinsic inputs during ontogeny or whether they are further evidence for endogenous programming. The point is that either conclusion could be supported as a function of the particular criteria upon which that conclusion is based. This is one of the reasons that questions of intrinsic versus extrinsic control are so difficult to resolve in a single unitary manner. As a second caution it must be emphasized that we are speaking here primarily of details in the performance of a given behavioral output. At higher levels of organization, such as in the control of basic motivational states, environmental factors that operate during various stages of ontogeny may be extremely important (Hinde, 1970). Thus we must take into account different levels of control in behavior, as well as differences that may underlie the distinction between different species.

THE QUESTION OF GENERAL PRINCIPLES

This leads directly to the question of how we search for general principles of behavioral and neurobiological organization. Not only is

FIGURE 7. Even following early postnatal amputation of the forelimbs in mice, well coordinated grooming movements develop with a striking degree of normality, including the coordination of limbs, head, tongue and eyes. This indicates a strong, but not necessarily exclusive, endogenous programming of movement. (From Fentress, 1973a.)

the diversity of animal species reflected in the diversity of underlying control mechanisms, but also within a given species different classes and levels of behavioral organization may reveal quite distinct properties of control. Hoyle (Chapter Two) and Bullock (Chapter Four) provide their own views about this question of general principles in the neural control of behavior. Three comments can be made at this stage. First, the degree of generality of a statement often coincides with the degree of superficiality of this statement. If, for example, we state that all animals eat, this does not in itself permit an appropriate evaluation of the diverse mechanisms for feeding that are found throughout the animal kingdom. Second, the degree of precision of a generalization may depend upon the level of analysis that is being investigated. Few, for example, would argue that basic principles of particulate inheritance based upon research with the fruit fly are irrelevant to particulate inheritance in man, nor would many challenge the importance of the squid axon to our understanding of basic principles of neuronal signaling in our own brains. The most simple way to put this is that we are operating within a scientific context that suggests that basic biological "building blocks" are similar for diverse species, even though the final architecture of these species may vary enormously. The other side of the question has not been explored as thoroughly. There may, for example, be common principles at higher levels of organization which are mediated by quite different mechanisms. The question of load compensation in vertebrate and invertebrate motor systems discussed in Chapter Five is a case in point. Is it necessarily true that our generalizations become more powerful and precise as we reduce our level of analysis? At the present time there is no satisfactory answer to this question, partially because it has not been examined in a critical manner. Finally, the power of our generalizations may depend in part upon the degree of abstraction in which they are framed. The number "2" is an abstraction which can be applied equally to individual nerve cells or organisms. Our search for abstract general principles of organization in superficially diverse neurobehavioral networks has not, however, achieved even a preliminary degree of satisfactory exposition.

CONCLUSIONS

Integrated patterns of behavior provide a dynamic linkage between individual organisms and their environment. Further understanding of the means by which this linkage is produced provides one of the most pressing challenges of modern science. Two distinct approaches have begun to draw together. The first involves analyses of integrated patterns of behavior at the level of the intact organism. This is the approach that characterizes most of ethology and psychology. The second approach concentrates upon the detailed analysis of *simpler networks* of neural elements which underlie behavior. It is with the latter approach that the present volume is primarily concerned.

However, the relations between levels of analysis in natural science are clearly reciprocal. Just as models of behavioral control are likely to be misleading which do not take into account principles of operation at the level of neuronal elements and their connection into functional networks, so, too, are models of neural networks likely to be incomplete and even superficial which do not take into account problems of behavioral integration at the organism level. Fortunately, there are a growing number of workers who, as did Donald Maynard, recognize the need for seeking synthesis from data gathered at a variety of levels of analysis in a way that does full justice to each.

From the perspective of networks defined at the behavioral level the major issue is to account for patterns of relationship between organism and environment in terms of short-term integration, development, and evolution. From the perspective of biological mechanism similar questions emerge, but these are most frequently viewed in terms of the extent to which one underlying system is independent in its operations from other biological systems. Here the simpler network approach to neurobiology and behavior has made a significant contribution by isolating clearly defined subcomponents in the control of behavior. The generality of operational features of these simpler networks, particularly when applied to the level of integrated behavior in intact organisms within diverse species, is an area that demands much future investigation.

CHAPTER TWO

Approaches to Understanding the Neurophysiological Bases of Behavior

GRAHAM HOYLE

INTRODUCTION

In 1961 I accepted an invitation from the University of Oregon to join Melvin Cohen in setting up a program of training and research in comparative invertebrate neurobiology. For some years the program was the only one of its kind, and we are proud to have trained, during those early years, so many of the outstanding young workers in this field. But by 1969 many other universities were following suit, and Mel had been attracted away to Yale. When I was given the task of seeking a replacement for him, the choice was not difficult, however, for, on all counts, Donald Maynard was an obvious substitute. We were highly pleased that he accepted our offer: although it was, alas, destined to be a short association, it was a highly stimulating and rewarding one; seeds

were sown then which will surely lead to the bearing of much fruit in the years to come.

Don and I shared a passionate interest in the study of invertebrate neurobiology. We both believed that an intensive study of simple systems, that is, of invertebrate ganglia, was the only way in which the basic rules underlying the complexities of neural organization required to control behavior could be unraveled. Our common goal was to understand the cellular substrates of behavior. It was Don's contention that a complete understanding of the role of every neuron in a miniganglion, comprising a small total number of cells and programming some easily understood motor act, was an essential starting point. He expected that any such study would automatically uncover previously unimagined physiological mechanisms and strategies of neural connectivity that would serve as guides in the search for subsystems operating in more complex ones. I am glad to see that this expectation is proving to be the case. He also expected that similar devices would be found to be used by higher nervous systems. As it is much easier to find a known mechanism than to discover a new one, the studies would be rewarding on a broader front than is implicit in their intrinsic interest alone.

Maynard's starting point was the nine-neuron ganglion that controls the heart rate of decapod crustaceans. Experience with this system, which has been intensively studied, had entirely supported his first general thesis. Although the properties of the five larger neurons quickly became known in detail, models that predicted the mode of action of the others failed to simulate the ganglion's operations. Only after the smaller neurons were penetrated with intracellular electrodes and data obtained from them incorporated did it become possible to simulate operation of the ganglion and to understand it fully at the cellular level.

The next ganglion in order of complexity in the Maynard search also comes from decapod crustaceans, the 30-neuron stomatogastric. Progress in the study of this ganglion is being aided by the introduction of intracellular dye-filling techniques on the part of Allen Selverston and his collaborators at San Diego (Selverston, 1974). With the aid of a computer graphics terminal, the reconstruction of individual identified neurons from serial sections is providing us with a level of understanding of the details of neural programming of the branching patterns of identified neurons that was previously impossible to obtain from any system. Two important new principles have already emerged from the work: first, rhythmicity can be produced by network properties alone (Selverston and Mulloney, 1974a, b); it does not require the presence of unstable, or "oscillator," neurons. Second, excitation by release from inhibition can play a role in generating neural patterns (Perkel and Mulloney, 1974). Thus are we enjoying continuing benefit from Maynard's wisdom and initiative. With his approach there was to be a progressive trend toward the use of more complex ganglia and the asking of more sophisticated questions. There is undeniable value to this approach. But he was a rare person

among neuroscientists, being willing to discipline himself to follow such a logic-prescribed course of action. Most of us who do not feel obliged to study vertebrates go straight to some preparation that offers easy technical feasibility. Large and easily visualized somata evidently provide irresistible attractions, for they have dictated the choice of experimental subjects in most laboratories; only after the work is under way is a serious attempt made to rationalize the choice. This is indeed a pity: what we are all most interested in is the neuronal basis of behavior, and we should therefore make every effort to allow behavioral considerations rather than ease of experimentation to determine our choices.

BEHAVIOR AND NEUROBIOLOGY

We should start with a definition of behavior. Behavior may be most simply equated with animal movements; the task of neurobiology in relation to behavior is to explain the control of movements. But this field is so vast that some subdivisions and restrictions of interest are essential for practical purposes. A detailed knowledge of muscle function and neuromuscular transmission may not be required to interpret behavior, but some knowledge of these phenomena is essential if the neuronal basis of movement is under examination. One possible approach to the study of the nervous system would be to follow the example of Bernard Katz in his detailed and thorough study of the frog neuromuscular junction. Step by cautious step we would gradually approach the central programming of behavior. But if all studies were carried out in such depth, on anatomically restricted test objects, it might take us many thousands of years before we could even begin to approach the problems of higher nervous function. Furthermore, if the example from rat psychology is any guide, the thrust could completely bypass the very areas of most importance.

Certainly it is important to have at least a sketchy comprehension of central integration. For, although the fine details cannot be of great relevance to the neurobiologist seeking to understand behavior, the overall principles of synaptic transmission are. In other words, it doesn't really matter to the neuroethologist whether the transmitter is acetylcholine or l-glutamate, whether it is released in quantal units, or whether these are contained in vesicles. These are interesting phenomena, but they need not occupy his attention experimentally. On the other hand, it is wholly relevant to single out from the vast field phenomena that are obviously of general interest, and to give them the status of subdisciplines. This was desirable, for example, in the Pavlovian study of conditioned reflex. It is valuable, however, to contemplate the extent to which the Russian inheritors of the magnificent Pavlov tradition came to exaggerate the relevance of the conditioned reflex in behavior, thereby completely losing sight of many other important aspects of neural function. Conditioned reflexes appear to play a minor role in the behavior of many invertebrates and none at all in some important phyla, which denies them the status of universal general phenomena. In the same way the post-Sherrington student of pure reflexology came to see all behavior as reflex actions or as chain sequences of reflexes and was therefore blind to the importance of endogenous programs.

The European zoological — experimental behavior school that came to call itself "ethology" arose from a systematic study of animal behavior in the field. Much of such behavior is unlearned, that is, instinctive. It clearly did not fit into the classifications of either the Russian conditioned reflex school or the American behaviorist and experimental psychologist schools. Many of the behavioral acts that attracted the attention of this school of acute field observers had at least a partial explanation in reflex action. But special terms became necessary to describe phenomena that, although perhaps known earlier, had not been studied systematically or even thought about intensively. "Reaction-specific energy," "releaser," "fixed-action pattern" (FAP), "displacement act," "drive," and "vacuum activity" were vivid terms added to the language of behavioral biology by this group.

The new concepts were summarized in a simple model that has become at once famous and infamous, the well-known hydraulic or "toilet" model, used by Konrad Lorenz in his article in Volume 4 of the *Symposia of the Society for Experimental Biology* (Lorenz, 1950). If there was any lingering doubt as to the significance of the independent thinking of the ethology school, it was presumably dispelled by the award to Lorenz, Tinbergen, and von Frisch of the Nobel Prize for Physiology and Medicine in 1973.

It is extremely apt that the Lorenz article was published in a symposium volume entitled *Physiological Mechanisms in Animal Behavior.* Ethological interpretation has been based on certain physiological principles. The relevant branch of physiology is, of course, neurophysiology. It is therefore appropriate to seek to interpret the descriptive phenomena of ethology in neurophysiological terms, and such a study would be designated "neuroethology." Reaction-specific energy and drive must have some physiological explanation, perhaps in terms of thresholds, firing frequencies, or synaptic efficacies. Releaser action must connote an interaction of specific spatiotemporal sensory inputs and a trigger, or "decision-making," population of nerve cells. The operation of a FAP is most simply achieved by the exact repetition of motor output patterns. Szenthagothai and Arbib (1974) use the term "output feature cluster" for the neural output that corresponds to a subroutine of a FAP. For ones that are inherited, genetic control of both connectivity and physiological features of relevant parts of the nervous system are implied. Some FAPs can also be learned, at least by vertebrates, and combinations of a simple inherent FAP with learning can occur, as in imprinting.

Obviously this material does not comprise the entire field of behavior. Ethology concerns itself primarily with the analysis of relatively complex acts of instinctive behavior, and not with simple reflexes, conditioned reflexes, operant conditioning, or cognitive processes. The single, most important aspect of ethological study is the inherited FAP. Much of the descriptive and analytical research on FAPs has been done on birds and insects, a happy combination of higher vertebrates and experimentally amenable invertebrates, though they also occur in mammals, including man, and other invertebrates. It seems a reasonable experimental goal to attempt to determine the neuronal basis of FAPs in suitable insects. Since the Lorenz summary of 1949 (Lorenz, 1950) I have regarded this as a very worthwhile, probably realizable, target. Its potential importance, both for ethology and for neurobiology, warrants its being the principal initial target of neuroethology. Subsidiary targets of the field include the cellular neuronal explanations of reaction-specific energy, drive, releaser, consummatory act, displacement activity, and vacuum activity. Their study will become possible when we have a detailed knowledge of some FAPs. All these phenomena occur in invertebrates that have been or probably can be brought into the realm of the practical for cellular analysis. In the course of such studies the investigator should be alert to the possiblity of encountering recurring variations in behavior during the execution of a FAP. Since genetically determined variance must provide the basis for evolutionary diversification of behavior, it follows that the discovery and analysis of any example will be of inestimable value in understanding the neural bases of behavior.

It may seem that some distinction needs to be made between simple reflex actions and FAPs, but in practice the dividing line is blurred. A true FAP in the ethological sense can always be reduced to a description in terms of a well-defined sequence of muscular contractions brought about by a discrete stimulus. However, the same applies to the scratching of a spot that is itching, which happens to be a well-known reflex. It is neither easy nor fruitful to try to define a FAP separately from reflex actions. The easiest FAPs to recognize are those which can occur spontaneously or as vacuum activities, in the absence of any external stimulations, but which perhaps require a high, internal level of a particular hormone or a particular "gestalt." Within this class the neatest are ones that have a fixed number of components but that overall are of some complexity. Yet we cannot restrict the term to endogenously generated movements. A single twitch contraction of an antennal muscle may cause an important biological signal but may also be a behaviorally irrelevant neural "noise" phenomenon. In behavior, the total context is always relevant. Only if the twitch is made with the biological "intention" of serving as a signal that in turn may cause another animal to respond, does it become of ethological relevance.

This raises questions regarding the relevance for understanding *behavior* of studies on involuntary and/or habitual activities, such as respiration or feeding movements. Are contractions of internal organs, notably the gut, the heart, and subsidiary circulatory devices, to be included in "behavior"? The act of procuring food is obviously behavior, and it may consist only of a simple act such as the periodic eversion of a proboscis. The detailed mechanics of feeding have not, however, interested ethologists, although the timing and releasing of feeding certainly have. What about sporadic events, especially locomotion – walking, swimming, or flight? Again, these are not intrinsically the stuff of ethology, but the stimuli that initiate and control them have been, and species differences are potentially interesting to neuroethologists. The musculature that subserves locomotion is also the substrate for FAPs. Furthermore, complex behavior of undoubted ethological interest is often built up out of subroutines of locomotion that are not themselves of direct interest: for example, flight machinery also causes stridulation in some grasshoppers and parts of the courtship sequence in others. The various mixes of standard subroutines are much more interesting in the behavioral context than the individual subroutines themselves. What especially interests ethologists are cases in which contraction sequences that involve components of locomotion have been put together in unique ways to subserve a specialized function: zig-zag swimming, fanning, swimming with the nose down or the tail up, and the like. The subroutines are common to large numbers of species, but the combinations are species-specific. Spiders, putting together standard locomotion and secretion modes, build characteristic webs by following procedures guided by sensory inputs. For this genetically programmed behavior to be successful, it is extremely important that a "species memory" of the appropriate sensory input be inherited, as well as the motor programs, and provide its important directing influence.

All movements of limbs, even the simplest reflexes, require the generation of neural output patterns, and surprisingly little is known about the quantitative aspects of the cellular characteristics that determine the patterns.

Even less is known about interrelationships among the neurons that control functionally related muscles. Knowledge sinks to zero when we consider how the nervous system programs different output patterns to the same muscle when it is used in different behavioral contexts.

It follows that detailed studies on motor output pattern generation for any kind of movement are likely to be of value as we work toward understanding how FAPs are controlled, how they evolve, and how genetic control fashions the developing neural circuitry.

The magnitude of the experimental effort involved in providing sufficient data for the satisfactory analysis of even one behavior of one animal is considerable. The question therefore arises as to whether or not the present fragmentary, as well as anarchistic, poke-and-hope approach applied to the whole animal kingdom, like bird shot from a blunderbuss, can be expected, with the aid of "inspired" selection or just plain luck, to provide quick and easy answers. I think not. We are blinded by our fascination with the ease of obtaining new information that our remarkably powerful electrophysiological tools permit. New preparations, providing diverse information, are appearing at a bewildering rate. Most are entertaining to those of us who love the whole animal kingdom. But almost all preparations have been chosen, especially the most popular ones, for reasons of experimental feasibility alone. The "rationalizing" process comes later. It is also already abundantly apparent that data obtained by somebody else on his pet preparation seldom affect the work one is doing on one's own. So far, in spite of the discovery of previously unknown cellular phenomena that have been discovered in invertebrate preparations, most invertebrate knowledge has become little more than parts of a not very useful information store. Referencing by prominent authors has already become minimal even across species lines, so that the one thing that might have given cohesion to the efforts has unfortunately been abandoned. There are, I submit, two reasons for this. The first is that we are not yet addressing ourselves to the more important questions. The second is that our approach is not yet sufficiently systematic. There must eventually come an end to this exploratory phase and we can only bring it about by disciplining ourselves. Sooner or later we must force ourselves to state our goals unequivocally, recognize the more worthwhile preparations, and then concentrate our efforts on them.

HOW DO WE STUDY NERVE CELL ACTION DURING BEHAVIOR?

I started my research, in 1950, with the idea that, in principle, an insect should provide the ideal subject for the study of the cellular neural substrates of behavior. The insect of my choice was the locust, part of whose behavior has been described in several of the books written since by such ethologists as Tinbergen (1951), Thorpe (1963), Hinde (1970), and Manning (1972). The behavior of this insect not only has important human and economic consequences, it is of interest to ethologist — an important criterion in making a choice of experimental subject. At that time glass capillary intracellular microelectrodes had just been brought into general use and were obviously, as they are today, the most powerful tool yet invented for neurobiologists. I learned how to use them from B. Katz and J. del Castillo and prepared to attack the locust. As I was in a laboratory that was intensively studying neuromuscular transmission, I decided to start with motor output, with the intention of gradually working into the central nervous system to try to find out how the output is programmed by the central nervous system. The first task was to establish the details of neuromuscular transmission.

Portents in this area were highly favorable; Pringle's (1939) work had shown that insect muscles were probably innervated by very few motor axons. This has turned out to be accurate, some muscles being innervated by but a single excitatory axon. In these cases, the details of the discharge pattern can easily be ascertained, for they comprise a digital sequence whose frequency controls the muscle's tension. This fortunate circumstance provided us with our first channel of communication with identified neurons during acts of normal behavior, because it proved to be easy to record these discharges while the insect went about its business. The trains can be recorded simply by implanting very fine wires (commonly 50 μm) into the muscle through the cuticle and cementing them in place with hard wax. The insect can then be set free in a large cage that permits considerable freedom of movement. The leads are brought together into a light harness on the pronotum to form a cable leading to pre-amplifiers via the top of the cage. In spite of the load, implanted insects perform the full sequence of courtship behavior, in the presence of a mature female, so that the investigator has, in effect, a window into the nervous system.

The same technique has been used to study the outputs to wing muscles of various insects during tethered flight (Kammer, 1967; Wilson, 1968a, b), of crickets during singing (Ewing and Hoyle, 1965; Bentley and Kutsch, 1966), leg muscles of locusts (Hoyle, 1964; Usherwood and Runion, 1970), and cockroaches (Pearson, 1972) during walking, running, and jumping.

The recordings serve as a starting point only for obtaining insight into the various ways in which the nervous systems program the motor output. Experimental intervention is made in a variety of ways, for example by forcing the insect to accept an added load, by removing a segment or limb, by changing environmental temperature or other external factors, by fixing a joint so as to prevent its moving, by applying forced movements, and by severing nerves providing specific sensory input. Already there is a body of literature based upon the use of the freely moving or nearly free, intact insect. There is less information than one would like, mainly because it is so difficult to make generalizations from the data.

During exploratory and routine loco-motory behavior I found that the output motor patterns are extremely variable: widely different patterns underlie even quite similar movements. But during flight or courtship behavior the movements are produced by extremely precisely repeated output patterns. What do these contradictions signify?

WHAT GENERAL PRINCIPLES MIGHT UNDERLIE BEHAVIOR CONTROL?

Before the ethologists' accounts of behavioral stereotypy it was universally assumed that behavior was due to chains of reflex actions in which the immediate sensory input causally determined the ensuing movement. The ethologists recognized that complex behavioral sequences, often merely "released" by briefly presented stimuli, can even occur spontaneously in the absence of any specific stimulus or can be elicited in times of stress by inappropriate stimuli.

Endogenous programs for the generation of behavior became an alternative possibility that had to be envisaged. But several tens of thousands of proprioceptive sense organs provide inputs for every limb, even of insects. Are they effective in some kinds of behavior but not in others involving the same limbs? And when the output is highly variable, does that mean that the animal is being subjected to constant modulation of a basically programmed output, for example, to achieve load compensation (Kennedy, 1974)? Or does it mean that the animal is programming for the achievement of temporal sensory inputs that indicate joint position, at appropriate times? Does the nervous system, then, have a series of memory stores of what inputs are appropriate to the relevant movement pattern, walking, for example, and does it constantly adjust motor output in an attempt to approximate closely to the appropriate form? Were these species memory stores inherited, and, if so, by what precise rules? By contrast, output during the execution of courtship patterns is prescribed in motor trains with precision to the ultimate level possible — the single impulse.

These apparently simple questions turn out to be surprisingly difficult to answer. In principle, there are two possible extreme ways in which an animal might deliver instructions to its muscles. At one extreme is the use of rigidly preplanned, invariant sequences of motor output patterns. Such a sequence could be produced entirely independently of sensory input once it had been initiated. All clockwork toys are models of such programming. Because there is no feedback from the ensuing movements, such a control system is termed "open-loop," or *motor-tape* control (see Hoyle, 1964). At the other extreme is motor output that is not preprogrammed at all but the direct reflex response to an immediately antecedent sensory input from the moving part. Each succeeding small step in the movement stimulates sense

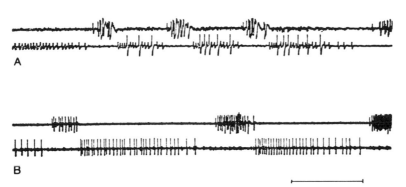

FIGURE 1. *Endogenously generated "walking" behavior in the cockroach* Periplaneta americana. *Reciprocal activity recorded from coxal levator and depressor motor nerves after removal of sensory input from leg receptors. Top traces are from levator nerve and lower traces from antagonistic depressor nerve. (A) was driven by stimulation of the lateral cercus. (B) was spontaneous. These discharges are too weak to drive walking but would do so if reinforced by positive feedback. Time: (A) 80 ms; (B) 200 ms. (From Pearson, 1972.)*

organs that activate the muscles to produce the next step. This is a closed-loop, chain-reflex system.

Between the two extremes there is a wealth of possible intermediates. A first preprogrammed sequence may control only a discrete fraction of the whole; the second fraction would be initiated only after sensory feedback results from the first; and so on. An important alternative to either of the extremes is one in which there is continuous computation of the output required to achieve the desired movement by comparison between the actual sensory input and a memory of that associated with correct performance of the relevant movements. I have termed this type of error-correcting system *sensory-tape* control.

Total deprivation of sensory input is required to test satisfactorily for the operation of a simple motor tape, and a negative result is not easily accepted because much sensory input serves as a general excitatory stimulus for the nervous system. Without it, the nervous system may lack both spontaneous and triggered activity.

Nevertheless, there is now evidence that at least a few behaviors have a strong basis in triggered motor-tape sequence. These include insect flight (Wilson, 1961) and the escape swimming FAP of *Tritonia* (Willows, Dorsett, and Hoyle, 1973a, b). Arthropod walking and swimming appear to be brought about by rather

weak, crude, motor-tape programs (Pearson, 1972); see Figure 1. The neural outputs from the motor tape are inadequate to cause the behavior unless they are reinforced by general feedback from proprioceptors that is positive (stimulatory) in nature. In addition, there may be timed negative feedback to terminate movements, especially where reciprocating antagonists are involved. Modulation, or trimming, of the reinforced output by the constant reflex action results in the final, perfected output. By contrast, patterns of neural activity generated in the isolated brain of *Tritonia* by a simple, brief train of electric stimuli applied to a cerebral nerve *of the isolated brain* exactly resemble those occurring in the intact animal during a swim evoked by contact with a starfish.

Although these may well turn out to be general principles of behavior, they are not to be found in textbooks of physiology, principally because students of mammalian movement have still not begun to think along similar lines as invertebrate neurophysiologists. They have not been influenced by the ethologists but have continued to follow Sherringtonian precepts. Almost the only experimental evidence that mammals use motor tapes has come from the work of Fentress (1972) on the grooming behavior of mice. Following denervation of both the forelimbs and the face, complete grooming movements take place at normal intervals. Even the stumps of amputated limbs perform the movements expected of the base of the limb in grooming behavior (Fentress, 1973a). The movements are relatively crude: no doubt sensory input is needed for perfect performance; but no major stage is missing, and manifestly this is the grooming behavior being turned on and played through to completion.

Most motor tapes for the endogenous control of behavior are inherited. Others are gradually developed by a trial-and-error and learning process. Even inherited tapes may be constantly modified, as a means, for example, of compensating for dynamic stress and strain changes associated with growth and development. Here we may be looking at a major function of proprioceptive sensory inputs — that is, to provide for the perfecting of the central neural program tapes. Certainly there are far too many sense organs in all animals, for their individual input to be greatly heeded during ongoing behavior. Well-studied invertebrate examples of motor-tape control of behaviors include cricket singing (Bentley and Kutsch, 1966) and grasshopper courtship (Elsner, 1973). In these cases, the output sequences are highly stereotyped, the intervals between impulses being timed to within a fraction of a millisecond and the number of impulses in a burst causing a twitch regulated to the ultimate level of the single impulse (Bentley, 1971).

By contrast, a locust climbing up a twig to reach its food source makes identical-appearing movements in sequence that nevertheless have very different impulse patterns underlying them (Hoyle, 1964). The sensory input is here playing a major role in determining output pattern details. If the insect were combining a weak motor tape for stepping with sensory reinforcement, the detailed patterns should be more similar than they are in practice. So perhaps the insect is computing continuously in this case.

Continuous computing is associated with the utilization of the alternative extreme type of control, that of the sensory-tape mode. Like the motor-tape system this requires a central store of information that is read out as a strict sequence of instruction which must be operated in real time to be useful. The evidence that there are sensory tapes that human beings can draw upon is self-evident, since memories of sensory sequences can easily be recalled into the conscious mind and utilized to control complex motor acts. The organist's trained feet and fingers flash accurately through tens of thousands of motor sequences that use combined audiovisual and proprioceptive sensory memory sequences as he plays a familiar toccata. This example represents the ultimate in sensory memory-controlled programming of motor acts. Relatively humble, but still complex counterparts exist in invertebrates, from purely inherited sensory control such as web building by spiders to the escalating program of larval feeding by digger wasps, which includes recent memory. These are also instinctive behaviors. There is a "species memory" of the appropriate sensory inputs and their sequence. The digger wasp adds to this true memories of its own environment and activities. Thus it combines inherited motor tapes with sensory tapes and 24-hour memory to achieve an instinctive act.

For complex behaviors that are learned, whether by vertebrates or invertebrates, there is a gradual perfection of the movements, and they must be constantly practiced to remain perfect. No serious studies appear to have been made on the kinds of neural processes that underlie the acquisition of these programs in invertebrates. Studies on the learning of motor tasks by primates, including man, suggest that animals rely heavily on sensory input to control new movements during acquisition, but that as they learn they shift progressively toward using motor-tape programs triggered by the appropriate stimulus.

General neurobiology is interested in these special problems, but its primary concern can be only with what the examples taken from different classes of animal share in common. Of course, in advance of a great deal of detailed knowledge about diverse invertebrate systems we cannot begin to be aware of what they might be. It has already been accepted that sodium—potassium current-switching channels form the universal basis for nerve-impulse propagation and that the quantal release of an enzymatically rapidly destroyed depolarizing chemical from terminals presynaptic to skeletal muscles is the universal mechanism for causing them to contract phasically. But that is more or less all that we have as general principles of neurobiology thus far; we have none at all yet for neuroethology.

STRATEGIES FOR THE FUTURE

The need, then, seems to be for eclecticism, as Bullock (1965) has strongly argued. Such an approach should work well as long as a sufficiently large number of people devote themselves to the field. Fortunately for this approach, which appears to have been adopted by most workers in the field, neurobiology has become phenomenally popular, and is growing at a fantastic rate. We do not know what the future will bring, but for the next few years, at least, some few hundred investigators around the world are well placed to tackle current problems in the field. At the time that Mel Cohen, Don Maynard, and I were planning our strategies, however, fewer than a score of persons was available to work on invertebrate preparations, and for all we knew it would always be thus. Faced with the enormous magnitude of the task, and the small size of the initial task force, I suggested that we should first seek a single "compromise" invertebrate that was as close to ideal as available and then agree to concentrate our limited experimental resources on various parts of it. This would have been analogous to the remarkably successful effort led by T. H. Morgan on *Drosophila* genetics in the 1920s and 1930s. Unfortunately for this approach, a *"Drosophila"* of neurobiology that was universally acceptable could not be found. Either that, or our field has lacked a leader with the powers that Morgan exerted on behalf of *Drosophila!*

The advantages of such a unified approach would have been manifold. It will be argued below that the first requirement for serious progress is a location map of identified neurons that are available to intracellular electrodes. For the classes of phenomena that must be studied, a detailed knowledge of mechanisms at the cellular level is demanded by an audience so comfortably familiar with cellular processes in axons and synapses. Leaders in the neurobiological sciences now must prepare the way for the training of, and the establishment of

long-term job security for, dedicated neuroscientists willing and able to work with identified cells for many years at a time. The new breed of electrode pushers must get to the point where they can plan to record simultaneously from three or more identified neurons, with a high probability of success.

The situation for the future of vertebrate studies is essentially similar, though in many respects worse. The most universally admired studies of recent years have been made by proceeding along essentially similar lines, not by identified-neuron work, which is possible only for the Mauthner cells, but by studies on specific cell types effectively isolated by anatomical considerations. We may single out, for example, analyses of the retina (Werblin and Dowling, 1969), the visual cortex (Hubel and Wiesel, 1968), the cerebellum (Eccles, 1973), and the olfactory bulb (Shepherd, 1972a).

The one advantage of vertebrate nervous systems is the multiplication of cell types: most of their individual neurons are not of critical importance, as they are in arthropods and mollusks. At the same time, the sheer volume of the nervous system makes many neuron types inaccessible to electrodes. Intracellular electrode studies are possible only for the small numbers of cell types present in relatively thin, peripherally located, layers. The more significant of the invertebrate findings of the last decade have all been dramatic and they should have had an influence on vertebrate studies as a whole, but there is as yet no evidence of this. Neuroscientists should bear in mind that *general principles* of neurobiological organization and cellular neuronal function are, by definition, those that apply to both the majority of invertebrates *and* to vertebrate animals.

Nevertheless it is unwarranted to believe *a priori* that vertebrate nervous systems function differently, in principle, from those of invertebrates. There are doubtless patterns of connectivity ("hardware") and system ("software") functions that are peculiar to specific invertebrates and specific vertebrates, or even to invertebrates as a whole or vertebrates as a whole, that therefore possess a restricted degree of generality. Students of exclusively vertebrate neurobiology are now seeking principles to collate the rapidly growing body of detailed information about selected neural elements. As evidence for their continuing lack of understanding of the principles both of ethology and of comparative neurobiology we may quote the "general principles for adaptive interaction of a complex system with its environment" enunciated by Szentagothai and Arbib (1974). *Principle 1*: Theory must be action-oriented. *Principle 2*: Perception is not only of "what" but also of "where." *Principle 3:* An adaptive system must be able to correlate sensory data and actions in such a way as to update an internal model of the world. *Principle 4*: Organization must be hierarchical with adequate "feedback loops" to coordinate the subsystems. *Principle 5*: The brain is a layered somatotopic computer.

With the first principle, as broadly conceived, we must concur. It is certainly the most important. Organisms can survive only in so far as they have inherited biologically useful reflexes and FAPs (Principle 1) that can be turned on in response to specific stimuli or environmental patterns. But they must also turn them on spontaneously. Without spontaneous intrinsic acts there can be no basis for behavior. Principle 2 is relevant only to free-living organisms with sophisticated visual or chemical sensory systems, and of course, perception is not applicable to most animals. The first part of Principle 4 is probably not true for most invertebrates, in which local ganglia operate independently and are only marginally influenced by others. The second part is only partly true. Feedback loops may improve the coordination of subsystems, but they may also be a hindrance to the execution of centrally programmed behavior. One reason is that they introduce a large requirement for information processing. At first, in evolution, nervous systems cannot possibly have provided the computing power. The feedback systems and the computing power must evolve in parallel. Second, signaling and data processing take time. One reason for efferent inhibitory output to proprioceptors is that the animals need to be able to shut off their complex inputs so that they do not interfere with simple command outputs. Open-loop coordinated commands provide the essence of quick action. Even higher animals that have both feedback systems

and learning mechanisms available to them use both to perfect simple motor tapes for important action patterns rather than continuous computing. The detailed functioning of invertebrate nervous systems shows that they employ a large number of parallel subsystems rather than a hierarchy.

Flexible computing and learning (Principle 3) have been able to advance only by superimposing these luxuries on the basics. Principle 3 essentially states that memory will be used if available. This point should be subdivided to indicate the important distinction between sequences of sensory memory and motor-tape memory, and their different roles in controlling behavior.

As a list of principles that applies broadly to invertebrates as well as vertebrates, I propose the following. *Principle 1*: Biologically useful actions must be generated spontaneously. *Principle 2*: Environmental inputs must be used to select appropriate FAPs from the animal's repertoire. *Principle 3*: Ongoing proprioception will be used to reinforce and improve the performance of FAPs. *Principle 4*: Species memory, or experiential memory of sensory sequences, will be used, if available, as a basis for computing motor output by comparison between actual input and stored input. *Principle 5*: Sensory (i.e., reference) input will be used to improve inherited or experientially developed motor output, pattern generation mechanisms (i.e., motor tapes and sensory tapes). *Principle 6*: Variation must occur in FAPs to permit evolution of nervous systems and behavior.

IDENTIFIED NEURONS AND BEHAVIOR

Let us recognize that wherever progress has been made in the last decade, it can be related to the use of identified neurons in invertebrates, and to studies of specified cell types in narrowly prescribed locations in vertebrates, which is equivalent. The pioneering invertebrate studies were those of Wiersma (1958) on interneurons of the connectives of the crayfish and the detailed analyses of the crayfish cord interneurons by Kennedy and Preston (1960). Wiersma realized that the large interneurons passing through the connectives of the crayfish can be studied selectively, mainly because their locations are constant in different specimens. But they are also recognizable either by the characteristic discharges that they carry when various sensory modalities are excited or by characteristic movements that some of them produce when stimulated. Some of these movements were clearly identifiable with normal behaviors of the crayfish, especially the startle response produced by the neuron termed by Wiersma, "Sherrington's interneuron." Such neurons are now called command interneurons. It is widely assumed that they must be pathways by which the brain actually causes the appropriate movement to occur. Command interneurons are now known that promote walking movements, both forward and backward, swimmeret beating (Bowerman and Larimer, 1974a, b), and stridulation in crickets (Bentley, personal communication).

A major weakness is that it has not yet been shown for any of the known command neurons that they are indeed the pathways via which the brain activates movements in the whole animal. This should not be too difficult to demonstrate technically; in the meantime, however, it remains a key question. For the lobster swimmeret system there is more than one neuron that can promote swimming (Davis and Kennedy, 1972). The majority of neurons cause movements only as long as they are stimulated. Another gives rise to a long sequence of movements following but a single brief burst. Because much behavior of ethological interest consists of relatively long-lasting output after but a brief presentation of a "releasing" stimulus, this phenomenon might serve as a neuroethological model.

In any event the discovery of these interneurons should have led to follow-up studies of both (1) the way in which natural sensory input leads to their firing, at the input, and (2) the way in which they cause coordinated motoneuron activation at the other end. There seem to be experimental difficulties in the way of making intracellular studies in crustaceans. Initial great success with identified motoneurons of the lobster by Davis (1969a, b, c, 1970, 1971) seems to hold much promise for cellular analysis of behavior.

The extreme demands of an integrated attack on arthropods will cause many investigators to "fall by the wayside," because it is extremely frustrating not to be able to see directly the nerve cell that one wants to record from. Even the most accurate neuron map is a crude guide when the cells are not pigmented, and a tough nerve sheath must either first be removed or directly penetrated by the ultra-fragile electrode tip, before the chance to record is taken. We now have a good test case for assessing the probability of success with an identified neuron. The soma of the locust metathoracic anterior adductor coxa (AAdC) was located and mapped as a result of penetrations and dye fillings in three preparations by Burrows and myself (Burrows and Hoyle, 1973). This 35-μm-diameter neuron is of special interest physiologically since it is tonically active and its firing rate can be raised or lowered by operant conditioning (Hoyle, 1965).

It has also afforded us a valuable opportunity to examine seriously the prospect for a detailed study of a specified, relatively small, invisible neuron. Marjorie Woollacott, whose thesis research involved pioneering a molluscan (visible) identified-neuron preparation (Woollacott, 1974), chose to study AAdC systematically in our laboratory, for an analysis of the basis of the learning phenomenon. She lacks neither skill nor patience, and now for two years she has attempted each day to record from this neuron, making an average of two preparations a day. Her success rate has peaked at two preparations a day but averages two to three per week, a figure that must now be taken as a probable upper limit for even a highly skilled and well-motivated identified-neuron specialist seeking to work with one small, selected, invisible neuron. Only some very large motoneurons, such as the fast extensor or flight neurons, are easier to work with than this. Many of the locust neurons will be much harder. When the time comes for combining penetration of this neuron with identified interneurons that synapse with it, the probability of success will go down dramatically.

Yet, for the serious participant in neuroethology no other way is possible and the success rate is clearly adequate for eventual scientific success. Information at the cellular level is essential if we are fully to understand the neurophysiology of FAPs.

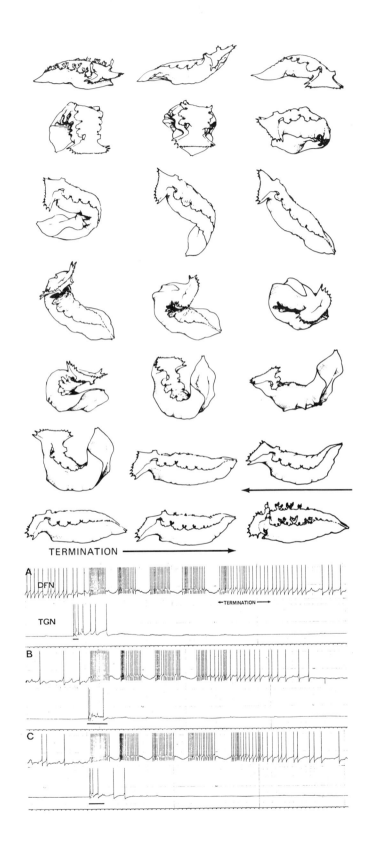

One behavioral act that I consider definitely to be a complex FAP in the ethological sense has been studied in an animal that also permits recording from relevant neurons intracellularly during behavior. This is the highly stereotyped escape swim, in response to a brief touch from certain species of starfish, of the nudibranch mollusk *Tritonia diomedia*. Also, Kater (1974) has recently applied the term FAP to the feeding behavior of a pulmonate snail, and analyzed it intracellularly. It may be that this type of vegetative act and indeed all cyclical behavior that subserves visceral activity require a different designation.

The behavior of *Tritonia* is not simply a succession of cyclical movements. It has a beginning and an end, each associated with complex, coordinated changes in posture. The characteristic, complex termination sequence occurs, as it were, in midswim, after a prescribed number of dorsoventral flexion cycles has been completed (Figure 2). Recently, a second swimming nudibranch, *Melibe*, has been brought into a similar analytical situation (Thompson, 1974). This creature shows simply a long sequence of dorsoventral swimming flexions in response to a brief chemical stimulus. The sequence stops only when the foot touches a solid object. The contrast with the briefer, but more complex, escape swimming behavior of *Tritonia* illustrates how a FAP may evolve. A principal, but simple, additional event has been added — an endogenous termination by *Tritonia* to a program otherwise terminated by a reflex action.

Willows and Dorsett (1975) have been able to make detailed comparisons between a North Atlantic species, *T. hombergi*, and the North Pacific *T. diomedia*. They point to the availability of at least six *Tritonia* species, so that a picture of the adaptive radiation at the neuroanatomical—physiological level may eventually be obtained. Many of the large neurons in the brain can be homologized with reasonable confidence on the basis of morphology alone. It is much more difficult to initiate an escape swim at all in *T. hombergi*, and this could be attributed to a combination in *hombergi* of fewer neurons in the trigger group (TGNs) and electrical coupling between the TGNs and their neighboring cells that somehow reduces the probability of their firing synchronously. TGNs in effect make the decision to turn on swimming by a synchronous spike in many neurons of the group. *T. hombergi*, like *T. diomedia*, has an active termination, but it is not obligatorily a dorsal flexion, as it is in the latter; 25 percent of cases examined ended in a ventral flexion. Unfortunately, this part of the behavior is one that is not yet understood in terms of underlying cellular mechanisms in *Tritonia*, but it is being worked on and once it is known we shall have a clue to a means by which evolution of a behavior mechanism has occurred. In order to understand it we must be able to determine the cause of the termination sequence. This does seem to be explicable on the basis of the connectivity and physiological properties of known neurons and so may be due to the intervention of specific neurons that remain to

---

FIGURE 2.   Top. *Escape swimming in* Tritonia diomedia. *An example of a strictly endogenously determined FAP in an invertebrate, for which the cellular neurophysiological basis is being intensively studied with intracellular recording. The behavior occurs spontaneously only rarely but can be evoked repeatedly simply by touching with certain starfish, or by dropping sea salt crystals on the animal. Behavior consists of an exactly repeated sequence, starting with preparation, followed by a series of flexions, beginning with a dorsal one. There is also a distinctive termination sequence comprising two weak dorsal flexions without ventral counterpart. Bottom: Patterned activity similar to that occurring in the same nerve cells in the intact animal during the swimming behavior shown above, but here recorded from the isolated brain. Simultaneous recordings were made intracellularly from a dorsal flexion neuron (DFN) and a trigger group neuron (TGN) (terminology of Willows, Dorsett and Hoyle, 1973) during three sequences (A, B, C) elicited by electrical stimulation of the nerve from the oral veil. Periods of stimulation are indicated by bars. Note the similarity of the details of the burst patterns. (From Hoyle, 1975.)*

be discovered. Again, this points out the need for a more complete knowledge of the functional roles of specific brain neurons.

In so many ways the optimal choice of organism for the concerted cellular attack that I advocate still seems to be an insect. It already seemed possible from the pioneering histological work of Zawarzin (1924) that at least some of the neurons of the large insects would permit the use of intracellular electrodes, and that the cell bodies probably had precise morphologies and cell body locations, so that cellular mapping, so important in principle for a serious neuroethological study, would be possible. In 1953, I made microelectrode penetrations of locust motoneurons, recording resting potentials of about 60 mV. But the neurons seemed to be dismally disappointing because they never gave the nice, overshooting action potentials that Eccles was finding in the ventral horn cells of the cat spinal cord. It was almost 20 years before I returned to the pitifully small active responses visible in these cells and found that they could be very useful after all (Hoyle, 1970; Hoyle and Burrows, 1973a, b).

In other respects the locust turned out to be admirable. The innervation pattern of functionally important muscles was simple, in many instances consisting of but a single or a pair of excitatory axons. The discharge could be picked up as a single train by simply inserting a fine wire into a muscle. The insect is so strong and its cuticle so tough that several of these leads could be inserted at the same time into a single insect, which could then be released. As it went about its business it gave off an accurate, quantitative, easily analyzable record of the firing patterns of its motoneurons. The ultimate success with this invaluable but simple technique has been achieved by Norbert Elsner, in Cologne, who implanted 30 fine-wire leads into different muscles of a male grasshopper barely 2.5 cm long (Elsner, 1968, 1973); see Figure 3. The insect is able, in spite of his load of wires, to make perfectly normal courtship movements and associated stridulatory songs. In the case of *Gomphocerippus rufus* and *Stenobothrus rubicundis* these courtship patterns are highly complex, representing a marked evolutionary advance over simple song patterns such as are displayed by the domestic crickets *Acheta* and *Gryllus*.

FIGURE 3. *Inch-long male grasshopper* Stenobothrus rubicundis, *with 30 fine-wire leads implanted in muscles to record electromyographic activity during courtship behavior. (Courtesy of N. Elsner.)*

A sequence for *Gomphocerippus* is an extraordinarily complex and beautiful FAP that starts with gentle head rocking and weak stridulation, proceeds through strong head rocking, and ends with a violent backward flick of the antennae and a loud song. A suitor cricket will play back this motor tape over and over to even the most unresponsive female, until either she consents to mate or he is exhausted by his frustrated efforts. He never uses a subroutine of this sequence in another context, or by itself, or in a sequence of different order. He does not try to force his attentions upon the female until she is good and ready. Contrast this superbly polite behavior with that of the Florida lubber grasshopper, *Romalea microptera*. When a mature male spots a mature female in his vicinity, he stalks her for a while, at a distance of 8 to 10 inches, then, at *his* convenience, makes a carefully calculated leap from the side or the rear that lands him squarely upon her back. A furious rocking movement follows. Whether this is a result of excitement, is part of the courtship pattern, or represents the attempt of the unwilling female to unseat the male has not been determined. But such represents the range of behavior patterns shown by different species of grasshopper. There is a wide range of analyzable behaviors in locusts, grasshoppers, and crickets. The analysis of representative types at the neurophysiological level is full of dramatic potential. The easily recorded myographs are already providing complete data about identified-neuron functions — the final common paths. An example of the myographic activity of muscles that cause stridulation in a *Gomphocerippus* courtship sequence, from Elsner's (1968) elegant work, is shown in Figure 4. Elsner has recently coined the nice descriptive term *ethogram* to designate these recordings made during natural behavior (Elsner, 1975).

The next step is extension of the work technically to a condition in which the ganglia are exposed and several intracellular electrodes are inserted into the relevant central nerve cells during the behavior. This is not an unrealizable dream; it was already achieved in part six years ago by David Bentley (1969) in a specimen of *Gryllus campestris*. He induced a single male cricket to sing continually by a fortunate brain lesion. It is now known how to produce these lesions routinely, though further studies have not yet been made. Hoyle and Burrows (1973a, b) started to identify neurons in *Schist-ocerca gregaria* ganglia systematically, starting with motoneurons. At the time of this writing, 185 neurons have been identified, including some inhibitory neurons and several inter-neurons (Hoyle, 1975). This work opens up the possibility that relatively complete cellular mapping and circuit analysis may now be feasible for selected insects. Examples of simultaneous recordings from three identified neurons by means of intracellular electrodes, are shown in Figure 5. Given sufficient skilled, highly motivated manpower and enough time, thorough analyses of both the anatomical networks and the dynamic integration could doubtless be made. Limited intracellular recording may also be achieved in the nearly intact, walking insect, from dorsal neurons of the brain and thoracic ganglia (Figure 6).

CONCLUSIONS

We now face a type of scientific problem new to man. Of primary importance is that issues be faced squarely instead of skirted. The

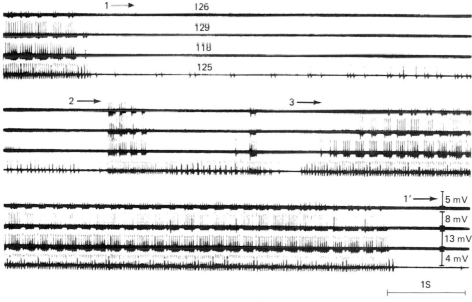

FIGURE 4.   *Excerpt from a recording of electromyograms of four flight muscles involved in a courtship pattern that includes singing — in male grasshopper* Gomphocerippus rufus. *Preparation was similar to that shown in Figure 3. A single, complete sequence is shown comprised of 3 subunits, 1, 2 and 3. It is repeated with exactly the same pattern, until the female shows interest. Numbers refer to specific muscles recorded. (From N. Elsner, 1968.)*

principal question is where, among 1.5 million species, the investigator should concentrate his efforts to resolve the questions of the neuronal bases of behavior. In Table I, I have compiled a "Michelin" guide to the animal kingdom for budding neuroethologists. In this guide, major animal groups are listed, and for each an assessment is made of categories relevant to neuroethology. Ratings are awarded on a scale from zero through five.

The list speaks for itself: larger insects qualify as most useful, receiving almost twice the number of pluses as birds, which are in second place, and gastropod mollusks, in third place. Although the majority of practicing neurobiologists feel that they should continue to study mammals rather than join the search for cellular integrative principles in invertebrates, an understanding of the full cellular details of intercellular communication during behavior is absolutely essential. Any other approach leads to the use of mere guesswork in interpretation and will be neither intellectually satisfying nor universally acceptable.

Questions will certainly arise as to the stage in accumulation of knowledge at which generalizations may be justly claimed. For example,

Aplysiologists were the first to obtain connectivity data, owing to the ease of working with *Aplysia*'s visceral ganglion cells. Once their findings can be proved to apply also to an arthropod ganglion, they can begin to gain acceptance as useful generalities. Certainly any potential claimant to the general, in either connectivity or physiological function, will have to be found in diverse phyla before it will be widely heeded. The pursuit is, in principle, very different from that in *Drosophila* genetics, because there is so much greater possibility of variation at the grosser morphological level represented by neural connectivity than at the level of cellular components represented by chromosomes. Both convergence – a similar function being served by different networks – and divergence – different functions being served by similar networks – already seem probable in nervous systems.

Students of exclusively vertebrate neurobiology should not fall into the trap, as they have in recent years, of closing their minds to principles derived solely from work on invertebrate animals. Otherwise, they may have to wait a long time before they have any "rules" to go by!

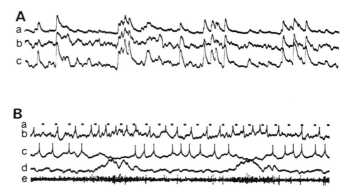

FIGURE 5.   *Excerpts from triple intracellular electrode recordings made from neuron somata of the locust* Schistocerca gregaria *during spontaneous activities. The recordings illustrate the potential for directly analyzing the neural mechanisms that underlie behavior. (A) Three fast-flexor tibiae motoneurons that are sometimes activated synergistically, sometimes independently. (B) a: time marks, 10 Hz; b: metathoracic expiratory ventilatory neuron; c: metathoracic inspiratory ventilatory neuron; d: wing elevator (tergosternal) neuron in mesothoracic ganglion; e: extracellular from thoracic–abdominal connective. The recording shows that excitatory input to a motoneuron can occur in synchrony with respiratory movements. [(A), courtesy of M. Burrows and A. Horridge; (B), courtesy of M. Burrows.]*

TABLE I

GUIDE TO THE OVERALL MERITS OF THE MAJOR ANIMAL GROUPS FOR STUDYING THE NEUROPHYSIOLOGICAL BASES OF BEHAVIOR. VALUE JUDGMENTS WERE OBTAINED BY QUESTIONING ADVANCED GRADUATE AND POSTDOCTORAL STUDENTS.

EXPERIMENTAL UTILITY

ANIMAL GROUP	Significance at a practical level for mankind	Individually identifiable central neurons (or vertebrate equivalent)	Intracellular analysis possible in whole animal during behavior	Intracellular analysis possible in isolated nervous system	Rich behavioral repertoire	Capability for plasticity (learning)	Possibility of chemical analysis of neurons	Breeding and genetic manipulation possible	Developmental stages accessible for experimentation	Animal easily obtained and maintained in lab	Analyzability of peripheral motor output pattern	Analyzability of sensory input	TOTAL MERIT POINTS for neuroethology
Primates	+++++	+	−	−	+++++	++	−	−	+	+	+	+	22
Other mammals	++++	++	−	−	+++	+++	+	+	++	+	++	++	24
Birds	+++	+	−	−	+++++	++	++	++++	++++	+	+	+	26
Reptiles	++	+	−	−	+	+++	+	−	++++	+	+	+	17
Amphibia	++	++	−	−	+	+	+	++	++++	+	++	++	22
Fish	++	+	+	+	++	+	++	+−	++++	+	+	+	21
Cephalopod mollusks	+	−	−	−	+++	+	−	−	+	−	+	−	8
Larger insects	+++	++++	+++	++	+++	++	++++	+++	+++++	+++++	+++	+++	43
Crustacea	++	++	++	++	+	+++	−	−	+++	+++++	+++	+++	23
Gastropod mollusks	+	+++	++++	++++	+	+++	+	+	+++	−	++	++	25
Smaller insects	++	−	−	−	++++	−	++++	−	++++	−	−	−	18
Annelids	++	+++	++	++	+	+	−	−	+++	+	++	++	19
Platyhelminthes	++	−	−	−	+	−	++	+	++++	−	−	−	11
Coelenterates	−	−	−	−	++	−	−	−	++	−	−	−	4

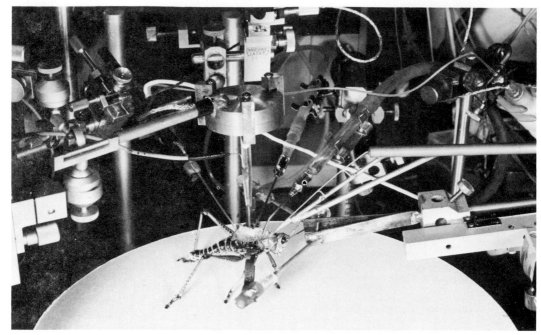

FIGURE 6.   *Intracellular recording during behavior of the Florida lubber grasshopper,* Romalea microptera. *In spite of the operation and removal of the heart and gut, the nervous system is still intact and limited behavior occurs.*

Many neuroscientists, even those working on invertebrate ganglia, consider their long-range goal to be the understanding of the human nervous system. With man but one species of animal among more than a million, this is most certainly not the goal of neurobiology at large. The important point to understand about research on an invertebrate nervous system is that in no case can it be considered de facto to serve as a model for what may be happening in vertebrates. Yet invertebrates will yield invaluable information. Sheer volume of the nervous systems of vertebrate animals, as well as astronomical numbers and inaccessibility of nerve cells, renders impossible the discrete cellular-level understanding of integration already being obtained for selected invertebrates.

CHAPTER THREE

Cellular Events in the Evolution of Behavior

MELVIN J. COHEN

INTRODUCTION

The relationship between neural organization and behavior was a central theme around which Don Maynard organized his life's work. In the hours of discussion that we had on this topic, starting as graduate students in T. H. Bullock's laboratory in the early 1950s, I can look back through the many arguments to what we both felt were essential requisites of a preparation for the examination of this problem: (1) the system should have a relatively small number of identifiable cells; (2) the cells should be open to electrical recording to permit the determination of the synaptic relationships between all the members of the group; and (3) the system should have a readily monitored output and the output should be open to modification from sources outside the immediate preparation. The classic preparations of the crustacean cardiac and stomatogastric ganglia developed by Don Maynard meet these requirements and are models for the study of simple integrative neural systems.

The functional synaptic relationships between identified cells are what Maynard's studies most beautifully illustrate. In this chapter I shall extend the examination of such identified systems into the structural realm, and particularly into the area of dendritic form. The enormously varied and complex structure of nerve cells, as manifest in the form of their dendritic arborizations, is intuitively felt to underlie the great variety of behavior generated by systems of neurons throughout the animal kingdom. Traditionally, the structure of the mature central nervous system has been considered rigid, and this stability of form has been related to stability of function. Within the lifetime of an individual, the stability of behavioral response may range from simple monosynaptic reflexes to the complex sequential behavioral patterns involved in courtship or the defense of territory. There is evidence for genetic stability where the same behavioral pattern appears from one generation to the next within members of a species (Bentley, 1971). The genetic component may extend

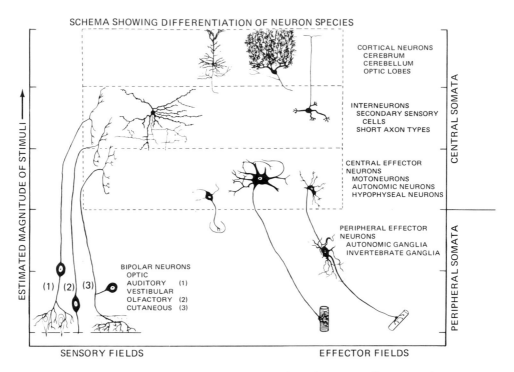

SCHEMA SHOWING DIFFERENTIATION OF NEURON SPECIES

ESTIMATED MAGNITUDE OF STIMULI

CENTRAL SOMATA

PERIPHERAL SOMATA

CORTICAL NEURONS
CEREBRUM
CEREBELLUM
OPTIC LOBES

INTERNEURONS
SECONDARY SENSORY
CELLS
SHORT AXON TYPES

CENTRAL EFFECTOR
NEURONS
MOTONEURONS
AUTONOMIC NEURONS
HYPOPHYSEAL NEURONS

PERIPHERAL EFFECTOR
NEURONS
AUTONOMIC GANGLIA
INVERTEBRATE GANGLIA

BIPOLAR NEURONS
OPTIC
AUDITORY   (1)
VESTIBULAR
OLFACTORY   (2)
CUTANEOUS   (3)

(1) (2) (3)

SENSORY FIELDS   EFFECTOR FIELDS

FIGURE 1.   *Summary of various neuron types found in the mammalian central nervous system. Note the variety and extent of the dendritic expansions that emerge from the cell bodies. (Modified from Bodian, 1967.)*

through phylogeny, as seen in the similarity of behavioral patterns exhibited by different but related taxonomic groups. A most striking demonstration of this is seen in the extraordinary likeness shown in certain aspects of social behavior for apes and man (van Lawick-Goodall, 1971).

In contrast to this stable aspect of the nervous system that may persist through phylogeny, there is the flickering network of neural activity made up from events of milliseconds in duration. This phase encompasses a series of changes that range from the molecular level through the integrated behavior of the entire organism. Action potentials wax and wane followed by transmitter release; there may ensue, within a fraction of a second, rapid movement of the whole animal, or a thought that reaches consciousness and then subsides.

These two aspects of neural function, stability and plasticity, may come together in a learned response, in which the behavior is modified as a result of a particular input. The newly acquired behavior is then stabilized and persists over the lifetime of the individual. The nature of this link between the transient events of synaptic transmission and the more stable parameters of neuron function has thus far proved elusive. However, one feels that it must manifest itself at some level within the synaptic connections of the dendritic tree. Understanding any of the factors that influence the form and stability of the dendritic tree may therefore go far in helping us understand the neural basis of both fixed and plastic behavior.

Our approach assumes that any major change that can be induced in dendrites and systematically examined may provide a clue to the neural substrate of behavior. We have investigated the response of dendrites in a variety of identified central neurons to factors known to affect dendritic structure and function such as axotomy and deafferentation. We have also asked whether a phylogenetic approach that makes use of known differences in behavioral potential as well as in the form of

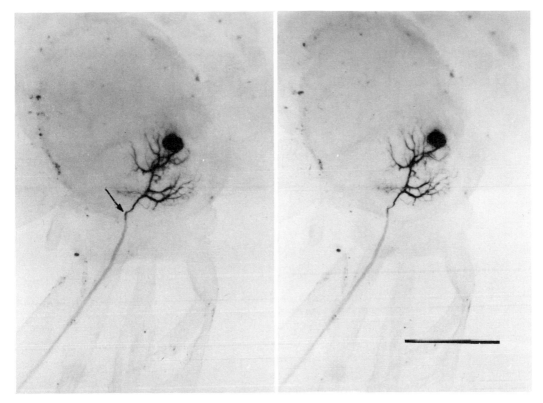

FIGURE 2. *Stereophotographs of the metathoracic ganglion of the cockroach* Periplaneta americana *show a motoneuron stained by iontophoretic injection of cobalt into the cell body. Dorsal view of the cleared wholemount. The ventrally placed soma is seen through the entire depth of the ganglion with the initial neurite running vertically toward the dorsal surface. The medial and lateral branches of the dendritic tree are seen throughout the 1-mm depth of the ganglion. The axon leaves the ganglion via nerve 5 at the point indicated by the arrow. Calibration: 0.5 mm. (Modified from Pitman, Tweedle, and Cohen, 1972a.)*

nerve cells may give us some idea of how the fixed and labile facets of neural function interact. Comparisons have been made between invertebrate and vertebrate central neurons with most of the information coming from arthropods and mammals. Recently we have examined central neurons of a relatively primitive vertebrate, the lamprey. The lamprey central neurons appear intermediate between the nerve cells of invertebrates and the higher vertebrates in that they share some characteristics of each group. In addition, their dendritic trees show a remarkable anatomical plasticity under certain experimental conditions, and it is to these particular dendritic changes

and their possible implications in the evolution of behavioral plasticity that the major part of this essay is addressed.

GENERAL COMPARISONS BETWEEN INVERTEBRATE AND HIGHER VERTEBRATE CENTRAL NEURONS

Several papers have dealt with the comparison between invertebrate and vertebrate central neurons in the past few years and only the major points of their arguments will be outlined here (Bullock and Horridge, 1965; Cohen, 1967a, 1970, 1974; Bullock, 1974).

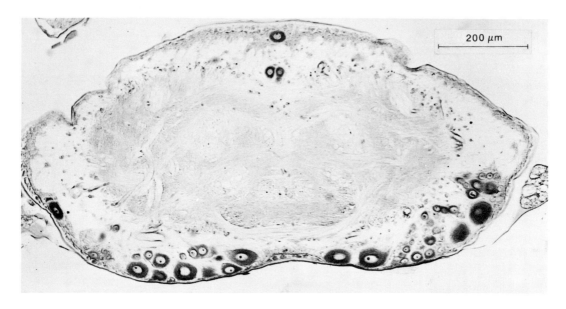

FIGURE 3. *Transverse section through the metathoracic ganglion of the cockroach* Periplaneta americana. *Note the peripheral distribution of nerve cell bodies and their absence in the central neuropil region. (From Cohen and Jacklet, 1967.)*

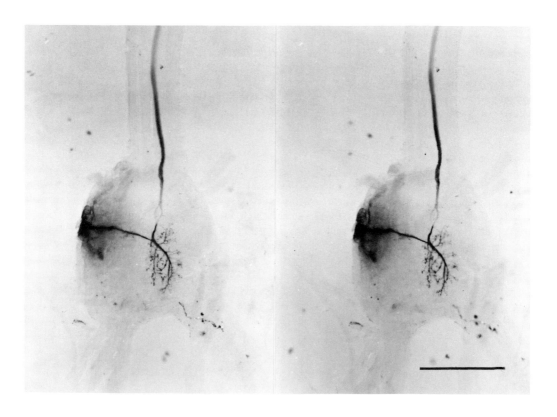

The Location of the Cell Body

A summary of neuron types found in higher vertebrates is shown in Figure 1 (Bodian, 1967). The highly branched dendritic tree that emanates from the cell body is characteristic of the vertebrate interneurons and effector neurons. In contrast, typical invertebrate central neurons are seen in Figures 2 and 4. The cell body is devoid of dendrites, and only a single neurite projects from the soma toward the core of the ganglion, where it branches extensively in the neuropile to form the dendritic tree. The axon then emerges from the dendritic tree. This neuron type differs fundamentally from the vertebrate central neuron in that the neuron soma is physically removed from the area of synaptic input and impulse initiation. In many instances the cell body is only slightly invaded electrotonically by either synaptic activity or the propagated impulse (Pitman, Tweedle, and Cohen, 1972b). This isolation of the soma from the sites of electrochemical activity is further demonstrated in Figure 3, where a cross section of a thoracic ganglion in the cockroach *Periplaneta americana* shows the cell bodies located round the periphery of the ganglion with the central regions of neuropile devoid of neuron somata.

The argument has been made (Cohen, 1970) that the multipolar and heteropolar attributes of the vertebrate central neuron place the soma, with its genetic apparatus that controls macromolecular synthesis, squarely in the path of the electrochemical events associated with synaptic transmission. This provides at least the possibility that some facet of synaptic transmission may affect the genetic apparatus and may be more permanently registered in the neuron by an induced change in macromolecular synthesis. Thus the basic configuration of the vertebrate central neuron may be responsible for the ability of selected regions of the vertebrate central nervous system to store some sign of their past activity and thereby modify subsequent behavior. In contrast, the monopolar configuration of the typical invertebrate central neuron places the soma far removed from the sites of synaptic transmission. In such a system there may be little opportunity for the genetic apparatus to be exposed to the events of transient neural activity, and the subsequent behavior of the organism may therefore be little influenced by past neural events. Thus the dominant thrust within the invertebrates has been toward complex but highly stereotyped behavioral patterns that tend to change little during the lifetime of the individual. Within the higher vertebrates, on the other hand, we see the remarkable capacity to modify behavior during the lifetime of the individual. This may be due in significant measure to the ability of the genetic apparatus of certain vertebrate neurons to encode molecularly some sign of past synaptic activity as a result of the strategic location of the genetic material within the cell body.

Dendritic Stability

This divergent evolutionary thrust that leads toward rigid stereotyped behavior in the invertebrates and to the highly plastic behavioral potential of the mammals may be reflected in the relative stability of the dendritic trees in the neurons of these two groups. The form of the dendritic tree in vertebrate central neurons is known to be affected either by removing presynaptic input (deafferentation) or by cutting the axon. Cerf and Chacko (1958) found a decrease in the number and diameter of dendrites of frog motoneurons following axotomy. A decrease in the dendritic spread of hypoglossal neurons in the rat after axon section has also been

---

FIGURE 4.   *Stereophotographs of the sixth abdominal ganglion in the cockroach* Periplaneta americana *show a giant fiber stained by iontophoretic injection of cobalt. Wholemount preparation shows the giant fiber running anteriorly toward the top of the picture in the right neural connective between the sixth and fifth abdominal ganglia. The cell body lies at the left edge of the ganglion and sends its initial neurite across the midline of the ganglion. A posterior branch of the initial neurite gives rise to the main dendritic tree of this neuron. Calibration: 0.5 mm. (Modified from Pitman, Tweedle, and Cohen, 1973.)*

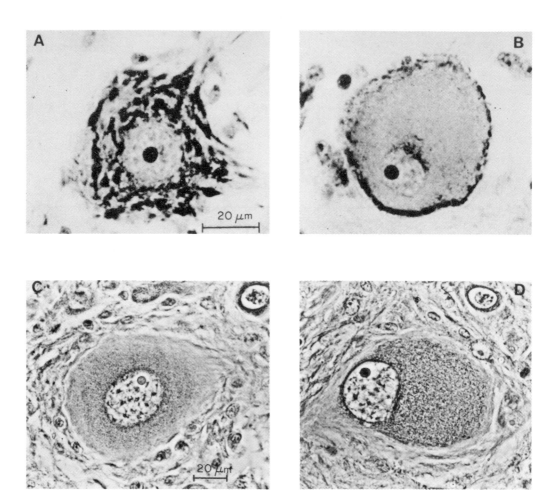

FIGURE 5. *Comparison of the response to axon section in central neurons of a rhesus monkey (A and B) and a cockroach (C and D). (A) Normal ventral horn cell shows the aggregates of Nissl bodies in the cytoplasm. (B) Ventral horn cell 7 days after axon section. Chromatolysis is indicated by the lack of Nissl bodies and the eccentric position of the nucleus. (C) and (D) are bilaterally matched cells from the same ganglion. (C) Normal cell with a uniform cytoplasmic basiphilia and a centrally located nucleus. (D) Cell with axon cut 4 weeks prior to fixation. The perinuclear basiphilic ring has already formed and then dispersed, but the nucleus has remained in an eccentric position. [Plate from Cohen, 1967a. (A) and (B) modified from Bodian and Mellors, 1945; (C) and (D) from Cohen and Jacklet, 1967.]*

reported (Sumner and Watson, 1971; Sumner and Sutherland, 1973). Other workers have reported a decrease in the number and length of dendrites after deafferentation of the cortex (Cowan, 1970; Jones and Thomas, 1962) or the olfactory bulb (Mathews and Powell, 1962). In contrast, studies on arthropod central neurons indicate that axotomy or deafferentation have no effect on the dendritic tree as examined with the light microscope. Tweedle, Pitman, and Cohen (1973) demonstrated the lack of effect of deafferentation on the dendritic tree of cockroach giant interneurons shown in Figure 4. They also showed that axotomy of the cockroach motoneurons shown in Figure 2 has no effect on the form of the dendritic tree. Wine (1973) demonstrated a similar lack of dendritic response to deafferentation in central

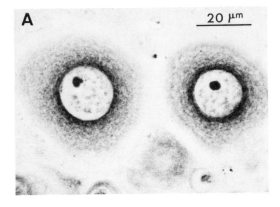

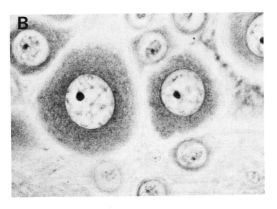

FIGURE 6. (A) Cockroach central neurons whose axons were cut 2 days prior to fixation and stained to show cytoplasmic basiphilia. Note the dense perinuclear ring of stained material, which is RNA. (B) Bilaterally matched control cells whose axons are intact. (From Cohen, 1967b.)

neurons of the crayfish. These differences in dendritic stability observed between the higher vertebrates and the invertebrates may be still another factor that contributes to the differences in behavioral plasticity apparent in these two groups.

Cytological Responses to Axon Injury

Nissl (1892) first described the cytoplasmic basiphilic masses characteristic of many vertebrate central nerve cell bodies. He demonstrated that these Nissl bodies dispersed during the first week following injury to the axon (chromatolysis). This may be accompanied by the nucleus shifting to an eccentric position within the soma, as seen in Figure 5 (Bodian and Mellors, 1945). If the neuron then regenerates an axon, there is a gradual reformation of the Nissl bodies and the nucleus returns to a central location. The Nissl bodies were later shown to be composed of laminations of rough endoplasmic reticulum (Palay and Palade, 1955).

In contrast, the cytoplasm of a normal adult cockroach central neuron shows a finely dispersed uniform distribution of basic material, as seen in Figure 5. There is a scarcity of rough endoplasmic reticulum and a relatively uniform distribution of ribosomes throughout the cytoplasm of the cell body (Young, Ashhurst, and Cohen, 1970). Within four days after cutting the axon of a cockroach motoneuron, a dense perinuclear basiphilic ring forms and there is a great increase in the amount of rough endoplasmic reticulum within the cell, as seen in Figure 6 (Cohen and Jacklet, 1965; Young, Ashhurst, and Cohen, 1970). At 7 to 10 days after axotomy, the perinuclear ring disperses and the axon begins to regenerate. This dispersal of the perinuclear ring could be considered similar to the breakdown of Nissl bodies during chromatolysis in the vertebrate neurons.

THE STRATEGIC PHYLOGENETIC POSITION OF LAMPREY CENTRAL NEURONS

The comparisons between vertebrate and invertebrate neurons made thus far have utilized primarily vertebrate neurons derived from the more highly evolved vertebrates. They also have not dealt with individually identified vertebrate nerve cells, and thus the studies that deal with dendritic change are sometimes difficult to interpret because of the heterogeneity of the cell population. In an effort to examine the possible phylogenetic development of the vertebrate charcteristics and also to develop a vertebrate preparation that could deal with individually identifiable central neurons, we investigated the giant reticular spinal neurons of the lamprey *Petromyzon marinus*. These Müller cells (Stefanelli, 1933; Rovainen, 1967) are

FIGURE 7.   *Dorsal view of a lamprey brain wholemount preparation shows two mesencephalic cells stained by intracellular injection of cobalt. M2 is the upper cell and M3 is below. The slender axons run posteriorly toward the lower left. Note the thick primary expansions of the dendritic trees in both cells. Calibration: 150 μm. (Modified from Fishman, 1975.)*

distributed from the mesencephalon through the medulla of the lamprey. Like the several available invertebrate simple systems described in this volume, these vertebrate central neurons have the attribute that individual nerve cells can be recognized from one animal to the next. The cell bodies of several bilateral pairs can be observed clearly in the living brain. When intracellularly injected with cobalt (Pitman, Tweedle, and Cohen, 1972a, 1973), their

dendrites are clearly visible in wholemount preparations of the brain. The lamprey studies described below are taken from the work of Fishman (1975).

The Cell Body and the Dendritic Tree

Two cobalt-filled mesencephalic Müller cells are shown in Figure 7. The thick primary

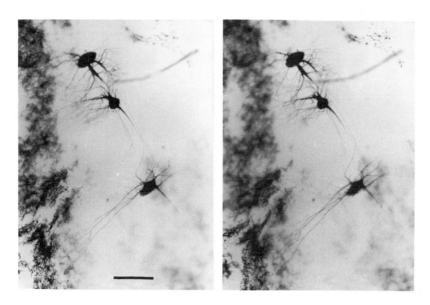

FIGURE 8.   Stereophotographs of the same preparation shown in Figure 7 show the Müller cells M2 (upper), M3 (middle), and an isthmus cell I1 (lower). In three dimensions, the initial stalk-like emergence of the major dendritic processes from the ventral surface of the cell bodies is apparent. This is seen particularly in the middle cell. Calibration: 300 μm. (Modified from Fishman, 1975.)

dendritic trunks emerge from the ventral surface of the cell bodies, and the slender axon runs posteriorly into the spinal cord, where it expands to become the giant Müller fibers of the cord. The two cells, M2 and M3, can be readily distinguished and recognized from animal to animal by the specific configuration of their dendritic trees and the constant location of their cell bodies as seen in the living brain. Figure 8 is a stereophotograph showing the above two mesencephalic neurons and in addition an isthmus cell, I1. In the stereophotograph it is apparent that the dendrites tend to emerge from the ventral surface of the cells as thick stalks that seem almost to be broad expansions of the soma itself. This is particularly apparent in the middle cell of the group, M3. The fine branches of the dendritic tree emerge from the few broad expansions of the soma rather than directly from the cell body as in higher vertebrates. In this respect, the lack of numerous fine dendritic projections from the soma resembles more the invertebrate neurons shown in Figures 2 and 4 than the classical vertebrate central nerve cells seen in Figure 1.

The Cytology of Lamprey Neurons

The Müller cells of the lamprey brain show a remarkable similarity to the insect central neuron in their cytological responses to axon injury. In the normal lamprey cell there is a lack of Nissl bodies and the cytoplasm shows the finely dispersed basiphilia when stained with pyronin dye that is seen in the insect cells (Figure 9). Approximately 3 weeks after cutting the axon of the Müller cell in the spinal cord, a dense perinuclear basiphilic ring forms in the soma similar to that seen in the insect cells (see Figures 6 and 9). In this respect, the lamprey central neuron is much more similar to the invertebrate nerve cell than it is to the central neurons of more highly evolved vertebrates.

Dendritic Changes of Lamprey Neurons to Axotomy

The dendritic tree of the lamprey Müller cell undergoes great change in its form follow-

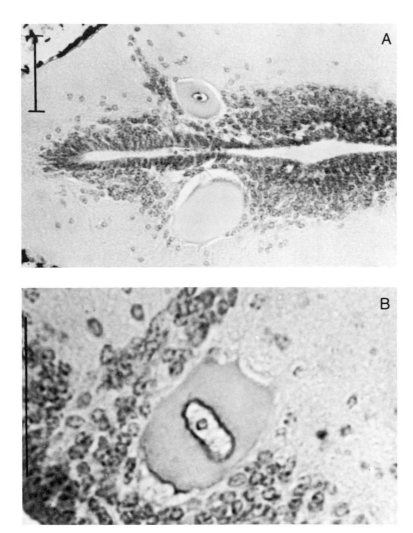

FIGURE 9. (A) Transverse section through the mesencephalon of a lamprey with a 5-week-old spinal hemisection; stained with pyronin–malachite green to show basic substances in the cytoplasm. The upper cell body is on the normal side of the animal. Note the uniform cytoplasmic basiphilia and the absence of Nissl bodies. The lower cell body is on the injured side, but the section does not pass through the nucleus. Note, however, the great swelling of the soma, characteristic of a cell whose axon has been cut. (B) Section stained as above shows a mesencephalic Müller cell whose axon was cut 24 days prior to fixation. Note the dense perinuclear ring of basic material similar to that seen in axotomized insect neurons. Calibration: 100 µm. (From Fishman, 1975.)

ing section of the axon in the spinal cord. At about 4 weeks after axotomy the fine dendritic branches of the Müller cells are no longer seen when the cell is stained with cobalt. The primary dendritic shafts appear smooth and largely devoid of fine higher-order branches, as seen in Figure 10. This is similar to the general phenomenon described above for higher vertebrates, except that here one can visualize the effect on single identified cells to allow a more

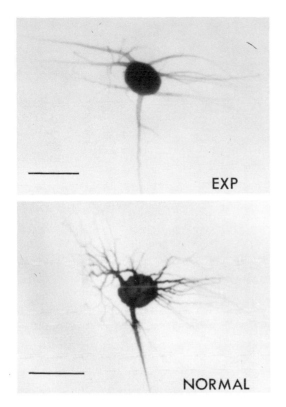

EXP

NORMAL

FIGURE 10. *Normal M2 cell in the lamprey brain seen in contrast to an experimental M2 cell whose axon was cut in the spinal cord 62 days prior to fixation. Cells were stained by intracellular injection of cobalt. Note the considerable reduction of fine branches emanating from the primary dendrites in the experimental cell. Calibration: 100 µm. (From Fishman, 1975.)*

embryonic development of dendrites, the appearance of the dendritic tree in the lamprey Müller cells at this stage following axotomy gives every appearance of profuse growth. The filamentous and bulbous types of dendritic growth cones described in neonatal mice (Hinds and Hinds, 1972; Vaughn, Henrickson, and Grieshaber, 1974) and embryonic chicks (Skoff and Hamburger, 1974) strongly resemble the structures described above in the lamprey cells. This is one of the few instances of profuse dendritic growth in vertebrate central neurons that have already differentiated.

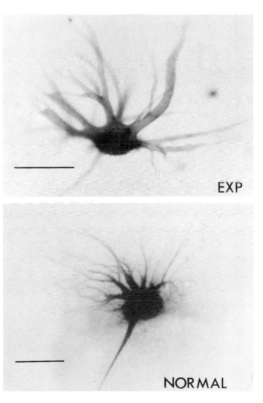

EXP

NORMAL

FIGURE 11. *Normal mesencephalic Müller cell (M3) in the lamprey compared with an M3 cell whose axon was cut 47 days prior to fixation (EXP). Note that the diameter of the dendrites has greatly increased in the experimental cell and that the two large dendrites on the left have long pointed tips. Calibration: 100 µm. (From Fishman, 1975.)*

precise evaluation of the dendritic retraction process.

Approximately 6 weeks after axotomy and up to about 4 months, the dendritic tree of the experimental cell now undergoes a radical change from the retracted state shown in Figure 10. The geometry becomes highly irregular with the dendritic shaft often increasing greatly in diameter all along its length. At the tips, the dendrites may either have sharp filamentous extensions, or they may be swollen and bulbous, as seen in Figures 11 and 12. From the small amount of information available on the

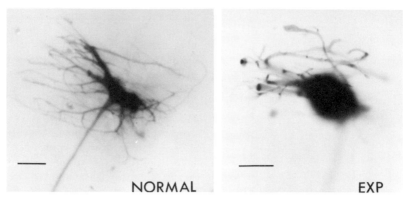

NORMAL   EXP

FIGURE 12.   *Comparison of a normal bulbar Müller cell in the lamprey brain and a bulbar cell whose axon was cut 126 days prior to fixation (EXP). Note the bulbous ending of some dendrites in the experimental cell. The experimental cell also shows an increase in the diameter of the dendrites along their entire length and a relative lack of fine higher-order branches. Calibration: 100 μm. (From Fishman, 1975.)*

SPECULATIONS ON THE EVOLUTION OF BEHAVIOR

The relative physical and electrical isolation of the invertebrate neuron soma from events occurring in the dendrites and axon leads to the general consideration of *intracellular* communication between different functional and structural regions of a nerve cell. The neuron may be considered divided into three structural compartments — soma, dendrites, and axon. Within the invertebrate neurons these compartments are structurally and functionally more separate than in vertebrate nerve cells. Synaptic transmission and spike initiation are relatively isolated from the cell body. Injury to the axon can initiate cytological changes in the soma but does not affect the morphology of the dendritic compartment. In crustacean central neurons this isolation seems carried to an extreme by the ability of the severed axon to remain viable and conduct action potentials for months after being separated from the soma (Hoy, 1970). The increased separation of these intracellular neuronal compartments in the invertebrate neuron might contribute to their stability of function by preventing activity in one region of the cell from influencing the structure or function of another region. This stability, especially at the dendritic level, may be related to a phylogenetic thrust within the invertebrates toward stereotyped behavioral patterns. The fixed action patterns related to arthropod walking (Wilson and Wyman, 1965), cricket song (Bentley, 1971), and molluscan swimming (Willows, 1967) are well-documented examples of behavioral stereotypy among invertebrates.

The lamprey appears to occupy an intriguing evolutionary position in regard to the degree of separation between the intracellular compartments of a neuron. It shares with the invertebrates a partial spatial isolation of the dendritic tree from the neuron soma. The cell body has a distribution of cytoplasmic RNA and a cytological response to axon injury that appears strikingly similar to that of the insect central neuron. And yet, in the lamprey, the signal initiated by axonal injury is not isolated from the dendritic tree as it is in arthropods but rather reaches the dendrites and initiates profound changes in their structure which involve retraction and subsequent growth. Here, the lamprey central neuron differs strikingly from that of the invertebrates, in which the differentiated dendritic tree appears structurally resistant to change in the face of factors that modify the form of vertebrate nerve cells. This *opening of the dendritic compartment* to events that occur elsewhere in the neuron may have been a requisite evolutionary change in the primitive vertebrate stock that signaled a final departure from the rigid behavioral repertoire to which most of the invertebrates are confined. It may have been the key that enabled a link to develop between the ephemeral events of synaptic transmission and the more permanent metabolic and structural changes that must underlie the extraordinary behavioral lability of the higher vertebrates, including perhaps even the far reaches of the human mind.

CHAPTER FOUR

In Search of Principles in Neural Integration

THEODORE HOLMES BULLOCK

INTRODUCTION

It is becoming increasingly clear that, even before we have many more neuron networks well worked out in living (not model) systems, the extrapolation of present findings will raise a serious question about the goals of "circuit-breaking" research. The limited number of cases of more or less analyzed living neuron networks now at hand has brought to light a plethora of parameters; variability along each of these and permutations of them provide immense numbers of degrees of freedom. If it should be the case that networks unraveled in the future merely show additional, unlimited permutations of the same variables, their interest will be ad hoc for the species and functions served, not for general neurobiology. Thus continued effort may require justification on such grounds as the following: (1) The explicit search for yet more variables is likely to be fruitful. There is no reason to believe that the steady flow of discoveries of elements, properties, and relations is about to stop. See Table I for a matrix of 46 variables available to the elements of networks. (2) The explicit search for rules, forbidden or favored combinations, correlations with function in a system-analytic sense or with habit of life, phylogenetic relationship, and behavioral or other adaptive significance is likely to be fruitful. There are now too many ways of designing plausibly realistic models; exclusions are needed. But rules will be difficult to discern in detailed studies of single cases. A partial list of neuronal (not model) networks known in considerable degree is given in Table II. Comparisons of series of cases by the same investigator are most likely to reveal rules and order in this greatest of reservoirs of scientific principles and discoveries.

CIRCUIT VARIABLES

That branch of neurophysiology devoted to circuit-breaking or unraveling the connections of neurons in organized systems is now

TABLE I

SOME VARIABLES AMONG THE ELEMENTS OF NEURONAL NETWORKS

PARAMETERS OF NEURONS AS UNITS *AND* IN ORGANIZED CONSTELLATIONS THAT PROVIDE
DEGREES OF FREEDOM IN ASSEMBLING NETWORKS

1. Spike threshold: high or low (depolarization from resting level necessary to fire)
2. Recovery cycle: slow or fast
3. Subthreshold local potential: steepness of nonlinear response function lower or higher
4. Safety factor: high or low, especially at axon branch points
5. Accommodation: large or small; fast or slow
6. Time constant: large or small
7. Space constant: large or small
8. Afterpotentials: magnitude, sequence, and duration
9. Iterativeness: tonic, phasic, or both; fast, slow, or both in succession
10. Autorhythmicity: silent or spontaneously active
11. Resting level: influenced by hormones, CO_2, temperature, etc.; direction and degree
12. Quantal, miniature junction potentials: more or fewer; larger or smaller
13. Synaptic transmission: chemical or electrical
14. Synaptic transmission: excitatory or inhibitory
15. Synaptic transmission: polarized or unpolarized
16. Synaptic transmission: high gain or low gain
17. Postsynaptic response: mainly potential change or conductance change
18. Postsynaptic potential: monophasic or biphasic
19. Postsynaptic response: slow or fast
20. Postsynaptic decay: only passive or partly active
21. Postsynaptic inhibition: with increased or decreased conductance
22. Postsynaptic inhibition: with discrete IPSPs or ILD (inhibition of long duration; up to many minutes)
23. Postsynaptic activity: does or does not exert influence back on presynaptic
24. Postsynaptic response: facilitating, antifacilitating, or neither
25. Facilitation: fast, slow, or both in succession
26. Firing rate: depolarization function steep or shallow

27. Firing rate: subject to autoinhibition or some form of saturation
28. Firing rate: regular or irregular; patterned or bursting
29. At end of input: postsynaptic response continues, rebounds, or neither
30. Electrotonic connection between cells: of low or high resistance
31. Electrotonic connection between cells: of low or high capacitance
32. Pacemaker units: can or cannot be invaded and reset by input
33. Synchrony between units in subthreshold potentials: weak or strong
34. Synchrony of spike firing: weak or strong
35. Recognition units: of lower or higher complexity of input requirements
36. Command units: of greater or lesser effectiveness (i.e., one or several units command a large musculature); sustained or triggering; high or low in responsibility
37. Central determinants or sensory determinants of time course relatively more important
38. Input sequence and interval: critical or not (e.g., "A *then* B" is critical, i.e., heterosynaptic facilitation)
39. Set point of a control circuit: adjustable or not known to be so
40. Kindling: present or not (1 second weak stimulus train per day gradually kindles afterdischarge in several days and finally leads to convulsion)
41. Potentiation: present or absent (see Bullock and Horridge, 1965: Glossary)
42. Recruiting response: present or not (see Bullock and Horridge, 1965: Glossary)
43. Augmenting response: present or not (see Bullock and Horridge, 1965: Glossary)
44. Evoked slow waves: large or small, early or late, simple or complex
45. DC and slowly fluctuating potentials across cells and masses form fields: of larger or smaller equivalent dipoles, simple or complex form, widely different power spectrum and coherence with other areas — the EEG and related states
46. Plasticity: greater or lesser

achieving such success that it may be time to look ahead and reexamine our goals. It is not that we have enough circuits, or even one circuit, of a complete act from receptors to effectors, with all the neurons and coupling functions involved. But the greatly accelerated pace of achievement, against a background that includes the classical contributions of Cajal and Sherrington among hundreds of others, promises to change the face of the problem.

The change is partly a result of the phenomenal expansion in the number of elements, processes, and degrees of freedom now known to be available to the nervous system. For many years after the neuron doctrine and the nerve impulse became familiar, our picture was essentially that crystallized in the McCulloch–Pitts (1943) model. Each neuron was an all-or-nothing element. A quiet revolution began with Hodgkin's (1938) demonstration of the subthreshold local potential and continued with the discovery of the muscle endplate potential (Eccles, Katz, and Kuffler, 1941) and synaptic potential (Eccles, 1946), confirmed intracellularly by Brock, Coombs, and Eccles (1952). There followed, in not so rapid succession, still more discoveries that added to the flexibility of the circuit elements. It became evident that junctions can be chemical and excitatory, chemical and

TABLE II

WELL-KNOWN NEURONAL NETWORKS

SOME ARE MUCH LESS FULLY KNOWN THAN OTHERS, BUT IF INFORMATION IS NOT REASONABLY FULL EITHER ON ALL THE NEURONS IN PARALLEL AT ONE OR TWO STAGES, OR ON SOME OF THOSE IN SERIES THROUGH SEVERAL STAGES, THE CASE IS OMITTED. MAINLY HYPOTHETICAL CIRCUITS AND SYSTEMS DIAGRAMS ARE NOT INCLUDED

Animal	Network or function served	Approximate number of neurons	Reference
Invertebrates			
Annelids			
Leech, *Hirudo*	Cutaneous mechanoreception	14	Baylor and Nicholls, 1969
	Swimming (11 pairs in each of 21 segments)	231	Ort, Kristan, and Stent, 1974; Kristan, 1974; Kristan, Stent, and Ort, 1974a, b
Arthropods			
Lobster			
Homarus	Cardiac ganglion	9	Alexandrowicz, 1932; Maynard, 1955; Hagiwara, 1961; Friesen, 1974
Panulirus	Cardiac ganglion	9	Bullock and Terzuolo, 1957
Crab, *Cancer*	Cardiac ganglion	9	Hartline, 1968
Lobster, *Panulirus*	Stomatogastric ganglion	30	Maynard, 1972; Selverston, 1974; Selverston and Mulloney, 1974a
Crayfish, *Cambarus*	Tail flexion; types of units (per hemisegment)	7	Zucker, 1972
	Tail flexion; all units from command to motor (all segments)	300	Kennedy, Evoy, and Hanawalt, 1966
	Tail extension; stretch receptor and motoneurons (6 per segment)	36	Fields, Evoy, and Kennedy, 1967
	Swimmeret control (6 segments)	38	Stein, 1971, 1974; cf. Davis, 1973b
Roach, *Periplaneta*	Walking (6 types, paired, 3 segments)	36[a]	Pearson, 1972; Pearson, Fourtner, and Wong, 1973

inhibitory, electrical and excitatory, or electrical and inhibitory. Electrical junctions can be one way or two way, low in resistance or not very low – and hence show low loss or high loss. Chemical synapses can be high gain or low gain, driving or modulating; they can be facilitating, antifacilitating, or neither. Several kinds of inhibitory synapses are known (Table I).

But the junction is not the only site of lability, integration, and possible plasticity. The locus concept (Bullock, 1958, 1959) emphasized the consequences of the newer understanding of the neuron by pointing as well to dendrites and their confluences, to spike-initiating zones, to the preterminal axon, and to

unknown, but apparently local, pacemaker loci in many neurons. More recently there has been added a class of potentially labile or integrative loci along the axon: regions of low-safety factor, especially at branch points. Here selective block can occur, affecting particularly those impulses that follow at short intervals; trains of certain frequencies or patterns may be filtered and different frequencies or patterns allowed to pass.

How common this – or others of the available possibilities – may actually be is not known and will only slowly and haltingly be assessed. In the meantime intellectual curiosity and scientific strategy compel us to consider

TABLE II: NEURONAL NETWORKS (CONTINUED)

Animal	Network of function served	Approximate number of neurons	Reference
Fly, *Calliphora*	Eye: receptors and second-order cells (22 for each of 1,500+ ommatidia)	33000	Trujillo-Cenóz, 1965; Trujillo Cenóz and Melamed, 1966; Kirschfeld, 1967; Braitenberg, 1967; Horridge and Meinertzhagen, 1970
Locust, *Schistocerca*	Metathoracic leg motoneurons and some of their inputs Flight mechanisms		Burrows and Horridge, 1974; Hoyle and Burrows, 1973 Burrows, in preparation
Mollusks			
Sea hare, *Aplysia*	Identified cells, unknown role	14	Kandel et al., 1967
	Control of circulation	8	Koester et al., 1973; Mayeri, Koester, and Liebeswar, 1974
	Gill, siphon, mantle withdrawal reflex	6	Kupfermann and Kandel, 1969; Peretz and Moller, 1974
Hermissenda	Interconnected photoreceptors	5	Dennis, 1967
Tritonia	Escape swimming[b]	11[a]	Willows, Dorsett, and Hoyle 1973b
Snail *Helisoma*	Feeding activity	28	Kater and Rowell, 1973; Kater, 1974
Vertebrates			
Electric knife fish, *Eigenmannia*	Jamming avoidance response of electric organ discharge, from receptor to motoneuron	7 orders	Scheich and Bullock, 1975
Mud puppy, *Necturus* (other vertebrates)	Retina	5 orders	Dowling and Werblin, 1969, 1971
Cat, *Felis*	Cerebellar cortex	6 orders	Eccles, Ito, and Szentagothai, 1967

[a] Some "units" are categories of unknown numbers of neurons.
[b] Partly hypothetical.

the possible consequences if all the known degrees of freedom are reasonably available to normal nervous systems. How does it change the nature of circuit-breaking studies, of modeling, and of theoretical neurophysiology if we must assume that, instead of synaptic junctions only, four or five classes of loci are significant sites of neuronal integration, lability, and plasticity? What if all degrees of electrotonic coupling from feeble to strong, from low pass to high, from linear to nonlinear may be common enough to reckon with? We must deal with the large variety of labile functions just mentioned, plus the permutations of these in all their dynamic alternatives.

The variables listed in Table I are surely not a complete list. They include mechanisms of lower and higher level; some of the latter may be the consequences of the former. They deserve independent listing because, like emergents, they could not be readily predicted even from a relatively full knowledge of the lower levels. The list does not include a number of phenomena that might soon be added to it, such as the following:

(1) Action potentials can in certain situations be both graded and decrementless (Zettler and Jarvilehto, 1971).

(2) Internal resistance in axon and soma can in certain situations be much higher than expected from the diameter owing to extensive and even branching invaginations of the surface membrane, often occupied by glial cell processes (Gorman and Mirolli, 1972).

(3) Synapses that were effective in firing the postsynaptic unit are claimed in certain circumstances to lose their ability to control that unit, yet to maintain electron-microscopical structure and the ability to regain control when the original circumstances are restored (Mark, 1974).

(4) Some transmission may become effective only when two presynaptic pathways from different sources converge and, within temporal bounds, coincide (heterosynaptic facilitation; "and" gates).

(5) A chemical synapse may be intimately associated with a potential electrical synapse and by the control of membrane conductance via the chemical transmitter effectively gate the electrical transmission (Bennett, 1973).

(6) Synapse formation and maintenance may be dynamic and under continued pressure from competition among presynaptic neurons, from a quasi-quota of terminals for given presynaptic neurons, and from a virtual trial-and-error contact process when opportunity permits, as in ontogeny and regeneration.

(7) A neuron may in some cases employ more than one transmitter.

In addition to these variables is the well-nigh indefinite variety of anatomical arrangements. Without attempting to detail a great number of these, it may be well just to mention a few. Neurons may have two axons with independent spike initiation, or one or none. An axon may have a single target neuron or collaterals and terminals on many thousands of neurons over a large volume of the brain; collaterals may be recurrent, feeding back on some of the population of neurons from which they came. Inputs to a neuron, defining its receptive field, may be extremely limited or wide. There are serial synapses, reciprocal synapses, synapses on axons, even on nodes of Ranvier, dendrodendritic, somatosomatic, and all the types and subtypes of light and electron microscopy — calyces, baskets, clubs, and so on; type I, type II, ribbon, triad, septal, and other synapses and many varieties of multiple, complex, or glomerular synapses. Dendrites in some places appear more than casually "bundled," which suggests some meaningful interaction (Scheibel and Scheibel, 1973).

In sum, the list of variables available to the nervous system is substantial. If we consider the range of possibilities within each variable and the combinations of these, the opportunities are immense.

FROM PARAMETERS TO RULES

So far, research on networks has documented that nature uses a very wide assortment of elements and combinations. The main question I want to raise here is how to justify continued circuit breaking. If it should be true that all neuronal circuits consist of unrestricted concatenations of these elements, then why analyze more and more circuits? The time is foreseeable when a skeptical panel member, aware of funding limitations, will say of a proposal for network analysis, "Isn't this going to be just another case? Won't the investigator find merely one more combination of the known array of elements? Will the findings be of interest beyond those concerned with this animal and this action? The first time that rhodopsin is found in a class of animals it is of general interest; the thirty-fourth time is data but not much real information."

The proposition I want to defend is that two principal justifications will remain, and research in this field will be judged on these criteria. The field I speak of is *circuit breaking*, neuron by neuron — not systems analysis, modeling, or cell physiology. First, it seems more than likely that still further parameters will be discovered which provide new degrees of freedom, additional complexity, and new phenomenology to be explained at lower levels. Discovery of emergent, qualitatively novel mechanisms, although it does not simplify our picture of how the nervous system works, makes it more realistic and accurate. Second, it seems likely that rules, regularities, tendencies, and generalizations will be found which limit the degrees of freedom with which the elements are combined. The discovery of rules, of forbidden or preferred combinations, will simplify our picture and permit inductions in a field that needs them — that of neuronal systems.

The first objective would be an extension to larger networks of the approach, traditionally on small parts of circuits, that gave us synaptic potentials, electrotonic connections, presynaptic inhibition, reciprocal synapses, spike train filters at axon branch points, hyperpolarizing responses, inhibition without conductance increase, spikeless neurons, and each of the presently known parameters. There is no end in sight, yet few workers will admit that they are explicitly seeking new mechanisms except incidentally. More than that, the methodology of most network analyses would hardly allow an unexpected novelty to make itself known.

The second objective would be in the tradition of true comparative physiology that gave us generalizations about the occurrence and correlates of diverse mechanisms for respiration, circulation, excretion, and the like. These may be phylogenetic or habit-of-life correlations, correlations with the function performed in a system-analytic sense, or biochemical or mechanistic correlations (e.g., "If A, then B"; "If C, then not D"; "E tends to precede F"; etc.) which themselves may become mysteries to be explained as well as helping to simplify rules. There is hardly a beginning in sight with respect to neural circuits, so little do we know about the incidence of the variables in our list (Table I). Few workers are explicitly looking for rules. More than that, the usual approach makes true comparison and hence generalization improbable and hardly a prime goal. Although this objective is therefore not at present a well-recognized reason for analyzing neuronal circuits, it could be, with a substantial gain in the generality of the value of any given research.

What is meant by rules in the combination of elements in neural circuits? There are few examples, and no systematic body of knowledge covers any substantial fraction of the known circuits. Maynard (1972) gave eight rules or tendencies derived from close study of the 30 cells and their connections in the lobster stomatogastric ganglion. I cite these, with special pleasure in this volume, as examples of a certain sort of generalization because they may become the basis for improved and extended formulations in this undeveloped aspect of neurobiology.

Several characteristics of the stomatogastric system appear to have more than incidental interest, and may have general significance.
1) Neurons of the system do not form a homogeneous population, but differ in functional properties that significantly affect the output of the system.
2) Neurons different physiologically also differ anatomically, and can be recognized on the basis of structure.
3) In addition to variation in physiological properties of neurons, the variety of synaptic types is large; slow inhibitory PSP, fast inhibitory PSP, excitatory PSP, non-spike inhibitory PSP, strong electrotonic

coupling, weak electrotonic coupling, and several transmitters seem indicated.

4) Neurons that discharge within the same temporal pattern (e.g., PD, LP, and PY neurons) are usually highly interconnected synaptically; they make almost no functional connections with other contiguous elements in the ganglion which discharge within a different pattern.

5) Excitatory synaptic activity in the ganglion appears to function primarily to bring component neurons to an appropriate discharge level, it does not determine pattern.

6) Inhibition plays a dominant role in carving out patterned output, and nearly all described chemical synapses between ganglion neurons are inhibitory.

7) Neurons that innervate the same or synergic muscles tend to be electrotonically coupled.

8) Regular rhythmic outputs do not result from reciprocal inhibitory connections, but from specific pacemakers that drive the output (Maynard, 1972).

Rules for the concatenation of elements (meaning both neurons and their properties, both structures and transfer functions) into circuits are distinct from rules in the behavior of elements, though it may sometimes be difficult or marginal to force the distinction. Rules for elements may be exemplified by a few familiar ones. (1) Impulse trains of higher mean frequency have coefficients of variation either equal to or smaller than those of lower frequency. (2) Smaller neurons tend to fire at lower physiological stimulus level, more tonically, and with lower maximum frequency than large neurons. (3) Most neurons seem to employ only one transmitter at all of their axonal terminals.

New forays into the search for physiological principles at the level of elements are extremely promising; the groundbreaking work of Thorson and Biederman-Thorson (1974) on the mechanism of adaptation may be mentioned. I cite these examples of regularities at the level of elements to clarify, by way of contrast, the sort of rules at the level of connectivity that I called a special opportunity for future circuit-breaking research. Other

examples at the level of elements are the well-known anatomical rules applicable more or less locally (e.g. those that characterize the destinations of classes of presynaptic terminals or specify the forms of dendritic arbors of classes of neurons). Some are more general, for example the rule that synaptic specializations with membrane thickening, clustered vesicles, and wide uniform cleft are always discrete, not of indefinite extent, nor more than a few square micrometers in area. Some generalizations that result from a comparison of vertebrate and invertebrate neurons have been given by Cohen (1970) and Bullock (1974). But the opportunity is still open to discern, collect, and systematize the rules especially germane to combining neurons into circuits.

These two objectives — discovering new parameters of integration and new rules of combination — are not the only good reasons for circuit breaking.

I grant that we need a series of well-worked-out examples. Each is a formidable task and a major achievement. I grant that we have only a few at present and that many of them are incomplete [Table II]. The list would look slightly more impressive if we included the anatomically nonaddressed class, in the nomenclature of Horridge (1961), such as the nerve nets of coelenterates; here, although the identity of the neurons is unknown, it is irrelevant and a few numerical values adequately characterize the system. These are approximately known in some examples. I grant that there is an intrinsic interest in how this and that species flies, walks, or eats and in differentiating between the performance or figures of merit in different cases by detailed knowledge of the circuits.

Especially few are the examples of networks with feedback; most of those at hand are open chains, at least as far as is known. Rarely have the receptors been identified for well-studied motor actions or the effector circuitry for well-studied afferent networks. I grant that the dilemma of our proposition — justifying additional cases — is rather far down the pike. Nevertheless, it can be foreseen. It is well to be forearmed. I would urge that every author be at some pains to make evident even now the novelty and significance for general neurobiology of each new case that we take up.

These remarks, it must be reiterated, concern that special branch of neuroscience, partly anatomical, partly physiological, partly behavioral, which aims at unraveling neuron networks. That means that the related but distinguishable systems-analysis and modeling approaches (e.g., Reichardt, 1961; Stark, 1968; Mittelstaedt, 1969; Dowling, 1970; Grüsser and Grüsser-Cornehls, 1972; Land and Collett, 1974) are not in view here. Systems analysis aims at subdividing or recognizing operationally defined components — which might be neurons — but which are usually larger or smaller, or might be many neurons in parallel.

Also not under consideration here is the large body of neurophysiology that reveals the relations that obtain between specific neurons — no doubt parts of circuits, but too restricted a portion of the whole network for inclusion in our list (see exclusions in the legend for Table II). The elegant physiology of spinal motoneurons, cerebellar Purkinje cells, Limulus eye eccentric cells, and many others provides essential understanding of the units and the proper ties but is for the present purpose too far from setting forth even a considerable fraction of the behaviorally significant circuit in which these neurons lie.

Are there then rules for the combination of elements in neural circuits? I can answer this question with a personal conviction — merely a confident hunch — that, yes, there are surely rules, correlations, exclusions, and favored combinations; there are surely generalizations, inductions, and principles waiting to be discovered. But it is difficult at present to formulate even some initial examples, let alone estimate whether the rules will mainly reflect zoological affinity or will really reduce uncertainty about how brains work. I am also quite sure that we will soon see the fruits of serious efforts to compare circuits and extract contrasts or generalizations.

A rider or corollary to this conviction is important because it appears that doubts persist in many quarters about the relevance for vertebrate brain function of single neuron analysis aimed at specified circuitry, largely an occupation indulged in by invertebrate physiologists. The invertebrate systems are sometimes said to be so vastly simpler as to offer little help or precedent for understanding mammalian systems. Even though I resist a sharp dichotomy and believe that specific units with low redundancy form reliable circuits in some parts of our brain, a good question does remain: Are there also rules and generalizations in the way in which elements are combined in the cell-rich vertebrate brain? Or is the wealth of anatomical variety and the 46 and more physiological variables concatenated without limitations, so that we have to think of "slugging" out every case and region of interest neuron by neuron? Perish the thought!

Network analyses with feedback and reciprocity and which account reasonably well for a significant piece of an animal's behavior are rather recent (Maynard, 1972, Selverston, 1974, and their colleagues on the lobster stomatogastric ganglion; Kater, 1974, on snail feeding; Ort, Kristan, and Stent, 1974, on the leech walking system; and Scheich and Bullock, 1975, on the jamming avoidance response of electric fish). These together with the simpler or behaviorally more fragmentary systems listed in Table II represent an advance over the previous state of our definite knowledge of nervous systems, whose significance is difficult to overstate. Even in 1965, when Horridge and I summarized the state of knowledge for invertebrates (Bullock and Horridge, 1965), only the nine-celled cardiac ganglion of lobsters and crabs — seemingly an exceptional, miniaturized peripheral ganglion, dubiously predictive of the organization of central nervous systems — was approximately worked out. One could still think of higher invertebrate ganglia such as the insect brain in much the same terms as we think of higher vertebrate brains today. Horridge (1961) said:

> From anatomical studies of neuropile no one has ever obtained anything which looks like a wiring diagram. ... Half a century of detailed work by the best methods on many favourable preparations has failed to demonstrate any pattern or circuit diagram which is evidently anatomically addressed.

The change in our views compelled by the many recent findings of specified connectivity, in an ever-expanding list of cases among higher invertebrates, is drastic. Although we do not assume that all neurons are unique or all connections specified, even a modest extrapolation of the curve of new cases in recent years makes a high degree of specification quite common. Evidence for this comes from many more places than those in Table II. The expanding list of identifiable neurons can only be mentioned (Cohen, 1970; Bentley, 1970, 1973; Kater, 1974; Altman and Tyrer, 1974; Tyrer and Altman, 1974; Burrows and Hoyle, 1973; Burrows and Horridge, 1974; Ort, Kristan, and Stent, 1974; Kandel, 1974; Willows, Dorsett, and Hoyle, 1973a; Davis et al., 1974). The pronounced increase in the number of distinguishable types of neurons in the optic ganglia of insects (Strausfeld, 1970a, b) over those known to Cajal and Sánchez (1915) is extraordinary. The same may be said for cephalopods (Young, 1971). A much higher degree of specification than heretofore realized is also clearly true for some well-studied parts of vertebrates, for example the retina (Dowling and Werblin, 1971), the cerebellar cortex (Llinás and Walton, Chapter Nineteen of this volume; Palay and Chan-Palay, 1974), and the neocortex (Colonnier, 1968; Szentagothai and Arbib, 1974). In many parts of the mammalian brain each new advance adds specifications. Hard-wired circuits of highly specified connectivity in higher centers are still not entirely plausible to many neurophysiologists, though we are gradually becoming adjusted to the astonishing degree of detail in the networks just mentioned.

The actual course of events that I foresee, however, is the extrapolation of trends that seem well established. There is not likely to develop any great dependence on, or targeted effort for, the discovery of new rules or new parameters, in spite of my feeble admonitions. To be sure, such discoveries will happen and add interest and complexity as well as significance to some researches. In general, however, the likelihood is that cases aimed simply at analysis will accumulate. In simpler groups and regions new examples of networks will be deciphered cell by cell and junction by junction, hopefully not so much redundantly as with an eye to comparison and contrast. In the more complex species and regions of the brain, classes of neurons will be subdivided and the subclasses further broken down on the basis of restricted connectivity and dynamics of

coupling functions. The fascinating question is: How far? In the cerebellum, inputs are still becoming more specified (Bastian, 1975), and Purkinje cells are being labeled by the exact destination of the deep nuclear axons to which they project (Courville, 1966; Brodal and Courville, 1973; Courville, Diakiw, and Brodal, 1973). In the mammalian visual system, area 17 orientation preference columns are now said to be only 50 μm wide and the extrapolation is not farfetched that within a column several gradients of properties exist, such as sensitivity, best stripe width, contrast, motion, disparity, and dynamics of discharge and recovery.

CONCLUSIONS

We may be moving toward a more general understanding. Perhaps the situation is analogous to that of a group of Martian sociologists studying a spectrum of colleges, who discover in some systems *identifiable* units such as the mail clerk or the chairman of philosophy and, in others, partly equivalent, partly *overlapping* units such as public relations, parking, and book-buying personnel. Such an understanding seems to be emerging for the brain.

Although the argument has been confined to one kind of research, it is important to recognize that such understandings as we may be gaining are being enriched, tested, and advanced by interaction between circuit breaking as one approach to asking how the brain works, and more theoretical approaches — systems analysis and simulation, for example. Analysis of circuit operations benefits also from interactions in another direction — that is, with the cell physiology of membranes and transmission mechanisms, and such concepts as mosaics, membrane fuzz, transmitter feedback, surface movement, and differential transport along axons. Such concepts and interactions add dimensions to the uniqueness of cells, parts of cells, and groups of cells. By the same token they add potentially important explanations of pathologic vulnerability and of plasticity, compensation, and "higher" functions.

The road is long and branching, distractions and obstacles are many, the goal is hazy and far away, pilgrims speak in many tongues. But we can look back and see progress, or look up and see some exciting peaks.

II

INTEGRATIVE
FOUNDATIONS

In Part II we explore the integrative foundations of neuronal function and behavior in greater detail, aided by a variety of specific examples. The term "integration" has several meanings. It is useful to start with a dictionary definition: "the act, process, or an instance of integrating: the condition of being formed into a whole by the addition or combination of parts or elements" (*Webster's Third New International Dictionary*, G. & C. Merriam Co., 1971). As integration lies at the heart of many basic problems in relating neuronal activity to behavior, one advantage of the "simpler networks" approach — in which both individual elements and their combined activity can be observed directly — becomes clear. In the behavioral literature the term "integration" also refers primarily to momentary and reversible changes of state, such as those which underlie the transitions between one class of activities and another (see Hinde, 1970). The issue of temporal pattern generation as reflected in behavioral output is a fundamental subdivision of this problem.

In Chapter Five, Kennedy stresses the importance of using organism behavior as the fundamental criterion for "system isolation," and like Hoyle (Chapter Two), he argues that motor output is a particularly useful focus for initial inquiry. There are two basic reasons for this. First, motor output is what we observe most simply and directly. Second, forces of natural selection also act most directly upon the integrated output of organisms. Sensory and interneuronal activity are indirectly selected for their role in producing adaptive patterns of integrated output.

It is important, however, not to oversimplify the relationship between neuronal activity and motor activity even in the production of relatively simple and stereotyped output patterns. For example, Kennedy notes that the same neurons may participate in several different behavior patterns, an example of operational divergence. Additional questions include: How stereotyped are particular action patterns when subjected to detailed quantitative analysis? To what extent are these patterns controlled by endogenous as opposed to exogenous factors? Can the basic patterning of neurobehavioral output be attributed to operations at the element (single neuron) level or does it entail necessary interactions in a more complex network sense? Each chapter in this part provides useful insights with regard to these and related questions.

Another important point is that both particular networks and particular neuronal elements may have quite specific and unique operational properties which must be studied directly. This warns against simple generalizations but does not preclude the search for more general operating principles at different levels. For example, Kennedy reviews a variety of literature, much of which has come out of his own laboratory, which suggests that during the execution of rapid motor activities in both invertebrates and vertebrates sensory inputs may be blocked at various stages of transmission, thus effectively isolating a previously activated motor system from extrinsic, and potentially interfering, sensory activity. Individual mechanisms of behavioral control may be quite divergent even though they serve common functions, as Kennedy illustrates in his discussion of load compensation in both invertebrate (e.g. Crustacea) and vertebrate species. This again raises the question at what level, and by what criteria, most useful general principles can be determined. The issue of hierarchical control is also raised by Kennedy, and it is useful to compare his comments on this matter with those of other authors in this volume.

In Chapter Six, Selverston provides a detailed analysis of one system of pattern generation, the lobster stomatogastric ganglion preparation pioneered by Donald Maynard (e.g., Maynard, 1972). He argues, as did Maynard (but somewhat differently from Hoyle and Kennedy), that cyclical activity is the most reasonable place to start detailed analyses. These differences of emphasis should not be overemphasized, however, for they reflect primarily individual strategies toward a common and well-defined goal. Selverston examines in detail the recurring question of pattern generation as a product of factors endogenous to individual neural elements as opposed to their combination into higher-order functional networks. Researchers in the field differ with regard to their positions on this point (compare, for example, Chapters Five and Twenty), but there is no question that individual investigators recognize that the diversity of biological organization along with our own current conceptual and analytical limitations should encourage, rather than detract from, a diversity of approaches (see Chapter Four).

Selverston argues strongly for the importance of combining intracellular recordings with more formalized network analyses as an approach to these issues. He has demonstrated that the precise rules of organization of rhythmic activity attributed to a single ganglion may be fragmented along the lines of particular functional end points subserved. The pyloric rhythm produced by the stomatogastric ganglion, for example, depends largely upon "bursty" activity inherent to the two PD cells and one AB cell, whereas the gastric-mill rhythm generated by the same ganglion is apparently more dependent upon superordinate network properties. An interesting feature revealed by the study of Selverston and others is that inhibition plays a particularly critical role in pattern generation. This is a direct confirmation of a main focus of Donald Maynard's last contributions and indicates an important reevaluation in our interpretation both of element properties and of their functional interconnections. (The importance of inhibition is also stressed in Chapter Eight.) Selverston points out that our understanding of neural circuitry involves an epistemological consideration as well as analytical details;

he makes the interesting point that, if vertebrate neurobiologists and behavioral scientists question the value of research on invertebrate preparations, it is their responsibility to assist in documenting precisely where generalizations are invalid.

In Chapter Seven, Pearson follows up on Bullock's and Selverston's documentation that a variety of specific mechanisms must be considered in neurobehavioral systems, including gating, mutual inhibition, and nonspiking inhibition. Pearson's major emphasis is upon neurons that function without action potentials. Graded (nonspiking) forms of neuronal activity and integration have only recently been documented, and Pearson provides a valuable review of their existence and possible role in a variety of systems. He points out that, although nonspiking neurons have most frequently been found in initial stages of sensory systems in invertebrates and vertebrates, they may also play a critical role in the more direct patterning of behavioral output. For example, there are nonspiking interneurons in the thoracic ganglia responsible for central patterning of insect locomotion, and in the subesophageal ganglia of lobsters and crabs that mediate patterns of ventilation.

In addition to the analyses of mechanisms (which, as Pearson notes, are still only understood in rudimentary fashion for synaptic transmission in nonspiking cells), Pearson points out various functional advantages of cells without action potentials in continually graded and precisely controlled output patterns. He then raises the important issue of what graded potentials, correlated with the observation that different anatomically defined regions of a given neuron may subserve separable functions, may indicate about traditional models of neurons as unitary functional elements. This question of defining the precise meaning of functional units in neurobiology and behavior is one that recurs repeatedly, and which deserves particular attention.

The role of hormones in the control of integrated patterns of behavior is introduced and discussed by Truman in Chapter Eight. He points out that hormonal mechanisms play a fundamental role in integration, such as in the release of activity patterns in previously established neuronal networks. His survey of vertebrate literature emphasizes the complexity of many hormonally mediated integrative systems and illustrates the value of looking at less complex networks. Truman's main focus is upon the preeclosion and eclosion behavior patterns of silkmoths. Truman's analyses demonstrate that *preeclosion* behavior in silkmoths involves two basic motor patterns that are combined into a temporal score of approximately 75 minutes in duration. He has shown, further, that the rotary and peristaltic movements are largely intrinsic to the circuitry of the abdominal ganglion, although sensory information can, to some extent, modulate temporal aspects of preeclosion behavior. The circuitry for *eclosion* movements develops before function is normally observed, as indicated to precocial movements consequent upon the peeling of pupal cuticle.

Truman also emphasizes the role of inhibition in these behavior patterns. One function of hormones, for example, is to release neuronal circuitry from its normally inhibited state, a consequence which in certain preparations can be mimicked by surgical ablation, such as decapitation in cockroaches. The importance of inhibition at the organism level has frequently been inferred by ethologists on behavioral grounds (e.g., Tinbergen, 1951; Hinde, 1970; Fentress, 1973b), and present neurobiological data support this basic contention.

Truman's data indicate the truly integrated nature of the organism and thus the importance of examining the interplay between various defined subsystems. For example, he reviews experimental data which indicate that shutting off motoneurons during eclosion produces degeneration of internal muscles which had previously formed a thick band lining the preemergent moth. Adult eclosion is in turn followed by degeneration of a large number of motoneurons in the abdominal ganglion. Many interneurons of the abdominal ganglion also degenerate, their total number in comparison to the preeclosion state being reduced from approximately 400 to 200. Thus, in addition to triggering integrated neural activity, hormones can produce irreversible consequences mediated through neuron death, a general issue previously alluded to in Chapter Three, and which will appear again in Part III.

CHAPTER FIVE

Neural Elements in Relation to Network Function

DONALD KENNEDY

INTRODUCTION

Three assumptions about the neuronal control of behavior form a useful starting point for a treatment of network properties. The first states simply that the generation of a pattern, like other important processes in the nervous system, depends upon interactions among neurons that are mediated by discrete (but not necessarily all-or-none or conducted) changes in potential. Some authors (see Chapter Four of this volume) refer to this assumption as the McCullough–Pitts doctrine. The alternative to it supposes the existence of emergent group processes not explicitly referable to events in individual neurons. Although this is an attractive prospect in many ways, no evidence now available supports it convincingly.

A second assumption is that a pattern of motor output is the most profitable place to start analyzing the origin of behavior in central nervous networks. We can infer a good deal from studies on sensory areas, and there is no denying that perception is as much a behavior as walking or courtship. But because motor acts are directly shaped by natural selection and can be described precisely in terms of the neuromuscular units of action, they give a more solid foundation on which to build.

Finally, I believe that analysis will progress further if it is undertaken in a system that is simple, in the sense that the number of participating elements and connections is as small as possible. Donald Maynard's last scientific paper (1972) argues lucidly for this proposition. So much about that paper and its author will be praised, here and elsewhere in this volume, that to take a single exception is surely permissible. Maynard holds the view that "system isolation" is an essential requirement. But behaviors, not anatomical entities, are the elements on which natural selection works in shaping neuronal organization. Thus the system we must complete is the behavioral act, not the anatomy of the control center. Elements in the neuronal ensemble may participate in other behaviors as well; or the anatomical unit may contain behaviorally irrelevant elements. Neither should matter as long as our inventory of the neurons and connections that participate in the behavior is complete

MOTOR PATTERNS

Animals execute many stereotyped movements in a complex but unvarying sequence, in which a number of parts are kept in a constant time relationship with one another. Among the examples of such behavior are the respiration of a mammal, the "singing" of a cricket, the beating of a lobster's abdominal appendates, and even the movement of a man's larynx during speech. We would like to know how the CNS commands the muscles to contract during sequenced motor output. What determines the order, the timing, and the relative emphasis of individual movements during such programs? What, in other words, are the properties of the neural *pattern generator*?

METHODS FOR DESCRIBING MOTOR PATTERNS

Motor output can be described at several levels. For the animal, the most relevant is the behavioral result of its neuromuscular work: in this sense, it would be preferable to have a record of the movement of its parts, or of some immediate result of that movement — such as one might obtain from a moving picture of the performance. Alternatively, a more intimate picture of what is going on might be gained by making electrical recordings (electromyograms) of the activity of all the participating muscles.

Some idea of the problems we face in describing behavior in terms of neural events can be gained by comparing these two methods. Both have been used to record and measure the movements of body parts in behaving animals and man.

To produce data from moving pictures that one can analyze readily is more difficult than it might appear. The scientific history of this problem is closely linked to the technological and artistic developments of instantaneous photography. The pioneers in this adventure were the Frenchman E. J. Marey and the American Edweard Muybridge; at the end of the nineteenth century, both had developed means of taking successive photographs of brief exposure with synchronized cameras. Marey developed an additional technique, "cyclography," whereby successive plots of the position of a light located on a moving part could be made. From such measurements the phase and velocity relationships in a movement could be reconstructed. Later developments included the perfection of rotating-prism cameras, which can now be used at speeds above 10,000 exposures per second, and electronic-flash photography, which permits the superimposition of briefly illuminated images on the same film without employing a shutter.

Electromyograms can be made by implanting fine-wire electrodes, insulated to their tips, into active muscles and then attaching them with adhesive cement to the body surface. The flexibility and thinness of the wire allows the ends to "ride" with the muscle, even though it moves; and, with appropriate external arrangements, the animal may be allowed to behave freely, even though the wires still connect it to the recording apparatus. Even very small muscles can be recorded over long periods of time by means of this technique.

Cinematographs (or torque measurements, or any other purely external measure) do not provide an entirely accurate portrait of the neural output program, because muscles in two different states of action can, in principle, produce exactly the same mechanical result. Flexion of a part, for example, can be accomplished by modest activity in flexor muscles accompanied by inhibition of extensors; the same movement, however, can equally well result from strong flexion opposing weak extensor outflow. No entirely external view of the behavior can discriminate between these two possibilities.

Neither, however, would a record of the neural output to the involved muscles — such as one can obtain by recording from all the motor nerves in an intact preparation — fully describe the behavior. The responses of muscles to a given frequency of motor-nerve discharge may depend upon their previous history of stimulation: we know of neuromuscular facilitation and depression processes that may last for over an hour following physiological frequencies of activation. Moreover, the muscle's response may depend on its own state. It now appears that a property termed "catch" — a tension change that outlasts the neural activation that produced it — occurs in a variety of muscles (Wilson and Larimer, 1968). The tension developed by a muscle is also affected by its initial length, by the load it is working against, and by the mechanical properties of the skeletal elements it moves. All these factors interfere with a successful prediction of behavior from a record of motor-nerve activity alone.

REFLEX CHAINS, MOTOR SCORES, AND SENSORY TEMPLATES

We can identify several alternative arrangements that might underlie a stereotyped sequence of muscular contractions. In the 1940s it was widely believed that information was returned from the periphery during the execution of each movement and then used by the CNS to initiate the next subroutine. According to this view, motor sequences depend for their phasing upon sensory feedback: the entire pattern is formed as the result of a *reflex chain.* We know of no motor systems that rely primarily upon this method, and of a great many that do not. The appendages of crustaceans employed in locomotion and ventilation, those of insects in flight and singing, and those of vertebrates in walking, all will produce the appropriate behavior patterns when each possible route of peripheral feedback has been cut — as long as adequate unpatterned excitation is fed to the CNS. Such findings eliminate another notion — that motor output could be programmed only to produce some appropriate sensory feedback (*reafference*) that matches a centrally stored version (*sensory template*) of what that feedback should look like. Such an arrangement would have the advantage of being able to compensate naturally for varying external conditions. It might produce very different motor output for the same behavior on any two trials and nevertheless satisfy the condition of producing an identical sensory feedback (Hoyle, 1964).

But for various motor output patterns, including ones involved in ventilation, feeding, locomotion, and acoustical communication, most of the program appears to be built into connections in the CNS; it is, in other words, a *motor score.* The pattern generator is subject to some influences from sensory feedback but does not obtain from it cues about sequence or phase relationships.

It was at one time doubted whether the concept of a motor score — even if it could be useful in explaining the behavior of insects and other invertebrates — was applicable to analogous processes in a vertebrate. New evidence, however, suggests that it may be. Properly ordered sequences of movements can occur in the deafferented limbs of toads, and investigators in the Soviet Union have devised a cat preparation in which the cat walks in an apparently normal way, even though the moving limbs have been deprived of sensory feedback.

PROPERTIES OF THE MOTOR SCORE

A useful analogy, first supplied by Donald M. Wilson on the basis of his studies of insect flight, compares the motor tape with a musical score. The analogy is appropriate because, like the score for a piece of orchestral music, the central program contains information about timing, intensity, and the relationship between different elements. One of the best-studied examples of a motor score is the beating of the abdominal swimmerets in lobsters and crayfish (Figure 1). This behavior is undoubtedly

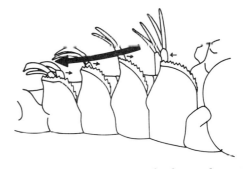

FIGURE 1.   *Swimmerets of a decapod crustacean. The anterior-most appendage, at left, is completing the power stroke, while the other three, as indicated by the small arrows, are in various phases of the return stroke. Heavy arrow shows the direction of water movement. (From Davis, 1969d.)*

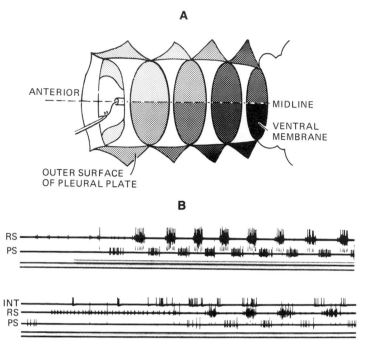

A

ANTERIOR

MIDLINE

VENTRAL
MEMBRANE

OUTER SURFACE
OF PLEURAL PLATE

B

RS

PS

INT
RS
PS

FIGURE 2. *Discharge patterns of swimmeret motoneurons and the role of command interneurons. Stimulating a single central interneuron, in the upper record of (B), produces alternating bursts of activity in the return- and power-stroke nerve (RS and PS). When the animal is mechanically stimulated in the receptive field diagrammed in (A), activity is evoked in this interneuron [top trace, second record of (B)]. Patterned output to the swimmerets accompanies interneuronal activity. (From Davis and Kennedy, 1971a.)*

derived from locomotor movements in lower crustacea, though in the lobster and crayfish it does not produce very much forward thrust. The output consists of alternating power- and return-stroke movements of each appendage. The two movements are not exact opposites: the two fringed blades of the swimmeret are spread during the power stroke, and other muscles are employed to produce a twist of the appendage that generates more thrust. Each movement cycle thus consists of several subroutines, each critically timed with respect to the others. For the moment, we can simplify them by classifying all as associated with either the power stroke or the return stroke. The neuromuscular basis of this behavior has been worked out in detail by Davis (1969a–c), from whose work much of the following description is taken.

The beating rate (expressed as the interval between corresponding points on successive cycles, or *period*) is variable, and can range from about 1 to 3 hertz. There is also a delay between adjacent body segments, so that the rhythm appears to begin at the most caudal point and progress forward. It is thus *metachronous*, like the beating of cilia in *Paramecium*, rather than *synchronous*, like the oars of a racing shell. The intersegmental delay is about 0.25 second at normal rates, so that typically when the rear segment is a third of the way through its power stroke, the segment ahead has just begun to make that same movement.

The relationships within a single segment are illustrated by the actual records, shown in Figure 2B, which were taken from a preparation in which electrical activity was recorded from the intact nerves going to the swimmeret muscles.

RELATIONSHIPS AMONG MOTONEURONS

In analyzing motor scores, we need to consider several relationships. First, what features determine the temporal differences in the discharge of different groups of motoneurons? Which groups are synchronous, and which ones are reciprocally related? Second, what governs the pattern of intervals as a function of period? For example, are the phase relationships between the activation of two different units preserved as the period of the rhythm changes? Third, how is intensity of response within any given segment of the program varied? Finally, what is the interrelationship, in a cyclic movement, between the period and the intensity of output in any given phase of the rhythm?

Fairly complete answers to these questions can be given for the swimmeret system. The conclusions also apply quite generally to other well-studied examples of stereotyped, coordinated behavior in arthropods, though it is, of course, not certain that they can be extended to other groups of animals.

Reciprocity

The motor discharge to certain pairs of muscles is always reciprocal for a given moment (i.e., always nearly 180° out of phase); in contrast, other pairs of motor units are related in a synergistic rather than an antagonistic fashion. These relationships are absolutely fixed in only a few special cases, however — for example, where muscles span a single joint that can move in only one plane. More commonly, a given muscle will have several different functions; the discharge to a given pair of muscles may therefore be characterized as synergistic or antagonistic only for a certain behavior, not for all possible kinds of movements. In those cases in which two muscles always behave as exact synergists, the motoneurons that innervate them can be considered to belong to a single pool. In arthropods, where most muscles receive peripheral inhibitory innervation, the inhibitory axon belongs to the antagonist pool because in most cases it is used reciprocally with the motoneurons that innervate the same muscle.

There is a rich (and growing) literature on the role of connections among motoneurons in determining synergism and reciprocity relations for the pattern generator. At the moment, it seems safe to say that such connections dominate the picture in networks that are relatively simple and that are concerned with a single function. Work on the stomatogastric ganglion, a small network of about 30 cells that controls the movements of the stomach in crustaceans, shows that nearly all connections critical to the rhythm are made at the motoneuron level (Maynard, 1972; Selverston and Mulloney, 1974a; Mulloney and Selverston, 1974a, b). This is perhaps the most complete reconstruction we have of a pattern-generating system, but the system is unusual in that it controls a single, continuous behavior exclusively. In insects, both inhibitory and excitatory connections between motoneurons play some role in generating the output rhythm to the major flight muscles (Kendig, 1968; Wyman, 1969a, b). In postural muscles of crustaceans, there are some mutual excitatory connections between motoneurons (Evoy, Kennedy, and Wilson, 1967; Tatton and Sokolove, 1975a, b); but these are relatively weak, and the main burden of reciprocity and synergism must depend upon interactions located presynaptic to the motoneurons. There is little evidence for strong motoneuron interaction in more complex systems that are capable of a variety of behaviors. This is not surprising because connections at the final level would fix the relationship between any given pair of motoneurons and prohibit their participation in behaviors that involve altered phase relations.

Phase Relationships

Like written music, a motor score should be playable over a range of speed without distorting its basic internal structure. Let us suppose that the three elements ("notes") a, b, and c at one speed have the temporal relationship

$$a \qquad b \quad c$$

If the three were generated by a mechanism that utilized a simple delay line between b and c, then increasing the speed with which the score is played would shorten the interval $a-b$ without affecting that between b and c. The pattern would in this way be altered to

$$a \quad b \qquad c$$

On the contrary, most motor scores adjust all intervals proportionally when the period is reduced, yielding, in our example,

$$a \quad b \quad c$$

The tendency is to maintain *constant phase*: in this case, b is two-thirds of the way between a and c (i.e., it has a phase position of 0.67 in the interval $a-c$), regardless of the period.

This is true of the phase relations between segments in the swimmeret system, although at the extremes of its dynamic range there is a weak dependence of phase upon period. In other motor scores, the same phase constancy is usual. For certain subroutines, however, latency constancy is observed. This arrangement seems particularly common in situations in which two movements are related, so that a fixed interval between them is desirable — for example, a preparatory movement followed by a strike in the feeding of a predator. Recent experiments show that delay lines function to generate the reciprocal phase relations between elevation and depression in insect flight (Burrows, 1973).

Recruitment

The strength of the discharge to a given muscle may be regulated by changes in the frequency of participating motoneurons or by recruitment of additional ones.

We are only beginning to appreciate the degree to which motoneurons belonging to a pool are individually specialized. Classically, the vertebrate motoneuron "pool" has been thought of as a population over which the threshold is distributed in approximately normal fashion. The work of Henneman and his co-workers (Henneman, Somjen, and Carpenter, 1965) and, more recently, Burke et al. (1971) has shown that for a number of motor acts the neurons in a pool are recruited in increasing order of size, with the smallest (and most tonically discharging) neurons having the lowest thresholds and the largest ones the highest. Since the largest motoneurons have the largest

(and, it now seems, the fastest) motor units in the muscle, peripheral recruitment must proceed in increasingly large steps as the intensity of drive on the motor system increases. A similar phenomenon has been shown for most inputs to power- and return-stroke motoneurons in the swimmeret system by Davis (1971). But it has also been found that particular inputs may recruit individual motoneurons selectively. Examples will be discussed below; at the moment, it should simply be pointed out that the concept of the motoneuron pool as a statistical array of unspecialized cells may be in error.

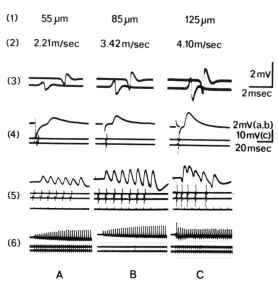

FIGURE 3. *Relationships between size and physiological properties of swimmeret motoneurons in the lobster. Three cells are compared in columns A, B, and C: as to soma diameter (1); axonal conduction velocity (2) and (3); intracellularly recorded responses in the muscle fiber in response to depolarization of the soma (4); ability to produce repetitive spikes in response to long depolarizing current pulses and muscle junctional potentials (5); facilitation of muscle responses (top trace, extracellular) in response to repetitive stimulation at 60 hertz (6). In (5) and (6), the top traces are extracellularly recorded junctional potentials; in (4), (5), and (6) the middle traces are extracellular records from the motor nerve. (From Davis, 1971.)*

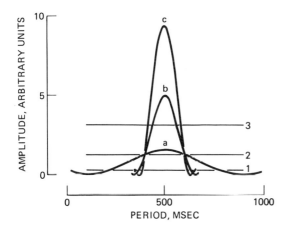

FIGURE 4. Scheme to account for the recruitment of motoneurons according to size, and for the relationship between burst duration and period. Levels 1, 2, and 3 correspond to thresholds for small, medium, and large motoneurons. This model predicts some surprising things — for example, an opposite effect of period on burst length in small and large motoneurons; but in fact these predictions are borne out. (From Davis, 1971.)

In general, the size principle predicts that the lowest-threshold motor units will be small and tonically discharging and that recruitment normally will proceed in ascending order of size. The motoneurons innervating crustacean swimmerets fit this rule (Figure 3), and for weak movements the output to return- or power-stroke muscles normally consists of a discharge in a few small motoneurons that waxes and then wanes in frequency during each burst. As the movements become stronger, the intervals decrease, and responses from larger motoneurons are also added. Since the smaller motoneurons tend to sustain a repetitive response better than large ones, the bursts become less "symmetrical" as the level of drive increases. The very largest motoneurons tend to fire only at the beginning of the movement. The details of recruitment are in agreement with the kind of model shown in Figure 4, where an underlying oscillation of approximately sinusoidal shape intercepts the thresholds of motoneurons successively, exciting the largest and most phasic ones last.

How is this pattern of recruitment related to the period of the rhythm? For natural movements, there is often a positive correlation between the strength of the movement and the frequency with which it occurs. In the swimmeret rhythm, the effects upon period and intensity are coupled, so that when the period decreases the intensity of motor output increases. This proportionality may reflect a basic property of the driving oscillation.

These conclusions, it will be noted, have all been drawn *entirely* by investigating motor elements without probing into the CNS itself. We may summarize them by suggesting that the motor score is generated by a series of segmental neurons or networks that behave like oscillators; these are located presynaptically to the motoneurons; a linkage between oscillators in the different segments holds a constant phase relationship between them. The excitability of oscillators and/or motoneurons may be controlled by various reflex inputs from sense organs associated with the moving parts and by elements within the CNS that are used to initiate movements. We may now turn to the CNS and ask what the relationship is between the pattern-generating network and these other elements.

MOTOR "COMMANDS"

In the CNS of arthropods and other invertebrates there are single nerve cells that, when stimulated, can release an entire pattern of coordinated behavior. Such "command" neurons, studied extensively in postural motor systems in the crayfish abdomen (Evoy and Kennedy, 1967; Larimer and Kennedy, 1969) and also in the control of the swimmeret system (Davis and Kennedy, 1972), have the following properties:

1) There are only a few of them. Most interneurons in the CNS of a crayfish, for example, respond to one kind of sensory stimulation or other; but they have no obvious motor effect when stimulated as single fibers. Less than 1 percent of the cells produce behavior, and often these cannot be shown also to respond to

specific kinds of sensory stimulation. Presumably, they have complex input requirements, as we might expect from a nerve cell that is very close to the motor side of the nervous system. But in some instances it is possible to show that their inputs are functionally related to their effects — that is, that they are driven by stimuli that produce actions identical to those produced by the command neuron. The cell that produces the rhythm in Figure 2B, shown in the bottom record, is such a command interneuron. Its receptive field is diagrammed in Figure 2A.

2) They produce coordinated activity in a great many motor elements. Some of the single command neurons that activate flexion or extension in the crayfish abdomen affect the discharge of over 200 motoneurons, all of them in proper reciprocal relationship. Command neurons for the swimmeret rhythm have equally widely distributed effects, which are much more complex because cyclical temporal patterning is involved.

3) Different elements may appear to produce similar behavioral results; but more careful analysis has always revealed differences between the outputs. For example, of several command interneurons that produce abdominal flexion, one may exert its most prominent effect upon the caudal segments, another may emphasize anterior flexion, and still another may produce an evenly distributed response. The difference in this case lies in how much influence the command cell has upon each segmental ganglion. Or command elements may sometimes differ according to which specific motoneurons in a given segment they excite most strongly.

In the swimmeret system, single command fibers can elicit the entire program of rhythmic movements involving all the segments (Davis and Kennedy, 1972). No single neuron, however, can take care of the entire performance range of the system. For example, the swimmeret beat in normal lobsters shows a range of periods that is much wider than can be evoked by varying the frequency at which any single command neuron is stimulated. We must presume that different elements are active over different portions of the output range. There are also command neurons that produce incomplete rhythms, in which either the power- or return-stroke is deficient. Such elements *must*, we suppose, be used with others in the control of normal behavior. It is found that, as in the abdominal postural system, command cells produce different segmental distributions of motor outflow.

Careful comparison of the responses produced by command fibers has shown that they closely resemble behaviors produced spontaneously by the intact organism. For abdominal postural changes and for swimmeret movement, as well as for a number of behaviors now being studied in mollusks, the activity evoked by stimulation of single neurons is indistinguishable from an element in the animal's natural repertoire. It also should be emphasized that, although some behaviors may require simultaneous activity in more than one command element, the system is not organized so as to depend on such control; despite the exception mentioned above, command elements do not *usually* code for parts of movements. One might have predicted that to move an appendage would require activity in several premotor cells, each one controlling a given set of muscles, or that there would be separate commands for the different segments in the swimmeret rhythm. This is not the case. Instead, each control unit seems to preside over a relatively complete, albeit somewhat specialized, behavioral routine. This pattern of control was aptly described by Hughlings Jackson, a pioneer British neurologist of the nineteenth century, who said of mammals that "the central nervous system controls movements, not muscles."

HIERARCHICAL ORGANIZATION

The opportunity to work with single neurons that elicit whole patterns of behavior has made it possible to think about the hierarchical organization of the elements in behavioral control. In the CNS, some neuron or group of neurons must generate the fundamental rhythmic excitation that underlies patterned output. We call this an oscillator but are still careful to avoid saying what it is exactly. It could be a single cell that is capable of pacemaker-like oscillations in potential, a group of cells sharing that property, or a group of cells lacking that property but driven by steady excitation, and connected in such a way that they convert unpatterned excitation into patterned output.

Evidence given already suggests that the motoneurons are not part of this pattern-generating network in most cases, so we believe that the oscillator is presynaptic to the motoneurons. The command neurons must form still another, higher layer. This conclusion is based upon the way in which command fibers affect the oscillation. In the swimmeret system, they increase the intensity of output and decrease the period simultaneously — just like cardio-accelerator fibers to the mammalian heart, which increase both the strength of contraction and the heart rate. In contrast, reflex inputs to the swimmerets often decrease or increase the strength of motoneuron discharge *without affecting the period of the bursts at all*. The latter result would be expected if the input were to the motoneurons directly; the former could occur only if the oscillator itself were activated.

The most difficult elements to place in the hierarchy are those that control the phase relations between different participating motor centers. This process has been directly studied only in the case of the swimmeret rhythm, in which separate segmental oscillators that can run independently are linked in phase. *Coordinating* neurons in the CNS that run between ganglia have been described by Stein (1971). They are neither sensory fibers nor motoneurons, since they are active in deafferented preparations and their discharge lags a little behind the motoneuron activity in the segment from which they come. What they do is to send a "copy" of the efferent discharge in one set of motoneurons to the next segment. If the pathway is cut, the two segments lose their phase relationship. Stein has shown that, when the coordinating signal arrives "early" (i.e., when the dependent member is delayed in phase), the effect is to add excitation and so advance the phase of the recipient oscillator. If, on the other hand, the coordinating signal arrives "late" and coincides with output from the recipient oscillator, the phase of the next and subsequent signals from the latter is retarded.

FAST MOVEMENTS

Quite unlike the rhythmic, intersegmentally coordinated movements that appendages make during the locomotion of segmented animals are escape or "strike" movements executed by single contractions of specialized sets of fast muscles. Various prey-capture movements, as well as certain kinds of locomotion, fall into this second category. In crustaceans such as crayfish and lobsters, most of the musculature of the abdomen is concerned with a behavior that the animal executes only occasionally, consisting of a rapid shortening of abdominal flexor muscles that propels the animal rapidly backward and out of danger. The innervation of these muscles and their control by the CNS was first studied by Wiersma (1947) and later by our group (Kennedy and Takeda, 1965a; Selverston and Remler, 1972). The basic facts are simple. In each abdominal segment, approximately 10 large motoneurons innervate the abdominal fast-flexor muscles of one side. One of these is a specialized "giant" motoneuron, which innervates every flexor muscle fiber in the segment. A second is an inhibitor, which also goes to each muscle fiber. The rest are nongiant motoneurons, and each of these innervates a smaller group of muscle fibers that occupy the more localized region. All these cells, except the inhibitor, are activated by two pairs of central command elements, the lateral and medial giant neurons. It now appears that the synaptic activation of motoneurons by interneurons is electrical in each case; this was first shown for the giant motor fiber by Furshpan and Potter (1959), but recently Zucker (1972c) demonstrated that the nongiant elements, although their synapses appear quite different, are activated in the same way.

The lateral and medial giant fibers are quite different from one another. The medials have their cell bodies and dendritic processes in the brain and only appear to receive input there; their axons extend for the length of the CNS. The lateral giant fibers, in contrast, are *septate*

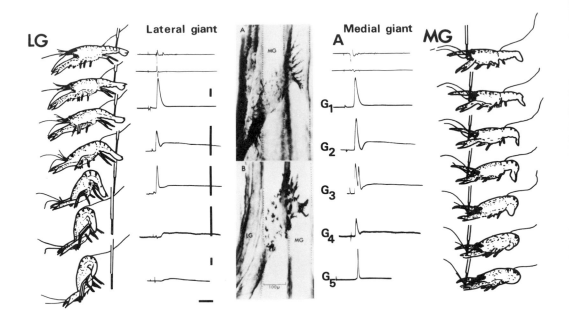

FIGURE 5. *Responses of crayfish to activity in the lateral (left) and medial (right) giant fibers. The sketches at extreme left and right are tracings from high-speed moving pictures of the behavior (Wine and Krasne, 1972); the recordings are from the postsynaptic motor giant neuron, recorded intracellularly in ganglia 1 through 5 (G_{1-5}) in response to stimulation of the central giant fibers, whose responses are shown in the top two traces of each panel. The center photographs show cobalt stains of the synaptic junctions between the lateral giant (LG) and medial giant (MG) fibers and the segmental motor giant neurons in an anterior segment (top picture) and in a posterior segment (bottom picture). Synapses show as dark tufts; in the top picture they occur on LG (extreme left) as well as both MG neurons; in the bottom picture, they are missing from LG. This correlates with the presence of postsynaptic responses to LG in the anterior ganglia, and accounts for their absence posteriorly. Calibrations: vertical, 20 mV; horizontal, 10 msec. (From Wine and Mittenthal, 1973.)*

elements; each segment contains a cell body and a length of axon, and the latter abuts against a similar axon in the adjacent body segment. Thus an uninterrupted chain of elements is formed from separate cells; only elements in the abdominal segments receive connections from input fibers.

Giant Fiber "Escape" Responses

At first it was believed that the two kinds of central giant fibers produced identical behaviors, because a single impulse in either produced rapid flexions of the tail. A more careful examination, carried out both in physiological preparations (Larimer et al., 1971) and in behaving animals (Wine and Krasne, 1972), showed that medial and lateral giants produce different behaviors (Figure 5). The former evoke contractions of the abdominal flexors in all segments, including the terminal ones, and the resulting movement carries the animal straight backward. The lateral giants, in contrast, fail to activate the main flexors in the terminal segments and also produce a different action on the last appendages, the uropods; the result is a sculling stroke that takes the animal upward, so much so that it often produces a complete somersault. The two kinds of movements are obviously adaptive responses to the different sorts of stimuli that activate these two command systems. Lateral giant activity is initiated only by mechanical stimuli that originate caudally, and it appropriately evokes escape in a headward direction; medial giant axons are activated in the head region and trigger backward escape.

Specific Connections of Giant Fibers and the Form of the Behavior

Recent evidence (Wine and Mittenthal, 1973) shows that these behavioral actions can be explained by directly visualized differences in the abdominal connections made between the central giant fibers and the segmental giant motoneurons. In the anterior segments, both lateral and medial receive branches from the postsynaptic motor cells; these form an unmistakable pattern when the motor axons are filled with cobalt ions by iontophoresis, and the latter are then precipitated as the sulfide (Figure 5). But in the last two segments, the synaptic branches to the lateral giant are clearly missing, whereas those from the median giant are present. This distribution correlates perfectly with the presence and absence of postsynaptic responses in the motor elements. In fact, this arrangement is exactly like the one proposed for the command interneurons that control slower movements: for a given class of actions, there may be a set of command elements each of which makes a slightly different set of segmental connections with output systems. In the case of the fast-flexor system, these differences can be reconstructed anatomically, whereas for the postural command elements it can so far only be postulated on the basis of physiologically recorded output patterns.

As command elements, the lateral giant fibers — about which most is known — differ in at least two respects from the interneurons that produce postural movements or multi-appendage locomotion. First, they have extremely high thresholds for activation by sensory input, as would be expected from the relative rarity of the behavior they produce; and, second, they can elicit the full behavioral act by discharging only a single impulse (repetitive tail flicks, or swimming, are quite different, and in any event do not depend upon repetitive activity in giant fibers). Both these properties relate to an attribute of the organization of output patterns described earlier under the general rubric of size principle: larger elements tend to have higher thresholds and to respond more phasically to continuous input. The lateral giant neuron and the behavior it evokes represent the extreme of a continuum: a system of phasic neural elements controls a ballistic movement, and at all levels (command elements, motoneurons, and muscles) it is arranged in parallel with a slow system for accomplishing postural movements of the same joints (Kennedy and Takeda, 1965a, b).

Excitation of the Lateral Giant Neuron

The lateral giant fibers are normally excited by activity in afferent fibers that connect with mechanosensitive hairs in the tail segments. The hairs themselves may be excited by direct touch or by near-field disturbances in the water around the animal; the primary sensory neurons connect with the lateral giant neurons directly *via* electrical synapses, but even simultaneous activity in all of them would be inadequate to excite the lateral giant neurons by this route. There is a more powerful indirect pathway, involving sensory interneurons that receive excitatory chemical input from the afferent neurons and in turn make electrical connections with the lateral giant neuron. These relationships, worked out mainly by Zucker (1972a–c), are illustrated in Figure 6.

Sensory Feedback from Fast Movements

The movement produced by a single impulse in a lateral giant fiber is a dramatic event: it can move the animal many centimeters through the water in 50 msec or less, and it produces violent activity in many of the sense organs that normally function to detect events of outside origin in the quiescent animal. The mechanoreceptor hairs that are involved in triggering the behavior are themselves powerfully excited by the movement. This raises interesting problems for the organism, and also serves to introduce a different perspective on the role that sense organs might play in the patterning of locomotor behavior. If receptors are excited during the execution of a movement, they may produce reflexes of their own

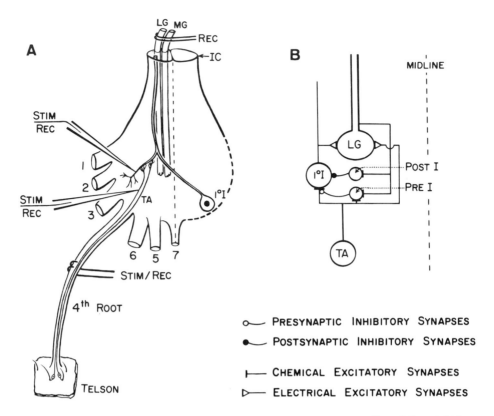

FIGURE 6. Cellular elements involved in the lateral giant escape reflex. LG and MG, central lateral and medial giant fibers; 1°I, primary interneurons; TA, tactile afferents; IC, interganglionic connectives. (A) shows the experimental arrangement for studies of presynaptic inhibition mediated by LG; (B) is a schematic diagram of the neuronal circuit. (From Kennedy, Calabrese, and Wine, 1974.)

that are inappropriate for the movement or that actually interfere with its completion. Muscle receptors in the crayfish abdomen, for example, respond strongly to flexion and produce reflex discharge to postural extensor muscles; if it occurred quickly enough, this response could interfere with full flexion. Similarly, many other resistance reflexes, including those mediated by vertebrate muscle spindles, might interfere with the completion of a movement. This does not happen in most cases because the excitability of these receptors is under the control of the CNS, through efferent innervation.

The animal also requires that sense organs retain their excitability following motor activity, when the rest position is resumed. If the mechanoreceptors that evoke the tail flick

lost their synaptic efficacy, the next stimulus appropriate for an escape might not produce one. From experiments by Zucker (1972b) we know that the synaptic sites between tactile afferents and nongiant interneurons are very vulnerable to habituation upon repetitive stimulation. These junctions are located at the first stage of the cascade that is essential to exciting the lateral giant neuron (Figure 6). If each escape rendered them ineffectual for many minutes, the animal would be in obvious difficulty.

Krasne and Bryan (1973) demonstrated that activity in the lateral giant neuron produces powerful inhibition of these synapses, and they offered evidence that the inhibition also offered "protection" against the habituating effects of repeated stimulation. Not only did the protecting effect seem to explain the utility of the inhibitory system; it also suggested strongly that the inhibition was actually exerted against the sensory terminals themselves, reducing the loss of transmitter they experienced as a result of the activity evoked by the tail flip (Figure 6A). Subsequently, we demonstrated directly by recording with microelectrodes from the afferent terminals themselves that the site of inhibition is presynaptic (Kennedy, Calabrese, and Wine, 1974). As in the vertebrate spinal cord, a depolarization of the afferent terminals is involved; in the crayfish, it is possible to show that the conductance change involved in the depolarization is large enough to reduce the amplitude of a propagating sensory inpulse. In this way presumably, the inhibitory input acts to reduce the amount of transmitter released and to husband more for subsequent periods of quiescence.

There is every reason to believe that such mechanisms will be important for any animal engaging in vigorous "voluntary" actions that might excite inappropriate reflexes or exhaust the sensory systems that are secondarily activated. In at least three other cases of rapid escape behavior, similar phenomena have been described. Crickets, for example, run rapidly forward when sensory receptors on their caudal cerci are stimulated with a puff of air. Murphey and Palka (1974) have shown that there is central inhibition of the synapses made by these receptors when the animal engages in spontaneous walking activity. In the frog spinal cord, presynaptic inhibition of afferents from the skin can be evoked by antidromic stimulation of motor nerves in the hind-limb segments. The inhibition is very powerful if the extensor muscle nerves are stimulated but weak if the flexors are stimulated (Carpenter and Rudomin, 1973). It seems quite likely that this inhibitory pathway is selectively involved with the major ballistic movement of the hind legs, the jump. Finally, in amphibians, rapid (but not slow) movements of the body musculature are normally preceded by inhibition of lateral-line mechanoreceptor afferents (Russell, 1971). In this instance, the inhibition is excited against the primary receptor cells — but in the periphery, because here the transducing elements are epithelial and not neural, and therefore lack an afferent process. The result is

the same: recurrent inhibition that prevents interfering reflexes and that preserves the sentience of the afferent system.

It may be that this is the primitive system for providing recurrent information about the output state of motor systems and that more sophisticated uses evolved later. One example has already been given: where intermember coordination is required, similar signals may be necessary in order to ensure preservation of the proper phase. Another function involves what we may call the signaling of expectation to sensory systems that will be excited by the movement. Instead of grossly inhibiting reafference, a quantified movement command could be used to deliver an amount of inhibition that would precisely cancel the amount of excitation expected to result from the movement. In this way the organism could in principle achieve a kind of world constancy, in which self-generated changes in primary orientation would be automatically compensated for. Such notions have been around for a long time under the labels "corollary discharge" and "efference-copy." There is now direct evidence for such an influence on the sensory discharge from the semicircular canals of fish, exerted by visual stimuli that presumably induced "intended" rotations (Klinke and Schmidt, 1970).

In a variety of movements, such as the crayfish tail flip, the execution is so rapid that sensory signals generated during the movement cannot provide critical information for the completion *of that movement*. This is true for such skilled human gestures as piano playing or speech. The rate at which the individual elements follow one another is too fast for reflex information about the state of the movement to be fed back to the CNS. Similarly, accurate single movements directed toward a goal — such as the strike of a praying mantis, an eye saccade, or the hockey player's slap shot — are executed without the chance of correction enroute.

For such ballistic movements, expectation must be critically important. An appreciation of the distances involved and the loads to be encountered requires complex sensory calculation and automatic compensation at the site of command. This mechanism simply prepares the central nervous command for the circumstances that will prevail in the actual movement. It seems likely that many skilled movements in man make use of highly automated predictions of this kind, fed forward to the motor centers and based upon a previously learned context for the movement. This may be one reason why so many motor systems, like those of the crayfish abdomen, have separate central locations for the control of slow and fast movements. Even in mammals, including man, there is growing evidence for such separation: the basal ganglia appear involved with the programming of slow movements, the cerebellum with fast ones.

THE ROLE OF PROPRIOCEPTION IN LOAD COMPENSATION

We cannot similarly rule out a directive action for sensory feedback in slower movements, because there is adequate time for it to play such a role. Yet evidence is available from a variety of locomotor systems, cited at the beginning of this chapter, that sensory feedback does not usually contribute to the basic patterning of the motor program. What, then, is its role? An important one appears to be correction for load and other unpredictable environmental variables encountered during the execution of a movement.

To accomplish load compensation, it is necessary to supply incremental excitation to a muscle in proportion to the load. The load may be detected by measuring the tension in the tendon of the muscle, and, in principle, such "series" receptors as Golgi tendon organs in vertebrates could be employed in load-compensating circuits. They would have to be arranged as in Figure 7, so that the response of the tendon receptor excites the motoneurons going to its own muscle. The trouble is that one particular length — the length that produced zero tension in the tendon — would be the permanent zero point for the system. It would be better if the zero point were adjustable, so that the amplitude of the desired movement could be started from any value of static tension. Perhaps this lack of flexibility explains why the tendon receptors known to date appear not to function in load compensation.

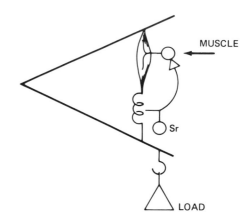

FIGURE 7. *Arrangement of tendon (series) receptors (Sr) in a load-compensating circuit. A command to the motoneuron (arrow) results in shortening; tension in the tendon is proportional to the load, and incremental excitation is thus fed to the motoneuron.*

Similar receptors located in the muscle may be equipped to accomplish load compensation by making the arrangement a little more complicated. Specialized muscle fibers, arranged in parallel instead of in series with the "working" muscle, are activated by the same motor program that drives the latter. A process of this kind occurs in mammalian muscle spindles. The small (gamma) motoneurons that innervate the specialized muscle fibers of the spindle are activated along with the large motoneurons to the muscle in voluntary human movements (Vallbo, 1971). Figure 8, which shows the muscle receptor organs found in the abdomen of crayfish and lobsters, illustrates another such circuit. In this case, activity of motoneurons that innervate both the receptor and working muscle fibers causes both to shorten together. The receptor is "in series" with its own special muscle, just like the tendon organ in Figure 7; it therefore discharges whether its muscle contracts or is passively stretched by a load. If a load is applied, the shortening of the receptor muscle will get ahead of that in the working muscle, and the receptor discharges more impulses. The heavier the load, the more the working muscle is impeded. This

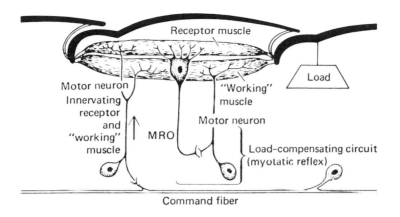

FIGURE 8. *Arrangement of muscle receptor organ (MRO) in the crayfish abdomen. The parallel receptor muscle shares innervation with the slow extensors, which are also innervated by a "private" motoneuron excited by the MRO. Commands to the shared motor pathway produce shortening of both muscles at once; but if there is a load, proportional excitation will develop in the MRO because tension is produced in the receptor muscle. This load-dependent excitation will activate the unshared motoneuron and add excitation to the muscle reflexly.*

produces a greater length difference between the receptor muscle and the working muscle, and leads to further discharge in the receptor. For this reason, the incremental excitation in the receptor is sometimes called an "error signal." This term, borrowed from control theory, merely expresses the fact that the load causes a length difference to develop between the two muscles as they shorten. The *difference* represents the amount by which the preprogrammed movement has fallen short of the point it would have reached if unloaded. Since the signal is proportional to this error, it is corrective when it is applied to the working muscle. This is done by central reflex connections between the receptor and motoneurons that innervate the working muscle.

There is good evidence that such load compensation takes place in the mammalian respiratory system (Corda, Eklund, and von Euler, 1965) and in abdominal extension in the crayfish (Fields, Evoy, and Kennedy, 1967; Sokolove, 1973). The experiments show convincingly that circuits involving efferently innervated muscle receptors function to oppose unexpectedly added loads. In both systems, stopping a movement from the outside produces a sudden burst of receptor activity and an increase in the motor output.

THE SIGNIFICANCE OF DISCHARGE PATTERNS IN SINGLE NEURONS

Single cells recorded in the intact CNS of an animal often display what is casually termed "patterned" activity. Most investigators use this term to describe distributions of impulse intervals that differ both from the constant-interval form of activity (Figure 9A) and from random activity that would yield an exponential interval discharge (Figure 9B). The former is characteristic of many "pacemaker" cells; the latter would be produced, for example, by a sensory element subjected to a source of "noise." Departures from these distributions could be produced by special membrane properties or by clustered arrival of input. Characteristically, these discharge patterns involve two or more peaks of preferred intervals, and can be called "bursty." Because such distributions can have very selective effects on the junctions that receive them and because they are often characteristic of elements that control output programs, they are commonly treated as a potential code by which single elements could yield information about the properties of their input.

To make the possibilities more explicit, we can consider what significance the discharge

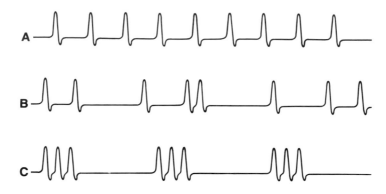

FIGURE 9. Patterns of impulse activity in neurons. (A) constant-frequency "pacemaker" discharge. (B) random-interval discharge. (C) "bursty" discharge with two interval modes.

pattern shown in Figure 9C might carry. It might simply be a way of exciting a postsynaptic neuron more effectively, by separating the discharge into periods of high activity and no activity and thus taking advantage of the properties of facilitation and summation that are characteristic of many junctions; in this way a kind of impulse economy might be achieved, because the pattern would be more effective than the same number of impulses distributed evenly over time. But there is a more tantalizing possibility: if the cell produced bursts in response to one kind on input but some other form of discharge in response to another, the pattern could serve as a label for identifying the two forms of input. To demonstrate that something of this sort was occurring, it would be necessary to show that the cell in question produced a different postsynaptic result when active in its two modes.

The latter proposition has been around for some time. It was once offered (though without direct experimental support) as an explanation of how some cutaneous receptors in mammals might differentially signal touch, pain, and other sensations. More recently it has stimulated a number of analyses of interval statistics in the discharge of central neurons. However, few situations have been found in which single neurons reliably signal input states by alterations in discharge pattern, and in no case has such a cell been shown to influence different populations of postsynaptic cells by such pattern changes.

The first proposal is supported by more evidence. Preferred intervals that occur naturally in some crustacean motoneurons appear to be optimal for exciting tension in the muscles that they innervate (Wilson and Davis, 1965). In another case, a burst pattern characteristic of a particular motoneuron activates muscle tensions equivalent to those that would be produced by constant-frequency discharges 10 to 15 percent higher in average frequency. In the latter instance, the discharge pattern is not a property of input timing; instead, it depends directly upon properties intrinsic to the motoneuron itself (Gillary and Kennedy, 1969a, b).

The capacity to discharge in such patterns makes neurons of this kind candidates for the basic cycle timers of such output rhythms as were described in the swimmeret system. Although we can now assign that role in a general way to the CNS, we still have not identified the pattern generator for any single case. It need not be assumed that single cells provide the basic rhythm; an attractive alternative is that the rhythm could be an emergent property of a multicellular network. One such model was originally proposed by Wilson and Waldron (1968) for insect flight. Two cells receive steady excitation of an unpatterned kind, and reciprocal inhibitory connections between them cause their discharge to alternate. Thus the pattern is characteristic of neither cell; it is a product of their association. Most studies on neuronal networks have focused upon the properties of connections as the source of their output pattern. In one of the most complete analyses of this kind, however, Maynard (1972) showed that the basic cycle timing was actually the property of a single cell in the network. The connections serve only in the "fine tuning" of phase relationships within the cycle. We do not now actually know of a single case in which connectivity — as opposed to the properties of isolated cells — is responsible for the most basic features of a motor output pattern. (See the next chapter (Six) for a more detailed discussion of this issue.)

A Model System for the Study of Rhythmic Behavior

ALLEN SELVERSTON

INTRODUCTION

Many kinds of behavioral activities in both vertebrates and invertebrates are cyclical in nature. Such activities include not only those which are vital to sustain life, such as the beating of the heart or the maintenance of respiration, but also those which are utilized intermittently as part of the organism's normal behavior patterns. It is known that, in many cases, the origin of such behaviors is centrally generated and can exist without continuous sensory feedback.

If we are to understand how nervous systems generate behavioral activities, cyclically repeating motor patterns are a good place to start. By their very nature, they allow repeated study of the basic mechanisms involved. In addition, since they can often be isolated from their central and peripheral inputs and still continue to operate, they provide a system that can be studied in more or less "pure" form.

The value of taking a comparative approach to the analysis of such cylical behavior patterns is that principles may well emerge from the study of simple networks which can be generalized to the more complex brains of vertebrates. Indeed, in a great many invertebrate preparations, progress toward determination of their functional circuitry is revealing more commonly shared properties than unique differences.

POSSIBLE MECHANISMS FOR THE PRODUCTION OF CYCLIC BEHAVIOR

The once generally accepted hypothesis that animal behavior was built upon a series of reflexes has been replaced by the idea of central pattern generation. With very few exceptions, the role of sensory feedback seems to be one of adjustment and modulation of the central score. The most convincing proof of this hypothesis was presented by the late Donald Wilson and has since been shown to be applicable to many invertebrate behavioral patterns (Wilson, 1966). Wilson based his ideas on extracellular recordings made from the nerves and muscles of the insect flight system. Since then, many workers have followed the general approach of correlating behavior with the activities of specific nerves and muscles and then tracing these activities back into the central nervous system, where they originate.

The problems involved in analyzing the synaptic circuitry of even numerically small central nervous systems has proved to be extremely difficult for those working on arthropods. Processes in the neuropile are usually too small to penetrate with microelectrodes and the cell bodies are either not visible or electrically unresponsive. Central connections have been established for molluscan systems, but usually the behavioral role of such circuits is not known. Despite the absence of intracellular data from insect neuropile, Wilson and his colleagues were able to suggest that the alternating bursts of activity in the elevator and depressor muscles could be generated by sets of reciprocally inhibitory neurons. One school of thought followed Wilson's belief that not only the bursting per se but also the correct phase relationships between bursts was a property of the network. A second group believed that within any network there was one or more cells that had the intrinsic capacity to burst and could act as the driving force for the entire network. Ingenious experimental evidence had shown that complete electrical isolation of some cell bodies by ligation or dissection did not interfere with their burst-generating mechanism (Alving, 1968).

We can state each hypothesis in a more formal way:

1) Endogenous bursting holds that within a particular subset of neurons there is contained one or more cells with endogenous burst capability. This cell or cells, by virtue of chemical synaptic and/or electrotonic connections, acts as the principal driving source for the rhythm, with the other cells acting as followers. Correct phase relationships are established by synaptic connections among the cells in the network.

2) Network bursting holds that no single cell has burst-generating capabilities but that bursting and correct phase relation-ships "emerge" as a property of the network and the cooperative interaction of its cells.

Many oscillatory networks are not active continuously and the way in which they get turned on and off is poorly understood at present. The network may be delicately balanced between an active and a nonactive state. If some of the neurons have spontaneous pacemaker activity (i.e., continuous firing but not in bursts), the transformation from one state to another may be triggered by an increase in the firing rate of these cells. Such an increased firing rate could result from either specific excitatory inputs or from a change in the level of some hormone to which the cells were sensitive. It is also possible that if sufficient external inputs are present, all the cells in the network could be completely silent when bursting is not present and thrown into activity by these external sources. Whether continuous input or a single burst of this input is required to start and maintain the rhythm would depend upon the global properties of the neurons and synapses present.

EXPERIMENTAL TESTS OF EACH HYPOTHESIS

If a circuit that produces bursting output can be described in relatively complete form, then each hypothesis is testable. With regard to the endogenous burster hypothesis, the primary experimental question is to determine whether or not there are cells which, if deprived of all synaptic input, continue to burst regularly. One way to remove such input is by altering the Ca^{2+}/Mg^{2+} ratios in a way that blocks synaptic transmission. Careful controls must be carried out to demonstrate that such ionic alterations have no effect on the endogenous burst-generating mechanism of the cell. A more definitive experiment is to isolate suspected somata mechanically and to examine their membranes for burst-generating capability. This has been accomplished both by ligating the neck of the cell and by removing the cell body totally from the ganglion.

If a cell is bursting endogenously, one would expect midburst hyperpolarizations or the addition of extra spikes to affect the bursting rhythm, whereas, if the bursts were the result of synaptic input, one would not expect such effects (Strumwasser, 1968). The rationale behind such an experimental design is that altering a cell's burst should not interfere with any synaptic inputs to it. If a cell that is postsynaptic to an endogenous burster is silenced or becomes free-running when the suspected burster cell is shut off by hyperpolarization, but not the reverse, a reasonable interpretation is that the "burster" cell is providing the driving force for the system. Of course, if there is more than one endogenous burster, care must be taken to ensure that all are completely shut off and that none are still contributing any rhythm to the nonbursting cells.

Further evidence that supports the burster cell hypothesis can be obtained from examining the response of a burster cell to slow ramps of depolarizing and hyperpolarizing current. As Arvanataki and Chalazonitis (1968) have so elegantly shown, endogenously bursty cells begin to fire in bursts when they reach threshold. As depolarization continues, the number of spikes per burst increases and the interburst interval decreases until the neuron fires steadily. In contrast, cells without such capability begin firing steadily at threshold, and only their interspike interval becomes shorter as depolarization progresses.

A final test, applicable to those bursty cells whose membranes show slow dc oscillations even when not firing, is suggested by evidence that implicates a time-variant electrogenic Na^+/K^+ pump. If such a pump is responsible for the oscillations, and there is no general rule regarding this, one might suspect that interference with the pump, by reducing external Na^+ to 0, or by adding dinitrophenol lithium, or ouabain, would eliminate the oscillations and any spikes that might result as a consequence of their membrane potential crossing threshold during the depolarizing phase (Willows, Getting, and Thompson, 1973). A more general experimental approach is to examine the ionic currents by means of a voltage clamp. Such a clamp would hold the cells voltage at a constant value by means of artificially applied current. The time course and amounts of such current would be proportional to any ion fluxes that cross the cell membrane during normal oscillatory activity. By means of ion substitutions, the identification of those ions responsible for the voltage variations may become known.

In some ways, oscillatory systems driven by endogenous bursters are easier to analyze than those in which no single cell or group of cells is responsible for generating the driving rhythm. The most serious problem is that it is often difficult to know whether or not all the cells in a particular circuit have been isolated and examined for spontaneous bursting.

If no cells with endogenous burst activity can be found within a given network and the network can still produce bursts when isolated from any external sources of input, the burst-generating mechanism must derive from the properties of the cells and their connections. What is the simplest form of neural connectivity which might produce alternating bursts? Wilson (1966) and others have shown that two reciprocally inhibitory cells are capable of alternate bursting if they are spontaneous pacemakers or driven by random excitatory input. Neither cell itself is capable of bursting, but the cooperative action of their synaptic connections confers this property upon them.

If more neurons and synapses are added to the circuit, more complex motor patterns can be generated, but it becomes increasingly difficult to explain them on the basis of each unit's interactions. Modeling of such networks, either with neuromimes, or digital computer simulations, is often helpful and can have predictive value experimentally. One such simulation, developed by Donald Perkel, is capable of modeling the complex interactions of up to several hundred neurons, and its use in some preliminary modeling studies of the lobster stomatogastric system will be described in a subsequent section.

Given the extremely wide range of nervous systems, how does one decide which one is the most analyzable in terms of securing a functional wiring diagram? The wiring diagram is simply a neural circuit in which identifiable nerve cells are treated as single units and any synaptic or electrical contacts they have with one another are so indicated. Conceptually, they have the same role as the schematic wiring diagram of the electrical engineer. Such wiring diagrams for neurons are usually limited to groups that subserve a specific functional role, such as the movement of an appendage. The wiring diagram for such specific groups is often called a network or circuit, the terms being interchangeable, for a particular behavior. In general, such wiring diagrams do not indicate the specific cellular properties of the neurons nor the quantitative effectiveness of the synaptic or ephaptic connections. To obtain the experimental evidence for the formulation of such diagrams the most direct approach is to study the effect of one neuron's activity on the activity of another by means of intracellular microelectrodes. What criteria give one preparation an advantage over another?

The advantages of invertebrate nervous systems are well known and need not be repeated here. But even with simple systems the sine qua non of establishing a network's circuitry is the ability to monitor the subthreshold integrative activity of the cell and not just its axonal spike patterns. We can learn a great deal about motor output by studying neuromuscular junctions and activity in peripheral nerves, but the mechanisms involved in pattern formation reside within the central nervous system and it is here that their detailed analysis must occur. If we can observe postjunctional potentials as well as spikes from the cell somata and this activity is not too distorted or attenuated by its distance from the actual postsynaptic loci, the pattern of connections can be ascertained with a high degree of reliability. If, in addition, the number of neurons involved in the generation of a particular behavior pattern is reasonably small, it is possible in many instances to work out the circuit in relatively complete form.

For an electrophysiological analysis to be meaningful, it is important that any network operate in near normal fashion when removed from the organism. In a few cases, intracellular recordings can be made from the central nervous system *in situ*, and synaptic activity can be studied while the animal is restrained but otherwise reasonably intact (Willows, 1968). In most instances, however, the central ganglia must be removed from the animal for intracellular recording and this abolishes not only its normal afference but also the effect of possible blood-borne factors which could effect

the network's activity. If the recordings of motor activity, sampled by EMGs or chronic peripheral nerve electrodes, have the same general pattern as that which is obtained from the isolated ganglion, one can assume that the isolation procedure, in and of itself, is not altering the basic pattern-generating mechanism. Hopefully, once a circuit is established for an isolated network, the influence of sensory input and/or "command" interneurons can be studied independently of one another.

If the oscillatory output is refractive to change by specific inputs, it becomes less interesting in terms of serving as a model. A very restrictive network, such as the cardiac ganglion of the lobster, has such a narrow range of activity that, even if all its connectivity could be established, it would not be a good representative of behaviors that have broader dynamic ranges. On the other hand, if the behavioral activity has such a wide range that many hundreds of neurons could participate in its genesis and modulation, it may not be experimentally tractable in terms of defining all the neurons involved in its production.

One final note with regard to some of the criteria necessary for an analysis of oscillatory-type circuits is the ability to examine the anatomical substrates of the cells involved. Such studies can not only help to confirm the electrophysiological data but can also suggest mechanisms not always apparent from a functional analysis. Although a combined study is probably the most fruitful in terms of a complete understanding, it is in the establishment of an anatomical basis for electrophysiological data that we are presently most deficient. New methodologies are being developed, particularly intracellular dye injections (Selverston, 1973), which will allow correlative studies, but a definitive structural analysis of any network remains to be accomplished.

A reasonable goal for such an analysis might be to substitute the actual anatomical connections of each cell in a network for the simplified labeled lines of a wiring diagram. Definitive anatomical proof for electrophysiologically determined connections have to be at the ultrastructural level, and, given the current sampling power of electron-microscopic techniques, the labor involved in such a task, even for a small system, would be enormous The introduction of intracellular staining technology has greatly increased the likelihood of making correlative anatomical and functional studies, and progress in this field suggest that the time is not far off when some circuits can be described in both functional and architectural terms.

THE LOBSTER STOMATOGASTRIC SYSTEM

Maynard's investigations of the lobster stomatogastric ganglion were prompted by many of the considerations just discussed (Maynard, 1972). This ganglion is responsible for the generation of the two complex rhythms that control the voluntary muscles of the stomach (unlike our own, the muscles are striated, not smooth). The 30 neurons contained in the ganglion are the only ones that innervate these muscles; the patterned motor output that they generate continues when the ganglion is completely deafferented and removed from the animal.

The lobster stomach consists of three separate regions: a cardiac sac for the storage of coarsely shredded food; a gastric mill, where the food is further macerated; and a posterior pyloric region (Figure 1). Maynard was concerned primarily with the pyloric region and its associated nerves and muscles. Movements of this part of the stomach are relatively simple. Strap-like extrinsic dilator muscles located between the pyloric region and the shell above and below contract simultaneously, causing dilation. This is followed by relaxation of the dilators and contraction of the intrinsic pyloric muscles, which causes constriction. The alternate contractions and dilations take place at a rate of about one per second in the isolated, deafferented preparation. In the intact preparation, the normal afferent input increases the frequency of the behavior to 2 or 3 per second, depending on the amount of food in the stomach.

The second rhythm generated by the ganglion controls the behavior of the gastric mill, a set of three calcified ossicles which function as teeth. The movements of the gastric mill are similar to the chewing movements of the vertebrate jaw and, in fact, perform the same function. Two lateral teeth open and close alternately, gripping the coarsely shredded food between them. As they come together, the single medial tooth is pulled over the food, effectively grinding it up. As the lateral teeth come apart, the medial tooth is reset and a new cycle begins. The backward and forward movement of the medial tooth as well as the opening and closing of the lateral teeth is caused by alternate contractions of antagonistic muscles. The two movements must be coordinated with each other for effective chewing. In the deafferented ganglion, however, movement of the lateral teeth can occur independently, as well as with different relative degrees of coordination with movement of the medial tooth.

The nerves which control the muscles that produce the gastric mill and pyloric movements originate in the stomatogastric ganglion. The ganglion itself is located within the lumen of the ophthalmic artery, the major vessel carrying blood from the heart to the brain. The motor nerves emerge from the artery near the ganglion and spread out along the dorsal surface of the stomach. The entire stomatogastric nervous system can be dissected free of the stomach and, when pinned out in a Sylgard-lined petri dish, continues to produce bursts of motor activity for up to 48 hours.

The desheathed ganglion is transilluminated to make the cells visible for intracellular recordings with glass microelectrodes. Peripheral nerves, traced to the muscles that they innervate, are used for recording or stimulating the motoneuron axons by attaching pin electrodes sealed with vaseline. The only conduit for information from the rest of the central nervous system to the stomatogastric ganglion, the stomatogastric nerve, was usually cut, but in some experiments was left connected to the anterior esophageal and commissural ganglia. The effect of leaving these other ganglia intact is to enhance greatly the overall activity produced by the stomatogastric ganglion.

EXTRACELLULAR ACTIVITY

Nerves that contain axons of the gastric-mill and pyloric motoneurons show two different bursting rhythms. The pyloric bursts occur at intervals of about 1 per second. The

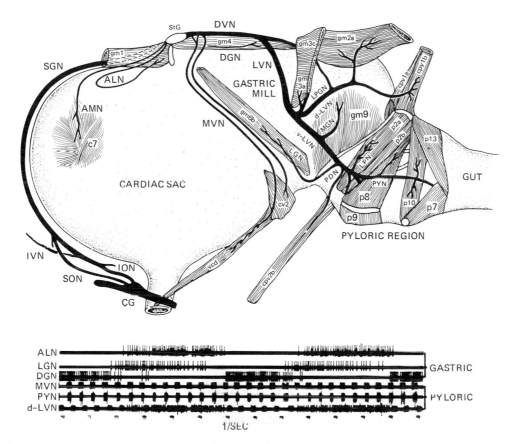

FIGURE 1. *Nerves and muscles of the lobster stomatogastric system are shown here diagrammatically. Nerves that innervate gastric-mill musculature are ALN, AMN, and DGN – medial tooth; and MGN, LGN, and LPGN – lateral teeth. Nerves to the pyloric musculature are d-LVN, PDN, and MVN – dilators; and LPN and PYN – constrictors. Abbreviations of the nerves are as follows: SON, superior esophageal nerve; ION, inferior esophageal nerve; IVN, inferior ventricular nerve; SGN, stomatogastric nerve; AMN, anterior median nerve; ALN, anterior lateral nerve; MVN, median ventricular nerve; DVN, dorsal ventricular nerve; LVN, lateral ventricular nerve; v-LVN, ventral branch of lateral ventricular nerve; d-LVN, dorsal branch of lateral ventricular nerve; LPGN, lateral posterior gastric nerve; MGN, median gastric nerve; LGN, lateral gastric nerve; PDN, pyloric dilator nerve; LPN, lateral pyloric nerve; and PYN, pyloric nerve. Abbreviations of the ganglia are CG, commissural ganglia; and StG, stomatogastric ganglion. An example of the two types of rhythms produced by the deafferented stomatogastric ganglion recorded extracellularly is shown also. The top three records are of gastric-mill motoneurons, while the bottom three are those of the pyloric region. Note that the pyloric rhythm is faster than the gastric. Also note the phase relationships present in the motor patterns of each rhythm. The bottom trace (d-LVN) contains both pyloric and gastric-mill units.*

activity corresponds to the behavioral observations and EMG recordings taken from the pyloric muscles. Bursts of activity in the pyloric dilator neurons alternate with bursts in the others. There is overlap of some of the bursts (Figure 1), but the total dynamic range of phase relationships is not very large.

Bursts of spikes in the gastric-mill motoneurons are much longer, about 3 seconds, and also correlate well with behavioral observations

(Figure 1). Bursts that go to antagonists of the lateral- and medial-tooth muscles alternate with slight overlapping of activity. Lateral teeth and the medial tooth also maintain a regular phase relationship although one that has a wider range than the pyloric elements. A detailed description of the gastric-mill activity has been published (Mulloney and Selverston, 1974a, b; Selverston and Mulloney, 1974).

INTRACELLULAR ACTIVITY

In most crustacean central ganglia, the experimentally accessible soma membranes are not only electrically inexcitable, but usually too far from the integrative region of the neuropile to reflect the synaptic activity that occurs there. Maynard was quick to realize the value of the stomatogastric ganglion as a model network when he discovered that the cell bodies did indeed show a considerable amount of subthreshold activity. The fortuitous occurrence of a network that produced two cyclical motor outputs and the ability to record subthreshold activity from the pre- and postsynaptic elements involved in their production suggested a valuable preparation for the study of how oscillatory motor patterns are produced.

THE PYLORIC CYCLE

Intracellular records made simultaneously from two or more pyloric units have the following characteristics:

1) The dc level of the membrane potential varies sinusoidly with spikes that occur during the depolarizing phase of the cycle (i.e., when the membrane is depolarized past threshold).
2) Passively attenuated spikes recorded in the soma are time-locked with peripheral axon spikes and can be used to positively identify each motoneuron.
3) Synaptic activity appears to be exclusively inhibitory in nature.
4) Some of the motoneurons are electrotonically coupled.

5) Monosynaptic connections can be established by the presence, after a short latency, of a unitary postsynaptic potential in a follower cell (Figure 2).
6) Electrotonic connections can be established by the passage of current between suspected cells.

The neuronal circuit established for the pyloric cycle units is shown in Figure 3. Two PD cells and a neuron called the anterior burster (because it exits the ganglion anteriorly via the stomatogastric nerve — its final destination is unknown) are electrotonically coupled and fire together. Their inhibitory connections suppress activity in the remaining cells. The phase relationship of the other cells to the PD follows from the distribution and strength of their synaptic and electrical connections (Figure 4).

For example, if we look just at the PD, LP, and PY cells (Figure 2), we see that both LP and PYs are inhibited by PDs and that the single LP inhibits all eight PYs and the two PDs. In addition, the PY cells inhibit the LP. During normal bursting the LP fires midway between the PD bursts, and the PY begins firing near the end of the LP burst and extends into the PD burst period. When the PD cells fire, they inhibit both LP and PYs. The LP can fire when this inhibition is removed, but since it inhibits the PYs, they do not begin to fire until the LP burst has been completed.

THE GASTRIC-MILL CYCLE

The intracellular activity of the gastric-mill motoneurons varies, depending upon whether or not the mill is active. When quiet, these motoneurons fire spontaneously (i.e., regularly, but not in bursts) or are quiet, showing only the inhibitory synaptic activity impinging on them from other cells. During periods when the gastric mill is bursting spontaneously, large dc shifts with spikes on the depolarizing phase occur among gastric rhythm cells. Connectivity patterns can be ascertained from this activity, although direct depolarization of nonbursting cells is somewhat easier from an experimental point of view.

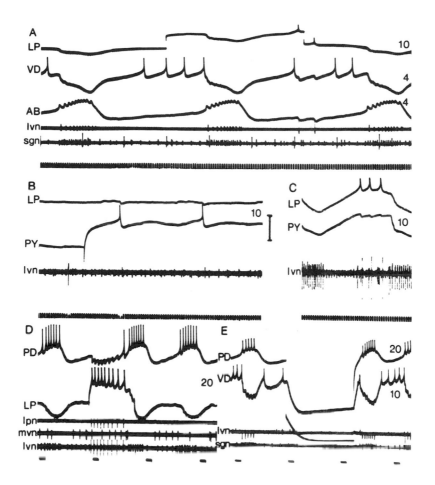

FIGURE 2. *Establishment of the connectivity between motoneurons of the pyloric cycle by direct polarization of one cell while examining others for signs of unitary postsynaptic effects. (A) Spontaneous activity, with only the VD and AB cells firing, shows simultaneous inhibitory hyperpolarizations of the LP and VD cells. Direct depolarization of the LP cell causes it to fire two spikes, one during the depolarization and one just afterward. These spikes can be seen to inhibit directly VD and AB by the appearance of unitary IPSPs on each cell. The lvn extracellular trace contains axons of the PD cells, firing concurrently with AB, and the LP. The sgn extracellular trace contains axons of the AB cell. (B) Direct depolarization of a PY motoneuron when the pyloric rhythm is not active puts an IPSP onto the LP cell. Note absence of bursting in the lvn extracellular record. (C) Continuous depolarization of an LP cell during slow pyloric rhythm activity causes firing of the LP and simultaneous IPSPs on a PY cell. The lvn trace shows PD, PY, and LP unit activity. (D) Similar depolarization of an LP cell to show the large IPSPs it puts onto a PD. The lpn trace contains the LP axon, the mvn contains a VD axon, and the lvn contains PD, PY, and LP axons. (E) A PD and a VD motoneuron during spontaneous bursting and with an applied hyperpolarizing pulse to show that they are electrotonically connected to each other. IPSPs from the PD to the VD can also be seen. The lvn shows the PD activity extracellularly, whereas the sgn shows that of the AB cell. All intracellular recordings were made from the somata of the motoneurons. Time marks for (A), (B), and (C) are 60 per second; for (D) and (E), one per second. Numbers by the intracellular traces are calibrations for the vertical bar in millivolts.*

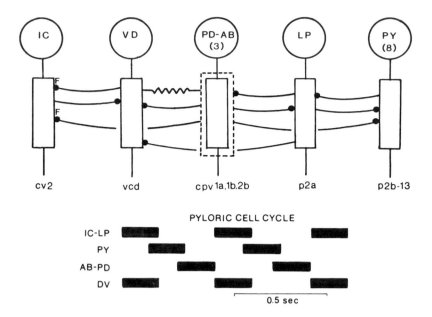

FIGURE 3. Complete neuronal circuit for cells producing the pyloric rhythm. The large open circles represent neuron somata; rectangles represent the lumped neuropile processes of each cell. Black dots are chemical inhibitory synapses and the resistor symbol represents an electrotonic junction. The dashed line around the PD−AB cells indicates that this group is electrotonically coupled and functions as a unit. The abbreviations at the bottom of each cell are for the muscles innervated and can be seen in situ in Figure 1. The symbol "F" signifies that these inhibitory connections are functional in nature and have not yet been shown to be monosynaptic. The sequential firing pattern for the bursts of activity generated by these neurons is shown in the block diagram.

Operationally, connectivity can be defined precisely only when discrete, unitary post-synaptic potentials follow a spike in a pre-synaptic cell (Figure 5). Because intracellular recordings are made distant from the actual postsynaptic loci, the unitary potentials in some cases electrotonically decay to below the noise level by the time they reach the soma. In some cases a burst of presynaptic spikes causes clear effects on other cells, firing even though unitary potentials cannot be observed. Such connectivity can be termed functional and the exact synaptic nature of these connections must at the moment remain obscure. Some examples of various kinds of synaptic interactions for the gastric-mill system are shown in Figures 5 and 7.

A synthesis of these data has resulted in the circuit shown in Figure 6. As with the pyloric circuit, most of the synaptic inter-actions are inhibitory. However, there are some excitatory connections present, and two putative interneurons appear to play a key role in the basic rhythm-generating mechanism.

There are several connections present between pyloric and gastric motoneurons, but they have not been completely worked out at this time. All but four of the cells in the ganglion have been accounted for. The role of these unidentified cells is unknown, although they have characteristic properties that makes them easy to identify. They do not participate in either gastric or pyloric rhythms.

MECHANISMS THAT UNDERLIE PATTERNED OUTPUT

As we have seen, there are two possible mechanisms that might form the basis of

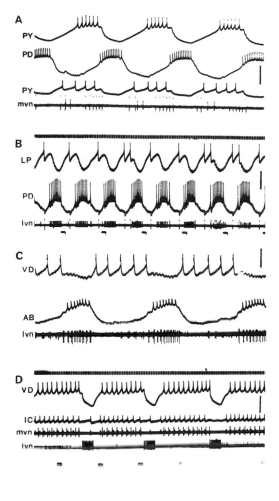

oscillatory pattern generation. The simplest mechanism consists of one or more cells that have the ability to generate bursts of impulses built into their membranes — that is, endogenous bursters. If such intrinsically bursting cells are connected to a spontaneously firing cell via an inhibitory synapse, the follower cell will be shut off or slowed down during the burst. Similarly, if an instrinsically bursting cell is connected to a silent cell with an excitatory synapse or via an electrotonic connection, that cell will be made to fire or be brought closer to threshold during the burst. If a silent cell happens to show strong postinhibitory rebound, it can be made to fire after a burst of inhibitory potentials has been delivered to it by the driver cell (Perkel and Mulloney, 1974). By the use of such combinations of synaptic input from the driver cell, it is not difficult to see how a group of cells connected to it can be made to fire properly phased bursts of motor output. Maynard recognized, on the basis of intracellular studies, that the PD cells were bursty cells which probably serve as the primary driving force for the pyloric rhythm. Hyperpolarizing or depolarizing the PDs has a powerful effect on the pyloric rhythm, whereas similar application of current to other cells of the pyloric cycle has much less of an effect (Maynard, 1972). Our investigation of the pyloric rhythm has tended to confirm Maynard's hypothesis. By terminating the PD burst with strong hyperpolarizing currents, other cells involved in the pyloric group loose their patterned activity (Figure 9). When the PD cells are hyperpolarized, the underlying membrane oscillations can be seen. These sinusoidal-like membrane shifts are similar to those reported by Mendelson (1971). Allowing the PDs to be depolarized slowly by passing a ramp current into their somata shows that, as the depolarizing phase of the membrane potential crosses threshold, the cell begins to burst (Figure 8). As the depolarization continues, the length of time that the membrane potential is above threshold increases, so that both the burst frequency and the number of spikes per burst increase. At a sufficient level of depolarization the membrane potential remains above threshold and the cell fires continuously.

Experimentally, it is clear that the PD cells are the strongest elements in the pyloric

FIGURE 4. *Examples of spontaneous intracellular activity among motoneurons of the pyloric cycle. (A) shows the PD cell inhibiting two PY cells as well as the VD and IC cells (shown extracellularly in the mvn trace). (B) shows the reciprocal inhibitory connections between PD and LP. The spike activity of both cells can be seen in the lvn. (C) shows inhibition of the VD by the AB–PD group. The PDs are the large units seen in the lvn trace. (D) shows simultaneous firing of VD and IC with inhibition from PD. Spike activity of VD and IC is shown in the mvn trace, that of the PD is the lvn trace; vertical calibration bars are A = 20 mV, B = 10 mV, C = 10 mV, and D = 20 mV. Time marks for (A) and (C) are 60 per second; for (B) and (D), one per second.*

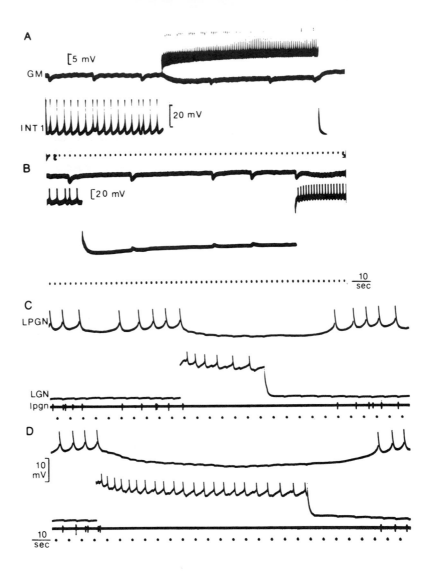

FIGURE 5. *Synaptic connections between interneuron 1 (INT 1) and a GM cell of the medial-tooth subsystem. In (A), INT 1 is firing regularly and is responsible for the small IPSPs on the GM. The large IPSPs are from INT 2 (see Figure 6). Depolarization of INT 1 greatly increases its firing rate, and the increase in IPSPs hyperpolarizes GM to a new level. In (B), INT 1 is hyperpolarized to below threshold. The small IPSPs disappear from the GM trace and the large IPSP is seen to be coincidental with the EPSP on INT 1, demonstrating an excitatory connection between INT 2 and INT 1. Note the postinhibitory rebound in INT 1 immediately after the hyperpolarizing current is shut off. (C) and (D) show direct monosynaptic connections between two lateral teeth motoneurons. Firing of the LGN cell by direct depolarization causes IPSPs to be put on the LPGN with complete cessation of its spontaneous firing. This recording was made when the system was not bursting and each cell was behaving as it normally does when this occurs — that is, the LPGN fires continuously with periodic interruptions due to inhibition from pyloric units. The LGN is silent, showing only the IPSP bombardment that it receives from interneuron 1.*

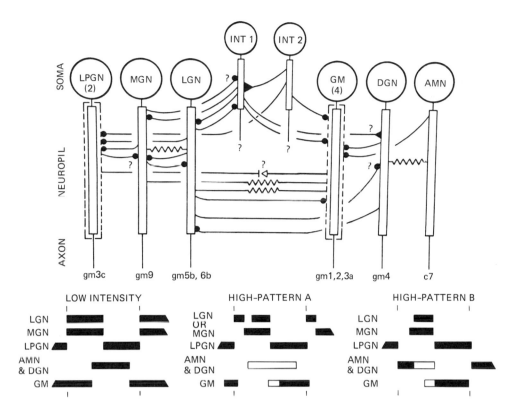

FIGURE 6. *Diagrammatic summary of the synaptic connections found among the gastric-mill motoneurons and the two interneurons in the stomatogastric ganglion. Symbolism is the same as that shown in Figure 5, except that functional connections are here indicated by question marks. In addition, there appear to be two excitatory connections (closed triangles) and one rectifying electrotonic synapse (diode). Three examples of the types of burst patterns generated by the gastric-mill network are shown in the form of block diagrams. The small vertical lines represent one complete cycle. Black rectangles represent periods when the neurons fire; open rectangles represent periods when firing may or may not occur.*

rhythm, bursting even when other elements are silent. As previously mentioned, if any pyloric cells are shut off by hyperpolarization, there is very little effect on the PD cell burst; however, any speeding up or slowing down of the PD burst by current injection has an immediate and powerful effect on the other pyloric cells (Figure 9).

In summary, the pyloric rhythm appears to utilize a mechanism that consists of a group of three inherently bursty cells (the two PDs and the AB) synaptically and electrically connected to eleven other cells in a way that produces their correct firing sequence.

A careful examination of all ten gastric-mill motoneurons as well as the interneurons involved in this rhythm has not produced an equivalent to the PD cell.

If no cells with inherent burst capability are present in a network but the network is still able to produce oscillatory patterned output without sensory feedback, we must examine the network itself for clues as to the mechanism involved.

It has been known for some time that if two artificial neurons which are firing regularly are connected with mutually inhibitory synapses, the two cells will oscillate in bursts

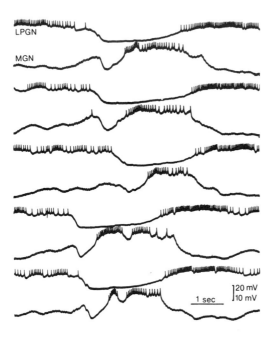

FIGURE 7. Spontaneous intracellular activity between two lateral-tooth antagonists, the LPGN and the MGN. Both cells have reciprocal inhibitory connections, and each is strongly affected by activity of the interneurons as well as by other cells in the gastric-mill subset.

results is that the "oscillator" for the gastric mill is the entire network of cells.

An examination of the gastric-mill circuit shows that, like the pyloric, it is made up of predominantly inhibitory synaptic connections. The total amount of connectivity between motoneurons and the two interneurons is much more extensive than that found among cells of the pyloric rhythm. An attempt at even a qualitative understanding of how such a neuronal circuit might operate the gastric-mill muscles, causing them to contract at the proper time, can be made only superficially. Among the more important questions that need to be answered are: (1) How does the gastric-mill rhythm get turned on? (2) What is its dynamic range? (3) Are some neurons more important to the rhythm than others?

A qualitative description of the burst-generating mechanism for the gastric-mill system falls far short of providing a complete explanation of how the system works. What we know about the network, however, is consistant with, and may in fact be one kind of explanation for, the observed behavior. For example, we can see in Figure 6 that activity in INT 1 turns on the DGN and the AMN neurons and

that are out of phase with one another (Reiss, 1962). It is not necessary to postulate a specific driver cell in this case; the oscillatory output "emerges" as a property of the network and its connections. Although numerous examples of modeling studies have exploited this basic theme of mutual inhibition, not many real networks with this property have been described. Gastric-mill (GM) cells show either pacemaker-type continuous firing or are silent during periods of gastric-mill inactivity. When the mill is active, the cells show alternate bursting among cells that operate antagonistic muscles. Current applied to the somata of any GM cell, whether a slowly depolarizing ramp or step, does not give any indication of bursty activity; instead, the cell fires when the membrane potential crosses threshold, and continues firing, usually with some accommodation, as long as the potential remains above this level (Figure 8). A reasonable interpretation of these

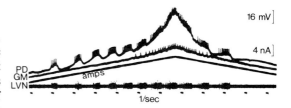

FIGURE 8. Responses of a bursty cell and a nonbursty cell to an applied ramp current. The PD cell of the pyloric rhythm begins to fire in bursts when its membrane potential crosses threshold. As the depolarization continues, the number of spikes per burst increases while the interburst interval decreases. The reverse happens when the ramp current begins moving in the hyperpolarizing direction. The GM cell of the gastric-mill subset, on the other hand, fires continuously when its membrane potential crosses threshold and stops firing when its potential becomes more negative. Spike activity of the two PD cells in the ganglion can be seen in the LVN trace.

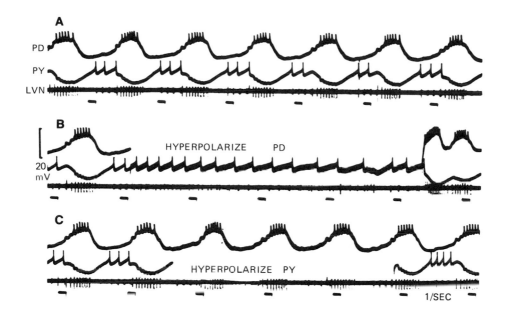

FIGURE 9. *The dominant role of the PD cells in maintaining the pyloric rhythm can be demonstrated by observing the effects of inhibiting PD discharge. In (A), normal alternation between a PD and a PY cell is seen. In (B), the PD cell is shut off by application of hyperpolarizing current. When this happens, the oscillatory bursting activity of the PY cell changes to a continuous firing pattern. In (C), the effect of hyperpolarizing the PY cell is seen to have no effect on the PD cells' bursting rhythm.*

inhibits their antagonists, the four GM cells. We can also see that the activity of the LGN cell inhibits INT 1 and that the reciprocal inhibitory connections between the LGN–MGN pair and the two LPGNs might form the basis for a sustained oscillatory rhythm. But to make such assumptions we have to suggest that some pathways are stronger than others and even ignore some of the connections entirely.

To say that we can really "understand" how a network, such as that shown in Figure 6, operates raises serious epistemological questions about just what constitutes understanding. A description of the network and the characteristics of each cell and synapse present may represent some level of understanding. A mathematical or electronic model that mimics the behavior of the system and has some predictive value represents a different level of understanding.

It will probably never be possible to determine a closed analytical solution for either the pyloric or gastric-mill network. There are

too many simultaneously occurring, nonlinear interactions to fit them into any known mathematical framework. But there are digital computer simulations available which can at least substantiate whether or not neuronal networks with electrophysiologically determined connectivity will behave in a way similar to that seen experimentally. Such modeling studies have a long history but, in general, have not been of much value to the experimentalist. A theoretical model builder can, if given unlimited degrees of freedom, produce a simulated network that exhibits almost any output desired. The experimentalist, however, has only a limited set of parameters with which to work and must attempt to explain the output patterns without violating these measurements. Probably one of the best simulations available, from the point of view of a physiologist, is one devised by Perkel at Stanford University. Its chief advantage is that, insofar as possible, it uses real parameters that can be determined experimentally. Each neuron is considered as a

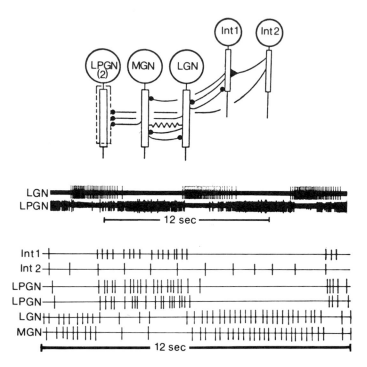

FIGURE 10. *Preliminary modeling studies of the gastric-mill rhythm by B. Mulloney and D. Perkel suggest that the alternating bursts of motoneuron activity can "emerge" as a property of the network and its connections. The part of the gastric mill which was simulated is shown in the upper part of the figure and consists of those neurons which control the lateral teeth as well as the two interneurons found in the ganglion. Actual activity of two of the neurons, the LGN and LPGN, is shown in the middle trace. The lower extracellular traces are the result of simulating the network with a digital computer model. No burst-generating cells are present, yet the synaptic connections are able to produce alternation of the LPGN cells and the LGN—MGN pair in a way which is quite similar to that observed in an actual wet preparation.*

point source, actually the spike-initiating zone. Real data are then supplied which flesh out the neuron in terms of resting potential, threshold, membrane time constants, and so on. These "neurons" can be connected to each other with "fibers" that terminate in various kinds of "synapses."

Errors are introduced into the model from both the experimental data and the construction of the model itself. Experimentally, the potential measurements are not made at the spike-initiating zone, but at the soma, some electrotonic distance away from it. The amount of attenuation produced differs for each neuron as well as for each synapse. In some cases, for example the PD cell, the size and shape of the synaptic potentials recorded close to the spike-

initiating zone in the neuropile appear quite similar to those recorded from the soma (Miller, unpublished observation). The model does not accurately simulate such phenomena as the rise time of synaptic potentials or electrotonic coupling. Even with such deficiencies, however, the Perkel model is extremely useful in studying the two rhythms of the stomatogastric ganglion.

In a preliminary modeling study Perkel and Mulloney (unpublished) have shown that by incorporating as many real parameters as possible into a simulation of the lateral-teeth subsystem, oscillatory bursting between antagonists could be obtained. It is important to point out that it was not necessary to incorporate a bursty cell into the network but only to give a

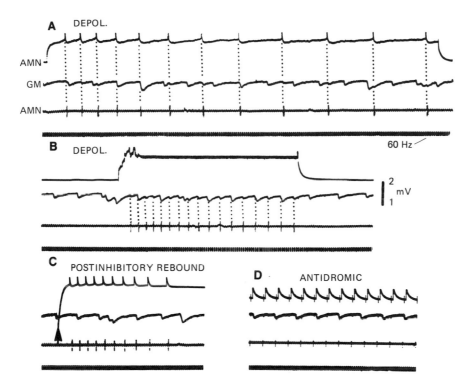

FIGURE 11. Gating of intraganglionic synapses is demonstrated by the AMN to GM inhibitory synapse. During depolarization of the AMN (A), unitary monosynaptic IPSPs are put onto the GM cell. At a higher level of depolarization, the intracellular trace goes offscreen, but the spike activity can be seen on the extracellular trace. When the AMN cell is made to fire by postinhibitory rebound (C), the shape of the soma-recorded potential not only has a faster rise time, but also no IPSPs are put onto the GM. Note that the main axon of the cell still fires. Similarly, in (D), antidromic firing of the axon causes the fast rise-time potentials to appear in the soma without activation of the inhibitory synapse to the GM cell.

slightly increased level of activity to cells that are spontaneously active when the gastric mill is not operating. Such an increase in frequency converted the network into one whose overall burst pattern looks surprisingly like the pattern observed experimentally (Figure 10).

SOME UNUSUAL PROPERTIES OF STOMATOGASTRIC NEURONS

The Gating of Cell Output

As indicated by the diagram of the synaptic connectivity for the gastric and pyloric networks, many of the motoneurons make inhibitory synaptic contacts with other motoneurons in addition to their excitatory neuromuscular synapses. In some cases these inhibitory intraganglionic synapses appear to have spike-initiating zones separate from the spike-initiating zone of the peripheral axon. In some cases, such as the AMN–GM connections, the inhibitory synapse onto the GM is only activated when the potential crosses the threshold of the second spike-initiating zone (Figure 11). In such cases, the second synapse can be said to be gated to this second level of membrane potential. It has already been shown that antidromic impulses are sometimes not strong enough to fire these secondary spike-initiating zones. For example, antidromic firing of the AMN fails to put IPSPs onto the GM cell, whereas direct depolarization does (see also Mulloney and Selverston, 1972). We do not know the precise nature of how such gating mechanisms operate during normal stomatogastric activity.

NON-SPIKING INHIBITION

Maynard and his colleagues have shown that the release of some inhibitory transmitters can occur in a graded fashion. In such cases, current spread from the soma or other parts of the neuron can invade the terminal and cause the release. The amount released and its subsequent effects on the postsynaptic cell are directly proportional to the amount of current that reaches the terminal (Maynard and Walton, 1975).

MUTUAL INHIBITION IN ELECTROTONICALLY COUPLED CELLS

There is one instance of combined mutual inhibition and electrotonic coupling between two gastric motoneurons. The LGN and the MGN control synergistic muscles and usually fire simultaneously. Electrotonic coupling between neurons is usually thought of as a way to ensure that two or more cells will fire together (Bennett, 1972). Why, then, do these two cells inhibit each other? The presence of weak synaptic inhibition between the cells appears to cause a momentary pause in the firing of whichever cell fires first. This inhibition is only transient and both cells are quickly brought into synchrony by the electrotonic junction. The behavioral significance of the pause is unknown at present and there has been only one previous description of such a circuit (Dennis, 1967). Whether or not the synaptic and electrotonic contacts are close enough to influence each other (Spira and Bennett, 1972)

in a dynamic way poses an additional interesting problem.

THE STOMATOGASTRIC GANGLION AND OTHER PATTERN GENERATORS

The stomatogastric ganglion can be considered to be a model network for studying the genesis of oscillatory rhythms. The majority of our data have initially been qualitative, showing only that the connections exist. A thorough analysis will need a quantitative description of the strength of each synapse as well if we are to understand the mechanisms involved in pattern generation. There are many invertebrate ganglia now being studied in which similar descriptions of networks are being obtained. The leech, *Tritonia, Pleurobranchia, Aplysia*, and *Helisoma*, among others, offer the hope of defining the neuronal connections in sufficient detail to suggest how the motor patterns they produce are generated. There is often criticism of such simple networks on the grounds that invertebrate neurons are different, both at a structural and network level, from those found in the more complex nervous systems of mammals. A similar argument concerning the generalizability of invertebrate networks to other systems is also made. With respect to basic differences in the functioning of invertebrate neurons, it is really the responsibility of vertebrate neurophysiologists to show how *their* cells are different from those found in simpler systems. The ability to extend any principles of neuronal functioning discovered among the invertebrates to more complex networks is a goal shared by many of us. The most important result of taking a comparative approach is that we are finding limited and characteristic ways in which neurons can be connected to produce particular kinds of behavior. It is a logical extension of these general principles to suppose that at least some will be basic to the functioning of vertebrate systems as well.

CHAPTER SEVEN

Nerve cells without Action Potentials

KEIR G. PEARSON

INTRODUCTION

The transmission of information in the peripheral nervous system, and between widely separated regions of the CNS, relies on the propagation of all-or-none action potentials along the axons of specialized nerve cells. The major advantage of encoding information in the temporal sequence of action potentials is that transmission can occur over long distances without attenuation. Since much of present knowledge about the integration of nervous activity, and information transmission within the nervous system, has come from studies of neurons with long axons, it is generally assumed (judging from modern texts in neurophysiology) that all communication between nerve cells is by action potentials. Moreover, current hypotheses for integrative mechanisms within localized regions of the nervous system are dominated by the idea that action potentials are generated in the interacting neurons. However, within the past five years strong experimental data have been obtained in a variety of vertebrate and invertebrate systems which show

that graded changes in potential in some neurons can influence the activity in other neurons and which demonstrate the existence of neurons that function normally without ever generating action potentials. The concept of graded interactions between neurons is not new. Fifteen years ago Bullock wrote: ". . . the possibility remains with us that in the most complex and finely textured higher centers, made up largely of very small neurons, perhaps most of the normal functioning is carried out *without nerve impulses. . .*" (Bullock, 1959). At that time, the only example of graded interaction between neurons was in the lobster cardiac ganglion, but it was also considered that some of the nerve cells of the vertebrate retina interacted in a graded manner (MacNichol and Svaetichin, 1958).

The purpose of this chapter is to review briefly the known examples of nerve cells that do not generate action potentials and the synaptic mechanisms for graded interactions between nerve cells, and to comment on some of the functional advantages of graded interactions between neurons.

OCCURRENCE OF NERVE CELLS WITHOUT ACTION POTENTIALS

Table I lists the systems known to contain nerve cells that function without generating action potentials. (Throughout this chapter these nerve cells will be referred to as nonspiking neurons.) Nonspiking neurons have been found mainly in the initial stages of sensory systems of both vertebrates and invertebrates. There are no examples of nonspiking neurons in motor systems of vertebrates, while only two invertebrate motor systems (crustacean ventilation and insect walking) have so far been found to contain this type of nerve cell. With the exception of the granule cells in the mammalian olfactory bulb there are no examples of nonspiking neurons in the vertebrate CNS. Clearly, then, nonspiking nerve cells have not yet been found to be widespread throughout the nervous system of any species of animal.

Vertebrate and invertebrate photoreceptors have also been included in Table I. Strictly, these receptors, as well as other specialized receptors (Steinbach, 1974), cannot be regarded as neurons. Nonetheless, despite their obvious morphological differences from nerve cells, there is a marked similarity between the electrophysiological and synaptic properties of photoreceptors and nonspiking neurons. Furthermore, vertebrate photoreceptors receive inputs from other retinal cells and are therefore members of an interacting network of cells. As such, they cannot be regarded simply as transducers of light energy. For these reasons, then, photoreceptors are included in this discussion of nonspiking neurons. Other specialized receptors which also function without generating action potentials have recently been well reviewed (Steinbach, 1974) and will not be considered in this chapter.

In this section the nonspiking cells in each of the systems listed in Table I will be described in turn; more general comments about the properties and functional advantages of these neurons are presented in sections which follow.

Insect Walking

During walking in the cockroach there are rhythmic reciprocal bursts of activity in slow motoneurons which innervate the flexor and extensor muscles of the legs. The basic rhythmicity and reciprocity in this activity

TABLE I

OCCURRENCE OF NERVE CELLS WITHOUT ACTION POTENTIALS

System	Location	Cell type	Reference
Motor			
Insect walking	Thoracic ganglia	Interneurons	Pearson and Fourtner, 1975
Crustacean ventilation	Suboesophageal ganglion	Interneurons	Mendelson, 1971
Sensory			
Vertebrate vision	Retina	Photoreceptors/ horizontal/bipolar	Tomita, 1970; Werblin and Dowling, 1969
Mammalian olfaction	Olfactory bulb	Granule	Rall and Shepherd, 1968
Invertebrate vision	Insect retina	Retinula/ monopolar	See Table III
	Crustacean and mollusk eyes	Photoreceptors	See Table III
Crustacean proproception	Coxal joints (crabs)	Stretch receptors	Ripley, Bush, and Roberts, 1968

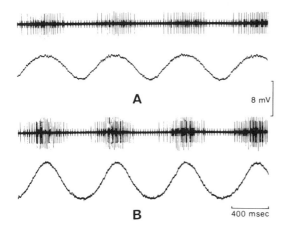

FIGURE 1. Excitation of flexor motoneurons (top traces) by applied depolarizations
(bottom traces) of a nonspiking interneuron
(interneuron I) in the cockroach metathoracic
ganglion. An increase in the amplitude of the
applied depolarization recruits additional motor
axons and increases the intensity of the flexor
bursts. The order of recruitment of identified
motoneurons is identical to that observed in
freely walking animals (from Pearson and
Fourtner, 1975).

depends on mechanisms located within the
thoracic ganglia, since patterns of activity
similar to those seen during walking are
observed after removal of all sensory input
from leg receptors (Pearson, 1972). Recent
studies using microelectrode and dye injection
techniques have shown that a system of nonspiking interneurons is responsible for centrally
patterning this motor activity (Pearson and
Fourtner, 1975). One nonspiking interneuron,
interneuron I, produces, when depolarized, a
very strong excitation of the flexor motoneurons (Figure 1) and inhibition of activity in
extensor motoneurons. Moreover, during spontaneous rhythmic leg movements the membrane
potential of this interneuron oscillates with the
slow depolarizing phase that occurs during the
burst of flexor activity (Figure 2). Since no
other interneuron (spiking or nonspiking) has
been found to produce a strong excitation of
the flexor motoneurons, it has been concluded
that oscillations in the membrane potential of
interneuron I are entirely responsible for producing the flexor bursts and therefore for

producing stepping movements during walking.
Apart from driving the flexor motoneurons,
interneuron I is also part of the rhythm-
generating system.

Three other types of nonspiking interneurons have also been physiologically identified
in the metathoracic ganglion. One of these
inhibits flexor activity when depolarized and
shows membrane oscillations during rhythmic
leg movements which are 180° out of phase
with those in interneuron I (Figure 2). This
interneuron has no effect on activity in the
extensor motoneurons and so probably functions to inhibit completely the flexors during
extensor activity. The other two types of
nonspiking interneuron specifically affect the
extensor motoneurons. One causes excitation
of these motoneurons when depolarized, while
depolarizations of the other inhibit extensor
activity. The function of the latter two nonspiking neurons is unknown.

The geometry of some nonspiking neurons
in the cockroach metathoracic ganglion has
been determined by means of the cobalt intracellular staining technique. None of these

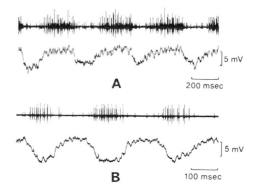

FIGURE 2. Oscillations in membrane potential of two nonspiking interneurons in the
cockroach metathoracic ganglion during rhythmic leg movements. Top traces, extracellularly
recorded activity from the axons of flexor
motoneurons; bottom traces, intracellular
records from nonspiking neurons. (A) Interneuron I: depolarizations of this interneuron
excite the flexor motoneurons. (B) A type II
interneuron: depolarizations of this interneuron
inhibit the activity of flexor motoneurons
(from Pearson, Fourtner, and Wong, 1973).

neurons has an axon and all their neurites are contained wholly within the metathoracic ganglion. Their neurites are very numerous, fine, and highly branched. The terminal neurites of interneuron I lie close to the main neurites of the flexor motoneurons that it excites, which suggests that the flexors are monosynaptically excited by interneuron I.

Crustacean Ventilation

Neurons that function without action potentials in the CNS of arthropods were first discovered in the ventilatory system of lobsters and crabs (Mendelson, 1971). Depolarization of a nonspiking neuron in the subesophageal ganglion of these animals strongly excited one group of ventilatory motoneurons and inhibited the antagonists. Hyperpolarizations produced the reverse effect. Since the timing of the ventilatory rhythm could be altered by passing brief current pulses into this neuron, it has been postulated that a single nonspiking pacemaker interneuron is entirely responsible for generating the rhythmic motor output. However, in the absence of structural data and more extensive intracellular studies, it remains possible that more than a single neuron is responsible for generating the rhythm.

Vertebrate Vision

Intracellular recordings made from retinal cells of many vertebrates have shown that the photoreceptors, the horizontal cells, and the bipolar cells do not generate action potentials

TABLE II

OCCURRENCE OF NONSPIKING CELLS IN THE VERTEBRATE VISUAL SYSTEM

Cell type	Animal	Reference
Photoreceptor	Monkey	Boynton and Whitten, 1970
	Cat	Brown and Wiesel, 1961
	Skate	Dowling and Ripps, 1972
	Carp	Tomita, 1965
	Turtle	Baylor and Fuortes, 1970
	Mud puppy	Werblin and Dowling, 1969
	Axolotl	Grabowski, Pinto, and Pak, 1972
	Gekko	Toyoda, Nosaki, and Tomita, 1969
	Frog	Toyoda et al., 1970
	Chordates	Gorman, McReynolds, and Barnes, 1971
Horizontal	Cat	Steinberg and Schmidt, 1970
	Skate	Dowling and Ripps, 1971
	Carp	Witkovsky, 1967
	Goldfish	Kaneko, 1970
	Dogfish	Kaneko, 1971
	Catfish	Naka and Nye, 1972
	Tench	Naka and Rushton, 1967
	Turtle	Baylor, Fuortes, and O'Bryan, 1971
	Mud puppy	Werblin and Dowling, 1969
	Frog	Matsumoto and Naka, 1972
Bipolar	Goldfish	Kaneko, 1970
	Mud puppy	Werblin and Dowling, 1969
	Frog	Matsumoto and Naka, 1972

(Table II). The amacrine cells show spiking characteristics, but it is possible that the slow-graded potentials that occur in these cells are also of importance in the integration of visual information. The graded nature of activity in cells in the outer plexiform layer was discovered some years ago (MacNichol and Svaetichin, 1958), but only recently have the cells from which graded potentials were recorded been unambiguously identified through use of intracellular dye injection techniques (Werblin and Dowling, 1969; Kaneko, 1970).

The response of photoreceptors to light is a graded hyperpolarization which is generated by a decrease in a steady inward current carried by sodium ions across the outer segments of the photoreceptors. Hyperpolarizing responses to light are also generated in one type of bipolar cell, whereas depolarizing responses occur in a second type. In fishes two types of horizontal cells have been identified physiologically. Type L responds with a sustained hyperpolarization to a light stimulus of any wavelength, whereas the polarity and magnitude of the response in the second type (type C) depends on the wavelength of the stimulus (Kaneko, 1970; Witkovsky, 1967). In other cold-blooded vertebrates, all horizontal cells hyperpolarize in response to light.

Mammalian Olfaction

From an analysis of extracellular field potentials evoked in the olfactory bulb of mammals it has been concluded that the granule cells do not generate action potentials, and that depolarizations of these cells produce a strong inhibitory effect on the mitral cells (Rall and Shepherd, 1968). The granule cells are small axonless neurons located wholly within the olfactory bulb, and their peripheral dendrites contact the accessory dendrites of the mitral cells. The dendrodendritic contacts between granule and mitral cells are reciprocal synaptic connections. Structural and electrophysiological data indicate that the mitral-to-granule connection is excitatory and the granule-to-mitral connection is inhibitory. Thus these reciprocal synapses provide a mechanism for local feedback inhibition to the accessory

dendrites of the mitral cells, while the spread of graded potentials within the granule cells can cause the inhibition of nearby mitral cells.

Invertebrate Vision

There are now many examples of non-spiking nerve cells in the visual system of invertebrates (Table III). The retinula cells in the retina of most insects respond to light with a graded depolarization without generating action potentials. The photoreceptor cells in the barnacle and some mollusks also respond to light in a graded manner. The only invertebrate photoreceptors so far found to respond with a hyperpolarization are the proximal cells in the scallop eye. However, not all invertebrate photoreceptors are nonspiking. Action potentials have been recorded from the retinula cells of the drone bee and horseshoe crab *Limulus* and from the photoreceptors in a number of mollusks (Chase, 1974). Even in some of these spiking receptor cells, graded potentials propagate for some distance, and it is possible that these potentials contribute to transmission of information to second-order neurons.

Apart from the many examples of non-spiking photoreceptors in the visual system of invertebrates, it has now been clearly demonstrated that second-order neurons in some insects transmit information in a graded manner (Table III). This graded transmission in second-order neurons has been studied most intensively in the visual system of the blowfly *Calliphora*. The monopolar neurons that leave the first optic ganglion receive direct synaptic connections from the retinula cells and respond to light with a graded hyperpolarization. This hyperpolarization is then propagated along the axon of the monopolar neuron for a distance of about 800 μm. Of considerable interest is that this propagated hyperpolarizing response does not decrement. Thus a mechanism other than passive electrotonic propagation must operate to transmit the hyperpolarization along these fine axons (2 μm in diameter) for such a long distance. The membrane mechanisms responsible for allowing this decrement-free conduction are not known.

Transmission of visual information over considerable distances without impulses also occurs in the photoreceptors in the barnacle. The axons of these receptors are up to 11 mm in length and 15 μm in diameter. The length constant for these axons has been calculated as 4.9 mm, assuming that propagation is electrotonic. Thus information can be transmitted along these axons with an attenuation of only a factor of 3 (Shaw, 1972). The reason for the large value of the length constant appears to be the exceptionally large value of the external membrane resistance.

The Crustacean Stretch Receptor

A specialized stretch receptor organ is located at the coxal joint in the legs of crabs and gives rise to two large axons which run to the CNS over a distance up to 5 mm. Stretching the receptor organ elicits graded depolarizations in these axons but no action potentials (Ripley, Bush, and Roberts, 1968). The conduction along these axons is purely electrotonic. The diameter of the axons is quite large (about

50 μm) and the membrane resistance is high. The length constant has been calculated to be between 3 and 5 mm. Thus there is not a large attenuation of signals as they propagate to the CNS. Depolarizations of the stretch receptors reflexly activate motoneurons that innervate the stretch receptor muscle and the synergistic muscles (Bush and Cannone, 1973). The gain of this reflex activity is high, for small changes in membrane potential in the receptor axons produce large changes in motoneuronal activity.

SYNAPTIC TRANSMISSION FROM NONSPIKING NERVE CELLS

Our knowledge of the mechanisms for synaptic transmission from nonspiking cells to other neurons is limited and is derived mainly from studies on the vertebrate retina. Nonetheless, there is little reason at present to believe that these mechanisms differ significantly from those which occur at junctions

TABLE III

OCCURRENCE OF NONSPIKING CELLS IN THE INVERTEBRATE VISUAL SYSTEM

Cell type	Animal	Reference
Retinula	Insects	
	locust	Shaw, 1968
	flies	Naka and Egughi, 1962; Jarvilehto and Zettler, 1970; Alawi and Pak, 1971; Scholes, 1969
	dragonfly	Laughlin, 1974
	cockroach	Butler and Horridge, 1973
	water bug	Ioannides and Walcott, 1971
	bee (worker)	Shaw, 1969
Monopolar (second order)	Insects	
	locust	Shaw, 1968
	fly	Zettler and Jarvilehto, 1971
	dragonfly	Laughlin, 1974
Ocellus receptor	Dragonfly	Chappel and Dowling, 1972
Photoreceptors	Crustacea: barnacle	Shaw, 1972
	Mollusks	
	Aplysia	Jacklet, 1969
	snail	Patton and Kater, 1972
	scallop	McReynolds and Gorman, 1970

where there are action potentials in the presynaptic terminals. Anatomical and physiological studies have shown that transmission at most junctions between nonspiking cells and other neurons is mediated chemically (Dowling, 1974; Dowling and Ripps, 1973; Laughlin, 1974; Nelson, 1973; Rall, Shepherd, and Reese, 1966). A few nonspiking cells have been found to interact via electrical junctions, for example the horizontal cells in fish retina (Kaneko, 1971) and invertebrate photoreceptors (Shaw, 1972). Interestingly, these electrical interactions have been found to occur only between identical types of cells.

It is now well known that, under certain conditions, graded transmitter release can be induced from junctions that normally function with presynaptic spikes. The best example is the squid giant synapse (Katz and Miledi, 1966). Under normal resting conditions at these junctions an insignificant amount of transmitter is spontaneously released. After treatment with tetrodotoxin to block action potentials, depolarizations of about 20 mV begin to cause the graded release of transmitter, and increasing amounts of transmitter are released with increasing depolarizations. By analogy with this system, then, it is conceivable that many junctions in which there are normally no presynaptic spikes function in a similar manner, except that under resting conditions the membrane potential is such that there is a continuous release of transmitter. Any changes in the presynaptic membrane potential will thus modulate the rate of this continuous secretion. Dowling and Ripps (1972) have recently found this to be true for transmission between the photoreceptors and horizontal cells in the skate retina. In the dark the photoreceptors are partially depolarized and the membrane potential of the horizontal cells is low (~25 mV). The response of both cell types to light is a graded hyperpolarization accompanied by an increase in membrane resistance. Increasing the external magnesium ion concentration, which inhibits transmitter release at conventional synapses, results in the hyperpolarization of the horizontal cells and a decrease in the response to light flashes. These observations can be explained by the reduction by magnesium of the continual release of a depolarizing transmitter, and they support the notion that

photoreceptor hyperpolarizations caused by light reduce the rate of continual release of this depolarizing transmitter. Although this interpretation is consistent with our knowledge of presynaptic mechanisms at more conventional chemical synapses, the postsynaptic processes may be unconventional, since, in the mud puppy at least, no clear reversal potential could be determined for the hyperpolarizing responses in the horizontal cells (Nelson, 1973).

Other junctions where graded presynaptic potentials seem to modulate the continuous release of either a depolarizing or a hyperpolarizing transmitter are at the bipolar-to-amacrine-cell junction and the photo-receptor-to-depolarizing-bipolar cells in the mud puppy (Nelson, 1973). For the latter junction, however, it is clear that the postsynaptic mechanisms are unconventional because the presynaptic hyperpolarization, which presumably reduces the transmitter released, causes an increase in the permeability of the postsynaptic membrane to sodium ions. One possible explanation for this phenomenon is that the transmitter acts postsynaptically by blocking sodium channels. This unconventional type of postsynaptic response has also been described in the frog sympathetic ganglion (Weight, 1974).

In contrast to the findings in the skate, the transmission from photoreceptors to horizontal cells in the mud puppy may not depend on the release of a chemical transmitter (Nelson, 1973). The hyperpolarizing response in the horizontal cells to light is only very slightly affected by membrane polarization, unaffected by injections of potassium and chloride ions, and not generated by changes in sodium ion permeability. Nelson (1973) has suggested that this response (and also the similar response in the hyperpolarizing bipolar cells) could be generated by light modulated changes in extracellular potassium concentration. Light causes a decrease in the outward potassium current at the photoreceptor terminals and thus may lower the external potassium ion concentration near the horizontal and hyperpolarizing bipolar cells. This, in turn, is postulated to produce a glial-like response in these cells. If this postulated mechanism is correct, the function of the presynaptic vesicles adjacent to the horizontal cell processes is not clear.

FUNCTIONAL ADVANTAGES OF NONSPIKING NERVE CELLS

Input–Output in Simple Systems

It is generally assumed that in simple nervous systems a single spiking presynaptic input can control, in a precise and continuous manner, the output discharge rate of a follower cell. Now, in many invertebrate systems the discharge rate of some follower cells (for example, motoneurons in arthropods) varies over a very wide range (20 to 350 impulses per second), and it is not obvious that a single spiking presynaptic input which is producing discrete excitatory postsynaptic potentials in follower neurons could precisely regulate the firing of the postsynaptic neurons over this wide range without 1 : 1 following or frequency division. We have resorted to computer modeling in an attempt to determine whether that is possible and have concluded that it is not (Pearson and DiCaprio, unpublished). A motoneuron was modeled by assuming that, following an impulse, the time course of recovery follows a hyperbolic time course described by α/t, where α is a constant and t the time following the impulse. When this recovery function is less than the input voltage but greater than the threshold, another impulse is initiated. The hyperbolic nature of the recovery gives a linear voltage–frequency relationship which has been found in insect motoneurons (Pearson and Fourtner, unpublished). The input to this model motoneuron was assumed to be a continuous train of EPSPs, the form of each individual described by

$$V_{\text{epsp}} = a\,\frac{t}{t_r}\exp\left(1 - \frac{t}{t_r}\right)$$

where a is the amplitude of each EPSP and t_r is the rise time to the peak. Thus five variables could be changed in the simple formulation of this model: (1) the frequency of the input, (2) the EPSP amplitude, (3) the EPSP rise time, (4) the rate of recovery of excitability of the motoneuron, and (5) the threshold for spike initiation. Nonlinear summation of the EPSPs was also built into the model, but this was found to have only slight effects on the input–output relation and did not qualitatively alter the general results of this study.

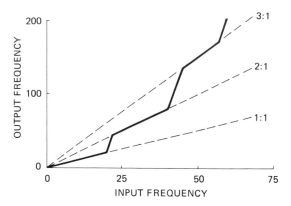

FIGURE 3.   An example of the input–output relationship for a model motoneuron excited by a single spiking presynaptic input, each presynaptic spike producing an EPSP of the form $V_{\text{epsp}} = a \cdot t/t_r \exp(1 - t/t_r)$ where a is the amplitude and t_r the rise time. The model motoneuron is described in the text. In this example the sensitivity of the motoneuron $(1/\alpha)$ was 18 impulses per second per mV, the threshold was 5 mV, and the EPSP parameters were $a = 10\ mV$ and $t_r = 10\ msec$. The input–output relationship shows regions where the output frequency is an integer multiple of the input frequency. The range of input frequencies for the transition between these regions is narrow. Qualitatively similar relationships were obtained using a wide range of values for a, t_r, and α and when nonlinear summation and facilitation of the EPSP were simulated.

Using a wide variety of the values for the various parameters in this computer simulation it was always found that the relationship between the input frequency and output frequency had a number of discontinuities (Figure 3). These discontinuities occurred such that the output frequency remained an integer (or sometimes a half integer) multiple of the input frequency. The sudden discontinuities in this relationship mean that a single input producing discrete EPSPs is unable to regulate the firing rate of the postsynaptic neuron in a continuous manner. For some systems the need for continuous regulation may be unnecessary, but for others it is clearly essential. For example, the sudden discontinuities in the discharge rate of motoneurons would not result in a continuous range of muscular contractions, which is necessary for the precise control of any movement. Again, it must be stressed that this conclusion applies only to a situation in which a *single* input is assumed to be entirely responsible for controlling the discharge rate in motoneurons. It is thus significant that for the two arthropod motor systems where it is known that the activity in certain motoneurons is produced by driving from a single interneuron (crustacean ventilation and insect walking), the driving interneurons do not produce action potentials. Slow oscillations in membrane potential in the driving interneuron in each system are responsible for producing rhythmic burst activity, and graded changes in the amplitude of these oscillations alter the intensity of motor activity in a continuous manner over a wide range (Figure 1). A third example of a single input precisely controlling motoneuronal activity is the nonspiking receptor organ in the legs of crabs. Graded depolarizations in either of the two axons from this receptor can precisely control the discharge rate of identified motoneurons. The conclusion from the above analysis is that this would not be possible if these axons produced action potentials and discrete EPSPs in the motoneurons.

Rather than having graded activity in single presynaptic neurons to control continuously the level of activity in postsynaptic neurons, it would be possible to produce graded changes in membrane potential in the postsynaptic neurons by having a large number of presynaptic input connections which discharge asynchronously yet each of which produces a small discrete EPSP. In the sensory systems of invertebrates this notion could explain why there are usually a large number of sensory axons arising from various groups of receptors. Clearly, action potentials must be generated in the afferents from these receptors since information is transmitted over long distances. Therefore, if this sensory information is to control precisely and continuously the activity of neurons onto which the afferents make connection, a large number of asynchronously discharging inputs are required.

We can conclude from the above discussion that in simple neuronal systems when the activity in a neuron is to be controlled by a single input it is advantageous that this input function is in a graded manner. There are clearly exceptions to this rule, but these occur only when there is 1 : 1 following, or when there is a significant reduction in the discharge rate between the input and the output.

Integrators of Neuronal Activity

In any neuronal system there is convergence of inputs from many regions of the CNS and perhaps from various groups of receptors. Because the information from these regions is transmitted over long distances these inputs are spiking. Now, if these inputs converge directly onto the output elements of the system, the temporal patterning of the spiking input may be reflected in the temporal patterning of action potentials in the output. In some circumstances this may be disadvantageous for example, where the output is to be related simply to the net level of input rather than the precise temporal pattern of the input. One solution to this need for integrating the activity of many spiking inputs is to have convergence onto nonspiking interneurons which in turn influence, in a graded manner, the activity of the output neurons of the system. Reese and Shepherd (1972) in their review of the olfactory system have described the input to the olfactory bulb from widespread areas of the CNS onto the nonspiking granule cells and not directly to the mitral cells, which are the output elements of the bulb. The graded activity in the granule cells then controls the degree of tonic inhibition to the mitral cells. Thus the overall sensitivity of the olfactory system is continuously regulated by the graded activity in granule cells. In two invertebrate motor systems the level of activity also appears to be regulated by graded activity in specific interneurons. Mendelson (1971) has described a neuron in the ventilatory system of crabs and lobsters which, when depolarized, initiated rhythmic burst activity in ventilatory motoneurons. The rate of occurrence of these bursts was directly related to the level of depolarization. We have found similar interneurons in the walking system of the cockroach (Pearson and Fourtner, unpublished). In these motor systems it is probable that there is convergence onto these control interneurons from a variety of descending and ascending command interneurons. The net level of depolarization then determines the rate of the rhythmic output.

The Isolation of Function
Within a Single Neuron

Many individual neurons within the CNS of vertebrates and invertebrates may have more than one function, with differing functions associated with anatomically separated regions of the neuron (Maynard, 1966; Shepherd, 1972a). For an effective diversification of functions within a single neuron it is obviously desirable for a large degree, or complete, electrical isolation of the different functioning regions. Clearly, the generation of large amplitude action potentials in any part of such a neuron would be disadvantageous because these large potentials would have a greater influence at distal sites in the neuron. Thus it would be useful if only small amplitude graded potentials were produced in each part of the neuron. One type of horizontal cell in the cat retina appears to function in this manner. The dendritic terminals of these cells connect only to cones and the axon terminals only to rods. Thus it has been suggested that the axon terminal system of these horizontal cells functions independently of the soma (Kolb, 1974). The thin axon that connects the axon terminals and soma may serve to isolate these two regions electrically rather than provide a pathway for communication (see Chapter Three).

Signal Detection

Two characteristic features of many specialized sensory receptors are (1) the very small amplitudes of the signals to which they respond and the corresponding small magnitude of the potential changes, and (2) the absence of spike activity (Steinbach, 1974; Laughlin, 1974). This correlation immediately suggests that the production of graded responses in specialized sensory cells is advantageous for signal detection. Perhaps the obvious advantage is that very small graded potentials could

modulate the release of transmitter and the signal thereby amplified in the postsynaptic neurons. Such amplification has been observed in the transmission from the retinula to monopolar neurons in the insect visual system (Laughlin, 1974). If action potentials were generated directly in the receptor cells, it is probable that very small signals would be insufficient to cause a detectable change in discharge rate.

In both vertebrate and insect visual systems the second-order neurons do not generate action potentials. The interactions of the photoreceptors, horizontal cells, and bipolar cells in the outer plexiform layer of the vertebrate retina have been discussed by Werblin (1974). The advantage of having graded interactions between these three cell types is that they provide a simple method for continuously repositioning the intensity—response relationship of the bipolar neurons so that the response in the bipolar cells remains maximal for small changes in light intensity around the background intensity. Thus small changes in light intensity near background always give a response in the bipolar cells irrespective of the absolute background intensity over a range of about $10^9 : 1$. In other words graded interactions between the cells in the outer plexiform layer provide a neuronal mechanism for continuous adaptation of the retina to an enormous range of ambient light intensities. In the insect visual system the advantage of graded potentials in second-order neurons may be to allow a higher rate of information transmission because the analog signal would not have to be integrated at output synapses (Laughlin, 1974).

CONCLUSIONS

The majority of nonspiking nerve cells have been discovered only within the past few years as a result of improved microelectrode and dye injection techniques. With the increasing use of these techniques in a variety of systems we can confidently expect that many more examples of this type of neuron will be reported in the near future. Moreover, we will probably discover that graded interactions occur via chemical synapses between neurons in many regions of the nervous system and that these interactions will be of primary importance in the integration and processing of information within localized regions. What are the indications that these predictions are reasonable? Perhaps the strongest is the relatively recent discovery of dendrodendritic synapses in widespread regions of the mammalian nervous system (Harding, 1971; Lieberman, 1973; Rall, Shepherd, and Reese, 1966; Ralston, 1971; Sloper, 1971). If we accept the conventional notion that, in general, dendrites do not generate action potentials, it follows that the transmission at these synapses is unlikely to depend on action potentials in the presynaptic dendrite. At present we have one clear example in the CNS of this type of interaction — the transmission from granule to mitral cells in the olfactory bulb. The synapses between these neurons are reciprocal and morphologically similar to reciprocal synapses in other regions of the CNS (Ralston, 1971; Lieberman, 1973). This structural similarity is thus another reason for believing that graded interactions between nerve cells is a widespread phenomenon. A third indication for the existence of other nonspiking neurons in the mammalian CNS is the discovery of axonless cells in different locations (Schiebel, Davies, and Scheibel, 1972; Lieberman, 1973; Valverde, 1973). We know that at least two other axonless neurons (bipolar and granule cells) do not generate action potentials. However, the lack of an axon does not necessarily mean that the cell functions in a wholly graded manner, as the axonless amacrine cells of the vertebrate retina generate action potentials. Nonetheless, the lack of an axon means that the neuron does not necessarily have to produce action potentials because the distances over which information is transmitted are short.

The factors that determine whether neurons in any animal will be spiking or nonspiking are likely to be distances over which the neuron must send information, the size of the neuron, the rate at which information is to be processed and transmitted, and so on. There can be extreme variation in these parameters in any single species, and consequently it is probable that both spiking and nonspiking neurons exist in the nervous systems of all animals. Rather surprisingly, then, nonspiking neurons have not yet been described in the CNS

of mollusks despite the considerable number of intracellular studies on these animals. However, intracellular recordings have not yet been made from the many relatively small neurons in these animals, and until this is done the likelihood of nonspiking neurons in these animals cannot be assessed. The fact that photoreceptors in some mollusks are nonspiking (Table III) and subthreshold graded interactions between spiking neurons are known (Kater, 1974) suggests that nonspiking neurons will eventually be found in these animals.

Based on the results to date, it is also highly probable that graded interactions between neurons is a widespread phenomenon in arthropods. Nonspiking interneurons have been found to be part of the rhythm-generating systems in crustaceans and insects (Mendelson, 1971; Pearson and Fourtner, 1975) and there are as yet no clear examples of patterned motor activity that depends on activity in spiking interneurons. This is not to say, however, that nonspiking interneurons are responsible for patterning motor activity in all arthropod motor systems. It is probable that the patterning of rapid phasic activity in arthropod motoneurons depends on the interactions of spiking neurons, whereas the patterning of slow burst activity in slow motoneurons is dependent on graded interactions between premotor neurons.

Finally, we must ask how the discovery of nerve cells without action potentials influences our general understanding of neuronal functioning. Clearly, the conventional notion that all information is transmitted between neurons in the form of action potentials is incorrect for some, and perhaps many, interactions. Even so, by itself this conclusion does not force us to alter radically our concepts of the function of certain types of multineuronal interactions (for example, reciprocal inhibition), provided we continue to regard single nerve cells as the functional units within the nervous system. It is just as easy, perhaps easier, to think of neurons transmitting information by graded potentials as by action potentials. But is it reasonable to regard single neurons as the basic functional units within the nervous system? Shepherd (1972) has eloquently argued that it is not. The discovery of dendrodendritic and, in particular, reciprocal synapses in many regions of the CNS leads to the conclusion that morphologically distinct regions of a single neuron may be involved in different integrative functions. Thus Shepherd has proposed that we must begin to regard the nervous system as being organized in terms of functional units, where a functional unit is the morphological substrate for a specific function. This new and important concept does not specify whether the synaptic interactions within a functional unit are by graded potentials or by action potentials, al-though it is implicit that graded interactions at many units would be advantageous for ensuring functional isolation (see the section "Functional Advantages of Nonspiking Nerve Cells"). Taken together, the discoveries of dendro-dendritic synapses and graded interactions between neurons are what I believe to be the beginnings of a revolution in our views about the integrative mechanism within the nervous system.

CHAPTER EIGHT

Hormonal Release of Differentiated Behavior Patterns

JAMES W. TRUMAN

INTRODUCTION

A student of animal behavior cannot help being impressed by the dramatic behavioral effects of certain homones. Undoubtedly, the most familiar example is the action of estrogen on the behavior of some female mammals. Under the influence of this hormone, the female displays behavior that is seen under no other conditions. Indeed, her behavior is often the complete opposite of what she would show in the unprimed condition.

The fact that hormones may exert their effects through a direct action on the central nervous system was first indicated by experiments such as those by Bard (1935), who showed that full estrus behavior was displayed by an estrogen-primed cat, even after complete denervation of the genital area. Harris, Michael, and Scott (1958) then directly demonstrated the central action of the hormone by implanting minute crystals of the estrogen mimic stilbesterol dibutyrate into the cat brain. Implantation of the crystals into the posterior hypothalamus elicited estrus behavior in the absence of the accompanying physiological manifestations. Experiments with the rat have similarly shown that estrogen implanted into the specific regions of the brain will elicit estrus behavior (Lisk, 1962). Moreover, these areas selectively concentrate systemically injected hormone, which indicates that they are indeed targets for estrogen action (Pfaff, 1972).

To determine how a hormone can change the behavior of an animal, one needs to identify the neural elements that are involved in the generation of the behavior. One must then find at what level in this circuitry the hormone-sensitive neurons reside and what properties of the neurons change to allow the performance of the behavior. It is very probable that the hormone ultimately changes the electrical properties of these selected target cells; but, clearly, these changes must reflect some deeper alterations in the biochemistry of the respective neurons.

The mechanism of hormone action is an area of intense research. It is firmly established that many steroid hormones exert their action by binding to cytoplasmic receptors in the target cell and then moving, as a hormone-receptor complex, into the nucleus (Jensen and De Sombre, 1973). Alternatively, many peptide hormones act through the "second messenger," cyclic-AMP (Butcher, Robison, and Sutherland, 1972). These studies on nonneural cells undoubtedly also have a bearing on how hormones affect neurons. The applicability of these mechanisms to hormonally induced differentiation of parts of the nervous system is obvious [such as the effect of testosterone in preventing the differentiation of the cyclic release center for luteinizing hormone in the hypothalamus (Barraclough and Gorski, 1961, Flerko, 1971)]. But how do these details of the molecular action of hormones relate to their relatively rapid effects on overt behavior (e.g., the induction of estrus behavior by estrogen)? One outcome of a study of the mechanism by which hormones influence behavior should be a better understanding of how changes in the biochemical state of specific neurons result in behavioral changes in the whole animal.

The recent review by Pfaff et al. (1974) shows that in vertebrates the identification of neurons that are central to the performance of a hormonally effected behavior is an awesome task, even for a deceptively simple behavior such as the lordosis reflex of the rat. Accordingly, we have taken the approach that is typified by many of the contributions in this volume. Our goal was to find a simple neural system that could be studied in isolation but which retained its sensitivity to hormones and generated a behavioral output similar to that seen in the intact animal. My choice of insects for this study was partly due to a long-abiding fascination with these animals and also to the wide array of hormonally influenced behaviors that this group displays (Truman and Riddiford, 1974). The work that we have done to date has involved a mixture of behavioral, anatomical, and physiological methods.

SILKMOTH ECLOSION

In insects that undergo complete metamorphosis, a quiescent pupal stage is interposed between the larval and adult stages. Meta-

morphosis is then completed with eclosion (emergence) of the adult insect from the pupal skin. In the moths, and very probably in other holometabolous groups, eclosion is triggered by a neurosecretory hormone released from the brain (Truman and Riddiford, 1970).

The behavioral effects of the eclosion hormone in silkmoths is best illustrated by a description of the behavioral changes that occur during emergence. Immediately prior to adult emergence, individuals of the Pernyi moth, *Antheraea pernyi*, show little in the way of adult behavior (Truman, 1971). When the confining pupal cuticle is manually peeled away from such animals, the insects continue to display pupal-like rotary movements of the abdomen but fail to show most of the behaviors characteristic of the adult. The moths neither walk nor climb, wing spreading does not occur, there is no righting reflex, and wing flapping movements can only rarely be elicited. Immediately after eclosion, the situation reverses itself. The adult behaviors are now expressed and the rotary movements of the abdomen disappear. Thus, prior to emergence, most adult behavior patterns are somehow centrally repressed; then, during eclosion, these behaviors are "turned on" and the pupal motor patterns are "turned off."

The fact that a hormone is involved in this behavioral change was revealed by a series of experiments aimed at elucidating the basis for the daily timing of eclosion. The emergence of the moth occurs only during a specific period of the day or night, the time of which is a function of the particular species and the environmental photoperiod. When the brain was removed from animals early in adult development, the resulting moths showed an abnormal emergence behavior and, importantly, emerged randomly without regard to time of day. This effect of brain removal could be repaired by implanting a brain into the abdominal hemocoel of a debrained animal (Figure 1). Upon completion of adult development these "loose-brained" moths emerged in a normal manner during the proper time of day. The synchronizing effect of the brain was further shown by exchanging brains between two species that had different emergence times. The resulting moths emerged synchronously during the time characteristic of the species

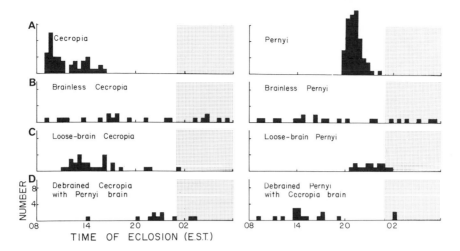

FIGURE 1. *(A) Normal eclosion of* Hyalophora cecropia *and* Antheraea pernyi *moths in a 17L:7D photoperiod regimen. (B) shows the effects of brain removal, (C) the transplantation of the brain to the abdomen, and (D) the interchange of brains between the two species.*

that donated the brain (Figure 1). Manifestly, the transfer of the brain between the two species served to transfer the time that the animals eclosed. Since the implanted brain could control emergence in the absence of neural connections with the rest of the nervous system, it was obvious that this control was exerted through hormonal means.

The hormonal triggering of eclosion and associated behavioral changes was directly confirmed by the injection of brain extracts into preemergence animals. Injections were typically followed within 15 minutes by the onset of the preeclosion behavior — a 1.25-hour-long stereotyped series of abdominal movements that immediately precedes eclosion — and culminated in the emergence of the moth. When brain extracts were injected into moths that had been freed manually of pupal cuticle, the animals performed the preeclosion behavior, then a pantomine eclosion, and then precociously assumed adult behavior (Truman, 1971).

Thus the eclosion hormone brings about a rapid behavioral change in the silkmoth. Within 15 minutes of injection, the insect begins the patterned preeclosion behavior which will be considered below. By 1.5 hours after injection, most of the adult motor programs have been switched on. This relatively rapid response to

the hormone made the silkmoth an ideal animal in which to study the influence of hormones on behavior.

THE PREECLOSION BEHAVIOR

As noted above, the preeclosion behavior is a stereotyped program of abdominal movements that lasts approximately 1.25 hours. We chose to study this behavior for a number of reasons: (1) it was the first behavioral response to the eclosion hormone; (2) it was a stereotyped motor response; and (3) it was performed by a part of the animal that was relatively simple in its musculature and nervous system.

The muscles responsible for the preeclosion movements are found primarily in segments 4, 5, and 6 of the abdomen. In the moth, prior to eclosion, these segments are essentially a muscle-lined tube with thick bands of longitudinal muscle arranged around the circumference of each segment. External to these, there is a second, weaker group of longitudinal muscles, the external muscles. Each segment is also supplied with a set of ventral oblique muscles and a dense band of transverse muscles along the lateral margin.

The abdomen has three simple ganglia that supply segments 3, 4, and 5. Segments 6 and

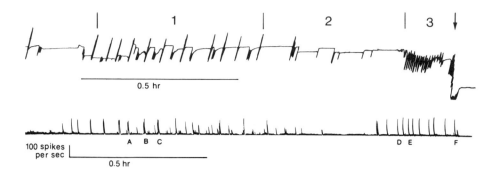

FIGURE 2. *Behavioral and electrical activity shows the three phases of the Cecropia preeclosion behavior.* Top: *Record of the abdominal movements obtained by attaching the tip of the abdomen to a lever that writes on a revolving drum. Rotary movements produced complete excursions of the trace. The downward deflections were produced by both ventrally directed twitches and peristaltic movements of the abdomen. (1) indicates the first hyperactive period; (2), the quiescent period; and (3), the second hyperactive period. Arrow identifies the moment of adult emergence.* Bottom: *Integrated motor activity from the right dorsal nerve of the fourth abdominal ganglion after addition of the eclosion hormone to the deafferented nerve cord. Letters refer to bursts represented in an expanded form in Figure 3. (From Truman and Sokolove, 1972; copyright 1972 by the American Association for the Advancement of Science.)*

beyond are innervated by a fused terminal ganglion. The ganglion that supplies segment 4, taken as a representative simple abdominal ganglion, contains about 500 neurons (Taylor and Truman, 1974). The entire abdominal nervous system probably consists of approximately 3,000 neurons.

The preeclosion behavior involves two major types of coordinated abdominal movements. The rotary movements of the abdomen are the result of the sequential contraction of the internal muscle groups around the circumference of the abdomen. The second type of movement is an eclosion movement that has two different forms, depending upon the species considered. In some moths, the eclosion movements are peristaltic waves of contractions along the abdomen. The movement starts with a strong, symmetrical contraction of the sixth segment and progresses anteriorly in a segment-by-segment fashion. The wave terminates in the thorax with a strong flexion of the wing bases. The eclosion movements shown by other species involve an extension of the entire abdomen accompanied by the wing flexion movements. Both the internal muscles and the lateral transverse muscles are likely to be involved in these eclosion movements. The two

motor programs are played off according to a stereotyped temporal score which lasts approximately 75 minutes. The temporal arrangement of movements in the score varies according to the species of moth.

The most complicated preeclosion behavior that we have studied belongs to *Hyalophora cecropia*. In the Cecropia moth, the behavior is divided into three distinct phases (Figure 2). The first phase lasts about 0.5 hours and consists of frequent bouts of rotary movements. This is followed by a 0.5-hour period of relative quiescence during which the frequency of rotary movements markedly declines. The end of the quiet period is signaled by the abrupt onset of peristaltic contractions. During this third phase, rotary movements are only rarely observed.

With respect to the preeclosion behavior, the site of hormone sensitivity, as well as the circuitry that generates the behavior, is contained entirely within the abdomen. Manifestly, injection of the eclosion hormone into abdomens that had been isolated from preemergence Cecropia moths results in the complete performance of the preeclosion behavior by these fragments (Truman, 1971). Thus the neurons in the abdominal nervous system can

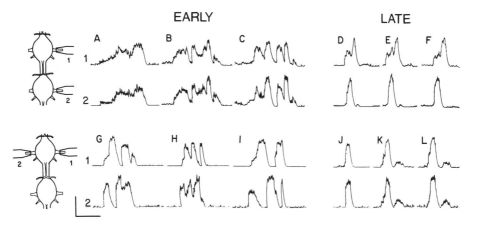

FIGURE 3. *Examples of integrated spontaneous bursts recorded from the deafferented abdominal ganglia after addition of the eclosion hormone.* Top: *Electrodes placed sequentially on the right dorsal roots of the fourth and the fifth abdominal ganglia.* Bottom: *Electrodes placed bilaterally on the right and left roots of fourth ganglion. Bursts (A) to (C) and (G) to (I) are of the rotational pattern typically observed during the first (early) hyperactive period. Bursts (D) to (F) and (J) to (L) are of the peristaltic pattern observed during the second (late) hyperactive period. Vertical line equals 100 spikes per second; horizontal line, 10 seconds. (From Truman and Sokolove, 1972; copyright 1972 by the American Association for the Advancement of Science.)*

respond to the eclosion hormone by the generation of a complex program of coordinated behavior.

THE NEURAL BASIS OF THE PREECLOSION BEHAVIOR

Thus far, electrophysiological studies on the preeclosion behavior have been designed to elucidate its neural basis and to demonstrate a direct action of the hormone on the silkmoth nervous system. The experiments have employed either a semidissected isolated abdomen in which all the peripheral nerves from the chain of ganglia had been severed (Truman and Sokolove, 1972), or a completely isolated chain of ganglia maintained in Ringer's solution (Truman, unpublished). In both cases, spontaneous motor activity was monitored by suction electrodes placed over the proximal stumps of the dorsal nerves. The latter nerves supply the longitudinal internal muscles and the lateral transverse muscles.

A nerve cord unstimulated by the eclosion hormone showed a low level of spontaneous motor activity, with an occasional rotary patterned burst. Addition of the eclosion hormone to either the semidissected or the isolated preparation dramatically changed this output (Figures 2 and 3). After a lag time of about 0.5 hours, the chain of ganglia began generating rotary bursts. Each burst consisted of multiple volleys of motor discharge which showed essentially identical patterning in the ipsilateral nerves from sequential ganglia but alternating volleys in contralateral roots. As seen in Figure 3, the patterning of the rotary bursts was quite variable even in the same individual. However, these bursts always maintained the character of bilateral alternation and ipsilateral synchrony among the various ganglia. Bursts having this rotary character occurred at relatively frequent intervals during the succeeding 0.5 hour, after which the frequency of bursts declined and the ganglia entered into a quiescent period. As with the behavior of the intact animal, the number of rotary bursts seen during this period was variable but it was always considerably less than was seen during the first 0.5 hour. The end of the quiet period was signaled by the abrupt resumption of motor bursts. These occurred at a relatively high frequency and showed a peristaltic patterning. The motor discharge typically consisted of one major burst. The dorsal nerves from each ganglion showed symmetrical discharges, and the activity began in the most posterior ganglion and then progressed anteriorly through successive ganglia. The peristaltic bursts were much more stereotyped than were the rotary bursts.

Thus, as one would expect from the work of Wilson (1961) on the patterning of locust flight, the rotary and peristaltic movements are prepatterned into the circuitry of the abdominal ganglia. In addition, the temporal sequence of movements, the quiet period, and the switch from one motor program to the next are also coded into the nervous system. We thus have an example of a motor tape (Hoyle, 1970) that can run for 75 minutes without the need of sensory information.

As with the flight of locusts (Wilson and Gettrup, 1963), however, sensory information appears to modulate some of the temporal aspects of the preeclosion behavior. When compared to the behavior of the intact animal, the first two phases of the preeclosion behavior in the deafferented nervous system appear to show the proper temporal arrangement of motor commands. However, this conclusion cannot be made with complete confidence because of the extreme variability seen in these phases of the behavior. But the need for sensory input is clearly apparent in the last part of the preeclosion behavior. In the intact animal, peristaltic contractions occur at a frequency of 2 to 3 per minute. The deafferented nerve cord generates peristaltic bursts that are separated by 2 to 5 minutes. Thus the overall pattern of the preeclosion behavior is centrally set, but certain aspects of the program can be modified by peripheral input.

ONTOGENY OF THE BEHAVIOR

The two motor programs that are included in the preeclosion behavior arise well before they are inserted in the species-specific temporal score. The final assembly of the completed "tape" then appears to coincide with the attainment of hormonal sensitivity. This can be best seen in the preeclosion behavior of the Pernyi moth. In this species, as well as all other moth species, rotary movements of the abdomen appear at the time of pupation and are seen throughout the 19 days of adult development. They occur spontaneously at 1- to 1.5-hour intervals and in response to vigorous prodding. Eclosion movements (which involve abdominal extensions in Pernyi) are normally not observed in the developing moth, but they can occasionally be elicited from an animal on day 15 of development by peeling off the pupal cuticle. Within a few minutes of peeling, day-15 moths show extensions of the abdomen accompanied by flexions of the wing bases. In slightly older animals these eclosion movements are stronger, occur at a frequency of about one per minute, and continue for well over an hour. It is of interest that at this time in development the eclosion movements are seen alone and not as a part of the preeclosion behavior. Also during this period, the preeclosion behavior cannot be elicited by eclosion hormone injection.

The completed preeclosion behavior appears to be assembled during the last 2 days of adult development. On day 18, removal of the pupal cuticle from developing Pernyi moths no longer elicits eclosion movements. The inhibition of this behavior presumably occurs when this program is incorporated into the hormone-sensitive circuitry responsible for the preeclosion behavior. After this time the moth becomes sensitive to the eclosion hormone, and injection of the hormone leads to the performance of the complete behavior.

THE POSSIBLE ROLE OF INHIBITION

Once the neurons involved in the generation of the preeclosion behavior have been identified and the interactions between the various components established, the question still remains as to how the circuitry is turned on by the hormone. In the case of some other hormonally controlled behaviors, it appears that in the unstimulated state, the relevant circuitry is functional but under neural inhibition. The hormone then serves to release this inhibition.

The hormonal release of inhibition over a motor program is most clearly seen in the control of copulatory movements of the male cockroach. Shortly after decapitation, males begin to show constant copulatory movements; there are peristaltic movements of the terminal abdominal segments, a bending of the tip of the abdomen, and coordinated rhythmic movements of the genitalia. In semidissected preparations, this effect of decapitation is also manifest by coordinated, rhythmic motor bursts in the phallic nerves (Roeder, Tozian, and Weiant, 1960). From these and other experiments, it was concluded that the motor centers responsible for the copulatory movements are normally inhibited by centers in the subesophageal ganglion. Decapitation accordingly removes the inhibition.

These effects of decapitation can be effectively mimicked by the application of extracts of the corpora cardiaca (the neurohemal organ of the brain). When these extracts were applied to the nerve cord or injected into the head capsule of semidissected cockroaches, the animals subsequently showed rhythmic bursting in the phallic nerves (Milburn, Weiant, and Roeder, 1960; Milburn and Roeder, 1962). The magnitude and time course of the hormonally induced response was the same as that elicited by decapitation, with the exception that the former treatment was reversible. Consequently, the "phallic nerve stimulating hormone" appears to trigger copulatory movements by removal of the inhibitory influence of the subesophageal ganglion.

The removal of neural inhibition may also be an important part of the action of the eclosion hormone. In the silkmoth *Automeris memusae*, Blest (1960) reported that certain fragments of adult behavior could be elicited during the latter part of adult development but that these then disappeared as development neared completion. We have seen a similar phenomenon in the eclosion movements of Pernyi moths. It would appear that in the preemergence moth, the adult motor programs are operational but under neural inhibition. The key to the action of the eclosion hormone would therefore appear to be in the changes that occur in these postulated inhibitory interneurons.

However, with a few notable exceptions, such as certain giant interneurons, it has been extremely difficult repeatedly to find and

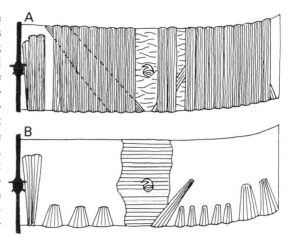

FIGURE 4. *Musculature of the fourth abdominal segment of a* Manduca sexta *male. Ventral midline is on the left, dorsal midline on the right. (A) Musculature of a newly emerged moth; (B) 3 days after eclosion.*

characterize specific insect interneurons. Consequently, we have turned our attention to large identifiable cells that are involved in the performance of patterned behavior but which most likely do not participate in the pattern generation itself. These cells are the motoneurons in the abdominal ganglia. As will be seen below, many of these cells undergo pronounced changes which can be attributed to the action of the eclosion hormone. Using these large cells, we hope to gain insight into how a hormone changes the properties of individual neurons.

CHANGES IN ABDOMINAL MOTONEURONS

As described above, the abdomen of the preemergence moth is lined with thick bands of internal muscles. After eclosion these muscles begin to degenerate and by 3 days after emergence they are gone (Figure 4) (Finlayson, 1956; Lockshin and Williams, 1965a). The muscle degeneration appears to be caused by changes in the respective motoneurons. Indeed, when the motor roots were continually stimulated either by application of the anticholinesterase, physostigimine, or by chronic

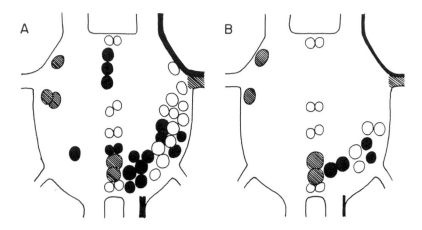

FIGURE 5.   Maps of the location of the cell bodies of motoneurons that send their axons to the periphery through the right lateral nerves. Cross-hatched, axons exit through dorsal nerve; open, through ventral nerve; filled, through dorsal nerve of next posterior ganglion. (A) Fourth abdominal ganglion prior to emergence; (B) 3 days after eclosion. (Modified from Taylor and Truman, 1974.)

electrical stimulation through implanted electrodes, the relevant muscles persisted (Lockshin and Williams, 1965b, c). Thus it was concluded that the muscles degenerated because their motoneurons "shut off" around the time of eclosion.

The fact that the triggering of muscle degeneration was associated with eclosion became more evident with the report by Lockshin (1971) that, when abdomens were isolated from preemergence *A. polyphemus* moths, the internal muscles were routinely retained, but that, if isolation occurred at the moment of eclosion or later, the internal muscles degenerated. Therefore, Lockshin concluded that some signal from the anterior end was required to trigger internal muscle breakdown. This signal proved to be the eclosion hormone. When the hormone was injected into Polyphemus abdomens that had been isolated prior to eclosion, internal muscle degeneration proceeded on schedule (Truman, 1970). Thus one action of the eclosion hormone on the silkmoth nervous system is the "shutting off" of certain abdominal motoneurons, which, in turn, leads to the degeneration of the corresponding muscles.

Since the moth abdomen has muscles that fall into two groups with respect to their fate

after eclosion (Figure 4), there must accordingly be two corresponding groups of motoneurons — one group that "shuts off" and another that remains active. In our initial attempts to identify which motoneurons innervate which muscle, we have used the technique of backfilling the appropriate motor root with cobalt chloride (Pitman, Tweedle, and Cohen, 1972a; Iles and Mulloney, 1971). Figure 5A shows the location of the cell bodies of the neurons that send axons to the periphery through the paired lateral nerves in the sphinx moth *Manduca sexta* (Taylor and Truman, 1974). In the moth, before eclosion, the muscles of the fourth abdominal segment are supplied by 70 motoneurons. The cobalt filling has allowed us to associate certain groups of neurons with various groups of muscles, but at this time we have not worked out connections between individual motoneurons and their specific muscles.

Adult eclosion is followed by the degeneration of a large number of motoneurons in the abdominal ganglia. Cobalt backfillings reveal that in 3-day old adult *Manduca* approximately one-half of the motoneurons have disappeared (Figure 5B). Serial section reconstructions of these ganglia similarly show the selective degeneration of specific motoneurons. The motoneuron degeneration proves to be more rapid than originally suspected (Taylor and Truman, 1974); by 24 hours after emergence, the relevant motoneurons already show obvious signs of degeneration (Truman, unpublished). Thus, in *Manduca*, degeneration is the ultimate response of certain motoneurons to eclosion. Figure 6 shows the location of the cells that degenerate after eclosion and those that remain functional.

Groups of interneurons also share the fate of the motoneurons. Prior to eclosion, the fourth abdominal ganglion contains approximately 400 small neurons, which are presumably interneurons. By the day after eclosion, the number has dropped to about 200, and it remains at approximately this number through the remainder of adult life. In the case of the interneurons, we cannot identify individual cells but undoubtedly, in these cells also, death is the response of specific neurons to the eclosion hormone.

Neuron death is an extreme response to a hormone. In many situations, a behavioral change elicited by a hormone is maintained for only as long as the hormone is present. With the disappearance of the hormone, the behavior of the animal reverts back to its original state. In such cases degeneration of the controlling neural circuitry would eliminate the option of reversibility. Even in eclosion, in which the behavioral change is permanent, degeneration appears to be an extreme response. In *Manduca*, neuron death is the final outcome of eclosion, but in the giant silkmoths the corresponding neurons do not degenerate, even though these moths exhibit the same types of behavioral changes and muscle degeneration as does *Manduca*. Thus neuron death is not an obligate result of turning off a neuron but only an extreme step that some species take to rid their nervous system of unneeded neural circuitry.

The study of the *Manduca* ganglion has identified which neurons turn off after exposure to the eclosion hormone (Figure 6). We are now turning to the homologous neurons in the silkmoth ganglion as subjects in which to examine how the properties of individual neurons change after hormone treatment.

With eclosion we have progressed to the point that we can work with an isolated portion of the nervous system and, by hormonal appli-

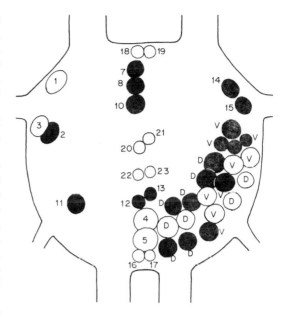

FIGURE 6. *Map of the location of motoneuron cell bodies in the fourth abdominal ganglion of* Manduca sexta. *Open cells are those that persist after eclosion; filled cells degenerate after emergence. D, unidentified neurons that exit to the periphery through the posterior dorsal nerve; V, unidentified neurons that exit through the ventral nerve. Numbering of remaining neurons follows Taylor and Truman, 1974.*

cation, cause it to generate a patterned behavior. Also, we have identified neurons that undergo specific changes presumably as a direct consequence of the eclosion hormone. We hope that this system will soon yield specific answers as to how hormones change the properties of neurons and how these changes are then reflected in the overt behavior of the animal.

NOTE ADDED IN PROOF

Three lines of evidence indicate that cyclic nucleotides are involved in the action of the eclosion hormone (Truman, Fallon, and Wyatt, in preparation). 1) Injections of cyclic AMP elicited the complete preeclosion behavior from *H. cecropia* abdomens.. 2) Administration of the eclosion hormone to isolated abdomens was followed within 10 minutes by a 2-fold increase in cyclic AMP in the abdominal CNS. 3) The effectiveness of a given dose of the eclosion hormone was enhanced by injection of theophylline, a drug that inhibits cyclic AMP degradation. Thus, in this instance it appears that the first step in the hormonal release of prepatterned behavior is an increase in cyclic AMP in the target neurons in the CNS.

III

PHENOTYPIC
FOUNDATIONS

In Part III, we consider the phenotypic foundations of neural networks and behavior from two complementary perspectives. Chapters Nine, Ten, and Eleven stress genetic mechanisms and various methods by which they can be studied. Chapters Twelve, Thirteen, and Fourteen place a greater emphasis upon the interplay between various factors during different stages of development. This distinction between genetic and developmental considerations is arbitrary, however, as will become clear when the present section is viewed as a whole. The very term "phenotype" refers to the indirect expression of genetic potential as released and molded by intrinsic and extrinsic environmental events during ontogeny (development). It is at this level that analysis of behavior as well as neural structure and function ultimately rest.

Chapter Nine, by Bentley, opens with an argument reminiscent of those previously proposed in Chapters Two and Five that an important starting place for the analysis of biological mechanisms of behavior is at the level of the behavioral system itself. Bentley notes, for example, that genes encode for the organism and its total functional characteristics rather than for neural mechanisms per se. He then goes on to demonstrate, however, that careful application of procedures and principles of neurogenetics can help us to link more precisely the substrates of operation of individual mechanisms to one another and to the functional characteristics of the organism as a whole. Two important principles in this investigation are *polygenic* expression, in which multiple genes converge in their effect upon a given trait, and *pliotropic* pathways, in which a given gene may exert multiple effects, both spatially and sequentially. This indicates that we must continue to think of dynamic interacting *networks* (rather than simple linear chains) in our considerations of phenotype. In this regard, Bentley discusses a variety of material relevant to such basic issues as *exclusiveness, directiveness, strength*, and *timing* of genetic factors in neurobiology and behavior. He shows, through his own work and that of others, that these issues can be approached by various strategies, such as alteration of the genome and rendering a given gene nonfunctional. Although Bentley, along with others in Part III, stresses the role of endogenous mechanisms, he is careful to note that intercellular communication, such as between the filiform sensory neurons and the medial giant neuron which mediates certain escape responses in crickets, can be of paramount importance. He also discusses problems of parsimony in encoding neural mechanisms and demonstrates how specific techniques such as the employment of "ring X-chromosomes" and temperature-sensitive mutants can bear importantly upon the clarification of possible general rules as well as specific instances.

Chapter Ten also starts with the general problem of organism–environment relationships, which make it possible to think of the nervous system as an information-processing machine. Like many other contributors to this volume, Ikeda stresses the limitations of previous emphases upon simple reflex models of integrated behavior that failed to take into account either (1) the role of inputs other than those isolated for investigation or (2) endogenous mechanisms of pattern generation. It is particularly with reference to the latter issue, along with consideration of genetic substrates, that Ikeda's research has contributed to current alterations in our thinking about mechanisms. For example, he helped to pioneer the concept of a "command neuron," which triggers highly specific species-characteristic activity patterns of largely intrinsic origin. Ikeda also discusses the problem of *hierarchy* in nervous system control, primarily with regard to the question of which neural elements lead and constrain the action patterns of others; his comments in this regard can usefully be compared to those expressed by other authors in this volume. The term "hierarchy" obviously has several different meanings, often but not necessarily including the concept of divergent control from a single superordinate controller. In constructing his arguments Ikeda follows three stages in logical progression: demonstration of "preprogramming," analysis of mechanisms of turning on and off the program, and genetic substrates. As pointed out in Chapter One, care must be taken not to draw inferences between stereotyped behavior, central control, and genetic predetermination in the absence of empirical data. Through his use of a variety of preparations, including *mosaic* and *gynandromorph* flies, Ikeda indicates one way in which these inferences may be supplemented by more direct empirical evidence.

In Chapter Eleven, Wyman introduces directly the problems of *determination* and *differentiation* in neurogenetics and behavior. This is the question of how cells with the same genome become phenotypically distinct, a question that obviously involves some consideration of cell–cell or cell–environment interaction. At this level the limitations of overly strict endogenous preformation models become apparent. Wyman is also particularly concerned with the problem of establishing *rules* of organization rather than merely examining each specific instance of neurobiological and behavioral expression in isolation. For example, as Wyman points out, there can be no way of accounting for the approximately 10^{15} neuronal connections in the human brain from an estimated 10^5 genes in the human genome without simplifying rules of combination and developmental strategy. The power of such rules and their importance is easily forgotten. For example, to many it is not immediately obvious that each of the 64 squares of a chessboard can be located uniquely with just 6 appropriately addressed "yes or no" questions (where each question is designed to divide the number of alternatives in half, i.e., $2^6 = 64$; see Attneave, 1959). Wyman explores several "simpler" systems, including the 250-cell nervous system of nematodes and the approximately 10,000-cell nervous system of

Drosophila (fruit fly). His own research has indicated that, for the latter, approximately two dozen neurons and muscle fibers can be effectively isolated for more detailed analysis. In this system the basic features of temporal patterning are produced at the level of the motoneuron itself rather than via a more complex circuit property. This assists in the integrative and genetic analysis, and Wyman approaches the question by considering principles of (1) resetting a given neuron after its own spike discharge, (2) shared input among neurons, and (3) mutual inhibition. These principles can help account for problems of pattern generation, and provide other basic questions at the level of genetic control. Wyman, like Bentley (Chapter Nine) and Ikeda (Chapter Ten), emphasizes the theme of *genetic determination*, although each of these authors is aware of potential developmental complexities. Given his emphasis upon genetic substrates, however, Wyman also shows how the use of various techniques, such as mosaics, somatic crossing over, and temperature-sensitive mutants, can be applied to clarify mechanism.

In Chapter Twelve, Edwards and Palka shift the emphasis to more direct developmental considerations. They start with an explicit interest in the distinction between invertebrate (particularly arthropod) and chordate phyla, and conclude with the consideration of possible general principles, such as the development of repeating modular units within the context of repetitive environmental gradients. The question with which these authors are particularly concerned is that of *pattern formation* at the neurobiological level, the necessary and presumed sufficient substrate for pattern in behavior. Toward this end they consider a variety of possible factors, such as spatial and temporal gradients, cell death, sprouting, and trophic relations. Like several other authors, Edwards and Palka emphasize the independence during development of many neurons, in terms of size and shape, from their immediate milieu, although they are careful to point out that general conclusions must at the present time be constructed with caution (see Meinertzhagen, 1973). They explore these issues primarily from the perspective of relationships between center and periphery in neural development. In this regard the authors cite a variety of useful examples, including the heteromorphic regenerates that occupied much of Don Maynard's attention. They make the general points that (1) regeneration studies, when applied with caution, can provide important insights into normal developmental processes, and (2) the restoration of apparently normal behavior after regeneration does not in itself justify precise conclusions about the detailed construction of a regenerated neuronal system (i.e., normal behavioral function can be restored even though individual neural connections retain abnormal characteristics). Along with the theme of gradients in development, Edwards and Palka provide evidence for increasing developmental rigidity (i.e., lack of flexibility) with age, which, when combined with judicious application of the hypotheses of environmental gradients and contact guidance, goes a long way in suggesting developmental rules of both neuronal and behavioral organization. Additional potential mechanisms in regeneration and development such as cell death, cell selection, clonal recognition, compartments, and "clock position" are critically evaluated in light of current experimental data on positional information and neuronal connectivity.

Chapter Thirteen elaborates upon these themes — for example, by providing evidence that simple gradient models are not in themselves fully sufficient for detailed understanding of the intricacies of neurobehavioral development. The authors of this chapter, Kimmel and Eaton, concentrate their attention on a single vertebrate example: the paired *Mauthner cells* of fish and amphibia, which mediate spinally controlled "startle" responses to sensory inputs over the acusticovestibular and lateral line systems. The data presented involve quantitatively combined approaches at the behavioral, neuroanatomical, and neurophysiological levels. Kimmel and Eaton stress in their analyses that a "cardinal rule" of determination of a cell during development is defined by its dependence upon its position in the embryo; this indicates a receptivity to extrinsic (defined at the cellular level) information sources. Subsequently, the rules of phenotypic expression become more or less fixed (i.e., intrinsically organized); this indicates an important shift between intrinsic and extrinsic rules with time (e.g., Bateson, 1976; Fentress, 1976). Their data also indicate that determination and differentiation can be widely separated along a temporal scale; the relations between these events deserve additional exploration (see below). Kimmel and Eaton also elaborate upon Wolpert's (1971) basic proposition that for a cell to be determined it must both receive the appropriate environmental signals and be in a state to "interpret" these signals correctly (commonly called *competence*). The authors are also careful to point out the role of intercellular interactions during differentiation; for example, unilateral removal of otic vesicles during development affects the form of ipsilateral Mauthner cell dendrites. Related considerations lead them to an evaluation of growth, migration, and specific interneuronal connections during differentiation. Chapter Thirteen is particularly useful in pointing out developmental shifts in behavioral control, such as in the ontogenetic sequencing of spinal, hindbrain, and midbrain phases of the Mauthner-cell mediated startle response.

In Chapter Fourteen, Provine adds the perspective that neurobehavioral systems at an early stage of development may often be "simpler," and thus easier to work with in terms of a variety of problems, than at later stages. Like several previous contributors, he emphasizes the usefulness of formulating initial questions of systems operation at the behavioral level and then proceeding systematically "downstream." This is complementary to an approach that starts at the level of "mechanism" with the intent of making inferences about higher levels of organization. Provine selects three preparations from his own research to illustrate the value of complementary levels of analysis. The first is an analysis of embryonic motility in chickens. Starting with the classic work of Preyer (1885) and the more recent work of Hamburger and associates (see the References), he provides both behavioral and electrophysiological evidence for a high degree of *autogenicity* of early motor systems. For example, motor systems in the chick become functional at an earlier developmental stage than do the sensory systems that eventually mediate reflex activities, and intrinsic neurogenic activity can be maintained following nerve section and curarization, which eliminate normal routes of exteroceptive and proprioceptive inputs, respectively. Provine also addresses the question of integrative versus segregative processes by examining the *coupling* of individual motor acts. Data are reviewed which indicate that early behavioral activities can have important structural consequences, such as sculpturing the joints (which in turn could modulate subsequent behavior, emphasizing the importance of looking at the integrative properties of the intact organism). Provine's second preparation concerns cockroach behavior development. He demonstrates the care one must take in inferences about autogenicity versus sensory influence by noting modifications in the duration and sequencing of movements that follow either experimental removal or cementing of the cuticle at the eclosion phase of development, and by examining the responses of embryos at this phase to tactile stimulation. Provine concludes by considering some advantages and disadvantages of tissue culture methods for revealing developmental mechanisms of both the neuro-biological and behavioral import. For example, with these methods it is possible to gain control over neuron types to be examined, their numbers, arrangements, and external environments, while of course eliminating potential sources of intercommunication that may operate in the intact organism.

Two closely related but distinguishable themes emerge from each of the chapters in this part, which also relate them to issues considered previously. These are, first, the balance between intrinsic and extrinsic control mechanisms, and, second, the relevance of "autogenicity," "preprogramming," and so on for consideration of genetic versus experiential substrates. Several general statements appear helpful at this point.

1) Generalizations between preparations and levels of analysis are suggestive but must be made with caution in the face of biological diversity as well as diversity (and limitation) of present techniques. For example, the "presensory" stage of spinal motor development seen in avian species does not occur in mammals.

2) Elimination of certain channels of extrinsic input (e.g., specific sensory connections) does not in itself permit the conclusion that no extrinsic variables are important (e.g., hormonal, temperature changes, etc.).

3) Observation of functional or structural consistency following the elimination of particular routes of extrinsic input does not in itself permit the conclusion that the system thus isolated is insensitive to *changes* in sensory input, even over the same channel. For example, if animals continue to show characteristic movements after elimination of proprioceptive input, this does not mean that they cannot normally respond to changes in this input, as through the application of phasic load.

4) At the functional (e.g., behavioral) level we must be particularly careful to recognize that lack of change in one measured parameter may reflect imprecision of recording technique, and in no case necessarily implies lack of change in other (presumably unmeasured) parameters. For example, adult grooming patterns in mice following dorsal root lesions appear unaffected by casual observation, but upon more detailed analysis certain movement components are noticeably slowed and less stereo-typed, and the sequential *coupling* between components is also modified (Fentress, 1972).

5) Evidence for endogenous patterning in adult animals does not in itself imply intrinsic organization from a developmental perspective. The two questions are logically distinct (see Chapter Twenty-Two).

6) Similarly, autogenicity, even in a developmental context does not imply simple genetic "preformation." The very processes of determination and differentiation which make genetically indistinguishable cells phenotypically distinct, for example, implies responsiveness of these cells to factors defined as extrinsic to them.

7) This indicates further that elimination of factors extrinsic to the organism as an intact entity does not in itself imply that mechanisms *within* the organism are not responding to factors extrinsic *to them* (i.e., to other factors within the organism).

Clearly the evidence of this section supports the previously underestimated importance of both intrinsic factors in developed ("mature") neural networks and behavior, as well as genetic contributions to development. The point to be emphasized is that to explore these issues further we must recognize the limitations of our present conclusions. It is worth repeating that scientific conclusions about causation are ultimately conclusions about observed *differences* and *similarities* between populations of events in the context of the limited set of factors that we have chosen to manipulate and the limited number of consequences that we have chosen to observe.

CHAPTER NINE

Genetic Analysis of the Nervous System

DAVID BENTLEY

INTRODUCTION

In 1973, the Nobel prize for Physiology and Medicine was awarded to Karl von Frisch, Konrad Lorenz, and Niko Tinbergen for their studies of ethology or animal behavior. The hallmark of their work is an emphasis on evolutionary antecedents of behavior, and along with many other workers in the field, they have firmly established a role for genetically transmitted information in behavior. Attention is now being directed to the mechanisms by which genetically stored information influences behavior, and particularly to the relationship between genes and neurons. Investigation of this relationship comprises the field of neurogenetics.

Neurogenetics is in an extremely nascent state. Few studies are available at present, and certainly no clear patterns or rules have emerged. Nevertheless, some illuminating pilot studies have been done, there is great and rapidly growing interest in the area, and the field promises important contributions to

biology in the future. At the moment, it is probably most useful first to give the current, very sketchy understanding of what the relationship between genes and neurons is likely to be; second, to describe present strategies of investigation; and, third, to review a selection of research which appears instructive.

THE GENETIC SUBSTRATE OF THE NERVOUS SYSTEM

Although little is known about genes and neurons, some general points can be made. First, genes encode for the organism, not for the nervous system or any other subsystem. We should not expect to find a set of genes which can be neatly labeled "for the construction and operation of the nervous system." Rather, it is more realistic to imagine each gene as lying somwhere in a multidimensional continuum that depicts effects on the nervous system. Some genes will have a powerful and intimate influence on the nervous system; others will have very weak effects. The relationship will not be all or none.

At least two dimensions of this hypothetical graph can be specified. One might be labeled *exclusiveness* of effect. Some genes that are critical for normal functioning of neurons, such as those whose products are involved in energy mobilization, will also be necessary for practically all cells. The activity of other genes, perhaps involved with potential-sensitive ionic membrane channels, will be restricted to excitable cells; the effects of other genes, such as those elaborating certain transmitter chemicals, will be confined to a subset of neurons. Thus there will be a gradient of exclusiveness of effect on the nervous system. Note that exclusiveness is independent of strength; genes with very widespread activity can still be absolutely necessary for neurons.

Another dimension that can be labeled is *directness* of effect. The action of a gene can be displaced either in space or time from the point of view of the completed nervous system. A gene with a very direct relationship — encoding, for example, for an enzyme participating in neurotransmitter production — would be active within the neuron itself and would also be continuously active throughout much of the life of the cell. Loss of such a gene might have an immediate effect on the neuron. Other genes critical for neural function will operate in nonneural cells and thus be displaced in space. Malfunction of a gene that controls availability of a metabolite or ion necessary for nerve cells might not alter the health of the cells expressing the gene at all, while dramatically effecting the health of neurons. The role of still a third type of gene could be displaced in time from the completed nervous system. If a gene product were involved in guiding the establishment of proper connectivity during morphogenesis of the nervous system, the gene might be active only within a brief period far removed from adulthood. Loss of such a gene in the adult might have no effect whatsoever, whereas malfunction during development could be lethal.

We can expect the genetic substrate of the nervous system to be enormously complex. Genes will vary greatly in the strength, exclusiveness, and directness of their role in generation and operation of the nervous system. The primary site of activity of many of these genes will not be in neurons at all. How will it be possible to unravel these relationships?

STRATEGIES FOR NEUROGENETICS

Three strategies for analyzing neurogenetics are generally employed. In one, a behavior generated by a particular portion of the nervous system is first selected for study. Then, the effect on this behavior of altering a large part of the genome by replacement with different, but still functional, genes is examined. The replacement can be accomplished by hybridization or by selective breeding. This approach provides information first on the degree to which the behavior is dependent upon genetically stored information. Second, careful analysis of variance among backcrosses and self-crosses indicates, within limits, how many genes are involved and on which chromosomes they are located. Third, comparison of the physiology and structure of homologous neural networks built according to different genetic specifications may reveal what aspects of the nervous system are the focus of genetic control mechanisms. The advantage of this technique is that you can select practically any feature of nervous function and produce a genetic effect upon it with relatively little difficulty; the disadvantage is that the role of any particular gene is very hard to isolate.

An alternative approach is based upon somatic cell hybridization. If different cell lines grown in tissue culture are mixed under appropriate conditions, some cells will fuse to form a single cell with chromosomes from both parental types (Ephrussi and Weiss, 1969). These hybrid cells can be isolated and cloned. In the hybrid lines, both sets of chromosomes are initially active, but with succeeding generations of cells some chromosomes are "lost." The opportunities offered by this situation are, first, that, since the generation time of the cells is short even when they come from animals with a long generation time, the genetic analysis of long-lived species can be greatly accelerated. Second, by correlating cell character losses with chromosome losses, genes can be mapped onto the different chromosomes. Third, large numbers of isogenic, differentiated cells are available for biochemical analysis and investigation of the regulation of gene expression. Finally, the conflict generated by fusion of cells that express different genetic programs may reveal something of the control of gene expression. In fortunate cases, a program of differentiation might be fractionated to expose the number and sequence of genes involved in producing a certain cell type.

The remaining strategy is to render a single gene dysfunctional and to examine the consequences of this lesion for the nervous system and behavior. Such lesions are produced by exposing organisms to a mutagenic regime and then screening offspring for behavioral anomalies. When mutant behavior is traced to a malfunction of the nervous system, two quite different kinds of analyses can be pursued. The most direct is a search for *serial* changes in the system. If, for example, malfunction of a certain synapse is detected, the consequences of the malfunction for the development of the postsynaptic neuron and also subsequent neurons in the circuit may be examined. The antecedents of the malfunction can also be followed and should eventually lead back to the gene itself. This approach attempts to trace out the chains of causality in the genesis and operation of the nervous system. It should be very revealing of the interdependence of the various elements and of how the system is put together.

Another line of analysis, once a neural malfunction has been detected, is to search *laterally* or horizontally for similar errors at different locations in the nervous system. If axons of a particular class fail to grow to their normal postsynaptic area, where else in the nervous system do axons show misguided growth? Lateral searching may reveal a general developmental scheme that employs the mutated locus in construction of different parts of the nervous system. This sort of parsimony is the genetic aspect of a developmental "rule." Hopefully, the discovery of frequently occurring serial and lateral relationships will impose some order on the mystifying complexity of development. Examination of a few case histories will illustrate how these research strategies have been followed and the support that they provide for this view of neurogenetics.

THE GENETIC SPECIFICATION OF A NEURAL NETWORK

Cricket calling songs are complex, highly stereotyped, species-specific behavior patterns that mediate intraspecific communication. What is the source of the information that determines this behavior? The patterns are generated by elements of the central nervous system, many of which have been studied anatomically and physiologically. In adults, sensory information is unnecessary for specifying the song pattern since it can be produced by an isolated central nervous system. Moreover, the pattern is not learned through practice because it can be elicited from nymphs, which lack wings and therefore have never been able to sing. Consequently, the song must reflect the structural and physiological features of the nervous system established during development. Extrinsic information available during development, for example songs heard by cricket nymphs, could influence these features. However, a variety of manipulations of extrinsic information, such as raising nymphs that hear no songs or only "incorrect" songs, have no detectable effect on patterns sung as adults. The remaining possibility is that information is stored in the genes. When crickets with altered genotypes are produced by hybridization, each new genotype generates a new and distinctive song pattern which reflects the proportions of different wild-type genes (Figure 1). This confirms the supposition that the source of information that specifies song pattern is genetic and that the information somehow directs the establishment of neural connections and network properties during development (Bentley and Hoy, 1974).

The number of genes involved in specifying calling can be estimated by analyzing the variance in song structure displayed by backcross individuals. If a feature of the pattern is controlled by a single, nondominant gene, crossing an F_1 cricket with a wild type will yield two distinct classes of backcross offspring, one like the F_1 and one like the wild type. With greater numbers of genes, larger number of classes would result from backcrossing. Examination of many song pattern features in backcrosses indicates that all are determined by at least two genes and possibly many more.

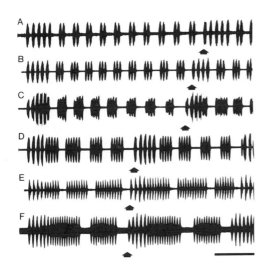

FIGURE 1. Calling song patterns of hybrid crickets shift according to the proportions of wild-type genes. Top and bottom traces show the wild-type songs: (A) Teleogryllus oceanicus; (F) T. commodus. Traces (C) and (D) are from reciprocal F₁ hybrids − (C) with T. oceanicus female and (D) with T. commodus female. (B) and (E) are from backcrosses between the F₁ and the wild type (B − C x A; E − D x F). Each trace begins with a chirp of about five sound pulses followed by two or more trills. Arrows indicate where the phrase repeats. Time calibration: 0.5 seconds. (From Bentley, 1971.)

Similarly, examination of reciprocal crosses reveals whether genes located on the X-, or sex, chromosome (the only unpaired chromosome) influence a behavior. In the case of calling song, some features are influenced by genes on the X-chromosome, whereas others are not. As expected, the portion of the genome involved in specifying the calling song neural network is complex, being both polygenic and multi-chromosomal (Bentley, 1971).

What is actually different about neural networks that generate diverse calling songs? The sites at which critical genetic control is applied may be revealed by examining the structure and physiology of homologous neurons built according to different genetic specifications. Recordings of impulse patterns in the same (homologous) neuron in various genotypes during calling song show an extra-ordinary level of genetic control over neuron physiology (Figure 2, I). During a certain segment of the song, the trill, wild-type, and backcross neural discharges differ by only a single impulse! By delving further into the nervous system, the cause of this alteration might be discovered. For example, in the wild type, a slight increase in the firing rate of the command interneuron which elicits the calling

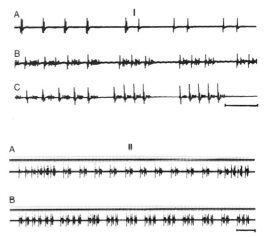

FIGURE 2. I. Song pattern is determined by the discharge pattern of motoneurons. Traces show muscle action potentials produced by impulses in a single, identified motoneuron. Patterns of the homologous neuron in three different genotypes, corresponding to Figure 1 (A through C), are illustrated. Genetically transmitted information exerts very fine control of discharge patterns so that, during a trill, the neuron from the backcross (B) fires only a single impulse more than its counterpart in the wild type (A). Time calibration: 100 msec. II. The difference between the wild-type and backcross discharge patterns can be induced in the wild type by manipulation of command interneurons for singing. Increasing the firing rate of the command interneuron (upper trace in each record) produces a shift in the song motoneuron discharge (lower trace in each record) from two bursts per trill (A) to three bursts per trill (B). Thus the command interneuron could be the neural element responsible for the difference in song pattern of the two genotypes. Time calibration: 0.5 seconds. (From Bentley and Hoy, 1974.)

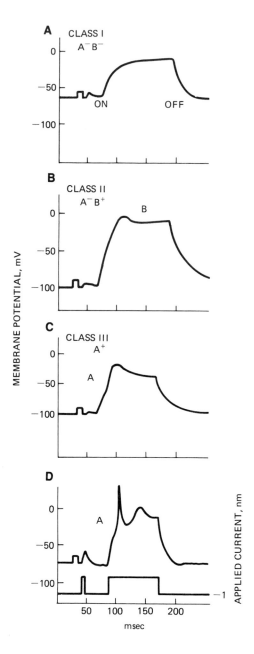

MEMBRANE POTENTIAL, mV

APPLIED CURRENT, nm

A CLASS I
A⁻ B⁻
ON   OFF

B CLASS II
A⁻ B⁺
B

C CLASS III
A⁺
A

D
A

FIGURE 3. Responses of different lines of neuroblastoma crossed with L-cell somatic hybrids to electrical stimulation. (A) Passive electrical response. (B) Delayed rectification (probably corresponding to K^+ conductance change). (C) Graded active response (probably corresponding to Na^+ conductance change). (D) Action-potential-type active response. The

song will switch the motoneurons from two impulses per trill, as normally seen in the wild type, to three impulses per trill, as seen in the backcross (Figure 2, II). Therefore, the consequence of the genetic change could be an increase in firing rate or synaptic efficacy of the interneuron, or in excitability of the motoneuron. Although numerous alternatives remain, it is at least possible to test directly the effects of genetic manipulations on the neural circuitry that underlies this behavior (Bentley and Hoy, 1974).

This study provides an example of what can be learned by extensive, but mild, alteration of genotype. Insights into the role of genetic information in a behavior can be obtained as well as some idea of the nature of the genetic system involved and the sites of genetic influence on the nervous system.

SOMATIC CELL HYBRIDIZATION

Mouse neuroblastoma cells maintained in clonal lines express 10 features diagnostic of neurons. These include extensive, branched processes which accept silver stain, high levels of acetylcholinesterase (AChE), and electrical excitability that exhibits both an active response to depolarization and delayed rectification. When the neuroblastoma cells were hybridized with L-cells and different hybrid clonal lines examined after several generations, these neural features were seen to be fractionated. Thus three levels of AChE activity were found as well as three classes of process formation. Cells in some clones had long, branched processes which silver-stained (correlated with neurofibrils); others had long, unbranched processes which did not accept silver; and some had no processes at all. Similarly, several classes of electrical activity were found: electrically passive cells, cells with delayed rectification but no active depolarizing response to depolarization, and cells with an active response and also delayed rectification (Figure 3). In all, seven distinct phenotypic

records show that different properties of excitable cell lines can be fractionated in different cell lines. (From Minna et al., 1971.)

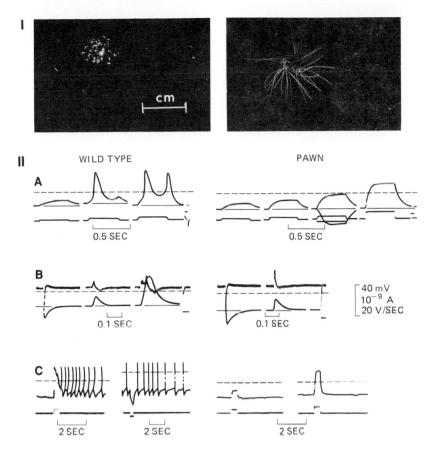

FIGURE 4. *I. Behavior of wild-type and mutant (pawn) Paramecia in a test solution that induces frequent ciliary reversals in normal individuals (fixed-time, dark-field photography). Reversals of wild types (left) keep the organisms in a small clump, while pawn individuals (right) disperse rapidly. (From Kung, 1971.) II. Electrical excitability of wild type (left) and pawn (right) in response to intracellular current injection in a barium test solution. Wild types show an all-or-none action potential in response to long (A) and short (B) stimuli, and also spontaneous afterdischarge (C). Pawns show no active response. (From Kung and Eckert, 1972.)*

classes were characterized (Minna et al., 1971; Minna, Glazer, and Nirenberg, 1972).

The fractionation of neural properties has not been clearly correlated with either gene loss or with regulatory events. However, the results show that the cells appear to be expressing a genetic program for neuron differentiation which involves several distinct steps. Moreover, there is some indication of the order in which these steps are expressed. For example, delayed rectification is displayed independently of an active response to depolarization, but the reverse sequence has not been observed. Since

large masses of cells with these features can be isolated through cloning, the somatic cell hybridization technique is very promising for investigation of the biochemistry and regulation of neuron differentiation, as well as the number and sequence of steps involved.

DIRECT EFFECTS OF A SINGLE-GENE LESION

Paramecia are single-celled organisms with surprisingly complex behavior. Their movement is controlled by the beating of cilia. After colliding with an object, they reverse the direction of ciliary beat, back off for some distance, and then resume forward motion at another angle. When touched posteriorly, they accelerate forward. The responsiveness of the cell as well as the direction and speed of ciliary beating are controlled by transmembrane ionic conductances which determine intracellular potential and ionic concentrations (Eckert, 1972). Anterior collision results in depolarization of the cell mediated by increased membrane conductance for Ca^{2+} ions. The calcium ions may directly modulate the ciliary mechanism. There is a strong regenerative component to the calcium conductance which can produce all-or-none spikes or even spontaneous after-potentials in barium solutions (Figure 4, II). Therefore, Paramecia share many critical features with other excitable cells such as neurons and muscle cells.

Several features, such as cloning, make Paramecia particularly suitable for genetic research and they offer an excellent opportunity for analyzing the genetic substrate of excitability. Among the single-gene behavioral mutants that have been isolated, one of the most intriguing is called pawn (Kung, 1971). This mutant fails to show ciliary reversal and backward movement in response to collision; like its namesake, it goes forward only (Figure 4, I). Although pawn has a normal resting potential, it displays no regenerative conductance change in response to depolarizing current pulses delivered through a micro-electrode. Even in barium solutions, it produces no action potentials or afterdischarge and remains electrically inexcitable (Figure 4, II). This situation could stem from (1) a low membrane resistance to potassium which would short circuit the effect of the calcium current on intracellular potential; (2) displacement in the hyperpolarizing direction of the potential to which the calcium-activation mechanism is sensitive, so that the mechanism would already be inactivated at resting potential; or (3) malfunction of the calcium-activation mechanism itself. The first of these alternatives was tested, and rejected, by injecting a range of depolarizing and hyperpolarizing currents into pawn and comparing displacement of potential to the wild type; pawn turned out to have normal membrane resistance. The second hypothesis was tested by artificially shifting the intracellular potential with hyperpolarizing current for a period sufficient to overcome inactivation, and then attempting to stimulate the cell with a depolarizing pulse. Since this still failed to elicit an active response, the remaining hypothesis appears to provide the correct explanation (Kung and Eckert, 1972). The mutant locus may encode for a membrane protein that forms part of the calcium-activation mechanism, or for some other intimately involved protein.

Pawn provides an example of a gene with a direct, highly specific effect on an excitable cell. Genetic dissection at this level should be useful in analyzing the molecular bases of membrane activation and of other poorly understood features of excitable cells, such as adaptation, postinhibitory rebound, and spontaneous discharge.

SEQUENTIAL EFFECTS OF A SINGLE-GENE LESION

Crickets have a pair of rear-end sensory appendages called cerci which are exquisitely sensitive to air movements, as anyone trying to catch one can testify. Stimulation of the cerci elicits an evasion response which is mediated by an intensively studied circuit, including cercal sensilla, sensory neurons, identified interneurons, and identified motoneurons (Edwards and Palka, 1974). There are four main types of cercal sensilla: filiform hairs (distance mechanoreceptors), clavate hairs (function unknown), bristle hairs (chemoreceptors and possibly contact mechanoreceptors), and campaniform sensilla (cuticular stress receptors). The evasion response to air puffs is mediated by the filiform hairs. These sensilla are innervated singly by sensory neurons whose axons terminate on interneurons in the last abdominal ganglion. One of these interneurons, the medial giant interneuron (MGI), sends an axon which passes through the thoracic ganglia, where the leg motoneurons are located, and continues on to the brain. In the thorax, it inhibits or excites other interneurons and is thought to provide a first step in organizing the evasion response.

Single-gene mutants that lack the normal evasion response have been found. One of

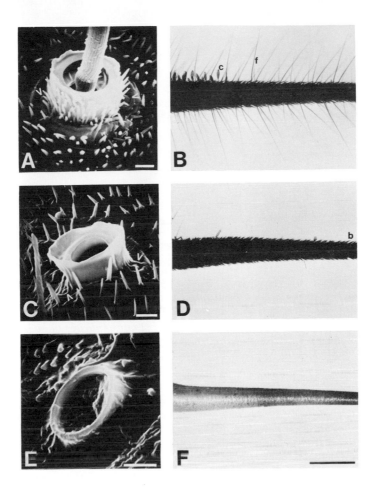

FIGURE 5. *Effects of* fl *mutation on cricket cercal sensilla. (A) Wild-type filiform hair and socket (arrows, campaniform sensilla). (B) Wild-type adult cercus (f, filiform hair; c, clavate hair). (C) Empty filiform socket of* fl *mutant. (D) Young adult* fl *mutant cercus (b, bristle hairs). Filiform and clavate hairs (save 1) are missing (long hairs at cercus base are a subclass of bristle hairs). (E) Empty bristle socket of mature adult* fl *mutant. (F) Mature adult* fl *mutant cercus. All hairs are missing. Calibration: (A), (C), and (E), 5 μm; (B), (D), and (F), 1 mm. (From Bentley, 1975.)*

these, *filiform* (fl), is lacking every filiform sensilla when it hatches (Figure 5) and throughout postembryonic development, although the other sensilla are present (after reaching adulthood, the other classes of cercal hairs are selectively lost). Filiform sensory neurons are found in the usual locations in the mutant, and, although their dendrites are truncated, they send axons with normal ultrastructure into the last abdominal ganglion. Judging from structural criteria, there is no reason to suppose that

these axons fail to form normal synapses with MGI, and this view is supported by the appearance of excitatory postsynaptic potentials in MGI following electrical stimulation of the cercal nerve. However, stimulation of the cercus itself with an air puff produces no response in MGI (Figure 6). Therefore, the absence of filiform hairs renders the sensory neurons inexcitable by the normal stimulus and in turn deprives MGI of normal synaptic activation throughout the developmental period.

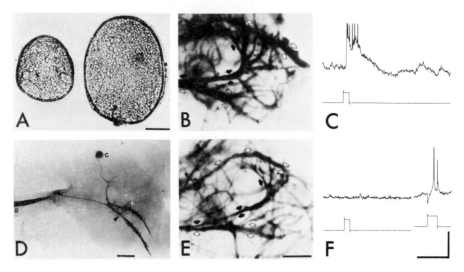

FIGURE 6.   Effects of fl mutation on neurons. (A) Cross sections of mutant (left) and wild-type (right) cercal nerves in adult crickets show degeneration of sensory axons accompanying the loss of bristle hairs (arrow, some remaining healthy axons). (B) Major dendrites of MGI (open arrows, two branches) and LGI (lateral giant interneuron, solid arrows) filled with cobalt dye show normal size in the wild type (ventrolateral aspect). (C) Intracellular recording in dendrites of MGI shows response to standardized air puff in the wild type. (D) MGI of adult fl mutant filled with cobalt through recording electrode (dorsal aspect: c, cell body; a, axon; arrow, third-order dendrite where measurements were taken: see text). (E) Major dendrites of MGI (open arrows) and LGI (solid arrows) in fl mutant show reduced diameter (same age, magnification, and aspects as B). (F) Intracellular recording in dendrites of MGI in fl mutant shows absence of response to standardized air puff stimulus. Inset (right) shows action potential in MGI elicited by current injection (lower trace) through the microelectrode. Calibration: (A), (B), and (E), 50 µm; (D), 100 microns; (C) and (F), 100 msec, 20 mV, 2×10^{-9} A. (From Bentley, 1975.)

Evidently, this deprivation results in a severe growth failure of the interneuron. Examination of MGI morphology with intracellular dye reveals a shriveled appearance, and measurements of key dendrites confirm that the cross-sectional diameter in the wild type is about 400 percent of the comparable diameter in the mutant. Therefore, MGI appears to be dependent for normal development upon its relationship with the filiform sensory neurons, and moreover this dependency is probably based on electrical activity rather than simply establishing connectivity (Bentley, 1975).

Tracing the consequences of the filiform mutation across two cell junctions has revealed something of the interrelationships between cells which result in normal construction of the cricket nervous system. The strategy of serial searching for the effects of lesions should be

produtive in unraveling the lines of communication in developing multicellular systems.

LATERAL EFFECTS OF A SINGLE-GENE LESION

The cerebellum is characteristic of many parts of the vertebrate nervous system in that it has highly organized layers of neurons. One type of cell, the granule cell, is found in a layer below that of the most characteristic cerebellar neuron, the Purkinje cell. This arrangement is secondary, however. Granule cells first arise from precursor cells in the layer dorsal or external to the Purkinje cells. Each granule cell soma then migrates through the Purkinje cell layer, leaving behind an axon that later elongates to form a T-shaped fiber parallel to

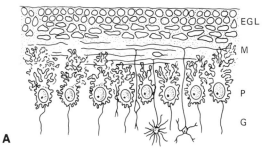

A

9 DAYS CONTROL (+/−)

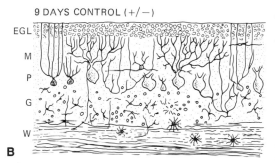

B

9 DAYS REELER (rl/rl)

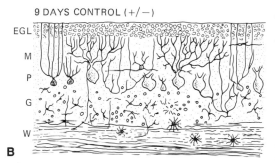

C

FIGURE 7. (A) Schematic drawing of a transverse section through the cerebellar cortex shows the migration of the granule cells (black) through the Purkinje cell layer (P) during the course of development. (From Sidman, 1972.) (B) and (C): Composite drawings from Golgi-impregnated preparations of mouse cerebellum show arrangement of cell layers in normal (B) and reeler mutant (C) littermates at 9 postnatal days. In reeler, cells are disarranged and the

the surface of the cerebellum (Figure 7A). The migration is apparently guided by another cell type, the Bergmann glial cell, which has a radially oriented fiber along which the granule cell soma moves through the Purkinje layer (Sidman, 1973).

Many behavioral mutations in mice have been examined and several with malfunctioning motor control can be traced to disorders of the cerebellum (Sidman, 1968). In one of these, *reeler*, granule and Purkinje cells are disoriented and migration of the former has largely failed to occur (Figures 7B and 7C). In addition to cerebellar cortex, there are only two locations in the mouse brain where a layer of late-forming neurons migrates through a layer of earlier-forming neurons with which synaptic contact will be established: these areas are cerebral isocortex and the hippocampal formation. In reeler, these two sites also show disarrangement of the cell layers evidently due to migration failures. No serial connection between these events can be detected; it seems likely that the same developmental strategy or mechanism is being used independently at the different brain sites and that in each place the product of the reeler locus is normally instrumental in effecting the strategy (Sidman, 1972).

Reeler provides an example of genetic parsimony in encoding information for construction of the nervous system. Multiple use of such information is the genetic aspect of a developmental "rule" or general mechanism. Lateral searching for the effects of mutations should reveal how genetic material is used repetitively in construction of the nervous system.

TRACING SPATIALLY DISPLACED GENETIC EFFECTS

It is evident that one of the main difficulties of working with single-gene mutations is discovering the site of a defect that results in a

granule cell migration has largely failed. G, granular layer; EGL, external granular layer; M, molecular layer; P, Purkinje cell layer; W, fibers of prospective white matter. (From Sidman, 1973.)

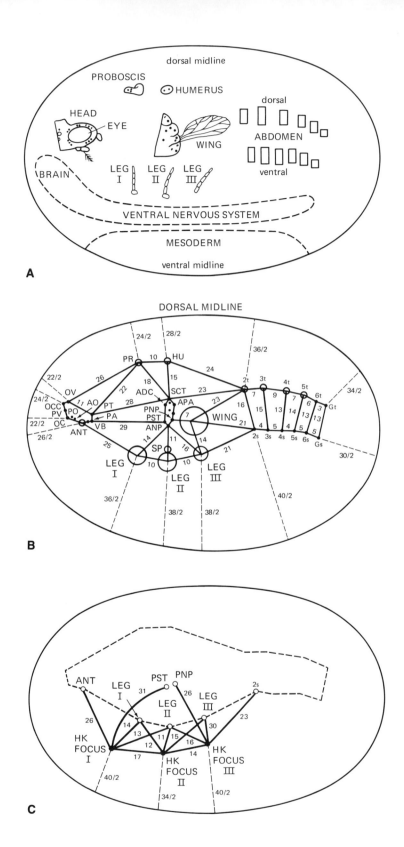

behavioral malfunction. On the other hand, one of the main benefits to be derived from this approach lies in tracing the consequences of a mutation as far as possible. In *Drosophila*, a method is now available for locating the primary effect of a mutation. The essence of this technique is the use of sex mosaics in conjunction with a fate map of the blastula (Benzer, 1973).

Drosophila have XX (female) and XY (male) sex determination. In normal development, the fertilized egg undergoes an initial series of divisions until sufficient cells are produced to form a single layer that covers the entire surface of the yolk. When this layer is completed, the embryo is called a blastula. A cell's position in the blastula determines its ultimate fate in construction of the organism. Therefore, the blastula can be viewed as a two-dimensional map of the organism; if a cell's position in the blastula is known, then the role it and its descendents will play in the adult can be predicted (Figure 8A).

This situation can be exploited by the use of an aberrant "ring X-chromosome" which is sometimes discarded during early (preblastula) cell divisions. In an initially female embryo, cells that have lost the ring X will become male, and cells that retain it will be female. In formation of the blastula, the male cells tend to remain contiguous as do the female cells. One can imagine the blastula girdled by a line separating the two groups of cells. The orientation of this line is random with respect to the axes of the blastula. Therefore, in different sex-mosaic individuals, different parts of the blastula will be male or female. Thus different parts of the adults will be male or female.

Given a behavioral malfunction caused by a recessive mutant gene on the X-chromosome, selective matings are arranged so that the mutant gene and a recessive body-color marker gene, such as *yellow*, are located on the normal

X-chromosome, and the dominant, wild-type alleles of the mutant gene and the marker gene are on the ring X-chromosome. Female embryos are now formed with one normal X-chromosome and one ring X-chromosome. In cells where the ring X is lost, the mutant gene and marker gene will be expressed, and, in cells where the ring X is retained, the wild-type allele will be expressed. In the adult, cells on the body surface with the mutant–marker phenotype will appear yellow, while those with the wild-type phenotype will appear dark.

To pinpoint the behavioral lesion, the next step is to score many such mosaics for the frequency with which the mutant behavior is expressed in conjunction with the marker color for several different sites on the body surface. For example, how often is the mutant behavior expressed when the head expresses the marker color or how often when the thorax expresses the marker color? This "conjunction index" reflects the probability with which the dividing line between male and female cells on the blastula falls between the cells that will form a particular part of the body surface and the cell(s) that determine the mutant behavior. Therefore, the index indicates the actual distance on the blastula surface between the cells that correspond to the parts of the body surface and the cells that will determine the mutant behavior. The location of the latter can then be calculated by triangulation if a conjunction index is obtained for three points on the body surface. Once the cells that must carry the mutant gene are located on the blastula, the cells in the organism which are the initial site of malfunction can be determined from the blastula fate map.

This technique has been employed to localize the primary defect in *Hyperkinetic* (HK^1), a behavioral mutant *Drosophila* which vibrates its legs when lightly etherized. Although the shaking results directly from

FIGURE 8.   *(A) Blastula fate map derived from embryological studies shows areas of the blastula which give rise to various parts of the adult* Drosophila. *(B) Blastula fate map derived from analysis of 703 sex-mosaic flies (1,406 sides). Distances between sites are indicated in* sturts *(one unit represents a probability of 1 percent that among the set of mosaics examined, the two structures in question will be of different type). (C) Fate map of the behavioral foci for the hyperkinetic mutant, Hk[1]. For each leg, there is a separate focus which lies in the area of the blastula that will give rise to the ventral ganglia. (From Hotta and Benzer, 1972.)*

abnormal oscillatory firing of thoracic moto-neurons, these neurons need not be the cells that express the mutant gene (Ikeda and Kaplan, 1970a). Using sex mosaics, the primary locus of the hyperkinetic effect has been restricted to the cells on the blastula surface which will provide the nerve cells in the thoracic ganglia (Figure 8B and C; Ikeda and Kaplan, 1970b; Hotta and Benzer, 1970, 1972). With the help of recently developed enzyme

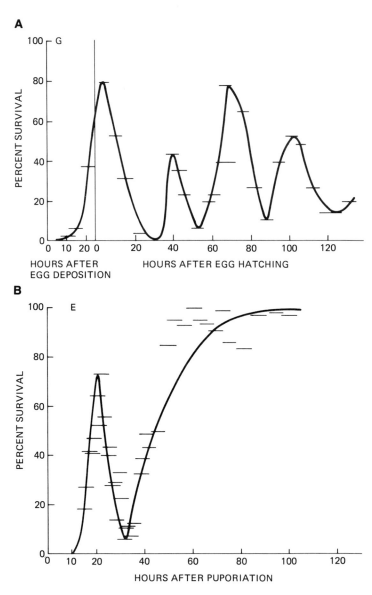

FIGURE 9.   Relationship of the time of inactivation of the Shibire[ts 1] locus to lethality during development of Drosophila. Shown separately for egg deposition to pupariation (A) and for pupariation to adult eclosion (B). The allele was inactivated with a 29 °C heat pulse for 6-hour periods. Evidently, the gene is active in a critical way only at certain times during development. (From Poodry, Hall, and Suzuki, 1973.)

marker genes, it may be possible to extend this approach to the single-cell level. The mosaic technique is an outstanding means of localizing genetic effects in space and also illustrates the versatility and power of genetic manipulation in biological problem solving.

TRACING TEMPORALLY DISPLACED GENETIC EFFECTS

Even when the cells that are the primary site of the effect of a mutant gene have been located, an additional complication remains. Many of the genes involved in the construction of the nervous system may be active only for a brief period during development. How can the duration and temporal location of a gene's activity be determined?

This problem can be approached with the use of temperature-sensitive (*ts*) mutants (Suzuki, 1970). In these cases, the wild-type phenotype is expressed in a certain range of temperatures, whereas a mutant phenotype is expressed in a higher range. Evidently, the mutant allele encodes for a protein that dissociates sufficiently at the higher temperature to become nonfunctional but can be restored by a return to the normal temperature. This makes it possible to turn the gene on or off at will. By switching it off at different times in development and examining adults for affected cells, the times at which a *ts* gene is active can be determined.

Shibire is a locus on the X-chromosome of *Drosophila* for which several temperature-sensitive alleles have been isolated. Behaviorally, these alleles all confer reversible paralysis in adults and larvae at higher temperatures (29 °C). The role of one allele, *shi^ts 1*, has recently been tested by applying brief heat shocks (3 to 6 hours) at different stages of development (Poodry, Hall, and Suzuki, 1973).

The gene is active at numerous sites in the organism and at several different times (Figure 9). However, each site has a single, well-defined temperature-sensitive period which is tissue-specific and to some degree structure-specific within the tissue. Therefore, the time in development when the gene is employed in determination of each of the effected structures can be defined. The technique thus provides a very powerful tool for establishing the temporal role of a genetic locus.

CONCLUSIONS

Neurogenetics is still in a very exploratory stage. The techniques, preparations, and systems that will shape the field are just beginning to emerge, and important new ideas and information are appearing with increasing frequency. It is already clear that genetic manipulation provides an opportunity for exquisite microsurgery with spatial and temporal precision unavailable through other methods. This should be an important tool for examining biochemical features of excitable cells and operational features of neural circuits. Analysis of the relationship between genes and neurons will be inextricably interwoven with the analysis of developmental mechanisms. Genetic encoding of the nervous system must be characterized by complex serial interactions between cells and by multiple use of information; it will involve many cells that are not neurons and features of neurons that are also expressed in other cell types. Although single-gene effects on neurons are known in several systems, there are still no cases where the effect has been traced back to the gene through its biochemical products (see Hotta and Benzer, 1969). Neurogenetics has a long way to go, but an attractive aspect of the field is that the most exciting years appear imminent.

CHAPTER TEN

Genetically Patterned Neural Activity

KAZUO IKEDA

INTRODUCTION

From the neurophysiological standpoint, a living organism can be considered as an information-processing machine: information from internal and external environments is processed mainly by the nervous system. Because the results of the processing are then expressed as coordinated behavior of an organism, it is thus natural that neurophysiologists are interested in understanding the nervous system in terms of stimulus—response, or input—output relationships. Since the introduction by Sherrington (1906) of the concept of synapse and the integrative action of the nervous system, the information-processing mechanism in the CNS has been investigated by observation of input—output relationships at a synapse or in a system. This approach has been explored by Eccles (1964) and co-workers with the support of more basic physiological knowledge at the synaptic and neural membrane levels. The great contribution of this approach to the understanding of the information-processing mech-

anism in the vertebrate CNS has resulted as well in many important discoveries concerning the spinal cord and cerebellum.

Specifically, basic strategy has been to observe the output pattern in response to an experimentally applied known input, and then to analyze the input—output relationship by which the processing mechanism is elucidated. This strategy is now traditional among neurophysiologists, especially those who are interested in investigating the processing mode on the basis of reflex.

This approach to the central nervous system may prove inadequate, however, when the system's activity is affected by inputs from pathways other than the one experimentally stimulated. Analysis becomes more difficult when the system includes its own endogenous activity. The strategy thus has a limitation, one which becomes especially apparent when the mechanism of the endogenously patterned activity itself is under investigation.

Because of the difficulties of analysis, investigation of the mechanism involved in endogenously patterned activity has not been well developed in classical neurophysiology. A question arises: Is it possible to understand the CNS's mechanism in terms of a combination of reflex chains, as classical neurophysiology appears to suggest? The essential part of the central nervous function may operate in other ways, and the reflex may play only the role of regulator.

This chapter is organized to answer this question by discussing (1) the endogenously patterned neural activity as a basis for patterned behavior, (2) the command interneuron for the control of endogenously active neurons, and finally (3) the genetic determination of the neural activity pattern. The answer will lead us to a new functional model of the CNS. This kind of research is possible when a reasonable question is submitted to a proper "simple neural system," as clearly stated by Maynard (1972). The construction of a functional model of the central nervous system is then possible on the basis of the firm experimental evidence obtained from that simple system. A generalization of the model thus obtained would not be limited to the invertebrate nervous system and could certainly cover the CNS of any animal, including mammalia, as discussed by Wiersma (1967).

Experimental evidence for endogenously patterned activity and the command interneuron has been taken from the original works of the author in collaboration with C. A. G. Wiersma at the California Institute of Technology (Ikeda and Wiersma, 1964; Wiersma and Ikeda, 1964), and that for genetic determination of neural activity is from the original works of the author in collaboration with W. D. Kaplan, City of Hope National Medical Center (Ikeda and Kaplan, 1969, 1970a–c; 1971, 1974; and Ikeda, 1974).

THE SWIMMERET MOTOR CENTER: A MODEL SYSTEM FOR A PATTERNED BEHAVIOR

The swimmeret motor center of the crayfish *Procambarus clarkii* provides a small and ideal system for investigation of the central nervous mechanism. A female crayfish has five pairs of swimmerets, one each on the ventral side of the first through fifth abdominal segments. Bilateral swimmerets in pairs usually beat synchronously with simple repetition of anteroposterior protraction and retraction. The five pairs of swimmerets beat metachronically in a coordinated fashion. The intersegmental coordination occurs sequentially, starting from the most posterior fifth pair and propagating anteriorly to the first with a delay of about 150 msec at each segment. The entire sequence repeats with an average frequency of 1.4 per second, for a period of 10 to 20 seconds, followed by a pause of several seconds or longer. Although the periods of beat and pause vary, depending on the conditions, the rhythmicity of each beat is regular and the propagation of the beat from posterior to anterior is in a fixed pattern.

The motor center that controls each pair of swimmerets is located in the abdominal ganglion of the corresponding segment. The motoneurons that innervate swimmeret muscles send their axons through the first roots of each ganglion.

The simplicity of each swimmeret movement allows quantitative analysis of the mechanisms, and the propagation of metachronic beat from posterior to anterior provides the opportunity for a study of coordination; therefore, the swimmeret motor system can be a simple, model-like system for study of the information-processing mechanisms in the CNS.

Prior to the work by Wiersma and Ikeda, Hughes and Wiersma (1960) had investigated the mechanism of the coordination of swimmeret movement. The neurons that they found to be responsible for the interganglionic coordination were later confirmed by both Wiersma and Ikeda (1964) and Stein (1971).

ENDOGENOUSLY PATTERNED ACTIVITY

In our study of the swimmeret motor system we first asked the following questions: (1) What is the mechanism for the rhythmicity? (2) How is coordination achieved among swimmerets in different segments?

In order to answer these questions, we recorded, at the first roots of each ganglion, the motor output impulses responsible for the

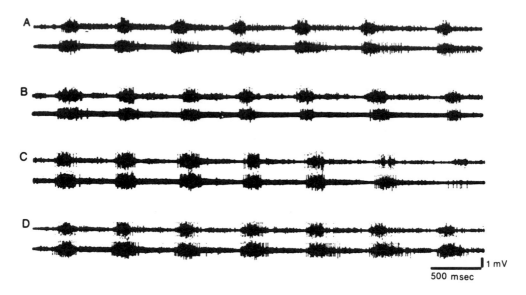

1 mV

500 msec

FIGURE 1. *Intraganglionic coordination of the burst obtained from the third abdominal ganglion. Upper trace: right first root. Lower trace: left first root. (A) Control. (B) After cutting all roots of all abdominal ganglia. (C) After cutting the cord between the thorax and abdomen. (D) After cutting the cord between the second and third abdominal ganglia. (From Ikeda and Wiersma, 1964.)*

swimmeret beating. In the experimental condition, with totally exposed abdominal ganglia, swimmerets beat spontaneously with normal rhythm and sequence. The nerve impulses monitored simultaneously from a pair of first roots of a ganglion showed synchronized bursts in both roots corresponding to each stroke of a pair of swimmerets of that segment. This bilateral coordinaton of motor outputs from a ganglion was usually quite stable. The frequency of bursting averaged 1.4 per second, which was similar to that of the swimmeret beating observed in intact animals (Figure 1A). When comparing the bursting discharges from different ganglia, we found a gradation in the duration of each burst from posterior to anterior ganglia: the more posterior the ganglion, the longer its bursting duration, ranging, on the average, from 300 msec at the fifth to 150 msec at the first ganglion.

The rhythmic activity of the same pattern as described above could be recorded from the first root even after its peripheral contact with the muscle was severed. The entire pattern of the first root activity remained unchanged even after severing all nerves originating from the

abdominal CNS (Figure 1B). The involvement of the peripheral system to the formation of this patterned activity was therefore eliminated; that is, the pattern formation mechanism did not require reflex from the swimmeret itself or any other sensory organs in the abdomen. This held true not only for the rhythmicity of each motor center but also for the sequential propagation of the rhythm from posterior to anterior ganglia. The activity pattern of the first through fifth ganglia did not change even after the sixth abdominal ganglion was separated by transection made on the connectives between the fifth and sixth ganglia, which indicated no involvement of the sixth ganglion. The occurrence of the initiation of beating was increased when the connectives between the fifth thoracic and the first abdominal ganglia were transected; in other words, the pause between bursting discharges was reduced. However, the activity pattern of the bursting discharges remained unchanged. The pattern formation mechanism was thus found to be endogenous in the abdominal ganglia (Figure 1C).

The activity pattern was not disturbed after cutting the first two abdominal ganglia

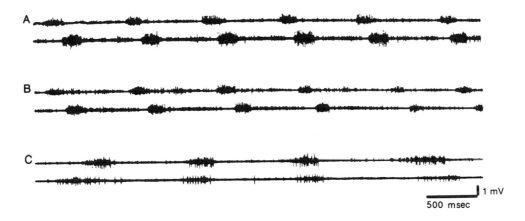

FIGURE 2. Interganglionic coordination and dissociation. Upper trace: the fifth ganglion, right first root. Lower trace: the fourth ganglion, right first root. (A) Control. (B) After cutting the cord between the fifth and sixth ganglia. (C) After cutting the cord between the fourth and fifth ganglia. (From Ikeda and Wiersma, 1964.)

(Figure 1D); and even after abdominal ganglia were separated from each other by transection between ganglia, the same activity pattern was obtained from the third, fourth, and fifth ganglia, although the phasic relationships among separated ganglia were disturbed. The first and second ganglia became inactive after separation from the third ganglion. In the chain of the first to fifth ganglia, the rhythmic discharge started from the fifth ganglion and propagated anteriorly. A coordinated pattern of rhythmic discharges could be obtained from every pair of first roots. When the fifth ganglion was cut, the sequence started from the fourth ganglion (now the most posterior) and propagated to the anterior ganglia with fixed delays at each ganglion. The third ganglion took the lead for the second and first ganglia when the fourth ganglion was cut. The patterned activity in the first and second ganglia stopped when they were separated from the third ganglion. Thus, it was clear that the fifth, fourth, and third ganglia had autogenicity for this particular motor output, and the activity was patterned endogenously in each of those three ganglia. When they were connected, however, the most posterior one took the leadership for coordination, revealing hierarchical order among the ganglia. The first and second ganglia did not have autogenicity and were followers of this hierarchy (Figure 2). The fifth ganglion took

the lead to the fourth ganglion in (A). The coordination was not disturbed by the separation of the sixth ganglion (B). After cutting the cord between the fourth and fifth, each ganglion exhibited its own rhythmicity (C).

In comparing rhythmicity of the fifth, fourth, and third ganglia, there was no significant difference in the frequency of bursts. The most commonly accepted concept for the pacesetting mechanism among autogenic centers is that the one which has the fastest rhythm becomes the pacemaker for the others because it can excite the slower ones before they get into action by their own rhythm. This Sherrington-type triggering mechanism, however, is not applicable to the mechanism involved in the swimmeret movement. On the other hand, we have already seen that there is a gradation in the duration of each burst from posterior to anterior, including the first and second ganglia, and the input from the more excitable posterior ganglion can bring the anterior ones to the threshold, resulting in the sequential propagation from posterior to anterior.

As a whole, the formation of rhythmicity did not require a reflex connection with the peripheral system. Even the coordination of activities in the different ganglia was established without reflex interaction, such as reciprocal inhibition. Instead, the entire neural activity basic for swimmeret movement — endogenously patterned activity — was programmed in the abdominal ganglia.

THE COMMAND INTERNEURON

The activity pattern of swimmeret movement proved to be preprogrammed, so we proceeded to the next question: How is this preprogrammed activity turned on and off? As stated before, the duration of the active period and the pause of swimmeret movement varied, in contrast to the fixed activity pattern shown during the active period. The fact that the occurrence of swimmeret beat became more frequent than normal after transection of the connectives between the fifth thoracic and the first abdominal ganglia, although the beating pattern remained the same, suggested that initiation of the patterned activity in the abdominal ganglia was controlled by the information coming from the superior ganglia.

An extensive search for the neuron that controls pacemaking activity in the abdominal ganglia has been performed at the connectives between the fifth thoracic and the first abdominal ganglia. Five pairs of interneurons were found to have a commanding action for initiation of the patterned activity in abdominal ganglia. Since these interneurons were innervating the neurons that had preprogrammed activity and gave an order for expression of the program stored in the latter, they were termed "command interneurons."

When a command interneuron (or, simply, command neuron) was stimulated with a series of pulses (optimum frequency, 30 per second), the swimmerets beat with normal rhythm and normal sequence of beating-cycle propagation from posterior to anterior.

When a preparation had all six abdominal ganglia or the first through fifth abdominal ganglia, swimmeret movements or rhythmic bursts of impulses in pairs of first roots always started from the fifth segment upon a command interneuron's stimulation and propagated to anterior segments; then the entire sequence was repeated. When the fifth ganglion was cut, the sequence started from the fourth ganglion. After the fourth ganglion was cut, the sequence began from the third ganglion. When the third ganglion was cut, the first and second ganglia did not respond to the command. Thus it was clear that the command interneuron innervated every pacemaking center in the fifth, fourth, and third abdominal ganglia. When a number of pacemaking centers existed, the one most posterior was always the first to respond to the command and thereafter took the lead. In other words, the command interneuron gave an order to the most potential one among the pacemaking centers and the others followed sequentially according to their hierarchical order. Once a command was accepted by the most potential pacemaking center, the command to the subcenter was ignored, resulting in perfect coordination.

Effective frequency of the stimulation for the command ranged from 20 to 100 per second. The rhythmicity of the patterned activity was slightly affected by the commanding frequency. A slightly increased rhythm was observed when the commanding frequency was higher, but the effect was small, suggesting that the role of command interneuron was only to trigger the patterned activity, whereas the pattern itself was endogenous in the pacemaking center. In contrast to the small effect on rhythmicity, the frequency of command interneuron firing had a large effect on latency from the onset of stimulation to the first discharge of the patterned activity (see examples in Figure 3): the higher the frequency, the shorter the latency — 2 seconds on the average at the threshold frequency (20 per second), 700 msec at the optimum frequency (30 per second), and 150 msec at the highest frequency (100 per second). This frequency effect on latency was suggestive of the triggering mechanism of the command interneuron. During the pause period, the potential pacemaker's excitability level was held below threshold. A command interneuron would bring a potential pacemaking center's excitability to the threshold. If the stimulation of command neuron had an effect of bringing the level above the threshold, the pacemaking action would be released and the latency would be frequency-dependent.

The pacemaking center oscillated with a patterned rhythm of its own after being brought above the threshold, so that the pattern was not frequency-dependent. This

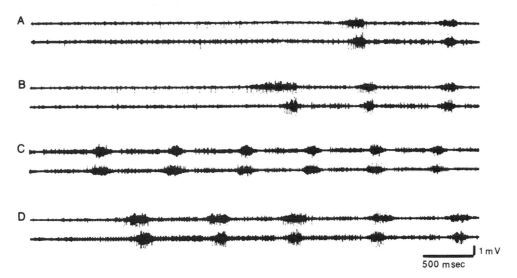

FIGURE 3. *Effect of the frequency of stimulation. The right interneuron B was stimulated. Upper trace: the third ganglion, right first root. Lower trace: the third ganglion, left first root. (A) 20 per second; (B) 25 per second; (C) 30 per second; and (D) 40 per second. (From Wiersma and Ikeda, 1964.)*

model also fits well with the mechanism for the hierarchical control among pacemaking centers. It there is a gradation in the excitability level from posterior to anterior centers, it is understandable that the most posterior is the first to respond to the command interneuron input; then the anterior will receive input from the former, resulting in sequential operation.

The swimmeret movements driven by a command interneuron functioning in the range of natural active period (10 to 20 seconds) or shorter usually stopped with two or three extra beats after cessation of the command interneuron firing. The extra beats might depend on the time constant of the commanding action. This suggested that the active state of a pacemaking center, once triggered, might be maintained by a lower frequency of command interneuron input than was necessary for triggering.

To see if this was the case, the command fiber was stimulated with optimum frequency (30 per second), after which the frequency was decreased to subthreshold (12 per second). Swimmeret movement was hardly triggered by such a low frequency (12 per second); but once brought into active state by higher frequency, activity was maintained with this low fre-

quency. After being maintained with the low frequency, the beating stopped immediately without extra beat when the stimulation was turned off. The rhythmicity stayed the same during the high- and low-frequency stimulation, indicating again that the mechanism that determines the rhythmicity is endogenous.

The command interneuron plays a role for initiating and terminating the endogenously patterned activity of the pacemaking centers.

It is certain now that the neural activity necessary for certain behavior is preprogrammed in neurons, and it can be monitored as endogenously patterned activity. The releasing and stopping of the endogenously patterned activity is controlled by the command interneuron, depending on the requirement of the environment.

The endogenously patterned activity must have been programmed genetically. There should then be a mechanism for the genetic programming of neural activity. Direct evidence for genetic determination of endogenously patterned activity is necessary before investigation of the mechanism itself. The following experiment was designed to confirm that the endogenously patterned neural activity is determined by a gene.

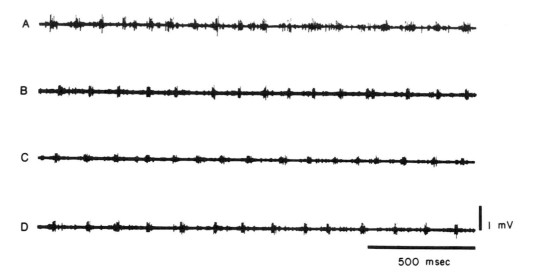

FIGURE 4.   Rhythmic bursts of nerve impulses corresponding to leg shaking of Hk[1] *mutant. Extracellular recordings from (A) right mesothoracic leg nerve, recorded at femotibial joint after cutting the cervical connective; (B) right mesothoracic motor region, CNS intact. Prothoracic and mesothoracic leg nerves were cut; (C) same preparation after cutting the cervical connective; and (D) same preparation after cutting all nerves from the thoracic ganglion. (From Ikeda and Kaplan, 1970a.)*

PATTERNED LEG SHAKING INDUCED BY A SINGLE-GENE MUTATION

Hk[1] is a single-gene mutant of the fruit fly *Drosophila melanogaster*, produced by feeding Canton-S wild-type stock with ethyl methane sulfonate. Detailed procedures for mutagenesis and control of the genetic background are described in Ikeda and Kaplan, 1970a. *Hk*[1] flies showed discretely patterned leg shaking in all three pairs of legs during anesthetization by ether, whereas Canton-S wild-type flies were completely paralyzed under the same conditions. The leg shaking of *Hk*[1] continued with a fixed pattern for more than 24 hours, when the concentration of ether was kept in the range of 3.5 to 5 percent vol./vol. The gene was located at 30.9 on the X chromosome, and the phenotypic expression was recessive. The neural mechanism underlying the leg shaking of *Hk*[1] was investigated.

Efferent impulses recorded from the tibial nerve of *Hk*[1] under the influence of ether showed bursting discharges with the pattern characteristic to this mutant (Figure 4A). Each burst corresponded to a stroke of tarsus. The impulses were stopped when severance occurred at the portion proximal to the recording site but remained with the same pattern when the severance site was distal to the recording site. This result suggested that the involvement of the peripheral system (muscle, neuromuscular junction, and sensory organs) was not likely (e.g., the cause of the activity could be solely dependent on a central efferent mechanism). The active site discharging with the same pattern as that recorded from the tibial nerve was located from three pairs of small areas near the bases of leg nerves on the ventral side of the thoracic ganglion (Figure 4B). Every burst corresponded to the stroke of shaking of the respective leg. The pattern of the discharge did not change after the transection of the connective between the cephalic and thoracic ganglia was made (Figure 4C). The pattern remained unchanged even after all nerves originating from the thoracic ganglion were cut (Figure 4D). Therefore, the possibility of the involvement of the cephalic ganglion and the peripheral system was eliminated, and the activity appeared to be endogenous in the thoracic ganglion. The localization of the

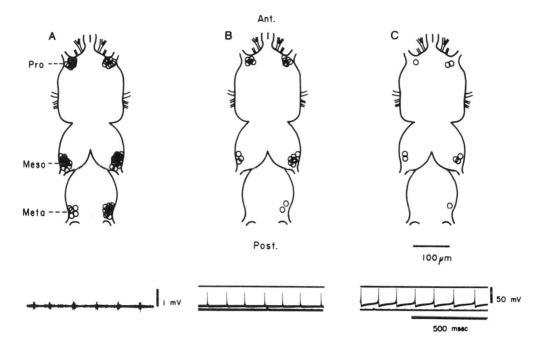

FIGURE 5. *Ventral view of the thoracic ganglion with superimposed recording sites of (A) extracellular recordings of the rhythmic bursts from* Hk[1]; *(B) intracellular recordings from motoneurons of* Hk[1]; *and (C) intracellular recordings from pacemaker neurons of* Hk[1]. *One circle represents one recording site. (From Ikeda and Kaplan, 1970a.)*

neurons responsible for this activity was mapped on the drawing of the ventral view of the thoracic ganglion (Figure 5). In this figure, the spot shown by ○ indicates a location from where a successful recording of the patterned activity was obtained. The marked spots in (A) indicate locations from where bursting discharges were recorded extracellularly. Those in (B) indicate locations from where the patterned activities of motoneurons were recorded intracellularly. Those in (C) indicate locations from where the activities of pacemaker neurons were recorded intracellularly. Examples of typical recordings are shown under each drawing. Thus the motor centers for leg shaking were located in these three pairs of limited regions. Every motor center expressed the activity pattern specific to Hk^1. However, there was no particular timing relationships between them. It appears, therefore, that each motor center has its own autogenicity, suggesting each motor center is directly affected by the Hk^1 gene.

In order to confirm the autonomous ex-pression of the genetic change induced by the Hk^1 gene at each motor center, however, we must answer the following questions. First, even after all neural connections were cut from the thoracic ganglion, the ganglion was still connected to the respiratory and circulatory system: Could genetic changes occurring in some other tissue send information to the ganglion via the humoral system which would result in the specific activity? Second, although each motor center was bursting asynchronously, might there be a particular area in the thoracic ganglion which was affected by the mutation and which indirectly caused the excited state at each motor center?

These possibilities were eliminated by our experiment in which we used gynandromorph flies that were also mosaic for the Hk^1 gene. It was proved that the genetic expression specific to the Hk^1 gene was autonomous at each motor center. The activity of the mutant motor center which was hemizygous for Hk^1 was found to be unaffected by the presence of the surrounding

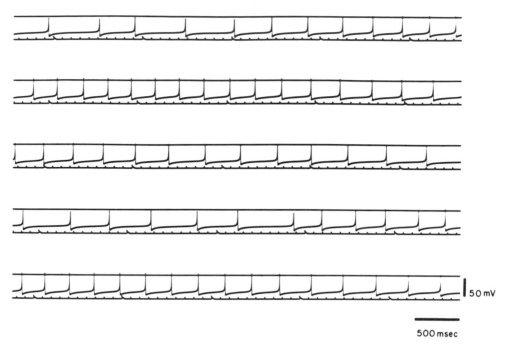

50 mV

500 msec

FIGURE 6. *Discharge pattern recorded intracellularly from a pacemaker neuron. Right mesothoracic region of 4-day homozygous* Hk[1] *female. Each action potential is preceded by slowly rising depolarization. (From Ikeda and Kaplan, 1974.)*

neural tissue of another genotype (heterozygous for *Hk[1]*). Explanation of the genetic techniques involved in this experiment is beyond the purpose of this book, but those interested in further details of that research should consult the original paper (Ikeda and Kaplan, 1970c).

The expression of the *Hk[1]* gene (e.g., the patterned activity specific to *Hk[1]*) was thus autonomous in each motor center. It was also found that the neural organization of each motor center concerning the leg shaking specific to *Hk[1]* was composed of at least one pacemaker neuron and several motoneurons whose activities were driven by the former. The mechanism of the formation of the patterned activity, then, must be sought in the pacemaker neuron.

GENETICALLY DETERMINED PACEMAKING ACTION

The activity of a pacemaker neuron responsible for the specific leg shaking of the *Hk[1]* fly

was intracellularly recorded. Figure 6 shows a typical recording. The activity pattern was a train of action potentials, each of which was preceded by a slowly rising depolarization. The frequency of firing of the action potential usually changed in a waxing and waning fashion within the range of 2 to 16 per second. The waxing and waning of frequency occurred every 10 to 20 seconds. The pattern was specific to *Hk[1]* and was matched by the leg-shaking pattern obtained separately by Trout and Kaplan (1973). This patterned activity usually continued for more than 10 minutes in the experimental condition, but the pattern sometimes gradually shifted to intermittent discharges. Such a case is shown in Figures 7 and 8. In these figures, (A), (B), (C), and (1) through (8) are continuous records. An exact, 3-minute period of the record was cut off from the original between the end of record (C) and the beginning of record (1). The pattern then shifted to intermittent. The discharge of action potentials stopped at the high level of membrane potential, leaving a large generator potential at the end. After repolarization, the

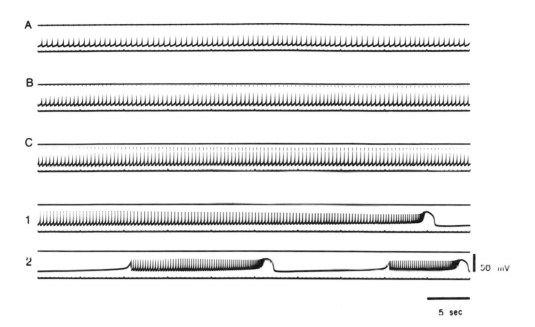

FIGURE 7. *Shift of discharge pattern from continuous to intermittent. Recorded intracellularly from a pacemaker neuron in the right mesothoracic region of 4-day homozygous* Hk[1] *female (A), (B), and (C) are continuous recordings. Between (C) and (1), an exact 3-minute period was cut off from the original recording. (1) and (2) are continuous recordings. (From Ikeda and Kaplan, 1974.)*

depolarization progressed slowly. When this slowly rising depolarization reached a certain level of the membrane potential, the next burst of action potentials occurred [Figures 7(2), 8(3), 8(4), and 8(5)]. The number of action potentials and their amplitudes and frequencies were dependent on the generator potential. As the generator potential became smaller, the number of action potentials and their amplitudes were reduced. No action potential appeared when the generator potential became smaller than a certain membrane potential level. The duration of the generator potential also changed gradually. The generator potential usually became larger and extended its duration again, and firing of action potentials was then resumed. The pattern then gradually shifted to continuous discharges, after which the entire sequence was repeated.

The generator potential occurred every 10 to 20 seconds, corresponding to the waxing and waning period of the continuous discharges. This suggested that the membrane potential change recorded here as the generator potential was the source of the waxing and waning pattern of the continuous discharges. In looking at a generator potential accompanied by firing of action potentials from it, one would notice the remarkable character of this neuron. The firing of the action potential stopped at a very high level of the membrane potential. The threshold for the action potentials became higher before the firing stopped. The recording electrode was impaled most likely into the soma, because other structures of the neuron were too small to be penetrated efficiently. Therefore, it is reasonable to assume that the generator potentials were elicited at the soma membrane, resulting in its large recorded amplitude. Although the action potentials appeared to be initiated somewhere on the axon away from the soma, the site of the action potential initiation seemed to move away from the soma when the threshold became higher, resulting in smaller action potentials and higher firing levels observed at the soma. Thus, besides the ampli-

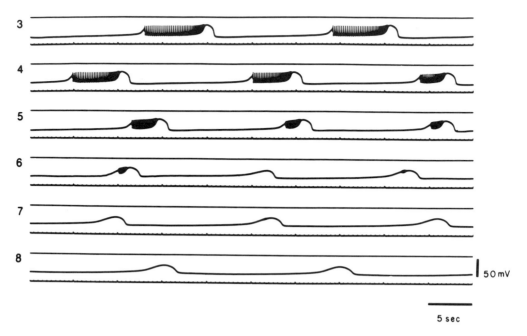

FIGURE 8. *Shift of discharge pattern from intermittent bursts to generator potential only. Continuous recording following (1) and (2) of Figure 7. Recorded intracellularly from a pacemaker neuron in the right mesothoracic region of 4-day homozygous* Hk[1] *female (same neuron and fly as in Figure 7). All recordings are continuous. (From Ikeda and Kaplan, 1974.)*

tude, duration, and periodicity of the generator potential, the shift of the site of action potential initiation seemed to be a factor determining the pattern. When the initiation site was closer to the soma, the pattern could be continuous with the fluctuation in frequency depending on the phase of the generator potential. When it was far from the soma, it could become intermittent. Thus the mechanism of the genetically determined pacemaking action of this neuron must be located in the generator mechanism. Further investigation of the mechanism is in progress.

MECHANISMS OF PATTERNED ACTIVITY

The combination of endogenously patterned activity and command interneurons disclosed in the swimmeret motor system serves as a model for the basic operation mechanism of the CNS. It is a model in the sense that as a compact system it represents the most essential mechanism of the CNS and presents the prin-

ciple of information-processing. Study of this model system has unveiled three important basic mechanisms for operation of the CNS.

1) An isolated ganglion such as the fifth, fourth, and third abdominal ganglia demonstrated that a complete rhythmicity necessary for the functioning of swimmerets is preprogrammed in the neurons of a ganglion.

The widely accepted Sherringtonian neurophysiological theory gives the impression that the CNS is a passive entity which responds only to the stimulation coming from external or internal environments, and that it is otherwise quiescent. The findings described in this chapter demonstrate that part of the nervous system has its own autogenic activity which is patterned for a specific purpose. The pattern is preprogrammed, with allowances for adjustment in the range of environmental variations. Programming has been achieved by the long process of evolution (genetic programming); therefore, the patterned activity is a genetically coded activity. The facts revealed by this study suggest that the basic function of the nervous system is preprogrammed, securing at least the necessary functions for survival of an animal. Regulatory functions such as reflex give flexibility to the basic function and probably evolved later phylogenetically. Roeder (1935, 1937) disclosed completely stereotyped movements in the sexual behavior of the praying mantis for which a built-in program of thoracicoabdominal ganglia released by disconnection from the brain was responsible (Roeder, Tozian, and Weiant, 1960). This demonstrates very well that even a mechanism that underlies a quite complex behavior is totally preprogrammed in the CNS. Coherent to the work by Roeder and his co-workers, Bullock (1961) stressed the importance of "patterned nervous discharge" for understanding of the central mechanism. Hoyle (1970) discussed the central mechanism for establishing certain behavior from his own view of the functional organization of the CNS. His "inherited motor program stores (tapes)" and "neural program store" appear to correspond to "autogenic activity" of Ikeda and Wiersma (1964) and "endogenously patterned activity" in this chapter.

The behavior of the Crustacea and the insect is known to be almost entirely instinctive; therefore, one might suspect them to be specific cases, and general principles derived from data obtained from them would not be applicable to other phyla, especially not to animals such as mammals with their great flexibility of behavior. The remarkable experiment reported by Fentress (1973a) clearly showed that the rather complex movement of forelimbs of the mouse was largely preprogrammed in the nervous system so that no feedback from sensory or effector organs was needed. This indicates that even in the Mammalia, in which the reflex control system is well developed, the essential neural function can be preprogrammed to a great extent.

2) The mechanism for the coordination between the swimmerets in different segments shows that the coordinated action among more than one endogenously patterned center can be achieved without reflex interaction with peripheries. Instead, a hierarchically arranged functional organization serves the purpose. The manner of coordination is less flexible when compared to reflex coordination, such as the

one depending on reciprocal innervation; on the other hand, the advantage is that the former has a smaller chance for failure. The coordinative action required for a basic nervous function (e.g., one necessary for survival such as the defense mechanism) does not permit failure. The preprogrammed mechanism for coordination rather than reflex action fits this purpose.

The mechanism of interganglionic coordination described in this chapter is further supported by the more recent, detailed works of Stein (1971, 1974).

3) Endogenously patterned activity must start and stop at the proper times in order to accomplish a defined role. The command interneuron that innervates the endogenously patterned activity center serves this purpose. The role of a command interneuron is to set the timing of the active period and the pause of endogenously patterned activity — but not the level of activity because the activity itself is preprogrammed. The command action can be achieved with experimentally applied stimulations of wide frequency range (20 to 100 per second). The frequency of command interneuron input to an endogenously patterned activity center, however, has little effect on the rhythmicity of the latter. Therefore, it is natural to expect that a command interneuron operates only in the range of the optimal frequency under ordinary conditions. Once a commanding action takes place, maintenance of the endogenously patterned activity can be performed with an input frequency lower than that necessary for triggering. This suggests that a command interneuron's natural firing pattern is not necessarily a regular train of impulses.

Only command interneurons that release bilateral, endogenously patterned activity have been described in this chapter. However, two kinds of command interneurons that suppress endogenously patterned activity bilaterally and ipsilaterally have also been found. As no command interneurons that have unilateral releasing action or contralateral suppressing action have been found, the unilateral command must be performed by the combination of two command interneurons that have releasing and suppressing functions.

The concept of "command interneuron," proposed by Wiersma and Ikeda (1964) with experimental evidence, opened a new way of looking at the functional organization of the CNS. Since then, the existence of command interneurons has been confirmed by other investigators with various materials [e.g., the swimmeret system of Crustacea (Davis and Kennedy, 1972); the abdominal muscle system of Crustacea (Kennedy, Evoy, and Hanawalt, 1966); the uropode system of Crustacea (Larimer and Kennedy, 1969); the stomatogastric ganglion system of Crustacea (Dando and Selverston, 1972); and the insect limb system (Elsner, 1969)]. Thus the idea of the command interneuron has been well established and ample evidence has been obtained, at least from the nervous system of the invertebrate. The idea is now being adopted to interpret the central mechanism of the mammalian nervous system (Roberts, 1972). It is quite certain that good evidence will be forthcoming in the future to establish the importance of the command neuron in the mammalian CNS.

The neural mechanism that underlies the coordinated movement of the swimmeret has shown that the basic function of the CNS is preprogrammed.

Many behavioral works in the past have indicated that the basis of instinctive behavior must be from the inherited program; however, the physiological evidence for the neural mechanism that links the inherited program and resulting behavior had not been presented until Ikeda and Kaplan's first work appeared. With evidence that the patterned neural activity is coded by a single gene, they have clearly shown that the neural activity basic to a certain behavior is genetically programmed.

The genetic programming must have been done phylogenetically through the evolution of the animal. The expression of genetically programmed neural activity in an individual animal must be activated at a proper time. The timing within a sequential series of patterned activity can be genetically programmed, as in the example shown with the interganglionic coordination of the swimmeret system. Of course, the timing of the release of the programmed action in response to the requirement coming from the environment cannot be genetically programmed.

This is where the command interneuron plays its role.

The leg shaking of Hk^1 was released only under the influence of ether. The effect of various anesthetics on the leg shaking has been explored (Ikeda, 1974). Among various volatile anesthetics investigated were chloroform, fluothane, penthrane, and trilene, all of which paralyzed the Hk^1 flies as well as Canton-S without inducing leg shaking. Diethyl ether, ethyl vinyl ether, and divinyl ether were the only ones that caused the leg shaking of Hk^1 flies and complete paralysis of Canton-S flies. This indicated that the leg shaking of Hk^1 was ether-specific. Hk^1 flies did not exhibit disorders in walking under normal circumstances; therefore, it can be speculated that the activity of the pacemaker neuron of Hk^1 is ordinarily suppressed by some neuron. When the suppressive action of the latter is blocked by ether, the endogenous activity of the pacemaker neuron can be released and results in the leg shaking. Under the same conditions, Canton-S flies remain paralyzed because they do not have the endogenous activity of the pacemaker neuron. This suggests that there is a command interneuron that controls the releasing and stopping of the activity of the pacemaker neuron and that the ether, which releases pacemaker activity, most likely affects the command interneuron. This point needs further investigation.

CONCLUSIONS

From this study, it can be stated that the endogenously patterned activity of some neurons is genetically programmed and plays an important role for the neural basis of behavior. The command interneuron controls the timing of the activity of the neuron which has the program in store.

The basic function of the CNS appears to be operated by the combination of the neuron that has genetically coded activity pattern and the command neuron. Reflex events appear to have regulatory action on the basic function determined by this combination.

CHAPTER ELEVEN

A Simple Network for the Study of Neurogenetics

ROBERT J. WYMAN

INTRODUCTION

Along with other bodily parts, the nervous system is built by the genes. Interacting with the embryonic and postnatal environment the genes specify the shapes and connections of the myriads of nerve cells in the nervous system. They specify the circuits that are responsible for "innate" behavior as well as the circuits that are capable of "learning."

The mechanisms by which the genes build the nervous system are as unknown as the mechanisms of differentiation in any other tissue. In no instance is it known how cells that have the same genome become so different during the course of development. Some cells are different because they are composed of different molecules; for instance, cells in the eye contain different molecules than cells in the finger. On the other hand, the cells in the forefinger probably have the same molecules as the cells in the thumb, yet the thumb is certainly different from the forefinger. We don't have even any reasonable guesses as to how this difference comes about.

The nervous system presents a problem much like the thumb forefinger problem. Each nerve cell cannot possibly make its own unique molecule because there is not enough DNA to code a unique gene for each neuron. Yet nerve cells have very different shapes and make very different connections. It is not very likely that any of the fundamental questions about differentiation will be answered for the terribly complex nervous tissue before they are answered for simpler cells. Thus we who work on the nervous system must use genetics to answer another level of question than that posed by developmental biologists.

Consider the human nervous system. It used to be estimated that there are 10^{10} nerve cells in a human. However, Braitenberg and Atwood (1958) found that there were 10^{10} to 10^{11} granule cells in the cerebellum alone. The total number of cells should then be more like 10^{12}. Each cell makes, and receives, 100 to 10,000 synaptic connections. Thus the total number of synaptic connections in the human nervous system is of the order of 10^{15}.

How many genes are there to code for

these connections? The total number of genes in the human genome is now estimated at something like 100,000 (Crow and Kimura, 1970). If the genes did nothing but code for neural connections, then, on the average, each gene would be responsible for the properties of 10 million neurons with 10 billion connections. There must then be regularities in the patterns of connectivity of neurons of at least that order of magnitude. The understanding of even a few of these gene-specified regularities would constitute a major advance in our understanding of the connectivity of the nervous system.

As a result of such arguments, the new field of neurogenetics has been burgeoning recently. Unfortunately, there are as yet almost no generalizable results. A host of papers show little more than that genes can affect behavior at many organizational levels, from defects in muscle proteins to defects in central circuitry. On the other hand, many investigators are developing systems and techniques that will allow significant advances to be made. The three systems that have been most studied are the mouse, the nematode worm, and the fruit fly.

Although some beautiful work has been done on the mouse cerebellum (see the excellent review by Rakic, 1974), many investigators (including myself) feel that, as in other experimental situations, there is no substitute for using the simplest possible system that still shows the property of interest, that is, a well differentiated nervous system.

The nematode worm, *Caenorhabditis elegans*, is by far the simplest preparation of the three. This worm has 600 cells in toto, of which 250 are nerve cells. The simplest repeat unit in its segmental nervous system is the 13 neurons of a body segment. Its genome is about two-thirds the size of *Drosophila* (Brenner, 1974). The disadvantages of the system are that its cells are too small to be studied electrophysiologically and that knowledge of its genetics, although developing rapidly, is far behind that of *Drosophila*. The advantages of extreme morphological simplicity may outweigh the disadvantages.

The major advantage of *Drosophila*, of course, is the great store of genetic knowledge that is already available. Recently there has been a tremendous reduction in estimates of

how many genes *Drosophila* has. There is now good evidence that *Drosophila* has only 5,000 genes, or, more accurately, 5,000 genetic complementation groups (Judd, Shen, and Kaufman, 1972). It is impossible to overestimate the conceptual impact of this small number. It means that development is carried out by a relatively few genetic instructions; it means that we may contemplate finding all the genes that are responsible for a given piece of developmental engineering.

Drosophila's nervous system is intermediate in complexity between the mouse and the worm. The total adult nervous system of *Drosophila* probably contains about 100,000 nerve cells. This is far too many cells to study. Thus it is necessary to study some subgroup of these cells.

Most attention in *Drosophila* has been focused on the visual system. The retina has a small number of cell types arranged in an array which repeats over the surface of the eye. The anatomy of the dipteran visual system is well studied (Strausfeld, 1971), and there are a host of mutants that affect visual function in *Drosophila* (Hotta and Benzer, 1969; Gotz, 1970; Alawi et al., 1973). Physiology, however, is the stumbling block. The electroretinogram, which is the summed electrical activity of all the cells in the eye, may be easily recorded. However, owing to their small size, it is exceedingly difficult, but not impossible, to record intracellularly or extracellularly from single units of the visual system (Alawi and Pak, 1971).

In my laboratory we have been developing an alternative system: the network of neurons that drive flight in *Drosophila*. This system has the advantage of involving only a small number of neurons, about two dozen, which directly shape a behavioral output, flight. These neurons are some of the largest in *Drosophila* and can be readily studied electrophysiologically. The disadvantage is that these cells are anatomically intermixed, in the thoracic ganglion, with a large number of other cells about which we know nothing.

The *Drosophila* work grew out of a continuing study in my laboratory on the flight neurons of larger Diptera as a simple network in which we could determine the neural basis of motor output pattern generation. We have largely succeeded in that task. In what follows,

I shall describe the physiology of the flight muscles and the electrophysiology of the neurons that drive these muscles. I shall concentrate on describing the interconnections of the flight neurons and how that network produces the motor output pattern. In the final section I shall describe our first steps in trying to figure out how the genes construct this network.

THE FLIGHT MUSCLES

In the several species of flies that we have studied, there are 26 giant muscle fibers which power the wing strokes during flight (Figure 1). These muscle fibers, which are single multinucleate cells, are very large, ranging from about 100 μm in *Drosophila melanogaster* to several hundred micrometers in the larger species. Six muscle fibers on each side of the midline form the right and left dorsal longitudinal muscles (DLMs) (Figure 1). These muscles pull the anterior and posterior walls of the thorax together. The wings are hinged to the thoracic walls in such a way that this contraction depresses the wings. When the dorsal and ventral sides of the thorax are pulled together, the wings are elevated, again via a complicated set of hinges. Seven muscle fibers on each side, forming three pairs of muscles called the dorsal-ventral muscles (DVMs), cause this wing elevation.

The wingbeat frequency in the species we have studied ranges up to 200 beats a second (other dipteran species have wingbeat frequencies of 1,000 per second, Pringle, 1957). Every muscle fiber contracts once in every wingbeat cycle. To achieve this rapid contraction and relaxation cycle, the muscles have evolved into a type termed "fibrillar." In this type of fiber each motonueron spike causes a muscle fiber spike, but the spike does not cause a twitch contraction of the fiber (Pringle, 1949, 1967; Roeder, 1951). These fibers contract only slowly to a series of spikes. However, if the muscle is rapidly stretched any time within several tenths of a second after a spike, then the muscle will pull back with a twitch-like contraction. The elevators and depressors are antagonists of each other; when one set contracts, it acts through skeletal linkages to

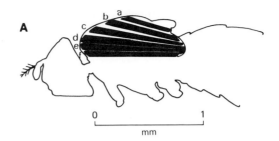

TERGOTROCHANTERAL MUSCLE

FIGURE 1.   (A) The fly is split at the midline and the right half is viewed. The six fibers (a−f) of the right dorsal longitudinal muscle are shown running the length of the thorax. (B) The dorsal longitudinal muscle has been dissected out and the more lateral dorsal-ventral muscles are seen. The seven muscle fibers that form the DVMs (I, II, III) are shown; the tergotrochanteral muscle is seen behind the DVMs.

stretch the other set. Hence, as long as nerve impulses occur each tenth of a second or so, the stretching of each group by its antagonist will keep the wings beating.

Since these fibrillar muscles twitch only when rapidly stretched, another mechanism is necessary to start their alternating action (see Mulloney, 1969). This is provided by the contraction of a nonfibrillar muscle, the tergotrochanteral muscle (Figure 1). A few impulses in this muscle at the beginning of flight cause it to twitch. This muscle pulls down the dorsal surface, elevating the wings and stretching the DLMs. This muscle is also attached to the middle legs; thus its twitch extends the legs, giving the fly a jump off the surface simultaneously with the first wing elevation.

The thorax of the flies is constructed like a stiff box whose walls can be set into vibration.

The box can be considered to have a resonant frequency for vibration which is higher when the box is made stiffer. The stiffness of the thorax is controlled by a pair of slowly contracting, tonically activated muscles running from the ventral midline to the lateral walls of the thorax, the pleurosternal muscles. Since the wings beat at the vibration frequency of the thoracic box, tension in these muscles is the major means of control of wingbeat frequency.

Other small muscles are directly attached to the wing base. These muscles control the plane of the wing stroke and the degree of wing folding. They thus control steering of the flight. They are also slowly contracting, tonically activated muscles (Nachtigall and Wilson, 1967; Heide, 1968).

Each fibrillar muscle fiber is innervated by a single excitatory axon (McCann and Boettiger, 1961); each axon innervates only one muscle fiber. The muscle fiber with its motoneuron is called a motor unit. The spike activity of these motor units is easily recorded by placing a wire or capillary electrode into the muscle fiber. The muscle fiber responds to each axon spike with an all-or-nothing spike of its own, which the electrode records. There is no electrical activity accompanying the individual twitch contractions. An electrode sitting in one fiber records the spikes of that unit at a greater amplitude than those of any other unit. Sometimes the insertion path of the electrode punctures the insulation of the fibers that it passes through; this permits multiunit recordings from a single electrode.

The flights may be studied in the following way (Figure 2). The fly is mounted on a phonograph cartridge and electrodes are placed in the thoracic muscles. The apparatus is set in the path of a windstream. When the support for the fly's legs is released, the insect starts to fly. The phonograph cartridge records the mechanical activity of each wingbeat while the electrodes register muscle spikes. The beginning of flight occurs (Nachtigall and Wilson, 1967) with activation of the pleurosternal muscles, followed by a burst of impulses in the tergotrochanteral muscle and in the fibrillar muscles. The tergotrochanteral muscle causes a jump and the first wing elevation. This elevation stretches the depressor muscles, which, since they have already been activated by a nerve impulse,

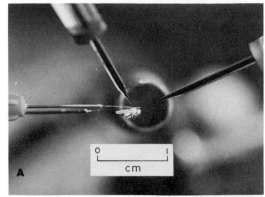

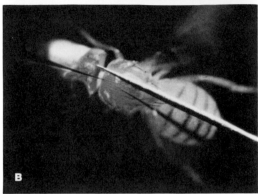

FIGURE 2. (A) Step in the preparation of a Drosophila melanogaster *for recording. The fly is glued onto a pin held in a hypodermic needle carried on a micromanipulator. Two glass microelectrodes, filled with the dye Niagara Sky Blue, have been inserted into the thoracic muscles. A ground electrode of sharpened tungsten is seen approaching the fly's abdomen from the rear just below and behind the support hypodermic. Two more dye-filled electrodes will be inserted before recording. (B) A fly as seen through the dissecting microscope. Insect is flying while rigidly mounted and with electrodes inserted. Notice the wingspread and the forelegs extended in flight posture.*

contract in response to the stretch. Following this, the wing-base muscles open the wings and set them to proper flight position. Thereafter, flight continues by alternating stretch and contraction of the elevator and depressor muscles. During flight the muscle units spike only once for every 10 or 20 wingbeats (Pringle, 1949; Roeder, 1951), even though each muscle unit contracts once during each wingbeat. This is possible because the muscle can contract as many times as it is stretched as long as it has been activated by a nerve impulse within the last few tenths of a second.

During flight, the nerve impulses come frequently enough to keep the muscle fibers continuously activated. As will be seen, each muscle fiber receives its nerve impulses at distinct times. Nevertheless, all the depressor muscle fibers contract simultaneously and alternate with the elevator muscle fibers, which also all contract simultaneously. This is because the timing of contraction is not set by the timing of the nerve impulses but by the times when the fibers are stretched.

Flight ends when the axons to the fibrillar muscles deliver their last spike. As shown by Machin and Pringle (1959), the amount of power delivered by a muscle in its contractile response to a stretch decreases with time from the last occurrence of a spike. Thus, after the last nerve impulse, successive wingbeats deliver less and less power, the vibration damps down and stops after 30 or so more wingbeats.

PATTERN GENERATION

The pattern of activity in the 26 motoneurons that drive the flight muscles have strong elements of similarity in all the fly species studied. The pattern, and the circuit generating it, were first understood in the blowflies and houseflies. The neurophysiology of these flies will be discussed first and then the special features of *Drosophila* will be described.

A typical record taken during flight, is shown in Figure 3. Three electrodes are in the animal, two of the electrodes are in the right dorsal longitudinal muscle (top two traces), while the third electrode is in a dorsal-ventral muscle. The spikes of four different DLM units can be distinguished. They are labeled (arbitrarily) W, X, Y, and Z. Throughout this section of the record these four units fire repeatedly in the sequence X, Y, W, Z. The unit in the DVM (U) fires at different times in the DLM cycle; in fact, it fires at a gradually later point in each cycle.

The first question that can be asked is whether there is a central pattern generator for this motor output. In a central pattern generator, the central nervous system contains a neural circuit capable of generating a reasonably proper output pattern without requiring timing cues from sense receptors. The alternative is that reflex sensory feedback determines the timing of the motor outputs. Most motor output patterns have some centrally generated components and some reflex influenced components. Thus the distinction between the two alternatives is blurred.

The reflex theory requires that nerve impulses, generated by proprioceptors at some point in the wingbeat cycle, set the timing of the motor outputs. From records that display both spike activity and wingbeat artifact, one can measure the points in the wingbeat cycle at which a given motor unit fires. When this is done it is seen that the motor unit fires at all phases of the wingbeat cycle (Wilson and Wyman, 1963, Figure 1). Thus it can be concluded that the timing of events in the output pattern is not rigidly dependent on sensory feedback, but is an example of a centrally generated pattern. Since flight can occur in a decapitated fly, and since the nerve cells that innervate both abdomen and thorax are collected in the thoracic ganglion, it can be concluded that the flight motor output pattern in Diptera is generated by circuits in the thoracic ganglion.

Even though a central pattern generator may not *require* timed sensory inputs, they may nonetheless be present. For the dorsal ventral muscles, although spikes do occur at every phase of the wingbeat, there is sometimes a preference for the motoneurons to fire at a certain phase of the wingbeat cycle. When this effect is present, it can cause up to a 30 percent difference between the number of spikes in one half of the wingbeat cycle and those in the other half (Heide, 1974). Thus wing proprioceptors probably do form part of the input to the dorsal-ventral motoneurons. The dorsal longitudinal muscles seem not to show this preferred phase of firing (Wyman, 1965; cf. Bastian and Esch, 1970), although this must be rechecked in the light of Heide's findings. No one has tried to ablate the wing proprioceptors or to replace their normally patterned input with random input and see the effect on the motor output pattern. This has been done for

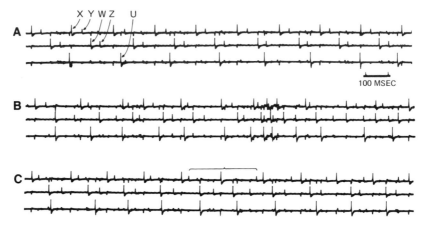

FIGURE 3. *Spike potentials from the flight muscles of the blowfly* Calliphora vomitoria *while in flight. Three electrodes are in the muscles. Each distinct spike shape is the record from a different motor unit. In each of (A), (B), and (C) the top electrode records two units, labeled X and Y. The second electrode records two units, W and Z. These two electrodes are in the right dorsal longitudinal muscle. The lowest trace is from an electrode in the dorsal-ventral muscle II; spikes from this motor unit are labeled U. (A) The pattern X, Y, W, Z repeats throughout, while U fires gradually later in each cycle. (B) Note how both the pattern X, Y, W, Z and the phase relationships between these units maintain themselves during large changes in frequency. The latency relationships change with the frequency. (C) A jump (at the brace) from the pattern X, Y, W, Z to Y, X, Z, W. (From Wyman, 1966.)*

locusts (Wilson and Wyman, 1965) and should be done for the flies.

Finding that a motor output is centrally patterned does not tell you very much about how the pattern comes about. It just establishes that the timing of the motor output pulses are not set by reflexes. In flies the pattern is established by the properties of the moto-neurons and their interconnections.

Resetting

Each motoneuron fires repetitively with a distribution of interspike intervals that is approximately a normal distribution (Wyman, 1965). The particular times of firing could be caused by bursts of excitation received from presynaptic neurons (interneurons). Alter-natively, the input could arrive continuously rather than in bursts. In this case the times of firing would be determined by the moto-neurons' own rhythm of accumulation of excitation, discharge, and resetting. The latter possibility is strongly indicated by the fol-lowing simple experiment. When a motoneuron

is firing rhythmically, a single extra spike is inserted into the rhythm by an antidromic stimulation. This single, extra spike always causes a resetting of the rhythm; the next orthodromic firing does not occur until at least a full normal interspike interval from the antidromic pulse (Mulloney, 1970; Harcombe, 1975). No other motoneuron's firing time is changed anywhere near that much. This indi-cates that the resetting is not a circuit property, but a property of the motoneuron itself. The probable reason for the resetting is that spikes invade the integrative membrane zone and reset its potential to resting level, requiring the full normal interspike interval to accumulate enough excitation to come up to threshold again. The time it takes to come up to threshold depends, of course, on the amount of presynaptic input.

Shared Input

Each of the motor units can fire with quite irregular variation about its average frequency (Figure 3B). The length of an interspike interval

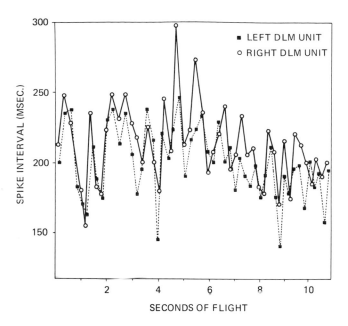

FIGURE 4. *From the blowfly* Calliphora terrae-novae. *Each spike in a short piece of record from two units is represented by a point. The abscissa of each point is the time of occurrence of a spike and the ordinate is the interval from the previous spike of the same unit. Notice how the units follow each other very closely through changes in frequency. (From Wyman, 1965.)*

can be double, or half that of the preceding interval. However, if graphs of the interspike intervals of any two units are superimposed (Figure 4), it will be seen that these two units undergo simultaneous variations in frequency of quite similar sign and amplitude. Hence the same varying excitatory input must be driving both cells. Since this is true for each pair of cells, the presynaptic excitatory input to the motoneurons must be largely the same for all cells.

This rapidly varying input must be composed of fibers that deliver only small synaptic potentials to the motoneurons. If any of the fibers delivered large excitatory postsynaptic potentials (EPSPS), it would deliver them simultaneously to several motoneurons and would tend to synchronize their firings. This is not observed. Two motoneurons in different muscles, although undergoing simultaneous frequency variations, fire with approximately equal *relations* to each other; there is minimal tendency toward synchrony (Wyman, 1965). However, the total effect of the small EPSPS is large on every cycle since the input can change

successive interspike intervals by a factor of 2. Thus there must be a large number of these EPSPS delivered by either a few fibers firing at high frequency, or many fibers firing moderately. The model that I think of (Wyman, 1969a) has each cell receiving as input similar, large numbers of small EPSPS from common presynaptic sources. Each motoneuron is gradually depolarized by this background, fires, and then repolarizes to start the process again. Thus each motoneuron can fire at completely independent times from the other motoneurons driven by the same excitation. When the rate of arrival of the EPSPS increases (or decreases), the rate of firing of all the motoneurons increases (or decreases), but they still can fire at independent times.

Inhibition

When some motoneurons are antidromically stimulated, they not only reset their own firing cycle but can also delay for a short time the firing of certain other motoneurons.

The period of delay is much shorter than the resetting effect. The delay is demonstrated in the following manner. During flight, one motoneuron is stimulated antidromically at a fixed frequency which is not close to the natural frequency of any of the motoneurons. As expected, the antidromic stimuli occur in all the possible time relationships to the firing of most motoneurons. However, it is found, for some pairs of motoneurons, say X and Y, that a spike in Y never occurs immediately after an antidromic spike in X. The period of time in which Y cannot fire ranges up to some 40 msec. The inhibitory effect begins very shortly after the antidromic pulse. Levine (1973) claims that the inhibitory effect begins with a latency of only 0.2 msec, implying that the inhibition is caused by a collateral of motoneuron X synapsing directly on motoneuron Y.

When the natural firing pattern (during flight without experimental stimulation) of these two neurons is examined, it is also found that Y never fires immediately after a normal (orthodromic) spike in X (Wyman, 1969a). Thus the inhibition that is experimentally induced by antidromic spikes is also caused by orthodromic spikes and is therefore part of the normal mechanism of pattern generation. When one neuron, X, is found to inhibit another, Y, it is almost always found that Y also inhibits X. Thus the inhibition between two neurons is usually reciprocal.

The Generation of Firing Patterns

We have now discussed the three major factors of pattern generation: the resetting of a neuron after its own spike, the sharing of input, and inhibition. In this section we shall see how these elements generate patterns of firing. Each set of motoneurons in each species fires in a somewhat different pattern. The patterns described in this section are presented in the order of increasing interaction among the motoneurons. It is not always easy to detect the presence of patterns when looking at the spike trains themselves, so I shall also describe a graphical technique by which patterns may be readily seen.

Consider two motor units, a and b. We define the "latency" of each occurrence of a

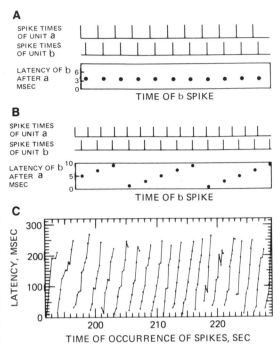

FIGURE 5. *(A) The two top lines represent spikes in two hypothetical motor units. a and b are firing at the same constant frequency. In the graph each spike of unit b is represented by a point. The spike's time of occurrence is plotted against the latency of its firing after the previous firing of unit a. Here all the latencies are the same and hence the points all lie in a straight horizontal line. (B) In this case a and b both fire with constant interspike intervals, but b has a slightly lower frequency than a. The latency now changes on each cycle. The points lie on a set of slanting parallel lines. (C) Real case from the housefly,* Musca domestica. *As in (B), the points lie on a set of slanting parallel lines.*

spike in b to be the time elapsed since the preceding firing of a. If the two units were firing at constant and identical frequency, the latency of each b spike would be constant, as seen in Figure 5A. If the two units are both firing at stable frequencies but each has a slightly different frequency, the latency changes at each firing. In fact, some pairs of units behave in just this simple way; see Figure 5B. Usually, however, the situation is not so

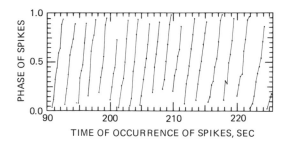

FIGURE 6. Musca domestica. *Again each point represents one spike, but here its phase with respect to the reference unit is plotted. Again the points lie on a set of slanting, parallel lines. This smooth progression of phases indicates that the two units are maintaining a constant percentage difference in frequency even during fluctuations in frequency. (From Wyman, 1969a.)*

straightforward. The frequencies are not constant but rapidly changing. However, if both units are undergoing the same changes in frequency, order can be regained in these graphs by dividing the latency by the current interspike interval (Wyman, 1969a). This gives the phase of each spike; the phase is equal to the fraction of the interval between successive a spikes at which a b spike occurs.

Figure 6 is a plot of the successive phases of one unit with respect to another. Even though the original record from which this figure was produced contained irregularly varying interspike intervals, these variations were the same for both units, as in Figure 4. Underneath the irregularity in frequency, the two units were maintaining a constant percentage difference in frequency and so are sliding smoothly in phase with respect to each other. This results in smooth lines in the graph of phases. This type of smooth, uninterrupted phase sliding holds for two units that only share their input and have no further connections between them.

When two units reciprocally inhibit one another, the smooth phase progression pattern is interrupted (Figure 7). Neither unit can fire for a short period after the other has fired. If the phases of Y firings in intervals of X is graphed, then Y can not fire at small phases because this is the time just after X has fired. When Y fires late in the cycle, it delays X's next

firing, prolonging the cycle. Thus Y is not seen to fire at very late phases. The phases at which a unit is inhibited from firing are called inhibition bands because of their appearance as bands running across the phase–time diagram.

When three units interact, each inhibiting the others, the effect of the third unit can be seen as a third inhibition band in the phase–time diagram; see Figure 8. In this flight two units fired in alternation – call them W and X as in Figure 3. A third unit, U, drifted in phase with respect to W and X. Both W and X exchanged weak reciprocal inhibition with U. In Figure 8 the phases of U in intervals of X are shown. Inhibition bands at very early and very late phases are shown reflecting the reciprocal inhibition of U and X. But W fires at a phase of 0.5 with respect to X, and it also inhibits U.

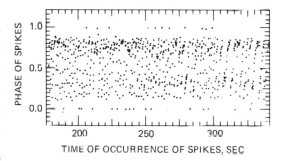

FIGURE 7. *Flight of* Eucalliphora lilaea *(blowfly) shows phase progression and reciprocal inhibition. If the figure is viewed edge on, from the bottom or the top, one can see the location of the points on a set of parallel lines, which indicates the regular phase progression due to input sharing. In contradistinction to Figures 3B and 4, however, the parallel lines do not extend through all phases. There is an empty band at small phases (0.0 to 0.15) and at large phases (0.85 to 1.0). This indicates that neither unit can fire within a certain period after the other has fired. However, the points at exactly phase 0.0 and 1.0 show that the two units can fire simultaneously, i.e., before the inhibition from either has had a chance to be transmitted to the other. The phase scale has been extended below 0.0 and above 1.0 to show the firing points at simultaneity, which would otherwise be obscured by the border lines. (From Wyman, 1969a.)*

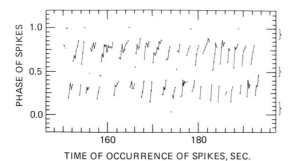

FIGURE 8. *From* Calliphora terrae-novae. *Phase–time plot shows phase progression and inhibition zones near simultaneity. A third inhibition zone, seen at about 0.6 phase, is caused by the firing of a third unit. (From Wyman, 1969b.)*

Therefore, U can not fire just after 0.5 phase either and a third inhibition band is seen.

In the dorsal longitudinal muscle of *Calliphora* and *Musca* there are four units, each of which strongly inhibits the others. Each unit contributes an inhibition band to the phase–time plots. In this case the inhibition bands are wide enough to overlap each other. Three wide overlapping inhibition bands allow only a small band of permitted firing for each unit. Each of the four units is restricted to firing in only one phase, each unit of course at a different phase (Figure 9).

Sequential Firing

The actual firing sequence for the units of Figure 9 appears as in Figure 1. The units fire sequentially, X, Y, W, Z, in a continuously repeated sequence. We can now put together the cell properties and interconnections and see how this repeated sequence is maintained. The neurons are receiving a continual barrage of incoming pulses. The average frequencies of these four neurons are almost identical. Let us break into the sequence at a time when a unit, say X, reaches threshold and fires. This resets its integrating region to resting level. Simultaneously, the other three motoneurons receive inhibition from a collateral of X. No neuron fires for a while. The neuron first to recover from X's inhibition will be the one that has

fired least recently and thus has had time since its last resetting to accumulate enough excitation to reach threshold. This is unit Y, which now fires and inhibits the other three. The cycle now continues. The unit that has fired least recently is always the next to fire. This explains how a sequence, once initiated, is maintained. The mechanism by which a particular sequence occurs rather than some other sequence is discussed later.

Sometimes after hundreds of cycles in one pattern the units abruptly shift their firing

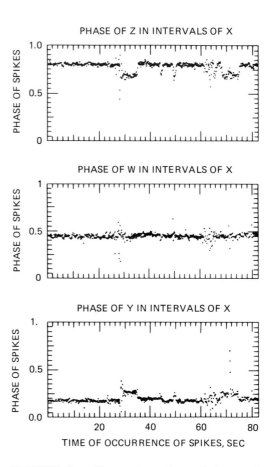

FIGURE 9. *Phase–time plots of three units in the right dorsal longitudinal muscle of* Calliphora terrae-novae *compared with a fourth. These four units were firing in a strictly repeated sequence during the hundred of cycles plotted here. The firing cycle is divided up among the units, each unit firing at a different phase. (From Wyman, 1969b.)*

pattern from one sequence to another (Figure 3C) (Wyman, 1966); we do not really know the cause of this. Usually, but not all the time, the sequence jumps occur during periods of large rapid frequency increases (Wyman, 1970). This suggests that a strong burst of presynaptic excitation can bring more than one cell up to firing threshold almost simultaneously. Either could fire first and inhibit the other; if the wrong unit fired first, the sequence would be permuted (Wyman, 1973).

OTHER PATTERNS

The motor output pattern has been studied in 10 species of Diptera so far (Wyman, 1969b, 1970; Mulloney, 1970; Levine and Wyman, 1973). In these studies all the possible combinations of the presence and absence of the input sharing and reciprocal inhibition were found. Thus pairs of units can be found that have neither input sharing, nor reciprocal inhibition; the phase–time diagram for these look completely random, as in Figure 10A. Other pairs have input sharing but no mutual inhibition, as in Figure 5B and 6. The converse, where the inhibition is present but not the input sharing, also occurs (Figure 10B). Finally, pairs are found that show both mutual inhibition and input sharing (Figures 7 and 8).

The main properties and interactions that lead to the observed motor output pattern are summarized above. It should be noted that the interactions causing the output pattern (i.e., the repeated cycling) are interactions between the motoneurons. This is rare among motor systems so far studied. In most other systems, the pattern is generated by interneurons and imposed upon the motoneurons. This system thus has the strong experimental advantage that in studying the motoneurons, which are *much* easier to study than interneurons, one is studying the pattern generating neurons themselves.

The structure of these neural circuits is undoubtedly genetically determined. The genetic differences between the species are expressed as different neural circuits with different resulting motor output. (For another example of this, see Chapter Nine.) The fact

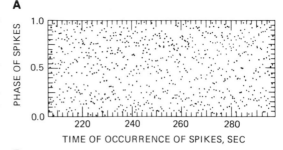

A

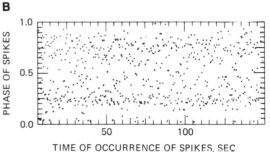

B

FIGURE 10. *From* Muscina stabulans. *(A) Two units in different muscles. No discernible pattern is present in the arrangement of the points. (B) Two units in the same muscle. Inhibition bands may be seen near phase 0.0 and 1.0, which indicates mutual inhibition. No linear array is seen, which indicates a lack of sharing of excitatory input. (From Wyman, 1969b.)*

that *Drosophila* was related to the species we had already studied encouraged us to attack directly the genetic basis of this wiring.

THE FLIGHT SYSTEM IN *DROSOPHILA*

The first step was to find out whether *Drosophila* had the same type of neural network to drive flight as did the other Diptera. Luckily, *Drosophila* turned out to be quite similar to the other flies.

The muscle fibers in *Drosophila* are large enough to allow multielectrode experiments. The fibers of the DLM are 0.5 to 1 mm long, with rectangular cross sections of approximately $150 \times 65 \ \mu m$. The dorsal–ventral muscle has a more circular cross section, with a diameter of 50 to 100 μm and a length near 700 μm.

Elnora Harcombe, a graduate student in my laboratory, has been able to perform a series of experiments in which she places four glass microelectrodes in specified muscle fibers and a fifth electrode in the abdomen. Through each electrode she can record, stimulate, and inject dye. Using these techniques, she measured the duration of the inhibition period caused in one unit by antidromic stimulation of another. The period of inhibition was the same as the naturally occurring interval between the firing of these two units. Thus she showed that the inhibitory connections were quantitatively responsible for the interunit timings during flight.

She also found that each of the DLM motoneurons had unique properties. Previously we had presumed, but not really checked, that the several motoneurons that innervate the different fibers of a given muscle had the same characteristics. The differences in strengths of inhibition have important consequences for the cyclic firing pattern.

The motoneurons to the four ventral DLM muscle fibers were each individually identified and labeled according to the anatomical designation of their muscle fibers (c through f, as in Figure 1). The four motoneurons maintain a cyclical firing pattern like that shown in Figure 3 and graphed in Figure 9. However, of the six possible sequences in which the four units could fire, only two sequences commonly occur. The sequences are c-e-d-f and c-f-d-e. Each motoneuron inhibits the others, which causes the firing times to be spaced out from each other. But the inhibitory interactions are not all the same. Neurons c and d inhibit each other strongly, and f inhibits e strongly. Thus, in the firing pattern, c fires at times most removed from the firing of d, and e fires as far away from f as possible. The two actually occurring sequences are the only ones that separate the firing times of both pairs.

Thus the repeated cycle of firing occurs in the following manner. One neuron fires, say c, and its integrating region is reset to resting potential. The next to fire will be one of the two neurons not strongly inhibited by c — that is, e or f. Say f fires, and it is reset. Next to fire is one not strongly inhibited by f — that is,

c or d. Neuron c has just recently been reset, so it is not yet up to firing threshold; thus d fires. The cycle continues in the obvious manner.

We have also begun to work out the neuroanatomy of the flight motor system in *Drosophila*. John Coggshall, a postdoctoral fellow in my laboratory, has found that when horseradish peroxidase is injected into a muscle fiber of a living fly, it is taken up by the axon that innervates that fiber, and after a few hours the peroxidase fills the whole motoneuron. After histochemically staining for peroxidase the whole motoneuron is stained a dense black which can be seen in both the light and electron microscopes. The motoneurons are confined to the middle part of the thoracic ganglion called the mesothoracic neuromere (Power, 1948). All the flight motoneurons have widespread dendritic trees branching ipsilaterally and contralaterally in the dorsal part of the neuromere. Motoneurons to the four most ventral DLM fibers have their four cell bodies in a cluster located in the most anterior corner of the ventral surface of the neuromere. This correlated with the physiological finding that these four neurons exchange the strongest inhibition and have the most precise firing pattern in the flight system. The two most dorsal DLM fibers have contralateral cell bodies. The cell bodies for all DLM neurons are about 12 to 15 μm in diameter, which means that microelectrode penetrations might be possible. The DVM motoneuron somas are much smaller, 5 to 6 μm in diameter and are less tightly clustered, which correlates with their weak physiological interactions.

We have begun some work on mutants of the flight system. These mutants are first picked up because of their abnormal flight behavior. Not all mutants with abnormal flight behavior have disturbed neural circuitry; many have defects in the muscles, wings, skeleton, or other organs.

As a beginning, we analyzed electrophysiologically a single locus mutant that disrupts the motor output pattern. This mutant is called "stripe" because of a black pigmentation stripe on its thorax. It is found at a map distance of 62 on the third chromosome. Individuals homozygous for the "stripe" mutation usually cannot fly. When they attempt to fly, the motoneurons fire in short (1 second) high frequency (100 per second) bursts, as compared to the normal, which fires at 3 to 10 per second for minutes of flight (Levine and Wyman, 1973).

Even though the motor output of the mutant appears markedly different from the wild-type output, the main features of the normal neural connections appear to have been retained in the mutant. This was seen by performing an analysis of the mutant's output similar to that used for the wild type output. Although the absolute rate of firing is increased in all motoneurons in stripe, the relative frequencies among the neurons are the same as in the wild type. Frequency covariation of the different motoneurons, indicative of input sharing, is clearly seen in the mutant as in the normal. Although the high-frequency firing may be due to reduced inhibition, the lateral inhibition network does exist in the mutant. The same neurons that inhibit each other in the wild type inhibit each other in the mutant. The altered motor output pattern is due to imbalance between excitation and inhibition. In the mutant, the balance is shifted drastically toward excitation. Whether this is caused by too much excitation, too little inhibition, or a lowered threshold of the motoneurons is the subject of ongoing research.

No anatomical alterations of the nervous system of "stripe" can be detected from light-microscope observation of silver-stained sections (Power, 1950). We are currently studying the anatomy of individual flight neurons with the peroxidase stain which allows study at both the light- and electron-microscope level.

GENETIC TECHNIQUES

Each gene that affects neuronal connectivity may be considered to be passing some instructions to the nerve cells. In order for us to read the instructions we need to know in what cells a gene is acting, at what time in development the gene is acting, and, if the gene is destroyed by a mutation, what will go wrong with development. The "reading" consists of learning what it is about the nerve cells, or their connections, that each gene specifies. In the end we would like to "read" the total sequence of gene actions that results in the connected nervous system.

Obviously, we have just begun to study mutations that affect the flight system. So far we have used only electrophysiological and anatomical techniques to describe the mutant phenotype. The real advantages of working with *Drosophila* only become apparent when one applies the sophisticated genetic techniques that are available. Some of the techniques that seem most useful in answering the above questions are described below.

Mosaics

When nerve cells are found to be affected by a mutation, it could be that the mutant gene has its action in the affected cells. Alternatively, the mutant gene could act in other cells (e.g., in a hormonal gland) and indirectly affect the nerve cells. Thus it becomes necessary to determine in what cells the mutant genes must act for the mutant phenotype to be expressed. A genetic tool for determining the locus of action of a mutant gene is the creation of mosaic animals. Mosaic flies have a different genotype in one part of their body from that in other parts. There are a number of genetic abnormalities in *Drosophila* that spontaneously generate mosaics (Hall, Gelbart, and Kankel, 1975). By examining a series of mosaic animals in which each tissue is sometimes normal and sometimes mutant, it can be determined just which tissues have to be of mutant genotype for the nervous system to be of mutant phenotype (Hotta and Benzer, 1972; Ikeda and Kaplan, 1970c; Suzuki, Grigliatti, and Williamson, 1971).

Somatic Crossing-Over

In one method of making mosaics, the time at which the animal becomes mosaic may be controlled. In *Drosophila* (and some other Diptera, but unlike virtually every other animal), homologous chromosomes pair in somatic cell mitoses. X-rays can induce crossing-over in these closely apposed chromosomes (Becker, 1956). The result is that a cell initially heterozygous at a particular genetic locus can divide and produce two daughter cells, each homozygous for one of the alleles at the initially heterozygous locus. After further divisions, this produces small patches of homozygous mutant tissue in an otherwise heterozygous adult fly. By varying the time of application of the X-rays in a series of flies, the period through which the normal gene function must be retained to ensure normal development in this patch can be determined.

Temperature-Sensitive Mutants

Some mutant alleles of a gene produce a completely defective gene product, or none at all; other alleles produce a product that is mostly normal. Some of these seemingly normal gene products malfunction at elevated (or lowered), but still physiological, temperatures. Members of this class are called temperature-sensitive mutations. Animals raised at a "permissive" temperature show normal phenotype; those raised at the nonpermissive temperature show mutant phenotype. An animal homozygous for the temperature-sensitive allele can be raised at permissive temperature except for a particular period at the nonpermissive temperature. If the gene product is not needed at the period of high temperature, and if it is not irreversibly denatured and needed later, the fly will still show normal phenotype. If, however, it is a time period when the molecule is needed, and is still labile, the fly will be of mutant phenotype. Temperature-sensitive mutants are thus another way to estimate the time of action of a gene (Suzuki, 1970).

By a combination of these three techniques, the time and locus of action of genes may be discovered.

The most exciting prospects for research arise when anatomical and electrophysiological techniques are combined with genetic techniques. For instance, consider a mutant fly whose motoneurons are anatomically and/or physiologically abnormal. A mosaic fly can be generated whose right half is normal and whose left half is mutant. All the motoneurons have branches in both right and left halves. The right-side motoneurons with ipsilateral cell bodies have normal nuclei and grow most of their dendritic tree in normal neuropile, but when they cross to the contralateral side, the tree grows through mutant neural tissue. The left-side neurons have the opposite situation and so serve as controls for the right side. The motoneurons with cell bodies contralateral to their axons furnish another arrangement of normal and abnormal parts. By this method, the effect on neuron morphology and electrophysiology of factors internal to the cell can be sorted out from those factors which are determined by the neuropile through which the cell grows.

CONCLUSIONS

At the beginning of this century, all that was known about the mechanism of gene action was that different genes resulted in different phenotypes; genes could produce wrinkled peas or smooth peas, curly hair or straight hair, yellow corn or white corn. It took a long time to reach the one gene—one enzyme hypothesis, which turned out to be the key to molecular genetics. Neurogenetics is not even at the stage of knowing the phenotypes produced by different alleles of the genes that affect the nervous system. We are a long way from any generalizable hypothesis that will explain how genes code the connections in the nervous system. In my mind the fascination of neurogenetics is precisely that we do not have any idea what the shape of the answers will be. It is a wide open territory just waiting to be explored, and possibly to be conquered.

CHAPTER TWELVE

Neural Generation and Regeneration in Insects

JOHN S. EDWARDS and JOHN PALKA

INTRODUCTION

There is a splendid diversity of architecture among the nervous systems commonly lumped together under the rubric "simple." Among these simpler systems, the arthropods, and particularly the insects, are useful for untangling the secrets of the nervous system, not so much because they are dubiously simple, but because they offer us a set of alternative solutions to the problem of constructing complex organisms to compare with our own chordate heritage. Recognition of the arthropods and chordates as fundamentally different engineering alternatives rather than as "primitive" and "advanced" puts the lessons of comparative neurobiology in a different and more significant light, for we are then able to see shared features as fundamental and necessary to an elaborate nervous system. Where we find evidence in the nervous systems of both groups for spatial and temporal gradients, cell death, sprouting, or trophic relationships, to mention only a few possibilities, we may argue

that they are fundamental and necessary processes. Thus the value of comparative studies comes as much from the degree of evolutionary divergence as from the scale of complexity. This is our rationale for looking at development and regeneration in the cricket nervous system and for comparing our findings with similar work on vertebrates.

Looked at structurally and developmentally rather than physiologically, the arthropod nervous system is certainly simpler than most chordate systems and has many design features that make for clean experiments. The peripheral location of sensory cell bodies, which allows for deafferentation by a pluck of the forceps, the prolonged cyclic postembryonic growth of the nervous system, the presence of individual, repeatedly identifiable interneurons, some of them very large, and the dramatic powers of regeneration have been the keys to our work on the rules of neural regeneration in insects. The abdominal cerci of the house cricket provide a good experimental system to exploit these features because they

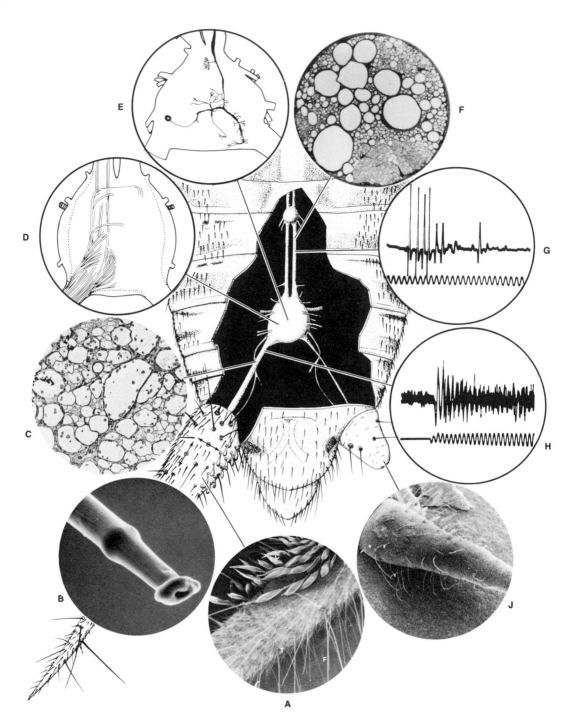

FIGURE 1. *Structure and function of the cerci and abdominal giant fibers of the house cricket,* Acheta domesticus. *Dorsal view of abdomen, with integument and viscera cut away to show terminal abdominal ganglion and paired ventral nerve cord. A normal cercus is shown at bottom left, and a regenerate at right, each with associated cercal sensory and motor nerves. Components of the system are illustrated in the surrounding sequence. (A) Scanning electron micrograph of*

are large, purely sensory structures of simple geometric form whose sensory fibers project to an abdominal ganglion, where they synapse with a small population of giant interneurons. Significant features of their structure and function are summarized in Figures 1 and 2.

A Background to Regeneration

Regeneration studies of vertebrates and arthropods have played such an important part in the emergence of current ideas about the formation of nerve connections that we should first look at some general aspects of regeneration to see how arthropods compare with chordates in this respect.

Flux of structural material is a fundamental property of living things. Molecules come and go, cells and tissues continually replace themselves, some, such as the gut, faster than others — for example, the skeletal system. Wound healing and regeneration of body parts lost in trauma may be seen as a homeostatic extension of this very basic function. In general, the simpler the organism, the better it replaces lost parts: coelenterates and flatworms regenerate entire animals from mere fragments,

the limitations seemingly being the capacity of the fragment to survive while regeneration processes are mobilized; annelids regenerate body regions; arthropods regenerate appendages and body parts. While chordates through Amphibia regenerate lost parts vigorously, birds and mammals have little power to do so. But the amniotes do repair damaged tissues. It seems that this broad pattern of regeneration responses through the Metazoa is a reflection of adaptive strategies rather than the necessary loss of capacity with increasing complexity (Bittner, 1973).

The pervasive capacity for repair and restoration depends, perhaps, upon the same class of phenomena that we recognize in developmental systems: the polarities and gradients that seem to regulate morphogenesis may also monitor the integrity of the organism. Is it possible that their disruption in trauma provides the information that evokes regeneration? How else could regenerating appendages cease their explosive growth as they approach symmetry with their intact partners? But, one may ask, why should regeneration vigor be unequally shared among quite closely related groups? Why is it that salamanders regenerate so well, while frogs are less adept, and why should crickets and

cercal sensilla. Three main types are present: freely articulated filiform hairs, F; clavate hairs, C; and deeply inserted trichoid sensilla, T. Campaniform sensilla are also present, always near the sockets of filiform sensilla (see also Figure 3D). (B) Filiform hairs are inserted on an ovoid base and thus have a preferred plane of oscillation in response to air movements. Dorsal and ventral hairs oscillate transversely relative to the cercus; lateral hairs oscillate longitudinally (arrows on cercus). The notch near the hair base marks the site of termination of the sensory dendrite and plays an important part in the molting process (see Figure 3D). The swelling on the hair shaft is opposed to a flange within the hair socket and serves to limit the excursions of the hair. (C) Axons from sensory cells (see Figure 2A) aggregate to form the cercal nerve, shown here in electron-microscope transverse section. The range of axon diameter is 0.05 to 7 mµ. All but a few fibers project to the ipsilateral side of the terminal ganglion. (D) Projection of the cercal nerve as determined by cobalt iontophoresis. Many of the primary afferent fibers synapse with dendrites of the giant interneurons. (E) Anatomy of a giant interneuron form a normal (symmetrical) ganglion reconstructed from serial sections of a cell filled with Procion yellow and from cobalt iontophoresis preparations. (F) Giant axon profiles in light-micrograph transverse section of ventral nerve cord. (G) Giant fiber spikes recorded in the connective in response to sound stimulation of the cerci. (H) Response of a whole cercal sensory nerve to a sound stimulus. Five repetitions are superimposed, showing a high degree of synchrony in the response of the primary sense cells. (J) Regenerating cercus. Initial regenerates have no or few sensilla, depending on when during the intermolt period the amputation is performed. Sensilla differentiate during subsequent instars, as shown in scanning micrograph [compare with adult cercus shown in (A)].

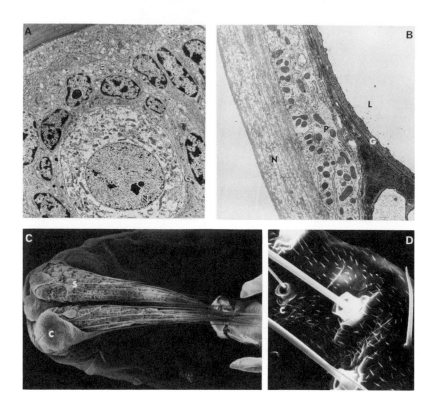

FIGURE 2.   (A) Sensory neuron cell body of a filiform sensillum. It is situated below the cercal cuticle, upper left, and has a characteristically light-textured cytoplasm and large nucleus containing prominent nucleolus, N. The cell is closely wrapped by a gial sheath, G, and surrounded by epidermal cells, E. (B) Transverse section of part of ventral cord which emphasizes the proximity of the lateral giant axon, L, to the periphery of the connective. The giant axon is closely wrapped by a layer of glial cell processes, G. A fibrous layer, the neurilemma, N, overlies perineural sheath cells, P. (C) Scanning electron micrograph of cerci of late-embryonic first unistar cricket shortly before hatching from the egg. The embryo is ensheathed by an embryonic cuticle, C, which has been peeled away over the cerci. Sensilla, S, are apparent on the rumpled cuticle, which will be expanded by inflation at hatching, thus erecting the sensilla. (D) Scanning electron micrograph of cercus of first instar cricket. Several filiform hairs and their sockets, with associated campaniform sensilla, C, are prominent. A single trichoid sensillum is present at right. The minute hairs (microtrichiae) are not sensory. Note small numbers of trichoid sensilla in comparison with those of adult (Figure 1A).

cockroaches have so much greater facility than locusts? Again, these small scale differences are doubtless due to the variation in adaptive strategies. Natural populations of arthropods are subject to surprisingly high levels of limb loss (see, e.g., Edwards, 1972). Many insects seem to be similarly vulnerable and we can assume a strong selection pressure for ability to regenerate limbs, antennae, and cerci during postembryonic development.

The capacity to regenerate functional appendages is tied to the events of the molt cycle by which arthropods grow and is lost in the adult except under experimental interventions which induce an extra molt. Regeneration processes interact with the endocrine control of development in many ways (Needham, 1965). For example, the duration of the molting cycle can be influenced by limb loss. In the best-studied case of the cockroach *Blatella germanica*, the molt may be hastened or delayed according to the time of appendage loss, and there is evidence that the information that mediates this control of developmental timing comes from limb proprioceptors (Kunkel, 1975). These effects seem to be more pronounced for motor appendages than for sensory appendages such as antennae and cerci. Many arthropods have an autotomy site built into their limbs [e.g., Crustacea (Bliss, 1960)] at a point where limb muscles do not overlap. A damaged limb may thus be sloughed and the hemocoel closed with minimum trauma. The regenerative response varies in gradient fashion according to the site of limb severance (Needham, 1965).

SOME GENERAL STATEMENTS ABOUT NEURAL DEVELOPMENT IN INSECTS

We shall consider neural regeneration in more detail below, but before doing so, we shall summarize some basic features of neural development in arthropods which provide the necessary context for regeneration studies.

1) *All sensory cells differentiate from epidermal cells; one cell transduces and transmits to the center.* The differentiation of sensilla from single epidermal cells is well documented (Wigglesworth, 1953; Clever, 1958), and the diverse pathways taken by the cells of the group which form the sensory unit afford an elegant example of differentiation (Figure 3).

2) *Sensory cells arise late in embryonic development, long after motor connections have been forged.* The development of insect embryos has been much studied (Counce and Waddington, 1973), but we have surprisingly little information on patterns of embryonic sensory differentiation in any species and no systematic study of the projection of axons from embryonic sensilla to the central nervous system. Our unpublished studies on *Acheta domesticus* suggest that sensory differentiation is one of the last events of embryogenesis. The

numbers of sensilla produced in the embryo are a minute proportion of the eventual adult population, which accumulates through successive additions in the series of molting cycles. In the cricket *Acheta domesticus*, for example, the embryonic cercal nerve carries about 300 axons, whereas the adult has some 10,000. The relative number of different sensillar types may change during development (Edwards and Palka, 1974; Schaeffer, 1973), and some sensilla present in the first instar may be lost, as in the locust *Schistocerca gregaria* (Bernays, 1972). It has been shown recently in a metamorphosing moth (Sanes and Hildebrand, 1975), embryonic orthopteran antennae and legs (Bate, in press) and cerci (Edwards, in preparation) that a small population of afferent fibers differentiate early and presumably provide a guide for subsequent functional sensory fibers, but these findings do not substantially alter the statement above about functional sensilla development.

Hair sensilla are unhooked from the central nervous system for an interval during each molt cycle. Of all the demands faced by a developing arthropod, one of the most exacting must surely be the transfer of sensitivity to new sensilla from their predecessors. The developing arthropod is, in effect, housed within two cuticles for part of each molt cycle — the rumpled new cuticle, which will expand at ecdysis, and, above it, the separated old cuticle (Figure 4). In this so-called pharate stage, the dendrite of sensillar hairs must pass *through* the new cuticle to their attachments on the previous cuticle. When the insect sloughs the old cuticle at ecdysis, the attachment is broken and lost (Moran, 1971), and the broken tip must now connect with the new sensillum, as has been superbly demonstrated by Schmidt and Gnatzy (1971) (see Figure 3). Does the process affect the responsiveness of the animal? Walcott and Salpeter's (1966) study of a spider's vibration receptor, the lyriform organ, shows that there is indeed a decline in responsiveness in the days before ecdysis but that it returns to maximum values shortly after sloughing off the old cuticle.

The mechanism that governs spacing of new sensilla during postembryonic development is an intriguing problem in pattern formation. Wigglesworth (1940), working with the evenly

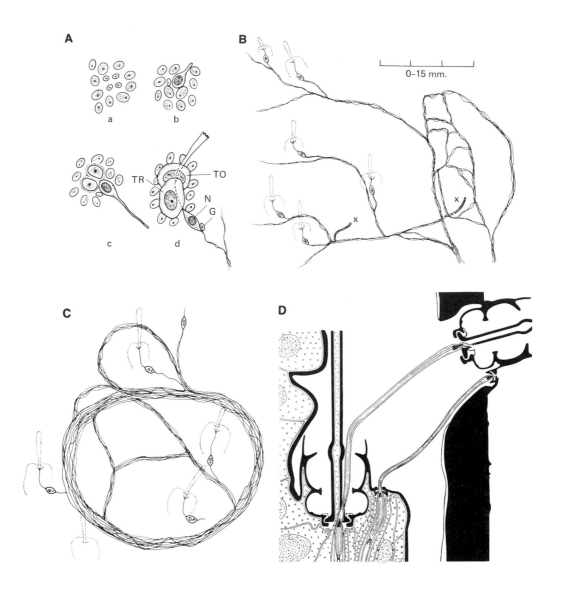

FIGURE 3. *Sensillar development in insects. (A) Differentiation of a sensillum from a single epidermal cell. The mother cell divides twice, giving rise to a quartet of cells of similar appearance, a. Each of these cells follows different developmental pathways, b and c, to form the functional sensillum d, composed of a bristle cell (the trichogen, TR); a socket cell (the tormogen, TO); a neuron, N; and a glial cell, G. (From Wigglesworth, 1953a.) (B) Pathways of sensory axons in regenerated epidermis of a late instar Rhodnius following a burn in an earlier instar. Axons elongate and travel between the epidermis and the underlying basal lamina, gathering, but not fusing, to form bundles that penetrate the basal lamina at points x. (From Wigglesworth, 1953b.) (C) An indication that contact guidance is involved in the directional growth of sensory axons comes from this well-known figure from Wigglesworth (1953b), which shows regenerating axons repeatedly following a loop of their own axons. (D) Molting of a sensillum. The formation of a new cuticle in developing insects requires separation of the epidermis (left) from the old cuticle (right), and the formation of new cuticular structures. The filiform hair and socket of the old*

spaced sensilla on the integument of the blood-sucking bug *Rhodnius*, found that the density remained constant as the animal grew, and proposed that each existing sensillum precludes the origin of closely neighboring sensilla. Only after increase in the separation of sensilla can new sites arise among the epidermis. Lawrence (in Counce and Waddington, 1973) has shown that a quantitative model based on the concept of inhibitory circles around existing hairs adequately describes the distribution of sensilla in several different insects.

3) *All interneurons, neurosecretory cells, and motoneurons arise from invaginated embryonic ectoderm.* The invaginated cells of the neural groove, or other areas of ectoderm in the case of holometabolan anlagen (e.g., the optic lobes), form the relatively small population of neuroblasts from which neurons are derived. Their pattern of divisions is remarkably uniform throughout the insects (see Figure 4; reviews: Edwards, 1969; Jacobson, 1970; and Pipa, in Young, 1973). The behavior of the newborn neuron in later stages of neurogenesis is less well known, but the potential is there for precise tracing of cell lineages from neuroblast to functional neuron, and, as Jacobson (1970) has also pointed out, to assess the hypothesis that clonal recognition may play a part in the development of connections.

Where the differentiation of ganglia has been followed in some detail, similar patterns of temporal and spatial sequence have been found (Meinertzhagen, in Young, 1973). This is so general among visual systems in both arthropods and chordates that one must suppose the general rule "a little at a time" to be fundamental to the creation of appropriate connectivity, perhaps by limiting the possible variety of connections at any given instant.

Such a pattern is by no means restricted to the visual system. The corpora pedunculata, or "mushroom bodies" of the insect brain, whose function intrigued Don Maynard (1965), are large structures, characteristically mushroom-shaped, which appear to be second-order antennal sensory-processing centers (Weiss, 1974). They add large numbers of cells throughout postembryonic development. The cockroach *Periplaneta americana*, for example, adds over 300,000 cells (Neder, 1959), while the 250 cells of the first instar *Drosophila* larva are augmented 10-fold through postembryonic development.

The pattern of cell addition has been followed radioautographically in both a hemimetabolan, the cockroach *Periplaneta americana* (Weiss and Edwards, 1975), and a holometabolan, the monarch butterfly, *Danaus plexippus* (Nordlander and Edwards, 1970; see Figure 4). In both cases centripetal movement of differentiating neurons from a central nest of neuroblasts produces a solid stalk of axons surmounted by a calyx of cell bodies. In his anatomical study of the corpora pedunculata of the cockroach *P. americana*, Weiss (1974) drew attention to the laminate neuropile of the stalks, which gives the appearance of growth rings. These prove to be cyclically laid down through postembryonic development, evidently in relation to the molt cycle, with the oldest axons at the surface and youngest at the core.

With the exception of some centers, such as the corpora pedunculata discussed above, central neuron populations of Hemimetabola are laid down in embryonic development, and few cells are added subsequently (Panov, 1966; Gymer and Edwards, 1967; Sbrenna, 1971). The central nervous system certainly grows in volume and adds great numbers of glial cells, but the neuronal machinery seems to be generally set up in the embryo, cells growing in volume and in ramification (Altman and Tyrer, 1974; see Figure 4) rather than number.

In the metamorphosing insects on the

---

cuticle (upper right) are replaced at the molt by the new structures, which become reoriented as the cuticle is expanded. Dendrites of the filiform hair and an associated campaniform sensillum traverse pores in the new sensilla to their insertions in the old cuticle. When the old cuticle is lost, the dendrite segment distal to the new sensillum is broken away. (From Gnatzy and Schmidt, 1971.)

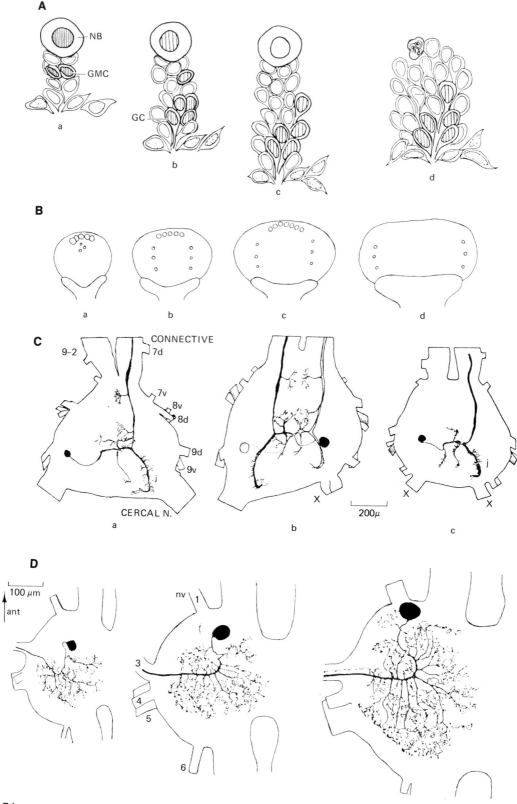

other hand, and that means the vast majority, the sequential polymorphism of larva and adult and the challenges of metamorphosis pose many tantalizing questions in neural development (Edwards, 1967; Pipa, in Young, 1973). The divergence of form and behavior between larva and adult, which underlies the success of the Holometabola and which reaches its peak in the Hymenoptera and Diptera, requires two successive nervous systems. How is an orderly conversion achieved?

Neuroblast clusters set aside during embryonic development are the source of most of the adult central nervous system. In the worker cast of the ant *Myrmica laevinodis*, for example, about 90 percent of all embryonic neuroblasts persist until metamorphosis (Stocker, 1974). Does that mean that all larval neurons are scrapped? It would not a priori be unlikely, especially in the Hymenoptera and Diptera, where all other larval cells except the Malpighian tubules are demolished in the pupal stage. But a clear answer is difficult to obtain, because the adult brain grows within the larval brain throughout postembryonic development, reaching a crescendo at metamorphosis, and the adult central nervous system is massive in proportion to that which was adequate for the larva. There is evidence that even those centers which are similar in volume and form in larva and adult, such as the olfactory lobes of the beetle *Tenebrio* (Panov, 1961), are replaced during metamorphosis. But we do have good examples of identified neurons in the nerve cord of Lepidoptera which do persist (Taylor and Truman, 1974). Of 74 motoneurons in the fourth abdominal ganglion of the larva of the tobacco hornworm, *Manduca sexta*, 12 neurons are lost and 8 new ones appear during transition to the pupal stage. The adult emerging from metamorphosis has 70 neurons, but thereafter 40 larval motoneurons and about 180 interneurons die.

4) *Arthropod giant interneurons are influenced by the periphery in the quantity of their growth but not in their form.* In the cricket *Acheta domesticus*, the dimensions of axons and cell bodies of the abdominal giant

---

FIGURE 4. *Development of central neurons. (A) Interneuron formation. A neuroblast, NB, divides unequally to produce ganglion mother cells, GMC, which may divide further before differentiating to ganglion cells, GC (interneurons). In the sequences shown, the material has been fixed at successively longer intervals after incorporation of isotopically labeled thymidine by the neuroblast nucleus. a: Fixed 2 hours after injection in the fourth instar. The neuroblast and a pair of ganglion mother cells are labeled, which signifies DNA synthesis at the time of injection. b: Fixed early in the following instar. The neuroblast has divided with consequent dilution of radioactive label. Labeled ganglion mother cells have divided further and differentiated to become interneurons. c: Fixed late in the fifth instar, label is no longer evident in the neuroblast, having been decreased by many divisions; interneurons are differentiating from later progeny of the neuroblast. d: The neuroblast nucleus is pycnotic and the cell is degenerating, having produced a number of ganglion mother cells. (B) Longitudinal sections show pattern of interneuron production during development of the corpora pedunculata of the monarch butterfly (Nordlander and Edwards, 1970). a: the position of neuroblast cells labeled by radioactive thymidine uptake in the third larval instar. b: at a later stage of larval development, the labeled progeny have been displaced laterally and the neuroblasts are again unlabeled following a number of divisions. c: A later stage. d: The adult stage, at which point neuroblasts have degenerated. (C) Effects of deprivation of input on the development of a giant interneuron in* Acheta domesticus. *a: The normal adult form of giant interneuron 9-2. b: Interneuron pair in a ganglion deprived of the right cercal sensory nerve throughout development. Note diminution of dendrties on deprived side. c: The same interneuron in a ganglion deprived of both cercal sensory nerves throughout development. Both ganglion and interneuron are reduced in size. (From Murphey, et al., 1975.) (D) Development of a motoneuron through later instars to adult in mesothoracic ganglion in the locust* Chortoicetes terminifera. *Note increasing terminal ramification as postembryonic growth proceeds. (From Altman and Tyrer, 1974.)*

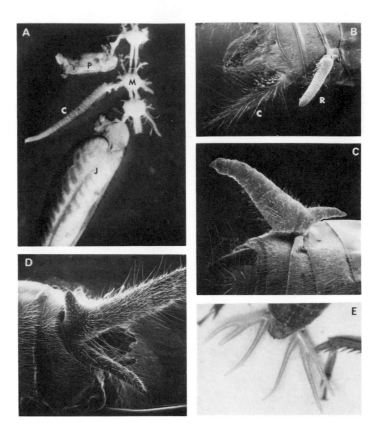

FIGURE 5.   *Cerci of crickets subjected to experimental surgery. (A) Light micrograph of cercal regenerate, C, transplanted to stump of left mesothoracic leg, sending its sensory nerve to the mesothoracic ganglion, M. Above and below are tibiae of prothoracic leg, P, and metathoracic (jumping) leg, J. (B) Scanning electron micrograph of cercal regenerate, R, transplanted ectopically to dorsal abdominal cuticle. Compare with normal cercus, C. (C) Scanning electron micrograph of another ectopic transplant. This particular cercus produced a branch, probably because of injury during surgery. The grafts in both (B) and (C) were placed in the middle of an abdominal segment, and distortion of segmental boundaries seems to have occurred. (D) Lateral view of cercus with supernumeraries dorsally and ventrally, modified by exchanging the animal's two cerci left for right and inverting them (scanning electron micrograph). Note that there is no evidence of any discontinuity between the dorsal supernumerary and the main shaft of the cercus, and that clavate hairs appear only on the medial side, as would be expected from cercal exchange and inversion. (E) Multiply branched regenerate cerci induced by damaging lateral tips of early bifid regenerates (light micrograph).*

fibers are not significantly smaller in animals that have been raised without cerci than in normal individuals. But the volume of the terminal ganglion, in which the dendrites are embedded, is reduced by some 30 percent (Edwards and Palka, 1971), and the dimensions of their dendritic branches are proportionally reduced, though they maintain the basic characteristics of their branching patterns, as recognized by cobalt iontophoresis (Murphey et al., 1975). Where the dendritic fields of a single cell lie on both sides of the ganglion midline, asymmetries in ganglion dimensions caused by rearing animals with a single cercus are reflected in corresponding differences in dendrite dimensions (Figure 5). Thus the instructions for growth need not apply uniformly throughout a single neuron.

The stability that we have found in the branching patterns of cricket giant interneurons is paralleled in the results of Tweedle, Pitman, and Cohen (1973), who detected no significant change in the form of deafferented interneurons and motoneurons in adult cockroaches, and of Wine (1975), who found giant interneurons of crayfish to be similarly stable. Development of the motoneurons output in the lobster *Homarus americanus* proved to be unaffected by loss of peripheral sense organs and target limbs. Davis (1973a) removed swimmeret limb buds from newly hatched lobsters and found normal patterns of rhythmic motor output at the fourth larval stage when swimmerets have normally become functional. Similar conclusions have been drawn by Kutsch (1974) in a study on the development of the flight motor system of locusts. All these observations conform with findings in the vertebrates, in which the shapes of large output cells seem to be governed more by genetic factors than by influences of their immediate milieu (Bodian, 1970, Jacobson, 1970; Rakic and Sidman, 1973).

The rules for the growth and form of small arthropod interneurons are virtually unknown, but there are signs that they are more responsive to their environment than are giant interneurons and motoneurons. Observations on the development of the eye and optic lobe of insects have yielded some conflicting views (critically reviewed by Meinertzhagen, in Young, 1973) as to the role of the periphery in the differentiation of interneurons, but the evidence from volumetric studies of neuropile strongly implies the need for peripheral contact in the differentiation of optic interneurons. Power (1943) found reduced olfactory center volume in the brain of *Drosophila* mutants with reduced eyes, the two centers showing a close size correlation; this may be a transsynaptic effect, or perhaps another case of Lebensraum. LoPresti, Macagno, and Levinthal (1973) have proposed that differentiation of neurons in the lamina neuropile of *Daphnia* is triggered by contact with incoming retinula axons. This is, again, reminiscent of vertebrate findings;

Sidman (1974) and others have pointed to the importance of interactions between certain interneurons during development.

SOME GENERAL STATEMENTS ABOUT REGENERATIVE GROWTH

1) *When sensory structures of any type are removed, the insect regenerates both sensilla and precise functional connections with the center.* This capacity can be repeatedly evoked. Axons from regenerates can reestablish functional connections even when development is delayed until late in postembryonic life (Edwards and Palka, 1971; Palka and Edwards, 1974), and they can reach and recognize their target cells of the central nervous system when transplanted to another part of the body (Edwards and Sahota, 1967; Palka and Schubiger, unpublished).

Nerves may reach a ganglion by devious, sometimes bizarre routes and their axons still form correct synapses (McLean, 1974; Kennedy, 1973; Palka and Schubiger, unpublished). They seem to locate correct interneurons even in remote locations, as if they recognize the cell per se and not the local dendritic milieu (Edwards and Sahota, 1967).

2) *The pattern of events in the growing regenerate is essentially a speeding of normal postembryonic growth.* Normal ontogeny is recapitulated, as judged by changing patterns of sensillar ratios. New sensilla are added through each molting cycle during normal development. This process takes place at an accelerated rate in the regenerate. The crux of sensory regeneration, then, is the directed growth of the first pioneer fibers from sensilla to ganglion.

In the case of regenerating cricket cercal nerves, the distance to be traveled by an axon tip setting out from the base of a regenerate appendage may be an order of magnitude greater than in the embryo. It must enter the ganglion, and once there must grow through a neuropile tightly wrapped and interlaced with glial cells to locate its target in a population of several hundred neurons. Since our tests reveal only the final connections of the regenerated cercal nerve, we can as yet only guess about the accuracy of the first connections formed during this target-seeking process. How many incorrect synapses might also be made? And what happens to faulty connections if they are indeed made? Do they remain as silent mementos of the search for a significant interaction? Or are they pulled away to leave no trace of what did not work? Just how labile are the connections?

In the regeneration of severed axons in the leech, sensory cells are highly selective in their connections with appropriate motoneurons, making few connections with other neurons (Jansen and Nicholls, 1972), but during this process, synapses within the nerve cord can undergo marked changes in effectiveness. We wonder whether annelids and arthropods also show the degree of synaptic plasticity that is being noted in vertebrate studies (Mark, 1974).

3) Regenerates usually re-create their predecessor, but this is not mandatory. Indeed, any appendage can be replaced by almost any other appendage, given the appropriate conditions. The similarity between the phenomena of homeotic regeneration, where an antenna, for example, is replaced by a leg, and of homeotic mutants, in which the product of imaginal discs is altered (e.g., antennapedia), cannot be fortuitous, and the implications for analysis of neural relationships between center and periphery are obvious. In fact, this facet of insect neurobiology may come to shed the clearest light on mechanisms of neurogenesis.

The possibility of learning important things about recognition in neurons from homeotic regenerates was clear to Don Maynard, as his studies on the spiny lobster, *Panulirus*, testify. His work brought the classic studies of Herbst into the context of modern neurobiology. Removal of optic ganglia when the eyestalk is cut is followed by the growth of an antennule. Whatever the cause of heteromorphic regenerates, the key question they pose for neurobiology is the addressing of their sensory fibres. Are they imbued with a regional specificity and do they follow local topographic cues to attain their central destinations? If so, they should report to the optic lobes. Or are they antennular in their identification and able to locate olfactory centers of the brain? Maynard and Cohen (1965) showed that the latter was so.

It is tempting to explain the crayfish antennule heteromorph as a consequence of the proximity of the antennule. Antennules are presumably more vulnerable to loss and damage than eyestalks; their vigor of regeneration may accordingly be more pronounced, and the heteromorph may then simply be the capture of a wound site by alerted antennular blastema cells. This explanation presumably applies to comparable heteromorphs in the cricket (Edwards, 1967). But heteromorph legs that spring from antennal stumps in stick insects can scarcely have such an explanation, and the rich repertoire of homeotic mutants and transdetermined imaginal discs in *Drosophila* offers a range of "misplaced sensilla" that are ideal for the study of specificity.

4) Regenerating sensory fibers follow precise rules of laterality. In the cricket cercal nerve-terminal ganglion system, fibers that form an ipsilateral projection during normal ontogeny do so during regeneration, and contralaterally projecting fibers behave equally precisely. Even the exchange, left for right, of the structures from which fibers are coming, as we have done with cricket cerci, does not produce large numbers of sensory fibers projecting erroneously across the midline (Palka and Schubiger, 1975).

We have found that several procedures increase the incidence of errors in laterality. (a) Unilateral cercal deprivation: axons cross the midline with increased frequency, and contralateral physiological responses are enhanced. (b) Left—right exchange of cerci: this procedure produces similar effects, but note that the great majority of fibers still terminate on the correct side. (c) Switched regeneration: in this procedure a cricket is raised with a single cercus for half its postembryonic development; then, that single cercus is removed and the opposite one is allowed to form. This last procedure produces the greatest amount of physiologically and anatomically recognizable crossing of the midline.

It is important to note that fibers which erroneously cross the midline nevertheless appear to synapse with the correct postsynaptic cells — the homologues of the ones they would have contacted on the correct side. The rule for laterality seems to be: discriminate ipsilateral from contralateral, not left from right. This rule is broken more readily than the unknown rules for seeking out the correct particular postsynaptic cells.

5) *Depriving a region of the central nervous system of a particular input leads to an enhanced effectiveness of the remaining inputs.* In a number of vertebrate cases (e.g., Cotman et al., 1974; Raisman and Field, 1973), the strengthening of remaining inputs has been demonstrated anatomically as well as physiologically. The cricket terminal ganglion seems to be the only arthropod (or invertebrate) case in which this possibility has been tested. The effect is clear on physiological criteria (Palka and Edwards, 1974); several possible anatomical bases for it have been found, but their relative importance is not yet understood (Murphey et al., 1975).

A corollary of this rule is that no totally new inputs to the deprived region are formed — only existing ones are strengthened. Jansen and Nicholls (1972) have recognized an apparently similar phenomenon following crushing of central connectives in leeches.

6) *Restoration of behavior that appears normal following regeneration does not necessarily mean that all neuronal connections have been restored to their original condition.* Reflex responses have often been used as an assay that is assumed to be sensitive for successful reconstruction of neuronal circuits, as in the classic studies of Sperry (reviewed in Sperry, 1963) on eye rotation in amphibians. However, there are recent studies indicating that this assay can yield a positive result in the presence of considerable alteration of circuitry. Jansen and Nicholls (1972) found a systematic change in the balance of excitatory and inhibitory components in intersegmental connections of identified neurons in leeches following regeneration of a crushed connective, even though the coordination of swimming movements appeared quite normal. And Sandeman and Luff (1974) found that stimulation of heteromorph antennules in crayfish elicited normal antennular reflexes in the presence of widespread wandering of antennular fibers in the brain, so long as one particular tract had reached its correct destination. Thus even behavioral assays of connectivity can give false positive results — that is, can fail to indicate errors if sufficient or particular correct connections have formed.

7) *Regenerating sensory fibers will, at least under some circumstances, pass over in-appropriate postsynaptic neurons in their path in order to reach the right ones.* The original evidence for this statement comes from the histological studies of Sperry and colleagues (Sperry, 1963) on regenerating goldfish retinal fibers. The level of resolution of these studies was only modest, but the experiment has been repeated recently on the chick retinotectal projection (Crossland et al., 1974) and the basic result has been confirmed.

There are no exactly analogous experiments in arthropods or, for that matter, in any invertebrate that we are aware of. This is largely because the postsynaptic elements are very few in number and highly individualized, so that there are no easily recognized *regions* which incoming neurons could bypass. However, there are strong indications that, except perhaps in heteromorphic regeneration, *numerous wrong connections are not made.* Anatomically, we have analyzed the axonal distributions of sensory neurons from regenerate cerci, using both a terminal degeneration technique (Palka and Edwards, 1974) and cobalt back filling (unpublished observations), and we have recognized many similarities in the details of the fiber distribution, while only rarely recognizing abnormalities. The best physiological evidence for the paucity of wrong connections comes from Jansen and Nicholls (1972) in their study of the leech. Many pairs of neurons in two adjacent ganglia were tested after regeneration of a crushed connective: only neurons that normally had connections were found to have them after regeneration, and no cases of new (erroneous) connections were found. However, (a) the restored connections were systematically different from the normal ones, as pointed out in (6) above; and (b) this test would not reveal connections that formed anatomically but failed to function (Mark, 1974).

8) *Many sensory surfaces and regions of the central nervous system have operationally definable polarities which appear to play a role in the establishment of neural connections.* This is a basic finding in vertebrate retinotectal systems, whose meaning is further enriched by the recent finding of Jacobson (1968a) and Hunt and Jacobson (1972), that there is a progressive increase in the rigidity of organization of the retina. If the eye anlage is rotated very early in development, the body imposes its axes upon it

and connections develop as if no rotation had been performed. Late in development both axes of the eye are found to project in reversed fashion upon the tectum. A variety of intermediate conditions have been found, indicating that the two axes are determined sequentially and that their strength, as measured by their resistance to the influence of the body axes, increases over time.

In arthropods, comparable data are available only for operations during postembryonic development. The most extensive study to date is from our own laboratory (Palka and Schubiger, 1975), reviewed in more detail below. In brief, we have found that, if cerci are rotated, their sensory fibers connect centrally according to the part of the cercus from which they come, not according to the orientation of that part relative to the rest of the body. When cerci are exchanged left for right, however, the new left cercus will project to the left hemiganglion and vice versa; there is *no* substantial crossing of fibers from a cercus to the side of the ganglion to which it originally projected. Thus the mechanisms that establish the laterality of a projection appear to be different from those related to orientation or to selection of particular pre-to-post-synaptic pairings.

9) *The trophic role of nerve in regeneration of arthropod appendages is equivocal.* This question is an old one, with opposing views as to the relevance of innervation to the origin and differentiation of the replacement appendages. We have no rigorous, adequately controlled study, partly because, as the following comments will show, a properly controlled experiment may not be possible. What, briefly, can we say from the work we do have?

a) *The integument or the blastema from which the regenerate develops is probably not dependent on specific innervation for the initiation of a regenerate.* There are claims that the insect regenerates require innervation (e.g., Rummel, 1970), just as vertebrates certainly do (Singer, 1974). We have found that cricket cerci regenerate normally after sources of local sensory and motor innervation have been removed, without doing extensive damage to other tissues (McLean, 1974). Details of the early differentiation of regenerates from the epidermal cells which cover the wound site of a lost appendage

are unknown, but the time course of blastema formation seems to preclude a need for innervation (Edwards, unpublished).

b) *The requirement for innervation to promote the development of the regenerate integument has not been proved.* Cut nerves regenerate, with varying degrees of vigor. It has been recognized since Bodenstein's (1957) pioneering exploration of limb regeneration in the cockroach that it is all but impossible to stem a flood of regenerating fibers into the site of limb loss in either nymph or adult, even when the operation also removes neighboring ganglia. Cutting nerves and implanting physical barriers to regeneration can cause many responses inseparable from direct effects of nerve on regenerates: wound responses, including effects on the molt cycle; accretion of hemocytes and clotting of hemolymph – both of which may impede or redirect circulation; loss of tracheation; and modification of other physiological functions due to loss of visceral innervation. All these effects can depress growth and differentiation of regenerates through nonspecific effects.

c) *A distinction can be made between the development of the integument of a regenerate and its mesodermal contents.* Although the integument probably does not need innervation, muscle differentiation clearly does. In metamorphosing insects, muscles simply do not develop in the absence of their nerves (Nüesch, 1968). This trophic dependence for growth at metamorphosis should be distinguished from a trophic role in muscle maintenance, which, as has been shown in Crustacea (Boone and Bittner, 1974), is not as important as stretch.

We tentatively conclude that nerve is needed for regeneration of muscle and not of integument, but we cannot assert that any regenerate in any experiment has ever regenerated in the complete absence of innervation, especially since neighboring multipolar subepidermal neurons are ubiquitous, and neurosecretory axons that supply the epidermis (Maddrell, 1967) are of wide occurrence. The response of these nerves to damage is unknown. But it may be that they exercise some function in regeneration, and the observation of Anwyl and Finlayson (1974) that neurons supplying regressed segmental muscle in *Rhodnius* carry spontaneous antidromic spikes may prove to have implications for such situations.

10) *While lost sensilla are readily regenerated from epidermal cells, central neurons are not replaced.* There may be some exceptions to this statement; for example, Drescher's (1960) studies of ablated cockroach brains suggest that regeneration is possible where postembryonic neuroblasts are available. This very limited capacity contrasts with the remarkable capacity of lower vertebrates (Guth and Windle, 1970) to replace cell bodies.

11) *Distal ends of cut motoneurons and interneurons can survive for remarkably long periods in some arthropods.* Distal segments of severed crayfish motoneurons remain physiologically active and can even knit with the proximal stump to restore functional connections (Bittner, 1973). Whether a similar process occurs in insects remains to be shown, but it is certain that cockroach motor nerves can specifically reinnervate muscles after severance (Pearson and Bradley, 1972) and that motoneurons will achieve specific innervation of homologous muscles in limbs transplanted to a neighboring segment (Young, 1973). Supernumerary grafted limbs receive motoneurons even when the innervation of the normal host limb is intact (Sahota and Edwards, 1968), but we know nothing of specificity in this case. Distal segments of severed interneurons can also survive for long periods in crustaceans and insects (Bittner, 1973; Tung and Pipa, 1971).

SOME POPULAR CONCEPTS OF MECHANISMS IN NEUROGENISIS AND THEIR MANIFESTATION IN SIMPLE SYSTEMS

Contact Guidance

The growth of sensory fiber populations of arthropods provides us with beautiful examples of what appears to be contact guidance as the axons migrate over the basal lamina below the epidermis "in search" for a pathway to the center (Figure 3) (Wigglesworth, 1953). How do new axons recognize the surface that they should follow? We do not know, but the mechanism for reaching the center need have

nothing to do with the process by which an axon tip finds its destination for synapse formation within the neuropile, just as a pigeon uses different cues to navigate home and to locate the door of its loft.

Where normal pathways are interrupted by wounding, an axon may be misled into endlessly following itself, like Fabre's column of caterpillars (Figure 3), and where regenerating neurons take multiple paths to the center, others follow them. In the embryo, initial contact between sensory elements at the surface and their central destinations requires spanning a gap of little more than 100 mμ. But when regenerating cercal axons of the cricket are allowed to approach the central nervous system for the first time late in postembryonic development they are still successful, though the distance they must travel through the hemocoel is an order of magnitude greater. They may take more than one path and give double cercal sensory nerves. The most efficient pathway would seem to be the cercal motor nerve which supplies the extrinsic cercal musculature, but this does not seem to be used, for the final product is always separate throughout its length.

New axons follow older axons to the center, but where do they synapse when they have reached their destination? Postembryonic growth of arthropods requires successive batches of new sensory axons to make their way to the appropriate ganglion and synapse with a fixed set of postsynaptic cells. Do new segments of dendrite grow to receive them, or are they accommodated among previous terminals in mosaic fashion? The question is very difficult to answer anatomically, but Kennedy (1973) has physiological evidence that the newest synapses are not farthest out on the dendrites.

Cell Death, Cell Selection, and Clonal Recognition

Paradoxical as it may seem, cell death is a widespread process in embryogenesis, and the nervous systems of both vertebrates and arthropods provide good examples. In the development of the ventral horn in the amphibian spinal cord (Prestige, 1970), the most thoroughly studied system, many more motoneurons grow out toward the periphery than are finally part of the functional system. Apparently, those axons that fail to make appropriate contact with muscle, die.

It has been known for many years that the cyclic growth of the insect epidermis involves a pattern of ebullient mitosis (Wigglesworth, 1954) followed by cell death. This is also true of imaginal disc development (Spreij, 1971) and of the developing optic lobe in the brain of the monarch butterfly, *Danaus plexippus* (Nordlander and Edwards, 1969), in which neuron production is followed in regular sequences by death of part of the population. Meinertzhagen in his thorough review (in Young, 1973) has drawn attention to conflicting interpretation of the role of receptor neurons in eliciting development of the optic neuropiles. One interpretation of cell death among interneuron populations holds that only those interneurons which establish functional connections with incoming retinula cells survive (Nordlander and Edwards, 1969). This would account for the temporal sequence of cell death, and is consistent with the recent observations reported by LoPresti, Macagno, and Levinthal (1973) that dendrites of the lamina, the outermost optic neuropile, are prompted to differentiate by the arrival of retinula cell axons. In vertebrates, too, dendrite growth may depend on availability of axons (Vaughn, Henrikson, and Grieshaber, 1974). It may turn out that the act of synapse formation saves cells from extinction in diverse nervous systems.

Clonal Recognition and Compartments

Clonal recognition, the capacity for cells of common origin to recognize their kinship, is a plausible candidate as a mechanism by which differentiating sensillar neurons might recognize their central target ganglion, for the primordial cells that will sink from the surface to form the neuroblasts of the central nervous system lie side by side with cells that will form the integument of the body and appendages from which sensillar neurons will differentiate. Arthropods seem ideal material for tracing such lineages, and major strides in this direction have been taken recently with the formulation of the theory of compartments (see the review of Crick and Lawrence, 1975).

Gradient Models

The notion that gradients of some kind are involved in morphogenesis and regeneration is a recurrent one in developmental biology (e.g., Child, 1941; Wolpert, 1971), and in recent years definitions have been sharpened (Bryant, 1974) and models quantified (e.g., Lawrence, in Counce and Waddington, 1973). These concepts are central to recent work on neurogenesis in vertebrate visual systems (Gaze, 1970; Jacobson, 1970).

Detailed analyses of gradient phenomena have been made with experimentally favorable pieces of insect integument and appendages, but very few studies consider corresponding neuronal connections. (Bate, 1973, and Palka and Schubiger, 1975, on sensory cells; Pearson and Bradley, 1972, and Young, 1972, on motor cells).

According to the gradient model, two factors govern the differentiation of a cell. First, a heritable tendency to become part of a particular structure, such as a leg, a wing, an abdomen, or a cercus, is established in unknown ways early in development and is called *determination* (e.g., Bryant, 1974). It is a rather rigid attribute of a cell, and, if the cell is transplanted to some other part of the body, for instance from a leg to the abdomen, it will form structures characteristic of the region from which it was taken. Second, it is postulated that the position of a cell in the coordinate system of its own part of the body, such as its position within the leg or within an abdominal segment, results from *positional information* received by the cell (Wolpert, 1971) and that this information specifies which of several alternative pathways of differentiation the cell should take. Positional information is thought to exist physically in the form of gradients of diffusible molecules.

Gradient models postulate a source of information-giving material or mechanism where the value of the gradient is highest and a sink where the value is lowest. For example, the anterior margin of a segment might be the source and the posterior the sink, as in the models derived from experiments on abdominal cuticle reviewed by Lawrence (in Counce and Waddington, 1973).

It is assumed that adjacent regions of the body will not tolerate gaps in the gradient, and growth of tissue following experimental interruption of the gradient will always be from high to low value regions. Thus ablation will be followed by regeneration, if the high point of the gradient is preserved. But if the original high point is removed, growth will be from the highest point remaining down along the gradient, producing a mirror-image duplication of the structures that the ablation spared.

Clock Models

Recently a class of models that present an alternative to gradient models has been proposed by French and Bullière (1975a, b). These models apply with especial clarity to tubular structures, such as appendages, and we can illustrate them in that context.

Clock models suppose that every point on the circumference of an appendage is identified by its own clock position, without reference to some special point, such as the high point of a gradient. They further suppose that when interruptions in the clock sequence occur, these are corrected by growth, which fills in the sequence by the shortest route. For example, if an ablation is made between 2 and 5 o'clock, regeneration of the missing region will occur; but if a large ablation is made in which tissue is removed from 11 to 7 o'clock, the shortest route is duplication of the tissue that remains.

Both gradient and clock models successfully predict many experimental consequences of ablation and grafting. How do they differ? Gradient models predict that the effects of surgery will be *location-specific*, because the high point of the gradient has properties shared by no other point. Clock models, on the other hand, predict *location-independent* consequences of surgery, except that it is often necessary to postulate uneven spacing of the clock hours on the body surface.

Positional Information and Neuronal Connectivity

Both gradient and clock models suppose that receptor cells distributed on a surface have available to them positional information. Receptor cells become receptor cells and not simple epithelial cells because of where they are. From a functional standpoint we would expect that they would also form central synaptic connections according to their location on the body surface, since this is a simple way of preserving information about the location of an outside stimulus relative to the body and is clearly a functional principle in the sensory systems of vertebrates. But can we find direct evidence that a cell's differentiation on the body surface, or within a sensory array such as the eye or ear, is governed by the positional information that it receives and that this same instructive mechanism (whatever its nature) also governs the synaptic pairings that the axon of the cell will establish? The question is particularly clear in arthropods, because the cell bodies of the sensory cells are in the epidermis and the first synapses occur far away in the central nervous system. Unfortunately, though the question may be clear, pertinent experimental data in insects are sparse and offer no more direct an answer than the much larger literature in vertebrates (reviewed, for example, by Jacobson, 1970, and Gaze, 1970).

1) *Some experimental findings.* In 1968, Horridge rotated the retinas of juvenile locusts by 180° and found no evidence for crossed visual connections in adults. His conclusion that axons from the rotated retina grow directly to the underlying synaptic region of the optic lobe to form synapses, just as they would have in their original locations, has been questioned because of the massive addition of new sensilla and optic lobe tissue during postembryonic development (e.g., Meinertzhagen, in Young, 1973). For the present, we must view the experiment as inconclusive relative to the role of positional information in neural circuit assembly.

Bate (1973) analyzed the central connections of the sensory hairs associated with gin traps on abdominal segments of privet hawkmoth pupae (*Sphinx ligustri*). Gin traps are hairlined pits that lie close to the anterior margin of the segment and are thought to protect against parasites and predators. When the abdomen is flexed sideways in response to stimulation of hair within the trap, the trap is closed by the cuticle of the next anterior segment. Bate showed that the closure response could be elicited by hairs outside the trap at the same anteroposterior level on the surface of each segment. More anterior and more posterior hairs, of apparently identical structure and giving identical sensory responses, did not participate in the closure reflex. Bate and Lawrence (in Young, 1973) interpret this as an indication of the action of an anteroposterior gradient in the segment. When receptor cells at the same level of the gradient receive the same positional information, they synapse centrally with neurons in the trap-closure reflex arc; similar receptor cells at at other levels, receiving different positional information, do not. This interpretation invites experiments in which strips of epidermis whose hairs elicit closure are exchanged with strips of epidermis whose hairs are ineffective; but this has yet to be done.

We have analyzed the central connections of the sensilla on cricket cerci following experimental translocation with the goal of interpreting them in terms of positional information (Palka and Schubiger, 1975). At first glance, the cerci appear to be radially symmetric structures, but the medial side of each cercus is easily distinguished by a small basal patch of about 65 specialized clavate hairs (Figure 4). The long, filiform hairs of the cercus occur in two distinct populations: the hairs on the dorsal and ventral surfaces vibrate transversely to the main axis of the cercus when stimulated by sound or low-velocity air movement (T-hairs), whereas those on the lateral and medial surfaces vibrate longitudinally (L-hairs). We find experimentally that (a) the giant fibers (MGI and LGI) are excited primarily, though not exclusively, by the ipsilateral cercus and are powerfully inhibited by the contralateral cercus; (b) their dominant input is from the T-hairs, and the morphologically similar L-hairs are much less effective; and (c) that the most powerful excitation comes from the most proximal regions of the cercus.

These characteristics make possible an analysis of geometrical factors in the establishment of neural pathways. When the two cerci

of a larval cricket are exchanged left for right, the great majority of regenerating axons (and those growing from sensory cells differentiated in subsequent instars) synapse on the side of the terminal ganglion which they enter; they do not cross the midline. When the orientation of a cercus is changed by $90°$, so that the T-hairs become lateral and medial and the L-hairs dorsal and ventral, the T-hairs again form the dominant input to the MGI and LGI. Cerci can also be grafted to various abnormal regions, such as leg stumps on the thorax (Edwards and Sahota, 1967; Figure 5A) or various positions on the abdomen (Schubiger and Palka, unpublished; Figure 5B and C). In such cases there is evidence, both anatomical and physiological, that connections with the giant fibers are reestablished; the details are presently under study.

2) *Interpretation.* The interpretation of the pioneering experiment of Horridge (1968) is made difficult by technical factors (see above). The findings of Bate (1973) are very suggestive, but no attempt was made to change the central connectivity of the hair receptors by manipulating their peripheral location. Thus his interpretation in terms of gradients is one of correlation only.

Our own work (Palka and Schubiger, 1975) appears to be the first in which manipulation of the periphery produced morphogenetic consequences interpretable in terms of gradient or clock models and in which the central connections of the receptors were also analyzed. It is a step in the right direction, but one limited by technical difficulties.

The responses of the cercal integument closely resemble those described by Bohn (1965) and by Bullière (1970) for cockroach legs (see the review by Lawrence, in Counce and Waddington, 1973). If an appendage is removed, rotated, and grafted back on its original site, it derotates at the graft margin by as much as $90°$ in a single molt. If it is grafted to the opposite side, it produces a pair of supernumerary appendages in predictable locations (Figure 5D): in cases of exchange and no rotation, the supernumeraries are medial and lateral; with exchange and inversion ($180°$ rotation) they are dorsal and ventral. Both these responses are viewed as being caused by a mismatch between the systems of positional information that prevail in the body and in the appendage. Where the two systems, misaligned as a result of surgical manipulation, meet, cellular responses are induced which bring them back into register; these effects are predictable from both gradient and clock models.

It is thus apparent that powerful interactions occur between graft and body tissues. Sensory axons will grow from the graft into the body: How will they behave? It is clear that they successfully reach and enter the terminal ganglion and synapse on the side that is closest. Recordings from the MGI and LGI indicate that the T-hairs always form the dominant input, irrespective of their location relative to the axes of the body; the more numerous L-hairs are consistently less effective. This could be regarded as an insect version of the famous eye rotation experiments in lower vertebrates (see Jacobson, 1970, and Gaze, 1970, for reviews), with the difference that body and nonneural cercal tissues interact dramatically, whereas there is only the barest hint of such an interaction in the amphibian work.

How, then, might the peripheral and central events be related? We have proposed the following argument: (a) T-hairs and L-hairs differ morphologically only in the orientation of their sockets; (b) they are distributed in mutually orthogonal arrays; and (c) a single mutation can cause the loss of the hair shafts of both populations (Bentley, 1975). It thus seems reasonable to propose that the filiform hairs all arise from the same differentiative pathway and that the orientation of the sockets is set by a gradient- or clock-based system of positional information which also directs back-rotation and formation of supernumeraries. It is economical also to take the next step and propose that the difference in the power of central connections made by the T-hairs and the L-hairs derives from a label imparted by these same peripheral systems.

The technical difficulty with this experiment lies in the fact that the giant fibers receive both T- and L-hair input. The former is strongly dominant but not exclusive. This complicates the interpretation of physiological responses in terms of anatomical connections. The studies of Pearson and Bradley (1972) particularly, and of Young (1972) on the innervation of leg muscles following regeneration and following translocation of the leg from one segment to another have employed more exact tests of connectivity, since both motoneurons and muscle fibers could be studied intracellularly and their pairwise relationships established. It appears that regeneration is very precise, even when mesothoracic neurons are asked to innervate a metathoracic leg; that is, the connectivity-establishing mechanisms are segmentally repeated. But in this case we do not yet know the response of the neurons in a situation where the positional information systems of body and appendage are set into conflict. Parenthetically, we also do not know to what extent sensory and motor systems will behave similarly in such situations.

CLOSING THOUGHTS

A basic similarity that underlies the very different architectures of arthropods and chordates is their metameric segmentation. It may well be that such a repetition of modular units, initially with repeating morphogenetic gradients, is a genetically economical way to build a complex organism, and it is tempting to suppose that such mechanisms regulate neurogenesis in both phyla. Given the relative simplicity of arthropod neural design — their small neuroblast populations, their two-dimensional, gradient-directed integument, their epidermal sensilla with spectacular powers of regeneration — and armed with powerful techniques in morphogenesis (e.g., somatic mutation), neuroanatomy (e.g., cobalt chloride iontophoresis), and electrophysiology (e.g., single cell recording), the time is ripe for a concerted effort to answer the question: "How does the nervous system get itself together?"

CHAPTER THIRTEEN

Development of the Mauthner Cell

CHARLES B. KIMMEL and ROBERT C. EATON

INTRODUCTION

In this chapter we shall analyze the development of a single identified neuron in the vertebrate central nervous system as an integral and probably essential part of a simple neural network that underlies an identified component of behavior. Our purpose is to look broadly at a number of features that make up neural development and to bring together information and ideas from several avenues of inquiry. We shall also emphasize current research, posing questions to which there are as yet no answers, so that the reader will be able to see where present studies are leading. Literature citations are largely limited to recent articles and general reviews.

A single pair of enlarged neurons, termed "Mauthner cells" (M-cells), are present at the level of the ear in the hindbrain of many species of fish and amphibians. The morphological appearance of these cells in young larvae of two representative species, the zebra fish and the axolotl, is shown in Figure 1. M-cells are func-

tionally connected with several classes of afferent neurons, whose axons synapse on the M-cell body and on its large and ramified lateral and ventral dendrites. A major source of input consists of axons from the acousticovestibular and lateral line systems. These fibers appear to synapse specifically with the M-cell lateral dendrite (Figure 1). The ventral dendrite projects into systems of fibers that descend from more rostral centers in the brain.

The axon of the M-cell is also unusually large. It emerges from the hillock region of the cell body, where its initial segment is surrounded by a dense neuropile termed the "axon cap" (Figure 1). The axon crosses the midline of the brain and courses caudally through the hindbrain and the whole of the spinal cord. A major efferent connection of the M-cell is with spinal motoneurons, through collaterals of the M-cell axon (Figure 1).

The M-cell is thus an interneuron, and it is normally an essential component in the excitatory reflex pathway that underlies a rapid startle response. In this response the animal,

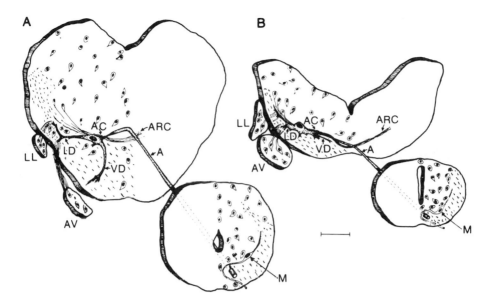

FIGURE 1. *Mauthner cell in young larvae of (A) the zebra fish,* Brachydanio rerio, *and (B) the axolotl,* Ambystoma mexicanum. *In each case, the drawings show transverse sections of the hindbrain, at the level of the M-cell bodies, and of the rostral spinal cord. Only the left M-cell is shown. The M-cell receives a major source of afferent excitatory connections through its lateral dendrite, LD, from axons of the acousticovestibular, AV, and lateral line, LL, systems. Its ventral dendrite, VD, connects with descending fibers. The M-cell is inhibited by synapses from arcuate, ARC, fibers in the axon cap, AC. Its axon, A, decussates and courses caudad into the spinal cord, where it effects excitatory connections with motoneurons, M, via collaterals. The M-cells were reconstructed from silver-stained paraffin serial sections, as described by Kimmel and Schabtach (1974) The dimension marker represents 25 μm for the drawing shown in (A) and 100 μm for that in (B).*

driven by vibratory stimulation, is rapidly displaced for a short distance through the water. Cinematographic records of adult and larval startle responses are shown in Figure 2. The major component of the behavior is a pronounced tail flip.

Synaptically connected and functional M-cells appear very early during development. This alleviates problems in a developmental analysis, for the system is not only phylogenetically primitive but also ontogenetically simplified.

In the following sections we examine different phases and features of M-cell development. Although studies have been carried out with several species, we have not emphasized species differences. The details that we discuss are peculiar to the M-cell system, but the problems raised are similar to those encoun-

tered in the development of any neuron. Study of the M-cell has served well as a model for other systems, and we believe that it will continue to yield useful general information applicable to neurogenesis.

ORIGIN OF THE M-CELL

During the late tailbud stage of development in the embryo a single cell in the mantle zone of each side of the hindbrain begins to enlarge and undergo a characteristic sequence of changes in shape, which culminates in the fully formed M-cell. Before the late tailbud stage there is no hint of any morphological specialization of cells in this region of the neural tube: they all have the appearance of simple epithelial cells, and many are undergoing

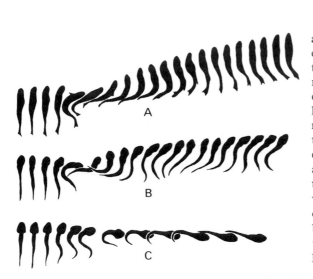

FIGURE 2. *Cinematographic records of startle responses to vibratory stimuli of (A) the adult zebra fish (about 30 mm in length), (B) the young larval zebra fish (about 4 mm), and (C) the young larval axolotl (about 14 mm). The series shown in (A) is from Kimmel, Patterson, and Kimmel (1974), and the methods are also described there. Frame-by-frame images are shown, with each image displaced a constant distance to the right in the drawing. In (A) and (B) the interval between frames is 6.7 msec. In (C) the interval is 10 msec; however, after the first six images, only every other one is shown.*

cycles of DNA synthesis and mitosis. However, although the cells look primitive and unspecialized, many of them have already undergone covert developmental changes that underlie later, particular types of specialization. Included in this population at the tailbud stage are the epithelial cells which will give rise to the M-cells.

Neurons do not divide but arise from dividing populations of germinal or stem cells (Jacobson, 1970). An early event in the developmental history of a neuron is its withdrawal from the cell division cycle. The time that this occurs — the "birthday" of the cell — has been shown to be determinate, such that distinctive populations of neurons have distinctive birthdays (Jacobson, 1970). An analysis of the birthday of the M-cell has recently been carried out by Vargas-Lizardi and Lyser (1974) for one

anuran species, *Xenopus laevis.* In this study, embryos received single injections of tritiated thymidine at discrete stages in early development and then were allowed to continue developing until the M-cell could be identified histologically. The thymidine selectively labels nuclei of cells that were replicating DNA while the thymidine was present in the system. The embryos were killed and the brains prepared for autoradiographic analysis. The analysis yielded the remarkable results that, if the thymidine were present during the *gastrula* stage of development, the M-cell nuclei were found later to be heavily labeled. If, however, the thymidine was not added until the early *neurula* stage or later, the M-cell nuclei were never labeled.

The interpretation of these data appears to be straightforward. The cells that will normally give rise to M-cells at a much later time cease DNA synthesis during the late gastrula stage of development. It has been shown that in *Xenopus* the M-cell contains the usual diploid amount of DNA (Billings and Swartz, 1969), and it follows that the prospective (i.e., undifferentiated) M-cells must enter cell division, probably shortly after their last replication of DNA. Evidence was provided in the birthday study that the pair of M-cells in an animal are not both daughter cells of the same final mitosis: the last division of a prospective M-cell must be an asymmetrical one, with respect to the later fate of the two daughters. Such a division must occur in at least two separate stem cells, each giving rise to one of the pair of M-cells that is found later.

These results suggest that a particular pair of cells have entered upon an M-cell developmental pathway at an exceedingly early time in development. One should now ask whether these cells are not *restricted* to this pathway, or if they can be made to abandon it and take up another. Embryological "determination," as we call this restriction, occurs according to the position of a cell in the embryo (see the following section), and a cell's position can be manipulated by microsurgery. Ideally one would like to be able to locate prospective M-cells early in development, excise these cells specifically, and reimplant them in a new position to see if they still gave rise to M-cells. This ideal test is presently impossible, because we lack precise knowledge of the positions of the prospective M-cells. Stefanelli (1952), however, removed small clusters of cells unilaterally from regions of the *Xenopus* embryo which were expected to contain prospective M-cells, and he allowed these clusters of cells to develop in isolation from the rest of the nervous system. He found that neurons developed in fragments isolated from embryos as early as the gastrula stage. However, only in cell clusters isolated from the early neurula, or from later stages, did an enlarged neuron develop which he recognized as an M-cell. This finding indicated that M-cell determination occurs about the time of, or very shortly after, the last division of a prospective M-cell. The timetable appears to be similar in salamanders: Jacobson (1964) has reported evidence that in the axolotl the M-cell is determined at least as early as the midneurula stage. It may well be more than coincidental that the time of M-cell determination is near that of the last mitosis, for Jacobson (1968b) has reported a similar correlation in the case of neurons in the retina.

The appropriate positions of the prospective M-cells in the neural plate of the midneurula, as discovered in these experiments, is shown in Figure 3B. Morphogenetic movements of cells in early stages of the embryo are well known (Jacobson, 1970), and Jacobson (1959) has constructed accurate maps of the prospective fates of cells in the neural plate. These make it possible to construct a sequence, shown in Figure 3, of locations of prospective M-cells from the late gastrula (or indeed earlier than this!) through tailbud stages, after which the M-cells begin to enlarge and can thus be recognized directly by their morphology. These maps indicate that prospective M-cells do not undergo any extensive migrations but move little, if at all, with respect to their neighboring cells. This is typical of other kinds of neurons in simple nervous systems.

MECHANISM OF DETERMINATION

As stated above, determination of cells occurs according to their positions within the embryo; this is a cardinal rule. Embryonic cells, transplanted surgically to a new location in the embryo before they become determined, specialize in accordance with cells in their new environment. Such systems are said to show "regulative" development, and the early prospective neural tissue of fish and amphibians is an excellent example of a regulative system.

Stefanelli's experiment (see the previous section) provided evidence that the prospective M-cell regulates its development if it is removed from its usual location in the gastrula, but if taken from the early neurula it no longer regulates. It is of considerable interest that the donor embryos, which provided the isolates at both of these stages, were often found to have a normal pair of M-cells (Stefanelli, 1952). This

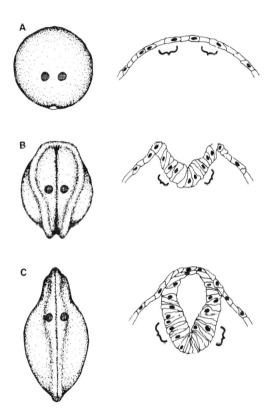

FIGURE 3. *Approximate positions of the pair of prospective M-cells in axolotl embryos, at (A) the late gastrula, (B) the midneurula, and (C) the early tailbud stage of development. M-cell positions are shown as crosshatched areas in the dorsal views of the embryos on the left. The drawings on the right are diagrams of a transverse cut through the ectoderm at the level of the M-cells. Curly brackets indicate the approximate M-cell positions.*

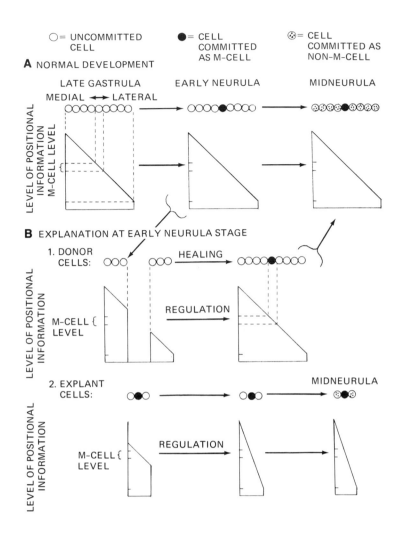

FIGURE 4.   *Application of Wolpert's theory to M-cell determination. For this treatment, which is entirely hypothetical, we consider a row of prospective neural cells (circles), at the rostrocaudal level of the M-cell, and extending from the midline laterally. We assume that by the late gastrula stage there is established a linear gradient of positional information for specification of cell type along this axis. Another gradient must exist in the rostrocaudal axis, but this is ignored here. During normal development (A) an uncommitted cell (open circle) interprets an intermediate level of positional information to become determined as an M-cell (black circle) at the early neurula stage. Cells that receive higher or lower levels of positional information become determined at the* midneurula *stage to be neuron types other than M-cells (dotted circles). Notice that the gradient does not change during this period. In (B), an experimental case, a group of cells is removed from the prospective M-cell region at the early neurula stage. In this case both the explant and the operated side of the embryo may produce an M-cell (Stefanelli, 1952). With respect to the donor embryo, healing of the wound occurs, and the cells interact to reestablish the usual gradient (regulation). An uncommitted cell is determined to be an M-cell, as noted above. Regulation might also occur in the isolate, such that the original boundaries could be reestablished in this smaller field of cells. The isolate contains a determined M-cell from the outset.*

shows that another cell left in the embryo regulated *its* development, in this case to form an M-cell. Probably this cell had migrated into the usual M-cell position in the neural plate during wound healing. This result was not obtained if the isolates were taken from the midneurula or later stages. The isolates, in such cases, contained an M-cell, but now an M-cell was absent on the operated side of the donor, although healing of the wound was normal. Some change had taken place within a few hours of the time of M-cell determination. The nature of this change is not known.

Wolpert (1969, 1971) recently proposed an important and very general theory which helps us see the problems involved in the question of how position influences determination. The theory postulates two separate mechanisms. First, there is a mechanism of position *signaling*, which occurs within a group of cells related by their proximity (a "field" of cells). Second, and operating in individual cells, is a mechanism of *interpretation* of this positional information. For proper determination a cell must both receive correct positional information and interpret it correctly. These two mechanisms can, in some cases, be studied independently from one another.

In a variety of systems (Wolpert, 1971), including the nervous system (Cooke, 1972; see also Meinhardt and Gierer, 1974), it can be shown that positional information appears to vary continuously across a field of interacting cells — that is, there is a gradient of positional information. A cell could thus compute its position in the field by determining the local level of the gradient of positional information, if boundary values remain fixed. In Figure 4 we show how this theory might be applied to M-cell determination.

A simple way to generate a gradient of positional information is by diffusion, between a source and a sink, of some informational molecule (e.g., a hormone). Thus a gradient of positional information, which is an abstract concept, could in reality be a chemical gradient (Crick, 1970; McMahon, 1974). In this context it is extremely interesting to note that embryonic cells undergoing determination have been found to be *coupled* to one another *via* gap junctions, which permit passage of smaller molecules between cells with very low imped-

ance (Bennett, 1973). This is true of the neural plate of the chick embryo (Sheridan, 1968), where, in the early neurula, cells are coupled to one another, as well as to the underlying mesoderm, which is thought to transmit positional information to the neural cells during embryonic "induction" (see Jacobson, 1970). Another interesting case is the retina, in which the cells are coupled to one another until the time of determination, when this coupling disappears (Dixon and Cronly-Dillon, 1972). Techniques are available for the study of the detailed history of such junctions between cells in the vicinity of and including the prospective M-cells, and this sort of study might be a productive beginning in learning the chemical cues that underlie its determination.

It is important to recognize that, although Wolpert's theory suggests chemical mechanisms, such as diffusion, it is not built from them and thus not dependent on any chemical mechanisms. It could well be that the chemical events in position signaling will turn out to be a good deal more complex than those in chemical diffusion but still follow the simple rules of Wolpert's theory.

Whatever the mechanisms that underlie position signaling and determination, a feature revealed in the M-cell system is the fidelity of these processes. We have examined several hundred zebra fish larvae, by visual observation of the M-cell axons (see Figure 9A), and have never observed an error in the number of cells present; we always see the usual pair. However, errors are more frequent in amphibian species, and unilaterally duplicated M-cells are sometimes observed. In *Xenopus* they occur at an estimated frequency of 2 percent (Vargas-Lizardi and Lyser, 1974).

DIFFERENTIATION

The changes during which a simple epithelial cell is transformed into a giant M-neuron fall under the general heading of "differentiation." These changes, once begun, occur rapidly during the late stages of embryonic development, such that in several species the hatched larva contains mature M-cells (see Eaton and Farley, 1973; Figure 5). After the time of hatching, M-cell growth and shape changes

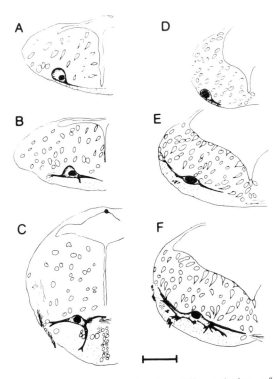

growth, to emphasize that the two phases are probably under very different kinds of control. A final series of dramatic degenerative changes occurs in the M-cell in anurans near the time of metamorphosis (Moulton, Jurand, and Fox, 1968). These lead to the cell's regression in the adult forms of these species.

When first identifiable because of its size, the M-cell has lost its epithelial form and occupies a position in the periphery of the neural tube. Both in the zebra fish (Figure 5A), and the axolotl (Figure 5D), it is already a monopolar neuron, oriented at right angles to the long axis of the embryo, with its neurite extending toward the midline among the very few fibers present at this stage (Eaton and Farley, 1973; Leghissa, 1941). This neurite will give rise to the M-cell axon. After a few hours, in the axolotl, the lateral dendrite begins to form as a second neurite oriented in the opposite direction (Leghissa, 1941; Figure 5E). Such a bipolar stage is also present in a number of species, including *Xenopus* (Billings, 1972) and the bullhead, *Ictalurus nebulosus* (Armstrong and Higgins, 1971). In the zebra fish the lateral and ventral dendrites appear at about the same time (Eaton and Farley, 1973; Figure 5B).

When the M-cell is first identifiable, its cytoplasm does not yet contain the oriented neurofibrillar material of the mature neuron but is homogeneous and basophilic. In the young bipolar cell of *Xenopus* the cytoplasm is packed with free ribosomes (Billings, 1972), which is a general characteristic of enlarging embryonic cells. Later, when dendritic ramification begins (Figure 5B and D), neurofibrillar material appears, and becomes abundant in the perinuclear area and in adjoining regions of the dendrites. In *Xenopus*, this reorganization is revealed both as extensive growth of the endoplasmic reticulum, which is sparse in younger cells, and by formation of cytoplasmic channels that contain microfilaments and microtubules (Billings, 1972).

Continued outgrowth of the M-cell axon occurs at the same time that these changes are occurring in the cell body and dendrites. In the axolotl (where development is relatively slow), the period of elongation is over 2 to 3 days. Leghissa (1941) was able to measure this period by identifying the swollen growth cone at the tip of the elongating axon. In the zebra fish,

FIGURE 5. *Stages in the differentiation of the M-cell in the zebra fish (A–C) and the axolotl (D–F). The drawings show outlines of half of a transverse section of the hindbrain and projections of the M-cell at successive stages of development: (A and D) the monopolar stage; (B and E) an intermediate stage; (C and F) the fully differentiated cell at the time of hatching (compare with Figure 1). Paraffin sections were stained either with the Rowell silver method (B and C) or with the Mallory triple stain (A, D–F). Photographs of the cells shown in (A) and (B) have been published (Eaton and Farley, 1973). The M-cell in serial transverse sections was traced with the aid of a camera lucida and the tracings stacked to give the projections shown. The stages are, for the zebra fish developing at 25°, (A) 40 hours; (B) 58 hours; (C) 98 hours; and, for the axolotl, (D) Harrison stage 36; (E) stage 38; (F) stage 42. The marker bar represents 43 μm (A–C) or 100 μm (D–F).*

continue. These are coordinated with the growth of the larval nervous system. Billings (1972) has termed the phase of differentiation as a period of "seeking" growth of the M-cell and the larval phase a period of "additive" elongation is more rapid, in keeping with the smaller size and faster development of this embryo, and is completed within about one day. The axon is initially very thin, and, after elongating, there is a rapid increase in its diameter, to a size of about 5 μm (Kimmel, 1972). Myelination occurs during this latter phase of axonal development.

SYNAPTOGENESIS

The M-cells are connected with a rich supply of synaptic knobs. These are diverse in structure and function, and arise from neurons at different locations within the central and peripheral nervous system. The knobs have been the subject of detailed study. Early light-micrographic descriptions, culminating with the classical study of Bodian (1937) of the fish, have been extended more recently to the ultrastructural level in fish (Robertson, Bodenheimer, and Stage, 1963; Nakajima, 1974) and amphibians (Kimmel and Schabtach, 1974).

An example of this diversity is shown in Figure 6, which compares two of the morphological types in the axolotl. The type in (A) arise from thin axons, and the synaptic knobs are swollen and twisted interconnected bulbs, exceedingly rich in synaptic vesicles. In (B), the knobs arise from axons nearly as large in diameter as the knobs themselves, and the synaptic vesicles are concentrated near their surfaces. These "club" synapses in (B) are restricted to the lateral dendritic surfaces of the M-cell (in the axolotl), whereas the large bulbs in (A) are largely localized in the axon cap, and connect with the initial segment of the M-cell axon and the adjoining axon hillock region of the M-cell. The origin of these two types is different. The axon cap synapses arise from neurons whose axons contribute to the system of arcuate fibers (Figure 1). The club synapses arise from cells in the peripheral ganglia of the acousticovestibular and lateral line nerves ipsilateral to the M-cell (Figure 1).

Some of the morphologically distinct types of synapses on the M-cell are also distinctive in their function (Nakajima, 1974). For example, in the fish, the club synapses on the lateral dendrite are the site of a strong, mixed electrical and chemical excitatory connection

(Diamond, 1971), and the axon cap is the source of a unique electrical inhibitory action on M-cell spike initiation (Furukawa and Furshpan, 1963; Faber and Korn, 1973; see Figure 9A).

When the young M-cell is first identifiable in tailbud embryos, it probably has not yet formed synaptic connections. Leghissa's thorough study with the light microscope (1941) revealed that in the axolotl the connections from various sources of input to the M cell appear during the period of the cell's differentiation. The first connections he recognized were those of ipsilateral acousticovestibular axons on the M-cell lateral dendrite at the stage when the cell is bipolar (Figure 5E). Presumably these fibers give rise to the club synapses discussed above. Later, other classes of fibers connect with other regions of the cell. From Leghissa's study, and from studies on fish (Eaton and Farley, 1973; Armstrong and Higgins, 1971), there appears to be a close correspondence in time between when a particular dendrite is formed and begins to ramify and when its first synaptic connections are encountered. Furthermore, these studies provide evidence that no extensive rearrangements of synaptic connections occur once they have been formed. Fibers from various sources might form stable connections in the region of the M-cell of their initial contacts.

Almost nothing is known about the development of the axonal connections of the M-cell itself. An extremely interesting proposal (Leghissa, 1941) is that the axonal collaterals originate from extensions of the axonal growth cone during the phase of axon elongation. This hypothesis remains untested.

A question of major interest in developmental neurobiology deals with the mechanisms that surround the emergence of orderly patterns of synaptically connected neurons in the brain. Currently many systems are being examined in a search for a general set of underlying principles (Gaze, 1970; Jacobson, 1970). In the M-cell system, and especially with reference to the afferent connections, we see synaptic ordering at the level of a single cell. This could be due to regional positional "specifications," in molecular terms, of the M-cell, such that for example the acousticovestibular fibers could recognize the lateral dendrite speci-

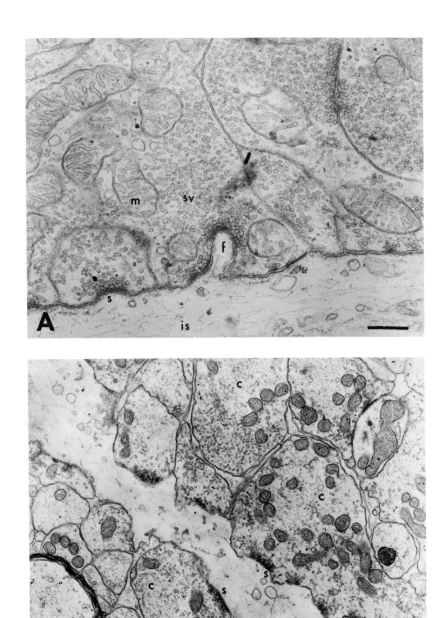

FIGURE 6. *Electron micrographs of synaptic knobs connecting with the M-cell in the young larval axolotl (stage 45; from Kimmel and Schabtach, 1974). (A) The twisted bulbs of the axon cap, which give rise to synapses, s, with the M-cell axon initial segment, is. The bulbs contain mitochondria, m, and are rich in synaptic vesicles, sv. Finger-like projections, f, increase the area of synaptic contact between the M-cell axon and this neuropil. The marker bar indicates 0.5 μm. (B) The large synaptic clubs, c, which connect with a dorsal process of the M-cell lateral dendrite, dld. Synaptic vesicles are peripherally located in the clubs, outside of radially arranged mitochondria. The bar indicates 1.0 μm.*

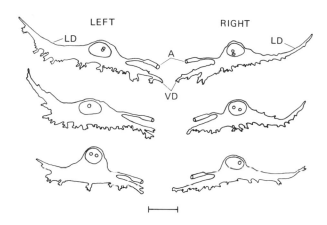

FIGURE 7.   Effect of removal of the ear on the size of the M-cell lateral dendrite. The drawings show the left and right M-cells from three of a series of experimental animals from which the right otic vesicle was removed in the late embryo (stage 34). The animals were killed 10 days later (development at 22°, stage 45), and the M-cells reconstructed from 5-μm epon sections, as described by Kimmel and Schabtach (1974). The drawings show projections, in approximately the transverse plane. Only the proximal portions of the finer dendritic branches are shown. A, M-cell axon; LD, lateral dendrite; VD, ventral dendrite. The marker indicates 50 μm.

fically. It may also be that the order is achieved without such a high degree of molecular recognition (see Kimmel and Schabtach, 1974). At present, the basis for patterning provides another focus for experimental work.

INTERACTIONS DURING DIFFERENTIATION

M-cells experimentally produced in abnormal environments are often misshapen and smaller than normal (Stefanelli, 1952). This suggests that normally there are interactions of the developing M-cells with their environment, both cellular and otherwise, during the period of differentiation, and that these result in an M-cell of normal morphology.

A most intriguing phenomenon related to this suggestion was discovered by Piatt in the salamander *Ambystoma maculatum*. He removed an otic vesicle from midtailbud embryos and found that the M-cell was absent on the same side of the brain, in one-fourth to one-third of a large series of experimental animals (Piatt, 1969, 1971). It is not known why all the animals did not respond similarly; this divergence could be due to genetic differ-ences among the embryos. The phenomenon itself is very unusual — since determination of the M-cell is completed well before the time that the operations were carried out. Piatt attributed the effect to the absence of the acousticovestibular nerve roots in these embryos (which are derived from the otic vesicle during subsequent development). It could also be that the interaction between the M-cell and cells of the otic vesicle itself during the tailbud period are essential for maintenance of the prospective M-cell.

Another role of the ear has recently been found (Kimmel, unpublished results). Otic vesicles were removed from one side of axolotl embryos at the late tailbud stage. After a period of development the ipsilateral M-cell was usually present but showed a characteristic change in its appearance. As compared with M-cells in normal animals, or with those on the contralateral (normal) side of the experimental animals, the M-cell lateral dendrite was thinner and ramified less extensively. Examples are shown in Figure 7. The acousticovestibular axons that normally connect with this dendrite were absent, or present in very reduced numbers here. This finding suggests that growth of the lateral dendrite is stimulated by interactions

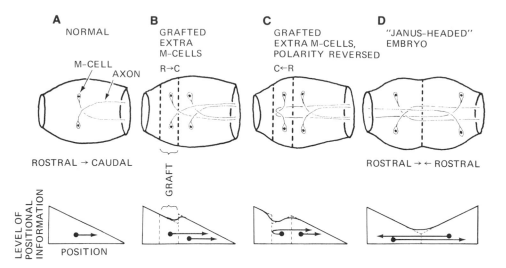

FIGURE 8. *Course of M-cell axons in (A) normal embryos, (B and C) the experimental embryos produced by Hibbard (1965), and (D) the experimental embryos produced by Swisher and Hibbard (1967). In (B) and (C) R = rostral; C = caudal. The figure is explained in the text.*

with the ingrowing fibers. Similar phenomena have recently been observed of other types of neurons (Globus and Scheibel, 1967; Kelly and Cowan, 1972; Murphey et al., 1975).

We have seen that dendritic growth and ramification during M-cell differentiation is correlated in time with the appearance of synaptic connections. It may be that many phases of the cell's morphogenesis are regulated *via* interactions with groups of growing fibers. More extensive experimental testing of this suggestion remains to be carried out.

Interactions between the M-cell and its environment have also been revealed in a number of experimental studies of the pathway through the central nervous system traversed by the M-cell axon. For example, the usual caudad course of the axon appears to be environmentally controlled. Hibbard (1965) grafted an extra section of hindbrain (containing prospective M-cell) just rostrad to the normal level of the M-cell. These operations were carried out in early tailbud embryos and the salamander *Pleurodeles waltlii*. The grafts were placed in either normal or reversed rostrocaudal orientation. The courses taken by the M-cell axons after a period of development were analyzed in sectioned material, and the results are diagrammed in Figure 8. The first drawing (A) shows

the course in the normal animal. The axons, after crossing the midline, coursed caudally. In animals bearing grafts with normal polarity (Figure 8B), both sets of axons showed the same course, even though the grafted pair have had to traverse an abnormal region of hindbrain tissue, rostrad to the host's own pair of cells. When polarity of the graft was reversed (see Figure 8C), the host axons took the usual course, but those in the graft initially take a course rostrad (i.e. in accordance with the polarity of the grafted tissue itself). Near the junction between the graft and rostral host tissue these axons abruptly turned about and coursed caudally, now in accordance with polarity of the host.

This finding shows clearly that the growing axons are responsive to directional cues in the environment, such that in the last example they reversed direction rather than proceeding rostrally against the polarity of the host tissue. As in our discussion of M-cell determination, we can think of these results in terms of gradients of positional information, to see if a set of consistent rules that explain axonal guidance can be derived (see the lower drawings in Figure 8). In the normal case (A) we can imagine that the axon follows the gradient "downhill." This rule is obeyed in the first experimental situation (B), and, further, we see that the axon can cross a discontinuous region (at the caudal end of the graft) without interrupting its course. In (C), after an initial downhill course, the axon arrives at a position where it can no longer obey the downhill rule: it can only go uphill. We can imagine that the axon, on reversing its direction, chooses the lesser of two "evils" — it appears to grow against the gradient of smaller slope.

Another situation was produced in the experiments of Swisher and Hibbard (1967). They grafted rostral halves of *Xenopus* tailbud embryos together to create monsters with two opposite heads and no tail ("Janus"-headed embryos; Figure 8D). More than 70 percent of M-cell axons in such embryos, after growing in accordance with the polarity in their immediate environment, crossed the grafted region and ascended past the opposite M-cell to terminate in the opposite head! Analysis of these results is perhaps more amusing than instructive. The rule that seems to emerge is: "If you can't beat 'em, join 'em."

In considering the results of these two sets of experiments, and also in experiments not discussed here (Jacobson, 1964; Stefanelli, 1952), we see that the simple gradient model *in itself* is not very useful. There is simply not enough experimental information about the nature of the polarity and the responses of the growing axon to its environment. A model is useful only insofar as it helps us to understand the experiments and show direction for future research. What is needed is a careful analysis of when directional cues are present in the environment, how stable these cues are in the experimental situations, and how sensitive the growing axon is to such cues.

FUNCTION DURING DEVELOPMENT

From recent studies on the zebra fish, it seems clear that the precocious determination and differentiation of the M-cell is a consequence of the fact that the cell plays a significant functional role in behavior of the embryo (Eaton and Farley, in preparation). Thus the system serves also as a model for studies in the ontogeny of behavior. Not only is the M-cell morphologically identifiable, but, as will be seen here, it is identifiable physiologically, and the behavior that it mediates during embryonic development is distinctive.

At the time of hatching, the zebra fish is only 3.4 mm in length and is nearly transparent. The M-axons can be visualized, under the compound microscope, if the embryo is embedded at the surface of a drop of gelatin (Figure 9A). This permits visual placement of microelectrodes for recording (Figure 9B). The animal has no difficulty obtaining oxygen by diffusion, and it can be maintained under these conditions for hours (Eaton and Farley, 1975). As in the adult fish (Furshpan and Furukawa, 1962), the larval M-cell produces a characteristic field potential that is readily identified in the extracellular record (Figure 9B). The relatively large amplitude of the spike allows placement of the electrode at a distance from the cell while still detecting the response.

The M-cell mediates startle responses of both adult (Diamond, 1971) and young larval (Eaton and Farley, 1975) fishes. Cinematographic analysis reveals some quantitative differences in these responses of the adults and larvae, but the latencies are similar and the net result of the behavior is the same: the adult and larva both move one body length in less than 100 msec after the stimulus (Kimmel, Patterson, and Kimmel, 1974; Figure 2). In electrophysiological experiments, the unanesthetized larva is capable of an appreciable amount of movement when embedded in gelatin. During the startle response, movements monitored with a phototransducer are quite similar in time course to those seen in free-swimming animals that are responding to a similar stimulus (Figure 10). In records such as in Figure 10, the M-cell fires only at the beginning of the response and does not appear to be involved in iterative movements of the tail which often follow the initial contraction of the contralateral trunk and tail musculature. These movements are rarely seen unless the M-cell fires first. Thus, in addition to mediating the initial tail flexion, the M-cell appears to act functionally as a "trigger cell" in much the same way as is seen in invertebrate systems, where certain cells initiate fixed action patterns (Willows, 1973) but play no role in the oscillatory mechanisms that subserve the behavior. In zebra fish, the cells that mediate this later

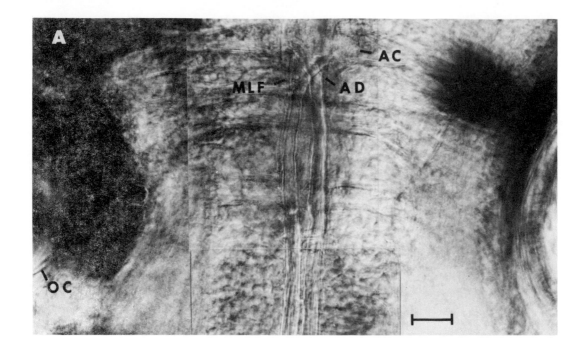

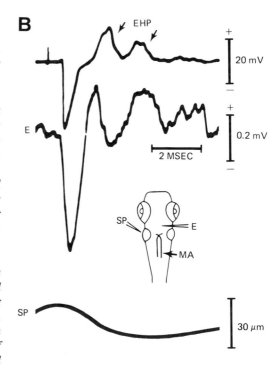

FIGURE 9. (A) Montage of photomicrographs (from Kimmel, 1972) of the living M-cell axons as they appear in experiments such as in (B). The micrographs were made by H. M. Howard, with Nomarski illumination, of a medaka (Oryzias latipes) larva, 14 days old. The axonal decussation, AD, is seen in the hindbrain at the level of the otic capsules, OC. The axon cap, AC, is also visible, as well as the much smaller fibers of the medial longitudinal fasciculus, MLF. The dimension marker equals 20 μm. (B) Comparison of the extracellular Mauthner cell potential in the adult goldfish (upper trace, from Furukawa and Furshpan, 1963) and in a larval zebra fish (middle trace, from Eaton and Farley, 1975). For the zebra fish recording, the drawing shows the M-cell axons, MA, the position of the recording microelectrode, E, and the stimulus probe, SP, which correspond to the middle and bottom traces, respectively. The stimulus consisted of an axial excursion of the glass probe positioned against the otic capsule. The positive potentials in the upper trace, EHP, are produced by neighboring cells with terminals in the axon cap. The EHP can block the M-cell spike without a concomitant change in its membrane conductance.

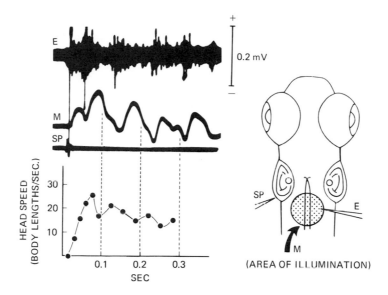

FIGURE 10.   Comparison of the startle responses in a free-swimming zebra fish (graph from Kimmel, Patterson, and Kimmel, 1974), and one restrained for electrophysiological recording (upper three traces from Eaton and Farley, 1975). The recording was made as in Figure 9A, but with the electrode, E, in the spinal cord (see drawing) and displayed at a higher gain and a slower sweep speed (indicated by the abscissa on the graph). Animal movements (trace M) were detected with a photocell placed in the optical system of the microscope. The excursion of the stimulus probe is indicated by the trace marked SP. In this recording the M-cell spike was approximately 0.4 mV, or twice the size evident in the record. The graph shows the relationship between head speed and time following a tactile stimulus. The data points were obtained from a cinematographic record.

function appear to be located in the hindbrain in the vicinity of the M-cell (Eaton and Farley, 1975).

Early development of behavior in the zebra fish (Eaton and Farley, 1973; Kimmel, Patterson, and Kimmel, 1974) is similar to that described for other species of teleost fish and amphibians (e.g., Coghill, 1929; Armstrong and Higgins, 1971) and appears to fit the general model of ontogeny of behavior proposed by Armstrong and Higgins (1971). This model was formulated on the basis of histological observations and of experiments that involved the stimulation and transection of the brain of the bullhead. According to this hypothesis, there are three distinct stages of "encephalization" in which regulatory control of swimming is progressively shifted from the spinal cord to the hindbrain and finally the midbrain. The model

relies heavily on the concept of M-cell mediation of swimming behavior, though, as mentioned above, this is unlikely in the zebra fish.

In the zebra fish, the spinal phase of motor control occurs toward the end of the first day of development (Kimmel, Patterson, and Kimmel, 1974), and it is characterized by spontaneous lateral contractions of the rostral myotomes, a behavior that later involves the entire trunk and tail. Before the end of the second day of development the spontaneous contractions become infrequent, but they consist of substantially faster side-to-side movements, which can result in some forward displacement of the animal. These movements are considered to be the precursor of swimming behavior (Coghill, 1929). It is possible that some components of this early behavior are mediated through epithelial conduction, as has

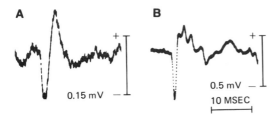

FIGURE 11.   Comparison of the extracellular M-cell spikes produced by the zebra fish at (A) 47 and (B) 99 h of development. The experiment was performed as in Figure 9A. In each case the electrode was placed at a constant distance from the M-cell to ensure recordings from the same region of the extracellular field.

been demonstrated in work on amphibians (Macklin and Wojtokowski, 1973; Muntz, 1964; Roberts, 1971).

The hindbrain phase begins at two days of development in the zebra fish (Kimmel, Patterson, and Kimmel, 1974). During the second day tactile stimulation elicits a sudden contraction of the tail, a behavior sometimes followed by iterative swimming movements. At this stage an M-cell spike can be elicited by vibratory stimulation of the body surface, and recorded (Eaton and Farley, in preparation; Figure 11). As the embryo develops, the initial contraction increases in strength, and the swimming movements begin to carry the animal several body lengths from the point of stimulation.

As seen in Figure 11, the embryonic M-cell spike is considerably smaller in amplitude and longer in duration than that recorded even at 4 days of development when the animal has hatched. This suggests that during the period between 2 and 4 days there is considerable maturation of the spike-generating mechanism of the cell membrane. It is also during the second day of development (Figure 5B) that the ventral and lateral dendrites have been first identified in light micrographs of the cell (Eaton and Farley, 1973). It appears that there are functional synapses on the M-cell even at these early stages of M-cell development, and perhaps from the very beginning of, or before, the formation of dendrites.

Zebra fish embryos begin to hatch during the hindbrain phase of development. Hatching

behavior probably involves M-cell activation in this species; tactile stimulation with a fine glass filament through the chorion elicits a strong tailflip, which can cause the chorion to rupture, allowing the embryo to escape (Eaton and Farley, 1973).

The midbrain phase of development begins at about 4 days of development, and is characterized by pronounced increases in the behavioral capabilities of the animal. The M-cell can now mediate acoustic (Eaton and Farley, 1973; Kimmel, Patterson, and Kimmel, 1974) as well as tactile startle reflexes. In addition, the animal is capable of spontaneous and sustained swimming, whereas, previously, swimming usually occurred only in response to stimulation. It is also at this stage that the zebra fish first uses its visual system in the capture of protozoa (Eaton and Farley, 1974).

Prior to the fourth day of development it is possible repetitively to elicit M-cell spikes by orthodromic sensory stimulation at rates of one per second. After the fourth day, though, it becomes progressively more difficult to elicit the M-cell spike repetitively, and the animals respond only to the first few of a series of stimuli. As seen in Table I, this failure to respond is not due to a developmental increase in response threshold, which does not change significantly during this time. Neither is it due to fatigue, since the inhibition can be overcome by increasing the stimulus intensity or by injecting strychnine (Eaton and Farley, in preparation). It is therefore due to an active inhibitory process which becomes functional during the fourth day of development. It is not yet known whether this inhibition originates in the midbrain, or from M-cell collaterals, which are thought to inhibit the cell in adult fish (Furukawa and Furshpan, 1963). However, the observations are consistent with the Armstrong—Higgins model, which, for the midbrain phase of development, predicts increased inhibition of M-cell mediated behavior.

CONCLUSIONS

We have seen that the known events surrounding the development of the M-cell occur within two discrete blocks of time during embryonic development. The first of these two times, revealed in studies of amphibians, is an interval of a few hours in the late gastrula—early neurula stages, during which epithelial cells are produced that have undergone embryonic *determination* toward an M-cell pathway of development. It now appears that the mechanisms underlying determination are extremely general ones, employed for any differentiated cell type in the animal.

The prospective M-cells stop DNA synthesis and cell division, evidently as a part of M-cell determination. This is followed by a "silent" interval, during which the cells neither divide nor differentiate.

The second interval of time is in the late embryo and marks the period of M-cell *differentiation*. During this time the M-cell becomes greatly enlarged, its axon and dendrites appear, and the cell acquires its definitive shape. The young M-cell shows a primary polarity, in that it is oriented at right angles to the major axis of the embryo. This simple geometry, as well as the secondary caudad course taken by its axon, suggests that the M-cell is responsive to axial gradients of positional information early during the period of its differentiation. Indeed, in certain experimental situations, the growing M-cell axon can be shown to be responsive to the polarity of its environment.

Differentiation of neurons that will give rise to synaptic connections with the M-cell also occurs during the interval of M-cell differentiation, and the growth of axons from these cells into the area occupied by the M-cell occurs simultaneously with the development of the M-cell dendrites. This correlation suggests that developmental interactions occur between the axons and the M-cell dendrites, which stimulate the latter to grow and ramify. This hypothesis is supported by experimental analysis.

In the zebra fish, the only species in which early M-cell function has been directly studied, M-cell action potentials can be recognized early in the period of the cell's differentiation, about the time that the M-cell dendrites appear and that neurofibrillar material is first seen in its cytoplasm. The spike can be obtained at this stage by orthodromic sensory stimulation, indicating that functional synapses are present. It appears weaker in the extracellular records than it will be later and matures during the latter part of the cell's differentiation. The functional maturation of the M-cell in the embryo is

TABLE I

DEVELOPMENT OF INHIBITORY CONTROL OF THE M-CELL STARTLE REFLEX.[a] THE EXPERIMENT WAS PERFORMED AS IN FIGURE 9B. ANIMALS IN THE HINDBRAIN AND MIDBRAIN PHASES OF DEVELOPMENT (14 ANIMALS EACH) WERE GIVEN TWO GROUPS OF FIVE TACTILE STIMULI AT INTERVALS OF 0.2 SECOND. THE DIFFERENCE IN THE NUMBER OF M-CELL RESPONSES IN THE TWO PHASES OF DEVELOPMENT IS HIGHLY SIGNIFICANT, WHEREAS THE THRESHOLD TO EVOKE AN M-SPIKE DID NOT CHANGE.

	Mean number of responses per animal	Number of animals	Mean stimulus threshold (μm)	Number of animals
Hindbrain phase, 2 to 4.5 days	8.50	14	12.0	14
Midbrain phase, 4.5 to 7 days	4.57	14	13.3	14
Probability of difference (t-test)	<0.005		>0.45	

[a] Eaton and Farley, in preparation.

closely tied to emerging patterns of behavior, and near the end of the cell's differentiation there is seen a marked functional change, indicated by active inhibition of the cell following repeated sensory stimulation. The change might be underlain by the appearance, during development, of new synaptic connections of the M-cells.

These studies of M-cell development show that a series of cell—cell or cell—environment interactions must occur during development to produce in the brain a single pair of cells that are of proper size, position, orientation, and shape; that are properly connected with other neurons; and that function correctly. The experimental work, however, is now incomplete, and some of these interactions are only suggested and not critically demonstrated. Other interactions could be more carefully defined, in terms of their components, and when they occur in development. Furthermore, nothing is known of the chemical and genetic mechanisms that underlie M-cell development. These will provide most interesting topics for study in the future.

CHAPTER FOURTEEN

Development of Function
in Nerve Nets

ROBERT R. PROVINE

INTRODUCTION

Developmental neurobiology is emerging as a major force in such diverse areas of neuroscience as anatomy and behavior. This interest is due in part to the fact that enthusiasts include both those primarily interested in neurogenesis and a growing group of individuals concerned with the application of such developmental methods as transplantation and tissue culture to basically nondevelopmental problems. Others are in search of a "simple" immature system to model some aspect of the adult. In the words of Ramón y Cajal (1937), "Since the full grown forest turns out to be impenetrable and undefinable, why not revert to the study of the young wood, in the nursery stage?" (p. 324). Students of such often-mentioned "simple" systems as invertebrates or tissue culture have equally diverse concerns; some are interested in the systems in their own right, whereas others see in them ideal models for some supposedly more complex and elusive process found elsewhere. The properties of invertebrates or developing organisms as models for other systems will not be emphasized here. Instead, behavior development and its neuronal bases will be evaluated in vertebrates and invertebrates. This approach, which is that of behavioral embryology, represents one of several different approaches to the development of function in nerve nets.

Behavioral embryology is both "naturalistic" and interdisciplinary. Throughout its relatively short history, it has emphasized viewing events, be they anatomical, physiological, or behavioral, *in vivo* or *in vitro*, within the framework of normal development *in situ* (Gottlieb, 1973; Oppenheim, 1974). The multidisciplinary emphasis accords with the example set by one of the pioneers in the field, George Ellett Coghill, in his now classic text *Anatomy and the Problem of Behavior* (1929). A common strategy begins by making behavioral observations to define the phenomenon to be studied and to determine critical periods to be examined in detail with higher resolution but more labor-intensive anatomical or electrophysiological procedures in an effort to specify mechanism. In this chapter, I shall try to remain within the bounds of the multi-disciplinary tradition of behavioral embryology and consider the development of movement from several different perspectives which sample widely the range of problems and variety of techniques that can be brought to bear upon the developing organism and its nervous system. Each topic (vertebrates, invertebrates, tissue culture) represents an analysis carried out at a different level of system complexity.

BEHAVIOR DEVELOPMENT
IN THE CHICK

The embryo of the domestic chicken provides an ideal object for developmental study. Eggs are easy to obtain and maintain and the embryos are large and hardy enough to permit dramatic experimental manipulation. The embryos are well suited for behavior analysis because they can be observed undisturbed through windows made in the shell. Another advantage is that the chick embryo is a traditional object for developmental study, which means that considerable supporting physiological, biochemical, anatomical, and behavioral evidence already exists. For these reasons, the chick embryo was selected as a representative vertebrate embryo against which we can compare other vertebrate and invertebrate findings.

There is generally good agreement concerning the course of behavior development of the chick embryo between the onset of movement at 3 to 4 days of incubation through hatching at 21 days (Preyer, 1885; Visintini and Levi-Montalcini, 1939; Hamburger, 1963; Hamburger and Oppenheim, 1967). The earliest movements are slight lateral flexions of the head. Other body regions become active later, in cephalocaudal order. With an increased participation of the trunk musculature, the early nodding movements give way to S-shaped flexions of the entire body. These rather slow flexions can be initiated in any region of the axial musculature and pass either rostrally or caudally, or they can be initiated in midtrunk regions and propagate in both directions simultaneously. At about 6 to 6½ days, the limbs

begin to move, trunk movements become more complex and the early wave patterns are replaced by generalized motility, which seems to involve all body parts capable of movement. In these last stages, body parts tend to be coactive, although they do not twitch in synchrony or show any particular ordering of movement. After the early wave movements break up, behavior becomes jerky and often convulsive-like, assuming what we shall call Type I pattern of movement (after the system of Hamburger and Oppenheim, 1967), which is most common up to 17 days. Thereafter, the jerky movements are interspersed with a qualitatively different pattern of smooth prehatching and hatching behaviors (Type III) which seem to involve the coordinated activity of different body parts. These late-appearing movements are the first to be immediately identifiable as similar in character to the normal awake behavior of the posthatch chick. Changes in the frequency and temporal distribution of embryonic motility also take place during development. The frequency of movement increases from its beginning up to a peak around 13 days, after which it declines (Figure 1). Up to the 13-day stage, movement occurs at regular intervals of roughly 30 to 60 seconds. The regular cyclic character of the movements is lost as the frequency of movement and the duration of activity periods increase until clear-cut inactivity periods disappear at around 13 days, when the embryo shows a relatively continuous pattern of activity.

A key observation concerning the mechanisms that underlie motility was provided by William Preyer (1885), one of the founders of behavioral embryology. Preyer noticed that the chick embryo was capable of overt movement several days before the time (7½ days) when a response could be evoked by exteroceptive sensory stimulation. On the basis of this "natural experiment," Preyer suggested that the motility of the chick embryo is autogenous, arising from physiological processes within the embryo, up to and possibly after the stage when the first evoked responses appear. Additional indirect support for the autogenous view of embryonic motility is provided by the observations that motility appears under relatively stable environmental conditions *in ovo* and that efforts to increase or decrease the level

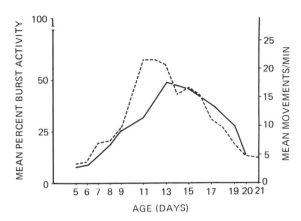

FIGURE 1. *Solid line represents the percentage of time during which polyneuronal burst discharges were present at different stages of development. Percent burst activity (solid line) is compared with the mean number of body movements (dashed line) reported by Oppenheim (1972). (From Provine, 1972a.)*

of stimulation received by the embryo have had little effect on the amount of movement (Oppenheim, 1972). Indirect evidence for an autogenous process is also provided by the presence of cyclic motility throughout much of incubation in the absence of periodic environmental stimuli; motility is periodic from its inception up to about 13 days, when it becomes aperiodic.

The first crucial experiment that demonstrated the spontaneous (nonreflexogenic) character of embryonic motility was conducted by Hamburger, Wenger, and Oppenheim (1966). This experiment is theoretically important because it deals with a fundamental issue in both psychology and neurobiology — that is, the role of exteroceptive sensory input in the ontogeny of behavior and the nervous system. These investigators extirpated several segments of the thoracic neural tube (immature spinal cord) of 2-day embryos. This procedure isolated the lumbosacral cord from input from the brain and rostral cord regions. At the same time, a second operation was performed which removed the dorsal half of the cord caudal to the thoracic spinal gap and the associated neural crest areas (the precursors of the dorsal root sensory ganglia), eliminating the possibility

of sensory input to the cord. Thus any movements of the legs of the operated embryos must be the product of neuronal discharges within the isolated lumbosacral cord segment that innervated them. The legs of the operated embryos were highly motile up to 15 to 17 days, which suggests that the embryonic motility was both nonreflexogenic and the product of endogenous discharges within the residual ventral half of the spinal cord. This experiment, along with earlier behavioral studies of spinal embryos (Hamburger et al., 1965), indicates a unique active role for the embryonic spinal cord in the production of movement; such a role is not characteristic of the adult cord.

The next step in the search for the neural mechanisms of motility involves the recording of electrophysiological activity within the spinal cord and motor nerves of the embryo. These experiments serve a dual purpose. They reveal the bioelectric correlates of embryonic motility and help clarify the correlation between neural and behavioral events. The latter objective is particularly important because we have no basis on which to assume a priori that there is a neurobehavioral parallelism in the developing embryo. A change in any one of numerous neural or muscular systems could radically modify the output of the developing motor system, which is reflected in overt behavior.

Electrophysiological studies of the spinal cord were first performed on embryos that were immobilized by the injection of curare, a neuromuscular blocking agent (Provine et al., 1970). The mobile embryos were paralyzed to facilitate the placement of microelectrodes. No artificial respiration of these curarized embryos is required, because pulmonary respiration does not begin until about 2 days before hatching. The electrophysiological results reinforce the earlier behavioral findings. Massive polyneuronal burst discharges were identified within the ventral cord region (Provine et al., 1970), shown by Hamburger, Wenger, and Oppenheim (1966) to support motility in deafferented embryos. Many parallels were also found between the patterning of the cord burst discharges and embryonic motility (Provine, 1972b). The amounts of cord burst activity (percent burst activity) and embryonic motility

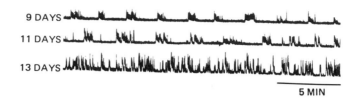

9 DAYS

11 DAYS

13 DAYS

5 MIN

FIGURE 2. *Periodicity of burst discharges. Regular phases of activity and inactivity are present at 9 and 11 days. This regular periodicity is lost by 13 days. (From Provine, 1972a.)*

were correlated throughout development. Both increase up to a peak at about 13 days and then decrease until hatching at 21 days. The close relationship between the number of embryonic movements per minute recorded by Oppenheim (1972) and percent burst activity is shown in Figure 1. Correlations were also found between the temporal distribution of cord burst activity and embryonic movements. Both are periodic up to 13 days, after which they occur at irregular intervals. Transitions in the periodicity of spinal cord burst discharges between 9 and 13 days are shown in Figure 2.

Simultaneous recordings of the unit activity from freely moving uncurarized embryos with "floating" electrodes demonstrated that the spinal cord burst discharges were the electrophysiological correlates of movement (Ripley and Provine, 1972). The spinal cord discharges recorded at a given site accompanied the movement of a wide variety of body parts in a reliable fashion (Figure 3). In a corollary experiment, motor outflow from the cord via peripheral nerves continued unabated even after curarization; cord burst discharges were synchronous with discharges in the ipsilateral radial and sciatic nerves which innervate the wings and legs. Thus movement-produced proprioceptive and/or exteroceptive stimulation is not necessary for the maintenance or production of embryonic movements. This point is more rigorously demonstrated in another study (Provine, 1973), which showed that there was no significant difference between the mean levels of spinal cord burst activity, the motility correlate, recorded before and after the curarization of twenty 15-day embryos. Furthermore, this result indicates that movement-produced injury discharges in the spinal cords of the delicate freely moving embryos were not responsible for

the high correlation between cord discharges and movements.

The electrophysiological studies show that embryonic motility in the chick is *neurogenic*, that is, the product of neuromuscular processes. We are not dealing with *myogenic* movements, which would be the result of spontaneous contractility of immature muscle. When we observe a twitch of the embryo, we are observing the consequence of a bioelectric event within the immature CNS. This finding takes the study of behavior development out of the realm of behavioral phenomenology and allows

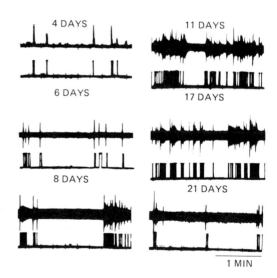

4 DAYS

11 DAYS

6 DAYS

17 DAYS

8 DAYS

21 DAYS

1 MIN

FIGURE 3. *Comparison of cord burst discharges (upper trace) with visually observed body movements (lower trace). Four-day cord activity was integrated to clarify the low-amplitude activity. Cord discharges were recorded from the lumbosacral region, except at 4 days, when the brachial cord was monitored. (From Ripley and Provine, 1972.)*

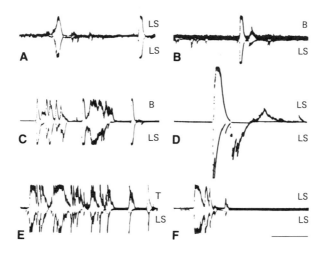

FIGURE 4. *Records of integrated polyneuronal burst discharges simultaneously recorded from pairs of spinal cord sites. Activity from one region is inverted and placed base to base with activity from the other region so that symmetry of the resulting composite trace indicates the similarity of the activity from the two sites. Correspondence (symmetry) is shown between burst discharges that appear in various pairs of spinal cord loci recorded from embryos of the following ages: (A) 6-day, bilateral: lumbosacral/lumbosacral, LS/LS; (B) 6-day, ipsilateral: brachial/lumbosacral, B/LS; (C) 9-day, ipsilateral: brachial/lumbosacral, B/LS; (D) 9-day, bilateral: lumbosacral/ lumbosacral, LS/LS; (E) 17-day, ipsilateral: thoracic/lumbosacral, T/LS; (F) 20-day, bilateral: lumbosacral/lumbosacral, LS/LS. The 9-day bilateral: LS/LS case (D) shows alternating region specific activity in the two cord halves after a common initial discharge. Time scale is 10 sec except in (D) where it is 2 sec. [Records are from Provine, 1971, except (D), which appears in Provine, 1973.]*

us to view the electrophysiological findings in a behaviorally relevant functional context.

Another phase in the investigation of the neural correlate of embryonic motility concerns the development of communication between different points within the embryonic spinal cord. On a gross level, this deals with whether the ontogeny of bioelectric activity involves a basically segregative or integrative process. Previous findings provide a few clues. It has already been established that multiunit bursting is present from at least as early as 4 days until hatching. This is within about a day of the onset of motility. Such synchronization requires that the bursting neurons in the vicinity of the electrode tip must either receive common input or be in communication. Further evidence of intracord communication is that the spinal cord burst discharges are the motility correlates of body parts both proximal and distal to the recording site. The behavioral

finding that many body parts are simultaneously motile during an activity period also suggests such a conclusion.

A more informative approach to the ontogeny of intracord communication used two electrodes simultaneously to sample burst discharges from two different cord loci (Provine, 1971). The surprising result was that nearly synchronous burst discharges were identified in regions as widely separated as the ventral brachial and lumbosacral cord in embryos ranging from at least as young as 6 days (2 to 3 days after the first movements and 1½ days before the first spinal reflex arcs) through 20 days of incubation (one day before hatching). The time of onset, duration, and envelopes of burst discharges recorded from such structurally and functionally disparate regions were highly similar (Figure 4). These findings indicate that burst discharges involve the integrated activation of neurons over a considerable expanse of cord tissue. Therefore, intracord communication is present throughout a major portion of embryonic development.

These results may explain the trunk flexures and S-shaped movements characteristic of embryos through about 6½ days. This behavior is the probable consequence of waves of neuronal discharges that sweep through the immature spinal cord. The precise nature of the correlations between CNS burst events and behavior becomes somewhat less clear once the wave movements break up, after about 6½ days. The behavior repertoire increases considerably at this time and the body parts no longer move in synchrony, although there are clear-cut activity periods during which all body parts capable of moving seem to do so. At this point, a limitation of using the burst as a motility correlate becomes apparent; we have only limited knowledge of what the consequences of the bursts are in terms of motor output to specific muscles. For example, the apparent synchronization of intracord burst discharges may be the result of summated excitatory and inhibitory discharges which may reflect very different functional processes at different cord levels. Thus the question arises of the level of reduction at which next to approach the developing system.

The level at which a system is studied must be attuned both to the experimental question and to the properties of the system under study. The first approaches to the embryonic motility problem involved the conjoint examination of gross body movements or peripheral nerve discharges and their CNS correlates within the spinal cord. Attention was directed to the multiunit burst discharges because they provide more direct information about behavioral events than would the isolated activity of single units, which may not be directly related to the production of movement. However, the burst discharges by themselves provide only a limited view of what the patterning of motor outflow to the muscles might be. For example, we cannot test whether embryonic movements are the result of electrical discharges that sweep through the embryonic spinal cord and indiscriminately activate all neuromuscular pathways, as suggested by Hamburger (1968), or whether some highly specific patterning of motor outflow from the cord is

present from the earliest stages. Even the recording of discharges in peripheral nerve trunks (radial and sciatic nerves) represent summated activity being directed to many different limb muscles (Ripley and Provine, 1972).

Evidence for a specific channeling of motor outflow to the muscles is presented in a recent series of electromyographic (EMG) studies performed by Beckoff (1974). By simultaneously recording EMG activity from the tibialis and gastrocnemius muscles, which are antagonists that activate the ankle joint, she was able to demonstrate reciprocal activation at least as early as 7 days. The presence of alternating activity in the muscles suggests that there is a pattern-generating circuit, probably involving excitatory and inhibitory elements, in the spinal cord which innervates them. This proposed circuit is already established within a few days of the time of appearance of the first embryonic movements.

An additional experiment by Narayanan and Hamburger (1971) suggests not only that pattern-generating circuits are present within the cord but that different circuits are specific to different cord regions. The methods of this experiment are as interesting as the results because they demonstrate a unique application of neuroembryological procedures to solve a behavioral problem. In 2-day chick embryos, the brachial spinal cord segments, which ordinarily innervate the wing, were transplanted in the place of the lumbosacral segments (which ordinarily innervate the legs) of another embryo, and vice versa (Figure 5). Therefore, two groups of experimental embryos were created; one set had two brachial cord segments (BL) and the other group had two lumbosacral segments (LB). The behavior of these experimental embryos was striking in several respects. At embryonic stages, the wings and legs moved in concert more frequently than is normal, which suggests that the homonymous spinal cord segments are receiving similar fiber tracts or that they are responding to (decoding) patterns of widely transmitted bioelectric signals in a similar fashion. Most dramatic was the posthatching behavior of the experimental chicks. In chicks with double brachial cord segments, the wings and legs moved together. They showed the synchronous abduction and

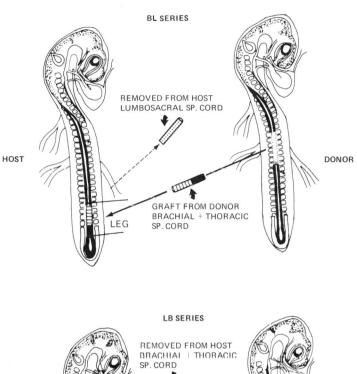

BL SERIES

REMOVED FROM HOST
LUMBOSACRAL SP. CORD

HOST

DONOR

GRAFT FROM DONOR
BRACHIAL + THORACIC
SP. CORD

LEG

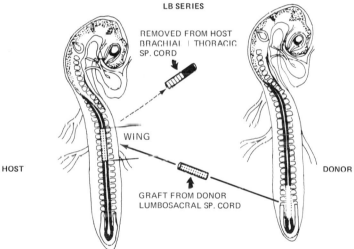

LB SERIES

REMOVED FROM HOST
BRACHIAL + THORACIC
SP. CORD

HOST

DONOR

WING

GRAFT FROM DONOR
LUMBOSACRAL SP. CORD

FIGURE 5.   *Transplantation of brachial spinal cord segments to lumbosacral level (BL series) and of lumbosacral segments to brachial level (LB series) in 2½-day chick embryos. (From Narayanan and Hamburger, 1971.)*

adduction movements typical of wing flapping. The embryos never showed the alternating movement characteristic of walking. Similar findings in posthatch chicks were reported by Straznicky (1963). Thus the circuits involved in the patterning of motor outflow to the muscle of a limb are specific to the adjacent spinal cord segment. These results show further that the circuits cannot be modulated by the appendages that they innervate, which suggests that the spinal or neural mechanisms that underlie these phenomena had been irreversibly determined at the time of the operation shortly after closure of the neural tube.

Taken collectively, the behavioral and electrophysiological studies of chick motor development show that embryos spontaneously behave before they respond (they "act" before they "react") and that exteroceptive and proprioceptive sensory input are not necessary for the development, performance, and maintenance of movement, at least until late embryonic stages. The finding of *motor primacy* is also characteristic of neurogenesis at the structural level. For example, cell proliferation in the embryonic spinal cord is completed in the ventral portion, which contains the motoneurons, several days before it terminates in the dorsal region, which contains the dorsal columns, and receives the afferent fibers from the dorsal root ganglia (Hamburger, 1948). These results do not suggest that sensory input and experiential variables play no role in the development and integration of embryonic motor patterns. Indeed, such a general position would be unwarranted. The problem is not one of whether experiential factors have an effect but of determining when, how, and to what extent such variables are active (Weiss, 1941). Unfortunately, the existing literature on the development of sensory processes, reflexes, and conditionability contributes little to our understanding of this problem. (Good reviews of these topics are provided by Carmichael, 1970, and Gottlieb, 1968, 1971b.) The literature deals primarily with the capabilities of the embryo at a given stage of development, only indirectly touching upon the issue of whether such capabilities are exercised in the course of normal behavior development. (Notable exceptions are Gottlieb, 1971a; Vince, 1973; and Impekoven and Gold, 1973.)

An instructive example of how environmental variables *in ovo* may adaptively influence an ongoing stereotyped motor pattern is provided by a study of shell-related factors in hatching (Provine, 1972b). Chick-hatching behavior has several components (Hamburger and Oppenheim, 1967), one of which is the back thrust of the beak tip, which serves to chip the shell. While series of these back thrusts are being performed, rotatory movements are made which propel the chick in a counterclockwise direction within the shell. When the shell is cracked around about two-thirds of its circumference, the shell cap breaks off and the chick emerges. However, if the shell cap is tapped down to prevent hatching, the distance that the

chick rotates can be increased up to twofold or more (Provine, 1972b). These results clearly show that the amount and duration of rotatory hatching movements are controlled by extrinsic mechanical factors associated with the shell and are not regulated by an intrinsic species-specific program. An analogous eclosion-hatching regulatory mechanism has been identified in the cockroach embryo (Provine, 1975).

That sensory input eventually becomes necessary for the successful performance of even centrally programmed motor behavior is obvious. To be maximally adaptive, behavior must be "tuned" to the ever-changing environment. Other chapters in the present volume deal with the varieties of often bidirectional central—peripheral interactions involved in the production of movement in a number of species (see also Gottlieb, 1973, and Hamburger, 1973). Also of interest in this regard is the work on bird song by Konishi (1965b), Marler (Chapter Twenty-Two), and others. These investigators provide beautiful examples of the complex and subtle interaction that can take place between central and peripheral variables in the ontogeny of a very sophisticated motor pattern at postnatal stages. In an equally interesting set of experiments that deal with visually guided behavior in kittens, Held and Hein (1963) demonstrate the significance of movement in the development of sensorimotor integration.

In concluding this section on the chick, the possible adaptive significance of the early embryonic movements will be considered. This issue is of particular interest because, until the appearance of prehatching and hatching movements starting about 4 days before hatching, the character of the embryo's behavior has no obvious resemblance to later adaptive function. It might therefore be hypothesized that the early movements are a simple epiphenomenon, a manifestation of the functional development of the CNS. Another view is offered by Corner, Bakhuis, and van Wingerden (1973), who suggest that embryonic motility is an early manifestation of the CNS state we know as REM sleep. Yet another possibility is suggested by Drachman and Sokoloff (1966), who showed that the immobilization of chick embryos for 1 to 2 days with curare resulted in ankylosis. The latter finding suggests that embryonic motility may play a role in the sculpting of joints. Thus the development of function may have an effect on the emergence of structure. In this regard, we should also consider what effect the presence of bioelectric activity within the embryonic spinal cord might have upon the differentiation of the immature system. No specific data are available concerning this point, although there is ample opportunity for such interactions to occur during the supposedly more plastic early developmental phases. The first bioelectric discharges in the embryonic cord are already present at least as early as 4 days, 3 days before the first reflex arcs are established and at a time when cell proliferation (Hamburger, 1948) and synaptogenesis (Foelix and Oppenheim, 1973) are still underway. Also relevant here are the often-quoted studies of Carmichael (1926) and others on the development of swimming behavior of amphibian embryos that have been chronically immobilized. Apparently normal swimming movements appeared in these animals after the removal of the paralyzing anaesthetic, which indicates that this behavior does not require movement-produced feedback for its maturation. However, since overt behavior was used as the dependent variable in these amphibian studies, it is not possible to rule out the presence of internuncial bioelectric activity during the period of behavioral quiescence. The question of whether functional (bioelectrical) development affects the emergence of structure (synaptogenesis) will be reintroduced in a later section in regard to the in vitro studies of Crain, Bornstein, and Peterson (1968).

Since the chick embryo was chosen as a representative vertebrate embryo, the question arises as to the generalizability of the chick results to other vertebrate species. The universality of spontaneous motility across species and its significance as a meaningful phenomenon for developmental study also comes into question. Hence, the evidence for other vertebrate species will be briefly considered.

All vertebrate embryos that have been investigated move when left undisturbed. The snapping turtle *Chelydra* performs movements much like those of the chick embryo. Early S-waves break up into total body movements during which the activity of various body parts seem uncoordinated (Decker, 1967). Behavior

of both the turtle and lizard embryos (Hughes, Bryant, and Bellairs, 1967) is cyclic, with alternating periods of activity and inactivity. As with the chick embryo, this finding is suggestive of nonreflexogenic motility. The identification of prereflexogenic motility periods in both the turtle and lizard provides more direct evidence for nonreflexogenic activity.

The lower vertebrates (teleosts and urodels) complicate the present story somewhat because their behavior remains smooth and integrated throughout development. No behavior pattern analogous to the jerky, uncoordinated (Type I) movements has been identified in these forms. However, spontaneous movements occur in both the salamander *Ambystoma* (Coghill, 1929) and the toadfish (Tracy, 1926), and a prereflexogenic period has been observed in the latter organism.

It is curious that little is known about spontaneous motility in mammalian fetuses (Hamburger, 1963). The work that has been done concentrates primarily on the problem of reflexogenesis and evoked movement. A recent report on the rat fetus by Narayanan, Fox, and Hamburger (1971) reviews the earlier literature and provides evidence of spontaneous motility in a representative mammalian. The rat fetus performs intermittent movements which are jerkier and less coordinated than those of the adult. While the nonreflexogenic nature of these movements has not been experimentally verified, their occurrence has been shown to be independent of at least one possible source of stimulation, uterine contractions. However, fetal behavior of the rat and other mammals differs from that of lower forms in at least two respects. Mammals do not have a prereflexogenic period, and their behavior has a relatively late onset in regard to body development and neuronal differentiation.

The considerable technical difficulties involved in working with mammalian fetuses has discouraged experimental studies. However, it is encouraging that several investigators have begun research on the role that sensory factors play in the ontogeny of behavior patterns at postnatal stages. Investigation at prenatal stages may not be far behind. Fentress (1973a) has found evidence for an endogenous mechanism involved in the face grooming of mice. Grooming sequences that involve the complex coordinated movements of the shoulders, tongue, and eyes developed in a remarkably normal manner in mice that had one or both forelimbs amputated at birth. This result is somewhat analogous to that of the previously described study of chick embryos in which disruption of the feedback loop between motor outflow and its behavioral consequences by curare had little effect on the level of activity in motor nerves (Provine, 1973). Also relevant here is the report that monkeys that had their arms and hands deafferented during the perinatal period did not develop fine arm and hand coordination, although gross locomotory movements of the limbs remained (Berman and Berman, 1973). These results suggest that some movement patterns survive deafferentation, whereas others may require sensory input to mature normally.

On the basis of these comparative considerations, embryonic motility is well established as a general developmental phenomenon. However, the absence of carefully controlled behavioral and electrophysiological studies of spinal and deafferented embryos of species other than the chick permits only speculation concerning the presence of common mechanisms.

BEHAVIOR DEVELOPMENT IN THE COCKROACH

The same characteristics that make invertebrates desirable for neurobehavioral analysis at adult stages commend them for studies of development. The limited behavioral repertoire and small number of anatomically and functionally identifiable neurons of many invertebrates encourage optimism that the mechanisms that underlie behavioral development may ultimately be resolved. After a long period of relative neglect, the neural and behavioral development of insects and other invertebrates is beginning to attract attention (Edwards, 1969; Bentley and Hoy, 1970; Young, 1973; Davis and Davis, 1973). Some of the most fruitful consequences of this recent trend are reported in Chapters Eight, Nine, and Twelve of the present volume. In this section, we shall describe preliminary findings on the behavioral embryology of the cockroach *Periplaneta*

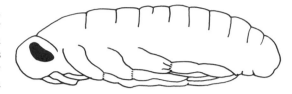

FIGURE 6. *Appearance of cockroach embryo during the latter portion of incubation. A brain and subesophageal ganglion are located in the head capsule and a ganglion is located in the ventral aspect of each thoracic and abdominal body segment. The eye appears and becomes larger during the last half of the embryonic period. The pigmented sensory hairs, which appear about 4 days before hatching, are not shown in drawing.*

americana (Provine, 1975; in preparation). These results, which are among the first concerning the behavior development of an insect embryo, will be compared with findings from other invertebrate and vertebrate species. The present discussion will be followed by a description of parallel *in vitro* studies of cultured ganglia from the cockroach embryo.

Twelve to sixteen cockroach embryos occupy a single communal egg case, the ootheca. The ootheca resembles a small brown bean with a notched ridge along one side. Within the ootheca, embryos are grouped in two opposed rows of six or eight, with the embryos of each row lined up side by side. Individual embryos are enclosed in capsule-like chorions. The embryos of both rows face inward toward each other and the center of the ootheca. The heads of the embryos are oriented toward the notched edge of the clam-like ootheca, which is pried open as the embryos escape during hatching. The embryos have soft, milky-white, translucent bodies about 8 mm in length. Their legs, antennae, and cerci are tucked beneath the body (Figure 6). Hatching and eclosion (the shedding at the embryonic cuticle) occur simultaneously in all 12 to 16 embryos at about 30 days of incubation at 29°C. The first instar nymphal cockroach that emerges at hatching has the characteristic adult locomotory gait and is a miniature of the adult, with the exception that it has no wings.

The cockroach embryo has much to recommend it as an object for developmental study. Unlike some insects that undergo metamorphosis, the body proportions of the cockroach embryo remain relatively stable during development and no dramatic fusion of ganglia takes place during the last half of embryonic development, with which we will be concerned. Therefore, the investigation of developmental phenomena is simplified. Electrophysiological and behavioral studies are facilitated by the relatively large body size (8 mm long) of the embryo. While this may be small by vertebrate standards, it is much larger than the tiny embryos of other commonly used invertebrate preparations such as the cricket.

Another advantage of the cockroach embryo is that it may be removed from the ootheca during the last half of embryonic development and be maintained on moistened filter paper in an organ culture dish without interfering with its maturation. This is equivalent to removing the chick embryo from its shell and placing it in a Petri dish, where it continues to develop. An embryo exposed in this manner is easy to observe and manipulate experimentally. A great deal of control over the environment of the embryo is also possible. The description of cockroach behavior development which follows is based upon observations of these *ex ovo* preparations unless otherwise noted.

The behavior repertoire of the embryo is limited by its soft body and the fact that the legs, antennae, and cerci remain folded beneath the body until eclosion or hatching (Figure 6). Therefore, twitches and depressions of the body wall are the only movements possible. The first movements of the embryo are minute slow depressions ("dimples") which appear in the anterior thorax about halfway through incubation. These dimples, which are the probable products of the contraction of single muscles, gradually appear in other body regions. As development proceeds, both the frequency and variety of different movements increase. After 20 to 22 days (hatching occurs on day 30), fast twitches appear as do the first clearly organized multisegmental contractions. These latter movements are dorsoventral "flattenings" of the abdomen which resemble the ventilatory behavior of posthatch cockroaches. Also appearing at about this time are

weak ripples of contraction which pass through the body and violent tremors ("shudders") which involve the simultaneous activation of all body parts. Overall embryonic movements increase up to 26 to 27 days and then decline until hatching—eclosion on day 30. However, if specific classes of movements are examined during this interval, local, uncoordinated movements drop out while the proportion of multisegmental movements increases in frequency. Even these multisegmental movements disappear shortly before eclosion—hatching movements begin.

The eclosion—hatching movements are a series of vigorous caudal—rostral peristaltic waves in the abdomen which are continued as ventral flexures when they reach the thorax and head. This behavior sequence is suddenly initiated at about 30 days of incubation and is maintained for 2 to 3 minutes or until eclosion is completed. While occasional movements of this type appear earlier, they are not maintained or performed with vigor. Air swallowing also accompanies the eclosion hatching movements and probably serves to increase body volume and stretch the cuticle (Sikes and Wigglesworth, 1931). The probable increase in body volume coupled with the peristaltic waves and ventral flexures stretches and eventually tears the cuticle along the dorsal thorax. Within minutes, the peristalsis carries the cuticle caudally and off the body. When *in ovo*, these same movements serve a second purpose of prying open the ootheca and propelling the embryos forward until they escape. Since all embryos in the ootheca perform the movements simultaneously, hatching is a "social affair."

A radical change of behavior takes place when the embryonic cuticle is removed from the body of the embryo and/or the embryo hatches. The now first instar nymphal cockroach immediately switches to an adult type of locomotory pattern and is capable of walking away. The walking movements seem to be performed perfectly on the first trial.

It is of interest that the eclosion—hatching behavior sequence is carried out by single embryos removed from the ootheca and incubated in organ culture dishes. Therefore, the initiation and performance of these behaviors are not dependent upon environmental factors associated with the ootheca and/or the presence of "litter mates." This does not rule out the participation of all sensory effects in the triggering of eclosion–hatching behavior. For example, some form of "communication" between embryos may be responsible for the synchronization of hatching in the 14 to 16 embryos in each ootheca. It has been shown that gentle tactile stimulation will trigger eclosion–hatching behavior in 30-day embryos (Provine, 1975). Therefore, it is possible that once eclosion has been initiated in one or several embryos in an ootheca, they rub against and trigger eclosion in their neighbors, producing the combined effort necessary to pry open the "spring-loaded" hinge of the clam-like ootheca and hatch.

Sensory factors play a definite role in the control of the stereotyped caudal to rostral eclosion movements (Provine, 1975). It was previously noted that the eclosion behavior was immediately terminated upon removal of the cuticle. This suggests that cuticle-related variables act to maintain or terminate ongoing eclosion movements. This possibility was tested by rapidly removing the cuticles of embryos that had just initiated eclosion. This procedure resulted in the immediate cessation of the behavior and the "switching" to the adult motor pattern. Conversely, by gluing the cuticles to the bodies of eclosing embryos with a rapidly drying adhesive, the eclosion behavior, which is typically completed within 2 to 3 minutes can be extended up to 10 to 15 minutes or more. These results indicate that, if we are dealing with a hormonally triggered readout of an endogenous central program, as suggested by Truman and Sokolove (1972) in their studies of silk moth eclosion, the termination and thus the time that the program runs is under peripheral (sensory) control. The peripheral feedback element of eclosion makes it maximally adaptive by assuring that the behavior will be maintained long enough to shed the cuticle or hatch and that the behavior will be terminated when its utility is exhausted. [A basically similar hatching "strategy" has evolved in the chick embryo (Provine, 1972b).] Unfortunately, in the present cockroach studies we were not able to remove the cuticle prior to the onset of eclosion in order to test whether the presence of the cuticle is necessary for the initiation of the eclosion–hatching behavior sequence.

The existence of early embryonic motility in the cockroach (Provine, in preparation) and in a few other invertebrate species (Berrill, 1973) indicates that movement is coincident with the differentiation of the segmentally organized invertebrate nervous system. Thus embryonic motility is not exclusive to vertebrates with their basically columnar CNS organization. However, further comparison between vertebrates and invertebrates would be premature because embryonic motility has not been shown to be neurogenic in any invertebrate species and because of the previously mentioned problem of interpreting the behavioral significance of the twitchings of the soft invertebrate exoskeleton. The latter problem also complicates comparisons between invertebrate species. Electrical recording from nerves or muscles of known behavioral significance may provide a solution to this problem.

Studies of the development of specific motor patterns at more mature larval stages do not encounter these interpretational problems, and cross-species comparisons can be made more easily. The finding that the first instar cockroach nymph is able to walk immediately on the first trial after eclosion–hatching has a parallel in the development of butterfly flight. Petersen, Lundgren, and Wilson (1956) note that the fundamental motor patterns for flight are already present when the butterfly emerges from the pupa. These studies show that practice is not necessary for the development of flight and walking behaviors in the examined species.

Recent electrophysiological studies have gone a step further and elegantly demonstrated that certain CNS motor patterns in invertebrates develop in the absence of various sources of peripheral input. Bentley and Hoy (1970) succeeded in evoking typical flight and stridulation (song) patterns in the muscles of nymphal crickets several instars (molts) before the development of the wings, which are necessary for the successful performance of these behaviors. Therefore, the neuronal circuits responsible for the production of these motor patterns are developed during nymphal stages without the benefit of exercise and are probably inhibited until the appearance of the wings and adulthood at the time of the final molt. Davis and Davis (1973) have also shown an independence of central and peripheral factors during development in the lobster. Presumptive swimmerets were extirpated prior to differentiation in newly hatched larva. In these experimental preparations, normal patterns of outflow remained in motoneurons which would ordinarily innervate the swimmerets. Therefore, the ontogeny of motor output is not dependent upon feedback normally received from peripheral muscles or sense organs. Results discussed in the previous section of this paper suggest that vertebrate behavior development may also be characterized by a high degree of motor autonomy.

TISSUE CULTURE STUDIES

Although tissue culture methods have not yet been effectively applied to the problems of behavioral embryology, tissue culture will be considered here because its potential is considerable and it deserves more than the near total neglect which it presently receives from behaviorally oriented investigators. The present essay examines the major evidence in support of this exemplary simple system and evaluates the limitations and pitfalls involved in extrapolating data obtained from isolated bits of CNS tissue in culture back to problems of CNS development in the intact organism.

Cultures are prepared by explanting small fragments of CNS tissue which vary in size from thin slices or small clumps down to single neurons. These explants mimic various aspects of neural development *in vivo* after being placed in a nutrient medium and incubated for periods up to several months. During the incubation interval, synapses are formed within individual tissue fragments, bioelectric discharges appear and increase in complexity, and outgrowing fiber processes may bridge distances up to several millimeters and establish functional synaptic contacts with adjacent explants (Crain, 1966, 1974).

The virtues of tissue culture preparations are many. The investigator has great control over the numbers and types of neurons and other tissues explanted as well as upon their environment (Crain, 1974; Provine, Seshan, and Aloe, 1974). Such conditions are ideal for the study of trophic interactions between tissues. Pharmacological studies are also facilitated because various agents may be flushed in and out of the culture medium with minimal attention being given to the blood−brain barrier or to the production of spurious results from nonspecific drug effects, which are more of a problem *in situ*. With dispersed cell cultures, it is possible to record the electrophysiological activity of a single neuron, which may be simultaneously visualized through a microscope. Such preparations are useful in establishing the discharge properties of specific classes of neurons which would otherwise be buried in a complex interconnected neuronal matrix *in vivo*. They therefore represent the ultimate "deafferentation" procedure. Single-cell cultures of neurons from the brains of nymphal cockroaches are shown in Figure 7. Culture techniques also make possible the assemblage of "custom-made" neuronal networks of diagrammatic simplicity. Some rather elaborate nonnaturally occurring neuronal patterns produced by fibers growing out of cultured abdominal ganglia of the cockroach embryo are shown in Figure 8. Although the latter cultures were prepared as part of a study of the emergence of patterns in neuronal networks (Provine, Seshan, and Aloe, 1974), they have a considerable esthetic appeal of their own.

The great experimental control over a neuron's environment which is possible *in vitro* is a mixed blessing. The experimenter has the considerable task of establishing a favorable physiological environment for an explant. That this task is formidable is suggested by the finding that up to 95 percent or more of the neurons in a given vertebrate CNS explant may die *in vitro*. If satisfactory culture conditions are not found and neural differentiation does not proceed in a reasonably normal manner, an *in vitro* study would have no true controls and every condition would be an experimental condition. These kinds of problems confound the interpretation of negative experimental results. Another criticism of neuron cultures which is often heard, although usually not supported, is that the usefulness of the preparations to model neural development *in vivo* is limited because of the dedifferentiation that is supposed to occur *in vitro*. Actually, a recent

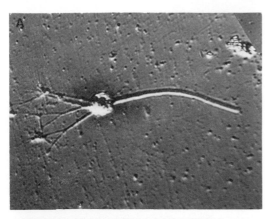

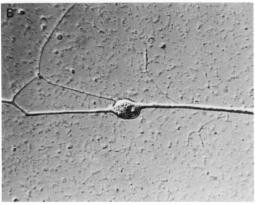

FIGURE 7. *Nomarski microphotographs of single living neurons removed from the medial neurosecretory cell region of the protocerebrum of nymphal cockroaches. (A) Thirty-three-day culture of a cell obtained from a seventh instar nymph. Note the stout axon-like process that grows out from one pole of the cell and the dendrite-like arborizations that emerge from the opposite pole. (B) Twenty-day culture of a cell obtained from a fifth instar nymph which assumes a bipolar configuration. (From Seshan, Provine, and Levi-Montalcini, 1974.)*

experiment supports the opposite notion — that neuronal specificity is retained *in vitro* and is reflected in selective synaptogenesis (Olsen and Bunge, 1973). Some of these problems are not necessarily inherent in the techniques of tissue culture and those that do exist will probably be lessened as procedural innovations are made. The application of *in vitro* procedures to the

developmental study of what may be called "behavioral nerve nets" will now be considered.

Parallel *in vitro* and *in vivo* studies of neuronal development and its bioelectric and behavioral correlates should be simultaneously carried out in order to make the *in vitro* results maximally useful. The *in vivo* study defines the nature of the correlate to be examined *in vitro* and provides an index against which the adequacy of the culture model can be evaluated. While this ideal situation has not yet been fully achieved, a number of findings of behavioral interest have been produced.

Single unit and polyneuronal burst discharges have been observed in small isolated fragments of the rodent brain and spinal cord *in vitro* (Crain, 1966, 1974). These results support the previously advocated position that spontaneous bioelectric activity is characteristic of differentiating CNS tissue. Furthermore, the polyneuronal bursts that are present in the cultured explants may be analogous to the spinal cord discharges, which are the correlates of motility in the intact chick embryo (Provine, 1972a; Ripley and Provine, 1972). However, a major problem arises in relating such *in vivo* and *in vitro* findings. Since there is no simple means of specifying the neuronal population being sampled *in vitro* (e.g., motoneurons), there is uncertainty concerning the behavioral significance of bioelectric events. This problem is in part alleviated in cultures that combine muscle and cord tissue (Crain, 1970). In these preparations, muscle twitches are often synchronous with bioelectric burst discharges in the cord explants which innervate them. This result, in conjunction with the finding that muscle twitches were eliminated by the addition of curare, indicate that the movements were neurogenic. While these simple twitches hardly qualify as interesting "behaviors," no concerted effort has been made toward exploiting the potential of the system. For example, the effect that explants from various brain regions have upon the frequency, rhythmicity, or duration of twitches or correlated bioelectric phenomena in attached cord—muscle systems may reflect the roles (i.e., excitatory, inhibitory, pacemaker) which these brain regions play in the unfolding of movement in the embryo. Combined nerve—muscle cultures have obvious utility for the develop-

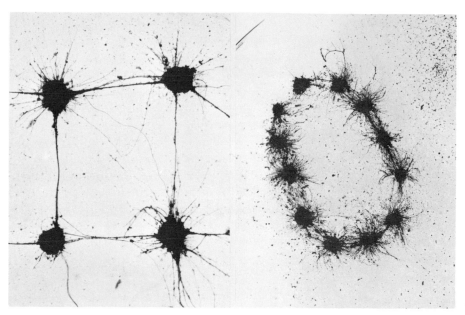

FIGURE 8.   Connections formed between embryonic abdominal ganglia after 3 to 4 weeks in vitro. (From Provine, Seshan, and Aloe, 1974.)

ment of neuromuscular coupling, a poorly understood phase of the behavior development story (Fischbach, 1972).

In a study designed to determine whether ongoing bioelectric activity is necessary for neurogenesis, Crain, Bornstein, and Peterson (1968) cleverly took advantage of *in vitro* procedures. Explants of fetal rodent spinal cord and cerebrum were grown in medium containing either Xylocaine or Mg^{2+}, which block bioelectrical activity. The neurons in these cultures continued to develop synapses as in control medium even though all bioelectric activity was absent. Furthermore, normal bioelectric activity reappeared within minutes after the blocking agent was removed. These results clearly indicate that some unspecified (and perhaps unspecifiable) types of complex synaptic interactions can develop in the absence of ongoing bioelectrical activity. These results also indirectly support and extend the findings of the previously mentioned *in situ* studies of Carmichael (1926) and others which showed that the paralysis of amphibian embryos during development did not prevent the later appearance of apparently normal swimming move-

ments after the removal of the paralyzing anesthetic.

One of the problems that arises in the preparation of virtually all vertebrate CNS cultures is the necessity of explanting small pieces of tissue. Only small explants permit sufficient diffusion of nutrients into and wastes out of their tissues to allow survival in culture. A consequence of dissecting small explants out of the host organism is that they are subject to both mechanical trauma and the loss of many neuronal contacts that may be necessary for their physiological maintenance *in vitro*.

Culture preparations of the CNS of the cockroach embryo (*Periplaneta americana*) avoid many of these problems (Chen and Levi-Montalcini, 1969). The CNS of the cockroach consists of a chain of segmental ganglia linked together by pairs of neuronal connectives. Each of these ganglia is a relatively complete structural and functional unit of the insect CNS (Bullock and Horridge, 1965). Therefore, the interganglionic connectives may be severed and the individual ganglia may be placed in culture with a minimal disturbance of the ganglionic neuropile and cell bodies. The

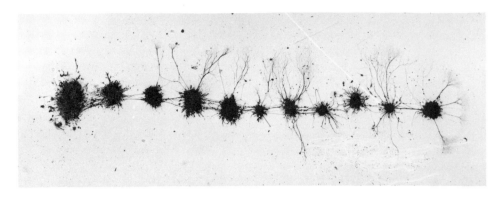

FIGURE 9.   *Four-week culture of a complete ganglionic chain of 16-day cockroach embryo which has reconnected* in vitro. *From left to right, the chain consists of a brain, a subesophageal ganglion, three thoracic ganglia, five abdominal ganglia, and a terminal abdominal ganglion. Silverstain preparation.*

small size of these ganglia, each of which contains from several hundred up to several thousand neurons (Cohen and Jacklett, 1967; Levi-Montalcini and Chen, 1971), probably also contributes to the excellent development and survival of neuronal structure, fiber outgrowth, and bioelectric activity (Provine, Aloe, and Seshan, 1973) for months in a chemically defined liquid medium (Levi-Montalcini et al., 1973).

Ganglionic chains that have been reconnected *in vitro* are a particularly interesting preparation from both neural and behavioral perspectives (Provine, Seshan, and Aloe, 1975). These cultures are made by dissecting apart the individual ganglia of 16-day cockroach embryos and reassembling them in rows on a cover glass submerged in a liquid nutrient medium *in vitro*. An attempt is made to retain the *in vivo* orientation of ganglia, with the exception that the interganglionic spacings are larger than normal to prevent the fusion of adjacent ganglia. The striking result is shown in Figure 9. After 3 to 4 weeks of incubation at 29°C, major nerve trunks were established between ganglia, producing a reasonable approximation of the original ganglionic chain *in vivo*. The reconnected chains often had lateral fiber processes that resembled their *in vivo* counterparts. It is particularly impressive that "organotypic" connectives were formed between ganglia that were growing out fibers on a glass surface submerged in a liquid medium, a milieu vastly

different and simpler than that encountered by outgrowing fibers *in vivo*. A developmental analysis indicates that these substantial connectives come about as a product of interactions between outgrowing fibers and that these interactions occur without regard to ganglion type or orientation (Provine, Seshan, and Aloe, 1975).

An electrophysiological analysis of the chain cultures shows that spontaneous single unit discharges and multiunit bursts are present in individual ganglia and that these discharges are propagated from ganglion to ganglion (Provine, Aloe, and Seshan, 1973). The presence of interganglionic propagation of burst discharges was established by simultaneously recording synchronous spontaneous bioelectric activity from the interiors of interconnected chain ganglia with two microelectrodes. Typical double electrode recordings are shown in Figure 10. These results indicate that communication is established between widely separated ganglia which become interconnected *in vitro*. The considerable interelectrode distances (up to 3.3 mm and six ganglia) argues against our recording from two ends of a single connective bundle, as does the finding that the amplitude and correlation between discharges in connected ganglia are often low and vary over time. Furthermore, the presence of very long lags (up to 500 msec or more) between discharges occurring in coupled ganglia suggests the presence of multisynaptic processes.

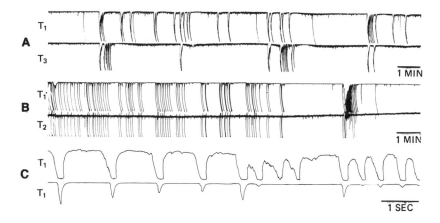

FIGURE 10. *Coincidence of integrated neuronal burst discharges in embryonic ganglia which became interconnected* in vitro: *(A) a loose coupling of bioelectric discharges is shown between the prothoracic,* T_1, *and mesothoracic,* T_3, *ganglia, which were part of a reconstructed ganglionic chain, such as that of Figure 9, which had been maintained for 3 weeks* in vitro; *(B) a high correlation is shown between discharges in* T_1 *and* T_2 *which were separated by three ganglia in a chain that consisted of recurring sequences of* $T_1-T_2-T_3$, *4 weeks in* vitro, *(C) note the fluctuation in both the coincidence and amplitude of multiunit discharges in a record obtained from two* T_1 *ganglia that were six ganglia apart and members of a chain of nine* T_1 *ganglia, 3 weeks in* vitro.

The cultures of the embryonic cockroach CNS have much to recommend them as models of insect neural development, as judged by both morphological and functional criteria. The cultures may also provide useful models of behaviorally significant phenomena. Numerous parallels have been found between the bioelectric discharges within the chains and the behavioral activity of the cockroach embryo reported in the previous section of this chapter. Much embryonic behavior consists of local segmental twitches and contractions. These local movements were interspersed with violent tremors that involved the entire body. Other multisegmental movements involved the smooth, orderly contraction of different body parts either in the form of propagated waves or synchronous abdominal contractions. An equally diverse range of activity was found in the bioelectrical activity of ganglionic chains which reconnected *in vitro*. Neuronal bursting discharges which would be the most likely candidates for neural correlates of motility ranged from local discharges of one or several units to massive discharges involving an entire ganglion. Wide variations between the coupling

of discharges in interconnected ganglia were also observed and varied over time. Furthermore, both bioelectric discharges and embryonic movements tended to cluster together into activity periods which occurred intermittently.

Although these correlations are found between ganglionic bioelectric activity and behavior, it is too early to comment with certainty on the adequacy of the *in vitro* system as a model of neurobehavioral development in the cockroach embryo. However, there is reason for optimism. Multiunit bursting discharges similar to those present in the cockroach ganglionic chains are found in the vertebrate embryonic nervous system both *in vivo* (Provine, 1972a) and *in vitro* (Crain, 1974). In the intact chick embryo, these neuronal bursts are correlated with body movements (Ripley and Provine, 1972).

Only one narrow aspect of the insect culture preparations has been considered in the present essay, that most relevant to behavioral embryology. The possible applications of this material to problems in insect physiology and developmental neurobiology are as numerous as the potential culture preparations, which may include sensory receptors, muscles (Aloe and Levi-Montalcini, 1972), and other organ systems. However, before proceeding with additional *in vitro* studies, it seems wise to return to the embryo for guidance. A comprehensive investigation of cockroach neural development should be undertaken in order to provide a better understanding of the system with which we are dealing *in vitro*. This project should be worth the considerable investment of time and effort that would be required. With the completion of this part of the puzzle, the embryonic cockroach CNS will be closer to fulfilling its considerable promise as a robust system for multidisciplinary developmental study. At present, it seems probable that the invertebrate nervous system which has already been so useful to contemporary neurophysiology will also be ideal for the *in vitro* analysis of developmental problems in neurobiology.

IV

PLASTICITY AND EXPERIENCE

Whereas Parts I through III have, on the whole, stressed principles of intrinsic organization and prepatterning, it is important to recognize that adaptive behavior also involves modifications in expression as a function of antecedent experience. This plasticity operates at many levels, including what we normally refer to as "learning." The biological approach to behavior emphasizes that learning does not operate on a blank slate but is ultimately constrained by the organism's genetic background and previous developmental history (e.g., Lorenz, 1965; Hinde and Stevenson-Hinde, 1973). Nevertheless, it is important to recognize that modification of behavioral output as a consequence of previous experience does occur, and provides the individual organism with a certain range of dynamic plasticity that can play a critical role in successful adaptation to a changing, and not always predictable, environment. Just as with the previously raised questions of integration, genetics, and development, it is often useful to employ simpler systems that display clear examples of behavioral plasticity to guide our thoughts in the analysis of mechanism. Chapters Fifteen and Sixteen indicate distinct ways that this strategy can be pursued. Although these two chapters have been compartmentalized for the sake of emphasis, their relevance to issues raised both previously and subsequently should be apparent.

Davis (Chapter Fifteen) initiates his thesis by pointing out that plasticity is a fundamental characteristic of living organisms and, when manifested within the lifetime of a single individual, can serve to broaden the range of habitats which can be exploited as well as to adjust to unexpected (novel) changes within a given habitat. He indicates that the question of plasticity can be examined at many different levels, ranging from the cellular to the organismic, and that a particularly important goal is to link these levels in a meaningful (nontrivial) manner. Like most other contributors to this volume, however, Davis stresses the advantage of concentrating upon relatively simple systems. His choice of animal group, as is that expressed in Chapter Sixteen, is the mollusks. The advantages he cites are (1) nervous systems with relatively small numbers of elements, (2) organization of these elements into discrete ganglia, (3) size of the elements, and (4) *individual* neural elements that can be specifically identified. From this perspective he then considers the basic problems of *habituation* (decline in response over time to a stimulus of little biological consequence), *choice* (the selection of particular activities from the organism's repertoire), and *learning* in its broader sense, including associative and nonassociative dimensions. From his own experiments and review of the literature Davis emphasizes the important point that changes in responsiveness (e.g., habituation) can persist over varying time periods, up to several weeks, and that cellular correlates can be determined by examining the responsiveness of individual interneurons (i.e., neurons that are neither sensory nor motor). A major mechanism of neuronal habituation in these preparations appears to be the depletion of transmitter chemicals of *individual nerve cells* (as opposed to emergent properties of neural networks). Similar phenomena may occur as a function of repeated stimulation in a variety of vertebrate as well as invertebrate systems (e.g., Fentress and Doty, 1971).

Like many other contributors to this volume, in his discussion of "choice" Davis refers to the problem of behavioral hierarchy. By demonstrating the interplay among different, functionally defined, classes of behavior Davis speaks to themes of direct ethological and psychological interest. For example, during egg laying, *Aplysia* become unresponsive to food stimuli that would otherwise evoke vigorous feeding. By combining studies of previous experience with the concept of behavioral hierarchies, Davis has also been able to demonstrate shifts in expressed output probabilities to given stimuli. This illustrates clearly that problems of behavioral integration at the level of the intact organism cannot be separated from problems of information "storage" in either the evolutionary or individual experience sense. Davis' chapter concludes with a particularly frank statement of the excitement and mystery of the search for mechanisms of behavioral plasticity, and his own conviction that simpler systems in neurobiology share basic common features with less simple ones.

In Chapter Sixteen Gelperin and Forsythe argue that the evolutionary emphasis of ethology can provide a useful perspective for the analysis of cellular mechanisms in learning, for example, its selective nature. The authors also stress the importance of obtaining preparations where the operation of isolated ganglia can be compared with the performance of a given circuit in situ. Toward this end they analyze properties of food aversion learning in a terrestrial slug (*Limax maximus*), as well as some of the neuronal circuitry that contributes to feeding in the intact animal. They raise the important evolutionary question of homology (commonality due to community of descent) of neuronal mechanisms and circuitry, and suggest that the metacerebral giant cells of gastropod mollusks are structures which deserve further investigation from this perspective.

Food-aversion learning, in addition to its obvious biological importance, is striking in terms of rapidity of aquisition, relative permanence, and the relatively long time delay possible between ingestion and its negative consequence (illness). The authors show that many of the characteristics of food aversion learning previously established for vertebrates can be replicated for *Limax* when a preferred food (e.g., mushroom) is followed by CO_2 poisoning. The method of yoked controls was employed subsequently to establish the role of association between antecedent feeding and subsequent reinforcement. From here the authors examine sensory (olfactory) and motor aspects of feeding, and as in several previous chapters they find that output patterns can be examined in isolated, in vitro, preparations. The metacerebral giant cell has formed a major focus for this research, but as acknowledged by Gelperin and Forsythe, further information is necessary to establish the precise role of this cell in behavioral integration and, possibly, learning. The cellular events that underlie learning in intact organisms remain elusive, but the simpler networks approach appears promising.

Learning is of course a concept derived through inference from observed long-lasting changes in an organism's behavior. The number of "classes" of learning and the extent to which they are mediated by common or unique mechanisms is a matter for continued investigation. Whether or not all forms of experience that alter behavior should be classified as learning is itself a moot point, for it is apparent that experience may not only "add" new information to the organism but may also "preserve" the functional properties of preexisting circuitry. Experience, in the broad sense, might also permit the organism to "gain access to" information of largely "endogenous" origin such as seen, for example, in a developmental context through mechanisms of determination and differentiation (see Part III). Although such relationships have been little explored up to the present time, they may provide useful insights when combined with a simpler systems approach. The power of our generalizations depend not only upon the precision and level of analysis employed, but also the boldness with which we recognize possible commonalities among apparently diverse material (e.g., learning and development) as well as the care with which we seek diversity in phenomena traditionally linked together under a single heading. Thus learning may share important features with other aspects of biological organization from which it is usually separated, as well as being a heterogeneous concept necessitating more than one form of explanation.

CHAPTER FIFTEEN

Behavioral and Neuronal Plasticity in Mollusks

WILLIAM J. DAVIS

INTRODUCTION

Biologists have long been preoccupied with defining that elusive property which we call life. As characteristics of living things, introductory biology texts list such properties as reproduction, motility, growth, metabolism, and irritability to stimuli. None of these defining features alone is adequate, however, for each applies also to inanimate objects. A crystal, for example, exhibits growth, and an automobile has motility. If any single quality distinguishes the animate from the inanimate, it is the capacity to modify behavior according to experience acquired during the lifetime of the individual. Such a capacity is called *behavioral plasticity*.

THE ADAPTIVE VALUE OF PLASTICITY

What survival advantages does plasticity confer upon a species? The first has to do with the distribution of a species throughout diverse habitats. The earth comprises an astonishing range of environments, from frozen desolation to equatorial lushness, from rarefied mountain chill to viscous desert heat, from pounding, salty coastal intertidals to quiet, freshwater ponds. Survival in each of these habitats requires not only different structural and functional endowments but also different behavioral strategies. Behavioral flexibility is one attribute that can encourage a species to colonize new and different environments. It follows that the species with the greatest plasticity should also exhibit the widest range of habitats, an expectation that is well confirmed by the radiation of the human species into all possible environments.

One adaptive value of behavioral plasticity, then, is that it broadens the range of habitats within which a species is likely to survive. The dinosaurs may well have become extinct precisely because they lacked such plasticity. But there is another and more significant advantage to plasticity. Even within a fixed environment, animals constantly encounter new circumstances in their day-to-day existence, including, for example, interactions with potential prey and predators, the discovery of a new route, the exploration of an unfamiliar range, the utilization of a different shelter or food source, and the finding of a new mate. Each new circumstance demands an appropriate behavioral response, and yet the possible range and combination of such circumstances is so vast that the number of potential responses quickly swamps the information-storing capacity of the genetic code. As a way around this impasse, evolution has selected for malleability in behavior. Once trial and error reveals an effective response to a new stimulus, there is then an obvious value to preserving the association between the stimulus and the response for future use. Seen in this light, plasticity is a tool for coping with the exigencies of daily existence and making use of the experience to guide future behavior.

AN APPROACH TO THE ANALYSIS OF PLASTICITY

Given that plasticity is one of the most important properties of animal life, how can we go about studying it? Plasticity may be investigated on many different levels, and the first step is to choose the level. The psychologist, for example, may study plasticity by training white rats to perform various ingenious tasks, such as running through a complicated maze in a way that avoids unpleasant electric shocks. Ethologists may analyze plasticity by studying an animal's learning capacity in its natural habitat. If we are interested in the physiological substrates of plasticity, however, we must eventually look to the nervous system and the cells that comprise it. Single nerve cells (neurons) have in fact been shown capable of altering their activity on the basis of experience, a phenomenon called *neuronal plasticity* (e.g., Bliss, Gardner-Medwin, and Lomo, 1973). Presumably such neuronal plasticity is responsible for behavioral plasticity, but in most instances we do not yet understand the connection; if only for this reason, the distinction between behavioral and neuronal plasticity must be carefully preserved.

If we wish to learn about the neuronal aspects of plasticity, we must first decide between two possible strategies: we may opt to study a "higher" organism that exhibits an enormous capacity for plasticity but that also has an immensely complex nervous system; or we may select a "lower" organism that exhibits a necessary minimum capacity for plasticity but that also has a relatively simple nervous system that can be unraveled with satisfying precision and completeness. In other words, we must come to grips with the capacity–complexity tradeoff. Many neuroscientists have chosen the latter strategy and selected experimental preparations from invertebrate animals, simply because this strategy has appeared more likely to succeed.

What are the advantages of invertebrate nervous systems for cellular analyses of behavioral plasticity? The answer, in a word, is simplicity. More specifically, we may identify four characteristics of invertebrate nervous systems that are especially useful (Figure 1). First, invertebrates possess a limited number of neurons. An advanced invertebrate such as a snail, for example, may contain but 10^4 central nerve cells, a crayfish, 10^5. In contrast the human central nervous system is estimated to contain from 10^{10} to 10^{14} nerve cells, most of which are concentrated in the brain. The number of single interconnections that is possible between 10^{14} neurons is a staggering 10^{28} $(n(n - 1) \cong n^2)$, and, if we allow more realistically for multiple connections between the neurons, the number of possible interconnections quickly exceeds the estimated number of atoms in the universe (10^{84} baryons in the finite-universe model). It is little wonder that Lashley's courageous and pioneering attempts to locate the memory trace (the engram) in the rodent brain were frustrated (Lashley, 1963).

As a second advantage, invertebrate neurons are not only few in number but also packaged in neatly separated bundles called ganglia. These ganglia may contain as few as nine neurons or as many as several thousand. In most invertebrate groups, the ganglia are spaced along ventral nerve connections, like beads on a necklace, with each ganglion bearing substantial similarities with others in the chain. In other words, and unlike vertebrates, the intelligence

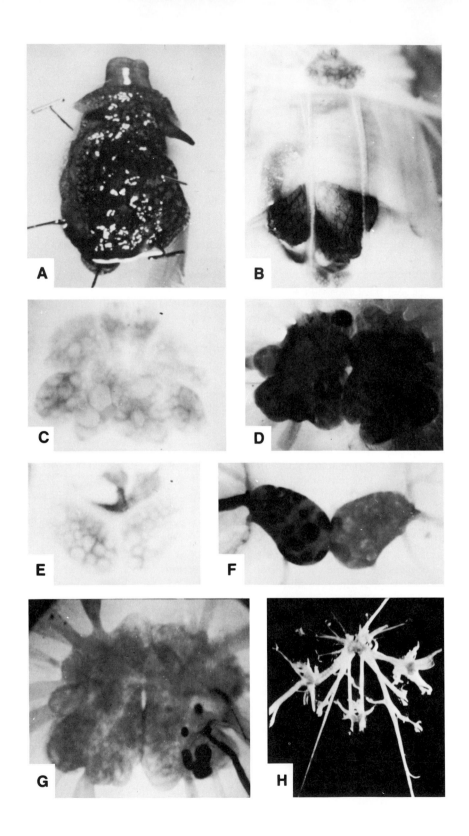

FIGURE 1. The nervous system of a representative invertebrate, the gastropod mollusk Pleurobranchaea californica, *which is the subject of experiments on the cellular basis of choice and learning. (A), dorsal view of an intact specimen. The anterior feeding proboscis is extended from beneath the oral veil at the top of the photograph. This specimen was 15 cm in length. (B), a view of the nervous system, exposed by a dorsal longitudinal incision in the anterior one-third of the animal. The anterior brain (top) is 1 cm wide and connected to the buccal ganglion by two nerves, the cerebrobuccal connectives. Note the many cell bodies, some of which reach 1 mm in diameter and are plainly visible with the unaided eye. (C), a living, unstained brain (dorsal view), showing the numerous, brightly-pigmented nerve cell bodies as they appear through the dissecting microscope. (D), a brain following back-injection of the left cerebrobuccal connective with cobalt chloride and subsequent precipitation of cobalt sulfide in the filled neurons. This technique has been used in this instance to anatomically identify and map the positions of interneurons that turn on the feeding behavior (Davis* et al., *1974), in preparation for electrophysiological studies. These interneurons may be the loci of physiological changes that underlie learning in this preparation. (E), a living, unstained buccal ganglion (dorsal view). Most of the cell bodies that are visible belong to motoneurons that supply feeding musculature (Siegler* et al., *1974). (F), a buccal ganglion following back-injection of the third buccal root, a nerve that supplies feeding musculature active during withdrawal of the feeding proboscis. Most of the filled cell bodies belong to identified feeding motoneurons. (G), a brain following back-injection of the right cerebrovisceral connective. (H), an isolated nervous system showing the brain (top), buccal ganglion (bottom) and lateral pedal ganglia. Neurophysiological experiments on associative learning are being conducted on this relatively simple preparation.*

of an invertebrate is not concentrated in one location but instead distributed into many simplified and smaller "mini-brains" that are much easier to understand.

As a third advantage, the individual neurons that comprise invertebrate nervous systems are often large and sometimes brightly pigmented (Figure 1C). The purpose of the pigmentation is unclear, but it makes the cells much easier to see and therefore to penetrate with stimulating and recording microelectrodes. Moreover, the large cell bodies of invertebrate neurons are typically located on the surface of the ganglion they comprise, from which position they send processes into the tangled central core called the neuropile. The most interesting integrative activity takes place in the central neuropile; fortunately, however, the electrical events within the neuropilar processes spread outward to the corresponding cell body on the surface of the ganglion, where the events can be readily recorded with microelectrodes. The cell bodies thus provide convenient electrical windows, through which we may view the integrative activity of the nervous system.

As a fourth and especially valuable advantage, invertebrates possess *identifiable* nerve cells. That is, the cell body of a given neuron always occupies the same position in the ganglion and has the same functional hookups with other cells. Since individual neurons are so distinctive in structure and function, the physiologist can identify and study a neuron in one animal, confident in the knowledge that the corresponding neuron can be found and studied again in the next animal. The possibility of such multiple access to the "same" neuron greatly extends the range of information that can be obtained from single cells and thereby permits a truly comprehensive cellular analysis of neuronal function.

The chief advantages of invertebrate nervous systems, then, relate to simplicity of organization and accessibility to cellular analysis. In the remainder of this article we shall see how these advantages can be used to learn about the physiological basis of plasticity. We shall consider four forms of behavioral plasticity that are especially amenable to cellular analysis: habituation, choice, sensitization, and learning. In the space available we can do little more than touch upon the highlights of this exciting subject; a more comprehensive review appears elsewhere (Davis, 1975).

HABITUATION

In terms of the procedure used to demonstrate it, the simplest form of plasticity is habituation, defined as the decline in behavioral response that is caused by repetition of a sensory stimulus. Habituation has long interested students of plasticity because it can be considered a primitive form of learning. As we shall see, however, the paradigm for associative learning, at least, is fundamentally different from that of habituation, and it seems likely that the underlying cellular mechanisms are also different. Habituation is nonetheless interesting and significant in its own right. Were it not for habituation, we would be constantly startled by small and unimportant sounds, unendingly surprised by sudden but trivial movements in our visual field, and continuously distracted by the feeling of clothes on our body. Habituation is the means by which harmless stimuli can be appropriately ignored.

Habituation has long been studied on the behavioral level, but it is only in the last few years that its cellular basis has been systematically uncovered by experiments on two invertebrate animals: the crayfish, and the gastropod mollusk, *Aplysia*. The crayfish flips its tail to escape from strong tactile stimuli and thus escapes from predators. In response to repeated tactile stimuli, however, this escape response habituates (for behavioral and cellular studies, see Bruner and Kennedy, 1970; Krasne, 1969; Krasne and Bryan, 1973; Krasne and Roberts, 1969; Krasne and Woodsmall, 1969; Wine, 1971; Wine and Krasne, 1969, 1972; Zucker 1972a–c; Zucker, Kennedy and Selverston, 1971). Similarly, the gill of *Aplysia* is defensively withdrawn when other parts of the body are touched. In both cases, the underlying neuronal mechanisms are similar, and hence only the molluscan example will be discussed here.

Aplysia may be thought of as an egg omelette with a nervous system. In the space between the two flaps of the omelette is the external mantle cavity, which contains a variety of organs, including the gill, the siphon, and the mantle shelf (Figure 2A). When the siphon is touched or stimulated with a jet of water, the gill undergoes a defensive withdrawal, contracting into a shadow of its former self (Kupfermann, Carew, and Kandel, 1974). Over the space of several seconds the gill relaxes and unfolds to its original shape. When the touch stimulus is repeated, the gill is still withdrawn, but with repetitive stimulation the response wanes and finally disappears altogether (Figure 2B). In other words, the gill withdrawal response habituates (Pinsker et al., 1970). Signs of this habituation persist for as long as several weeks (Carew and Kandel, 1973; Carew, Pinsker, and Kandel, 1972), a time course not unlike that of long-term learning.

To study this form of behavioral plasticity on the cellular level, it was first necessary to identify the neurons that control the gill. It is here that the many advantages of invertebrate nervous systems become especially apparent. Large nerves supplying the gill and the siphon can be readily traced to the abdominal ganglion, which thus appeared a likely locus for the cellular events that underlie habituation. To expose the abdominal ganglion, a small hole was cut in the anterior, dorsal surface of the animal, and the ganglion was pinned to a micromanipulated stage without damaging its nerves. Using this relatively intact preparation, stimulating microelectrodes were inserted in one cell body after another until neurons were identified that caused the gill to contract. These cells, which are identifiable from one preparation to the next (Figure 2C), were then subjected to more rigorous tests which proved that they were the motoneurons supplying the gill musculature (Kupfermann and Kandel, 1969; Kupfermann et al., 1971; Kupfermann Carew, and Kandel, 1974).

One of the gill motoneurons identified in these studies, named L 7, has been studied particularly closely in connection with habituation. When the siphon is touched in the semi-intact preparation, the tactile information is carried along many axons in the siphon nerve to the abdominal ganglion, where it causes a compound excitatory postsynaptic potential (EPSP) in motoneuron L 7. In response to repeated touch, this compound EPSP declines in amplitude, and the decline exactly parallels

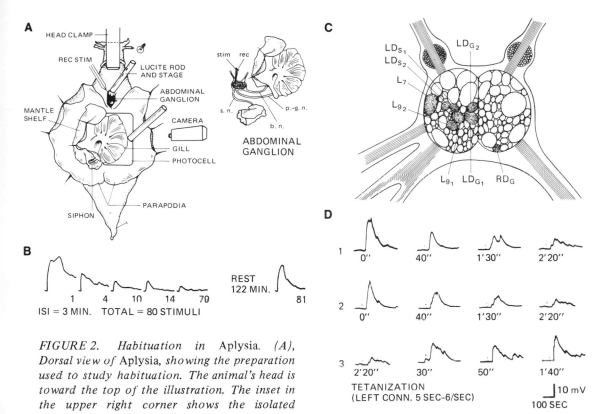

FIGURE 2. Habituation in Aplysia. (A), Dorsal view of Aplysia, showing the preparation used to study habituation. The animal's head is toward the top of the illustration. The inset in the upper right corner shows the isolated abdominal ganglion/siphon/gill preparation.
(From Kupfermann, Carew and Kandel, 1975.) (B), Behavioral habituation of the gill withdrawal reflex. To produce these records, a force transducer was attached to the gill of an intact animal so that gill contraction caused an upward deflection of the recording. The siphon was then touched every 3 minutes to a total of 80 stimuli, followed by a two hour rest (before trial 81). Note habituation as well as recovery. (From Pinsker et al., 1970.) (C), Dorsal surface of the abdominal ganglion of Aplysia, showing some of the central neurons in which neurophysiological correlates of behavioral habituation have been studied. (From Kupfermann, Carew and Kandel, 1974.) (D), Neurophysiological correlates of behavioral habituation in Aplysia. All traces are intracellular recordings of the compound EPSP in motoneuron L7, in response to electrical stimulation of the siphon nerve at one per 10 seconds. In 1, repeated stimulation causes decrement, seen at the indicated time intervals from the first stimulus. In 2, the EPSP recovers after a 15 minute rest and is then again decremented. In 3, the left connective from the left ganglia was stimulated tetanically to increase the EPSP amplitude from siphon nerve stimulation, a presumed neural parallel to behavioral dishabituation. (From Schwartz, et al., 1971.)*

the behavioral habituation seen earlier (Figure 2D; Kupfermann et al., 1970; Carew and Kandel, 1973). Neither the gill musculature nor the sensory receptors mediating the touch stimulus show any response decrement, and the motoneuron itself shows no change in responsiveness (e.g., Carew, Castellucci, and Kandel, 1971). Therefore, the physiological process(es) that underlie habituation reside in the central nervous system presynaptic to the motoneurons.

From these studies we may reasonably infer that a decline in EPSP amplitude in gill motoneurons is responsible for behavioral habituation. We must next ask what causes this decline. A number of possibilities exist, but none has been definitely proven. The simplest explanation that fits with the available data is that the amount of chemical synaptic transmitter substance released by the afferent neurons to the gill motoneurons declines with repeated stimulation. In other words, behavioral habituation may result simply from the depletion of transmitter chemicals from synapses located in the central circuits that mediate the behavior.

If such a cellular explanation for behavioral habituation seems almost disappointingly simple, we may remind ourselves that the most universal truths are nearly always simple. Moreover, the analysis of habituation in both the crayfish and *Aplysia* has left us with an important take-home lesson. These studies have shown for the first time that at least a simple form of behavioral plasticity can be analyzed on the level of single nerve cells in invertebrate animals. Behavioral plasticity may represent an emergent property of central nerve networks, that is, a property that resides in no single nerve cell; but we can no longer believe that the physiological substrates of plasticity are distributed throughout so very many neurons that the causal events in single cells are too subtle to detect. In other words, these studies on habituation furnish every reason for optimism in our quest to learn about the cellular foundation of more complex forms of behavioral plasticity.

CHOICE

At one time or another we are all moved to ask ourselves why we choose to do the things that we do. Why go to school when we could be working? Why study about plasticity when we could be writing a poem? To avoid behavioral conflicts, organisms have evolved internal "priority lists," or *behavioral hierarchies*, that guide their choice of activities. It is these hierarchies that explain why an animal does what it does, with the implied exclusion of alternative possibilities. The fundamental features of behavioral hierarchies are no doubt inherited, but especially in "higher" animals, the lists may be in large part learned. Even in "lower" animals, the lists can be modified by experience, and it is in this sense that

behavioral hierarchies are relevant to the topic of plasticity.

A behavioral hierarchy is formally defined as the organization of unrelated acts of behavior into a priority sequence that governs behavioral choice (Davis, Mpitsos, and Pinneo, 1974a, b). For example, the marine mollusk *Pleurobranchaea* normally turns over within 20 to 30 seconds when turned onto its back. If a specimen is turned onto its back and then fed, however, righting is delayed until the food is gone, sometimes for more than an hour. That is, feeding occupies a higher position than righting in the behavioral hierarchy of *Pleurobranchaea*.

Feeding behavior also dominates other acts of behavior in *Pleurobranchaea*. For example, specimens normally withdraw their heads when touched on the anterior oral veil. If the animal is feeding, however, the touch stimulus is ignored. The animal is thus "programmed" to avoid the mistake of withdrawing from food. Surprisingly, feeding in these mollusks even dominates mating behavior. *Pleurobranchaea* is hermaphroditic, and specimens normally mate in a reciprocal, side-by-side position. If one member of such a mating pair is offered a morsel of food, it immediately abandons its friend to pursue the food. These mollusks may have the sophisticated capacity to make choices, but the choices that are made are apparently not guided by a well-developed sense of esthetics!

There is one behavior, however, that takes precedence over feeding, and that is egg laying. During egg laying, specimens are unresponsive even to their favorite food, fresh squid. In *Aplysia*, egg-laying behavior is induced by a hormone that is released into the blood by specialized "bag" cells located in the abdominal ganglion (Kupfermann, 1967, 1970; Toevs and Brackenbury, 1969). To test the hypothesis that a similar egg-laying hormone is used by *Pleurobranchaea* not only to turn on egg laying but also to turn off feeding, blood was withdrawn from egg-laying animals and injected into nonlaying specimens. Within 24 hours the specimens showed both egg laying and suppression of feeding. Crude extracts of the central nervous systems of egg-laying specimens was even more effective, causing egg laying and suppression of feeding within 2 to 4 hours.

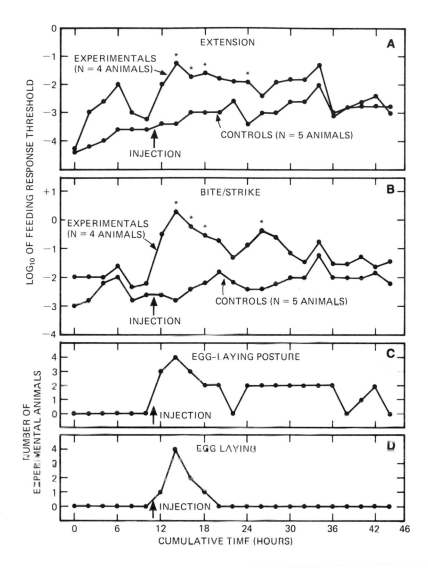

FIGURE 3. *Graphs showing mean thresholds or the extension (A, upper curve) and bite-strike (B, upper curve) feeding responses in animals induced to lay eggs by injection of crude extract from nervous systems taken from egg-laying specimens. Asterisks designate experimental means that were different from corresponding control means at the 0.05 level (multivariate ANOVA). (C) and (D) show indexes of egg-laying behavior measured simultaneously with feeding response thresholds. (From Davis* et al.*, 1974b.)*

(Figure 3A and B). In contrast, control animals, injected with extract from nonlaying nervous systems (Figure 3C) or with seawater (Figure 3D), showed no such changes. Unpublished experiments (performed in collaboration with Jeffrey L. Ram) in which each ganglion of egg-laying animals was bioassayed indicate that the hormone is contained only within the brain and two pedal ganglia, and biochemical analyses indicate that the hormone is a polypeptide with a molecular weight of around 6,000.

Why is feeding behavior relatively dominant in the behavioral heirarchy of *Pleurobranchaea*, and why is it subordinate to egg

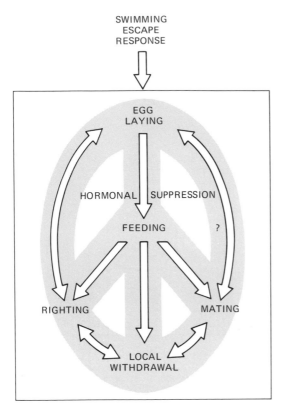

SWIMMING
ESCAPE
RESPONSE

EGG
LAYING

HORMONAL | SUPPRESSION

FEEDING   ?

RIGHTING   MATING

LOCAL
WITHDRAWAL

FIGURE 4. *Major aspects of the behavioral hierarchy of* Pleurobranchaea. *Unidirectional arrows from one behavioral act to another signify dominance of the former over the latter. Bidirectional arrows between behavioral acts signify mutual compatibility, i.e., behavioral acts that can occur simultaneously. Escape behavior is dominant over each behavioral act enclosed within the box. The question mark designates a probable but undemonstrated relation. (From Davis* et al., *1974b.)*

laying? The answer presumably lies in the fact that *Pleurobranchaea* is a carnivore and thus depends upon a relatively limited and sporadic food supply. Thus opportunities to feed must be met with an immediate and decisive response if the species is to survive. The suppression of feeding during egg laying presumably prevents the species from self-destructing by consuming its own eggs, literally eating itself out of existence.

The behavioral hierarchy of *Pleurobranchaea*, summarized in Figure 4, is thus the

means by which this species decides between alternatives in any circumstance requiring choice. We might well wonder, however, whether this hierarchy is predictive of the animal's behavior regardless of the individual's experience. For example, if the swimming response were habituated, would it still dominate all other behavioral acts? And if specimens were fed to satiation, would feeding still occupy its usual position of dominance? To explore the effects of experience on the behavioral hierarchy, we examined the effects of food satiation on the dominance of feeding over righting and over local withdrawal of the oral veil and head in response to tactile stimuli. We found that in satiated specimens, application of squid homogenate to the oral veil still suppressed righting behavior, but no longer suppressed the oral veil withdrawal response (Davis et al., in preparation 1975). In other words, the dominance of feeding over righting persisted, but the dominance of feeding over the withdrawal response was abolished. The hierarchy can therefore be modified by a relatively potent form of experience, food satiation. Whether other forms of experience also alter the hierarchy (e.g., learning) remains to be studied.

The cellular mechanisms that underlie choice and its modification by experience are not yet known. It is easy to speculate that feeding behavior is dominant because chemosensory inputs that excite feeding inhibit other behaviors. This possibility is supported by the finding that chemosensory influences suppress righting even when specimens are satiated. Alternatively, the central circuitry that controls feeding may itself inhibit the neurons that control subordinate behaviors. This possibility is supported by the finding that when specimens are satiated (and thus no longer feed), chemosensory inputs for feeding do not suppress oral veil withdrawal. Egg laying may dominate feeding simply because egg-laying hormone makes the neurons that control feeding behavior less susceptible to excitation from their normal sensory influences. *Pleurobranchaea*'s nervous system is accessible to cellular studies (Davis and Mpitsos, 1971; Davis, Siegler, and Mpitsos, 1973; Davis et al., 1974; Siegler, Mpitsos, and Davis, 1974), and these speculations should be relatively easy to test on the cellular level.

The kind of "choice" that is exercised by *Pleurobranchaea* is, in an operational sense, just like the kind of choice we make in deciding, for example, to study plasticity instead of writing a poem. Perhaps we have a greater awareness of the alternatives than the slug, but even this notion is debatable. The exercise of choice implies the capability to ignore certain sensory commands, which in turn implies the capacity for attention and selective perception. Choice also implies the pursuit of one behavior to the exclusion of others, which is what we mean by drive and motivation. I think that by studying behavioral hierarchies, we can gain a unified understanding of a variety of psychological and ethological phenomena, and eventually hope to understand these phenomena on the cellular level.

SENSITIZATION

Once, while I was descending on a scuba dive in a murky, storm-tossed sea off the coast of northern California, a gigantic animal, hovering an arm's length away, crashed into my awareness. My initial fright subsided somewhat when I recognized the creature as a curious sea lion, but a minute later in the descent, when the bottom loomed unexpectedly from the murk, I experienced a second jolt of fear that was even more intense than the first. I had been "sensitized" by the encounter with the sea lion, so that the normally pleasurable sight of the seafloor became frightening. To generalize from this instance, sensitization is an increase in the behavioral response to one sensory stimulus caused by previous delivery of another sensory stimulus. The paradigm for sensitization resembles that of classical conditioning (see below), except that the behavioral modification in sensitization does not require the pairing of the stimuli. That is, sensitization is non-associative, resembling a general "arousal."

Behavioral sensitization has been analyzed in *Aplysia* using the same preparation employed to study habituation, that is, the gill withdrawal response. Touching the siphon in an un-habituated preparation causes the normal withdrawal response described earlier. If the touch stimulus is preceded by touching another body region (e.g., the head), the gill withdrawal response is sensitized; that is, the gill contraction is much stronger than usual (Carew, Castellucci, and Kandel, 1971).

The physiological basis of sensitization has been studied by recording from the identified gill withdrawal motoneuron, L 7, in the abdominal ganglion of the semi-intact preparation (e.g., Figure 2A). As might be expected, the compound EPSP caused by touching the siphon increases in size during behavioral sensitization (Carew, Castellucci, and Kandel, 1971). Experiments on the isolated abdominal ganglion have shown that the increase in EPSP amplitude results from a cellular mechanism known as heterosynaptic facilitation — that is, the increase in the efficacy of one presynaptic pathway caused by prior stimulation of another presynaptic pathway. The biophysical basis of heterosynaptic facilitation is unknown — indeed, homosynaptic facilitation is not yet completely understood — but at least we are again able to point to a specific cellular mechanism as responsible for a particular form of behavioral plasticity in at least one preparation.

LEARNING

Learning is the most diverse, advanced, and intriguing form of plasticity. The debate over how to define learning could fill volumes, but the reading would be dry. Briefly, we may recognize two general classes of learning: associative and nonassociative. Associative learning may be simply defined as a behavioral modification caused by reinforced (rewarded or punished) experience; it includes such familiar categories as classical (Pavlovian) and instrumental (operant) conditioning. Nonassociative learning, the acquisition of a new behavior pattern in the apparent absence of reinforcement, is presently impossible to define in a way that distinguishes it from simpler forms of plasticity, such as habituation and sensitization. It is for this reason that some workers prefer to think of habituation as a form of learning, even though the underlying physiological mechanisms are probably fundamentally different. Nonassociative learning includes such phenomena as imitation learning, language learning, and place learning. (These distinctions

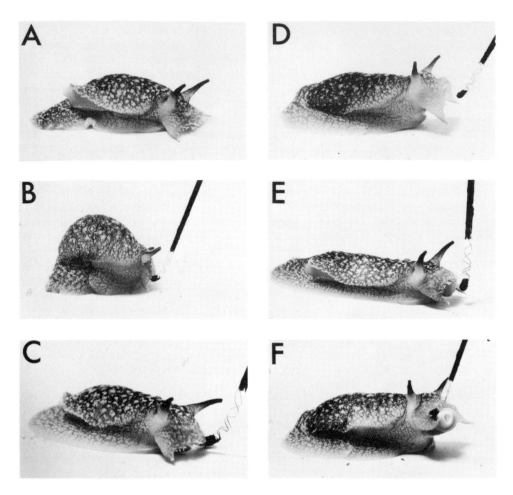

FIGURE 5. *Behavioral responses of* Pleurobranchaea. *(A), Animal viewed from right side; the anterior oral veil and fused lateral tentacles are on the right. (B), Withdrawal in response to tactile stimulation of the oral veil with a glass probe. The probe is partially wrapped to make it visible for photography. (C to F), Components of the feeding behavior, illustrated in a classically conditioned animal, are (C), no withdrawal; (D), orientation and following movements; (E), extension of the proboscis; and (F), the bite-strike feeding response. (From Mpitsos and Davis, 1973.)*

depend in part on the definitions of reinforcement discussed below.) Memory, the conversion of experience to an "engram" that is stored in the central nervous system for later recall, is presumed to underlie all forms of learning.

There has been considerable debate over whether invertebrate animals can learn at all, occasioned in part by the relatively strict definitions expounded by vertebrate psychologists and, sad to say, in part by the occasionally loose standards of invertebrate psychologists. These considerations aside, it is an empirical

fact that invertebrate animals are often hard to teach anything. This reluctance to learn is hardly to be blamed upon the animal; instead, the human experimenter commonly chooses stimuli that are tantalizing to a human but irrelevant to a snail or a worm. We now know that animals cannot form associations between any and all stimuli (the "equipotentiality" premise of Pavlov; Pavlov, 1927) but only between those stimuli for which evolution has prepared them (the "preparedness" principle of Garcia; see Seligman and Hager, 1972, for an

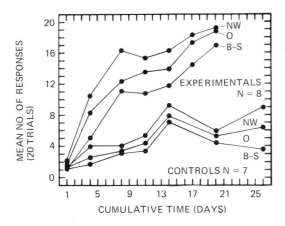

FIGURE 6. *Classical conditioning of the feeding response of* Pleurobranchaea. *The number of positive responses per 20 test trials (touch alone) is plotted against time. Conditioning trials occurred daily beginning after the measurements on day 1 and were stopped on day 13. NW, no withdrawal to touch; O, orientation to touch; B-S, bite-strike, feeding response to touch. (From Mpitsos and Davis, 1973.)*

excellent analysis and documentation). Such selective associability favors combinations of stimuli that have special survival value to the animal, and it is often difficult for a human being to guess what might turn on a worm. As a general rule, the most successful attempts to condition invertebrates have relied upon their well-developed chemical senses.

That invertebrates possess well-developed learning capabilities is now documented by dozens of studies (e.g., Corning, Dyal, and Willows, 1973a–c). Among the most convincing examples are studies on insects (Nelson, 1971; Quinn, Harris, and Benzer, 1974; Horridge, 1962a, b, 1965; Hoyle, 1965), crustaceans (Chow and Leiman, 1972) and mollusks (Chapter Sixteen, this volume; Mpitsos and Davis, 1973). In order to illustrate the type of approach that can be taken with invertebrate animals, and to illustrate the two major forms of associative learning (classical and instrumental conditioning), I shall discuss our work on learning in the mollusk *Pleurobranchaea*.

In classical conditioning, two sensory stimuli are presented together until the re-sponse caused originally only by the first stimulus becomes associated with the second stimulus. For example, Pavlov presented dogs with food and sound until the animals "learned" to salivate in response to the sound. A similar procedure has been used to classically condition *Pleurobranchaea*. Touch was paired with food stimuli until the formerly aversive touch stimulus became capable of causing the feeding response (Figures 5 and 6). Such conditioned behavior persisted for as long as 2 weeks without reinforcement before extinction was complete. Control experiments were performed by giving specimens touch alone and food stimuli unpaired with touch. Neither procedure caused the same behavioral modifications as classical conditioning, and hence the modification caused by conditioning represents true associative learning rather than sensitization. The control procedures in this experiment were not entirely satisfactory, because the food stimuli were delivered to the control animals in a slightly different way than to experimentals. It seems unlikely, however, that this difference was responsible for the results.

Instrumental conditioning differs from classical conditioning in that reinforcement is delivered only when the subject performs a "spontaneous" or "voluntary" act. In other words, the delivery of reinforcement is not inevitable, as it is in classical conditioning. A special kind of instrumental conditioning is avoidance conditioning, in which an act of behavior is suppressed by punishing its occurrence. Avoidance conditioning is usually considered a blend of classical and instrumental conditioning, but we need not worry about such details here (see Davis, 1975). As a general rule, avoidance conditioning is more rapid but less permanent than classical reward conditioning; in other words, positive reinforcement yields a more permanent form of learning than does punishment, a lesson we might well heed in raising our children.

Avoidance conditioning has been studied in *Pleurobranchaea* by shocking classically conditioned specimens whenever they exhibited the classically conditioned feeding response to touch. Specimens quickly learned that touch was associated with aversive shock and ceased feeding to the touch stimulus alone. Control specimens, in which shock and touch were unpaired, continued to exhibit the classically conditioned feeding response to touch alone. Thus the behavioral modification caused by avoidance conditioning is again attributable to associative learning rather than to generalized inhibition ("sensitization").

A new form of learning has recently been demonstrated in *Pleurobranchaea* (Mpitsos and Collins, 1975). Specimens that were presented with squid homogenate and simultaneous electric shock soon learned to suppress the feeding response to the squid homogenate, and this learned response persisted for more than 8 days. Control specimens that received unpaired squid homogenate and shock also showed suppression of the feeding response (shock-induced sensitization), but this behavioral modification disappeared after a day or two. In other words, although sensitization occurs in this paradigm, there is also a strong learning component. Perhaps this form of learning represents a facilitation of sensitization.

STRATEGIES FOR THE NEURONAL ANALYSIS OF PLASTICITY

Given that invertebrate animals do learn, how can we take advantage of their relatively simple nervous systems to study the neurophysiological substrates of learning? The strategy that has proved so effective in analyzing habituation and sensitization in *Aplysia* involves exhaustive analysis of the neuronal circuitry of the specific motor system that exhibits plasticity (i.e., the gill withdrawal motor system), followed by examination of specific neurons in that circuitry (i.e., motoneuron L 7) for the electrophysiological concommitants of plasticity (i.e., changes in the size of EPSPs). Only then is it possible to design meaningful experiments aimed at revealing the biophysical mechanisms that underlie plasticity.

Precisely the same strategy can be used to study more complex forms of plasticity, such as the modification of choice by experience and learning. For example, the feeding system of *Pleurobranchaea*, which exhibits choice and various forms of associative learning, is now reasonably well understood from the viewpoint of neuronal organization. The isolated nervous system (Figure 1H) can be made to generate

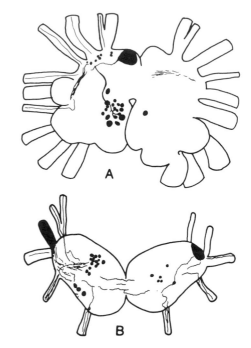

FIGURE 7. *Tracings of cobalt-chloride filled neurons in the brain (A) and buccal ganglion (B) of* Pleurobranchaea, *showing the major classes of interneurons that participate in the control of feeding. The brain cells, including the large metacerebral giant cell (A), sent axons through the cerebrobuccal connectives to the buccal ganglion, where they synapse on identified feeding neurons and initiate feeding behavior. The buccal ganglion cells (B) include small "corollary discharge" interneurons and the large "efference copy" neuron. The former help to coordinate the brain and the buccal ganglion during feeding. These back injections were made in collaboration with Melody V. S. Siegler.*

"feeding" activity simply by stimulating the appropriate nerve, thus facilitating analysis of the feeding circuitry (Davis, Siegler, and Mpitsos, 1973). The physiological machinery that controls the feeding behavior consists of several identified feeding muscles (Davis and Mpitsos, 1971), the motoneurons that supply the feeding muscles (Siegler, Mpitsos, and Davis, 1974), coordinating interneurons in the buccal ganglion (Davis et al., 1974), and a population of 40 to 50 putative "command" interneurons in the brain (Davis et al., 1974; Figure 7). All the central neurons of the feeding circuitry have been identified by means of intracellular dye injection (Figure 7), and many have been analyzed by means of intracellular microelectrodes (Davis and Mpitsos, 1971; Siegler, Mpitsos, and Davis, 1974). Stimulation of the metacerebral giant neuron of the brain (Figure 7), for example, activates the feeding rhythm and causes postsynaptic potentials in neurons of the buccal ganglion (experiments performed in collaboration with H. R. Gillette). This cell and the remaining putative command interneurons are thus especially interesting, because they appear to play the crucial role of turning on the motor networks that control the feeding behavior. It does not require a great stretch of the imagination to speculate that the cellular events that underlie choice and learning should be sought within these interneurons.

CONCLUSIONS

Near the beginning of this article we spoke of Lashley and his unsuccessful search for the memory engram, a search that occupied the better part of his productive life. Students of plasticity owe a debt of gratitude to Lashley; if I may be forgiven a cosmic metaphor, he groped unsuccessfully in a relatively uncharted universe, and thereby showed us that we should instead explore a single galaxy or even map a single solar system. Our search for the engram has not progressed much beyond Lashley's, but at least we know where and how to look. We have developed a successful experimental strategy, which involves the use of relatively simple invertebrate animals whose nervous systems can be mapped with unprecedented precision. Once behavioral plasticity is demonstrated and the nerve cells that control the behavior are identified, then, unlike Lashley, we know precisely where to search for the physiological substrates of plasticity.

I wish that words could convey how exciting this search is. Often in writing about science I am reminded of Antoine de Saint-Exupéry's "children's" book, *The Little Prince*, in which he writes:

If I have told you these details about the asteroid, and made a note of its numbers for you, it is on account of grown-ups and their ways. Grown-ups love figures. When you tell them that you have made a new friend, they never ask you any questions about essential matters. They never say to you, "What does his voice sound like? What game does he love best? Does he collect butterflies?"

Similarly, I often feel that in scientific papers, the essential matters are skirted and only the figures are presented. Not that the figures are unimportant; indeed, without them, our fellow scientists could neither believe nor repeat our work. But with figures alone, how can we communicate the essential humanness of the scientific enterprise? How can we tell about the playfulness of scientific experimentation and the susceptibility to error? How can we express the frustration that Lashley must have occasionally felt? How can we convey our gratitude to Lashley and other colleagues on whose work and ideas we build? And, above all, how can we express the fullness, the wonder, and the reverence that comes in seeing a little glimpse of nature for the first time, and sharing that vision with a friend?

At its best, science encompasses all the above sentiments. Also at its best, science uncovers truths that are as simple as they are universal, and we may well ask what generalities are likely to emerge from research on a worm, a crayfish, or a snail. The answer is exemplified in the success of genetics and molecular biology. In studying sweet peas, an Austrian monk first revealed to humanity the rules that govern its own heredity. And in studying protein synthesis in bacterial cells, molecular biologists have uncovered the mechanisms by which our own brain cells synthesize proteins. Time and again we are shown that common biological problems have generated common solutions at all levels in the animal kingdom. How can we believe that the neurosciences are exempt from this evolutionary reality? Time and again we are shown that on the most basic levels, life has a unified oneness. To think otherwise is, in my view, an egocentric denial of humankind's evolutionary legacy. Because of this principle of "evolutionary conservatism," we can be assured that studies on snails will have general relevance. I feel certain that the next few decades of research on invertebrates will have us understand the cellular basis of such funda- mental properties of life as choice and learning, and that, in the process, we cannot fail to learn something important about ourselves.

CHAPTER SIXTEEN

Neuroethological Studies of Learning in Mollusks

ALAN GELPERIN and DAVID FORSYTHE

INTRODUCTION

The essence of the neuroethological approach is the synergistic combination of the viewpoints of ethology and cellular neurophysiology. Ethology contributes an evolutionary perspective and a sensitivity to the critical importance of specific environmental stimuli from the *Umwelt* of the animal. The impetus from cellular neurophysiology is to select an animal whose neural machinery is maximally accessible to modern intracellular recording and staining techniques. The animal should also permit use of the full range of physiological preparations from isolated brain *in vitro* to semi-intact to intact with implanted electrodes, all of which are needed to establish the link between the biophysics and biochemistry of cell—cell interactions and behavior of the intact animal.

The utility of the neuroethological approach in studies of the physiological basis of learning in simple systems is expressed at several levels. Initially, a behavioral paradigm is needed which gives consistent and unequivocal learning. The ethological literature contains several examples of very rapid and long-lasting learning among invertebrates, such as wasp nest-site recognition (Van Iersel and van den Assem, 1965), honeybee food-site recognition (von Frisch, 1967), and octopus visual discrimination tests (Sanders, 1975). The realization that animals are genetically programmed to learn selectively (Seligman and Hager, 1972; Hinde and Stevenson-Hinde, 1972) guides the search for an appropriate learning task in terms of the ethology of the particular animal.

The neuroethological perspective also demands explicit demonstration that the detailed synaptic interactions established in isolated ganglia operate in essentially the same manner when the circuit is *in situ*. Elegant examples of the necessary types of experiments are provided by the analysis of circuitry for gill withdrawal in the opisthobranch mollusk *Aplysia californica* (Kandel, 1974) and for swimming in the medicinal leech *Hirudo medicinalis* (Kristan, Stent, and Ort, 1974). In both cases the behavior under study could be elicited when the controlling ganglion was externalized and stabilized for intracellular penetrations but retained its central and peripheral connections.

The evolutionary aspect of ethology prompts the neuroethologist to investigate the homology of neural structures and patterns of connectivity. The metacerebral giant cells of gastropod mollusks are especially favorable for this type of study (Senseman and Gelperin, 1973; Kupfermann and Weiss, 1974a). Similar comparisons have been made for molluscan neurosecretory cells (Kupfermann and Weiss, 1974b; Gainer, 1972), the Retzius cell of the leech (Lent, 1973) and the neurons that mediate branchial tuft withdrawal in *Tritonia* (Dorsett, 1974). In systems where the genetics can be directly manipulated, such as *Drosophila* (Hotta and Benzer, 1972), *Daphnia* (Levinthal, Macagno, and Tountas, 1974) or *Caenorhabdita* (Brenner, 1974), the available neurophysiological data are more limited. The gains from comparative studies will be much greater when entire neural circuits can be compared; studies of molluscan feeding mechanisms now underway in a number of laboratories may fulfill this role.

FOOD-AVERSION LEARNING

One of the most striking examples of selective learning is taste aversion learning in vertebrates. Rats quickly learn to associate the olfactory and gustatory cues associated with novel foods with aversive or paliative consequences of ingesting the food (Garcia, McGowan, and Green, 1972; Kalat and Rozin, 1972). Taste aversion learning is distinctive in that typically it occurs in one trial, extinguishes very slowly, and can occur with delays of one hour or more between sensory input and internal consequence. Birds also learn taste aversions very rapidly but use visual cues associated with the novel food (Wilcoxon, Dragoin, and Kral, 1971). The Atlantic cod has recently been shown to form conditioned food aversions (MacKay, 1974). A clear example of taste-aversion learning in an ethological setting is provided by blue jays (*Cyanocitta cristata*

bromia) learning to avoid ingestion of monarch butterflies (*Danaus plexippus*) (Brower, 1969).

To the ethologist it is clear that animals are genetically programmed to learn selectively. This is particularly true of invertebrates. As neurophysiologists seeking to understand the synaptic basis of plasticity in simple systems, we require robust and reliable learned modifications so as to maximize the possibility of locating the responsible synapses. It is clearly of advantage to use selective learning mechanisms such as food aversion learning whenever the behavioral paradigm can be exploited for neurophysiological analysis.

Encouraged by initial experiments using the terrestrial slug *Limax maximus* as a neurophysiological preparation (MacKay and Gelperin, 1972; Chang, Gelperin, and Johnson, 1974; Senseman and Gelperin, 1973) and as a behavioral subject (Gelperin, 1974; Prior and Gelperin, 1974), we asked the question: Can *Limax* learn taste aversions? This animal is a generalized herbivore (Gain, 1891; Frömming, 1952) confronted by plants containing a wide variety of noxious and potentially toxic chemicals (Kingsbury, 1964). If a large number of plant species are offered to *Limax*, only 20 to 30 percent of them will be sampled. Of the acceptable species, mushroom (*Boletus edulis*), carrot root (*Daucus carota*), potato tubers (*Solanum tuberosum*), and cucumber seed pods (*Cucumis sativa*) are most highly preferred. Since *Limax* can live 3 to 4 years (Quick, 1961), the increased fitness conferred by learned modifications of food preferences would have ample time for expression.

Experiments to test for food-avoidance learning in *Limax* were conducted in the following way. Slugs were fed individually and their intake measured by weighing the food before and after a one-hour access to the food. Animals were fed potato once per day for 7 days to establish it as a safe food. On the eighth day animals were given access to a very palatable food, mushroom (*Agaricus campestris*), 4 hours after their normal meal of potato. Half the slugs ($N = 8$) were poisoned with CO_2 for 5 minutes immediately after they finished their meal of mushroom. The other half of the group ($N = 8$) were poisoned with CO_2 3 hours after the termination of their mushroom meal. The 3 hour interval should

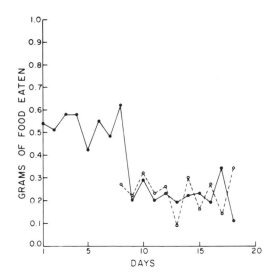

FIGURE 1. *Average daily intake of potato (solid line) and mushroom (dashed line) when mushroom intake is measured 4 hours after potato intake. CO_2 given after 3 hours if mushroom is eaten.*

obviate the possibility of learning but serve as a control for nonspecific effects of CO_2 poisoning. Dual feedings were continued for an additional 10 days with the stipulation that CO_2 poisoning was applied to animals in both groups if and only if a meal of mushroom was eaten. The data for these two groups of slugs are shown in Figures 1 and 2. Mushroom intake of the learning group was depressed on the second day of dual feedings and remained depressed for the duration of the experiment.

Two types of statistical tests have been performed on these data, both of which give the same answer in somewhat different form. For the 10 days on which learning could be expressed (days 9 to 18), mushroom intake was compared to potato intake for each animal day by day. For the control group mushroom intake was not different from potato intake (Wilcoxon matched-pair, signed-rank test, $p = 0.3$), whereas for the learning group mushroom intake was very significantly less than potato intake (Wilcoxon test, $p < 0.0001$). Comparison between the groups was done using potato-intake-minus-mushroom-intake differ-ence values so that variations in feeding which influenced both foods would not in-

fluence the comparison. The potato–mushroom difference values were very different for the learning versus control group (Mann–Whitney U test, $p < 0.00003$). Since the control-group animals received gas with greater frequency than the learning group (43 percent of mushroom trials versus 28 percent for learning group), the nonassociative effects of CO_2 have been more than adequately con-trolled. These data have been more fully presented elsewhere (Gelperin, 1975a).

Two additional groups of slugs have been examined. A control group was run with no CO_2 poisoning applied at any time. These animals ate equivalent amounts of mushroom and potato once dual feedings commenced. Another learning group was trained with a one-hour delay between the mushroom meal and CO_2 poisoning. These animals decreased their mushroom intake. Between-group com-parisons showed that the one-hour delay of CO_2 poisoning still promoted significant learning. Further comparisons are found in Gelperin (1975a).

An additional replication of the food-avoidance learning experiment has been carried out using a yoked-control procedure. Each member of the control group ($N = 15$) was

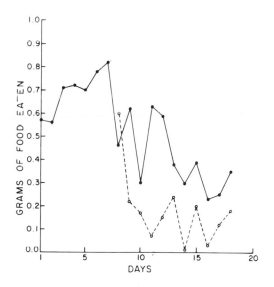

FIGURE 2. *Average daily intake of potato and mushroom. CO_2 given with no delay if mushroom is eaten.*

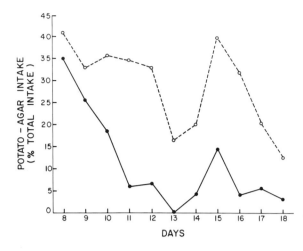

FIGURE 3. *Potato-agar intake for experimentals (solid line) and yoked controls (dashed line). See text for details.*

randomly paired with a member of the experimental group ($N = 15$). Carrot-agar was the safe food and potato-agar the unsafe food. Slugs were fed a preweighed piece of carrot-agar once each day for 18 days and their intakes measured. On the eighth day and for the following 10 days we offered each animal a piece of potato-agar 4 hours after the carrot meal. Animals in the experimental group who ate the potato-agar diet were exposed to CO_2 for 5 minutes immediately after completing the meal. A control slug received CO_2 if its counterpart in the experimental group received CO_2 but independent of its own response to the potato diet. CO_2 administration to control slugs was delayed three hours from the presentation of the potato diet. This delay eliminated the possibility of one-trial learning in the control group due to the chance pairing of potato ingestion closely followed by CO_2 administration. The yoked-control procedure resulted in two groups of animals with identical schedules of CO_2 exposure, but only in the experimental group was CO_2 exposure contingent on potato ingestion and timed to permit its association with potato ingestion. The results are shown in Figure 3. The experimental group had significantly depressed potato intake relative to the control group on 6 of the last 10 days.

A striking feature of food-aversion learning by the slug, as in the several vertebrate species, is its rapid onset. Of the total population of slugs trained, 40 percent completely avoided mushroom for 6 days after one or two training trails. As Figure 4 shows, some animals do even better. None of the animals in either control group showed such behavior.

SENSORY AND MOTOR ASPECTS

Olfaction is of prime importance in the orientation of slugs (Gelperin, 1974). Odors are important both for navigation relative to the home site and for identification of potential plant prey. The superior tentacles bear olfactory receptors at their tips served by the digitate (i.e., tentacular) ganglion. A distinctive patch of sensory epithelium is served by the digitate ganglion. Electrical potentials recorded from the external surface of the sensory patch resemble the electroolfactogram (EOG) recorded from frog nasal mucosa. The negative-going EOG and simultaneously recorded action potentials in the olfactory nerve are elicited by plant odors as well as by artificial odorants, such as amyl acetate. Animals with bilateral section of the olfactory nerve show greatly

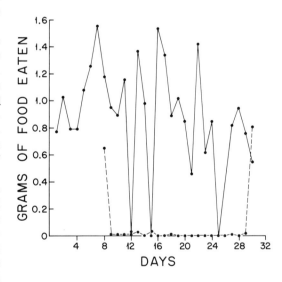

FIGURE 4. *Intake of potato (solid line) and mushroom (dashed line) by individual slug. Mushroom meal punished by CO_2 exposure.*

impaired food selection and homing behavior (Gelperin, 1974).

When a hungry slug contacts a palatable food, it opens and expands its lips and begins rhythmic feeding movements. The motor program for feeding behavior in *Limax* comprises coordinated rhythmic output from the buccal and cerebral ganglia. The buccal ganglia are situated on the posterior face of the buccal mass just ventral to the esophagus. The muscles of the buccal mass accomplish rhythmic protraction and retraction movements of the radula by which food particles are rasped from the substrate and ingested. Rhythmic movements of the lips aid in grasping the food and pressing it against the radula. Motor nerves 1, 2, and 3 show phasic, coordinated activity during feeding activity. A preparation of the isolated buccal mass, buccal ganglia and CNS will show vigorous feeding movements *in vitro*, particularly if the animal is starved before the preparation is made. Recording *en passant* and from cut central ends of motor nerves 1, 2, and 3 during such *in vitro* feeding has established a 1 : 1 correlation between the coordinated phasic bursting in these nerves and actual feeding movements.

The intensity and frequency of feeding movements in such *in vitro* preparations varied greatly, but rapid, rhythmic, high frequency bursting of large numbers of buccal efferents was invariably associated with vigorous buccal movements indistinguishable from those of normal feeding. Units in buccal nerves 1 and 3 were predominantly in phase with each other and in alternation with units in buccal nerve 2. Recordings from the salivary nerve reveal that activity in the salivary nerve burster, an autoactive motoneuron to the salivary duct, is phase-locked to the protraction–retraction cycle (Gelperin, 1975b; Prior and Gelperin, in preparation). This output pattern represents the motor pattern for feeding. The details of the motor program will be dealt with elsewhere (Gelperin, Forsythe, and Bernstein, in preparation).

The patterned motoneuron activity underlying feeding can be produced spontaneously by a single isolated buccal ganglion or from a preparation like that shown in Figure 5. The lips are sequestered in separate chambers with their innervation from the cerebral ganglia

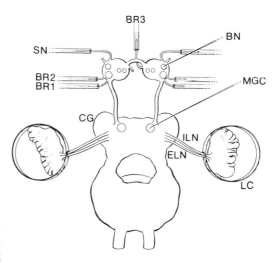

FIGURE 5. *Preparation used to elicit feeding motor program by chemical stimulation of lips. Suction electrodes are shown recording from buccal roots (BR 1, 2, and 3) and the salivary gland nerve (SN). Microelectrodes are shown in the metacerebral giant cell (MGC) and a buccal neuron (BN). CG, cerebral ganglion; ELN, external lip nerve; ILN, internal lip nerve; LC, lip chamber.*

intact. Food-derived or chemically-defined solutions can be applied to the lips while recording intracellularly from cerebral and buccal cells and extracellularly from buccal motor roots so as to detect unequivocally the release of the feeding motor program. Figure 6 shows the activation of feeding motor output by potato juice applied to the lips.

Analysis of buccal motor programs for feeding is progressing for a number of gastropod mollusks (*Pleurobranchaea* — Davis, Siegler, and Mpitsos, 1973; Siegler, Mpitsos, and Davis, 1974; *Helisoma* — Kater and Rowell, 1973; Kater, 1974; *Aplysia* — Gardner, 1971; Kupfermann and Cohen, 1971; *Tritonia* — Willows, personal communication; *Navanax* — Spira and Bennett, 1972; Woollacott, 1974; *Planorbis* — Berry, 1972; *Ariolimax* — Senseman, in preparation; *Limax* — Gelperin, Forsythe, and Bernstein, in preparation). These systems offer abundant opportunities to study novel cellular and synaptic phenomena, and

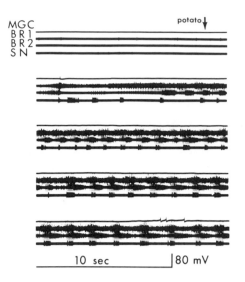

MGC
BR1
BR2
SN

potato↓

10 sec   80 mV

FIGURE 6.   Recording from the metacerebral giant cell, buccal nerves 1, 2, and the salivary gland nerve before and after application of potato juice to the lips. Potato juice is applied at arrow.

eventually to understand their full functional and evolutionary meanings.

The neuromuscular organization of gastropod feeding is simple in comparison with other molluscan motor systems. Centrally-located motoneurons make direct monosynaptic junctional potentials onto muscle fibers, and the contribution of peripheral motor elements to muscle activation appears to be small. Central sensory neuron cell bodies have been tentatively identified in *Navanax* (Spray and Bennett, 1975) and *Pleurobranchaea* (Siegler, Mpitsos, and Davis, 1974). It is therefore possible that easily accessible central neurons and their interconnections may largely account for the patterning of feeding activity.

Synaptic inputs to buccal ganglion motoneurons and synaptic interactions among these cells can be readily determined by intracellular recording. In some systems, substantial progress has already been made in identifying buccal interneurons which may be responsible for the coordinated activation of motoneurons (Kater, 1974; Gardner, 1971). Chemical synaptic control of electrical coupling among such interneurons may be important in modulating the

ability of sensory inputs to trigger or terminate feeding in *Helisoma* (Kaneka, Kater, and Fountain, 1974). It may eventually be possible to account for many aspects of molluscan feeding behavior, including learned modifications, in terms of the action of sensory inputs and central interneurons on pattern-generating premotor interneurons.

INTERNEURONS

Study of feeding interneurons in *Limax* has focussed primarily on a pair of large neurons in the cerebral ganglia, the metacerebral giant cells (MGCs). These identifiable interneurons have been found in over a dozen species of opisthobranch and pulmonate mollusks (Senseman and Gelperin, 1973). In *Limax*, the MGC exhibits the characteristic histofluorescence of a serotoninergic neuron (Osborne and Cottrell, 1971). Each MGC sends one or more axons to the periphery via a lip nerve and also sends a major process to the buccal ganglion via the cerebrobuccal connective, where it branches to exit in several buccal motor roots and the salivary gland nerve. The MGC receives excitatory synaptic input from the olfactory nerve and provides excitatory synaptic output to buccal motoneurons and salivary effector cells.

The nature of the synaptic inputs and outputs of the MGC led us to examine the possible involvement of this cell in the activation of the feeding motor program. In preparations consisting of isolated cerebral and buccal ganglia, the MGC has been observed to fire during buccal bursting activity. Firing rates of 1 to 2.5 spikes per second may be sustained for many seconds in cells not yet penetrated by microelectrodes. Both slow, smooth depolarizing potentials and discrete, rhythmic bursts of inhibitory post-synaptic potentials modulate MGC firing and cause the cell to fire most often immediately before and after the major portion of buccal root 1 and 3 bursts. Buccal cell B7 is an identified protractor mononeuron to the supralateral radular tensor muscle. Activation of B7 is coincident with the barrage of IPSPs in the MGC (Figure 7).

A preparation such as that shown in Figure 5 was used to record from the MGC while food stimuli were applied to the lips so as to elicit

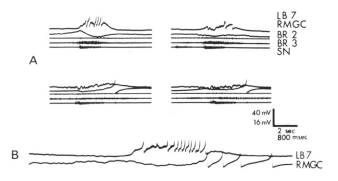

FIGURE 7. *Recordings from isolated buccal ganglia-cerebral ganglia preparation. A. Four segments from a continuous record showing coincident synaptic inputs to a left buccal motoneuron (LB7) and the right metacerebral giant cell (RMGC) during four successive cycles of buccal nerve bursting of decreasing vigor. Simultaneous extracellular records show efferent buccal nerve activity in buccal roots 2, 3, and salivary nerve. B. Higher sweep speed record from same experiment. Tops of intracellular spikes are not visible. Calibrations for intracellular records: LB7, 40 mV; RMGC, 16 mV. Time: A, 2 sec.; B, 800 msec.*

the feeding motor program. A single spike was elicited from the MGC soon after stimulus application (see Figure 5). Thereafter the MGC was sporadically active during release of feeding output. A more compelling experiment would involve implanting electrodes on a peripheral nerve containing an axon of the MGC under conditions where the extracellularly recorded action potential of the MGC could be recognized in recordings from unrestrained, feeding animals. This was accomplished by implanting monopolar cuff electrodes on the salivary gland nerve (Forsythe, unpublished observations). Animals recovered quickly and locomoted and fed normally. These experiments suggest that the MGC probably fires at most one to two spikes per feeding cycle, which is equivalent to an average rate of 0.5 to 3 spikes per second. This amount and timing of MGC activation would be insufficient to account for activation of the feeding system as judged by experiments in which the MGC is activated by intracellular current pulses at low rates while monitoring buccal motor roots.

The function of the MGC remains to be determined. It is unlikely that the cell is a command neuron for feeding in *Limax*, although it may be coactivated with the command cells for feeding. The large size, distinctive biochemistry, and ubiquitous occurrence of the MGC among opisthobranch and pulmonate gastropods make it a very attractive focus for comparative studies on behavioral evolution at the cellular level. These studies must include the full range of analyses from *in vitro* to *in vivo* monitoring of neural activity.

STRATEGIES FOR FURTHER WORK

The existence of rapid food-aversion learning by *Limax* raises a host of questions. The interplay of food palatability and hunger level is critical in determining whether the novel aversive food will be rejected after the initial experience. These and other parametric features of the learning remain to be established in detail. Aversive stimuli more closely related to food plant toxicosis may prove more effective than CO_2 poisoning in promoting learned food aversions. Comparative studies of food-aversion learning by other herbivorous gastropods may clarify the factors that determine whether learned or "hard-wired" circuits are used for plant prey selection. The testable prediction can be made that oligophagous herbivores will not demonstrate food-aversion learning, as they have learned over evolutionary time that a few plant species are safe and hence restrict their food plant selection to these few species. Other long-lived, polyphagous herbivores, such as *Limax*, should show food-avoidance learning.

The neurophysiological analysis of food-aversion learning in *Limax* requires initial studies to establish the relevant sensory input and motor output pathways. These are currently in progress. A neurophysiologically tractable aversive stimulus, such as nerve shock, must be found to replace CO_2 poisoning. In *Pleurobranchaea*, shock is effective in eliciting a modified form of food-aversion learning (Mpitsos and Collins, 1975). Previous results from *in vitro* studies of brains from trained *Pleurobranchaea* provide encouragement that a learned modification will survive the surgical trauma necessary for intracellular study (Mpitsos and Davis, 1973). It may be possible to capitalize on the one-trial learning aspect of food aversion learning in *Limax* so as to induce the synaptic modification *in vitro*.

VERTEBRATE

BRAIN

In Part V, we discuss basic problems of integration in vertebrate brain, with particular emphasis upon neural processing in mammals. The authors of Chapters Seventeen through Nineteen concentrate upon mechanisms involved in the production of species-characteristic and acquired sequences of motor output. In Chapter Twenty, emphasis is on quantitative patterns of integration in a sensory system, with reference to neural systems in a much more general sense. Each of these authors is faced with problems of "system isolation" and "simplicity" discussed by Maynard (1972) and by various authors in previous chapters. The diverse approaches provide useful comparison. Understanding the integrative properties of vertebrate (e.g., mammalian) brain is a basic challenge of modern science which can, and perhaps must, be approached at many different levels and via many different preparations.

In Chapter Seventeen, Doty focuses his discussion on the concept of "neural centers," which are viewed as operationally definable (but not necessarily tightly localized) populations of nerve cells that serve a common function upon being activated by appropriate afferent information. The extent to which a center thus defined reflects tight patterns of intrinsic organization determines its utility as an organizational and simplifying concept. In addition to the question of its *unitary* nature, it is necessary to ask how *separate* a center is from its surround. Doty notes that in a strict sense this is often an issue of conceptual abstraction whose utility is dependent upon the particular question being asked. Convincing evidence is presented that, when carefully applied in this way, the abstraction of neural "centers" can help clarify basic control mechanisms of direct relevance to species behavior patterns. Doty's approach provides a particularly interesting combination of concepts of ethology and invertebrate neurobiology. Like the majority of previous authors, Doty concentrates upon relatively simple "stereotyped" patterns of behavioral expression to help clarify the operation of mechanism. He is thus able to isolate movements, such as feeding, deglutition (swallowing), and vocalization, that are, to a large extent, released and patterned by mechanisms intrinsic to a given population of neural elements. The comparison to invertebrate material discussed previously is obvious. Doty isolates questions of afferent code, central excitatory state, intrinsic organization, efferent control, feedback, and hierarchical organization as being applicable to a variety of specific instances. He reviews evidence for a progressive encephalization of control during ontogeny for stereotyped movement sequences, which is often revealed dramatically following neural insult (e.g., cortical atrophy). One implication of Doty's review is that patterns of behavior are often blocked from expression by inhibition until "released" through disinhibitory processes, a conclusion that ties in well both to previous inferences by ethologists (e.g., Tinbergen, 1951) and experimental documentation in invertebrate neurobiology.[1]

Using his research on deglutition as an example, Doty points out that "center" concepts may be valuable in accounting for the fact that the same muscle groups can be employed in several distinct acts but with quite different rules of coordination. This approach can be used as a supplementary feature in the definition of hierarchical control. In addition to a largely intrinsic pattern of organization Doty shows that control centers may "isolate" themselves from disturbance by corollary inhibition when activated. These specific examples illustrate that general "rules" of neurobehavioral organization may be beginning to emerge in a variety of diverse preparations, although possible limitations to these generalizations must also be examined critically.

Evarts, like other contributors to this volume, discusses the concept of reflex and shares the conclusion that the distinction between reflex and nonreflex activity blurs upon closer inspection. Evarts' particular concern, however, is with the distinction between reflex and acquired "voluntary" behavior. This is an issue of long metaphysical debate which Evarts successfully approaches (or, perhaps, circumvents) through an analysis of how "higher centers" in primates participate in the control of particular acquired movements. By combining "instructions" which tell the monkey *what* to do (i.e., push or pull a lever) with subsequent perturbations of the manipulandum toward or away from the monkey, the interplay between reflex activation and prior motor set is examined directly. It is clear that preceding instructional "sets" can modify spinal reflexes as measured between synergistic and antagonistic relations and between instructional commands and independently applied lever movement. By recording changes in muscle (e.g., biceps) activity, it becomes possible both to separate and recombine tendon jerk reflexes and "voluntary" responses. A comparison of altered excitability of biceps motoneurons and sensitivity of biceps stretch receptors can be formulated in this way. The data indicate that each plays an important role in the interface between reflex and voluntary movements. Thus a system that is not intrinsically *simple* can be *simplified* with the aid of careful experimental dissection. The interlocked roles of *alpha* and *gamma* motoneurons, for example, is thus clarified, along with the important conclusion that prior instruction can differentially affect these two populations of cells, with increased excitability but not actual discharge of the alpha motoneurons being a common consequence. Since it is the alpha motoneurons which exert the main contractile force upon muscles (gamma motoneurons work primarily at the level of the spindle apparatus, a major route of reflex activity), it is reasonable to

---

[1] The reader must take care here, however, to recognize that "inhibition" defined at the behavioral and neurobiological levels are logically distinct in the sense that neither one alone *necessarily* implies the operation of the other (see Fentress, 1972, 1973b, 1976).

conclude that prior instructions may affect behavioral set without any concomitant overt muscular activity.

From this perspective it becomes possible to evaluate behavioral set independently from overt movement patterns (see Fentress, 1968a, b). Mechanisms are clarified further by Evarts through his recordings of pyramidal tract (motor output) neurons of cortical origin. What happens is that instructions can modulate the excitability of pyramidal tract neurons of cortical origin, which in turn differentially affect alpha and gamma motoneurons of the spinal cord, the traditional site for reflex responses. Thus, as clearly appreciated by Maynard (1972), spinal reflexes represent systems that are only partially separable from other (e.g., cerebral) influences; Evarts shows clearly how these dimensions of vertebrate behavior may be linked together.

At the conclusion of his chapter, Evarts considers briefly the possible role of the cerebellum in the control of skilled movement. This theme is picked up in Chapter Nineteen, by Llinás and Walton, who emphasize that the highly specific neural connections between climbing fibers and Purkinje cells of the cerebellar cortex provide a relatively simple network structure that is particularly amenable to detailed analysis. For example, through the use of intracellular current injection techniques, the authors demonstrate that the form of climbing fiber excitatory postsynaptic potentials is importantly influenced by geometrical properties of distributed junctions on the membrane surface of the Purkinje cell. From this they discuss possible functional advantages of such distributed synaptic connections, most importantly with respect to stereotyped activation of the postsynaptic neuron. This emerges as relevant to models of behavioral control when combined with the consideration that the climbing fiber—Purkinje cell synapse is an integral part of the olivocerebellar system, which in turn participates in the generation of movement. The cells of the inferior olive (which gives rise to climbing fibers that in turn synapse upon cerebellar Purkinje cells) are also electronically coupled, with the result that they probably activate motoneurons in stereotyped patterns. One consequence of the arrangement of the inferior olive system and its cerebellar projections is to provide a vertebrate analogue of command systems studied in invertebrates. Further, the degree of coupling between inferior olive neurons appears modifiable by chemical synaptic action. This provides a possible route for limited functional variation in motor expression. For example, Llinás and Walton provide evidence that cells of the inferior olive may play an important role in motor compensation following neural insult. The authors conclude that the inferior olive—cerebellar system provides a circuit of sufficient precision and simplicity to permit detailed examination of mechanisms of movement patterning in vertebrates. By blocking segmental afferents as well as activating motoneurons, the inferior olive system may act to isolate intrinsic pattern generation mechanisms in a way analogous to that previously discussed for other invertebrate as well as vertebrate preparations.

Freeman starts Chapter Twenty with the proposition that neural systems of apparent complexity may become "elements" when rules of combined action are determined. From this initial position he seeks ways for defining and analyzing neural *macrostates*, which can be considered functional entities not directly reducible to the individual elements of which they are composed. This combines aspects of thinking often referred to in terms of "emergent properties" with notions of functionally integrated "centers" but within a more dynamic context. Freeman sees this strategy as a way to return to the framework of "simpler networks" in complex neural systems, although now the "elements" of the system would be neural *masses* rather than single neurons. Questions of interaction would then focus upon relations between one defined neural mass and another.

Freeman pursues these and related issues in conjunction with detailed quantitative analyses of activity patterns in the vertebrate olfactory bulb. A key step in these analyses is the arrangement of neurons into operationally defined "sets" which in turn are arranged hierarchically. Once this is done, Freeman argues, we can treat resulting macrostates without knowing the detailed activity of each neuron within a given set, much in the same manner that we can perform chemical analyses without reference to individual particles. Macrostates thus defined are postulated to occupy both a greater volume and operate over a longer time scale than are their more elemental constituents. Further, only a relatively small number of neurons within a set are expected to be active at any one time, the precise timing of a given pulse being unpredictable either from the neuron's preceding history or activity in a small number of neighboring cells. The activity level of each neuron in a set is viewed in the context of activity levels of neurons in its surround, to which it both responds and contributes. Freeman presents these views as a conceptual bridge to permit the modeling of cortical dynamics that would otherwise be sought at the unit level. From here he emphasizes interaction strengths represented by feedback gains as the major variables that underlie the dynamic relations between macrostates and behavior. Freeman postulates that structures such as the cortex and basal ganglia may send packaged bursts of neural activity (controlled by macrostates) to brain stem and spinal cord with resulting coordination of motoneural activity necessary for behavior. The thrust of this chapter is to provide an alternative way to conceptualize the problem of dynamic pattern, an issue clearly relevant to the definition of both behavior and neural functioning but primarily at the level of macroscopic sets of elements, which in themselves display properties of intrinsic organization and interaction that are not necessarily apparent at more elementary (or molecular) levels of organization. As such, Freeman's views provide a different perspective on the problem of "simpler networks."

The four chapters in this part provide the reader with a variety of perspectives and strategies in the analysis of systems which are at least superficially much less simple than those found in most invertebrate studies. There are signs that these divergent perspectives and strategies are beginning to converge toward commonly defined problems even though their formulation differs in detail.

CHAPTER SEVENTEEN

The Concept of Neural Centers

ROBERT W. DOTY, Sr.

INTRODUCTION

I use the term "center" to signify a group of neurons whose coordinated action produces a stereotyped movement or series of movements (Doty, 1951, 1960, 1968). Three essential features of a center are (1) a detector mechanism at its afferent portal which will assure the activation of the center if and only if a specific pattern of input occurs; (2) an inherent organization that reproducibly yields the appropriate temporal and anatomical distribution of excitation and inhibition each time the center is activated; and (3) preemptory command of the required motoneuronal system.

This degree of precision has not always prevailed in defining the term. Sherrington (1900), among others, protested a certain "laxity" in its use (e.g., a "convulsion" center in the medulla), and he generally eschewed use of the term "center." In the context of neural activity this designation appears to have arisen

with Bouillaud (1825),[1] who astutely inferred from clinical material the existence of "centers" in the cerebral cortex controlling the movements of speech. Flourens (1842), in his work on the neural control of respiration, occasionally used the term "center" to describe the area at the junction of medulla and spinal cord which was essential to this function. He carefully insisted, however, that such a center must not be considered as a sharply delimited "point" in the nervous system but rather that some anatomical dispersion of the controlling

---

[1] "It would be wrong to believe that the limbs are the only participants in movements for which there exist special *centers* in the brain .... I shall subsequently endeavor to determine the site of the neural center which controls the mechanism of the organs of speech." ("On aurait tort de croire que les membres soient les seules parties pour les mouvemens desquelles il existe dans le cerveau des *centres* particuliers. ... Je tâcherai de déterminer ensuite le siège du centre nerveux qui tient sous ses lors le mécanisme des organes de la parole.")

system was likely even though it was difficult to reveal experimentally. He also identified and succinctly stated a cardinal difficulty in all efforts to divide the nervous system into discretely operating units, concluding: "(1) that despite the diversity of action of each of the parts constituting the nervous system, it is nevertheless uniquely a system; [and] (2) that independently of the specific action of each part, each exerts a common action on all the others, as they in turn do upon it; . . ."[2] (Fluorens, 1842, p. 212). In other words, centers are embedded within an interactive network and only in the abstract can they be considered as independent functional units.

In the ensuing years the implications of the term "center" were significantly broadened. Siminov (1866a, b), the first experimenter to use implanted electrodes for electrical stimulation of the brain and for making discrete electrolytic lesions, described the action of what he called "inhibitory centers" (probably caudate nucleus) in the forebrain of dogs. Shortly thereafter, Fritsch and Hitzig (1870), in their extraordinarily important but largely accidental (see Doty, 1969) discovery of the electrical excitability of the cerebral cortex, not only vindicated Bouillaud's concept of cerebral centers but broadly extended it. In the concluding words of Fritsch and Hitzig: "... *in their entry into matter, or their origin from it, apparently all individual mental functions are localized to circumscribed centers in the cerebral cortex.*"[3]

This uniquely challenging proposal of Fritsch and Hitzig, that certain cortical centers operate in a transcendental manner, may yet have merit (Doty, 1976). However, neither it nor an emphasis on anatomical discreteness is presently helpful in elucidating the operation of centers, or in using the concept of centers to clarify the neural basis of behavior. From the

definition offered in the opening paragraph, it is obvious that a "center" corresponds in part to the neural substrate for a "reflex." If one wishes to maintain with Sechenov (1866) that essentially all behavior is reflex, this is enough. The classification of the behavior, however, is not of as great interest as the fact that so much of it can be explained by the operation of neural centers. Thus the sight-reading of music, the typing of a manuscript, the braking of the motorist upon sight of the red light, are governed by the same principles of operation of neural centers as is the dog's raising its paw in a conditioned reflex upon presentation of a tone or the bird's preening of its feathers upon the occurrence of appropriate sensory cues. In each case there is an output, precisely reproducible, triggered exclusively by an equally precise afferent input, and occurring only when the proper setting of the central components is present (i.e., the passenger does not raise his foot to a nonexistent brake any more than the bird preens while flying).

The manner in which such behavior is organized and controlled by the central nervous system (i.e., how "centers" operate) is most readily set forth by discussing specific examples. Analysis of the operation of each center revolves around six questions:

1) The afferent code: What is the spatio-temporal pattern of nerve impulses required to trigger or "release" activation of the center?

2) The setting of the central excitatory state: What are the neural or neurohumoral background conditions that favor or preclude the activation of the center? There are actually several problems here: the manner in which concurrent activation of incompatible movements (e.g., preening and flying, or breathing and swallowing) is avoided; the sequencing of movement by means of antecedent components, providing an appropriate excitatory background for subsequent components; the more general settings, such as hunger or satiety in relation to feeding responses or hormonal levels relevant to sexual activity, or "intellectual" set, such as with the motorist or the dog in the conditioned reflex situation; and finally, whether these

---

[2] "(1) Que, malgré la diversité d'action chacune des parties constitutives du système nerveux, ce système n'en forme pas moins un système unique; (2) Qu'independamment de l'*action propre* de chaque partie, a une *action commune* sur *tous les autres*, comme toutes les autres sur elle."

[3] "... *einzelne seelische Functionen, wahrscheinlich alle, zu ihrem Eintritt in die Materie oder zur Entstehung aus derselben auf circumscripte Centra du Grosshirnrinde angewiesen sind.* "

settings are effective only via action on the triggering complex or whether they also intrude in later stages of operation of a center. (See Chapters Fifteen and Twenty-One.)

3) The intrinsic organization: How is the precise spatiotemporal sequence of the output generated?

4) Efferent control: How is the output of the center guaranteed effective command of motoneurons?

5) Feedback: Does the movement controlled by the center, once begun, proceed independently of proprioceptive or other afferent guidance? This is, indeed, the usual case and many striking examples exist. The neural output that generates escape swimming in the gastropod, *Tritonia*, remains the same when initiated from a brain isolated *in vitro* as it was in the intact animal (Dorsett, Willows, and Hoyle, 1973). Once initiated, certain egg retrieval movements of a goose continue without interruption even if the egg is removed from beneath the beak (Lorenz and Tinbergen, 1938). Preening reactions proceed in the absence of tail feathers to be preened (Lorenz, 1955). The inferred discharge pattern of a "center" can even develop quite normally in the absence of feedback: for example, in mice deprived of forelimbs at birth, "grooming" occurs with head bobbing, licking of the missing limbs, and blinking of the eyes in time with their expected passage (Fentress, 1973a); and macaques, blind from birth, groom their fellows by carefully brushing the hair, "peering" at, seizing with thumb and forefinger, and "eating" imaginary particles (Doty, unpublished).

6) Hierarchical organization: To what degree can the output of the "center" be fractionated, incorporated into other synergies, or linked in various behavioral sequences?

FEEDING RESPONSES

As is apparent from Table I, man is born with a set of innate responses to various gustatory stimuli (Steiner, 1973). Each type of stimulus triggers a unique constellation of orofacial behaviors which, from the fact that they are present in anencephalic monsters, can be inferred to be organized entirely at rhombencephalic and mesencephalic levels. It is of considerable interest that normal adults display highly similar, "reflex" expressions to these stimuli. The presence of these responses in the infant thus seems likely to be more related to nonverbal, intraspecific communication (Steiner, 1973) than to feeding responses per se; particularly as *in utero* the infant has been imbibing amniotic fluid at a rate of 500 ml/day (Pritchard, 1965), scarcely a bland concoction, and postnatally will normally long subsist exclusively on milk. As a consequence of experience, such gustatory reactions can be wholly suppressed, in animals as well as man — for example, the learned acquisition of a preference for bananas by cats, a food innately provoking strong rejection (Wyrwicka, 1974). It can thus be seen that the afferent code for triggering the action of a center, in this case a constellation of centers (smiling, licking, sucking, etc.), can be altered by learning.

Another response of infants is opening the mouth and rooting for the teat upon circumoral touch. This cutaneous control of mouth opening gradually passes in both man and ape to opening upon sight of approaching objects (Pilleri, 1971), then to objects brought to the mouth by the hand (Figure 1); and finally, in late infancy, the adult feeding pattern is established wherein the mouth opens in conjunction with feeding only as food is brought to appropriate position, not as an automatism coupled to an approaching hand or object. Note that Figure 1 demonstrates the existence of a center in primates that couples hand, mouth, and tongue movements; for the posture in child and monkey is identical, even to that of the tongue, and the same response has been elicited in macaques from stimulation near the rhinal sulcus (amygdala? Delgado, 1959).

Such progressive "encephalization" of the afferent control of a center, as just exemplified with the mouth-opening feeding response, is probably characteristic of most brain stem centers. A particularly clear demonstration of this principle was found by Bignall (1974) with the righting reflex of rats. In normally matured rats more than 10 days old the mesencephalon is required for righting. In rats 3 to 4 days old, however, decerebration at the medullary (!) level does not abolish righting, and, as such an animal matures, its skill at righting improves in a nearly normal manner. Thus there is a medullary or spinal righting center which, if deprived of pontine and mesencephalic control, remains essentially self-sufficient but, if once controlled by higher centers, cannot function in their absence.

Release rather than depression of brain stem centers consequent to loss of rostral control is sometimes observed, and again can be exemplified with elements of the feeding response in man, cat, and toad (Figures 2, 3, and 4). In this regard, patients with severe cortical atrophy regress beyond the point of the child shown in Figure 1 to that of a 4-month-old infant that opens its mouth to approach of an object (Figure 2). In other cases, such patients display mouth opening to circumoral touch (Pilleri, 1971), part of the still earlier rooting reflex. Similar release from dependence on forebrain control for oral centers activated by trigeminal input is seen in Figure 3. In this instance, certain components of prey-capture behavior in the cat have been released by destruction of mesencephalic pathways (Randall, 1964). The presence of such centers at lower brain stem levels for hunting behavior was demonstrated by Bignall and Schramm

TABLE I

FREQUENCY OF OCCURRENCE OF FACIAL RESPONSES TO GUSTATORY STIMULI IN NEONATES[a]

	Normal (Age 3 to 7 days) N = 100	Anencephalic (Age 1 to 19 days) N = 4
SWEET: 2.5% sucrose		
Retract corner of mouth	87	4
Expression of satisfaction resembling a "smile"	73	3
Eager sucking, with licking of upper lip	97	4
SOUR: 2.5% citric acid		
Pursing of lips	98	4
Wrinkled nose	73	2
Quick, repeated blinking	70	2
Increased salivation	65	4
Flushing of face	64	1
BITTER: 0.25% quinine		
"Arch-like" lips with depression of mouth angles	96	4
Protrusion of flat tongue	81	3
Salivation and spitting	87	4
General expression of "anger" and "dislike"	86	3
Vomiting	52	3

[a] Steiner, 1973, pp. 255–278.

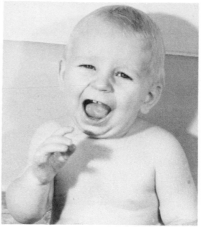

FIGURE 1. *Output of center which coordinates part of primate feeding behavior: arm flexion with mouth opening. For* Macaca fascicularis, *on the left, the stimulus was 50 1-msec, 0.2-mA pulses applied to left precentral gyrus for 1 second. The stimulus is unknown for the 13-month-old child on the right, but the response is nearly identical with that on the left, even to retraction and flattening of the tongue. (From Doty, 1960.)*

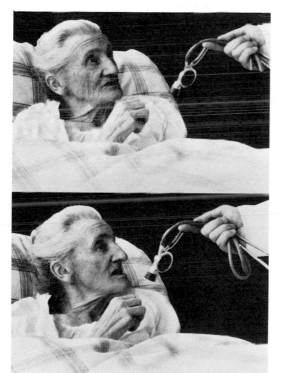

FIGURE 2. *Patient with severe loss of cerebral tissue consequent to Alzheimer's disease opens her mouth and endeavors to make*

(1974). They found that chronically decerebrate kittens, hearing a scratching noise, would flatten their body to the floor, tread, then pounce upon the source of the sound, biting vigorously any object placed there. Such attack behavior, when elicited in the intact cat by electrical stimulation of the hypothalamus, is strongly dependent upon trigeminal input (MacDonnell and Flynn, 1966). The same is true for mouse killing by rats (Thor and Ghiselli, 1975). In this connection it is of interest that as the hunting cat springs, the vibrissae are directed forward and downward, thus assuring contact with the prey (Figure 23 in Leyhausen, 1973). This requirement for trigeminal input for the killing bite provides an example of operation of the center's being controlled by afferent feedback, an effect also readily seen in the esophageal stage of deglutition (Roman and Tieffenbach, 1972). Trigeminal input in the pigeon, on the other hand, seems to provide a background excitatory state necessary for normal operation of the feeding but not the drinking center, in addition

oral contact with the approaching object. As with the toad in Figure 4, this represents release of center normally inhibited by tonic action of the forebrain. (From Pilleri, 1971.)

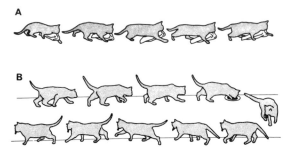

FIGURE 3. *Uninhibited components of prey-capture behavior in a cat that has extensive lesions of midbrain. In (A) the cat inappropriately seizes and carries a towel as though it were prey. (B) shows the prey-carrying behavior applied to food from a dish, the sequence being repeated for each mouthful that the cat ate. (From Randall, 1964.)*

to being necessary for manipulating food with the beak and tongue (Zeigler, 1974).

A release highly similar to that seen for the patient in Figure 2 can be obtained for the toad, as in Figure 4, by cutting the commissural connections at the mesodiencephalic junction. A normal toad will not strike at objects greater than a certain size, and a toad lacking forebrain will never strike (Ewert, 1967a). Cutting the intertectal connections apparently alters a balance of mutual inhibition between the two sides so that the "striking center" is triggered by any moving visual stimulus of sufficient size (Figure 4) and shows no inhibition with increase in size (Ewert, 1967a).

Figure 5 shows the normal feeding behavior of the toad and its fractionation into four components under control of visually

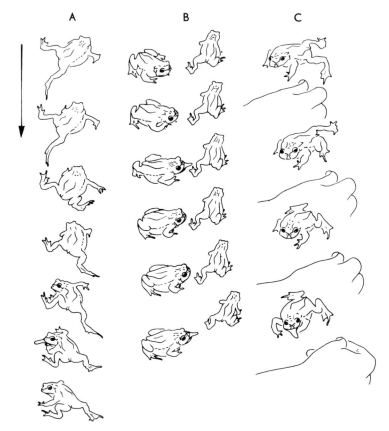

FIGURE 4. *Release of prey-capture, feeding behavior in the toad by a sagittal knife cut for about 2 mm at the junction of the midbrain and thalamus. Drawings from motion picture frames show that the toad will orient toward, fixate, and strike (note tongue flick) anything that moves: in (A), its own leg; in (B), another toad; in (C), a human hand. (From Ewert, 1967a.)*

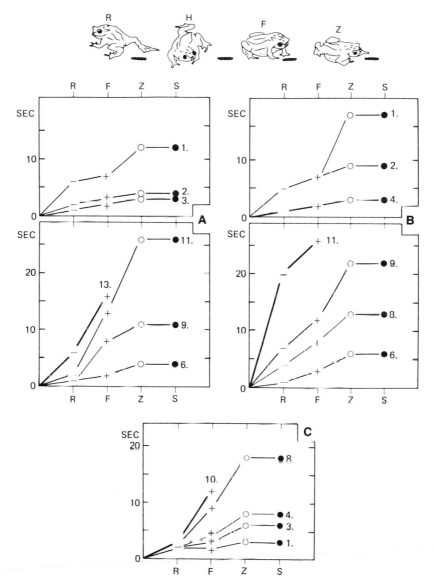

FIGURE 5. *Components of feeding behavior in three toads (A, B, C) upon repeated presentation of meal worms. R, orientation; H, approach; F, visual fixation; Z, striking (with tongue); S, swallowing. Latencies to each component are shown on the abscissa for the first worm up to the thirteenth (in A). Latency between striking and swallowing is constant, but other components have progressively longer latencies until the toad ceases to strike, although it will always orient and approach. (From Ewert, 1967b.)*

guided centers: orientation, approach, fixation, and striking. The fifth reaction, swallowing, is triggered by the presence of the worm in the gullet and always follows this stimulus after a constant latency (Figure 5). An increasing degree of adaptation of the earlier components is apparent with the progressively increasing latency prior to their release (Figure 5), the varying latencies demonstrating the independence of action of these centers. It is the frequency of repetition, not the degree of satiety, which determines these latencies; and once prolonged for stimuli through one eye they are equally prolonged through the other (Ewert, 1967b). The automatic nature of such responses, as with that in Figure 2, is further apparent from the fact that the toad continues to orient to the stimulus even after 1,000 presentations. Just as with the killing response of the cat (MacDonnell and Flynn, 1966) or the seizure of "butterflies" by macaques (Doty, 1967), the prey-capturing sequence in toads can be elicited by electrical stimulation of appropriate loci in the central nervous system (Ewert, 1967b).

Since most components of the stalking, prey-capturing response are present in decerebrate kittens (Bignall and Schramm, 1974), it is apparent that the fixation, slinking, crouching run, pounce, and killing bite of the hunting cat are executed under the control of brain stem centers, sequenced and activated by forebrain command. The major function of the cerebral cortex in relation to movement may thus consist not in controlling motoneurons directly but in selecting and sequencing the activation of brain stem centers which are inherently organized to produce the needed patterns of muscular contraction. Some centers, such as those involved in generating the crossed, alternating rhythm of walking or the bilaterally congruent rhythm of running, seem to be present even in the spinal cord (e.g., ten Cate, 1965; Forssberg and Grillner, 1973).

Ingeniously, in accord with the phenomena of "release" described above, Roberts (1974) has suggested that some of the cortical control exerted on lower centers, rather than being phasically excitatory, may instead be tonically inhibitory, their activation thus reflecting a brief disinhibition.

DEGLUTITION AS A PARADIGM OF THE ACTION OF A CENTER

The foregoing examples are weakened by the fact that understanding of the neural operation of the controlling centers is rudimentary at best. A more extensive effort has been made to define the neural characteristics of the mammalian swallowing center. Swallowing can be elicited by stimulation of peripheral nerves, hence is readily accessible for study. It is also the most complex "all-or-none" reflex known, involving a precise bilateral sequence of excitation and inhibition for more than 500 msec, distributed from upper cervical cord to mesencephalon.

Figure 6, in one sense, demonstrates why centers are necessary. The six synergies illustrated there demand activation of the same group of muscles, but in strikingly different temporal relation to each other. Such activity would obviously become impossible if dog or man had to compute the synergy anew each time swallowing or coughing was required (e.g., to "remember" to contract mylohyoideus early and vigorously, to delay thyropharyngeus, . . . , to swallow — but to give a weak, late contraction of mylohyoideus, having begun with concurrent, rather than sequenced, contraction of hyo- and thyropharyngeus, to cough, etc., etc.).

The muscles participating in deglutition have been identified electromyographically (Doty and Bosma, 1956; Kawasaki, Ogura, and Takenouchi, 1964; Hrycyshyn and Basmajian, 1972), and are shown in Figure 7, together with their innervation, the input to the swallowing center, and the interrelations that can be inferred to exist between the swallowing and other centers.

Actually there are two swallowing centers, or half centers, one for each side. The medulla can be split down the midline, and swallowing then proceeds with its normal repertoire of muscular performance, but independently on the two sides for concurrent bilateral stimulation (Ishihara, 1960; Doty, Richmond, and Storey, 1967). Transections at pons and obex eliminate participation of certain motoneurons, but the basic pattern of swallowing activity survives, thus indicating that it is organized exclusively within the medulla (Doty, 1968). However, further identification of the locus of the center is difficult. Central electrical stimulation or lesions both are subject to misinterpretation because of their various nonspecific actions as well as their local effects on axons of distant neurons; and the discharge of single units cannot readily be distinguished as to its relevance in the activity of the center per se, since it can only be correlated with afferent or

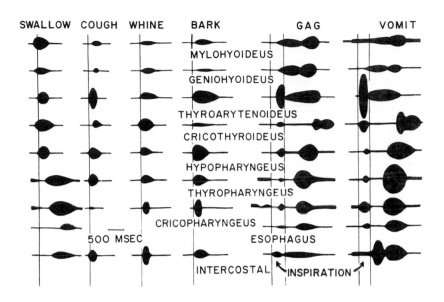

FIGURE 6.   Schedule of muscle activity in the normal, alert dog as seen electromyographically in nine muscles engaged by the output of six different centers. Note the great variation in order and intensity of the muscular participation in the various synergies. (Modified from Kawasaki, Ogura, and Takenouchi, 1964.)

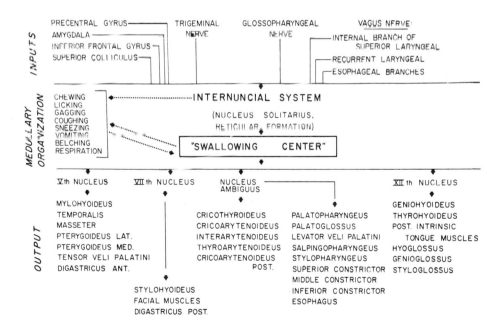

FIGURE 7.   Outline of afferent and efferent systems involved in deglutition, and suggested central interactions with other medullary centers. (From Doty, 1968.)

efferent events. Work with lesions suggested that a critical area lay in the medial reticular formation just rostral to the inferior olive (Doty, Richmond, and Storey, 1967). Exploration of this region with microelectrodes, however, has failed to detect any activity associated with deglutition and has instead revealed significant "anticipatory" activity only in or around the nucleus solitarius (Jean, 1972a).

The nucleus solitarius is probably the site where decoding of the afferent input occurs. Some mechanism certainly must exist for selecting sensorial access to the various centers, and it must be rather subtle to distinguish stimuli which produce swallowing from those which produce gagging. As anyone knows who has ever endeavored to give a small child a pill, some of the selection may be attributed to a central setting of the system, but this is clearly not the only feature that makes selective triggering possible. Using electrical stimulation of the superior laryngeal nerve, which is highly effective in eliciting swallowing, extensive studies have shown that the afferent mechanism is rather sharply selective for different stimulus frequencies or patterns (Doty, 1951; Miller, 1972a). Since these same optimal and limiting frequencies are found for eliciting swallowing by stimulation of the frontal cortex in the rabbit (Sumi, 1969a) and sheep (Car, 1970), it seems likely that the cortical command is exerted at least to some degree via the same portal as used by peripheral afferents. This gains further credibility from the fact that the cortical stimulation which is capable of eliciting swallowing also evokes potentials in the region of nucleus solitarius, and that these potentials interact with those evoked via the superior laryngeal nerve (Car, 1973).

One of the notable features of centers is their ability to organize a complex motor output independently of regulation by afferent feedback. Thus, with the swallowing center, the basic act is undisturbed by a great variety of manipulations such as cutting afferent and efferent nerves, stretching or fixation of muscles, and anesthetizing reflexogenic areas (Doty and Bosma, 1956; Miller, 1972b). Complete paralysis of striated muscles by curariform agents does not disrupt the neural output (Sumi, 1964, 1970; Car, 1970; Tieffenbach and Roman, 1972; Miller, 1972b). In the kitten,

however, curarization does abolish the coordination (Sumi, 1967). There is also evidence in human infants that their organization of swallowing differs significantly from that in adults (Tulley, 1953).

It must not be inferred that because swallowing is independent of feedback it is not subject to some degree of modification by continued afferent influences. It has long been recognized that voluntary swallowing becomes difficult or impossible if there is nothing to swallow. The characteristics of the material swallowed also influence the duration of discharge in most participating muscles (e.g., Hrycyshyn and Basmajian, 1972; see Doty, 1968), and this is especially true for the esophageal stage, where afferent feedback provides a very powerful influence (Roman and Tieffenbach, 1972). The focus for at least some of these influences is seen to lie in the parasolitary area, for Jean (1972a) has shown here a strong effect upon unit discharge by the presence or absence of distension of the pharynx.

The swallowing center is remarkable in its ability to expand or contract proportionately the timing of discharge in each motoneuronal group as the overall duration of swallowing is altered, either by peripheral conditions or by anesthesia. This is difficult to explain; for example, an increase in anesthesia which changes the threshold from 12 to 240 volleys at 30 Hz applied to the superior laryngeal nerve, thus clearly evidencing a profound depression of central excitability, may merely halve the duration of mylohyoid action and leave unaffected the timing of hyopharyngeus, which peaks its discharge in each case just as action in mylohyoideus is terminating (Doty and Bosma, 1956).

That the motoneurons are being driven by a common center is often clearly evident in concurrent, brief, bilateral pauses in activity of muscles whose motoneurons are widely separated — for example, fifth and twelfth motor nuclei (Doty, Richmond, and Storey, 1967; see also Figure 58 in Faaborg-Andersen, 1957, and Figure 3 in Hrycyshyn and Basmajian, 1972). Pauses identical to these can also be seen in simultaneous recordings from units in the medullary respiratory center (Figure 19.4 in Merrill, 1974).

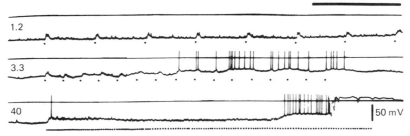

FIGURE 8. *Intracellular recording from a hypoglossal motoneuron during electrical stimulation of superior laryngeal nerve at 1.2, 3.3, and 40 Hz, the latter inducing swallowing (and loss of neuron) at the end of the lower trace. Note the EPSPs produced by stimuli at 1.2 and 3.3 Hz, forming the basis for "elementary" reflexes. The nature of the activity in the latter half of the trace at 3.3 Hz is uncertain, but might be licking, which commonly precedes swallowing. At 40 Hz, the first few pulses yield EPSP's and a spike, but elementary reflexes cannot follow this frequency. Swallowing is accompanied by large, sustained depolarization, leading to numerous spikes. The dots indicate stimuli; the upper lines, zero potential. (From Sumi, 1969b.)*

Figure 8 shows that the swallowing center is capable of controlling motoneurons by a powerful, sustained depolarization. Frequently this depolarizing action is preceded in hypoglossal motoneurons by a briefer hyperpolarization (Sumi, 1969b), and inhibition of background activity before and after the discharge in swallowing is observed in many muscles (Hukuhara and Okada, 1956; Doty and Bosma, 1956; Doty, Richmond, and Storey, 1967). It is thus possible that the excitatory control that the swallowing center exerts upon motoneurons is bracketed by inhibition, in this manner assuring the absence of interfering action.

Of course, some of the inhibition exerted by the center is more prolonged and functionally necessary to the proper mechanical action of the reflex. This is the case with the constrictor musculature of the lower pharynx (hyopharyngeus, thyropharyngeus, cricopharyngeus — see Figure 6), and it was thus of great interest to learn that the excitatory control of each half center upon these muscles originates contralaterally, whereas that for all the other muscles in swallowing is ipsilateral (Doty, Richmond, and Storey, 1967). This "crossed constrictor" arrangement is certainly unexpected if one endeavors to explain the existence of decussating systems in the brain as

arising consequent to the optical inversion of the lens system of the vertebrate eye, as suggested by Ramón y Cajal and many others. Actually, the "optical" explanation of decussation is not overly convincing, since Insecta, which have an entirely different solution to the optical inversion problem (Braitenberg, 1967), have large, decussating axons emanating from their optic lobe to ventral cord (Bullock and Horridge, 1965). The reason for decussation thus still remains mysterious. The proposal that it might be necessitated neurochemically by the sequencing of inhibition and excitation in the constrictor motoneurons (Doty, 1968) is now complicated by the fact that Merrill (1974) has found decussation to be the rule for axons passing from the medullary respiratory center into the spinal cord. Although "antecedent" inhibition is common in respiratory motoneurons (Sears, 1964), it is not "antecedent" in the same sense as the inhibition applied to constrictor motoneurons by the swallowing center. Some axons from the medullary respiratory center actually ramify bilaterally within the spinal cord (Merrill, 1974), but they could, of course, ultimately be producing excitation in motoneurons on one side and inhibition on a functionally different set contralaterally.

It can be seen in Figure 8 that each pulse applied to the superior laryngeal nerve at lower frequencies evokes an EPSP in the hypoglossal motoneuron. More complex action is often observed (Sumi, 1969b). This emphasizes the fact that peripheral input, in addition to influencing various centers, also elicits "elementary" reflexes through more direct pathways into the motoneuronal system. The elementary reflexes interact with the output from a given center but generally are overwhelmed by it (Figure 8). Perhaps it is this interaction with elementary reflexes which obscures a possible orderliness in the recruitment of motor units by the swallowing center (Doty and Bosma, 1956). There is also a random order of recruitment in certain circumstances in motoneuronal pools for simple reflexes in the spinal cord (Wyman, Waldron, and Wachtel, 1974), but the more general rule appears to be that order of recruitment is inversely related to size of the motoneurons, that is, the smaller the neuron the earlier its discharge in a given synergy (see, e.g., Barillot and Dussardier, 1973). On the other hand, Miller (1974) has found that units which fire with high regularity in respiration discharge with unpredictable interspike intervals in swallowing.

The question of fractionating the operation of the swallowing center cannot be adequately answered. Electrolytic lesions do seem to be able to eliminate various components (Doty, Richmond, and Storey, 1967; Jean, 1972b) and thus should provide a valuable means of analyzing the organization of the center. Human beings are capable of modifying or selecting components of the act of swallowing in performing such feats as esophageal speech or glossopharyngeal breathing (Weinberg and Bosma, 1970). The latter, however, may simply constitute reactivation of a preexisting synergy, since the newborn infant inflates its lungs initially by "swallowing" air with larynx open and cricopharyngeus closed (Bosma and Lind, 1962). There have been suggestions that the movements of speech are derived from components of several different reflex configurations in the oral, pharyngeal, and laryngeal areas, swallowing among them. The idea has some appeal, but the evidence is not yet at hand.

VOCALIZATION

One of the most remarkably constant arrangements in the evolving vertebrate brain has been the maintenance of a midbrain focus for organizing socially relevant behaviors such as vocalization. Thus in the toadfish (Demski and Gerald, 1974), frog (Schmidt, 1974a), alligator (Goodman and Simpson, 1960), birds (see Brown, 1974), and all mammalian species tested [e.g., cat (Kanai and Wang, 1962; Testerman, 1970), squirrel monkey (Jürgens and Ploog, 1970), and chimpanzee (Graham Brown, 1915)], electrical stimulation of this area can elicit normal vocalization, often of an aggressive or "threatening" nature (although in the chimpanzee it was "laughing"). Localized destruction in the dorsal tegmentum renders animals or man mute.

In fish, frogs, and birds, much of the vocalization elicited from stimulation of the midbrain areas is relevant in reproductive behavior. Neurons in this restricted area in the chaffinch have a high affinity for circulating testosterone (Zigmond, Nottebohm, and Pfaff, 1973). In several instances, excitability of the vocalization center is seen to be set by the hormonal level when natural stimuli are used for eliciting the vocalization (e.g., Schmidt, 1966; Zigmond, Nottebohm, and Pfaff, 1973). Male patterns of vocalization can be produced in female frogs by removing the ovaries and implanting testes and anterior pituitary glands in their body cavity (Schmidt, 1966). It is thus apparent that the neural organization for male vocalization is present in females, even though in normal circumstances it would never be activated.

The same is true for the clasping reflex in which the male amphibian during mating grasps the female with his forelegs. The females normally do not clasp, but if the brain stem is transected at the midmedullary level, the forelegs of both females and males assume the clasping posture for several minutes to several hours (Koppányi and Pearcy, 1924), a further example of release of a lower center, and of the sexually selective suppression of a center by rostral mechanisms. The clasping reflex is normally evoked and maintained by cutaneous stimuli from the inner surface of the forearm, particularly as reinforced by the respiratory

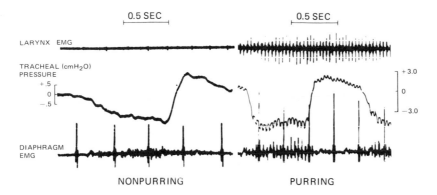

LARYNX EMG

TRACHEAL (cmH₂O)
PRESSURE

DIAPHRAGM
EMG

NONPURRING   PURRING

FIGURE 9.   Electromyographic and respiratory pressure records during purring and nonpurring states in a normal, alert cat. Upper trace, EMG from cricothyroideus, but it records from other muscles as well. Note that, with purring, the high-frequency EMG in both the larynx and the diaphragm (lower trace) is reflected in oscillations of pressure in the trachea (middle trace), and that it continues throughout both phases of the respiratory cycle. (From Remmers and Gautier, 1972.)

movements of the clasped female (Lullies, 1926). In such circumstance the clasp of the male amphibian on the female may be maintained for many hours or even several days. On the other hand, if the male clasps another male, the latter emits a release call which effects an inhibition of the clasp reflex in the clasping frog or toad. Actually, the vocalization is merely a by product. The effective stimulus for inhibiting the clasp reflex is the cutaneously perceived vibration of the body wall of the clasped, vocalizing, and hence vibrating male (Schmidt, 1974c). The clasp reflex thus offers a clear example of how tactile input can produce different effects upon a center, depending upon (1) the hormonal setting and (2) the temporal and possibly spatial encoding of the stimulus.

While the vocalization may be merely a means of achieving an effective tactile code, its production nevertheless involves some elegant efferent coordination, the output of the "release-call center." This center in turn is, of course, hormonally controlled, and it is activated by tactile input. Its investigaton has a long history from the last century, the famous *Quackversuche* of Goltz and many others. Schmidt (1966, 1972) has now defined the output of the center electromyographically, and has located a midbrain focus of electrical activity which correlates with the discharge of the center (Schmidt, 1974a, b). The central

correlate remains unchanged by total denervation of the brain stem, from which it can be evoked, as can the release call, by central electrical stimulation at the appropriate locus (Schmidt, 1974b). The output of the center is thus, again, essentially independent of triggering stimulus and of afferent feedback.

The electromyogram of the various glottal and pharyngeal muscles during the release call shows a strong tendency of motor units to be phase-locked in activity at about 30 Hz (Schmidt, 1966, 1972, 1974b). A highly similar pattern and frequency appears in the diaphragm and laryngeal muscles of the cat during purring (Figure 9). The peculiar feature in purring is that the activity in the larynx continues uninterrupted throughout both inspiratory and expiratory phases (Figure 9). The phase locking of the motor units is extremely precise (e.g., within 1 msec), and when the diaphragm is active during inspiration, its motor units discharge with a fixed delay after the laryngeal units, during the few milliseconds when the glottis is open (Remmers and Gautier, 1972). Just as with release calling, purring proceeds wholly under central control, for various relevant forms of deafferentation have no effect on the motor discharge, nor do elimination of diaphragmatic or laryngeal activity have any effect upon the pattern of the other.

Although the mammalian larynx is well

supplied with proprioceptive afferents (see Doty, 1968), their role must lie with the protective reflexes of the airway rather than with laryngeal control in vocalization. Testerman (1970), eliciting vocalization in the cat by electrical stimulation of the midbrain, found the pattern of discharge in the laryngeal muscles was unaltered by stretching or deafferenting the larynx. On the other hand, inflating the lungs, or any other maneuver such as stimulating the vagus nerve, which called into play the Hering—Breuer reflexes, had a very powerful influence on the laryngeal performance during vocalization. The Hering—Breuer reflexes are organized at the pontine rather than medullary level (Kahn and Wang, 1967), and are thus clearly distinct from the organization of the respiratory center per se (e.g., Merrill, 1974). It is conceivable that such separation of the Hering—Breuer reflexes from the respiratory center arises because their activity is relevant to the organization of other centers as well as to respiration [e.g., to vocalization (Testerman, 1970) or to coughing].

Little is known of the actual location and details of operation of the vocalization center or centers. The site of effective midbrain stimulation is unlikely to be the center per se, because (1) electrical stimulation applied directly to a center should disrupt its timing and organization (Doty, 1969), and (2) a variety of vocal and other effects are obtained from stimulation of single loci. Thus, in the cat, vocalization ranges from gentle hissing, through growling, to sharp, crescendoing cries — all ultimately combined with piloerection, lashing of the tail, rolling, and striking repeatedly with claws fully extended on the forepaw (Kanai and Wang, 1962). In other words, the full spectrum of the defense reactions of the cat can be obtained by stimulation at a single point, even in the decerebrate animal (Doty, unpublished). This undoubtedly means that an afferent system has been engaged which activates a group of centers in a coordinated, hierarchical manner. The variety of vocal responses from midbrain stimulation in the squirrel monkey is even greater than in the cat (Jürgens and Ploog, 1970; Doty, unpublished), and in the frog both the release call and the mating call can be elicited from a single site (Schmidt, 1974a). In

the cat a pathway for the vocalizing response can be traced, independently of other components of the defense reaction, into the pons and medulla (Kanai and Wang, 1962). A medullary locus also seems likely in the frog (Schmidt, 1974a), since activity in the midbrain which is correlated with vocalization is lost after medullary transection.

In both frogs (Schmidt, 1971) and birds (Newman, 1970) acoustically evoked activity can be recorded from midbrain sites intermingled with or immediately adjacent to those which yield vocalization upon electrical stimulation. This close association of auditory input and vocal output is found behaviorally as well as anatomically. The mating call of the frog is commonly evoked by the call of another frog, and similar conspecific elicitation is observed for singing and calling in birds. An extraordinary precision is present in the neural categorization of these auditory inputs (Capranica, 1965; Gerhardt, 1974a; Todt. 1974), which again manifests the selectivity of the afferent portal to a center. It is probably because of the complexity of the "feature extraction" process in the auditory midbrain that stimulation of sites that yield acoustically evoked potentials is ineffective in eliciting vocalization (Newman, 1970), whereas stimulation of adjacent sites (the output of the auditory analyzer and input to the vocalization center?) is effective in this regard.

Some of the selectivity is achieved by peripheral mechanisms of the auditory system (Capranica, 1965), but in any event this selectivity plays a significant role in the reproductive isolation of closely related species (e.g., Gerhardt, 1974b).

CONCLUSIONS

A "center" is defined as a functionally linked set of neurons which are activated only by appropriately encoded stimuli and which are interrelated in such a manner that their combined activity yields a predetermined and reproducible pattern of behavior. This concept of centers explains in outline practically the entire neural basis of the instinctive behaviors recorded by ethology, as well as a wide range of learned behavior.

I have defined six problems that arise with respect to centers: (1) decoding the afferent input which triggers the center, (2) the central excitatory state of the center as set neurally or hormonally, (3) the intrinsic organization, (4) how the center preempts the control of motoneurons, (5) autonomy of the center once activated (i.e., common lack of proprioceptive guidance), and (6) hierarchical arrangement of centers and the possibility of fractionating their activity. Numerous examples are available, particularly in relation to feeding, swallowing, and vocalization.

A recurring theme is that higher centers of the forebrain operate in large measure via their command of phylogenetically stable centers in the brain stem and that much of this control is exerted as tonic suppression, giving rise to phenomena of release upon loss of rostral tissue (Figure 2, 3, and 4). The possible reasons for decussating control merit consideration.

CHAPTER EIGHTEEN

Neuronal Representation of Acquired Movement Patterns in Primates

EDWARD V. EVARTS

INTRODUCTION

Sherrington (1906) believed that voluntary movement involved control of segmental reflex arcs by descending pathways. According to this view, there should be no sharp demarcation between reflex and acquired patterns of muscular contraction, but instead the two categories of movement should interact and merge, one into the other. An instance of such interaction was described by Hammond (1956) in a brief paper entitled "The Influence of Prior Instruction to the Subject on an Apparently Involuntary Neuro-muscular Response." In Hammond's experiments, subjects were instructed to "resist" or "let go" in response to a sudden pull on the flexed forearm. The sudden pull stretched the biceps and evoked a biceps EMG response (the so-called tendon jerk) with a latency of 18 msec. A second phase of muscular activity began at a latency of about 50 msec in subjects who had been instructed to resist but was absent in subjects who had been instructed to let go. The short latency of the

50-msec EMG response suggested that it was a reflex, but Hammond noted that ". . . this must be reconciled with the fact that prior instruction to 'let go' can interfere so rapidly and effectively with the subject's response." Here, then, was a movement exhibiting interaction between voluntary and reflex factors, a movement that could neither be classified as *all* reflex or as *all* voluntary.

EXPERIMENTAL PROCEDURES

Investigation of the ways in which higher centers control movements such as the one described by Hammond have been carried out by my colleague Jun Tanji and myself, using a technique for recording activity of brain cells in monkeys performing learned movements (Evarts and Tanji, 1974). Figure 1 illustrates the use of this technique. Details of the microelectrode assembly used to pick up the action potentials of motor cortex neurons are illustrated in Figure 2.

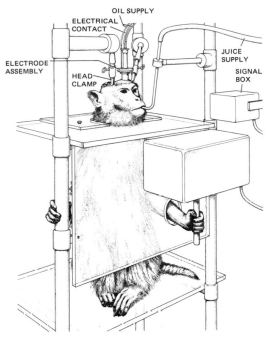

FIGURE 1. Recordings of the activity of single nerve cells in the brain are obtained while a monkey performs a learned task in this primate chair. The monkey's head is painlessly immobilized so that the microelectrode in the brain does not change position during the experiment. The monkey has been trained to move the rod when it is perturbed by a torque motor in the box from which the rod protrudes. The direction in which the handle must be moved is indicated by an "instruction" (red or green lamp) flashed from the signal box. Thus the signal box tells the monkey how to move and the handle's movement tells him when to move. If the monkey makes the required movement within a specified time, it receives a reward of fruit juice through the tube in its mouth. Signals from the microelectrode in the brain, along with data from the signal box and transducers connected to the rod, are fed into a computer for analysis. (From Evarts, 1973.)

In the setup pictured in Figure 1, the monkey is rewarded for making the correct motor response after receiving one of two possible instructions. A red or green lamp tells the monkey what to do (red lamp means that

the monkey should pull and green lamp means that he should push), but the monkey must delay doing anything until the rod in his hand is perturbed by a torque motor. There are two possible directions of perturbation (toward or away from the monkey). The perturbation serves as a "trigger" which tells the monkey when to carry out the movement called for by the prior instruction.

RECORDINGS OF MUSCLE ACTIVITY

Figure 3 shows EMG records from the biceps muscle for the four possible combinations of the two instructions and the two perturbing stimuli. In addition to the EMG records, Figure 3 shows potentiometer traces that indicate movements of the handle grasped

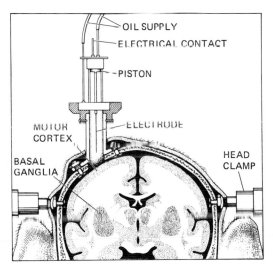

FIGURE 2. The microelectrode assembly consists of a fine platinum–iridium wire attached to a hydraulically actuated piston. A stainless-steel cylinder permanently attached to the monkey's skull provides access to the brain. The bolts on the sides of the skull are also permanently implanted. They are attached to clamps during the experiment to prevent head movement. After the electrode assembly is bolted to the cylinder, the electrode is lowered by pumping oil into the inlet on the right and raised by pumping oil into the inlet on the left. (From Evarts, 1973.)

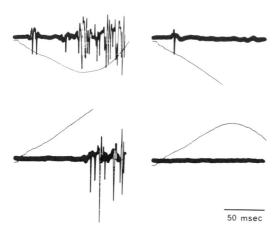

FIGURE 3. *Biceps activity for different instruction–stimulus combinations. Instructions to* pull *or* push *and perturbations* toward *or* away *from the monkey could be combined in four possible ways, as shown in the four pairs of traces in this figure. Each pair of traces shows biceps EMG activity and the output of a potentiometer coupled to the handle, with upward deflection of the potentiometer trace indicating movement of the handle* toward *the monkey and downward deflection of the potentiometer trace indicating movement of the handle* away *from the monkey. For the set of traces at upper left, the prior instruction was pull, calling for biceps contraction, and the perturbing stimulus (indicated by the potentiometer trace) moved the handle away from the monkey, thereby stretching the biceps. At lower right the instruction was push and the initial perturbation was a movement of the handle toward the monkey, resulting in biceps shortening. For further explanation, see text. (From Evarts and Tanji, 1974.)*

by the monkey. Upward deflection of the potentiometer trace indicates movement of the handle toward the monkey (with consequent shortening of biceps), and downward deflection indicates movement away from the monkey (with biceps stretch). Each trace begins at the time when power was applied to a torque motor whose shaft was coupled to the handle. The lag between energization of the torque motor and the beginning of handle displacement was about 4 msec. In the two sets of traces at the top of Figure 3, the perturbation

moved the handle away from the monkey, stretching the biceps and evoking a short latency EMG response ("tendon jerk"). In the two sets of traces at the bottom of Figure 3, the perturbation was a movement of the handle toward the monkey. This perturbation shortened the biceps, so there was no tendon jerk. For the two sets of traces at the left of Figure 3, the prior instruction was red, meaning pull, which required that the biceps contract. For the two sets of traces at the right of Figure 3, the prior instruction was green, meaning push, which did not require biceps contraction. Of these four instruction–perturbation combinations, the one at the upper left of Figure 3 was associated with maximum biceps activity: the perturbation (biceps stretch) elicited a tendon jerk and the instruction called for biceps contraction. Thus the perturbation and prior instruction reinforced each other, both favoring biceps activity. The condition of minimum biceps activity is seen at the lower right in Figure 3, where neither the perturbation nor the prior instruction called for biceps activity: a perturbation that shortened the biceps was paired with a prior instruction to push. In this situation, as in the first, the perturbation and instruction reinforced each other, but now both called for biceps quiescence rather than for biceps activity.

For the two remaining parts of Figure 3, the perturbation and prior instruction were antagonistic. At the lower left is shown the case in which the instruction (red) called for biceps contraction but the segmental reflex effects of the perturbaton (biceps shortening) tended to silence biceps activity. Here the tendon jerk is absent, as one would expect. In addition, the biceps contraction called for by the prior instruction has a longer latency than it had had when the perturbation was biceps stretch.

The last of the four instruction–perturbation pairings is shown at the upper right of Figure 3, where the perturbation involved biceps stretch (tending to elicit biceps contraction) but the prior instruction was push (green), which did not call for biceps contraction. Here again there is antagonism between the perturbation and the instruction, and this antagonism results in a reduction in the tendon jerk elicited by biceps stretch: the tendon jerk elicited by biceps stretch is smaller when the stretch is coupled with a prior instruction calling for push (green) than when coupled with a prior instruction calling for pull (red). It is thus apparent that the two different instructions give rise to differential presetting of spinal cord reflex mechanisms that mediate the tendon jerk.

The results shown in Figure 3 are for only one muscle, whereas behavior for which the monkey is rewarded requires the coordinated activity of many muscles. In considering neural mechanisms that might underlie the effects of prior instruction, however, one need not consider *all* muscles, since the mechanisms that operate for one muscle are probably common to a number of muscles. Consideration of changes of the biceps response to perturbation as a result of prior instruction may be divided into two parts, one part concerned with changes in the tendon jerk and a second part concerned with changes in the second phase of muscular activity, the phase that occurs regardless of whether the triggering perturbation shortens or stretches the muscle. In this consideration it will be useful to keep in mind that stretch is a necessary and sufficient condition for the occurrence of the tendon jerk (with the amplitude of this reflex being modified by the prior instruction). In contrast, it is the prior instruction "pull" that is necessary and sufficient for the second phase of biceps activity (with the latency and amplitude of this phase of the response varying, depending on whether the triggering perturbation had stretched or shortened the biceps).

The enhancement of the biceps tendon jerk by the prior instruction "pull" might be due to (1) increased excitability (i.e., a lower threshold) of biceps motoneurons; or (2) increased sensitivity of biceps stretch receptors (the muscle spindles) as a result of discharge of gamma motoneurons innervating their intrafusal fibers. Figure 4 illustrates the neural pathways that might be involved in these two sorts of modifications of the tendon jerk. Studies in man (Paillard, 1955; Landau and Clare, 1964; Clare and Landau, 1964; Kots, 1969; Dietrichson, 1971) have shown that both sorts of modifications (i.e., increased motoneuron excitability and increased spindle sensitivity) occur prior to voluntary movement, and it seems likely that the "pull" instruction to the

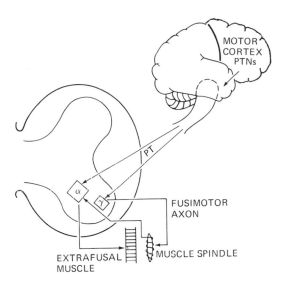

FIGURE 4.   The "tendon jerk" is a response ("jerk") of extrafusal muscle in response to stretch of its tendon. It is a two-neuron reflex arc involving the 1A afferent and the α-motoneuron. An increase of this reflex may be due either to increased sensitivity of the 1A receptor (as a result of increased α-motoneuron discharge) or to heightened excitability of the α-motoneuron, or to some combination of the two. PTN axons end on both α- and γ-motoneurons and could play a role in either or both of these processes.

monkey sets up these two processes concurrently in relation to biceps motoneurons and biceps muscle spindles. A central mechanism that might serve to set up these two processes is known as "alpha–gamma linkage," a term proposed by Granit (1955) in reference to the coordinated central control of α- and γ-motoneurons. The outflow from motor cortex to spinal cord via pyramidal tract neurons (PTNs) provides a route for α–γ coactivation (Koeze, 1973) and the synaptic connections of PTNs onto α- and γ-motoneurons are such that thresholds of γ-motoneurons are lower. As a result of this lower threshold of γ-motoneurons, it is possible for PTNs to discharge at frequencies sufficient to cause discharge of γ-motoneurons but merely raise the excitability of α-motoneurons (without causing their dis-

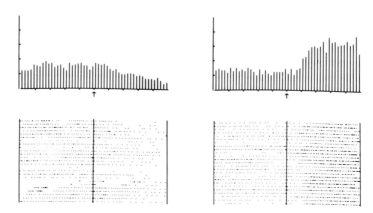

FIGURE 5.   *Instruction-evoked motor cortex activity. This figure shows rasters and histograms corresponding to 2 seconds of activity of a precentral PTN. In the rasters the central line represents the time of occurrence of the instruction (red or green light); dots to the left of the central line represent neuronal discharge occurring during 1 second when the animal was waiting for the instruction. The arrow at the center of each histogram indicates the time of occurrence of the instruction; histogram bin width is 40 msec. About 200 msec after the instruction to push (green), there was an increase in discharge (right raster and histogram). In contrast, after the instruction to pull (red), there was a decrease in discharge (left raster and histogram). (From Evarts and Tanji, 1974.)*

charge). This differential effect of PTN output on γ- as compared to α-motoneurons could explain the observed effects of prior instruction of the monkey's tendon jerk. That the intruction raised the excitability of motoneurons without causing their *discharge* is important, because the instruction itself did not evoke any EMG discharge.

RECORDING OF MOTOR CORTEX NEURON ACTIVITY

Records of the effects of instruction on motor cortex PTN activity show effects that are consistent with the hypothesis put forward above. An example of the effect of instruction is shown in Figure 5. For the neuron whose activity is displayed in this figure, the instruction green (push) was followed by an increase in activity, whereas the instruction red (pull) led to a decrease of neuronal activity. Many precentral neurons were influenced by the instruction, this effect appearing from 200 to 500 msec after the onset of the red or green light. Both PTNs and non-PTNs showed clear responses to the instruction. Many neurons in

motor cortex showed a differential effect for the two instructions, so that by the time the perturbation of the hand occurred (0.6 to 2.0 sec following the instruction) the motor cortex was in a different state, depending on which of the two instructions had been received. It seems clear that impulses that descend to the spinal cord as a result of the modification of motor cortex activity set up 200 msec following the instruction might serve as a basis for the presetting of spinal cord reflexes by increased γ-motoneuron discharge and/or increased α-motoneuron excitability.

The finding that PTN activity changes following an instruction, together with the previously known fact that PTN axons excite α- and γ-motoneurons, provides an explanation for the observed changes in the tendon jerk. But from the standpoint of the monkey's goal of getting the fruit juice, the tendon jerk is quite unimportant. This mono-synaptic reflex is so brief that it hardly influences the arm displacement caused by the torque motor. It is the *second* phase of muscle activity that underlies the monkey's execution of what the lamp has instructed him to do. To determine the possible role of the motor cortex in this second

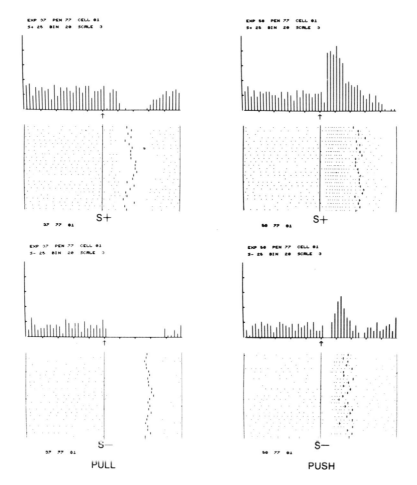

PULL   PUSH

FIGURE 6.   Effect of prior instruction on PTN response. This PTN was most active (upper right) when a prior instruction to push was triggered by an opposing perturbation, that is, one which moved the handle toward (S+) the monkey. The effect of prior instruction on this PTN response to perturbation may be seen by comparing upper right with upper left, where the same handle movement (S+) failed to evoke discharge when there had been a prior instruction to pull. At lower right, the instruction (push) but not the perturbation (S−) called for discharge of this PTN, and at lower left neither the instruction (pull) nor the perturbation (S−) called for discharge, and the neuron became almost totally silent within 20 msec of the perturbation (S−). The perturbation occurs at the center line in rasters and at the arrow in histograms, and activity is displayed for 500 msec before and after the perturbations. Histogram bin width is 20 msec. The short solid lines in the right half of each raster row indicate completion of the motor response, following which the monkey would return the handle to the central holding zone and await a new instruction. (From Evarts and Tanji, 1974.)

phase of muscle discharge – the phase that Hammond found to be so dramatically modified by prior instruction in man – one must look for changes in motor cortex response to the perturbation, depending on the prior instruction.

For this reason, a major point of interest in analyses of motor cortex neuronal responses was the interaction between the prior instruction and the subsequent motor cortex output triggered by the perturbation. Figure 6 illustrates a case of this interaction for a precentral

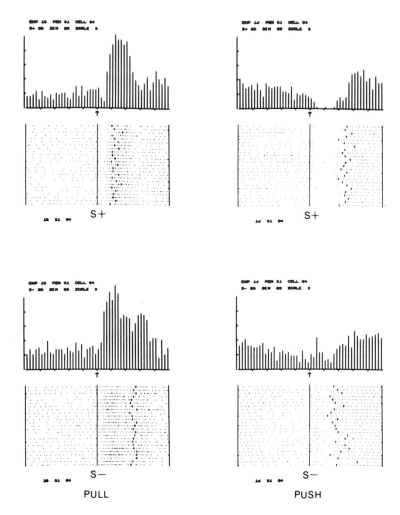

FIGURE 7. Effect of prior instruction on non-PTN response. This non-PTN was most active (lower left) when a previously instructed pull was triggered by an opposing perturbation (S−). For further details of this figure, see the text. (From Evarts and Tanji, 1974.)

PTN. This neuron was active in association with the push movement, and, in addition, the neuron discharged in response to externally produced handle movements toward the monkey (S+). The magnitude of the PTN response to handle movement differed considerably, depending upon whether the prior instruction was push or pull. The PTN shown in Figure 6 had its most intense response when an instruction to *push* (green) was paired with a perturbation that moved the handle toward (S+) the monkey (upper right of Figure 6), whereas the PTN was almost totally silenced when an instruction to pull (red) was paired with a stimulus that moved the handle *away* (S−) from the monkey (lower left of Figure 6). Note the analogy between this situation and that observed for muscle in Figure 3. The muscle was most active when the direction of the perturbation was *opposite* to the direction of instructed movement. So, too, with this PTN: the PTN was active with voluntary push and responded to an oppositely directed external perturbation. The analogy between muscle and PTN is again seen in the instruction–perturbation pairing associated with minimal

PTN activity: when a perturbation that moved the handle away from the monkey was paired with a prior instruction to pull (red), the PTN became totally silent almost immediately after the perturbation. These analogies between the muscle and PTN activity are consistent with Phillips' (1969) proposals concerning a transcortical servoloop.

Figure 7 shows another motor cortex neuron (a non—PTN) whose activity in the four different stimulus—instruction pairings was analogous to biceps recordings shown in Figure 3. This cell was active with voluntary pull and was activated by an *opposite* external perturbation, that is, a perturbation that moved the arm *away* from the monkey. Like biceps muscle, this unit was maximally activated when an instruction to pull (red) was paired with a perturbation that moved the arm *away* from the monkey. Again in analogy with biceps muscle, the cell was silenced when an instruction to push was paired with a stimulus that moved the arm toward the monkey. In this neuron the "reflex" response evoked by the "excitatory perturbation" was enhanced after the "excitatory instruction," just as the tendon jerk of a muscle was enhanced after an instruction calling for activation of the muscle.

CONCLUSIONS

Studies of brain and muscle activity in monkeys performing acquired movements support Sherrington's view that more complex patterns of muscle activity associated with volitional or learned movement involve control of reflex responses. Actually, the notion that there is continuous gradation between "higher level" and "lower level" processes has been widely recognized since the monumental contributions of the British neurologist, Hughlings Jackson. Jackson's ideas in regard to levels of nervous organization have been reviewed by Phillips in his Hughlings Jackson Lecture (1973). In this lecture, Phillips puts some of Jackson's ideas into modern terminology:

> In the jargon of today we might speak of hierarchical series of "executive programmes" (higher level) and "sub-routines" (lower level), without being able to identify or to localise their neural "hardware" or to trace the sequences of "sensorimotor processes" which emerge as patterns of excitatory and inhibitory synaptic action upon the output neurons of the Middle Level. ... Of the "sub-routines" of movement, the "lowest" would be those which must link up the muscles in the varying but relatively stereotyped combinations.

The middle level would include the motor cortex PTNs, and even in 1897, Phillips points out:

> Jackson had already fastened on the importance of the cerebellum in relation to the middle level — on the status it occupies in our thinking today. He adopted Gowers' hypothesis that "the cerebellum exerts a restraining influence on motor centres of the cortex cerebri and that the cerebellum coordinates movements by intermediation of these centres."

CHAPTER NINETEEN

Neuronal Systems in the Cerebellum

RODOLFO LLINÁS and KERRY WALTON

INTRODUCTION

Among the obstacles in the development of a general conception of central nervous system (CNS) function from invertebrates to higher vertebrates has been the supposed absence of the so-called "simple" neuronal circuits in the latter forms. This supposition has been implicitly supported by the fact that the number of cells and neuronal circuits in the higher vertebrate CNS is orders of magnitude larger than in most invertebrates and that the connectivity in the vertebrate brain is thought to be rather grossly specified. The latter point is especially clear when comparison is made with such impressive examples as the segmental ganglia of the leech, *Hirudo medicinalis*, in which synaptic junctions may be specified to the level of single neuronal elements (Jansen and Nicholls, 1972).

It was in the light of this type of supposition regarding the grossness of specificity in CNS connectivity in higher vertebrates that

Ramón y Cajal's discovery of the cerebellar climbing fiber (CF) Purkinje cell synapse appeared, to him, as something of a revelation (Ramón y Cajal, 1899, pp. 70–71). He was led by two observations to the conclusion that such a synapse is unique in the vertebrate nervous system First, the CF Purkinje cell synapse has a somewhat special embryogenesis, the fiber coming into contact with its Purkinje cell very early in the development of the cerebellar cortex. This intimate relation is such that, as the dendrites of the Purkinje cell develop towards the molecular layer, the CF follows and twines over most of the surface of the smooth dendritic tree. Second, he observed a striking one-to-one relationship between the CF and Purkinje cell. This anatomical description, which has been confirmed many times (see Palay and Chan-Palay, 1974), was put into a functional context by the physiological characterization of this synapse as a powerful excitatory junction (Eccles, Llinás, and Sasaki, 1966).

CF EPSPs OF PURKINJE CELLS

The activity of single Purkinje cells following CF activation may be recorded intra- or extracellularly in the cerebellar cortex. Extracellularly, this response is characterized by a stereotyped repetitive firing of the Purkinje cell which can best be described as a burst of action potentials having an all-or-none property and a high frequency of firing. Intracellularly, this form of activation generates prolonged action potentials which rise from a large, unitary EPSP.

The chemical nature of the CF Purkinje cell synapse was demonstrated by its reversal with depolarizing current pulses (Eccles, Llinás, and Sasaki, 1966). Recent experimentation by Llinás and Nicholson (1975) has shown in more detail the reversal properties of this EPSP. As illustrated in Figure 1, the EPSP is generally reversed in a biphasic manner, with the rising phase reversing at a more negative membrane potential level than the falling phase.

The biphasic reversal of the synaptic potential during current injection at somatic level was intuitively regarded to be due to the unequal development of potential between the site of current injection (the soma) and different portions of the dendritic tree. This conjecture was tested on a computer model of a Purkinje cell which included a CF-like distributed synaptic conductance on the soma and two proximal dendritic compartments (Figure 2). Direct calculation of the potential generated by a point-source current injection into the soma in this model indicates that the dendritic tree is far from isopotential. Moreover, at a current injection level capable of reversing the somatic components of the synaptic potential, neither the proximal nor the distal dendritic EPSP was reversed. In order to reverse the second component, enough current had to be injected to raise the somatic potential to +40 mV. For the third component, several hundred millivolts had to be generated at the somatic level. These results demonstrate that the biphasic character of the reversal of the CF EPSP can be explained by the geometrical distribution of the junction on the surface of the soma—dendritic membrane of the Purkinje cell.

Functionally, in those cases in which the postsynaptic element must be fired with a high

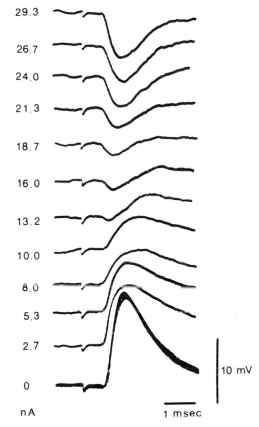

FIGURE 1. *Intracellular recording from a cat Purkinje cell showing characteristic CF-EPSP activated by electrical stimulation of underlying cerebellar white matter. Records show the biphasic properties of the CF-EPSP reversal with application of extrinsic depolarizing direct current. Example taken at high sweep speed. Note that at levels 13.2 to 18.7 nA, synaptic potential reverses in such a manner that the fast rising phase of the normal EPSP is the first to reverse while the falling phase reverses later. (Modified from Llinás and Nicholson, in press.)*

degree of reliability, distributed synapses have several advantages over punctiform synaptic inputs. First, distributed synapses provide sufficient transverse membrane current to minimize the longitudinal current needed to charge the membrane capacity of the dendritic tree and thus can produce a very rapid depolarization of the postsynaptic element. Second, since the gap resistance of the synaptic terminal is kept to a

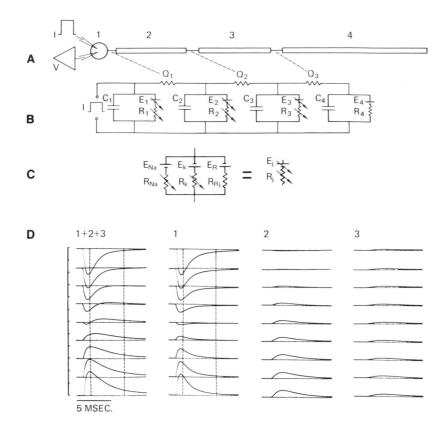

FIGURE 2.   Compartmental model of Purkinje cell. (A), Cable model for a Purkinje cell. The soma compartment 1 corresponds to a sphere 30 µm in diameter and is connected to the dendrites 2–4 which are lumped into a cable of uniform diameter (3.2 µm) divided into three compartments (150, 150, and 300 µm in length). Synaptic inputs are introduced at the soma and the two proximal compartments. The potentials generated by this synaptic input are measured at the soma V. Modifications of the membrane potential along the length of the cable are produced by current injections through a second microelectrode in the soma I. (B), Electrical diagram of the model. The four different compartments 1–4 represent the soma and the three dendritic segments. The compartments are separated by resistances Q_1, Q_2 and Q_3, the longitudinal dendro-plasmic resistance. Potential across each compartment is indicated by a variable battery, E_j, and a variable resistor, R_j, to simulate synaptic input in parallel with the membrane capacitance, C_j. The resistance of the extracellular medium is neglected. The last compartment 4 has a constant resting e.m.f., E_4, and resistance, R_4, in parallel with the membrane capacitance, C_4. In (C) the meaning of the variable battery and resistance is further described. E_j and R_j consist of three compartments: 1) a sodium battery, E_{Na}, having a potential of +60 mV; R_{Na} representing the conductance of the sodium channels; 2) a potassium battery, E_K, with a potential of −90 mV, and a potassium conductance, R_K; 3) E_R is the resting potential, −70 mV, and R_{Rj} is the resistance of the plasma membrane. (D), Computer display of somatic potentials following synaptic activation of the three different compartments in the cable model. The first set of records to the left illustrates EPSP at normal resting potential and its reversal as the membrane is depolarized to +50 mV. The EPSP is generated by superposition of synaptic inputs to compartments 1, 2 and 3. The next set of records (labelled 1) is produced by synaptic input restricted to the first compartment, while 2 and 3 are restricted to compartments 2 and 3 respectively. Note that when synaptic input is restricted to compartment 1, the EPSP reversal (at approximately −15 mV) is a mirror image of

minimum, distributed synapses allow more synaptic current to be injected across the postsynaptic membrane. This is possible because, as shown by Eccles and Jaeger (1958), synaptic boutons have a maximum possible size beyond which no further synaptic current is gained by increasing the area of the contact. Third, because this distributed synapse extends over a large area of the dendritic tree, excessive closeness of the actual junctions on the postsynaptic element is prevented. This special arrangement reduces the nonlinear summation of synaptic potentials due to shunting and reduced electromotive force. On the other hand, such input does not utilize the integrative properties of the Purkinje cell, since all the cable properties of the cell are nullified by the simultaneous depolarization of the dendritic tree. In short, a distributed synapse is the most appropriate mechanism to produce a step voltage transient in an electrotonically large cell and the best way to ensure a stereotyped activation of the postsynaptic neuron. Using this type of argument, it has been proposed that the stereotyped output generated by the CF Purkinje cell synapse may be regarded as part of a "preemptory" pathway (Llinás, 1974) of the kind that has been demonstrated in invertebrates (Wiersma, 1958; Wilson, 1962).

THE OLIVOCEREBELLAR SYSTEM

The specificity and potency of the CF Purkinje cell synapse have suggested a large number of hypotheses about its possible functional role (see Llinás, 1970). Several recent studies on the origin of the CF system (Desclin and Escubi, 1974; Sotelo et al., 1975) have demonstrated that, as postulated by Szentágothai and Rajkovits (1959), the CFs arise for the most part from the inferior olive (IO). This nucleus also sends axon collaterals to Deiters' and to the cerebellar nuclei, all of these structures constituting the olivocerebellar system (Figure 3). It has in fact become clear that the CF Purkinje cell synapse must be understood as part of an olivocerebellar pathway and that this understanding will be an important step in clarifying the function of the cerebellum as a whole.

Several new results promise to advance considerably the understanding of the functional meaning of the olivocerebellar system. First, it is clear from studies of the action of drugs such as harmaline on the IO that the olivocerebellar system is capable of generating movement (Montigny and Lamarre, 1973; Llinás and Volkind, 1973). This movement requires the integrity of the olivocerebellar nuclear connections, the olivo-Purkinje-nuclear portion of the system being more modulatory than generative. Through the action of the olivonuclear and olivo-Deiters' pathways, spinal motoneurons may be activated with high priority and in the absence of segmental sensory input. In short, anatomical and physiological studies have demonstrated that the IO exercises an indirect but powerful excitatory action on motoneurons at brain stem and spinal levels.

Second, the olivocerebellar system has, besides the distributed synapse, a second intriguing specialization that sets it apart from the general theme of neuronal organization in vertebrates. Several studies of the IO have recently shown that the cells in this nucleus have an unusual type of synaptic organization, the cells being electrotonically coupled to each other via a specialized glomerulus (Llinás, Baker, and Sotelo, 1974; Sotelo, Llinás, and Baker, 1974). Being electrotonically coupled, these IO neurons probably activate motoneurons in stereotyped clusters. On the other hand, the possibility of dynamic uncoupling of IO cells by chemical synaptic action on the IO

its depolarized counterpart. The potential generated by an input to compartment 2 reverses at approximately +40 mV. Input to compartment 3 does not reverse at all at the same current level. When 1, 2 and 3 are activated (with progressive delay of 0.2 msec between compartments to allow for CF propagation time), the reversal is biphasic as in the experimental data. Current injection levels increase from zero at lowest record to 40 nA at the uppermost level, in 5 nA steps. (Modified from Llinás and Nicholson, 1976.)

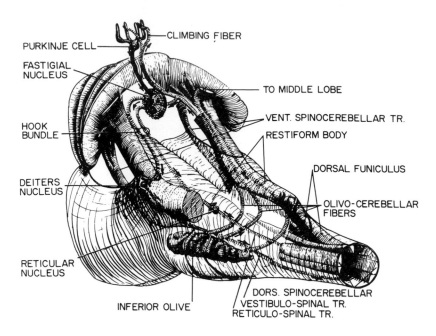

PURKINJE CELL

CLIMBING FIBER

FASTIGIAL NUCLEUS

TO MIDDLE LOBE

VENT. SPINOCEREBELLAR TR.

RESTIFORM BODY

HOOK BUNDLE

DORSAL FUNICULUS

DEITERS NUCLEUS

OLIVO-CEREBELLAR FIBERS

RETICULAR NUCLEUS

DORS. SPINOCEREBELLAR

VESTIBULO-SPINAL TR.

RETICULO-SPINAL TR.

INFERIOR OLIVE

FIGURE 3.   Stereogram of brain stem and cerebellar white matter, including the fastigial nucleus. Through the olivocerebellar pathway, the olive activates fastigial nuclear cells and, via climbing fibers, the Purkinje cells. The latter project back to the cerebellar nuclei. The output of the fastigial nucleus activates alpha motoneurons through the Deiters' and reticular nuclei. Arrows indicate direction of pathway conduction. (Illustration kindly modified by Prof. W. J. S. Krieg, from his book Functional Neuroanatomy, *Blakiston, 1953. From Llinás and Volkind, 1973.)*

glomeruli gives this system the possibility of subtle functional variability (Llinás, Baker, and Sotelo, 1974).

Although the concept of preempting systems in vertebrates may be criticized, it is used here to illustrate the similarities that exist between some high-priority nerve nets in vertebrates and those of invertebrates (see Chapter Four). For the olivocerebellar system to be a high-priority network, all neuronal links in the pathway from the IO to the motoneurons would have to have a high transmission safety factor. It has been possible to demonstrate this for the olivonuclear (Llinás and Volkind, 1973) and olivovestibular (Bruggencate, Teichmann, and Weller, 1972) projections since the IO afferents generate distinct synaptic potentials in the cerebellar and Deiters' nuclei. Furthermore, it has been demonstrated that activation of these nuclei through the olivocerebellar system is capable of producing phasic activation of motoneurons. This provides a functional basis

for the so-called harmaline tremor and may also contribute to the modulation of reflex clonus in decerebrate cats (Clendenin, Szumski, and Astruc, 1974).

On the other hand, it has been suggested recently that the function of the olivocerebellar system may not be restricted to generating stereotyped movement but may also be required for a certain type of motor learning. In a set of behavioral experiments, Llinás et al., (1975) have shown that, following chemical IO destruction, motor compensation from unilateral labyrinthine lesion does not occur. In the normal animal, damage to one labyrinth produces a clear motor deficiency characterized by vigorous body rotation to the side of the lesion. This motor anomaly is, however, compensated for within 24 hours unless, as stated above, the IO has been damaged. This finding is significant because it has been assumed that the CF system may be involved in motor learning in the cerebellar cortex (Marr, 1969).

However, the more significant finding here concerns the effect of olivary lesion on those animals that had already compensated for unilateral labyrinthine lesion. In these animals, IO lesion produced an immediate reversion to the uncompensated state; thus, as opposed to what would be expected from Marr's hypothesis (Marr, 1969), no transfer of learning occurred at the cerebellum itself. Whether this situation may be considered as a learning paradigm is of course of great importance. It has been known that the reversion to an uncompensated state following IO lesion can also be produced by total surgical removal of the cerebellum (Magnus and De Kleijn, 1930). In contrast, disruption of the cerebellar cortex, without damaging the olivonuclear and olivovestibular projections, does not produce a reversion to the uncompensated state (Llinás et al., 1975). This finding strongly suggests that motor compensation is lacking because the IO motoneuronal pathway is interrupted rather than as the result of the CF deafferentation of Purkinje cells.

The mechanism for this IO effect in motor compensation is not yet clear. Apparently, specific neuronal changes that involve the olivonuclear motoneuronal pathway must occur for the animal to compensate. Whether the dynamic or anatomical modifications that must underlie this compensation occur at a pro olivary level, or at the IO itself, is not known.

PROBABLE ROLE OF THE OLIVOCEREBELLAR SYSTEM IN MOVEMENT

On the basis of the results reviewed above, a hypothesis may be advanced regarding the function of the olivocerebellar system in movement. It seems evident that the IO is capable of generating organized synchronous activation of spinal motoneurons. There appears to be a strong descending modulator of extensor motoneurons, as would be expected from the excitatory action of this nucleus on the Deiters' complex. Besides the activation of motoneurons, it seems clear that the IO is capable, through its activation of brain stem nuclei, of producing a gating type of phenomenon at spinal cord level. Thus, segmental information, which could interfere with descending commands onto the motoneuronal pool, is blocked in order to prevent motor conflict. This implies, then, that the olivocerebellar system is a truly supraspinal pathway — one capable of organizing and generating movement in the sense of a prespecified set of motor orders or scores (Wilson, 1968a) and of being "simple" in the sense of well specified and functionally secure connectivity.

It is probably fruitful to consider the IO as mediating motor synergies, as described by Brown (1914) and further elaborated by Bernstein (1967) and by Gelfand and Tsetlin (1971). It is expected that the olivocerebellar system may serve to allow the forebrain and brain stem to organize motor responses via descending pathways by modifying "hardwired" motor subroutines stored in the spinal cord (see Grillner, 1975). Although this olivocerebellar path strongly involves the cerebellar cortex, the damage observed following cerebellectomy is actually not due to the CF Purkinje cell disruption, but rather to the disruption of the olivocerebellar input to cerebellar nuclei and the vestibular nucleus. If this is so, then the main path for the organization of movement would be through the cerebellar nuclei, the nuclei in fact being the part of the pathway that conveys the signals to generate movement, while the cerebellar cortex acts as modulator for such activity.

CHAPTER TWENTY

Quantitative Patterns of Integrated Neural Activity

WALTER J. FREEMAN

INTRODUCTION

It is salutary to recall that our interest in simpler neural networks began historically with an interest in our own nervous system and, in particular, the cerebral cortex as the principal organ of our behavior. From time to time we should reappraise our knowledge of the simpler forms of cortex to determine whether we may take additional small steps toward our ultimate goal in neurobiology on the basis of new techniques, data, and concepts that derive from simpler networks. At the same time, we should be alert to the possibility and even likelihood that in some crucial aspects the neurophysiological dynamics of cortex may differ from those of other parts of vertebrate central and peripheral nervous systems and from those of invertebrate nervous systems.

In this regard the three strategies of research proposed by Maynard (1972) should be recalled. When faced with exceedingly complex nervous systems, we may (1) constrain ourselves to the study of functional subcomponents, such as the nerve axons or dendrites; (2) artificially isolate subsystems, such as the spinal cord; or (3) search for complete, simpler nervous systems with small numbers of neurons which comprise neural networks. To this list I wish to add a fourth strategy. Nervous systems with very large numbers of neurons may work by different "principles of combination" (Maynard, 1963) than presently known simpler systems, and they may be reclassified as "simpler" (in Maynard's meaning) if those principles can be learned. My purpose here is to introduce an alternative set of principles which arise out of the neuron doctrine but transcend it and which may lead to an explanation of cortical dynamics that is not foreseen by neural network theory.

We may begin with the very properties that make the vertebrate cortex so formidably resistant to analysis: the immense number of neurons, the high local density of synaptic interconnection, and the highly nonlinear[1] dynamics of each of the myriad of neurons. From studies in a broad variety of complex physical and chemical systems we know that, when a large number of nonlinear elements influence each other diffusely and thereby become interactive, a new entity emerges which we call macroscopic. Its properties depend as much on the interactions as on the elements and cannot be reduced to the properties of the elements. Then, simply from the above properties, we can predict that forms of neural activity may exist in cortex, which we shall call macroscopic active states or macrostates.

If we could predict the forms of these active states, we could devise appropriate experimental systems to observe and measure them. By this means, in each appropriate area of cortex that forms a neural mass we might comprehend the conjoint activity of millions or hundreds of millions of neurons in a single statement. Further, we could describe the main connections among neurons at two levels: those among neurons within a mass, which sustain the interactions that lead to macrostates, and those between masses that form a network of neural masses. Given the active state of one mass, which describes the activity that it transmits to a second mass, and given the active state of the second mass, we could describe the operations performed by the second mass on its input to give its output. In this way we could return to the heuristic concept of the simpler network, but the element in the network instead of being a neuron would be an interactive neural mass.

[1] The term "linear" when applied to a system means that the output is proportional to the input and that the outputs for two or more overlapping inputs are added to give the total output. For example, suppose that a stimulus is given first to one afferent nerve and then to another so that two successive subthreshold EPSPs are evoked in a target neuron. Then let the two stimuli be given together. If the result is a larger subthreshold EPSP equal to the sum of the first two, then the neural dynamics can be described with a linear differential equation. If the result is an all-or-none action potential, then nonlinear differential equations such as the Hodgkin–Huxley equations (Katz, 1966) are required to describe the dynamics. However, if the departure from proportionality and additivity is sufficiently small, as when the sub-threshold EPSP for two stimuli is somewhat smaller or larger than the sum of the two separate EPSPs, we may still use a linear differential equation to describe the dynamics, which we call a linear approximation.

The concept of the macrostate should not be confused with a cooperative state, though it constitutes a form of cooperativity. Like a digital computer, a neural network that contains a numbered set of neurons and trans-mission channels has system properties based on interaction, but not macrostates based on ensemble averaging. Further, the macrostate should not be confused with the Sherringtonian central excitatory or inhibitory state (c.e.s. or c.i.s.), which is the average of activity over a pool of neurons and is not predicated on interaction among the neurons in the pool (1929). And it is not a matter of convenience for description, or, as Barlow (1972) puts it, "the globalists' despair" (p. 382). If neural macrostates exist, they must be reckoned with in the same manner that we now deal with action potentials and synaptic potentials; with the ionic currents and membrane conductance changes that underlie them; and with the yet underlying protein, lipid, and transmitter chemistries and biophysics.

We pursue the concept of macrostates in cortex by raising the following questions: Which properties of neurons are significant at the macroscopic level and which are not? What are the conditions necessary for macrostates to exist in a mass of neurons? How can their forms be predicted, measured, and interpreted in terms of properties of neurons and their inter actions? How are macrostates manifested or observed? How might they play a role in the organization of behavior? Some proposed answers are based on studies primarily of the vertebrate olfactory bulb, which is the simplest form of cortex.[2]

PROPERTIES OF NEURONS

The existence of a macroscopic active state depends on locally dense interaction within a mass of neurons. I postulate that each neuron transmits to other neurons in a distribution

[2] Some anatomists might object to this classification, but it is justifiable because the bulb consists (as does the cortex) of laminated neuropil with a well-developed columnar organization. It comprises a part of the cerebral hemisphere which is contiguous with areas of paleocortex that extend onto neocortex and which is embryologically derived from a swelling in the wall of the neural tube precursor of the forebrain.

around itself, depending on the connections of its own fibers with those of its neighbors. We are concerned with the average size of the distribution, the time required for transmission, and the strength of transmission. The mode of transmission, whether by impulses, synaptic currents, or diffusion of transmitter substances, is unimportant, and the variations in single neural geometry, type or chemistry of synapse, and specific sites of connections are submerged in the averages. I assume that transmission from each neuron to others is *only by synapses* and not by extracellular chemical or potential gradients.[3]

The dendritic tree of each neuron provides for local convergence and the axonal tree for local divergence. Both provide for translation and time delay, which are described with space coefficients and rate coefficients in appropriate descriptive equations. The dendrites sustain activity (in the main) in the form of synaptic current, which I shall call the wave mode, and axons sustain activity (again in the main) in the form of trains of pulses, which I shall call the pulse mode. Synapses are the sites of conversion of activity from the pulse to wave mode, and trigger zones are the sites of conversion from the wave to pulse mode. Translation and delay are operations in the space and time coordinates, and the conversions are instantaneous point processes.

Each of the three types of operation supposes an input and an output. If the output is proportional to the input over a range of output and if the outputs for two or more inputs are simply added to give the total output, we say that the operations are linear. We find in general that the operations of translation and delay are linear in both the pulse and wave modes, and we describe them with linear differential equations. The two conversions are in general nonlinear, pulse to wave because of the ionic mechanisms of the EPSP and IPSP in dendrites, and wave to pulse because of the thresholds and refractory

periods of axons. The nonlinearities take the form of bilateral (two-sided) saturation. There is a relatively narrow range for each conversion in which pulse rate is proportional to transmembrane current, and vice versa, and a relatively broad range in which the proportionality fails.

The principal determinants of macroscopic states are the topology and density of functional interconnection, which provides for interaction. To simplify the description of neural masses we introduce the concept of a hierarchy of neural sets. The simplest set is called the KO set. It consists of a collection of neurons that receive input from a common source, that have a common sign of output (they are either all excitatory or all inhibitory), and that have no synaptic interaction. An example is the set of olfactory receptors, each of which has an axon without collaterals extending from the olfactory mucosa to a part of a glomerulus in the olfactory bulb (Figure 1). It is designated KO_R.

The KI set consists of neurons that have input from a common source, a common sign of output (excitatory or inhibitory), and dense interaction. An example of a KI_i set is the lateral eye of *Limulus*. An example of a KI_e set is formed by the periglomerular neurons in the olfactory bulb (Figure 2), which receive input from the KO_R set and are mutually excitatory; it is designated KI_P. Other examples of KI sets are the KI_M set of mitral-tufted cells in the bulb (Figure 2), which receive excitatory KO_R input and are mutually excitatory, and the KI_G set of granule cells in the bulb, which receive excitatory KI_M input and are mutually inhibitory.[4]

---

[3] This assumption is not always necessary and in some interactions it is not valid. In one such instance (e.g., Freeman, 1974) the mass actions involve multiplicative rather than additive combinations of neural activity, and therefore they conform to a different model (Chapter 5 in Freeman, 1975) than those for synaptic interactions being considered here.

[4] There is no direct electrophysiological evidence for synaptic transmission between granule cells. The assertion that they do interact is based on analysis of the dynamic properties of the bulb reflected in the evoked potential (Freeman, 1972b, 1975) and on the existence of stellate cells (Figure 2) that have synaptic connections in the granule cell layer (Figure 1).

Again, there is no direct electrophysiological evidence that granule cells generate action potentials, and it is clear that, if they do, the action potentials are not extracellularly detectable. However, that fact can be explained by the geometry of the dendritic spines of granule cells. The spines are indistinguishable from axonal *boutons terminaux* under electron microscopy and may generate action potentials asynchronously over each granule cell. In any case, the measurements

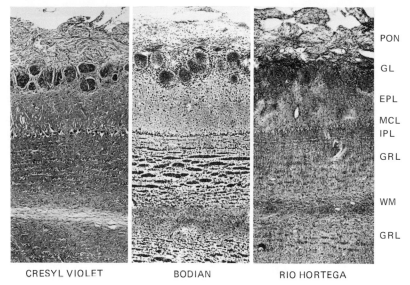

GL

EPL

MCL
IPL

GRL

WM

GRL

CRESYL VIOLET   BODIAN   RIO HORTEGA

FIGURE 1. Histological cross sections of the olfactory bulb with different stains. PON, primary olfactory nerve; GL, glomerular layer; EPL, external plexiform layer; MCL, mitral cell layer; IPL, internal plexiform layer; GRL, granule cell layer; WM, white matter containing axons entering the lateral olfactory tract (LOT). (From Freeman, 1972c.)

The KI_G set also transmits to the KI_M set and is inhibitory (Rall and Shepherd, 1968; Shepherd, 1972b). The dense interaction of a KI_e set and a KI_i set forms a KII set, in this case the KII_{MG} set. By these definitions, the channels of interaction in the neural mass of the bulb can be reduced to a network or flow diagram (Figure 3), which consists of the input tract from the KO_R receptor set (the primary olfactory nerve or PON), the KI_P periglomerular set, the KII_{MG} mitral-tufted-granule set, and the outflow tract from the KI_M set in the bulb (the lateral olfactory tract or LOT).

Each bulbar neuron has unique afferent and efferent connections, geometry, and perhaps chemistry, but at the macroscopic level these attributes do not appear. We are concerned only with its membership in a set and its location in that set. Within the set the neuron performs a continuing local integration[5] over

its dendritic tree in the wave mode, a continuing transmission over its axonal tree in the pulse mode, and serial nonlinear conversions between the two modes. The details of these operations are not known for any single neuron, but we can estimate the average transmission distances, delays, and strengths for local subsets within each set of neurons.

THE CONDITIONS FOR MACROSTATES

We proceed here by drawing on our knowledge of other systems that have both microstates and macrostates and in particular on an analogy from theoretical chemistry. Katchalsky (Katchalsky, Rowland, and Blumenthal, 1974) was the first to perceive a very deep isomorphism between interactive neural masses and diffusion-coupled chemical reaction systems, in recognition of which I have designated K-sets in

---

on the macroscopic properties of the KI_G show that it has essentially the same amplitude-dependent input–output nonlinearity as the KI_M set, in which the neurons generate action potentials.

[5] The term "integration" has different meanings at several levels of brain function, as shown in Sherrington's (1906) best-known work, *The Integrative Action*

of the Nervous System. Here I use it to mean the weighted summation of infinitesimals – by a dendritic tree, by a neural subset, or by the experimenter in solving an equation representing those operations. The outcome is "integrated neural activity."

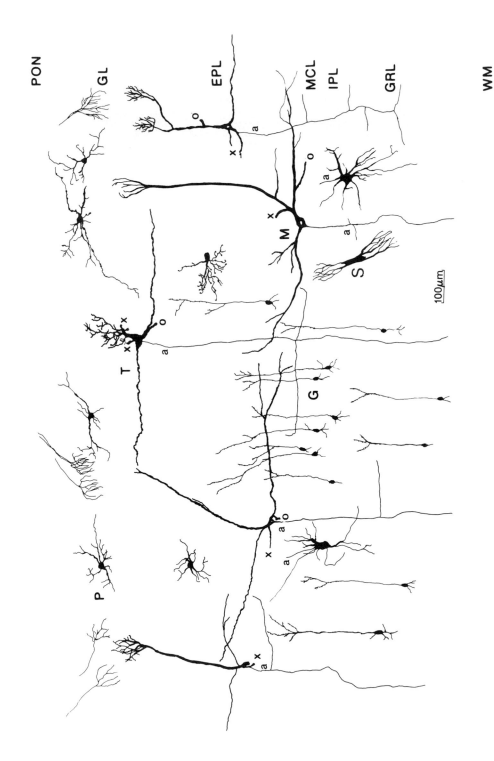

FIGURE 2. Camera lucida drawings of types of bulbar neurons in Golgi preparations placed in their respective layers (see Figure 1). P, periglomerular; M, mitral; T, tufted; G, granule cell; S, stellate cell. (From Freeman, 1972c.)

his name. Accordingly, we may characterize cortical neural activity in ways that are analogous to particles in a reaction complex by assuming the following conditions.

First, each neuron in a KI set transmits to and receives from a large number of neurons in its neighborhood. We cannot know the levels of activity of every neuron at all times nor the precise synaptic channels through which transmission takes place. To characterize macrostates we do not need to know. Similarly, in a chemical system we do not know or need to know the history of every particle.

Second, there exists in the neighborhood of each point in a KI neural set a level of activity which is the average of the levels of activity of the neurons in that neighborhood. In other words, there can be defined for each set a volume or surface element containing a subset of neurons which is sufficiently large to support the formation of an ensemble average over the activities of the neurons in the subset and which is sufficiently small to allow the average to hold over the entire subset when the level of activity over the set is not homogeneous. This is analogous to the assumption for a chemical system that a volume element exists which is large enough to allow a concentration to be defined at each point and small enough to allow the concentration to be treated as uniform in the element in the presence of a concentration gradient.

It seems likely that the size of the neural volume element in the bulb may be a column on the order of 0.1 mm in radius and that the numbers of neurons in each set in such an element may range from 10^7 to 10^6. These numbers would seem rather low if we were attempting to express pulse density in each element as a continuous function, but activity in the pulse mode is continuously transformed into the wave mode and back again. As the cable properties of the dendrites have a powerful smoothing effect in both space and time, the assumption of continuity of a macroscopic activity level in a neural set over time and space is reasonable.

Further, a macrostate is defined for a set and must exist in a volume or over a surface area of cortex which greatly exceeds the dimensions of the volume or surface element that comprises the subset and also the dimensions of lateral connectivity in the cortex for single cortical neurons, probably ranging considerably upward from 10 to perhaps several hundred square millimeters.

Third, the time scale for macroscopic events is much longer than the time scale for events in single neurons, which have time durations on the order of 1.0 msec for pulses and time constants on the order of 5.0 msec for PSPs. The durations of macroscopic events are typically on the order of 100 to 500 msec. This is analogous to the existence of two time scales for describing chemical reactions: very short times in which two particles react, and relatively long times describing the rates of the macroscopic reactions. Changes in the macroscopic state of a neural set may be conceived as occurring rapidly, but each state in a sequence of states must, in order to be defined, have some minimum duration on the order of 0.1 second, corresponding, for example, to an evoked potential or a pattern in the EEG. It cannot be observed or measured over time durations on the order of the duration of an action potential.

Fourth, the fraction of the neurons in a set that is generating pulses at any moment is always relatively small, and the time of occurrence of a pulse in each neuron is not predictable from its history or the history of any small number of its neighbors. Though each neuron continually receives pulses from its surround, it seldom gives a pulse. Most cortical neurons fire at rates less than 10 per second, and at random with respect both to previous firing in the same neuron and to firing in other neurons in the cortex. This condition is analogous to chemical systems, in which there is predominance of elastic collisions over reactive collisions between particles, so that most ions most of the time are not reacting even though macroscopic reactions are taking place. We infer from this assumption that we can construct differential equations to describe macroscopic interactions in either the wave or pulse mode without explicit reference to the threshold, the refractory periods, adaptation, accommodation, and related phenomena. It is largely on this basis that we can separate the amplitude dependency of neural mass actions from both space and

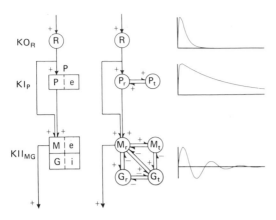

FIGURE 3. *Schematic diagram of bulbar topology in terms of KO, KI, and KII sets. The characteristic forms of the impulse responses are shown at the right. R, receptors; P, periglomerular cells; M, mitral-tufted cells; G, granule cells;* r, *receiving subset;* t, *transmitting subset;* e *and* +, *excitatory;* i *and* −, *inhibitory.*

time dependencies, which is not the case, for example, in the Hodgkin–Huxley equations (Katz, 1966).

Fifth, the level of activity of each neuron in a set is locally determined by an ensemble average of the activity levels of neurons in its surround, and on the average it must be consistent with that average, because it is itself a part of the surround and contributes to it. By this assumption we can at every instant divide a KI set into a transmitting subset, *t*, which is giving pulses and a receiving subset, *r*, which is not giving pulses. Membership in the two subsets continually changes at random for each neuron, and the density of distribution of the two subsets is uniform over the set by assumption. Because a new transmitting subset continually emerges from the receiving subset, we can describe the interaction within the KI set by an equivalent feedback loop between two KO sets (Figure 3). Differential equations describing the KI or higher set can be written as feedback equations. The strength of interaction can be expressed as a nonlinear function that holds for each point in the set and for the time duration of a macroscopic event. We replace the nonlinear function by a linear approximation. A sigmoid curve is replaced by a straight line approximating the curve, the slope of which we

shall call the feedback gain (Chapter 3 in Freeman, 1975).

When these five conditions are reviewed, they may be seen as a kind of conceptual bridge on which we move from consideration of the more pervasive properties of cortex to a position where we can begin to construct some detailed models of cortical dynamics. The references to chemical kinetics serve as guidelines on what to look for, but they are not essential. What is essential is the recognition that we are no longer speaking about neurons or about collections or networks of individual neurons, but about macroscopic entities that transcend the neurons. This concept is not likely to be comprehensible after one reading, and the reader is advised to proceed and return after suitable reflection.

THE FORMS OF MACROSTATES

At this point, the reader might reasonably ask to see a neural macrostate, because we are conventionally taught that facts are the basis for theory and must speak for themselves. This is like going to city hall and asking to see the government. One needs some good questions beforehand, which is to say some testable hypotheses. Unguided observation and the neuron doctrine are not sufficient for prediction beyond the level of single neurons. From the definitions and assumptions already given, we must construct some precise predictions of what to look for.

We shall use four steps (Chapter 1 in Freeman, 1975) in constructing each prediction. The reader will already be familiar with the basic rules of construction from his knowledge of the properties of nerve membrane. The membrane consists of a lipid layer that separates inner and outer aqueous compartments. Events in the membrane consist of complex space–time fields of current and of potential, which in general reflect dynamics that are highly nonlinear in the sense already defined. For simplicity, we shall use for illustration only some special cases for membrane and for K-sets as well which involve just the time dimension (so-called lumped circuit approximations) and a narrow range of current-potential relations that allow the use of linear approximations.

Suppose that we place a pair of electrodes, one on either side of the membrane, for passing a transmembrane current impulse[6] (the input, $\delta(t)$ at $t = 0$), and another pair nearby, on either side of the membrane, for measuring the transmembrane potential difference [the output, $v(t)$ or simply v]. Within the linear range, we observe that v jumps to a new value during the pulse and then decays monotonically back to the baseline that existed before the pulse, say $v = 0$. We note that the response waveform seems to conform to an exponential curve:

$$v = v_0 e^{-a_1 t} \qquad t \geq 0 \qquad (1)$$

We know that this equation is the solution to a first-order linear differential equation, using $\dot{v}$ to denote dv/dt:

$$\dot{v} + a_1 v = k\, \delta(t) \qquad (2)$$

where k and a_1 are constants to be determined. From our knowledge of physical systems in general, and of the chemical and anatomical structure of membrane in particular, we construct a model in which the membrane is represented by a resistance, R, in parallel with a capacitance, C. We define a time constant, $\tau = RC$. We assert that $\tau = 1/a_1$ and that $v_0 = k = 1/C$. Then we fit the theoretical curve,

$$v = \frac{1}{C} e^{-t/\tau} \qquad t \geq 0 \qquad (3)$$

to our experimental curve by linear regression[7] in order to measure τ and C. Finally, we interpret R and C to mean the existence in the membrane, respectively, of pores through which ions may pass and of bound charge on or in the lipid layer acting as a dielectric.

In review, the four steps are (1) constructing a topology[8]; (2) making an observa-

tion of an event (the waveform); (3) constructing, solving, and evaluating a differential equation; and (4) interpreting the parameters of the equation in terms of subsystems of membrane. We shall use the same four steps in each of the following four illustrations.

Let us consider the dynamics of a KO set. By instituting appropriate experimental controls (Chapter 4 in Freeman, 1975) we use a lumped circuit approximation.

Suppose that we place a stimulating electrode on the LOT and stimulate the axons of the KI_M set antidromically, so that a volley is delivered directly to the KI_G set. In the appropriate experimental conditions (Chapter 4 in Freeman, 1975) we can record the response of the KI_G set in the wave mode with a monopolar electrode on the bulbar surface and a distant reference electrode. In waking or lightly anesthetized animals the impulse input initiates prolonged interactions, but under very deep anesthesia the interactions are suppressed, and the KI_M and the KI_G sets are reduced to the KO_M and KO_G state.

With the impulse input, $\delta(t)$, we observe a rapid increase in surface-negative potential followed by a less rapid decay (Figure 4A). For simplicity, we shall not consider the factors of afferent temporal dispersion in the input tract and the late positivity or dendritic afterpotential. By appropriate stimulation with pairs of stimuli to test for additivity, we establish a linear range for observation (Biedenbach and Freeman, 1965). Then we postulate that the response can be fitted with an equation in the form

$$v = v_0 e^{-a_1 t} - v_0 e^{-a_2 t} \qquad t \geq 0 \qquad (4)$$

The first term represents an initially upward exponential curve, $v = v_0$ at $t = 0$, and conforms to the decay of the response. The decay rate is

[6] The symbol $\delta(t)$ denotes the Dirac delta function.

[7] Regression is a procedure for fitting curves to data points. If the fitted curve is a straight line or can be converted to a line as an exponential curve is linearized by semilogarithmic transformation, then linear regression is used (see any statistics textbook). If the fitted curve is the sum of two or more exponential curves, then nonlinear regression must be used (e.g., Chapter 2 in Freeman, 1975).

[8] I use the word "topology" to mean specification of the elements of which a system is constructed and the channels or functional connec-

tions and interconnections by which the elements act on each other, including the input and output elements and channels. Here, for example, we have the membrane represented by a network of resistive and capacitive elements, the input and output electrodes, and the current paths, which are commonly represented by a lumped circuit diagram. Note that the geometry is not specified by the topology and that both must be given in order to construct the differential equation in step (3), as in constructing the lumped circuit approximation.

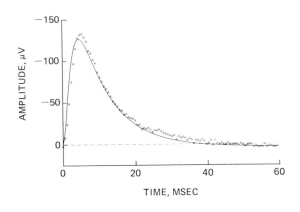

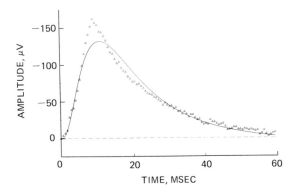

FIGURE 4. *Predicted (curves) and observed (symbols) bulbar responses (averaged evoked potentials or AEPs) under deep pentobarbital anesthesia (the open-loop state) on single-shock LOT (A) or single-shock PON (B) electrical stimulation. (From Freeman, 1972a.)*

a_1. The second term represents an initially downward exponential curve, $v = -v_0$ at $t = 0$, and the coefficient a_2 determines the rate of rise. When the second curve is subtracted from the first, the amplitude at $t = 0$ is of course zero, and the peak latency is seen to depend on both a_1 and a_2. This is the characteristic form of an EPSP as well as the simplest form of cortical evoked potentials, and because the form corresponds to the sum of two exponentials, we must fit the curve to the data using nonlinear regression.

Equation (4) is the solution to a linear second-order differential equation,

$$\ddot{v} + (a_1 + a_2)\dot{v} + a_1 a_2 v = k\,\delta(t) \qquad (5)$$

where $\ddot{v}$ means d^2v/dt^2, and k is an arbitrary constant. We construct a model in which we represent the KO_G set by a large number of neurons in parallel, each of which performs three operations on its input: pulse to wave conversion represented by k, combined synaptic and cable delay represented by a_2, and passive membrane decay represented by a_1.

We can fit Equation (4) to the observed response to evaluate k, a_1, and a_2. Of course, the values may hold only in the range of the linear approximation. If we change the input strength sufficiently, the value for k changes, but we find that the values of a_1 and a_2 and the form of the equation do not change. This is an important result because it means that the rate constants (reciprocals of the time constants) are invariants — a major reason why we can use linear approximations in this as well as in more complex constructions.

We interpret the KO model as equivalent to an average neuron in which the passive membrane model is one of its parts, and we interpret $a_1 = 220/\text{sec} = 1/4.5$ msec and $a_2 = 720/\text{sec} = 1/1.4$ msec as the average rate constants for, respectively, the passive membrane decay and lumped synaptic and dendritic cable delay.

We can repeat the procedure under quite deep anesthesia (what we call the "open-loop state," because interactions are suppressed), but this time with stimulation of the KO_M set orthodromically by way of the PON. The output is still that of the KO_G set in the wave mode, but the rise time of the response to the impulse is slower. This reflects the delay contributed by the synaptic, cable, and passive membrane properties of the KO_M set. Then we construct a system of two second-order linear differential equations:

$$\ddot{v}_M + (a_3 + a_4)\dot{v}_M + a_3 a_4 v_M = k\,\delta(t) \quad (6a)$$

$$\ddot{v}_G + (a_1 + a_2)\dot{v}_G + a_1 a_2 v_G = k_M v_M \quad (6b)$$

Equation (6a) says that the input $k\,\delta(t)$ to the KO_M set is an impulse and the output of the KO_M set v_M has the form specified by Equation (4). Equation (6b) says that the input $k_M v_M$ to the KO_G set is the output of the KO_M set v_M times a coefficient k_M, and the output of the KO_G set v_G can be predicted by solving Equations (6a) and (6b) for v_G.

The solution gives a curve, which we fit by nonlinear regression to the observed waveform to evaluate a_3 and a_4. We find experimentally that $a_3 = a_1$ and $a_4 = a_2$, so that the equation for the fitted curve (Figure 4B) takes a peculiar form:

$$v_G = v_1 e^{-a_1 t} + v_2 t e^{-a_1 t} + v_3 e^{-a_2 t}$$
$$+ v_4 t e^{-a_2 t} \qquad t \geqslant 0 \qquad (7)$$

The mathematical basis for this form need not concern us here.

We are now ready to predict the form of the response of the KII_{MG} set under light anesthesia or the "closed-loop state" when interactions are present. For simplicity, we shall consider only what we shall call the "reduced" KII_{MG} set, in which we assert that the interactions within the KI_M and KI_G sets cancel each other. The proof that this occurs and the relevant experimental conditions are described elsewhere (Freeman, 1975). We shall again take the output from the KI_G set in the wave mode and now also from the KI_M set in the pulse mode. For PON stimulation, the differential equations are

$$\ddot{v}_M + (a_1 + a_2)\dot{v}_M + a_1 a_2 v_M = -k_G v_G + k\,\delta(t) \tag{8a}$$

$$\ddot{v}_G + (a_1 + a_2)\dot{v}_G + a_1 a_2 v_G = k_M v_M \tag{8b}$$

Equation (8a) says that the input to the KI_M set is the sum of an impulse $k\,\delta(t)$ and the output of the KI_G set v_G times a coefficient k_G. The KI_G output is inhibitory, so it is subtracted. Equation (8b) says that the input to the KI_G set is given by the output of the KI_M set times a coefficient k_M. The sign is positive because the KI_M output is excitatory. For LOT stimulation the input term $k\,\delta(t)$ is added to Equation (8b) instead of Equation (8a).

This pair of equations describes a negative feedback loop[9] (Figure 3). The solutions consist of damped (exponentially decaying) sine and cosine waves with frequency ω (in radians per second) and decay rate α in (seconds^{-1}):

$$v_M = v_{0M}[\cos(\omega_1 t + \phi_1)e^{-\alpha_1 t}$$
$$+ \cos(\omega_2 t + \phi_2)e^{-\alpha_2 t}] \qquad t \geqslant 0 \quad (9a)$$

$$v_G = v_{0G}[\sin(\omega_1 t + \phi_1)e^{-\alpha_1 t}$$
$$+ \sin(\omega_2 t + \phi_2)e^{-\alpha_2 t}] \qquad t \geqslant 0 \quad (9b)$$

Equation (9a) predicts the closed-loop output of the KI_M set, and equation (9b), that of the

[9] Negative feedback should not be confused with the various forms of recurrent inhibition. For example, the neurons in the compound eye of *Limulus* are mutually inhibitory and form a positive inhibitory feedback loop. As noted below, the periglomerular neurons are mutually excitatory and form a positive excitatory feedback loop. Feedback is negative only when interaction occurs between excitatory and inhibitory neurons, as in the bulb. The spinal motoneuron–Renshaw cell network is commonly cited as an example of negative neural feedback. However, in the usual conditions of observation each motoneuron acts through Renshaw cells to inhibit other motoneurons in its surround. Unless the initiating motoneurons are then shown to undergo oscillatory activity, which is characteritic of negative feedback and would show that in fact the loop is closed, this network should be considered as an example of parallel forward inhibition and not feedback.

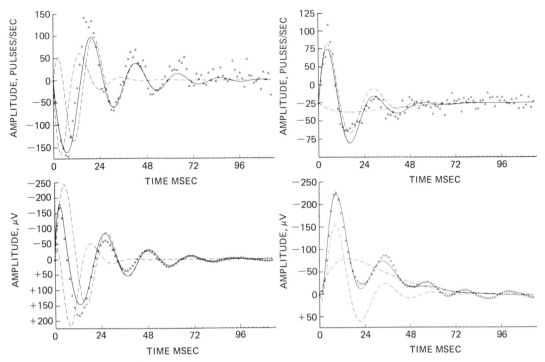

FIGURE 5. *Predicted (curves) and observed (symbols) bulbar responses under light anesthesia to single-shock electrical stimulation of LOT (left) and PON (right). (A) Poststimulus time histograms (PSTHs) from mitral cell (KI_M set). (B) AEPs from granule cells (KI_G set). The interaction of the KI_M and KI_G sets forms the KII_{MG} set. (From Freeman, 1972b.)*

KI_G set. We predict that the activities of the KI_M and KI_G sets should oscillate at the same frequencies and decay at the same rates but with a 90° phase lead for the output of the KI_M set over that of the KI_G set. This should hold for PON and for LOT input as well, and the values for ϕ_1 and ϕ_2 should depend on the site of input (Figure 5).

The basis for the oscillation and for the KI_M phase lead is intuitively explained as follows. Excitation of the KI_M set excites the KI_G set, which then inhibits the KI_M set. Inhibition of the KI_M set disexcites (inhibits) the KI_G set, which disinhibits (excites) the KI_M set. The cycle repeats with a time period that depends on the rate constants, a_1 and a_2, and on the product of $k_M k_G$, which we shall call the negative feedback gain, K_N. If we know a_1, a_2, ω_1, and α_1, then we can evaluate K_N, which is the numerical estimate or measurement of the strength of interaction between the KI_M and KI_G sets.

For contrast, we can predict the form of the response in the pulse mode of the KI_P set to impulse stimulation of the PON. The neurons are mutually excitatory, so we have a case of positive feedback (Figure 3). By our fifth assumption, we divide the set into two subsets having the active states p_t and p_r. The differential equations are

$$\ddot{p}_r + (a_1 + a_2)\dot{p}_r + a_1 a_2 p_r = k_p p_t + k\,\delta(t) \quad (10a)$$

$$\ddot{p}_t + (a_1 + a_2)\dot{p}_t + a_1 a_2 p_t = k_p p_r \quad (10b)$$

Equation (10a) says that the input $k\,\delta(t)$ to the KI_P set is received by a subset with active state p_r that is not transmitting at the time of $\delta(t)$ at $t = 0$, and that this subset also receives from the transmitting subset with active state p_t. Its output is p_r. Equation (10b) says that the input to the transmitting subset is the output p_r of the receiving subset times a coefficient k_p.

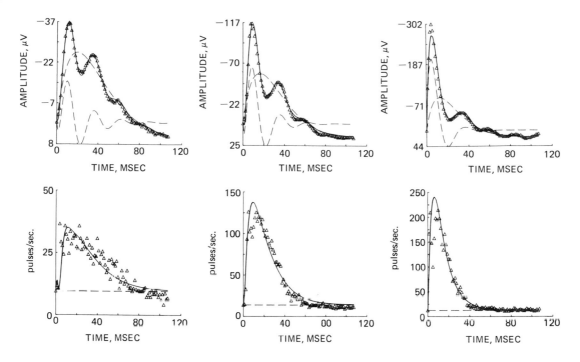

FIGURE 6. *Predicted (curves) and observed (symbols) bulbar responses under light anesthesia to single-shock electrical stimulation of PON. Dashed curves in upper frames show the components of the AEPs. Each pair of frames (left to right) shows the changes in bulbar responses with increasing stimulus intensity. (A) AEPs from field potential recordings at the bulbar surface, which show the output of the KI_G set. (B) PSTHs from single unit recordings in the glomerular layer, (GL) in Figure 1, which show the output of the KI_P set.*

The solutions for the outputs of the two subsets are

$$p_t = p_{t1}e^{-\alpha_1 t} + p_{t2}e^{-\alpha_2 t}$$
$$+ p_{t3}e^{-\alpha_3 t} + p_{t4}e^{-\alpha_4 t} \quad (11a)$$

$$p_r = p_{r1}e^{-\alpha_1 t} + p_{r2}e^{-\alpha_2 t}$$
$$+ p_{r3}e^{-\alpha_3 t} + p_{r4}e^{-\alpha_4 t} \quad (11b)$$

where p_{tj}, p_{rj}, and α_j ($j = 1, \ldots, 4$) are real or complex. The four rate coefficients α_j result from the combination of two second-order differential equations, and they are identical in Equations (11a) and (11b). The total output of the KI_P set is $p = p_t + p_r$.

The predicted output (Figure 6) consists of a sharp increase in pulse density followed by a very slow decay to the prestimulus baseline without overshoot. The rate of increase depends on whether or not the subset under

observation receives the PON input volley. The decay rate to the baseline, say α_1, depends on a_1, a_2, and the square of k_p, which we will call positive excitatory feedback gain, K_E. Knowing a_1, a_2, and α_1, we can calculate the strength of interaction, K_E, in the KI_e set.

Our ability to predict the forms of macrostates is crucially important in several respects. First, we must know clearly what to look for amid the complexites of cortical electrophysiology. Second, we must have good reasons to accept proposed models and be able to reject inadequate models firmly, and this can best be done by quantitative comparison of predicted curves and observed wave forms. Third, we must be able to measure our experimental data, which can best be done by fitting curves to the data. And, fourth, we must be able to interpret our measurements in terms of rate constants and strengths of interaction, or we have engaged in empty curve fitting. The most important parameters are the interaction strengths represented by feedback gains, because they are the determinants of the existence and forms of neural macrostates, and there are many indications that they are the principal and perhaps sole variables that underlie the continually changing relations between the forms of macrostates and behavior.

OBSERVABLE ASPECTS OF MACROSTATES

We assume that each macrostate exists in the form of an organized pattern of neural activity for a limited time interval over a limited area of cortex comprising a neural mass. We analyze the mass into a network of KO, KI, and KII sets (and perhaps higher-order sets based on feedback between KII sets). We define a level of activity in the subset of neurons at every point in each of the component KO and KI sets over a definite time interval, say Δt, starting at t_0. We shall call that level of activity the activity density at every point. We represent the activity density by p or v in equations such as those in the preceding section. The activity densities for all points in one KO or KI set constitute the activity density function (a.d.f.) of the set, $p_j(t, x, y, z)$ or $v_j(t, x, y, z)$, $t_0 \leqslant t < t_0 + \Delta t$, respectively, in the pulse and wave modes. The macrostate of the mass over Δt is given by the a.d.f.'s for all the KO_j and KI_j sets in the mass, $j = 1, 2, \ldots$.

In the olfactory bulb and mucosa we can describe each of the neural sets in a two-dimensional surface, because the interactions occur in the directions parallel to the surface and orthogonal to the main trajectory of transmission. The macrostate of this system is given by four a.d.f.'s in time and the surface coordinates for the KO_R, KI_P, KI_M, and KI_G sets. The input to the bulb is defined by the a.d.f. of the KO_R set in the PON at the glomerular layer, $p_R(t, x, y)$, and the output of the bulb is defined by the a.d.f. of the KI_M set, $p_M(t, x, y)$, in the mitral cell layer of the bulb (Figure 1). The operation, O, of the bulb is given by the function relating the a.d.f.'s of the KO_R and KI_M sets, $p_M(t, x, y) = O[p_R(t, x, y)]$.

The activity density of each subset is manifested or reflected in either the pulse mode, the wave mode, or both — that is, in the pulse trains and dendritic currents of neurons in the subset. There are three difficulties here. First, the activity density is the ensemble average of neural activities over the entire volume of the subset *and over the entire duration* of the macrostate. Therefore, the macrostate is reflected only in time and space averages over electrical measurements made at each point in a set. An example may be the measurement of an EEG wave at a point on the cortex, which in certain conditions is mainly the spatial average of extracellular dendritic potentials of neurons in the vicinity, and which is identified by its frequency and amplitude distribution or its configuration over a definite time interval. Another example is the pulse probability conditional on EEG amplitude and frequency for a unit cluster recorded with an extracellular microelectrode (Chapter 3 in Freeman, 1975).

The duration of observation of macrostates at one or a small number of points in a mass is generally too short to give an adequate basis for averaging, so we often resort to periodic electrical stimulation and time-locked ensemble averaging of electrical responses with respect to the time of the stimulus, on the assumption that each stimulus initiates a macrostate that differs from the others in a series only because of the presence of random variation that we commonly call "noise." In the wave mode this yields an averaged evoked potential (AEP), and in the pulse mode it yields a poststimulus time histogram (PSTH). The procedure has limited value, but at present it is the mainstay for macroscopic observation.

Second, the reflections of a macrostate can be observed only at a small number of sample points over its spatial extent (at present 10 points in the pulse mode or 64 points in the wave mode). We must have very precise predictions of the spatial characteristics of a.d.f.'s to use such small samples for effective testing. The simplified examples in the preceding section predict only the temporal characteristics, so we cannot consider the spatial characteristics here. In experimental testing it is feasible to arrange the conditions of observation so that homogeneity of the a.d.f.'s can be inferred to hold in the vicinity of a test point. These are the conditions in which measurements of AEPs, PSTHs, the EEG, and conditional pulse probabilities are best made at present.

Third, the activity density at a point in a KO or KI set is not identical to the AEP, PSTH, or EEG recorded at or near the point. The connection between an observable event and an active state is made from extensive knowledge of the neural geometry, cytoarchitecture, and functional properties of the neurons and the set. The same problem exists at the level of single neurons, though in less acute form. For example, the pulse rate of a neuron may not accurately reflect the state of a neuron (its output to other neurons), because the effectiveness of each pulse may increase or decrease with decreasing pulse interval. For another example, the relation between membrane potential at the soma and pulse rate in "spontaneously" active neurons is notoriously obscure. The difficulties at the level of sets are compounded by the overlap of extracellular potential fields of sets in the same mass or adjacent masses and by the admixture of pulse trains from differing sets in unit clusters. Some detailed examples of analyses of these problems are given elsewhere (Chapter 4 in Freeman, 1975).

Another difficulty is that surgical or pharmacological isolation of a neural mass (as by anesthesia) may dramatically alter the dynamics of the mass (as in reduction to the open-loop state). Mass actions are best observed in intact animals, preferably in conjunction with normal behavior. In these cases, we can use our predictions to design filters to isolate the components of observed events having interest for us. For example, the bulbar AEP on either PON or LOT stimulation has multiple frequency components (Figure 5). We predict that the KII_{MG} set should generate a damped sine wave, and intuitively we expect that positive feedback within the bulbar KI sets (as well as feedback from the cortex) can lead to multiple superimposed low-frequency components, all reflected by activity in the KI_G set in the wave mode. For signal isolation and measurement we design a matched filter with two parts. One is matched to the damped sine wave and the other is matched to the "clutter" introduced by the other circuits still not analytically understood (Chapters 2 and 5 in Freeman, 1975). The filters are, of course, adaptive to the changing characteristics of the signal, and even more to those aspects of an event that we wish to isolate. More complex forms of isolation can be achieved by use of spatial analyses or by factor analysis combined with behavioral control (Chapter 7 in Freeman, 1975). The details are not important here. What is important is that macrostates must not be confused with observables such as the EEG.

MACROSTATES AND BEHAVIOR

From peripheral and central unit recordings we already know or infer that patterned sensory stimulaton leads to the formation of space–time patterns of activity of neurons in the brain, and that space–time patterns of action potentials in the array of motoneurons are the basis for even the simplest motor activity. It is easy to see intuitively that coordinated patterns induced by sensory stimulation may be transformed by locally dense interactions into macrostates. Such macrostates would control the forms of bursts of activity transmitted from one neural mass to another in the brain by KI sets, each burst being described by an a.d.f. in the two dimensions of the cross section of the efferent tracts of a KI set and in the time dimension of the burst duration. The cortex and basal ganglia may continually send packaged bursts to the brainstem and spinal cord, which could provide the basis for widespread coordination of the activities of motoneurons.

The difficulty in substantiating this intuition lies in the complexity of predicting the spatial forms of macrostates. The dynamics of KI and KII sets can be described by means of coupled nonlinear partial integrodifferential equations with deterministic or stochastic state variables (Glansdorff and Prigogine, 1971; Wilson and Cowan, 1973). General solutions of these equations do not exist, though in some instances the existence of classes of solutions can be proven analytically (Ahn and Freeman, 1974). Particular solutions can be obtained by computer simulation, which are useful if the initial conditions and boundary conditions are realistically structured to represent anatomical and physiological inputs and constraints. There is a rich field here for collaboration between neurobiologists and mathematicians with the appropriate backgrounds.

Some special properties of solutions to this class of equations have already been explored in connection with diffusion-coupled chemical reactions and other related thermodynamically irreversible systems (Glansdorff and Prigogine, 1971; Katchalsky, Rowland, and Blumenthal, 1974). When a distributed system containing multiple-feedback channels among nonlinear elements with time decays is isolated, it stabilizes in a steady state with minimal entropy production, similarly to the way in which an isolated cortical slab becomes "silent" (Burns, 1958). Such steady states are said to be at equilibrium, and they are typically spatially homogeneous. But if energy is steadily fed into the system, it is driven away from equilibrium. If driven far enough, it crosses one or more thresholds, and entirely new properties emerge based on interactions. These include oscillatory or limit cycle activity, and spatial inhomogeneities in the concentrations of the reactants. These dynamic patterns are called "dissipative structures" to distinguish them from "equilibrium structures," such as crystals (Prigogine, 1969), because they require a continuing influx of energy and by definition occur only in open systems. Considerable progress has been made in predicting the spatial forms for some relatively simple chemical systems (Herschkowitz-Kaufman and Nicolis, 1972; Nicolis, 1974).

It is likely that the same techniques will be useful in predicting the forms of dynamic patterns in neural macrostates, because the basic assumptions and appearances of events are so similar. For example, when the input to the cortex is withdrawn as by deep anesthesia or by surgical undercutting, the cortex tends (Burns, 1958) to be electrically silent, and its responses to electrical pulses decay to the rest level without oscillation.[10] This open-loop state, with zero feedback gain is equivalent to an equilibrium state. In the normal cortex and bulb there is continual synaptic input, which raises the feedback gains in the KII set above zero in proportion to the amplitude of input. If the continuing input is strong enough to raise the negative feedback gain above a certain threshold value, the KII set in the bulb or cortex becomes unstable and breaks into oscillation (Adrian, 1950). The frequency and amplitude of the oscillation are stabilized by the nonlinearity in the KII set, giving rise to a limit cycle. Specifically, during each inspiration, there is a sustained burst of unit activity from the KO_R set to the KII_{MG} set, which excites it and also raises its feedback gains. The sinusoidal burst in the EEG with each inspiration (Figure 7[11]) is not "ringing" in response to the change in level of input, in the way that a bell rings when it is struck. It is the manifestation of an instability due to the high negative-feedback gain (Chapter 6 in Freeman, 1975). A similar phenomenon is heard in audioamplifiers when the gain is too high, but whereas there it is pathological, in the bulb there is experimental evidence that the induced oscillation is spatially inhomogeneous and might carry olfactory information (Freeman, 1975). If we combine mathematical prediction with electrical recording of bulbar activity during stimulation with odors, we may be able to describe macrostates fully for the first time and explore them in relation to the problem of olfactory signal processing. One might suppose that this should be tried first in the visual or auditory cortex with better stimulus control, but the critical problem is mathematical prediction of responses and in this respect the dynamics of the bulb appear to be simpler than those of neocortex.

---

[10] The bulb and cortex differ in their responses to surgical isolation. In the bulb, EEG activity disappears but unit activity persists, whereas in the isolated cortex both are almost entirely suppressed. The difference can be attributed to the presence in the bulb of a stable excitatory state in the KI_P set (Ahn and Freeman, 1974).

[11] EEG records as in Figure 7A (and evoked potentials as well) from the deep pole of the KI_G dipole field are positive (downward) during increased KI_G activity due to PON input, whereas records from the surface show negative potential (upward) during KI_G excitation. This rule may not hold for other input, such as from the anterior commissure (Rall and Shepherd, 1968). Sinusoidal bursts tend to begin at or after the positive crest of the respiratory wave (maximal mean KI_G excitation). This coincides also with the maximal mean pulse rates in the KI_P and KI_M sets, where the means are oscillating at the respiratory rate.

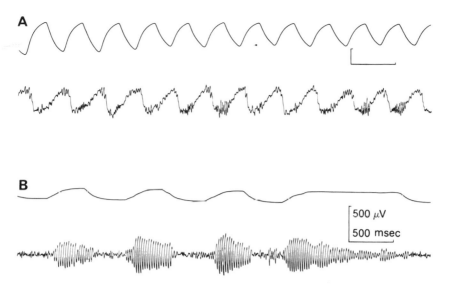

FIGURE 7. *EEG waves in a waking minimally restrained rabbit recorded with implanted electrodes from the depth of the olfactory bulb (lower trace in each pair, negative upward) showing the relation of burst activity to the respiratory cycle (upper trace, inspiration upward) recorded with a thermocouple in the external nares. (A) Normal breathing room air. Half-amplitude low-frequency filter set at 0.1 hertz. (B) After tracheotomy with nasal air flow (room air) controlled by a push–pull air pump attached to the pharyngeal end of the trachea. Pump rate: 1 per second. Stroke volume: 15 ml. Breathing rate was about 2 per second.*

We conclude by considering whether this concept of bulbar function is consistent with Maynard's view of simpler systems. It is not, if his view is taken to mean that the neurons in a simpler network are to be analyzed like components in a digital computer, conceptually assembled, and put into controlled operation according to deterministic equations. It is consistent, if allowance is made for the intermediary assembly into sets of certain parts of nervous systems, and in particular the neuropil of vertebrate cortex and perhaps of invertebrate ganglia, which then function as elements at the macroscopic level that are embedded within discrete networks of neurons.

The assumption is often adopted in macroscopic modeling that the *neurons* in a set are identical except for location. This is not required and is demonstrably untrue. We assume that the macroscopic properties of *subsets* in a set are uniform, or that they vary in a predictable way with the location of the subset in the set, but the uniqueness of the neurons in each subset is not sacrificed. Rather

it is obviously required for read-in and read-out of the specific neural information subserving sensory and motor events, which is mediated in the neuropil. The problem is to identify the operations at the interfaces between neural networks and macroscopic elements so that Maynard's stringent requirements for simpler systems may be more closely approached.

CONCLUSIONS

The vertebrate cortex seems intractable to analysis in terms of "properties of single neurons and their principles of combination" (Maynard, 1963) because of their immense number, locally dense connectivity, and highly nonlinear dynamics. Yet these very characteristics provide the basis for predicting the existence of widespread dynamic patterns of neural activity which emerge by integration from locally dense interactions and which we call macrostates. The properties of an interactive neural mass that sustains macrostates can be derived from our knowledge of the input–output dynamics of single neurons and the main synaptic interconnectivity patterns in the mass, which are described as networks of interactive neural sets.

From a set of assumptions based on empirical observations of activity in neural masses and on analogies with diffusion-coupled chemical reaction systems, we can construct differential equations to represent the dynamics of interactive neural sets. The solutions to the equations by integration constitute predictions of the forms of macrostates, which we can use to guide our experiments, test our models, measure our data, and evaluate the strengths of interactions. We find that macrostates cannot be observed directly, but their forms are to be inferred from averages of measurements on dendritic and action potentials.

It is reasonable to intuit that neural macrostates represent forms in which information is processed and carried between sensory and motor systems. The mathematical prediction of the forms is very difficult, but a solid basis for attempting this has already been laid principally in the field of irreversible thermodynamics. Additionally, the problems of read-in and read-out of specific information in sets have not been solved. The neurons in interactive sets do not lose their unique attributes, and it appears that neural sets may be best treated as specialized elements embedded in the central terminals of the motor and sensory neural networks.

VI

ORGANISM
BEHAVIOR

The three chapters in Part VI deal primarily with problems of behavioral organization at the level of the intact organism. It is well to remind ourselves that organism behavior is the raison d'être of neurons and neural networks, and what we ultimately wish to explain by analyses of functional subunits within the organism. At the same time it is clear that adaptive patterns of behavior follow rules that can be described and analyzed at the behavioral level. Often it is these rules which set the most basic problems of investigation at the neurobiological level.

In Chapter Twenty-One, Heiligenberg takes a classical concept in behavior, motivation, and demonstrates how it can be approached precisely through systematic and quantitative examination of the interplay between factors intrinsic and extrinsic to the organism. The basic idea of motivation in ethology stems from the observation that animals do not respond in an invariable manner to repeated external circumstances, a fact that permits inference of change in internal, or "motivational," state. This inference about the importance of intrinsic factors in the organization of species-typical behavior led ethologists to abandon simple reflex or stimulus–response views of behavior in favor of a more balanced emphasis upon intrinsic processes, or more accurately, the relationship between intrinsic processes and the animal's responsiveness to external events. We have already seen that this emphasis upon intrinsic control in behavior has caused a major change in our conceptualizations of nervous system operation. The approach to "motivational" analysis is operationally similar to that utilized in the study of neural units and nets, except that the unit of emphasis is the organism as an intact entity. Thus at each level the question is asked, for example, whether external factors may release a given response whose threshold is changed and whose patterning is coordinated largely by intrinsic mechanisms; and there are many data at each level to the affirmative (although one must be careful not to overgeneralize at this stage). At the organism level, changes of intrinsic state may result in qualitatively as well as quantitatively different responses to a constant stimulus, and a major set of questions currently being pursued is the interplay between different classes of behavior once each is defined independently by formal input—output criteria.

Heiligenberg reviews much of the ethological literature relevant to these themes and to issues discussed previously in this volume (e.g., "central patterning," "genetic control," "feedback"). He then reviews basic methodological issues in "motivation" research and shows that it can be useful to treat the animal as a probabilistic system with a number of more or less discrete behavioral outputs. One can then match changes in output probability with (1) changes in stimulus input and (2) changes of internal state. The relations of (1) to (2) as measured by response can then be determined. He illustrates this approach with experiments under constant external conditions and then with experiments involving short pulses and prolonged step functions of stimulus presentation. To do this he also asks questions about the *sequential* distribution of acts in behavior, where the influence of a given act upon the relative probabilities of subsequent acts is assessed. Heiligenberg's data with adult male cichlid fish exposed to a population of juveniles indicate the importance of evaluating both short-term and long-term fluctuations in calculations of dynamic changes of internal state leading to temporally patterned response distribution, both of individual acts and their various possible pairings. From these data Heiligenberg is able to construct a causal "network" between derived internal processes and behavioral outputs. Heiligenberg's data also demonstrate that brief stimulus presentations may produce long-term changes in behavioral state, in addition to any immediate responses, which must be examined for a critical assessment of dynamic processes that contribute to functionally organized behavioral sequences. Stimulus patterns with separable "positive" or "negative" effects on a given behavior (e.g., attack) can be combined for evidence of arithmetic summation, both at the moment of stimulus presentation and as a function of possible differential decay time. An important point about these experiments is that relatively "simple" quantitative rules emerge at the organism level which not only provide useful explanations for observed behavior but fundamental questions about nervous system operation.

Whereas the chapter by Heiligenberg focuses upon *integrative processes* in species behavior, Chapter Twenty-Two, by Marler, emphasizes its *phenotypic substrates* — that is, the interplay between genetic (evolutionary) and experiential factors that operate during ontogeny in the construction of what has previously been referred to as behavior's "musical *score*" as opposed to its momentary performance. The analogy is particularly apt here, since Marler concentrates upon the foundations of birdsong, with subsequent comments upon the phenotypic foundations of human speech. Marler briefly reviews three models of performance discussed elsewhere in this volume: central patterning with automaticity, central patterning with external triggering, and patterned sensory feedback interacting with central mechanisms. He then pursues the question of sensory feedback during development and points out the need to distinguish "score" construction from performance. For example, certain bird species must hear their own voices to *develop* species-typical song, but once established the mature performance may be maintained in the absence of vocal feedback. This indicates clearly that sensory factors can play a critical role in the development of central processes that subsequently operate in a relatively autonomous fashion. Marler is careful to point out basic species differences in this regard, which cautions for a limitation in our generalizations, at least at the level of specific detail. He also cautions about generalizing from highly stereotyped movement patterns, such as occur in many (but not all) forms of animal communication, and more variable "graded" movements.

The basic mechanism postulated by Marler for the ontogeny of birdsong is the *auditory template*. Stated briefly, the auditory template is viewed as a mechanism that sensitizes the animal to certain classes of sounds, from which a model of species vocal behavior is formed and against which motor performance (vocalization) is compared and perfected. Three general statements can be made at this point. First, both genetic and experiential factors contribute to the formation of this auditory template. Second, birds display a high degree of selectivity in the stimuli they "allow in" to template formation. Third, these stimuli must occur during relatively specific developmental stages for the bird to benefit from them. The bird is then presumed to compare its own vocalizations with its auditory template, and to perfect its vocal output accordingly. These general conclusions are supported by a variety of isolation, deafferentation, and stimulus playback experiments in several species. The song in general becomes more tightly crystalized (stereotyped) with practice.

It is of interest that the sensitive period for song learning may (in some species) precede the onset of singing by several weeks or even months, in some ways an analogous situation to the time gap between determination and differentiation in other biological systems. The extent to which song might be "released" through experiences other than direct imitation might be worthy of further consideration, although, at this point, the available data suggest limitations in the analogy with purely biological development. At the behavioral level, Marler concludes his chapter by drawing parallels between certain features of birdsong development and the development of human speech. For example, recent research has demonstrated a high degree of selectivity of human infants to specific sounds, combined with an early capacity to respond to particular vocal boundaries that are subsequently employed in language. Possible mechanisms for categorical processing and signal matching are discussed.

The concept of "template" represents an abstraction based upon behavioral data which serves not only to summarize a diverse body of previously obtained information but which also suggests further experiments. However, it is important to recognize that such behavioral constructs are in some sense metaphorical in their construction. Thus, as analyses proceed, their utility may be limited, as is the case for such behavioral constructs as "drive." (Hinde, 1970). In the final chapter of this volume, therefore, Fentress attempts to provide a framework for our examination of problems of neurobehavioral integration that can be applied with equal utility across quite different specific forms and levels of analysis.

The major theme discussed by Fentress (Chapter Twenty-Three) is the balance between interaction and self-organization in neurobehavioral control systems. He introduces his chapter with a general consideration of systems and mechanism approaches to behavioral biology. The systems approach stresses the spectrum of interrelationships among a total population of underlying elements or dimensions of control, while the mechanism approach stresses presumed unitary states that intervene between specified antecedent and consequent conditions within a causal framework. Fentress argues that classical definitions of *mechanism* may be limited in the analyses of biological systems. The dual principles of interaction and self-organization suggest a dynamic framework for bridging diverse material presented in previous chapters. The basic idea is that, as systems become activated during integration, or formed during development, they frequently increase in the autonomy of their organization, with the result that responsiveness to, and dependence upon, surround states are diminished. In this sense the systems become self-isolating, thus simplifying the range of factors which must be examined in analysis of their control. The chapter concludes with the argument that relationships between three major themes can help guide future research at complementary analysis levels: (1) intrinsic—extrinsic balance, (2) continuous—discontinuous functions, and (3) dynamic—stable time referents.

CHAPTER TWENTY-ONE

A Probabilistic Approach to the Motivation of Behavior

WALTER HEILIGENBERG

INTRODUCTION

Ethology started with the discovery that animals perform certain behavioral patterns which are species-typical and which thus may be considered part of the general morphology of a given species. The fact that two species commonly show greater similarities in corresponding behavioral patterns the closer they appear to be related anatomically led to the assumption that such patterns are under genetic control and that the notion of "homology" should hold for behavioral as well as for anatomical features (Lorenz, 1941, 1958),[1]

Even though a given behavioral pattern may be performed with varying "intensities" or degrees of "completeness," it is commonly sufficiently identifiable and distinguishable from others to be labeled as a discrete event (e.g., head bobbing, fin spreading, and

chirping). A striking stereotypy is found particularly in patterns of communication (Hazlett, 1972b; Wiley, 1973) which, because of their function in sex and species recognition, were naturally selected for discreteness and conspicuousness. Such patterns were of central interest to early ethologists and gave rise to the notion of fixed action patterns.

Whereas certain behavioral patterns occur without any known external cause, others are commonly performed in response to certain stimulus patterns. In contrast to simple reflexes, such responses cannot be elicited with certainty, and even the kind of response to be expected may be uncertain, since the overall behavioral state of the animal may determine which of several possible behaviors will be released by a given stimulus. Whereas a rather elaborate stimulus pattern is required to elicit a particular response at times when its probability of occurrence is low, most rudimentary forms of this stimulus pattern, or even no such stimulus at all, are sufficient to elicit the same response when its probability of occurrence is

---

[1] References in this chapter are intended neither to be exhaustive nor to reflect priorities. Rather, they represent a sample of publications that the student is recommended to read.

high. This led to the assumption that stimulus patterns mainly release centrally coordinated processes rather than control the manner of coordination itself (Lorenz, 1937; Tinbergen, 1951). This view was supported by von Holst's (1935) claim that rhythmic patterns of locomotor coordination are programmed centrally rather than by afferent signals.

Certain behaviors, particularly those which serve physiological needs such as feeding and drinking, are more likely to be elicited after they have not been released for longer periods of time. This state of "deprivation" will eventually lead to growing restlessness, referred to as "appetitive" behavior. As soon as the animal is then given the opportunity to perform those "long wanted" behaviors, restlessness will again subside. Since these particular behaviors terminate episodes of restlessness and arousal, they are called "consummatory" behaviors. Early ethology interpreted this phenomenon by postulating action-specific drives which accumulate during nonperformance of the associated behavior and eventually evoke appetitive behavior. The performance of the consummatory behavior itself, rather than afferent feedback associated with it, was believed to lower the particular drive again (Lorenz, 1937).

Notions of early ethology, such as genetic control and central patterning of behavior, were often criticized (e.g., Lehrman, 1953, 1956; Hinde, 1959; Barlow, 1968), particularly with respect to the general validity of such concepts and theoretical categories developed in studies of stereotyped behavioral patterns in particular groups of animals. On the background of more recent studies, particularly in the field of simpler nervous systems, the present state of these controversial issues can be summarized as follows.

Bentley's studies (1971) on the motor control of chirping in crickets have demonstrated the significance of the genome in the ontogeny of behavior, down to such minute details as the timing and number of spikes in single motor unit discharges. In addition, the neuronal circuitry that generates the chirping pattern is completed long before the elytra — that is, the "tools" of this behavior — are developed. A central inhibition suppresses the activity of this circuit until the animal has emerged from its final molt (Bentley and Hoy, 1970). On the other hand, studies by Konishi and Nottebohm (1969) on the song development in birds have demonstrated how environmental factors contribute to the ontogeny of behaviors and how widely their impact and significance may differ among species of animals.

The notion of "central patterning" found support by Wilson's (1961) analysis of the locust flight system. Even though sensory feedback contributes to the general excitation and, to some extent, provides phasic input, which affects the actual pattern of the motor output (Wendler, 1974), central pacemakers have been shown to be capable of coordinating output without afferent input. Naturally this will not hold for all patterns of behavior, and one would expect that sensory feedback will contribute to motor patterning to a larger extent the more a given behavior depends on continual adjustment to environmental conditions (e.g., as in the case of "walking across obstacles" as compared to "flying in open air space" or "pelagic swimming"). Similar differences could hold for more complex behavioral patterns as well. Chirping in crickets, for example, which is not oriented toward a particular receiver and commonly occurs in isolated animals, may depend very little on feedback and thus be largely programmed in a feed-forward manner. In contrast, the patterning of copulatory movements may depend heavily on continual feedback. Lorenz (1937) tried to tackle this problem by splitting behavioral performances into an orienting taxis component and an "instinctive act" (*Erbkoordination*) and considered only the latter to be strictly centrally generated. Even though this distinction is very appropriate in some cases, it can hardly be maintained in others. The notions of genetic control and central patterning of behavior have thus found support from neurophysiological studies, and both principles may hold, even though only to varying degrees, for many more patterns of behavior.

Contrary to these two early concepts of ethology, the drive hypothesis remains rather dubious, and a generally accepted theory concerning the causation of behavior is still lacking. No proof has been provided that the causation of social behaviors, such as aggression, is governed by similar principles as the causation of behaviors linked to obvious physiological needs, such as feeding and drinking; in particular, there is no proof that in social behaviors nonperformance will necessarily lead to increased responsiveness. Further, the probability of responses does not seem to be reduced by the performance of the "consummatory behavior" itself rather than by the sensory feedback – that is, the "consummatory situation" – provided by a successful performance (Boll, 1959, Dethier, 1966). In cases that were considered to demonstrate the build-up of drives not related to immediate physiological needs, the processes of habituation and recovery from habituation appear to be sufficient to explain increasing responsiveness during periods of stimulus deprivation (Heiligenberg and Kramer, 1972).

The complex of causal factors which determines the probability of occurrence of a particular behavior is often referred to as its "motivation." To explain and eventually to predict fluctuations of these probabilities on the basis of such factors is the goal of "motivation analysis."

METHODOLOGICAL CONSIDERATIONS IN THE STUDY OF MOTIVATION

Probabilities of particular behaviors fluctuate even under standardized environmental conditions. This suggests that internal factors govern a fluctuating state of "readiness" to perform a certain behavior. This readiness can be defined operationally by stating that it is measured by the number of performances of the associated behavior in a standardized test situation. Whereas in the case of "spontaneously" occurring behaviors, readiness can obviously be measured by the number of occurrences under a standardized condition, particular difficulties are encountered in the case of behaviors that require releasing stimuli: to measure the readiness of the animal to respond as a function of time, a standardized test stimulus has to be presented repeatedly. Unfortunately, however, animals commonly habituate to repeated presentations of a given stimulus pattern, and thus fewer and fewer

responses are elicited during a longer series of stimulations.

Certain behavioral patterns can be elicited by at least two different stimulus patterns, A and B. Often after A has been presented until it fails to elicit responses, B is still found to be a sufficient releaser. The same may hold if the sequence of presentations of A and B is reversed (Prechtl, 1953; Curio, 1967). The animal can thus habituate separately to different stimulus patterns which all release the same behavior. Most interestingly, the animal may also habituate to a stimulus pattern if it is presented at such a low intensity that responses are not elicited from the first presentation on. It is thus not necessarily the actual performance of the behavior which leads to habituation (Curio, 1967).

If one were to disregard habituation and measure readiness by the number of responses elicited by a test stimulus, regardless of previous exposures to this stimulus, one might obtain a zero readiness for a given behavior, even when stimulus patterns other than the test stimulus still elicit strong responses. Here habituation is stimulus-specific rather than behavior-specific; it seems advisable to exclude habituation from the phenomenon of "readiness" and to base measurements of readiness on a constant level of habituation to the test stimulus. Under this condition two alternative ways of experimentation can be chosen. First, one may limit the temporal resolution of the measurement by presenting the test stimulus at intervals large enough to allow for sufficient recovery from previous habituation. This method is not feasible in cases where days are required for recovery. Second, the test stimulus may be presented continually and measurements may be taken if, after an initial period of habituation, a steady state is obtained at which no further habituation leads to the total cessation of responses. This method was successfully applied in studies of readiness to attack in cichlid fish (Heiligenberg, 1965, 1974a) and will briefly be described later in this chapter.

In some rather fortunate cases the state of readiness for a particular behavior expresses itself in such features as the momentary coloration of the male guppy (Baerends, Brouwer and Waterbolk, 1955) or the front-leg posture of the water insect *Ranatra* (Cloarec, 1972) and can thus be monitored continually without the need of test stimulus presentations.

Apart from releasing behavioral responses, stimulus patterns are also known to affect states of readiness over varying periods of time following their presentation. While the readiness of a given behavior is measured by the rate of responses elicited by a continually present test stimulus, A, a short presentation of a particular stimulus pattern, B, may instantly raise this readiness. The increment in readiness will again decay with a time constant typical for the kind of stimulus, B. Another stimulus pattern, C, may be found to lower the same readiness in a similar manner. Half-time constants of such "excitatory" and "inhibitory" processes vary from seconds to days (Heiligenberg, 1965, 1974a; Leong, 1969).

One may thus conceive of an animal as a probabilistic system with more or less discrete behavioral outputs and a number of patterned stimulus inputs. Probabilities of different behaviors will partly fluctuate "spontaneously" and partly be affected by certain stimulus inputs. To investigate the probabilistic structure of this system, one may proceed in two steps. First, one may eliminate stimulus transients and thus study inherent fluctuations in probabilities and their mutual correlations under steady external conditions. Second, to study linear response characteristics of this system, certain stimulus patterns may be presented, either briefly in the manner of a short impulse or for a prolonged period in the manner of a step function, and their effects on probabilities of different behaviors be analysed. These two steps are demonstrated in the following two sections.

The Temporal Patterning of Behavior Under Steady External Conditions

Behavioral events tend to follow each other in particular sequences. The performance of the present behavior thus affects probabilities of subsequent behaviors. Different random-process models have been proposed to describe this phenomenon and various conclusions drawn from these models with respect to the motivation of behavior (Baerends, Brouwer

and Waterbolk, 1955; Wiepkema, 1961; Delius, 1969; Hauske, 1967). Wiepkema, for example, postulated that two behaviors, *a* and *b*, can be considered to represent similar motivational states the more their transitional probabilities for subsequent behaviors are alike. By means of factor analysis he demonstrated that the tendencies of the bitterling, *Rhodeus amarus*, to perform any of most of its behaviors could be mapped in a three-dimensional vector space, the main axes of which were aggressive, sexual, and nonreproductive factors or "tendencies." The relative strength of these factors was considered to determine behavioral outcomes. Since Wiepkema's analysis considered pairs of subsequent behaviors, to calculate transitional probabilities, his statements were based only on the short-term structure of behavioral sequences.

Apart from short-term patterns of organisation, long-term fluctuations and particular mutual correlations can be detected in the rate of occurrences of various behaviors. Most striking are negative correlations between the occurrences of two behaviors, which lead to the assumption that animals pass through long-term states during which certain behaviors have higher priorities and thus higher probabilities than others. A territorial cichlid fish, for example, will readily attack rather than avoid intruders and hardly ever join a group of schooling conspecifics. The opposite relation is found before an animal enters the behavioral state of territoriality or after it has been driven from its territory by a still stronger conspecific or by adverse environmental conditions (Heiligenberg, 1963). Studying long-term fluctuations in probabilities of different behaviors, ethologists have speculated about the minimum number of separate processes necessary to explain the diversity of correlations between different behaviors (e.g. Fentress, 1973b).

The following analysis attempts to assess both short- and long-term processes in the occurrence of behavioral events and to draw most general conclusions with respect to the motivation of behavior. Details of this approach and, in particular, mathematical procedures are given elsewhere (Heiligenberg, 1973).

A territorial male cichlid fish is placed in an aquarium together with 10 juveniles, which serve as randomly distributed, continually present targets to elicit attack and courting responses in the male. The particular advantage of such juveniles is that they represent rather weak stimuli, in contrast to adult conspecifics, which commonly elicit strong attack and courting behavior and thus, depending on the outcome of such encounters, may affect the behavioral state of the male for long periods of time. Juveniles are therefore suitable test stimuli to measure continually attack and courting readinesses without much affecting the behavioral state of the male. A total of at least seven behaviors can readily be recorded over hours of observations.

1) *Feeding.* The fish takes up small amounts of substrate into its mouth and spits out indigestible parts. This behavior also occurs in the absence of food particles. To maintain a standardized situation the animal should be fed in the evening. Only enough food should be given so that none is left the next morning when observations are resumed.

2) *Digging.* The fish digs deeply into the bottom of the aquarium and takes up a large amount of substrate which it usually carries away before spitting it out somewhere else. This behavior occurs preferentially at a certain site of the aquarium and results in a deep pit which later becomes the "spawning site" in the male's territory.

3) *Attacking.* The animal rushes at another fish and bites if the victim does not escape in time.

4) *Courting.* The male swims up to another fish, bends its head away to the side, and quivers. This behavior is often followed by ostentatious swimming to the pit. A pregnant female would follow and spawn.

5) *Approaching.* The male approaches another fish quickly, without directly facing it, and halts. This behavior may be followed by courting or sudden attacking.

6) *Chafing.* The fish chafes its body on the bottom or the walls of the aquarium as though it were trying to rub and shake off parasites. This behavior is often accompanied by fin flickering.

7) *Yawning.* The animal opens its mouth wide and spreads its gill arches.

All these patterns can be easily identified and are of short duration, on the order of approximately one second. They can therefore be recorded as yes—no events with a temporal resolution of one second. Occurrences of behavior j can be coded by a variable $x_j(i)$ which is "one" if behavior j occurred in the ith second of observation and "zero" otherwise.

The cross-correlation functions, $r(x_j, x_k, \tau)$, of pairs, x_j and x_k, of these time series are plotted in line j and column k in Figure 1A, with each abscissa covering a time-shift range, τ, from -1 to $+1$ minute. A particular function has to be interpreted as follows. With behavior j occurring at $\tau = 0$, which is the center of the abscissa, behavior k is more likely to occur at a given interval, τ, the farther the corresponding value of the correlation function, r, reaches into the positive range of the ordinate. Behavior k is less likely to occur at this interval the farther the corresponding value of r reaches into the negative range. These ranges are limited by $+1$ and -1, respectively, which indicate certainty of occurrence and nonoccurrence, respectively. A correlation value of 0 indicates statistical independence between the occurrences of j and the occurrences of k separated by an interval, τ. Positive values of τ refer to the future; negative values refer to the past with respect to the occurrence of behavior j, and $r(x_j, x_k, \tau) = r(x_k, x_j, -\tau)$.

Particular diagrams in the matrix of Figure 1 can thus be interpreted as follows:

1) Behavior 1 (feeding) is likely to occur in bouts. In contrast to this, the occurrence of behavior 7 (yawning) does not affect the probability of this behavior occurring within the next minute.

2) The occurrence of behavior 1 (feeding) raises the probability of behavior 2 (digging) occurring within the subsequent seconds.

3) The occurrence of behavior 7 (yawning) is preceded by a slow decrease in probability of behavior 3 (attacking). This probability, however, returns to its normal level immediately after behavior 7 has occurred.

4) The occurrence of behavior 3 (attacking) is preceded by a quick drop and followed by a gradual recovery of the prob-

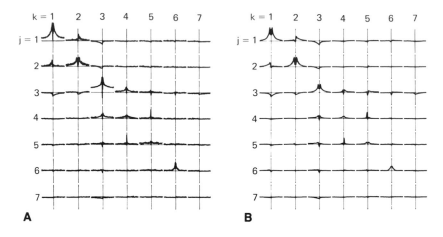

FIGURE 1.   (A) Empirical and (B) theoretical cross-correlation funtions between occurrences of behavior j *(lines) and occurrences of behavior* k *(columns). Each of the 49 functions in either matrix is plotted on intersecting coordinate axes (fine lines), the ordinate ranging from −0.05 (bottom) to +0.05, the associated abscissa ranging from −60 seconds (left) to +60 seconds with respect to the occurrence of behavior* j. *The +1 peaks of the correlation functions with* j = k *at time 0 were left out for space reasons. The theoretical correlation functions were calculated from interval distributions. Owing to computer core-storage limitations, these distributions had to be based on a 3-second time resolution rather than a 1-second time resolution. For this reason some peaks in the theoretical correlation functions are less pronounced than in their empirical counterparts. Behaviors 1 through 7 are feeding, digging, attacking, courting, approaching, chafing, and yawning. (From Heiligenberg, 1973.)*

ability of behavior 1 (feeding). The reverse time course holds when the probability of behavior 3 is considered with respect to the occurrence of behavior 1.

After a correlation pattern, such as that shown in Figure 1 has been obtained, one may speculate about general random-process models that could furnish such data. In his analysis of two behaviors in a related cichlid species, Hauske (1967) demonstrated that renewal processes provide a suitable description. Such processes are defined by a set of functions that describe the probabilities of certain events as functions of time, t, since the last event. These processes are therefore "renewed" by each event, in that their probability functions are reset to their initial values at time $t = 0$. As a consequence, the probability of a particular event to occur depends on the kind of and the time since the last event *only*, and inter-event intervals are thus statistically independent. The validity of a renewal-process model can therefore be tested by calculating theoretical cross-correlation functions on the basis of interval distributions, under the assumption of statistical independence between intervals. A close similarity between theoretical functions and their empirical counterparts (Figure 1) will thus support the renewal-process model.

In behavioral terms, a renewal-process model would imply that each behavioral performance takes the animal into the beginning of a new state or situation and simultaneously erases aftereffects from previous performances. Proprio- and exteroceptive feedback associated with the last behavioral performance could thus determine probabilities of subsequent actions and thereby override aftereffects from previous events. In the case of the seven behaviors in Figure 1, which represent routinely occurring patterns in the stationary daily schedule of a territorial male, this model indeed gives satisfactory results.

With a few exceptions, all correlation functions in Figure 1 level off at zero within

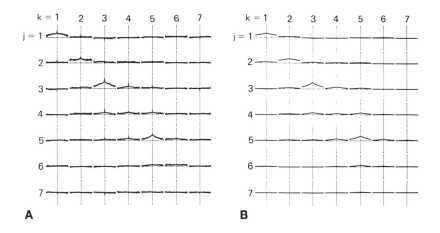

FIGURE 2. *(A) Empirical and (B) theoretical cross-correlation functions between the per-minute rates of behavior* j *(lines) and behavior* k *(columns). Each of the 49 functions in either matrix is plotted on intersecting coordinate axes (fine lines), the ordinate ranging from −0.5 (bottom) to +0.5, the abscissa ranging from −120 minutes (left) to +120 minutes. The +1 peaks of the correlation functions with* j = k *at time 0 were left out for space reasons. The theoretical correlation functions were calculated under the assumption of linear combinations of four basic slow processes that underlie long-term fluctuations in the rate of occurrences of different behaviors. The seven behaviors are numbered as in Figure 1. (From Heiligenberg, 1973.)*

one minute. This implies that a behavioral event hardly affects probabilities for subsequent behaviors over periods longer than one minute. The exceptions in Figure 1 can be shown to be due to long-term fluctuations in the mean rate of certain behaviors. These fluctuations also lead to discrepancies with the original renewal-process model. As briefly mentioned above, a renewal process is defined by a set of probability functions that describe the probability of behavior k following behavior j as a function of time, t, since the occurrence of j. In a stationary situation, such as in the case of a territorial male, these probability functions have constant parameters from which the mean rate of a particular behavior can be calculated. To cope with long-term fluctuations in the mean rate of certain behaviors, a renewal-process model has to be extended by introducing variable rather than constant parameters. Long-term fluctuations in certain probabilities of occurrences can then be formulated in terms of corresponding fluctuations of such parameters. This extended renewal-process model could also cope with drastic changes in behavioral probabilities

found in connection with such significant events as spawning or parturition.

Long-term fluctuations can be studied by analyzing per-minute frequencies of different behaviors over periods of hours and days. With $f_j(i)$ being the number of performances of behavior j within the ith minute of observation, cross correlations, $r(f_j, f_k, \tau)$, of pairs of these functions, f_j and f_k, were calculated and plotted in line j and column k of Figure 2A, with each abscissa covering a time-shift range, τ, from −2 to +2 hours. A particular correlation function in this matrix has to be interpreted as follows. With a high (low) rate of behavior j given at time $\tau = 0$, a high (low) rate of behavior k is more likely to be found at an interval, τ, the farther the corresponding value of the correlation function, r, reaches into the positive range of the ordinate. The opposite, a low (high) rate, is more likely the farther the corresponding value of r reaches into the negative range. These ranges are limited by +1 and −1, respectively, which indicate maximal positive or negative coupling, respectively, between $f_j(i)$ and $f_k(i + \tau)$. Finally, a correlation value of 0 suggests statistical indepen-

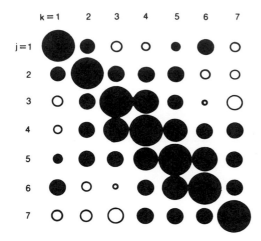

FIGURE 3. *Empirical correlation coefficients of order 0 between the per-hour rates of behavior* j *(lines) and behavior* k *(columns). The absolute value of each coefficient is symbolized by the area of the corresponding circle. Open circles indicate negative, filled circles indicate positive coefficients, their values on the diagonal being +1 by definition. The seven behaviors are numbered as in Figures 1 and 2. (From Heiligenberg, 1973.)*

dence between these terms. Positive values of τ refer to the future; negative values of τ refer to the past of behavior k with respect to behavior j, and $r(f_j, f_k, \tau) = r(f_k, f_j, -\tau)$.

The matrix of correlation functions shown in Figure 2 reveals long-term and mainly positive correlations within particular groups of behaviors over periods of one hour or longer. This pattern becomes even more apparent when the zero order ($\tau = 0$) cross correlations between the per-hour frequencies of these behaviors are plotted (Figure 3). The fact that, for example, behaviors 2 to 5 show considerable positive correlations among themselves suggests that they may share the influence of a certain slow process that affects their mean rates of occurrence. In a similar manner, another process could be shared by behaviors 1 and 2, and still another process could influence behaviors 4 to 7.

On the basis of such assumptions the following linear model was conceived. Long-term fluctuations, $l_j(t)$, in behavior j are considered to be a linear combination of several slow processes, $v_1, \ldots, v_m$, so that $l_j(t) =$

$c_{j1} \cdot v_1(t) + \cdots + c_{jm} \cdot v_m(t)$, with constant coefficients, c. By a mathematical procedure, similar to factor analysis, the matrix of coefficients $(c_{j\mu}), j = 1, \ldots, 7$ and $\mu = 1, \ldots, m$, and a minimum number, m, of orthogonal processes, v_μ, were determined to approximate the correlation functions in Figure 2A as closely as possible. Four slow processes, v, were found to be sufficient, since additional processes did not improve the approximation further. Figure 4 represents a diagram of this model. The thickness of the line that connects the slow process, v_μ, with behavior j was chosen proportionally to the value of the coefficient $c_{j\mu}$, and c-coefficients with absolute values smaller than 0.05, which included all negative coefficients, were discarded.

The model presented interprets long-term fluctuations, $l_j(t)$, of behavior j as a vector in a four-dimensional space with coordinate axes, $v_1, \ldots, v_4$. The coefficient $c_{j\mu}$ is the projection of l_j upon v_μ. Unfortunately, however, the coordinate axes, v, are not uniquely determined, since any orthogonal transformation of this space, which yields new axes and new coefficients, c, will not affect the cross correlations between the behaviors. This analysis only tells us that we have to assume at least four basic slow processes, most probably located in the animal, to explain the diversity of correlations in Figures 2 and 3. The identification of these processes in terms of particular hormone concentrations and/or other physiological variables still has to be achieved. Suitable experiments are suggested elsewhere (Heiligenberg, 1974b).

The behavioral analysis in this section has demonstrated that the probability of a particular behavior occurring can be considered to recruit itself from two different sources: long-term processes that cause slow fluctuations in the mean rate of occurrences and short-term aftereffects from preceding behavioral events which lead to preferred sequences of behavioral performances.

The Effect of Stimulus Patterns on the State of Readiness

Whereas many behavioral studies have focused on the response-releasing function of

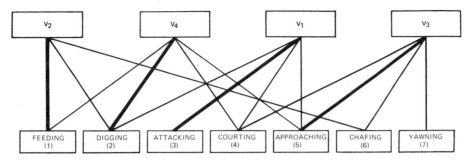

FIGURE 4.   Long-term fluctuations in the rates of occurrence of seven behaviors represented as linear combinations of four basic slow processes, $v_1, \ldots, v_4$. The thickness of the line that connects process and behavior is proportional to the influence of the process on that behavior. (From Heiligenberg, 1973.)

stimulus patterns, less attention has been paid to the fact that stimulus patterns may change the behavioral state of an animal for considerable periods of time following their presentation. Often a stimulus pattern may not even release a particular overt response in an animal and still affect its future readiness to perform certain behaviors. A territorial cichlid male, for example, after brief exposure to the view of a territorial male conspecific, will attack familiar fish in his environment more frequently than expected without this exposure. This effect can also be achieved by presenting a dummy resembling a male conspecific, as demonstrated in the following experiment.

The experimental situation described in the previous section is modified by inserting a glass partition which divides the aquarium into two compartments, a large compartment for the territorial male and the juveniles and a small compartment into which different dummies can be lowered from above. At half-hour intervals a certain dummy is presented behind the glass partition for a period of 30 seconds. Whereas this dummy can hardly be designed to look so natural that it elicits overt aggressive responses in the male, the presence of certain color patterns may nevertheless affect the animal's readiness to attack. Since the juveniles are to serve as a constant test stimulus to measure the readiness to attack before and after the presentation of the dummy, they should be prevented from seeing this stimulus. By severing their optic nerve, juvenile cichlids can be blinded for several weeks until regeneration of

this nerve restores their vision. An additional advantage of such blinded juveniles is that they never form a school and thus stay randomly distributed.

By recording the rate of attacking over several minutes before and after the presentation of the dummy and then averaging 50 to 100 of these recordings, one will find that particular dummies will affect the rate of attacking for at least a few minutes following their presentation.

Figure 5 demonstrates a case in the cichlid, *Pelmatochromis kribensis*. Figure 5A shows an instantaneous poststimulatory increment in attack rate which decays again with a half time of approximately 1.5 minutes. Figure 5B demonstrates that the size of the mean initial increment does not depend on the prestimulatory level of attack rate and can thus be described as a constant *additive* increment (Heiligenberg, 1965).

Cichlid fish show various color patterns, some of which can appear and disappear within seconds and are commonly correlated with certain behavioral states such as "high aggressiveness" or "strong fear" (Figure 6). By presenting different color patterns on separate dummies, Leong (1969) demonstrated that only two of all color patterns in *Haplochromis burtoni* affect the state of attack readiness. A vertical black eye-bar, which is part of a black head coloration, was found to raise the rate of attacking (Figure 7), and a field of orange spots above the pectoral fins was found to lower the rate of attacking (Figure 8). When both

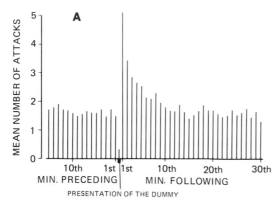

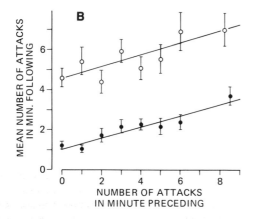

FIGURE 5. *The presentation of a dummy that resembles a conspecific male raises the rate of attacking in a male cichlid fish,* Pelmatochromis kribensis. *(A) Mean rate of attacking in consecutive minutes preceding and following stimulation (average of 150 experiments). (B) Open circles show mean rate of attacking in first poststimulatory minute as function of rate in last prestimulatory minute. Filled circles represent values obtained in the absence of stimulation. Standard errors are indicated by vertical bars. Since prestimulatory attack rates larger than 6 per minute were rare, they were pooled and their averages plotted on the abscissa. (From Heiligenberg, 1965.)*

patterns were presented simultaneously, their combined effect emerged as the arithmetic sum of the effects associated with each pattern separately. Since the increment caused by the black eye-bar is larger than the decrement

caused by the orange spots, the total effect is still positive.

A comparison of the time courses in Figures 7A and 8A reveals different half times, approximately 3 minutes in the case of the "excitatory" process in Figure 7 and approximately 11 minutes in the case of the "inhibitory" process in Figure 8. Figures 7B and 8B show that the size of the increment and decrement, respectively, does not depend on the prestimulatory level of activity, as has already been demonstrated in Figure 5. The mean rate of attacking to be expected after presentation of a certain stimulus pattern thus differs by a constant amount from the mean rate of attacking predicted from the prestimulatory level without stimulation.

The data presented in Figures 5, 7, and 8 suggest that changes in readiness, caused by a particular stimulus pattern, decay again in an exponential manner with a half time typical for the particular stimulus. However, a closer analysis may reveal that more than one exponential process is involved and that the approximation by only one exponential function is insufficient. The black eye-bar pattern, for example, was found to cause, in addition to the short-term effect shown in Figure 7, a very weak long-term increment which decays with a half time of approximately 7 days (Figure 9). The

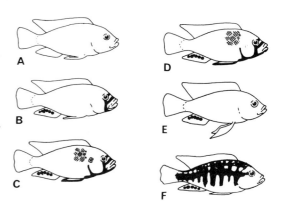

FIGURE 6. *Color pattern of male* Haplochromis burtoni. *(A) Juvenile; (B) adult ready to establish territory; (C) territorial; (D) spawning; (E) fleeing in open water; (F) hiding on substrate. Crosshatched areas are orange. (From Leong, 1969.)*

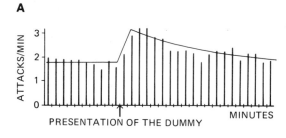

A

PRESENTATION OF THE DUMMY — MINUTES

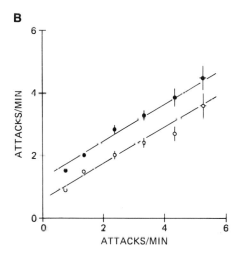

B

size of this increment, however, is so small that it cannot be detected in single experiments. Only long sequences of repeated stimulus presentations will lead to a gradual build-up of this process, and its decay can then be followed over days after stimulation has ceased (Heiligenberg and Kramer, 1972).

Different stimulus patterns may thus initiate different excitatory or inhibitory processes that are characterized by different initial amplitudes and time constants of decay. Such processes appear to be added upon "spontaneous" long-term fluctuations in a particular readiness \ so that the level of readiness to be expected after stimulation differs by a certain amount from the level predicted without stimulation (Figure 10). Processes of this nature may be very common.

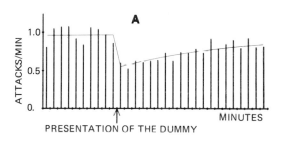

A

PRESENTATION OF THE DUMMY — MINUTES

FIGURE 7   Presentation of a dummy that resembles a male conspecific with a black vertical eye-bar and no orange spots above the pectoral fins raises the rate of attacking in a male Haplochromis burtoni. *(A) and (B) as in Figure 5, with the following exceptions. The data used in (B) represent mean rates of attacking within the 5-minute periods preceding and following stimulation, respectively. These data were divided into classes according to different ranges on the abscissa and, within each class, means were calculated with respect to both coordinates. Standard errors are indicated by vertical bars and horizontal bars, respectively, many of which were too small to show in the diagram. The regression lines were calculated according to the original data rather than on the basis of the averages shown in the figure. Open circles indicate controls; filled circles indicate experiments (total of approximately 400).*

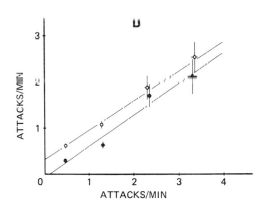

FIGURE 8.   Presentation of a dummy that resembles a male conspecific with orange spots above its pectoral fins and no vertical black eye-bar lowers the rate of attacking in a male Haplochromis burtoni. *(A) and (B) as in Figure 7, total of approximately 260 experiments.*

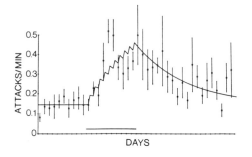

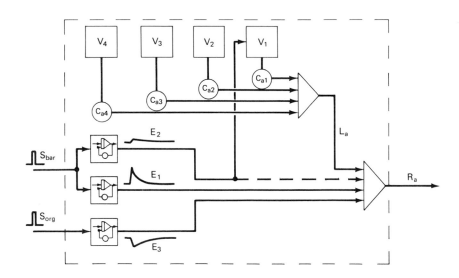

FIGURE 9.   Long-term increment in attack rate of male Haplochromis burtoni. *Bar above the abscissa indicates 10 days during which a dummy with a vertical black eye-bar was presented for 30 seconds every 15 minutes. Given are average data of four animals that had not been stimulated for several weeks preceding the experiments. This long stimulus deprivation resulted in a very low prestimulatory level of attacking. Vertical bars indicate standard errors. The continuous line represents a theoretical long-term build-up of attack readiness which rises during each day of stimulation and then*

They can also be found in animals as far related to fish as insects (Heiligenberg, 1969, 1974a).

The physiological nature of these processes is still obscure. Excitatory processes such as those shown in Figures 5 and 7 resemble the phenomenon of "dishabituation" or "sensitization" studied in simpler systems (Groves and Thompson, 1970; Carew, Castellucci, and Kandel, 1971). In terms of this phenomenon, the presentation of the dummy would dishabituate the animal, habituated to the continual presence of the juveniles. Both short- and long-term processes have been demonstrated for habituation and dishabituation. Lehrman (1964) gave evidence that certain stimulus patterns may ultimately affect the hormonal state in an animal and thus simultaneously cause long-term changes in behavioral and certain identified physiological states.

decays again with a half time of 7 days overnight and during the whole poststimulatory period. (From Heiligenberg and Kramer, 1972.)

FIGURE 10.   Analog computer flow diagram represents attack readiness (R_a) *in* Haplochromis burtoni *as a sum of inherent long-term fluctuations* (L_a) *and excitatory* (E_1, E_2) *and inhibitory* (E_3) *processes caused by the appearance of the black eye-bar pattern* (S_{bar}) *and the orange spots* (S_{org}), *respectively.* v_1 *to* v_4 *are basic slow processes of Figure 4 which form* L_a *as a linear combination,* $L_a = c_{a1} \cdot v_1 + \cdots + c_{a4} \cdot v_4$. *The same processes control inherent long-term fluctuations in other behaviors by different sets of coefficients,* c. *The long-term excitation,* E_2, *demonstrated in Figure 9, is not exclusively found in the rate of attacking but also, to some*

CONCLUSIONS

As mentioned previously, stimuli may release particular responses on the one hand and affect the readiness to perform certain behaviors on the other. However, the distinction between these two functions appears difficult and both phenomena may well be extreme expressions of one fundamental process. A cricket, for example, commonly chirps spontaneously. When a chirping cricket is exposed to chirps of a neighbor, it will raise its own chirp rate. If the same cricket happens to be silent while being exposed to this stimulus, it very likely will start to chirp for a brief period (Heiligenberg, 1969). Therefore, if a cricket commonly were silent, one would state that certain acoustical stimuli *release* chirping. If a cricket were always chirping, one would prefer to say that these stimuli *raise the readiness to* chirp. We thus tend to use the word "release" in the case of a short and drastic increase in probability of occurrence, whereas the term "raises readiness" is used in the case of long and less conspicuous rises in probability. Since the first is a more striking phenomenon than the second, it has naturally attracted more attention.

On the basis of these results one may propose the following general model to represent the causation of behaviors. For reasons of simplicity, the behavioral pattern should approach the ideal of an all-or-none event, and stimuli may only release but not modify this behavior. This behavior is assumed to occur whenever a physiological variable, e, reaches a critical threshold, e_0. In the case of a spontaneous behavior this threshold will be reached as a consequence of inherent fluctuations in e. In the case of a response-type behavior, however, certain stimuli are required to elevate e up to its threshold, e_0. A short and strong elevation of e will promptly trigger a performance. A slight and long-lasting elevation of e will not yet necessarily cause a performance but will certainly enhance its probability of occurrence. The opposite will be achieved by a long-term depression of e. Different stimulus patterns thus contribute different, and quite possibly additive, changes in e, and their summed input will determine the probability of e reaching e_0. In the case of the experiment described in this section, a juvenile fish appearing in the attacking range of the territorial male would represent a stimulus with a strong but rapidly decaying increment in attack readiness, e, whereas the stimulus pattern of a male conspecific would yield a low but longer-lasting rise in e. According to this hypothesis, the short but drastic increment in e caused by the appearance of a juvenile may elicit an immediate attack, whereas the weaker but longer-lasting increment in e caused by the dummy only raises the probability of attacking without necessarily eliciting an instantaneous attack. A detailed discussion of this model and its mathematical consequences are given elsewhere (Heiligenberg, 1974a).

In studying any system one can choose a probabilistic approach for various reasons. First, as exemplified in quantum mechanics, events may inherently be unpredictable and a probabilistic formulation thus be the only adequate description of the phenomena encountered. Second, a basically deterministic system may be so complex that mathematical predictions become unfeasible. We thus describe gambling machines in terms of probabilities of certain outcomes rather than try to predict outcomes on the basis of initial conditions. Third, ignorance about the system may force us to use a probabilistic language until increasing knowledge will allow more deterministic statements. The third category certainly applies to our present situation in the study of complex behaviors. Further studies may reveal whether use of a probabilisitic language will remain a necessity and, if so, whether the reasons will be of the first or the second category.

---

extent, in a few other behaviors. E_2 thus appears to be added on the higher level of a v-process (solid arrow) rather than on a lower level (dashed arrow) directly into R_a. Stimulus presentations are symbolized by square pulses; excitatory and inhibitory functions are generated by integrator circuits with negative feedbacks (inserts in square boxes). Habituation was disregarded in this diagram but could be added on the level of the stimulus inputs.

CHAPTER TWENTY-TWO

Sensory Templates in Species-Specific Behavior

PETER MARLER

INTRODUCTION

Insofar as behavioral movements reflect patterns of neuromuscular activity, ultimately owing what specificity they may possess to the particular patterns of physiological activity they are associated with, explanations of behavioral development are ultimately best expressed in physiological terms. Ethological studies can play a valuable role in delineation of the functional properties that are required of the underlying machinery. Inevitably these inferred properties will be defined in general terms. This is a permissible and indeed a productive practice provided the likelihood is recognized that a conceptually similar functional organization of sensory—motor relationships may be underlain by very different physiological mechanisms in different organisms (see Chapter 5).

I concentrate on the ontogeny of avian vocal behavior in this chapter, because I believe the general principles to be relevant in understanding the development of vocal be-havior in other organisms. With specificity as an underlying theme some detail must necessarily be presented to establish that general principles do in fact emerge from the particular cases under study. I shall develop the argument that sensory templates are significantly involved in the development of birdsongs, in cases where learning plays both major and minor roles, and that the principle has relevance to the development of human speech.

Some of the logically alternative physiological mechanisms for maintaining patterned movements have been outlined by Bullock (1961), Wilson (1964), Konishi (1965b), and most comprehensively by DeLong (1971). As the latter indicates, the basic requirements for the central nervous system to produce coordinated movement are (1) the appropriate muscles must be selected, (2) each participating muscle must be activated or inactivated in proper temporal relationship to the others, and (3) the appropriate amount of excitation and/or inhibition must be exerted on each muscle. This approach is useful, even though imprecision of the terms "appropriate" and "proper," still leaves much to be defined. A classical question has always been: What is the role of sensory stimulation in the development and maintenance of such patterns of muscular activity? At least three possibilities must be considered.

The first is central patterning with automaticity. A typical case is the motor output from the central nervous system of a locust controlling the basic pattern of flight movement, in which patterned activity adequate to maintain the basic locomotor rhythm is instigated and maintained in the absence of any patterned sensory input, though tonic input is necessary (Wilson, 1964).

The second possibility is centrally patterned movement with external triggering. As Bullock (1961) has indicated, many actions come into this category, including reflexive actions, with abundant vertebrate and invertebrate examples. External stimuli are necessary for triggering but not for patterning the internal structure of the movement. An example is swallowing in the dog, studied by Doty (1967), in which a complex sequential coordination that involves 18 different muscles seems to be centrally patterned without any requirement of sensory feedback from one phase to evoke the next. However, the entire sequence requires an external trigger — in this case tactile stimulation in the mouth and pharynx. The purring of cats seems to be a similar case (Remmers and Gautier, 1972).

The third possibility is patterned sensory feedback interacting with central nervous control. In reviewing illustrations of this category, DeLong (1971) notes that

> while the contribution of central patterning is enormous in almost every instance, it is striking how varied is the role of proprioceptive feedback — in some instances exerting only a nonspecific tonic effect (wingbeat — frequency control in the locust flight system), in other cases providing phasic reinforcement of discrete phases of the movement (lobster's swimmerette), and elsewhere providing timing clues for the overall patterning (dogfish swimming).

The care with which conclusions about central patterning and sensory control must be made at the behavioral level in mammals can be seen in the study by Fentress of face grooming in mice (e.g., Fentress, 1972). While sensory feedback resulting from movement can have obvious and powerful influences on actions that follow, especially on their orientation and power, few cases are discussed in which sensory feedback plays a basic role in development of the patterned coordination of a movement. I shall show that the vocal behavior of birds provides an unusually clear and novel demonstration of this type of motor control.

The focus in the present discussion is on problems of behavioral ontogeny. There is a need to distinguish control of development from mature performance. Evidence will be presented which demonstrates that the capacity of certain birds to hear their own voice controls the development of their vocal behavior. However, once mature performance is attained, this dependence of the motor coordination upon auditory feedback is reduced or eliminated. A case in point is the white-crowned sparrow in which male song is highly abnormal if birds are surgically deafened in youth. However, once singing behavior is fully developed and stable, deafening has little or no immediate effect on the fine structure of the motor coordination (Konishi, 1965b). Only over a period of months is a gradual drift away from the original pattern detectable (Figure 1) In other bird species auditory feedback seems to retain its importance into maturity, as in the cardinal (Dittus and Lemon, 1970) and the canary (Nottebohm, in press). One could easily be misled in inferring the role that auditory feedback plays in ontogeny from the result of adult deafening on song performance. While there are explicitly ontogenetic studies of the role of sensory feedback in the development of motor skills, such as spatially coordinated hand movements (e.g., Held, 1974), many of the examples in the literature of centrally patterned movement derive from study of adult subjects. The possibility of a more intrusive role for sensory mechanisms in development remains to be explored. It is not hard to imagine that repeated performance of a stable motor coordination gradually reduces reliance on sensory feedback control, leaving a centrally patterned motor outflow in increasing control of the pattern of behavior.

BEHAVIORAL SPECIES SPECIFICITY AND SOCIAL COMMUNICATION

In a review of recent research on the genetic control of acoustic behavior in crickets, Hoy (1974) draws attention to the stereotypy and species specificity of the calling song of his subjects with the remark that these properties make it an ideal preparation for some kinds of physiological and genetic analysis. For communicative behavior to be effective, the participation of at least two individuals is required, often many. Some behavioral rules must be held in common by the participants if the interaction is to be orderly and predictable. Biological constraints on the development of communicative behavior, as manifest in both sender and receiver, are likely to be especially prominent, making such behaviors as the calling song of male crickets, and the responsiveness of female crickets to it especially instructive for study. Avian communication has also provided illuminating illustrations of different strategies involved in the ontogeny of species-specific behavior (Marler, in press).

Ethologists have long emphasized the stereotypy of many of the motor patterns found in the natural behavior of animals, as is embodied in the term "fixed action pattern" (Lorenz, 1935; Tinbergen, 1951). The fixity of some behaviors is indeed remarkable (Schleidt, 1974), as documented in a variety of organisms such as crustaceans (Hazlett, 1972a), birds (Wiley, 1973), and mammals (Marler, 1973). In some cases the stereotypy is so marked that one is tempted to postulate special mechanisms detecting and compensating for inevitable perturbations in development that must occur, especially at the behavioral level.

Much of what follows is concerned with such stereotyped motor patterns, which lend themselves to ontogenetic analysis. It should be noted, however, that highly stereotyped actions are probably a special case. Highly variable actions have been described in the signaling behavior of a number of organisms in recent years, and "graded" rather than "discrete" repertoires of motor signaling behaviors seem to be especially characteristic of species with a complex social organization, particularly primates (e.g., Marler, 1972, 1975; Marler and Tenaza, in press). The ontogeny of such vari-able motor patterns is harder to analyze and interpret than that of stereotyped behaviors. While more invariant species-specific actions are suitable subjects for broaching the analysis of ontogeny of species-specific behavior, eventually an understanding of the development of variable motor patterns, and how they are responded to, may prove to be of even greater interest.

Given a requirement that members of a population share rules for the production, perception, and mode of response to signaling behaviors, there is a special interest in developmental strategies that might serve to guide both motor and sensory development. Sensory templates, as they have been postulated to explain the process of selective auditory responsiveness and vocal learning in birds have this dual potential to influence both motor and sensory aspects. A similar point is again illustrated by studies of the development of vocal communication in crickets.

Calling songs of hybrid male crickets were found to be intermediate between those of their parents in a number of respects (Bentley and Hoy, 1970, 1972; Hoy, 1974). Tests of the phonotactic response of hybrid females revealed that their behavior was also intermediate between that of females of the parent species (Hoy and Paul, 1973). While females are normally more attracted to homospecific than to heterospecific song, hybrid females find the calling song of their male siblings more attractive than either parental calling song. Hoy goes on to speculate that, while the coupling of song transmission and song reception might result from two mechanisms evolving in parallel, it would be neurophysiologically economical if both were controlled by a common mechanism.

The demonstration in studies by Walker (1957, 1962) that temperature-dependent variation in properties of male cricket calling songs is paralleled by changes in female responsiveness is consistent with the idea that a common mechanism controls both. The possibility that species-specific song templates might somehow control both male singing and female responsiveness in crickets remains to be studied. The fact that male cricket calling songs develop without the need for auditory experience of song stimulation suggests that direct control of song development by a template mechanism is

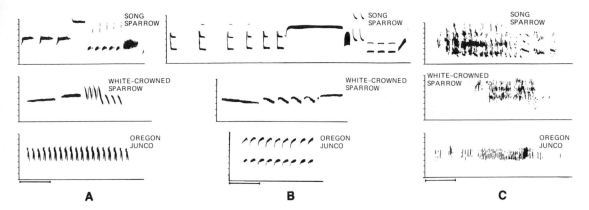

FIGURE 1. *Songs of sparrows developed under three conditions: (A) in the wild; (B) after rearing in isolation from conspecific song: hearing intact; (C) after deafening before the onset of singing. The three species illustrated, song sparrow, white-crowned sparrow, and Oregon junco are close relatives, all members of the subfamily Emberizinae. There is a loss of species specificity from (A) to (B) in the white-crowned sparrow and the junco, but not in the song sparrow. All are subject to a further loss of species specificity in (C). (After Konishi, 1964, 1965b; Kroodsma, 1975; Marler, Kreith, and Tamura, 1962; Marler, 1970; Mulligan, 1966.)*

unlikely, though a proprioceptive channel might still be involved. In birds there is more secure evidence that the shared mechanism underlying both male singing and female responsiveness does involve species-specific sensory templates.

THE ONTOGENY OF MALE BIRDSONG

Extensive studies on the effects of deafening on vertebrate vocal development by Konishi (1963, 1964, 1965a, b) lend support to the hypothesis that species-specific auditory templates are involved in the ontogeny of birdsong. This involvement extends to the imposition of constraints on processes of vocal learning, which underlies the development of song in many bird species, and to the development of female responsiveness to conspecific song. The kind of evidence that implicates a sensory template mechanism is best conveyed by the pattern of song development in one of the best-studied species, the white-crowned sparrow (Marler and Tamura, 1964; Konishi, 1965b; Marler, 1970).

A young male white-crowned sparrow usually begins to sing when a little over 100 days of age, first at irregular intervals, then becoming more continuous until full song emerges, usually after about 200 days of age in *Zonotrichia leucophrys nuttali*. If such a bird is deafened between 40 and 100 days of age, before singing behavior has developed, he will subsequently begin to sing on a more or less normal schedule, but the structure of the song produced will be very abnormal. The song of such an early deafened male is amorphous and variable in structure, scratchy or buzzy in tone, with components that change rapidly in frequency or even have a click-like quality. An example is illustrated in Figure 1, together with an example of normal male white-crowned sparrow song. The noisy, amorphous structure of the former is clearly evident.

Figure 1 also illustrates normal male songs of two close relatives of the white-crowned sparrow, the song sparrow (A) and the Oregon junco (C). Songs of these three species differ in many respects without overlap, as careful descriptive studies have shown (Marler and Tamura, 1962; Marler, Kreith, and Tamura, 1962; Mulligan, 1963; Konishi, 1964). By contrast, the songs produced by males deafened early in life, illustrated in Figure 1C have lost the species-specific traits that distinguish them from one another. Only the duration and range of frequencies persist clearly as species-specific qualities (Konishi, 1964, 1965b; Mulligan, 1966). This result demonstrates that audition plays a critical role in the development of species-specific characteristics of sparrow song. Similar gross abnormalities in the song of early-deafened males have been demonstrated in the chaffinch (Nottebohm, 1967, 1968), the cardinal (Dittus and Lemon, 1970), the robin and the black-headed grosbeak (Konishi, 1965a), and the red-winged blackbird (Marler et al., 1972). Further study reveals that the role of audition in development in all these species is a complex one.

If a young male white-crowned sparrow is taken from the nest prior to fledging and raised by hand in isolation from normal conspecific song but able to hear its own voice, some of the abnormalities that characterize the song of early-deafened birds are eliminated. The song now assumes a definite controlled morphology with relatively pure and sustained tones, longer in duration at the beginning than at the end of the song, thus sharing several characteristics with wild white-crowned sparrow singing. As can be seen in Figure 1, which also presents illustrations of the songs of a male song sparrow and an Oregon junco reared in isolation from normal conspecific song but with hearing intact, in each case and especially in the song sparrow more species-specific traits emerge than in an early-deafened bird. Thus one could arrange the songs of all three species in a series, with the normal song showing the highest degree of species specificity, the song of early-deafened males the least species specificity. The songs of intact but socially isolated males fall somewhere between — closest to normal in the song sparrow and farthest from normal in the white-crowned sparrow. Evidently, audition is involved in the ontogeny of some of the species-specific qualities of birdsong that develop in males reared in auditory isolation from normal conspecific song. The degree of dependence on auditory stimuli varies both with age and with the species investigated.

Further experiments reveal yet another role for audition in the ontogeny of birdsong in males. Not only does it permit the bird to hear its own voice, but it also gives access to patterned stimulation from other birds. This stimulation may have both generalized and highly specific effects on subsequent singing behavior of the subject. The former have been considered elsewhere (e.g., Marler and Mundinger, 1971). Here we are more concerned with cases in which the consequences are specific, as for example in the white-crowned sparrow. Although a male white-crowned sparrow taken as a nestling and reared thenceforth in isolation from normal conspecific song will develop singing with certain normal characteristics, some critical properties of the normal song are still lacking. Figure 2 shows the songs of nine male white-crowned sparrows reared together as a group but in isolation from normal conspecific song (Marler, 1970). These particular subjects came from three different areas in California. A typical example of normal white-crowned sparrow song from each of these areas is also illustrated (AN, BN, and CN). A comparison clearly reveals the abnormalities of the songs of intact but isolation-reared males, especially in the second part of the song. There are two significant kinds of abnormality. On the one hand, although the second part of a typical isolate song is broken into a train of separate notes, shorter in duration than the introduction, these notes are never as short in normal song, and lack all the fine detail usually present. In nature, these details have the further property of exhibiting local dialects, each unique to one area, the second or "trill" portion of the song being especially diagnostic (Figure 2). In addition to lacking certain species-specific properties, characteristics of the home dialect are also absent from the songs of intact male white-crowned sparrows reared in isolation from normal song.

If a young male white-crowned sparrow taken as a nestling is placed in individual isolation and exposed to 4 minutes of normal white-crowned sparrow song at a rate of six per minute for a period of 3 weeks somewhere between 7 and 50 days of age, his song will subsequently develop normally and will in fact be a copy of the model to which he was exposed. This copy will include the dialect characteristics of the model, though it may differ in some characteristics of the introduction (Marler, 1970).

There is a sensitive period for this learning. Equivalent exposure to a model between 50 and 71 days of age had only minor effects on

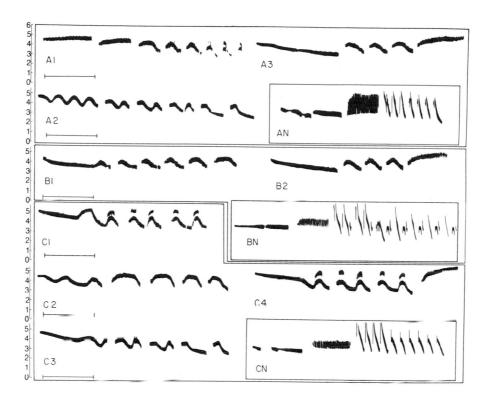

FIGURE 2. Songs of nine male white-crowned sparrows taken as nestlings in three different areas of California and reared as a group in a large soundproof chamber. Illustrations of the three home dialects are given in the boxes (AN, BN, and CN). The songs lack characteristics of the home dialect and some species specific traits also, especially in the second part of the song. (From Marler, 1970.)

subsequent singing, and exposure after about 100 days of age has none at all. Sensitive periods have also been demonstrated for song learning in other birds such as the chaffinch (Thorpe, 1958) and the zebra finch (Immelmann, 1969; Arnold, 1975a, b). In both these species a male reared without experience of normal song will sing abnormally. Exposure to normal song during the sensitive period restores not only the general characteristics of normal conspecific singing but also results in imitation of specific properties of the model used. In the song of wild chaffinches, dialects are again marked (Marler, 1952).

The learning ability manifest during such sensitive periods has the further significant characteristic that it is selective with regard to which models are acceptable. A male white-crowned sparrow given playback of both conspecific song and that of another related species during the sensitive period will learn only the conspecific song. Young males exposed to alien song and nothing else at this time — the alien model was song sparrow song in this case — develop songs like those of untrained social isolates (Marler, 1970). Although I was surprised at the time to discover how selective song learning is in white-crowns, further reflection on the natural history of this species might have suggested its existence.

In the environment where a young male white-crown spends the early phase of its life, many other bird species are present, all generating sounds to which the young male is exposed. Imitation of these other species rarely occurs in nature. Interspecific learning would be highly dysgenic, for we have shown in other work that females are also responsive to conspecific song, and probably base their initial selection of a mate upon song recognition. Thus a male learning the song of another species would experience both communicative and reproductive difficulties with females and males of his own species. His fitness would surely be reduced as a result. Thus it is not surprising that the evolution of a capacity for song learning has been coupled with genetically based mechanisms that constrain the learning to conspecific models. The song template hypothesis provides a potential explanation for this selectivity.

CONSTRAINTS ON THE SONG-LEARNING PROCESS: SENSORY TEMPLATES

Various lines of evidence point to the existence of constraints imposed on the process of song learning. There are constraints in time, such that there are sensitive periods when learning takes place most readily. There are also stimulus constraints in that some acoustical patterns are learned more readily than others. In addition some species exhibit contextual constraints, as will be described later. However, in the white-crowned sparrow and also in the chaffinch (Thorpe, 1958) restrictions on the type of sound that is most readily learned are not attributable to contextual influences, such as the social situation, since they are manifest in a bird making a selection from sounds coming through a loudspeaker. In these cases there must be constraints that are in some sense endogenous to the male bird. We can imagine a wide spectrum of neural and neuromusclar mechanisms that constrain the learning process. One obvious possibility is a limit on what sounds the syrinx can produce.

The structure of the sound-producing equipment of birds — involving the respiratory machinery, the syrinx and its associated membranes, muscles and resonators — clearly imposes restrictions on what sounds can be produced. Recent research has greatly clarified the mode of operation of the avian syrinx (Greenewalt, 1968; Nottebohm, 1971; Gaunt and Wells, 1973; see the review in Nottebohm, 1975). While the syringes of phylogenetically distant bird species operate in different ways, those of close relatives seem to be very similar in both morphology and mode of operation.

Indeed, the structure of the avian syrinx is known to be a conservative trait that changes only slowly in the course of evolution. This conservatism has to lead to extensive use of syringeal structure as a taxonomic character at the higher levels of phylogenetic classification.

The likelihood that differences in syringeal structure are responsible for the differences in learning selectivity that we are considering here is reduced by demonstrations that species with similar syringeal structure can produce very different vocalizations. Thus a chaffinch and a bullfinch have very similar syringes, but a bullfinch, which is a species in which song learning seems to be guided only by social constraints, can be trained to imitate a great variety of unnatural sounds, including musical instruments (Nicolai, 1959; Thorpe, 1955). As a further point the resemblance that we have already noted between the songs produced after early deafening by a white-crowned sparrow, a song sparrow, and a junco suggest that the output of the syringes of these three species is very similar when freed from auditory control. Limitations on the sensory side, such as are invoked by the sensory template hypothesis, provide a more plausible explanation, although restrictions on the motor side deserve more study even in close relatives.

The loss of species specificity in singing behavior that results from auditory deprivation, partial in the case of isolation from exposure to adult song, and extreme in the case of early deafening, points to a sensory mechanism involved in the maintenance of song species specificity. It is in this context that the notion of auditory templates has arisen. These are visualized as lying in the neural pathways for auditory processing, sensitizing the organism to certain patterns of stimulation, thus embodying information about the structure of vocal sounds, and with the capacity to guide motor development. As such, they are conceived as having a more dominant influence on vocal development than either the structure of the sound-producing equipment or the characteristics of hearing in general, although both are also involved (Konishi, 1970). According to this view, as the young male begins to sing he strikes a progressively closer match between his vocal output and the dictates of the auditory template. As described in a moment, this is just the impression you get listening to a young male as he passes through the stages of subsong, plastic song, and finally full song.

As indicated in Figure 3, which diagrams the pattern of song development in the male white-crowned sparrow both under normal conditions, when reared in isolation from normal song, and when deafened early in life, it can be seen that the time of song learning, between 10 and 50 days of age, precedes the onset of singing by several weeks. The male thus sings from memory. He must be able to hear his own voice to translate into song this remembered "engram" of the song, learned earlier in life. This is implied by Konishi's demonstration that a male deafened after training but before singing has the same highly abnormal, unspecific song as a male deafened without training (Konishi, 1965b).

When the male white-crowned sparrow begins to sing, typically after about 100 days of age in the *nuttalli* subspecies we studied, the imitation of the model experienced earlier does not spring forth immediately in complete form. Instead the male goes through a series of vocal transformations such as one might expect if the task confronting the male were now to acquire skill in matching its vocal output to the dictates of the auditory template. A bird that has been exposed to normal song previously soon manifests syllables in its subsong that resemble those of the model. However, they are variable, and jumbled in order. As subsong develops into plastic song, the form of the syllables becomes more stereotyped and the matching to the model becomes clearer. Finally, with the transition from plastic song to full song, the syllables become properly ordered, and an accurate imitation of the model emerges — a model that has not been heard for several weeks.

The temporal separation of the first stage of auditory song learning from the onset of singing performance is known in other species, such as the zebra finch (Immelmann, 1969), but is not universal. In the chaffinch, for example, the two phases overlap in time. Nevertheless, chaffinch song development has much in common with those in which the overlap does not occur. By deafening young males at various stages in the transition from subsong to full song, Nottebohm (1968) found that, while birds deafened early in the sequence

reverted to a very simple pattern of singing, after delaying deafening beyond a certain point the bird retained some of the normal characteristics of singing that had been achieved. Finally, a male whose song is fully crystallized shows little deficit after deafening, a result obtained in other species as well (Konishi, 1965b). Thus, while auditory feedback is critical in the early stages of song development in certain species, it seems to become redundant once song has fully crystallized. This is not the case with others, such as the cardinal and the canary, where song regression occurs after deafening even in adulthood (Dittus and Lemon, 1970; Nottebohm, 1975).

Conceived as sensory mechanisms embodying species-specific information that guide vocal development, auditory templates obviously vary in their competence to generate fully natural song without access to a model from the environment. That of the male white-crowned sparrow is the least competent of the three species displayed in Figure 1, in the sense that the song of an intact, isolated male is most different from the natural song in this species.

By contrast, an isolated, intact male song sparrow produces songs which, though somewhat variable, are often hard to distinguish from those of wild birds (Mulligan, 1966; Kroodsma, in press). Yet most of these normal song characteristics are lacking from the song of an early-deafened song sparrow, which suggests that a species-specific auditory template is involved in their ontogeny. Unlike that of a white-crowned sparrow, however, which must be extensively modified by environmental learning to produce natural song, a song sparrow template is capable of guiding virtually normal development without any opportunity to learn an environmental model. Correspondingly, learning from other birds seems to play a less intrusive role in the development of song sparrow song. Dialects, though present, are much less well marked than in white-crowned sparrow song as a result (Harris and Lemon, 1972), and neighboring song sparrows show much less conformity in their singing behavior than white-crowned sparrows that live together.

The Oregon junco resembles the song sparrow more than the white-crown, in that dialects in its song are probably either subtle or

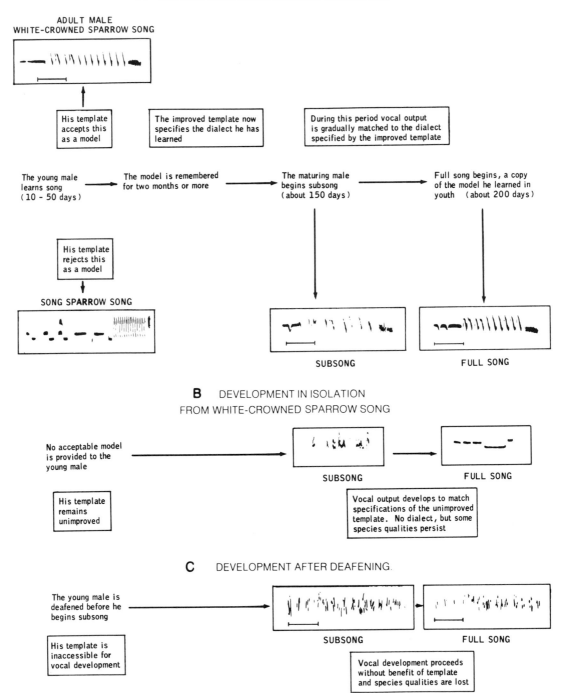

A DEVELOPMENT UNDER NORMAL CONDITIONS

ADULT MALE
WHITE-CROWNED SPARROW SONG

His template accepts this as a model

The improved template now specifies the dialect he has learned

During this period vocal output is gradually matched to the dialect specified by the improved template

The young male learns song (10 - 50 days) → The model is remembered for two months or more → The maturing male begins subsong (about 150 days) → Full song begins, a copy of the model he learned in youth (about 200 days)

His template rejects this as a model

SONG SPARROW SONG

SUBSONG

FULL SONG

B DEVELOPMENT IN ISOLATION
FROM WHITE-CROWNED SPARROW SONG

No acceptable model is provided to the young male →

SUBSONG → FULL SONG

His template remains unimproved

Vocal output develops to match specifications of the unimproved template. No dialect, but some species qualities persist

C DEVELOPMENT AFTER DEAFENING.

The young male is deafened before he begins subsong →

SUBSONG FULL SONG

His template is inaccessible for vocal development

Vocal development proceeds without benefit of template and species qualities are lost

FIGURE 3.   Song development of male white-crowned sparrows: (A) under normal conditions; (B) reared in isolation from conspecific song from the early nestling stage; (C) after deafening early in life. (From Marler, 1975.)

absent. Also, an intact, isolated Oregon junco produces a song which, although abnormal in several respects, is closer to the natural song than that of a white-crowned sparrow reared in similar circumstances (Marler, Kreith, and Tamura, 1962). Thus the sensory template for song of a naive Oregon junco might be thought of as intermediate between the other two species in its competence to generate normal song. It is modifiable through experience of normal song stimulation, though apparently only in its specifications for overall pattern. Juncos are less prone to slavish imitation of a song model to which they are exposed than are white-crowned sparrows. Instead each male tends to produce individually distinctive morphology of the notes from which the song is constructed, although conforming in overall pattern. It is as though males of this species are prone to improvise individually within rather broad limits set by the auditory template. Thus dependence on a sensory template to guide song development is not incompatible with a significant role for the "invention" of individually distinctive patterns of motor activity. Indeed, such a process has been invoked to explain how new birdsong dialects may arise (Lemon, 1971).

It is clear, then, that species differ in the particular pattern of auditory stimulation specified in the auditory template of a naive individual. It is sometimes sufficient to generate virtually normal song. In other cases it requires more or less extensive learned modification before normal singing can develop, though it still suffices to focus the learning bird's attention upon conspecific song models. Species also seem to differ in the latitude allowed for motor development within the constraints set by the sensory template. In some species, such as the white-crowned sparrow, the constraints are narrow, although even here, with such accurate imitation of the dialect represented by models heard during the sensitive period there is individuality in the introductory part of the song. In species with broader constraints there is less conformity to the models that are heard and correspondingly more latitude for individuality. This is an important point, for most birdsongs have strong individualistic components, and there is evidence that songs mediate individual recognition in several bird species. Further comparative study of the transitions from subsong to full song that accompany song ontogeny is needed if we are to learn more about how the delicate balance between conformity to species-specific properties of song and individuality in other properties of the same song is achieved and maintained in different bird species.

THE SIGNIFICANCE OF SUBSONG

As already noted in many of the species we have been considering, the male song does not suddenly appear in complete form. It develops over a period of weeks, passing through several distinct stages. The first is known to ornithologists as subsong (Thorpe and Pilcher, 1958; Lanyon, 1960), and differs from full song in a number of respects. It is not as loud as full song, and the components are often given in long irregular sequences. In addition to fragments of song, other sounds from the repertoire are often included. The frequency of its components tends to fluctuate erratically, giving subsong a wider range of sound frequencies than occurs in full song. The variability is such that it is hard to discern with any great precision units that are repeated.

As development proceeds, the subsong becomes louder and in many cases more clearly segmented. Finally, the patterns crystallize into stereotyped themes, thus completing the development of full or primary song.

The significance of subsong is uncertain. On the one hand, it may be regarded as a by-product of increasing androgen levels, without any intrinsic significance. On the other hand, it is conceivable that subsong serves to aid the bird in acquiring skill in the use of its sound-producing equipment as a necessary stage in the accomplishment of full song. There are reasons for thinking that the latter may be true in at least some cases. Male chaffinches and white-crowned sparrows cycling in and out of song in their second or third year of age pass through the stages from subsong to full song more quickly than young males coming into song for the first time. This might be expected after the adult song pattern has been fully established, although it could also be argued that rates of hormone production or sensitivity to hormonal effects might be enchanced in older birds that have already experienced one annual cycle.

A comparison of development in trained and untrained male white-crowned sparrows is illuminating in this regard (Marler, 1970). Males that have been trained with a normal song usually pass through the subsong stage rather quickly. Full song is generally crystallized within a few weeks after the onset of subsong. On the other hand, birds raised in social isolation, or unsuccessfully trained either with presentation of conspecific song outside the critical period or exposure to alien song, often remain much longer in this transitional stage of song development. It may take months for full song to become completely crystallized. Thus a bird that is destined to produce abnormal song may persist with variable patterns for a major part of the singing season. If we think of effective training as providing the bird with a clear goal toward which vocal development should then proceed, it is perhaps understandable that the transitional stages of subsong should be passed over more quickly than in a bird which is lacking such specific instruction.

Careful study of the structure of the components of subsong reveals another difference between white-crowns that have and have not heard normal song during a critical period. Although the subsong of the former shares many formal properties with that of untrained birds, the resemblance between the structure of the earliest components produced and those of the training song is apparent. Thus some of the basic acoustical components are established early in the course of song development. However, these fragments are produced in a very disorderly fashion at first, and the complete match with the training song is only achieved gradually as the syllables become organized into the appropriate order and timing.

These results are not inconsistent with the auditory template hypothesis advanced earlier to explain song development. Although a bird trained with normal song during the critical period is assumed to possess a highly specified "template" already, the accomplishment of a perfect match between this template and the vocal output will take time. Novel and complex operations of the sound-producing equipment are required. The sequence of development observed in a trained bird is what one might expect if, by engaging in subsong, it thus acquires more proficiency in matching vocal output to the specified pattern of auditory feedback.

To explain development in a male white-crowned sparrow that has been prevented from hearing normal song during the critical period, we have postulated a cruder template which provides only a rough specification for song development. This will allow considerable latitude, and it might be anticipated that in development guided by this crude template, crystallization of song patterns will take longer than in a trained bird which possesses more highly specified instructions. Untrained birds show every sign of vacillation, sometimes changing major patterns several times in the course of development. It will be recalled that an adult male white-crowned sparrow possesses only one song type. Some untrained males had two song themes at intermediate stages of development, subsequently rejecting one of them. This was never recorded in birds that had been subjected to effective training.

If we carry this line of argument still further, one might predict that birds deafened early in life, thus deprived of access even to the crude template of an intact untrained bird, would show an even more attenuated and variable sequence of song development. This is precisely what happens. Apart from their abnormal quality and pattern, the most striking characteristic of the songs of male white-crowned sparrows deafened in youth is their instability (Konishi, 1965b). The same is true of other species deafened early in life (Konishi and Nottebohm, 1969). Some deaf birds even pass through their entire first singing season without a stereotyped theme emerging. Many show some degree of crystallization but nevertheless vary much more in successive repetitions of a theme than a normal bird. Even successive units within a single song vary widely. The deaf birds seem to have difficulty in maintaining a steady tone. Many of these traits are reminiscent of an early stage of normal subsong development. These birds behave almost as though deafening arrests their development at this stage, in at least some respects, even though the rhythm of song

EMPHASIS IN ORIGINAL CONCEPT RETAINED	SELECTIVE FILTERING OF EXTERNAL STIMULI
INITIAL SELECTIVITY DEVELOPS WITHOUT PRIOR EXPERIENCE OF A MODEL	MODIFIABILITY OF SELECTIVITY BY EXTERNAL STIMULATION
DEVELOPMENT OF CONCEPT REQUIRED	INCORPORATION IN MOTOR DEVELOPMENT

FIGURE 4.   Relationships between "innate release mechanisms" and "sensory templates."

delivery and the singing posture do continue to develop in the normal fashion. We have already noted that a male chaffinch deafened in youth, but after some subsong experience, develops a more advanced song than a male deafened still earlier and lacking such experience (Notte-bohm, 1968).

It thus seems probable that the subsong of young males does have developmental significance, perhaps providing opportunity both to learn new operations with the sound-producing equipment and to employ trial-and-error learning to match the output with a particular pattern of auditory feedback specified by an auditory template. The recurrence of subsong at the start of each singing season in adult males remains unexplained.

SENSORY TEMPLATES AND "INNATE RELEASE MECHANISMS"

An attractive feature of the auditory template hypothesis is its provision of an economical explanation for the initial select-ivity of the song-learning process. While the auditory template for song of an untrained male white-crowned sparrow is thought of as only an elementary specification of species-specific song, such as is manifest in the singing of an intact but untrained male, it may nevertheless be sufficient to serve as a kind of filter for external auditory stimuli. In this sense it has much in common with the classical ethological concept of the innate release

mechanism, serving to focus the attention of the male on patterns of external stimulation that have assumed a special valence in the course of phylogenetic history of species (Lorenz, 1950; Tinbergen, 1951). The present conception differs in that the sensory template is subsequently involved in motor development (Figure 4).

An analogous function to that of an innate release mechanism is apparently served by the auditory template of a female. It is known that females are especially responsive to normal male song at the time of sexual pairing (Milligan and Verner, 1971). By injecting females with exogenous testosterone, Konishi derived supporting evidence for the hypothesis that the mechanism underlying responsiveness of females resembles that which guides male song development. Provided she has experienced normal song early in life, such a female will not only sing under the influence of testosterone, but will reproduce the particular dialect to which she was exposed earlier, demonstrating that she is in possession of the same information about song as a trained male, though this information is normally manifest in the process of mate selection rather than song development.

Although auditory templates for song development in birds are conceptualized as single functional mechanisms, they may actually involve several physiological components that together serve as filters both for external stimuli and for stimuli derived from the animal's own performance. It might be that components that are modifiable are separate from those which underlie the selective perception of a naive, untrained male. Mechanisms might operate in series or in parallel, with control shifting from one to the other after training. Thus the term should not be taken to imply the existence of single unitary mechanisms. The underlying mechanisms may be several and complex, and may also differ in their nature, number, and mode of coupling from species to species. As with other "feature detectors" and indeed with several mechanisms postulated on the basis of ethological evidence, such as "sign stimuli and releasers" and "innate release mechanisms," one should be prepared for the likelihood that similar behavioral ends are achieved in different organisms by entirely distinct physiological means (Marler and Hamilton, 1966; Chapter Five, this book).

SENSORY TEMPLATES IN HUMAN SPEECH DEVELOPMENT

Like such birds as the white-crowned sparrow, human infants are able to discriminate between conspecific, communicative sounds and other sounds at a very early age, probably within a few days after birth (Moffitt, 1971; Morse, 1972; Trehub and Rabinovitch, 1972; Trehub, 1973; Palermo, 1975). There is no evidence that this ability depends upon prior experience of speech sounds by the infant, although careful studies are needed to exclude the possibility of rapid learning after birth, and of intrauterine learning of sounds of the mother or of others. Nonetheless, the point seems well established that speech sounds are recognized as a class prior to the development of speaking.

Another line of research has specified more precisely some of the critical acoustical properties of speech sounds. The results of experiments with synthetic speech sounds, in which continuously varying series of intergradations are presented, show that listeners segmentalize such speech continua at particular boundaries, and find it difficult even to discriminate between sounds that fall on the same side of the normal boundary between two such speech sounds as [ba] and [pa] (Liberman et al., 1957; Liberman et al., 1961; Liberman et al., 1967). While the same is true of recorded

sounds of natural speech, the point is made more forcefully with synthetic stimuli in which all parameters are under complete control.

In itself, the demonstration that we are especially sensitive to variations in speech sounds close to critical boundaries is not surprising, and perhaps of more interest to psychologists than to biologists. However, two additional findings draw the phenomenon firmly and irrevocably into the biological realm. Having defined the critical boundaries for some acoustically adjacent speech sounds, Abramson and Lisker, in a long series of comparative studies, have demonstrated recurrence of very similar boundaries in one language after another. This is true, however different the languages may be in other respects, to the extent that one may begin to think of some of these critical boundaries as universals in all human speech (e.g., Abramson and Lisker, 1965, 1970, Lisker and Abramson, 1970). Thus, in addition to the features of grammar that structural linguists and students of early speech development believe to be shared by all languages (e.g., McNeill, 1966; Chomsky, 1967; Lenneberg, 1967; Brown, 1973), some more superficial aspects of the acoustical structure defining categorical boundaries in speech may also be shared by all human speakers. The existence of such species-specific features is an invitation to the biologist to explore the role of genetic factors in their determination.

It appears then that, in either natural or synthetic speech, we perceive the phonemic components of words as discretely different from one another even when they are not. While one may speculate that such features of speech as pitch, intonation, loudness, and tempo, along with other aspects of speech that convey variations in the speaker's mood and intent, are processed in continuous rather than categorical fashion, much of the content of speech is obviously processed segmentally. The work of Eimas and his colleagues (Eimas et al., 1971; Eimas, in press; Cutting and Eimas, 1975) shows that such segmental processing of speech sounds occurs at normal boundaries in infants as young as 4 months, or even one month, of age, long before they have begun to speak or even to babble. Working with related speech sounds such as [pa] and [ba] or [bae], [dae], and [gae], distinguished by adults according to acoustical criteria that are broadly similar in all languages studied so far, Eimas has found that infants process them in essentially the same way as adults.

The demonstrations rest on a habituation technique. Using sucking as an operant for delivering recorded sounds that catch the infant's attention, habituation with repetitions of one sound pattern to a given criterion is followed by substitution of the sound with another. The extent of revival of the response is used as an index of the degree to which the pre- and posthabituation sounds contrast with one another. Working along series of synthetic speech sounds, Eimas found little or no evidence of contrast between within-category sound pairs until approaching that part of the series where an adult discerns a sharp boundary. In roughly the same area the infant shows a sudden revival of response as the boundary is crossed. Responsiveness to several such boundaries has been demonstrated in infants at ages young enough that it becomes plausible to postulate that certain speech sounds can be processed in the appropriate categorical manner without the need for prior exposure to them. The analogy with innate release mechanisms and with the auditory templates that we have postulated to explain the perception and development of bird song is highly suggestive.

Auditory templates for certain speech sounds could serve a prespeech child well in two respects. First, they would focus an infant's attention on the appropriate class of external stimuli for social responsiveness, much as the auditory templates of some birds are thought to restrict responsiveness to members of their own species when they are living in a community with many others present. Second, auditory templates for certain speech sounds could be of value in providing an orderly frame of reference for the infant's developing responsiveness to speech patterns in the culture in which it grows up, drawing its attention to the particular subset of the myriad, complex properties of speech that retain valence into adulthood (Mattingly, 1972). As postulated for birds such as the white-crowned sparrow, so the templates that a child possesses for guiding some of the initial steps in the perceptual analysis of speech are presumably modified in the process of such analysis. In the human case

they would also be multiplied as the infant acquires more competence in the perceptual analysis of additional sounds of the language in which it participates.

One may even take a further step and postulate that an additional function for speech-sound templates might lie in the development of speaking itself. Evidently, the sensory mechanisms for speech perception precede motor development, much as occurs in the white-crowned sparrow (Palermo, 1975). Could it be that some of the early stages of speech development depend upon a process of matching vocal output to sensory templates by auditory feedback? Improvements in a child's babbling, as with a bird's subsong, might reveal a growing skill in achieving this kind of a match. By the time an infant reaches the age at which the first exercises in speech begin, these hypothetical templates for the sounds of speech would now be greatly modified and enriched compared with those of early infancy, as a result of the intervening experience with the speech of adults and siblings. No doubt this elaboration of the perceptual processing of speech sounds interdigitates extensively with the onset of speaking, with the result that in the adult there is extensive and intimate correspondence between the motor performance of speaking and the perception of speech sounds (Liberman et al., 1967).

This interpretation implies that the physiological mechanisms that underlie the perception of speech sounds are to some extent distinct in their mode of operation from those associated with auditory perception of other kinds of sounds. There is evidence that points to this conclusion from a variety of sources (Liberman et al., 1967; Studdert-Kennedy, 1975). Dichotic listening studies in which competing sounds are presented to the two ears demonstrate that speech sounds are more readily perceived when the sounds arrive at the right ear than the left, whereas the opposite is true for nonspeech sounds (e.g., Kimura, 1961, 1964; Studdert-Kennedy and Shankweiler, 1970).

Electrophysiological studies of averaged evoked potentials given in response to speech and nonspeech sound stimuli confirm this tendency for separation of the processing of the two classes of sounds in the two hemispheres

(Wood, Goff, and Day, 1971; Molfese, 1972). The method also provides an independent demonstration of categorical processing (Dorman, 1974). Molfese (1972) finds stronger responsiveness of the left hemisphere than the right by dichotic testing with speech sounds, even in infants as young as one week of age.

Thus the distinctive attributes of the perceptual processing of speech sounds as compared with other kinds of auditory stimuli seem to include a tendency toward categorical rather than continuous processing, and a tendency for the processing to be associated more with the dominant, left hemisphere of the brain than with the right. The converse tends to be true of nonspeech sounds.

If sensory templates for speech sounds are to be invoked as a factor in the development and operation of speech perception and development, a tendency toward categorical rather than continuous processing is to be expected. The notion is an intriguing one for ethologists, already implicitly accustomed to thinking in terms of categorical modes of perceptual processing whenever innate release mechanisms are invoked. The present tendency for researchers to concentrate on stereotyped species-specific behaviors in developmental studies has already been noted. Yet there also exists an extensive repertoire of highly graded motor actions with signaling significance in many species. It will be a challenge of some magnitude, both theoretical and practical, to achieve some understanding of the perceptual and neurophysiological correlates of communicative stimuli that are graded rather than discrete.

CONCLUSIONS

A case has been made, largely on the basis of ethological data, that the concept of a sensory template is heuristically useful in understanding the ontogeny of the vocal behavior of both birds and man. The concept derives from the ethological term "innate release mechanisms" (Lorenz, 1950; Tinbergen, 1951) and seeks to retain the emphasis so implied on species-specific genetic constraints. As applied to avian and human vocal learning, these genetic constraints are viewed as modifi-

able as a consequence of experience. They impose a general species-specific direction on subsequent behavioral development by sensitizing the young organism to certain classes of external stimuli.

Sensory templates provide a structural framework for the perceptual analysis of arrays of stimuli that is both plastic and yet constrained. After more or less extensive modification by experience, with their number added to or subjected to attrition, and changed in specification so that their properties may now be both species-specific and also population-, group-, or even individual-specific, they then guide motor development by a process of sensory feedback. Phases of this multistage process may interdigitate in time or they may be temporally separated, proceeding most readily at particular developmental stages or "sensitive periods."

Temporal requirements will vary greatly according to the sociobiology of the species, with such species-specific variables as tendencies for family cohesion or dispersal, seasonal patterns of migration, and community composition, all bearing on the optimal timing for each stage. Since temporal optima may vary even in closely related species, the physiological determinants of sensitive periods for the employment, modification, and motor involvement of sensory templates may prove to vary between species, exploiting opportunistically whatever hormonal, neural, and behavioral events coincide with particular temporal requirements. The same may tend to be true of sensitive periods in other kinds of behavioral development, though the lack of physiological unity so implied need not necessarily undermine the heuristic value of the sensitive period as a concept.

The hypothesis that species-specific, modifiable, sensory templates guide the development of certain kinds of motor behavior has been developed to explain some of the complexities of vocal learning. The sensory equivalence between auditory stimulation from another individual and auditory feedback from one's own voice makes it easier to picture how the process operates in vocal development than in behaviors engaging other sensory modalities. An organism may hear its own voice in somewhat similar terms to those in which it hears another's voice, with opportunities to compare the two in short-term memory and, as suggested here, by reference in long-term memory to a remembered "schema," such as a modified sensory template may provide.

It is harder to imagine a similar process guiding development of visually signaling behavior such as a facial expression, except by use of a mirror. However one should bear in mind that the feedback loop mediating a template-matching process could be internal to the animal. Even in the present case, bone-conducted sound is surely important in guiding our own vocal development. People are usually surprised when they first hear a sound recording of their own voice.

There is growing evidence that patterned neural commands to motor effectors can be accompanied by collateral patterned inputs to parts of the brain not in the direct line of motor commands (Evarts, 1971). If patterned neural activity of exteroceptive sensory origin converged on the same parts of the brain, an organism might then be able to engage in a matching process, with changes in behavior designed to reduce any mismatch, as von Holst and Mittelstaedt (1950) visualized in their original formulation of the "re-afference principle." For evidence on such internal channels for matching sensory templates to feedback from motor activity, the ethologist must necessarily turn to the physiologist. Even with external channels such as have been postulated here for the control of vocal learning by modifiable auditory templates, the ethologist is working on the edge of his competence, and must eventually give way to the skills of the neurophysiologist. Hopefully the latter will find the task easier if the ethologist has already defined the problem area, specified its evolutionary context, and made some progress in defining relevant parameters of motor activity and stimulus control.

CHAPTER TWENTY-THREE

System and Mechanism in Behavioral Biology

JOHN C. FENTRESS

INTRODUCTION

In this volume the problems of neural networks and behavior have been examined from a variety of perspectives. My aim here is to draw together some major similarities and differences in data and strategy as I see them. I shall do this by focusing initially upon the relations between two distinct yet complementary approaches to natural science: the systems approach and the mechanism approach. Subsequently, I shall present a framework of interactive/self-organizing systems which may help us seek a partial synthesis in a manner that does justice to the diversity both of biological material and of our strategies of understanding.

SYSTEM AND MECHANISM

Before providing a formal definition of system and mechanism, let us see how these terms are traditionally used. In his general analysis of adaptive control systems in biology,

Reiner has stated: "it is of the utmost importance to keep in mind that analysis analyzes something which is a *system* of parts, and that one must, after isolating and studying the parts, also study the *relations* that hold the system together" (Reiner, 1968). The similarity of this position to Maynard's comments about the analysis of "simpler networks" is obvious. At one level we can say that *system* emphasizes relationships, whereas *mechanism* emphasizes component dimensions.

The term *mechanism* also implies causal connection. In simple terms we can say that a mechanism is the means by which an effect is produced, or the means by which cause and effect are related. If I state that an animal responds to a flash of light by blinking, I might then go further and state that the mechanism by which this blink is produced is the electrochemical translation of photons into generator potentials, or the transmission of spikes down the axon, or the activation of neuromuscular junctions in the animal's eyelids. In this sense the mechanism is defined as "a single part of the system which appears to mediate the connection between other parts" with which we are concerned. Since we can postulate and examine a great number of mechanisms between "input" and "output" in this and most other cases of biological organization, it is apparent that we are not necessarily trying to account for the system in its totality; in other words, we are simply attempting to link a subpopulation of components within the system into a causal framework.

This is valuable, and essential, as long as we do not overly interpret what we have done; that is, other mechanisms may be participating as well in the more complete picture. If we use larger categories for mechanism, such as "hippocampus" or "basal ganglia," we may incorporate a greater number of intervening processes, but upon subsequent refinement in analysis our mechanism itself becomes a complex system of interacting parts. The point here is that system and mechanism are relative terms: a mechanism at one level of analysis is a complex system at a different level of analysis. One approach, advocated strongly in work with simpler networks, is to reduce the complexity of the material to a level at which basic *units* of organization can be found (e.g., individual neurons). As pointed out clearly by Pearson in Chapter Seven, however, the assumption of cellular "units" may be an oversimplification if we examine these cells in greater detail. The other side of the coin is that stressed particularly by Maynard: in the very process of simplifying we may be dealing with but a part of what is really a much larger total system, thus limiting the statements we can make about the system as a whole. Less obvious, perhaps, but not less important is that information gathered even "within" a partial system can be distorted if the elements within that partial system are affected by events in their surround. A fourth issue is that if we do work with truly *simple* systems that can be examined in greater detail, then we may lose our ability to extrapolate meaningfully to more complex systems. There are no obvious answers here, but the problem must at least be recognized.

The question of elementary "units" implicit in the term mechanism is based upon a model in classical physics in which, for example, elementary particles move mechanically according to certain laws of inertia and forces of interaction. The view of Newtonian mechanics is, in current theoretical physics, considered a convenient abstraction in which clusters of events develop sufficiently stable and unitary properties of expression that they can be treated "as if" they are indivisible building blocks. But such abstractions, of course, can be treated at a variety of levels of analysis, from protons, to molecules, to individual cells, or even to networks of cells. It is perfectly appropriate, therefore, for the behavioral scientist to treat a given act of behavior as a "unit" for certain purposes, and then to treat that "unit" as an explanation for (mechanism of) change observed in another "unit" of behavior. In this sense mechanism becomes an abstract simplification for the generation of causal inference.

Bohm (1969) has recently argued that current physical theory leaves the biologist with a dual problem. The first is that it may often be an error to attempt reduction to too fine a level of analysis, for in doing so the link to the phenomenon itself may be lost. This is basically the position advocated by Hoyle in Chapter Two of this volume. Second, Bohm points out that *if* we wish to be truly reductionistic in our explanations, even in terms of future goals, the language of mechanism may be misleading since it has been largely abandoned by physics. In both statistical mechanics, and particularly in quantum theory, systems of interlocking dimensions have replaced unitary mechanisms, or units, of operation. In Bohm's words,

> It does seem odd, therefore, that just when physics is thus moving away from mechanism, biology and psychology are moving closer to it. If this trend continues, it may well be that scientists will be regarding living and intelligent beings as mechanical, while they suppose that inanimate matter is too complex and subtle to fit into the limited categories of mechanism (p. 34).

What is being argued here is largely a perspective of conceptual stance. Most individual contributors to this volume, for example, find the idea of mechanism satisfactory for their problems, whereas Freeman (Chapter Twenty) clearly does not. This returns us to the

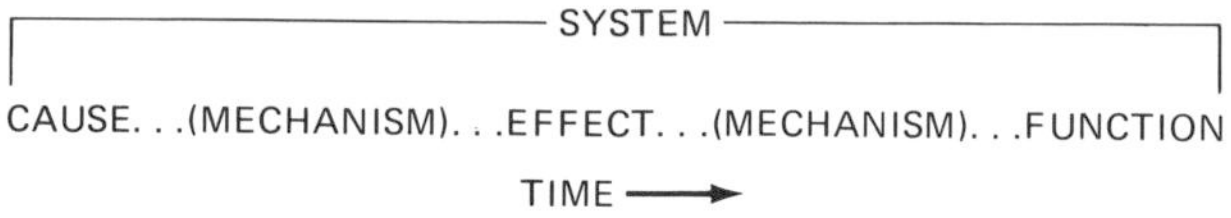

```
┌──────────────────── SYSTEM ────────────────────┐
│                                                 │
CAUSE. . .(MECHANISM). . .EFFECT. . .(MECHANISM). . .FUNCTION
                      TIME ──────▶
```

FIGURE 1.   Schematic representation of the relation between system *and* mechanism *as commonly employed in biobehavioral research. The term "mechanism" refers basically to intermediary processes in a causal sequence, whereas the term "system" typically refers to a larger range of component processes which together form a functional unit.*

questions raised by Maynard (1972) and in the first chapter of the present volume: How and when is it useful to separate off a chunk of the universe as a focus for our attention? What are the consequences of doing this?

I suggest that "mechanism" is primarily a *functional* concept, using function here to indicate the intervening means (operations) by which components that would otherwise be separate are linked together within a causal framework. Structures are mechanisms only insofar as they have demonstrable functional properties. Further, the term mechanism can be employed without explicit reference to structure as long as the criterion of intervening processing stage is met. I can, for example, state that ongoing behavior is a mechanism that mediates qualitatively different responses of an animal to the same external stimulus (e.g., Fentress, 1968a, b). This usage fits the basic logic of experimentation, and avoids the difficulties of excessive interpretation noted by Bohm. It is, anyway, what most biologists do.

We can summarize the basic sense of mechanism and system with a simple diagram (Figure 1). The figure indicates the three basic time referents in the analysis of a biological control system: cause (antecedent condition), effect, and function (consequence of the effect). I can state, for example, that increased day length "causes" an increase in birdsong, which in turn functions to promote pair bonding and reproduction. If I then note that day length produces its effect upon singing by generating an intermediate effect upon testosterone levels, I can speak of this altered hormonal state as the mechanism (or to be more precise, *a* mechanism) by which light produces its effect. Similarly, if I show that singing in a male songbird alters the endocrinological state of a female who is a potential mate, then I can cite this as the (*a*) mechanism which connects singing of one bird and receptivity of the other.

This is obviously a highly simplified representation, and, as analysis proceeds, a greater number of intervening and interlocking steps may be uncovered; that is, one's mechanism at this level of analysis becomes a system of interlocking subcomponents at a more refined level of analysis. For other purposes, such as an analysis of population dynamics, the various stages outlined in this system may be combined and treated as a unitary mechanism. Mechanism at any level implies a unitary intervening causal step when viewed in terms of the higher-order system within which it participates. Thus mechanism is a heuristic principle by which we order our thoughts in causal analysis, and should be interpreted within that limited sense. Questions such as "Is that a mechanism?" taken in the abstract sense can be applied to particular instances only when the precise context of examination is determined. Although when these points are outlined they seem simple and obvious, failure to recognize their implications is at the heart of much confusion, both in neurobiology and behavior, and particularly in the relationship between these disciplines.

HIERARCHICAL ORGANIZATION AND OPERATIONAL PRINCIPLES

The issue of practical importance, raised by nearly all the contributors to this volume, is the problem of relating in a precise manner hierarchically divergent levels of organization in biobehavioral systems. For example, there is the question of whether patterned activity in networks is basically attributable to patterned activity of single units within that network (e.g., "burst generators") or an "emergent" property of the network as a whole. On one hand, the answers seem to depend upon the particular system under investigation (e.g., pyloric versus gastric-mill systems in Crustacea); on the other hand, they depend upon the style of questions that we are asking and the types of measurements that we produce. I submit that this will remain a basic conceptual challenge for some years to come (see Chapter Six).

The importance of different styles and strategies of analysis cannot be emphasized too strongly. I recall a discussion that I once had with a good friend in molecular biology who made the claim that the goal of molecular biology is "to understand the biochemical nature of birdsong," to which I responded that I thought it was carbon! This was obviously not his point, for he was referring to complete dissection of biological molecules of major complexity. But the question of what understanding means becomes the important point here. For example, are we to take his statement to imply a miniature replica of song within a single molecule, as if upon the construction of an appropriate model the song could be elicited by placement of a phonograph needle? Such a form of reductionism would be indistinguishable from the homunculus in the head of the sperm that haunted the early days of developmental biology! What about the fact that some species of bird must have particular experiences during particular stages of ontogeny to perfect their song (Chapter Twenty-Two)? What about seasonal changes in the tendency to sing, or the fact that even during the peak of reproductive season a given bird may sometimes sing, then fly, then feed, then perch, then sing again, etc.? Is this what one expects to find "within" the molecule? Obviously not; there are important questions at many complementary levels of organizatiion.

We tend today to "explain" higher levels of organization by reference to lower orders of organization, and the heuristic value of this approach cannot be denied. But this is an asymmetry which we have imposed upon nature and which, particularly for biological systems, has some potential dangers. On one hand, it is a moot point whether "hydrogen" and "oxygen" *explain* the nature of H_2O more than H_2O and related compounds *explain* the nature of H_2 and O_2. Historically, certainly,

the explanation went the other way; that is, atomic structure was derived from detailed analysis of higher-order configurations. There may be something of relevance here to our consideration of nervous systems and behavior, for constraints at the behavioral level may tell us important facts about the properties of individual elements as well as the other way around. The three-part theory of color vision, for example, was generated through psychophysics; the behavioral data told the neurobiologist what *must be* the case in terms of "mechanism." It is a severe challenge to other behavioral scientists to set the stage as precisely.

The other obvious biological reason for bringing this consideration to the fore at the present time is that behavioral units are the primary focus of evolutionary selection; behavior is the phenotypic expression of the nervous system. From the more general perspective of physical systems, rules of interrelationship among component dimensions may generate stable properties of organization at higher levels which are much more clear, and in that sense "simple," than properties at lower levels. The gas laws in physics are illustrative. Whether it is fair to expect stabilities in behavioral expression at the organism level to be mediated by equally obvious stabilities of operation at the neuronal level is a legitimate subject for debate.

If we merely stop with the conclusion that natural phenomena are complicated, the present exercise can serve no useful purpose. It is much more practical to ask whether there are "themes" of organization at the neurobiological *and* behavioral levels which might help us to link them together. Such a *thematic* position demands that we step away from the *details* of individual elements and seek rules of relationship between elements by several levels and forms of analysis. In a relatively simple form there do appear to be cases of evolutionary convergence in which selection pressures have apparently produced similar operational principles at the organism level even though the details of underlying machinery are vastly different. The example, cited earlier, of load compensation in vertebrates and arthropods is a case in point (Fentress, Chapter One; Kennedy, Chapter Five).

A THEME OF INTERACTIVE/SELF-ORGANIZING SYSTEMS

Drawing from the chapters in this volume we can start with the premise that biological systems display two fundamental modes of organization: interaction and self-organization. It is clear that it is the balance between these two modes of organization which sets the stage for many of the basic problems at both the behavioral and neurobiological levels. Our purpose here is to see whether these two modes can be viewed within a dynamic context in a manner which will suggest ways to look for principles of organization that can be applied to diverse specific instances at complementary levels.

The basic position I wish to suggest is that, *as systems of a variety of specific types and at a variety of levels become activated through interactions with their surround, they become more tightly and intrinsically organized, and as a consequence reduce their interactions with their surround.* This suggests a dynamic stability of organization both within and between systems. I suggest further that the output characteristics of a given system can also be referred to this basic principle of dynamic stability. This in turn can affect our very definition of system boundaries. I recognize that at this level of abstraction the ideas are not immediately clear. The illustrations that follow are aimed at clarification.

Kennedy (Chapter Five) cites a number of examples in which motor output can be elicited by extrinsic factors, but once this output becomes activated the systems sculptor themselves away from further external input. Similarly, Doty (Chapter Seventeen) and Llinás and Walton (Chapter Nineteen) suggest means by which specific neural systems in mammals can, through such mechanisms as collateral inhibition, protect themselves from disruption once activity within the system is initiated. At the purely behavioral level there are numerous parallels. It is useful first to take cases in which a given behavioral system interacts with and isolates itself from sensory input defined at the organism level. Subsequently, we can ask questions about the relationships between systems which underlie different classes of behavior. A third consideration is whether similar problems of interaction and self-organization can be found in development. Finally, we can ask whether operational rules at the organism level suggest novel ways to link properties of integrative dynamics and phenotypic capacities.

Intrinsic–Extrinsic Factors at the Organism Level

It is well known from the ethological literature that a variety of action patterns can be elicited by environmental stimuli but, once triggered, continue in a relatively fixed course in spite of removal or change in these external stimuli (e.g., reviews in Tinbergen, 1951; Hinde, 1970). Other behavior patterns have graded forms of expression, often grouped under the heading of "intensity" (Fentress, 1973b). In these cases rapid and vigorous forms of expression frequently display a greater autonomy from both extrinsic and proprioceptive input than do these same general classes of behavior when expressed more slowly. Lashley (1951) long ago pointed out that in the execution of very rapid movement sequences there is simply insufficient time for each act in the sequence to trigger the next via proprioceptive loops; in other words, a degree of central programming must be postulated here.

A well-known theme in animated cartoons is the rapid chase, in which one or more participants in the chase collide repeatedly with an object that has been moved into their path. It is possible to observe similar phenomena in animals by altering the placement of objects in their environment. When the animals are moving about slowly, they adjust to these changes, whereas upon being chased or frightened they may collide with objects that are placed in their path and avoid objects that have previously been removed (Fentress, 1976). A simplified illustration of this can be found in the perseverant cage stereotypies that too frequently accompany the housing of wild animals in captivity.

For example, I once placed a chain, approximately 0.8 meters high, across the path of a figure-eight stereotypy that had developed in a Cape hunting dog (*Lycaon*) at the London Zoo. The aim was to block this aberrant form of behavior. The animal, however, simply relocated its path and continued pacing in a figure eight. This was the case when the pacing movements were relatively slow. However, upon being "excited" by external disturbances, the animal reverted back to its old path, tripping frequently on the chain. Gradually, over the course of several days the animal returned to its former path and jumped the chain with ease. The chain remained in place for 3 months. When it was subsequently lowered to the ground, the animal soon ceased jumping *until* it was again disturbed. Now when disturbed it would jump the chain *as if it were still raised.* I observed similar phenomena in voles (*Microtus, Clethrionomys*) who had been isolated for long periods of time in small cages. These animals developed species-characteristic movement stereotypies around and/or over the glass waterspouts that protruded into their cages. When these waterspouts were removed, the animals ceased their stereotypies until disturbed. They then performed the stereotyped movements at high speed, jumping or spinning about the waterspouts that were no longer there. In these admittedly abnormal forms of behavioral expression the animals acted as if they were progressively less influenced by external stimuli as the vigor of their motor performance increased.

Similar phenomena can be documented in normal behavior. Face-grooming sequences in mice, for example, become less influenced by, and less dependent upon, both tactile and proprioceptive input during periods of vigorous expression (Fentress, 1972). The animals are also less easily interrupted during these periods. The point I wish to make here is that once the behavioral control system becomes vigorously activated, it shuts itself off from a variety of external factors, including those which may have initially activated the behavior (see Fentress, 1976, for more extensive review).

In this sense the system, once activated strongly, becomes more autonomous or self-organized in its expression. It is as if the control boundaries by which we define the system become more tightly focused during high levels of activation. One can argue further that mechanisms of motor control discussed by Kennedy (Chapter Five), Doty (Chapter Seventeen), and Llinás and Walton (Chapter Nine-

teen) are compatible with the basic premise of increasing system autonomy with activation; that is, the system shifts from a basically interactive to a self-organized state.

It is of interest that a variety of systems at the biophysical level appear to follow similar general operational principles (e.g., Eigen, 1971; Katchalsky, in Katchalsky, Rowland, and Blumenthal, 1974). Freeman's comments on macrostates (Chapter Twenty) may reflect similar properties. In the other direction, there are also data that indicate that well-established and rapidly performed movement sequences in man may be much more "intrinsically" controlled than are less well-established and/or more slowly performed sequences (e.g., Konorsky, 1967; Keele, 1968). The shift between interactive to self-organized states as a function of system activation may thus provide a useful framework for fuller investigation at a variety of levels of analysis. It provides a dynamic perspective on the problem of "system isolation" discussed by Maynard (1972).

One additional feature of interest at the level of movement sequencing in animals is that rapidly performed sequences are frequently more stereotyped (i.e., contain more predictable relations between component elements) than less rapidly performed sequences (Fentress, 1976, and in preparation). This would be expected if responsiveness to extrinsic inputs that normally add to the variability of output expression is reduced during phases of rapid execution. A variety of mechanisms could be envisioned, ranging from direct inhibition through occlusion due to limitations in processing capacity. This should provide a ripe field for future analyses at the neurobiological level.

Relations Between Systems Within the Organism

If the above principle of interactive/self-organizing systems has any generality, we should expect to find that similar phenomena occur between systems defined within the organism. Here, however, we are faced with the difficulty recognized by Maynard that the boundaries between behavioral control systems, unlike the boundary between organism and environment, must in general be inferred rather than observed directly. One way to do this is to determine the range of inputs which are normally associated with different classes of behavioral output, and then to ask how elements within these separately defined systems interact with one another as measured by change in output. Specifically, how do factors normally classed with one type of output influence the expression of another? One can apply several methodological tricks to clarify possible shifting relationships between systems thus defined. First, through careful observation it is possible to determine the behavioral "set" of the animal – that is, to predict accurately that, if the animal is going to perform a behavioral act, it will most probably be act X rather than Y or Z. Second, one can apply the inputs at different intensities, or again through careful experimentation infer under what set of conditions a behavioral system is likely to be strongly or weakly activated. Third, one can trace the temporal relations between events as a means for inferring increases and/or decreases of system X, Y, or Z activation over time (see Heiligenberg, Chapter Twenty-One).

When this approach is followed, several common rules of relationships between systems are found. First, a given input and/or intervening control system may have more diffuse excitatory influences when activated at a low level than at a high level. This can be measured, for example, by the range of outputs that this input and/or intervening system will facilitate. A simplified example can be used to illustrate this. When mice recover from an anesthetic dose of barbiturates, they can be made to perform a variety of movement patterns in sequence. At early stages of recovery, the animals can be induced to show scratch reflexes by placing them on their backs and gently twisting the spine. Later they will gnaw on a pellet that touches their mouth. Still later, they will show face-scratching movements. In this sense we can say that the animals sequence through three distinct behavioral "sets" during the course of recovery from barbiturate anesthesia.

The question now is what happens if we introduce an input (e.g., tail pinch) that is not obviously associated with any one of these classes of behavioral output. The answer is that low-intensity tail pinches will *facilitate* the expression of each of these three classes of motor activity in turn. Stronger tail pinches, on the other hand, will *block* these same behavioral outputs, at least during application of the pinch. After the strong pinch is terminated, a poststimulus facilitation is frequently observed. This illustrates that during low levels of activation the "tail-pinch system" has a relatively diffuse excitatory field as measured by the range of output classes that it will facilitate, whereas at higher levels of activation the "tail-pinch system" becomes more tightly focused, thus blocking the expression of these diverse outputs (which are replaced by specific defensive orientations). A second point is that the aftereffects of a strong tail pinch are also relatively diffuse in their focus of behavioral excitation.

This is a highly simplified illustration of properties found in a variety of behavioral systems – that is, diffuse excitation at low levels of activation and specifically focused excitation at high levels of activation. Perseverant motor stereotypies provide another simple demonstration; for example, zoo animals will increase their pacing in response to a great variety of factors at moderate intensity, such as food deprivation and the distant approach of school children. At higher levels of disturbance, pacing is replaced by specific orientation toward or away from the source of disturbance. Animals that are recovering from central nervous lesions provide a third simplified illustration. For example, animals with surgically produced aphagia can be made to eat when placed in the appropriate set and when activated by light pinches of the tail (Wolgin, Cytawa, and Teitelbaum, 1975). In less constrained circumstances a variety of behaviors such as fighting and mounting can be facilitated during various disturbances of moderate intensity, or after disturbances of higher intensity (e.g., Hinde, 1970; Hanby, 1974; Archer, 1976). I have reviewed these data in greater detail elsewhere (Fentress, 1972, 1973b, 1976). The principal point to retain is that the excitatory boundaries of a given behavioral control system are often broadly defined (1) *during* periods of low activation, and (2) *after* periods of high activation. During periods of high activation the system is more restricted, or tightly focused, in terms of the outputs that it will facilitate rather than block.[1]

The second major consideration is the extent to which a given behavioral system isolates itself from external influences — as a function of the degree to which it is activated. The evidence, from a great number of sources, is clear: as activation of a system increases, the system becomes more independent from the external surround in its expression. This process is mediated in part by active inhibition of potentially disruptive influences from other control systems, which has long been recognized by behavioral researchers on a largely intuitive basis. Levels of motivation are frequently inferred by the ease with which an animal is disrupted from its course of behavioral expression (Hinde, 1970; Fentress, 1973b, 1976). Mice that are grooming vigorously, for example, can actually be turned with a probe into a better position for filming, whereas mice that are grooming less vigorously are disrupted by much milder manipulations (Fentress, 1972).

A relatively simple summary statement can be made from these diverse examples: *as behavioral control systems become activated, they progressively restrict the range of output classes[2] that they will facilitate*; the outputs facilitated occur in a much more tightly organized (e.g., stereotyped) pattern; the system becomes more dependent upon intrinsic as opposed to extrinsic factors for its expression; and extrinsic factors may be actively blocked. In a word, I believe that the degree of intrinsic organization of a variety of neurobehavioral control systems may shift as a function of the degree to which these systems are activated. If this is true, then possible bridges between the organization of qualitatively different systems, and systems examined at different levels of analysis, can be explored within a common dynamic context.

One way to visualize the main features of

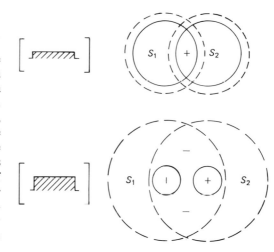

FIGURE 2. *Schematic representation of partially overlapping control systems (*S_1 *and* S_2*) in which each system is visualized in terms of an excitatory core and inhibitory surround. The model presented suggests an increased system focus with activation as well as increased tendency to block factors of extrinsic origin. (A) and (B) represent low and high levels of activation, respectively. (From Fentress, 1973b).*

this framework is in terms of partially overlapping control systems with excitatory centers and inhibitory surrounds in an "information space" sense (see Katchalsky, Rowland, and Blumenthal, 1974). As the systems are activated, they become more tightly self-organized (the core of positive control becomes constricted) and reduce the influence of extrinsic factors on the expressed output (e.g., through expanded inhibition). This type of dynamic shift in system boundaries would account both for reduced influence of extrinsic factors with activation, and an increased tendency to block the expression of other control systems (Figure 2).

It is important that such models be recognized as *abstract* representations of system properties at the phenomenological level. Their value is that they can suggest new ways to organize our search for mechanisms, as well as general organizational principles of a more abstract nature, within an explicitly dynamic context (see Fentress, 1973b, 1976).

---

[1] Remember that the use of "system" here is based upon inference from observed connections between specified inputs and outputs; in other words, no direct implication in terms of anatomically localized "mechanisms" is implied.

[2] *Class* is defined here in terms of functional endpoints; see Fentress, 1973b, 1976.

Developmental Considerations

I would next like to suggest that the question of interactive/self-organizing systems can be usefully applied to the development of neurobehavioral control systems. In this context the most obvious variable for discussion is that of developmental stage. For example, Kimmel and Eaton (Chapter Thirteen) stress the critical importance of interactions of cells with their environment for early stages of determination, but once this determination has occurred intrinsic factors predominate. Provine (Chapter Fourteen) makes a similar point. Hoyle (Chapter Two) notes that skill acquisition may depend upon feedback from the external environment and/or proprioception, but that once acquired, skilled movements may continue independently of these same sensory channels. Similarly, Marler (Chapter Twenty-Two) provides extensive evidence that, although the ontogeny of birdsong may depend upon specific sources of sensory information, the production of song in adult birds appears much more independent from these sensory inputs. A general principle worth pursuing is the increase in intrinsic control of behavioral and neurobiological networks as development proceeds. Perseverant movement stereotypies, referred to above, may be useful to pursue in this context.

The main point I wish to convey here is that the balance between intrinsic and extrinsic control factors in living systems is not a constant one. This balance may be altered not only as a function of momentary (and reversible) dynamic states of the organism but also during the course of ontogeny (and certainly phylogeny as well, although here our knowledge sinks to zero). A final question remains. Are there any guidelines by which we can combine the short-term expressions of behavior with the problem of underlying phenotypic structure?

The Construct of Processing Capacity

The idea that the organism as a whole has phenotypically set limitations in its capacity to process information has become an important focus in experimental psychology (e.g., Broad-bent, 1971). This idea of limited processing capacity, defined at the organism level, has not up to the present time made much impact on research in either neurobiology or ethology. Yet there are reasons to expect that it may be an important principle.

We all know that it is impossible to perform more than a limited number of activities at any one time. We also recognize that our ability to handle multiple tasks simultaneously depends in part upon the complexity of these tasks, and the degree to which we have practiced them. For example, it is blatantly foolish to attempt to carry on an esoteric conversation with a novice driver when he or she is faced with a complex flow of traffic; either the conversation or the driving will leave something to be desired.

My point is that phenotypically derived capacity limitations may provide important clues about the classes of behavior that are expressed under different conditions of processing load defined at the organism level. When animals or people, for example, are operating under conditions of reduced capacity, those behavioral activities which place minimal loads upon processing capacity are most likely to occur. There is considerable evidence that frequently repeated and relatively simple forms of behavior can persist under a variety of conditions (such as fatigue, stress, neural insult) which block the full expression of less well-established and/or more complex forms of behavior (e.g., Broadbent, 1971; Fentress, 1976). The concept of "displacement activity" in the ethological literature provides a case in point, for the motor patterns that appear in states of apparent conflict between major tendencies are frequently those which are relatively stereotyped and well established in the organism's response repertoire – in other words, patterns that appear to be capable of "self-organized" expression. In higher vertebrates these stereotyped output sequences appear largely under the control of subcortical (including brain stem) mechanisms (e.g., Luria, 1966; Andrew, 1974; Antelman and Szechtman, 1975; Vanderwolf, 1975; Wolgin, Cytawa, and Teitelbaum, 1975; Fentress, 1976; Valenstein, 1976).

By examining further the effects of reduced processing capacity upon different classes of behavioral expression, it may be possible not only to speak about problems of interaction and self-organization independently for integrative expression and phenotypic substrates of behavior, but to draw together aspects of dynamic processes and structural capacities at the organism level.

CONCLUSIONS

In this final chapter I have attempted to review some of the basic themes that underlie the systems and mechanism approaches to behavior and neurobiology. In the first place, it is important to recognize that these approaches provide complementary perspectives and that, when employed together, they can provide insights and conceptual connections between levels of analysis that might be missed by concentrating upon either approach alone. Second, it is necessary to explore possible abstract themes that can both guide specific research inquiry and suggest possible routes of synthesis across forms and levels of analysis. One such theme is the balance between interaction and self-organization in biological systems. The balance between these modes of organization appears to shift both as a function of integrative dynamics and developmental history. If we can find ways to link the dynamic and structural aspects of behavior together within a common framework, considerable advances in our knowledge will be forthcoming.

It is valuable from time to time to stand back from the immediacy of individual details of our particular projects and ask how we might draw these details together into a more unified conceptual framework. This can be done in part by reminding ourselves of organizational themes that appear to apply to many levels of analysis. In closing, I repeat three such themes (Figure 3). The first is the *balance* between *intrinsic and extrinsic control factors*. This can be defined in the same operational terms at levels of analysis that range from the organism and its environment to relations between subcellular components and their surround. The second theme is a more abstract refinement, that of *continuity versus discontinuity*. This theme has both spatial and temporal components, and refers to how clearly separated

one dimension of the universe we choose for study is from another. The third theme is that of *stability versus change*. For example, we have in this volume spoken of behavior and neural function from the dual perspectives of dynamic process and phenotypic structure, with a major question being how we relate these time perspectives to each other (see Cohen, Chapter Three).

In conjunction with these themes I argue that it is useful both to divide a given phenomenon into its *component dimensions* (the usual definition of analysis) *and* to examine the broader *context* within which these dimensions are expressed. This involves a two-way translation between levels of analysis rather than unilateral reductionism. This perspective can be summarized under the dual headings of component analysis and contextual analysis.

It is important to recognize that these basic organizational perspectives can be applied with equal utility at various levels of analysis. In moving from one level to another, however, our perspectives may change. For example, as we raise our level of analysis, such as can be symbolized by raising the sphere in Figure 3 within its framework, variables that were initially defined as extrinsic to a given system may be incorporated within it, dynamic properties may appear more stable because of our change in perspective, and discontinuites may be treated as a graded population. These changes in perspective are represented in the figure by shifts in the position along the various arrows in reference to the frame as the sphere is raised and lowered.

There are obviously many additional general issues that arise when we attempt to relate specific analyses, such as the question of species diversity. The dimensions outlined here are designed primarily to provide the reader with a conceptual overview that may aid these comparisons, and may also be applied to questions along such different time scales as integration and development. It is clear, for example, that the idea of interactive/self-organizing systems involves the interplay between each of the dimensions I have outlined. It is precisely at the level of *interplay between dimensions* that we may gain some of our most useful fruitful insights. Many of these

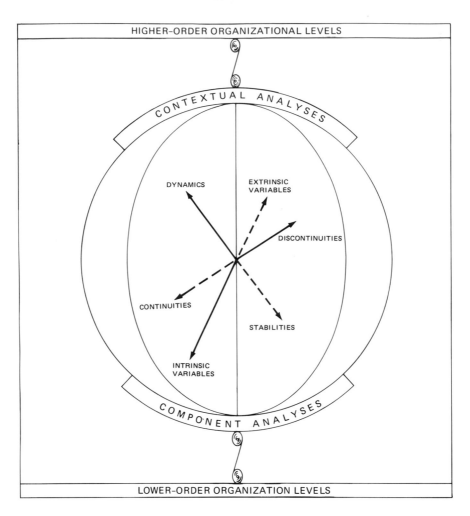

FIGURE 3.   *Summary diagram of three basic dimensions relevant to the analysis of behavioral and neural networks. These dimensions, and their relationships, can be examined both in terms of the context of their expression and the subcomponents of which they are composed. Perspectives can vary as one moves between organizational levels (represented here by movements of the sphere within the frame).*

insights will certainly come from research at the level of simple networks. These, however, will have to be related to phenomena at both higher and lower levels of organization before any truly general principles, if they can ever be found, will emerge.

Acknowledgments

Chapter Four

The work reported in this chapter was aided by grants from the National Science Foundation and the National Institutes of Health.

Chapter Seven

The work reported in this chapter was supported by National Science Foundation grant GB-40112. I thank Lynn M. Riddiford for a critical reading of the manuscript.

Chapter Twelve

The work reported in this chapter was supported by grants from the National Institutes of Health. Its preparation was supported by grant NB-07778.

Chapter Thirteen

The work reported in this chapter by one of us (R.C.E.) was supported by U.S. Public Health Service grant ES-00084. Drawings are by S. K. Sessions. We thank our associates in this work, particularly R. D. Farley and E. Schabtach; D. L. Kimmel, Jr., provided many helpful comments on the manuscript.

Chapter Fifteen

The work reported in this chapter was supported by National Institutes of Health research grants NS-09050 and MH-23254, National Science Foundation grant GZ-3120, and University of California Faculty Research Grants.

Chapter Sixteen

The work reported in this chapter was supported by National Science Foundation grant BMS 74-03572, United States Public Health Service grant 1-T01-MH-13445-01 and a grant from the Spencer Foundation.

Chapter Seventeen

The work reported in this chapter was supported by grant NS-03606 from the National Institute of Neurological Diseases and Stroke.

Chapter Nineteen

The work reported in this chapter was supported by Public Health Service research grant NS-09916 and training grant NS-05748, both from the National Institute of Neurological Diseases and Stroke.

Chapter Twenty

The work reported in this chapter was supported by National Institute of Mental Health grant MH-06686.

References

Abramson, A. S., and Lisker, L. (1965). Voice onset time in stop consonants: acoustic analysis and synthesis. *Proc. 5th Int. Congr. Acoustics* (D. E. Commins, ed.). A51, Liège.

Abramson, A. S., and Lisker, L. (1970). Discriminability along the voicing continuum: cross-language tests. *Proc. 6th Int. Congr. Phonetic Sci., Prague, 1967*, 569–573. Academia, Prague.

Adrian, E. D. (1950). The electrical activity of the mammalian olfactory bulb. *Electroencephalogr. Clin. Neurophysiol., 2*, 377–388.

Ahn, S. M., and Freeman, W. J. Steady-state and limit cycle activity of mass of neurons forming simple feedback loops: I. Lumped circuit model: II. Distributed parameter model. *Kybernetik.* (In press.)

Alawi, A. A., and Pak, W. L. (1971). On-transient of insect electroretinogram: its cellular origin. *Science (Wash. D.C.), 172*, 1055–1057.

Alawi, A. A., Jennings, V., Grossfield, J., and Pak, W. L. (1973). Phototransduction mutants of *Drosophila melanogaster*. In "The Visual System: Neurophysiology, Biophysics, and Their Clinical Applications" (G. B. Arden, ed.). Plenum, New York.

Alexandrowicz, J. S. (1932). The innervation of the heart of the crustacea: I. Decapoda. *Q. J. Microsc. Sci., 75*, 182–250.

Aloe, L., and Levi-Montalcini, R. (1972). Interrelation and dynamic activity of visceral muscle and nerve cells from insect embryos in long-term culture. *J. Neurobiol., 3*, 3–23.

Altman, J. S., and Tyrer, N. M. (1974). Insect flight as a system for the study of the development of neuronal connections. In "Experimental Analysis of Insect Behaviour" (L. Barton Browne, ed.). Springer-Verlag, New York.

Alving, B. (1968). Spontaneous activity in isolated somata of *Aplysia* pacemaker neurons. *J. Gen. Physiol., 51*, 29–45.

Andrew, R. J. (1974). Arousal and the causation of behavior. *Behaviour, 51*, 135–165.

Antelman, S. M., and Szechtman, H. (1975). Tail pinch induces eating in sated rats which appears to depend on nigrostriatal dopamine. *Science (Wash. D.C.), 189*, 731–733.

Anwyl, R., and Finlayson, L. H. (1974). Peripherally and centrally generated action potentials in neurons with both a motor and a neurosecretory function in the insect *Rhodnius prolixus. J. Comp. Physiol., 91*, 135–145.

Archer, J. The organization of aggression and fear in vertebrates. In "Perspectives in Ethology" (P. P. G. Bateson and P. H. Klopfer, eds.), Vol. 2. Plenum, New York. (In press.)

Armstrong, P. B., and Higgins, D. C. (1971). Behavioral encephalization in the bullhead embryo and its neuroanatomical correlates. *J. Comp. Neurol., 143*, 371–384.

Arnold, A. P. (1975a). The effects of castration on song development in zebra finches (*Poephila guttata*). *J. Exp. Zool., 191*, 261–278.

Arnold, A. P. (1975b). The effects of castration and androgen replacement on song, courtship, and aggression in zebra finches (*Poephila guttata*). *J. Exp. Zool., 191*, 309–326.

Arvanataki, A., and Chalazonites, N. (1968). Electrical properties and temporal organization in oscillatory neurons. In "Neurobiology of Invertebrates" (J. Salanki, ed.), 169–199. Plenum, New York.

Attneave, F. (1959). "Applications of Information Theory to Psychology." Holt, Rinehart and Winston, New York.

Baerends, G. P., Brouwer, R., and Waterbolk, H. T. (1955). Ethological studies on *Lebistes reticulatus* (Peters): I. An analysis of the male courtship pattern. *Behaviour, 8*, 334–349.

Bard, P. (1935). The effects of denervation of the genitalia on the oestrual behavior of cats. *Am. J. Physiol., 113*, 5–6.

Barillot, J. C., and Dussardier, M. (1973). Modalités de décharge des motoneurones laryngés inspiratoires dans diverses conditions expérimentales. *J. Physiol. (Paris), 66*, 593–629.

Barlow, G. W. (1968). Ethological units of behavior. In "The Central Nervous System and Fish Behavior" (D. Ingle, ed.), pp. 217–232. University of Chicago Press, Chicago.

Barlow, H. B. (1972). Single units and sensation: a neuron doctrine for perceptual psychology? *Perception, 1*, 371–394.

Barraclough, C. A., and Gorski, R. A. (1961). Evidence that the hypothalamus is responsible for androgen-induced sterility in the female rat. *Endocrinology, 68*, 68–79.

Bastian, J. (1975). Receptive fields of cerebellar cells receiving exteroceptive input in a gymnotid fish. *J. Neurophysiol., 38*, 285–300.

Bastian, J., and Esch, H. (1970). The nervous control of the indirect flight muscles of the honey bee. *Z. Vgl. Physiol., 67*, 307–324.

Bate, C. M. (1973). The mechanism of the pupal gin trap: I. Segmental gradients and the connexions of the triggering sensilla. *J. Exp. Biol., 59*, 95–107.

Bateson, P. P. G. Rules and reciprocity in behavioural development. In "Growing Points in Ethology" (R. A. Hinde and P. P. G. Bateson, eds.). Cambridge University Press, London. (In press.)

Baylor, D. A., and Fuortes, M. G. F. (1970). Electrical responses in single cones in the retina of the turtle. *J. Physiol. (Lond.), 207*, 77–92.

Baylor, D. A., and Nicholls, J. G. (1969). Chemical and electrical synaptic connexions between cutaneous mechanoreceptor neurons in the central nervous system of the leech. *J. Physiol. (Lond.), 203*, 591–609.

Baylor, D. A., Fuortes, M. G. F., and O'Bryan, P. M. (1971). Receptive fields in cones in the retina of the turtle. *J. Physiol. (Lond.), 214*, 265–294.

Becker, H. J. (1956). On X-ray-induced somatic crossing over. *Drosoph. Inf. Serv., 30*, 101–102.

Beckoff, A. (1974). Patterned motor output in the 7-day chick embryo. *Proc. Soc. Neurosci.,* 4th Annual Meeting, St. Louis, Mo. p. 136.

Beer, C. G. (1973). A view of birds. In "Minnesota Symposia Child Psychology, Vol. 7" (A. Pick, ed.), pp. 47–86. University Minnesota Press, Minneapolis.

Bennett, M. V. L. (1972). A comparison of electrically and chemically mediated transmission. In "Structure and Function of Synapses" (G. Pappas and D. Purpura, eds.), pp. 221–256. Raven, New York.

Bennett, M. V. L. (1973). Function of electrotonic junctions in embryonic and adult tissues. *Fed. Proc., 32*, 65–75.

Bentley, D. R. (1969). Intracellular activity in cricket neurons during the generation of song patterns. *Z. Vgl. Physiol., 62*, 267–283.

Bentley, D. R. (1970). A topological map of the locust flight system motor neurons. *J. Insect Physiol., 16*, 905–918.

Bentley, D. R. (1971). Genetic control of an insect neuronal network. *Science (Wash. D.C.), 174*, 1139–1141.

Bentley, D. R. (1973). Postembryonic development of insect motor systems. In "Developmental Neurobiology or Arthropods" (D. Young, ed.), pp. 147–177. Cambridge University Press, London.

Bentley, D. R. (1975). Single-gene cricket mutants: effects on behavior, sencilla, sensory neurons, and identified interneurons. *Science, 187*, 760–763.

Bentley, D. R., and Hoy, R. R. (1970). Postembryonic development of adult motor patterns in crickets: a neural analysis. *Science (Wash. D.C.), 170*, 1409–1411.

Bentley, D. R., and Hoy, R. R. (1972). Genetic control of the neuronal network generating cricket song patterns. *Anim. Behav., 20*, 478–492.

Bentley, D. R., and Hoy, R. R. (1974). The neurobiology of cricket song. *Sci. Am., 231*, 34–44.

Bentley, D. R., and Kutsch, W. (1966). The neuromuscular mechanism of stridulation in crickets (*Orthoptera: Grillidae*). *J. Exp. Biol., 45*, 151–164.

Benzer, S. (1973). Genetic dissection of behavior. *Sci. Am., 229*, 24–37.

Berman, A. M., and Berman, D. (1973). Fetal deafferentiation: the ontogenesis of movement in the absence of sensory feedback. *Exp. Neurol., 38*, 170–176.

Bernays, E. (1972). The intermediate moult (first ecdysis) of *Schistocerca gregaria* (Insecta, Orthoptera). *Zeits. Morphol. der Tiere, 71*, 160–179.

Bernstein, N. (1967). "The Coordination and Regulation of Movement." Pergamon, Oxford.

Berrill, M. (1973). The embryonic behavior of certain crustaceans. In "Studies on the Development of Behavior and the Nervous System" (G. Gottlieb, ed.), Vol. 1, "Behavioral Embryology," pp. 141–158. Academic, New York.

Berry, M. S. (1972). A system of electrically coupled small cells in the buccal ganglia of the pond snail *Planorbis corneus. J. Exp. Biol., 56,* 621–637.

Biedenbach, M. A., and Freeman, W. J. (1965). Linear domain of potential from the prepyriform cortex with respect to stimulus parameters. *Exp. Neurol., 2,* 400–417.

Bignall, K. E. (1974). Ontogeny of levels of neural organization: the righting reflex as a model. *Exp. Neurol., 42,* 566–573.

Bignall, K. E., and Schramm, L. (1974). Behavior of chronically decerebrated kittens. *Exp. Neurol., 42,* 519–531.

Billings, S. M. (1972). Development of the Mauthner cell in *Xenopus laevis:* a light and electron microscopic study of the perikaryon. *Z. Anat. Entwicklungsgesch, 136,* 168–191.

Billings, S. M., and Swartz, F. J. (1969). DNA content of Mauthner cell nuclei in *Xenopus laevis:* a spectrophotometric study. *Z. Anat. Entwicklungsgesch, 129,* 14–23.

Bittner, G. D. (1973). Degeneration and regeneration in crustacean neuromuscular systems. *Am. Zool., 13,* 379–408.

Blest, A. D. (1960). The evolution, ontogeny, and quantitative control of settling movements of some New World saturniid moths, with some comments on distance communication by honey bees. *Behaviour, 16,* 188–253.

Bliss, D. (1960). Autotomy and regeneration. In "The Physiology of Crustacea" (T. H. Waterman, ed.), pp. 561–590. Academic, New York.

Bliss, T. V. P., Gardner-Medwin, A. R., and Lømo, T. (1973). Synaptic plasticity in the hippocampal formation. In "Macromolecules and Behavior" (B. Ansell and P. B. Bradley, eds.), pp. 193–203. Macmillan, New York.

Bodenstein, D. (1957). Studies on nerve regeneration in *Periplaneta americana. J. Exp. Zool., 136,* 89–116.

Bodian, D. (1937). The structure of the vertebrate synapse. A study of axon endings on Mauthner's cell and neighboring centers in the goldfish. *J. Comp. Neurol., 68,* 117–159.

Bodian, D. (1967). Neurons, circuits, and neuroglia. In "The Neurosciences: A Study Program" (G. C. Quarton, T. Melnechuk, and F. O. Schmitt, eds.),
pp. 6–24. Rockefeller University Press, New York.

Bodian, D. (1970). A model of synaptic and behavioral ontogeny. In "The Neurosciences: Second Study Program" (F. O. Schmitt, ed.), pp. 129–140. Rockefeller University Press, New York.

Bodian, D., and Mellors, R. C. (1945). The regenerative cycle of motoneurons, with special reference to phosphatase activity. *J. Exp. Med., 81,* 469–488.

Bohm, D. (1969). Some remarks on the notion of order. Further remarks on order. In "Towards a Theoretical Biology" (C. H. Waddington, ed.), Vol. 2, pp. 18–60. Aldine, Chicago.

Bohn, H. (1965). Analyse der Regenerationsfähigkeit der Insektenextremitat durch Amputations und Transplantations versuche an Larven der afrikanischen Schabe (*Leucophaea maderae* Fabr.). IO. Mitt. Achsendetermination. *Wilhelm Roux' Arch. Entwicklungsmech. Org., 156,* 449–503.

Boll, A. C. A. (1959). A consummatory situation. The effect of eggs on the sexual behavior of the male three spined stickleback (*Gasterosteus aculeatus*). *Experientia (Basel), 15,* 115.

Boone, L. P., and Bittner, G. D. (1974). Morphological and physiological measures of trophic dependence in a crustacean muscle. *J. Comp. Physiol., 89,* 123–144.

Bosma, J., and Lind, J. (1962). Upper respiratory mechanisms of newborn infants. *Acta Paediatr. Suppl., 135,* 32–44.

Bouillaud, J. (1825). Recherches cliniques propres à démontrer que la perte de la parole correspond à la lésion des lobules antérieurs du cerveau, et à confirmer l'opinion de M. Gall sur le siège de l'orange du langage articulé. *Arch. Gén. Méd., 8,* 25–45.

Bowerman, R. F., and Larimer, J. C. (1974a). Command fibres in the circumoesophagial connectives of crayfish. I. Tonic fibres. *J. Exp. Biol., 60,* 95–118.

Bowerman, R. F., and Larimer, J. C. (1974b). Command fibres in the circumoesophagial connectives of crayfish: II. Phasic fibres. *J. Exp. Biol., 60,* 119–134.

Boynton, R. M., and Whitten, D. N. (1970). Visual adaptation in monkey cones: recording of late receptor potentials. *Science (Wash. D.C.), 170,* 1423–1426.

Braitenberg, V. (1967). Patterns of projection in the visual system of the fly: I. Retina-lamina projections. *Exp. Brain Res., 3,* 271–298.

Braitenberg, V., and Atwood, R. P. (1958). Morphological observations on the cerebellar cortex. *J. Comp. Neurol., 109,* 1–33.

Brenner, S. (1974). The genetics of *Caenorhabditis elegans. Genetics, 77,* 71–94.

Broadbent, D. E. (1971). "Decision and Stress." Academic, New York.

Brock, L. G., Coombs, J. S., and Eccles, J. C. (1952). The recording of potentials from motoneurons with an intracellular electrode. *J. Physiol. (Lond.), 117,* 431–460.

Brodal, A., and Courville, J. (1973). Cerebellar corticonuclear projection in the cat crus: II. An experimental study with silver methods. *Brain Res., 50,* 1–23.

Brower, L. P. (1969). Ecological chemistry. *Sci. Am., 220,* 22–29.

Brown, G. S. (1969). "Laws of Form." Allen & Unwin, London.

Brown, J. L. (1974). Brain stimulation parameters affecting vocalization in birds. In "Birds, Brain and Behavior" (I. J. Goodman and M. W. Schein, eds.), pp. 87–99. Academic, New York.

Brown, K. T., and Wiesel, T. N. (1961). Localization of origin of electroretinogram components by intraretinal recording in the intact cat eye. *J. Physiol. (Lond.), 158,* 257–280.

Brown, R. (1973). "A First Language, the Early Stages." Harvard University Press, Cambridge, Mass.

Brown, T. G. (1914). On the nature of the fundamental activity of the nervous centers, together with an analysis of the conditioning of rhythmic activity in progression and theory of the evolution of function in the nervous system. *J. Physiol. (Lond.), 48,* 18–46.

Bruggencate, G. ten, Teichmann, R., and Weller, E. (1972). Neuronal activity in the lateral vestibular nucleus of the cat: III. Inhibitory actions of cerebellar Purkinje cells evoked via mossy and climbing fiber afferents. *Pfluegers Arch. Eur. J. Physiol., 337,* 147–162.

Bruke, R. E., Levine, D. N., Zajac, F. E., III, Tsairis, P., and Engel, W. K. (1971). Mammalian motor units: physiological–histochemical correlation in three types in cat gastrocnemius. *Science (Wash. D.C.), 174,* 709–712.

Bruner, J., and Kennedy, D. (1970). Habituation: occurrence at a neuromuscular junction. *Science (Wash. D.C.), 169,* 92–94.

Bryant, P. J. (1974). Determination and pattern formation in the imaginal discs of *Drosophila.* In "Current Topics in Developmental Biology" (A. A. Moscona and A. Monroy, eds.), Vol. 8, pp. 41–80. Academic, New York.

Bulliere, D. (1970). Interpretation des regenerats multiples chez les Insectes. *J. Embryol. exp. Morph., 23,* 337–357.

Bullock, T. H. (1958). Parameters of integrative action of the nervous system at the neuronal level. In "Symposium on Ultramicroscopic Structure and Function of Nerve Cells" (H. Fernandez-Moran and R. Brown, eds.), *Exp. Cell Res. Suppl., 5,* 323–337.

Bullock, T. H. (1959). The neuron doctrine and electrophysiology. *Science (Wash. D.C.), 129,* 997–1002.

Bullock, T. H. (1961). The origins of patterned nervous discharge. *Behaviour, 17,* 48–59.

Bullock, T. H. (1965). Strategies for blind physiologists with elephantine problems. *Symp. Soc. Exp. Biol., 20,* 1–10.

Bullock, T. H. (1974). Comparisons between vertebrates and invertebrates in nervous organization. In "The Neurosciences: Third Study Program" (F. O. Schmitt and F. G. Worden, eds.). MIT Press, Cambridge, Mass.

Bullock, T. H., and Horridge, G. A. (1965). "Structure and Function in the Nervous Systems of Invertebrates." W. H. Freeman, San Francisco.

Bullock, T. H., and Terzuolo, C. A. (1957). Diverse forms of activity in the somata of spontaneous and integrating ganglion cells. *J. Physiol. (Lond.), 128,* 341–364.

Burns, B. D. (1958). "The Mammalian Cerebral Cortex." Williams & Wilkins, Baltimore, Md.

Burrows, M. (1973). The role of delayed excitation in the co-ordination of some metathoracic flight motoneurons of a locust. *J. Comp. Physiol., 83,* 135–164.

Burrows, M. (1975). (In preparation).

Burrows, M., and Horridge, G. A. (1974). The organization of inputs to motoneurons of the locust metathoracic leg. *Philos. Trans. R. Soc. Lond. B Biol. Sci., 269,* 49–95.

Burrows, M., and Hoyle, G. (1973). Neural mechanisms underlying behavior in the locust *Schistocerca gregaria*: III. Topography of limb motorneurons in the metathoracic ganglion. *J. Neurobiol., 4,* 167–186.

Bush, B. M. H., and Cannone, A. J. (1973). A stretch reflex in crabs evoked by muscle receptor potentials in non-impulsive afferents. *J. Physiol. (Lond.), 232,* 95.

Butcher, R. W., Robison, G. A., and Sutherland, E. W. (1972). Cyclic-AMP and hormone action. In "Biochemical Actions of Hormones" (G. Litwack, ed.), pp. 21–54. Academic, New York.

Butler, R., and Horridge, G. A. (1973). The electrophysiology of the retina of *Periplaneta americana* L. *J. Comp. Physiol., 83,* 263–278.

Capranica, R. R. (1965). "The Evoked Vocal Response of the Bullfrog: A Study of Communication by Sound." MIT Press, Cambridge, Mass.

Car, A. (1970). La Commande corticale du centre déglutiteur bulbaire. *J. Physiol. (Paris), 62,* 361–386.

Car, A. (1973). La Commande corticale de la déglutition: II. Point d'impact bulbaire de la voie corticifuge déglutitrice. *J. Physiol. (Paris), 66,* 553–576.

Carew, T. J., and Kandel, E. R. (1973). Acquisition and retention of long-term habituation in *Aplysia*: correlation of behavioral and cellular processes. *Science (Wash. D.C.), 182,* 1158–1160.

Carew, T. J., Castellucci, V. F., and Kandel, E. R. (1971). An analysis of dishabituation and sensitization of the gill-withdrawal reflex in *Aplysia. Int. J. Neurosci., 2,* 79–98.

Carew, T. J., Pinsker, H. M., and Kandel, E. R. (1972). Long-term habituation of a defensive withdrawal reflex in *Aplysia. Science (Wash. D.C.), 175,* 451–454.

Carmichael, L. (1926). The development of behavior in vertebrates experimentally removed from the influence of external stimulation. *Psychol. Rev., 33,* 51–58.

Carmichael, L. (1970). The onset and early development of behavior. In "Carmichael's Manual of Child Psychology" (P. H. Mussen, ed.), Vol. 1, pp. 447–563. Wiley, New York.

Carpenter, D. O., and Rudomin, P. (1973). The organization of primary afferent depolarization in the isolated spinal cord of the frog. *J. Physiol. (Lond.), 229,* 471–493.

Cate, J. ten (1965). Automatic activity of the locomotor centres of the lumbar cord in lizards. *J. Exp. Biol., 43,* 181–184.

Cerf, J. A., and Chacko, L. W. (1958). Retrograde reaction in motor neuron dendrites following ventral root section in the frog. *J. Comp. Neurol., 109,* 205–216.

Chang, J. J., Gelperin, A., and Johnson, F. H. (1974). Intracellularly injected aequorin detects transmembrane calcium flux during action potentials in an identified neuron from the terrestrial slug *Limax maximus. Brain Res., 77,* 431–442.

Chappel, R. L., and Dowling, J. E. (1972). Neuronal organization of the median ocellus by the dragonfly: I. Intracellular electrical activity. *J. Gen. Physiol., 60,* 121–147.

Chase, R. (1974). The initiation and conduction of action potentials in the optic nerve of *Trituria. J. Exp. Biol., 60,* 721–734.

Chen, J. S., and Levi-Montalcini, R. (1969). Axonal outgrowth and cell migration *in vitro* from nervous system of cockroach embryos. *Science (Wash. D.C.), 166,* 631–632.

Child, C. M. (1941). "Patterns and Problems of Development." University of Chicago Press, Chicago.

Chomsky, N. (1967). Appendix A: The formal nature of language. In "Biological Foundations of Language" (E. H. Lenneberg, ed.). Wiley, New York.

Chow, K.-L., and Leiman, A. L. (1972). The photosensitive organs of crayfish and brightness learning. *Behav. Biol., 7,* 25–35.

Clare, M. H., and Landau, W. M. (1964). Fusimotor function: V. Reflex reinforcement under fusimotor block in normal subjects. *Arch. Neurol., 10,* 123–127.

Clendenin, M. A., Szumski, A. J., and Astrug, J. (1974). Proprioceptive influences on inferior olivary neurons during phasic reflex movement in cat. *Exp. Neurol., 44,* 198–208.

Clever, U. (1958). Untersuchungen zur Zelldifferenzierung und Musterbildung der Sinnesorgane und des Nervensystems in Wachsmottenflügel. *Z. Morphol. Oekol. Tiere, 47,* 201–248.

Cloarec, A. (1972). A study of the postural variations in the foreleg of *Ranatra linearis* (Insecta, Heteroptera). *Behaviour, 48,* 89–110.

Coghill, G. E. (1929). "Anatomy and the Problem of Behavior." Cambridge University Press, London. (Reprinted in 1964 by Hafner, New York.)

Cohen, M. J. (1967a). Correlations between structure, function and RNA metabolism in central neurons of insects. In "Invertebrate Nervous Systems" (C. A. Wiersma, ed.), pp. 65–78. University of Chicago Press, Chicago.

Cohen, M. J. (1967b). Some cellular correlates of behavior controlled by an insect ganglion. In "Chemistry of Learning" (W. C. Corning and S. C. Rotner, eds.), pp. 407–424. Plenum, New York.

Cohen, M. J. (1970). A comparison of invertebrate and vertebrate central neurons. In "The Neurosciences: Second Study Program" (F. O. Schmitt, ed.). Rockefeller University Press, New York.

Cohen, M. J. (1974). Trophic interactions in excitable systems of invertebrates. *Ann. N.Y. Acad. Sci., 228,* 364–380.

Cohen, M. J., and Jacklett, J. W. (1965a). The functional organization of motor neurons in an insect ganglion. *Philos. Trans. R. Soc. Lond. B Biol. Sci., 252,* 561–569.

Cohen, M. J., and Jacklett, J. W. (1965b). Neurons of insects: RNA changes during injury and regeneration. *Science (Wash. D.C.), 148,* 1237–1239.

Cohen, M. J., and Jacklett, J. W. (1967). The functional organization of motor neurons in an insect ganglion. *Philos. Trans. R. Soc. Lond. B Biol. Sci., 252,* 561–569.

Colonnier, M. (1968). Synaptic patterns on different cell types in the different laminae of the cat visual cortex. An electron microscopic study. *Brain Res., 9,* 268–287.

Cooke, J. (1972). Properties of the primary organization field in the embryo of *Xenopus laevis*: II. Positional information for axial organization in embryos with two head organizers. *J. Embryol. Exp. Morphol., 28,* 27–46.

Corda, M., Eklund, G., and Euler, C. von (1965). External intercostal and phrenic α motor responses to changes in respiratory load. *Acta Physiol. Scand., 63,* 391–400.

Corner, M. A., Bakhuis, W. L., and Van Wingerten, C. (1973). Sleep and wakefulness during early life in the domestic chicken, and their relationship to hatching and embryonic motility. In "Studies on the Development of Behavior and the Nervous System" (G. Gottlieb, ed.), Vol. 1, "Behavioral Embryology," pp. 245–279. Academic, New York.

Corning, W. C., Dyal, J. A., and Willows, A. O. D., eds. (1973a). "Invertebrate Learning: Protozoans Through Annelids," Vol. 1. Plenum, New York.

Corning, W. C., Dyal, J. A., and Willows, A. O. D., eds. (1973b). "Invertebrate Learning: Arthropods and Gastropod Mollusks," Vol. 2. Plenum, New York.

Corning, W. C., Dyal, J. A., and Willows, A. O. D., eds. (1973c). "Invertebrate Learning," Vol. 3, "Cephalopods and Echinoderms." Plenum, New York.

Cotman, C. W., Matthews, D. A., Taylor, D., and Lynch, C. (1974). Synaptic rearrangement in the dentate gyrus: histochemical evidence of adjustments after lesions in immature and adult rats. *Proc. Natl. Acad. Sci. U.S.A., 70,* 3473–3477.

Counce, S., and Waddington, C. H. (1973). "Developmental Systems: Insects," Vols. 1 and 2. Academic, New York.

Courville, J. (1966). Somatotopical organization of the projection from nucleus interpositus anterior of the cerebellum to the red nucleus. An experimental study in the cat with silver impregnation methods. *Exp. Brain Res., 2,* 191–215.

Courville, J., Diakiw, N., and Brodal, A. (1973). Cerebellar corticonuclear projection in the cat. The paramedian lobule. An experimental study with silver methods. *Brain Res., 50,* 25–45.

Cowan, W. M. (1970). Anterograde and retrograde transneuronal degeneration in the central and peripheral nervous system. In "Contemporary Research Methods in Neuroanatomy" (W. J. H. Nauta and S. O. E. Ebbesson, eds.), pp. 217–251. Springer, New York.

Crain, S. M. (1966). Development of organotypic bioelectric activities in central nervous tissues during maturation in culture. *Int. Rev. Neurobiol., 9,* 1–43.

Crain, S. M. (1970). Bioelectric interactions between cultured fetal rodent spinal cord and skeletal muscle after innervation *in vitro*. *J. Exp. Zool., 173,* 353–370.

Crain, S. M. (1974). Tissue culture models of developing brain function. In "Studies on the Development of Behavior and the Nervous System" (G. Gottlieb, ed.), Vol. 2, "Aspects of Neurogenesis," pp. 69–114. Academic, New York.

Crain, S. M., Bornstein, M. B., and Peterson, E. R. (1968). Maturation of cultured embryonic CNS tissues during chronic exposure to agents which prevent bioelectric activity. *Brain Res., 8,* 363–372.

Crick, F. H. C. (1970). Diffusion in embryogenesis. *Nature (Lond.), 225,* 420–422.

Crick, F. H. C., and Lawrence, P. A. (1975). Compartments and polyclones in insect development. *Science (Wash. D.C.), 189,* 340–347.

Crossland, W. J., Cowan, W. M., Rogers, L. A., and Kelly, J. P. (1974). The specifications of the retinotectal projection in the chick. *J. Comp. Neurol., 155,* 127–164.

Crow, J. F., and Kimura, M. (1970). "An Introduction to Population Genetics Theory." Harper & Row, New York.

Curio, E. (1967). Die Adaptation einer Handlung ohne den zugehörigen Bewegungsablauf. *Verh. Dtsch. Zool. Ges.,* 153–163.

Cutting, E. J., and Eimas, P. D. (1975). Phonetic feature analyzers and the processing of speech in infants. In "The Role of Speech in Language" (J. F. Kavanagh and J. E. Cutting, eds.). MIT Press, Cambridge, Mass.

Dando, M. R., and Selverston, A. I. (1972). Command fibres from the supra-oesophageal ganglion to the stomatogastric ganglion in *Panulirus argus*. *J. Comp. Physiol., 78,* 138–175.

Darwin, C. (1872). "The Expression of the Emotions in Man and Animals." John Murray, London.

Davis, W. J. (1969a). The neural control of swimmeret beating in the lobster. *J. Exp. Biol., 50,* 99–118.

Davis, W. J. (1969b). Reflex organization in the swimmeret system of the lobster: I. Intrasegmental reflexes. *J. Exp. Biol., 51,* 547–563.

Davis, W. J. (1969c). Reflex organization in the swimmeret system of the lobster: II. Reflex dynamics. *J. Exp. Biol., 51,* 565–573.

Davis, W. J. (1969d). *Proc. R. Soc. Lond. B Biol. Sci., 170,* 435–456.

Davis, W. J. (1970). Motoneuron morphology and synaptic contacts: determination by intracellular dye injection. *Science (Wash. D.C.), 168,* 1358–1360.

Davis, W. J. (1971). Functional significance of motoneuron size and soma position in swimmeret system of the lobster. *J. Neurophysiol., 34,* 274–288.

Davis, W. J. (1973a). Development of locomotor patterns in the absence of peripheral sense organs and muscles. *Proc. Natl. Acad. Sci. U.S.A., 70,* 954–958.

Davis, W. J. (1973b). Neuronal organization and ontogeny in the lobster swimmeret system. In "Control of Posture and Locomotion" (R. B. Stein, K. G. Pearson, R. S. Smith, and J. B. Redford, eds.). Plenum, New York.

Davis, W. J. Plasticity in the invertebrates. In "Research Approaches to Learning and Memory" (E. L. Bennett and M. R. Rosenzweig, eds.). MIT Press, Cambridge, Mass. (In press.)

Davis, W. J., and Davis, K. B. (1973). Ontogeny of a simple locomotor system; role of the periphery in the development of central nervous circuitry. *Am. Zool., 13,* 409–425.

Davis, W. J., and Kennedy, D. (1972). Command interneurons controlling swimmeret movements in the lobster: I. Types of effects on motoneurons. *J. Neurophysiol., 35,* 1–12.

Davis, W. J., and Mpitsos, G. J. (1971). Behavioral choice and habituation in the marine mollusk *Pleurobranchaea californica* MacFarland (Gastropoda, Opisthobranchia). *Z. Vgl. Physiol., 75,* 207–232.

Davis, W. J., Mpitsos, G. J., and Pinneo, J. M. (1974a). The behavioral hierarchy of the mollusk *Pleurobranchaea*. I. The dominant position of feeding behavior. *J. Comp. Physiol., 90,* 207–224.

Davis, W. J., Mpitsos, G. J., and Pinneo, J. M. (1974b). The behavioral hierarchy of the mollusk *Pleurobranchaea*: II. Hormonal suppression of feeding associated with egg-laying. *J. Comp. Physiol., 90,* 225–243.

Davis, W. J., Siegler, M. V. S., and Mpitsos, G. J. (1973). Distributed neuronal oscillators and efference copy in the feeding system of *Pleurobranchaea*. *J. Neurophysiol., 36,* 258–274.

Davis, W. J., Mpitsos, G. J., Siegler, M. V. S., Pinneo, J. M., and Davis, K. B. (1974). Neuronal substrates of behavioral hierarchies and associative learning in *Pleurobranchaea*. *Am. Zool., 14,* 1037–1050.

Davis, W. J., Pinneo, J. M., Mpitsos, G. J., and Ram, J. L. (1976). The behavioral hierarchy of the mollusk *Pleurobranchaea*: III. The effects of food satiation on the dominance of feeding behavior. (In preparation.)

Decker, J. D. (1967). Motility of the turtle embryo, *Chelydra serpentia*. *Science (Wash. D. C.), 157,* 952–954.

Delgado, J. M. R. (1959). Prolonged stimulation of brain in awake monkeys. *J. Neurophysiol., 22,* 458–475.

Delius, J. D. (1969). Stochastic analysis of the maintenance behavior of skylarks. *Behaviour, 33,* 137–178.

DeLong, M. (1971). Central patterning of movement. *Neurosci. Res. Program Bull., 9,* 10–30.

Demski, L. S., and Gerald, J. W. (1974). Sound production and other behavioral effects of midbrain stimulation in free-swimming toadfish, *Opsanus beta*. *Brain Behav. Evol., 9,* 41–59.

Dennis, M. J. (1967). Electrophysiology of the visual system in a nudibranch mollusc. *J. Neurophysiol., 30,* 1439–1465.

Desclin, J. C., and Escubi, J. (1974). Effects of 3-acetylpyridine on the central nervous system of the rat, as demonstrated by silver methods. *Brain Res., 77,* 349–364.

Dethier, V. G. (1966). Insects and the concept of motivation. *Nebr. Symp. Motiv.,* 105–136.

Diamond, J. (1971). The Mauthner cell. In "Fish Physiology" (W. S. Hoar and D. J. Randall, eds.), Vol. 5, pp. 265–346. Academic, New York.

Dietrichson, P. (1971). Phasic ankle reflex in spasticity and Parkinsonian rigidity. *Acta Neurol. Scand., 47,* 22–51.

DiStefano, J. J., Stubberud, A. R., and Williams, I. J. (1967). "Feedback and Control Systems." McGraw-Hill, New York.

Dittus, W. P., and Lemon, R. E. (1970). Auditory feedback in the singing of cardinals. *Ibis, 112,* 544–548.

Dixon, J. S., and Cronly-Dillon, J. R. (1972). The fine structure of the developing retina in *Xenopus laevis*. *J. Embryol. Exp. Morphol., 28,* 659–666.

Dorman, M. F. (1974). Auditory evoked potential correlates of speech and discrimination. *Percept. Psychophys., 15,* 215–220.

Dorsett, D. A. (1974). Neuronal homologies and the

control of branchial tuft movements in two species of *Tritonia*. *J. Exp. Biol., 61,* 639–654.

Dorsett, D. A., Willows, A. O. D., and Hoyle, G. (1973). The neuronal basis of behavior in *Tritonia*: IV. The central origin of a fixed action pattern demonstrated in the isolated brain. *J. Neurobiol., 3,* 287–300.

Doty, R. W. (1951). Influence of stimulus pattern on reflex deglutition. *Am. J. Physiol., 166,* 142–158.

Doty, R. W. (1960). Neural hierarchies and behavior. In "The Central Nervous System and Behavior" (M. A. B. Brazier, ed.), pp. 414–421. Josiah Macy, Jr. Foundation, New York.

Doty, R. W. (1967). On butterflies in the brain. In "Electrophysiology of the Central Nervous System" (V. S. Rusinov, ed.), pp. 96–103. Science Press, Moscow. (Translation available: Plenum, New York, 1970.)

Doty, R. W. (1968). Neural organization of deglutition. In "Handbook of Physiology, Sect. 6, Alimentary Canal" (C. F. Code and C. L. Prosser, eds.), Vol. IV. American Psychological Society, Washington, D.C.

Doty, R. W. (1969). Electrical stimulation of the brain in behavioral context. *Annu. Rev. Psychol., 20,* 289–320.

Doty, R. W. Consciousness from neurons. *Acta Neurobiol. Exp. (Warsaw).* (In press.)

Doty, R. W., and Bosma, J. F. (1956). An electromyographic analysis of reflex deglutition. *J. Neurophysiol., 19,* 44–60.

Doty, R. W., Richmond, W. H., and Storey, A. T. (1967). Effect of medullary lesions on coordination of deglutition. *Exp. Neurol., 17,* 91–106.

Dowling, J. E. (1970). Organization of vertebrate retinas. *Invest. Ophthalmol., 9,* 655–680.

Dowling, J. E. (1974). Synaptic arrangements in the vertebrate retina: the photoreceptor synapse. In "Synaptic Transmission and Neuronal Interaction" (M. V. L. Bennett, ed.), pp. 87–103. Raven, New York.

Dowling, J. E., and Ripps, H. (1971). S-potentials in the skate retina. *J. Gen. Physiol., 58,* 162–189.

Dowling, J. E., and Ripps, H. (1972). Adaptation in skate photoreceptors. *J. Gen. Physiol., 60,* 698–719.

Dowling, J. E., and Ripps, H. (1973). Effect of magnesium on horizontal cell activity in the skate retina. *Nature (Lond.), 242,* 101–103.

Dowling, J. E., and Werblin, F. S. (1969). Organization of retina of the mudpuppy, *Necturus maculosus*: I. Synaptic structure. *J. Neurophysiol., 32,* 315–338.

Dowling, J. E., and Werblin, F. S. (1971). Synaptic organization of the vertebrate retina. *Vision Res. Suppl., 3,* 1–15.

Drachman, D. B., and Sokoloff, L. (1966). The role of movement in embryonic joint formation. *Dev. Biol., 14,* 401–420.

Drescher, W. (1960). Regenerationsversuche am Gehirn von *Periplaneta americana*. *Z. Morphol. Öekol. Tiere, 48,* 576–649.

Eaton, R. C., and Farley, R. D. (1973). Development of the Mauthner neurons in embryos and larvae of the zebra fish, *Brachydanio rerio*. *Copeia, 1973,* 673–683.

Eaton, R. C., and Farley, R. D. (1974). Growth and the reduction of depensation of zebra fish, *Brachydanio rerio*, reared in the laboratory. *Copeia, 1974,* 204–209.

Eaton, R. C., and Farley, R. D. (1975). Mauthner neuron field potential in newly hatched larvae of the zebra fish. *J. Neurophysiol., 38,* 502–512.

Eccles, J. C. (1946). Synaptic potentials of motoneurons. *J. Neurophysiol., 9,* 87–120.

Eccles, J. C. (1964). "The Physiology of Synapses." Springer-Verlag, Berlin.

Eccles, J. C. (1973). The cerebellum as a computer: patterns in space and time. *J. Physiol. (Lond.), 229,* 1–32.

Eccles, J. C., and Jaeger, J. C. (1958). The relationship between the mode of operation and the dimensions of the junctional regions at synapses and motor end-organs. *Proc. R. Soc. Lond. B Biol. Sci., 148,* 38–56.

Eccles, J. C., Ito, M., and Szentágothai, J. (1967). "The Cerebellum as a Neuronal Machine." Springer-Verlag, New York.

Eccles, J. C., Katz, B., and Kuffler, S. W. (1941). Nature of the "endplate potential" in curarized muscle. *J. Neurophysiol., 4,* 362–387.

Eccles, J. C., Llinás, R., and Sasaki, K. (1966). The excitatory synaptic action of climbing fibres on the Purkinje cells of the cerebellum. *J. Physiol. (Lond.), 182,* 268–296.

Eckert, R. (1972). Bioelectric control of ciliary activity. *Science (Wash. D.C.), 176,* 473–481.

Edwards, J. S. (1967). Some questions for the insect nervous system. In "Insects and Physiology" (J. W. L. Beament and J. E. Treherne, eds.), pp. 163–174. Oliver & Boyd, Edinburgh.

Edwards, J. S. (1969). Postembryonic development and regeneration of the insect nervous system. *Adv. Insect Physiol., 6,* 97–137.

Edwards, J. S. (1972). Limb loss and regeneration in two crabs: the king crab *Paralithodes* camtschatica and the tanner crab *Chionoecetes bairdi*. *Acta Zool. (Stockh.)*, *53*, 105–112.

Edwards, J. S., and Palka, J. (1971). Neural regeneration: delayed formation of central contacts by insect sensory cells. *Science (Wash. D.C.)*, *172*, 591–594.

Edwards, J. S., and Palka, J. (1974). The cerci and abdominal giant fibres of the house cricket *Acheta domesticus*: I. Anatomy and physiology of normal adults. *Proc. R. Soc. Lond. B Biol. Sci.*, *185*, 83–121.

Edwards, J. S., and Sahota, T. S. (1967). Regeneration of a sensory system: the formation of central connections by normal and transplanted cerci of the house cricket *Acheta domesticus*. *J. Exp. Zool.*, *166*, 387–396.

Eigen, M. (1971). Molecular self-organization and the early stages of evolution. *Q. Rev. Biophys.*, *4*, 149–212.

Eimas, P. D. (1975). Speech perception in early infancy. In "Infant Perception" (L. B. Cohen and P. Salapatek, eds.). Academic, New York. (In press.)

Eimas, P. D., Siqueland, E. R., Jusczyk, P., and Vigorito, J. M. (1971). Speech perception in infants. *Science (Wash. D.C.)*, *171*, 303–306.

Elsner, N. (1968). Die neuromuskularen Grundlagen des Werbeverhaltens der roten Kenlenheuschrecke *Gomphocerippus rufus* (L.). *Z. Vgl. Physiol.*, *60*, 308–350.

Elsner, N. (1968). Kommandofasern im Zentralnervensystem der Heuschrecke *Gastrimargus africanus* (Oedipodinae). *Zool. Anz.*, *33*, 465–471.

Elsner, N. (1973). The central nervous control of courtship behavior in the grasshopper *Gomphocerippus rufus* (L.) (Orthoptera: Acrididae). In "Neurobiology of Invertebrates" (J. Salanki, ed.). Akadémiai Kiadó, Budapest.

Elsner, N. (1975). Neuroethology of sound production in biomthocerine grasshoppers (Orthoptera: Acrididae): II. Neuromuscular activity underlying stridulation. *J. Comp. Physiol.*, *97*, 291–322.

Ephrussi, B., and Weiss, M. C. (1969). Hybrid somatic cells. *Sci. Am.*, *220*, 26–35.

Evarts, E. V. (1971). Feedback and corollary discharge: a merging of the concepts. *Neurosci. Res. Program Bull.*, *9*, 86–112.

Evarts, E. V. (1973). Brain mechanisms in movement. *Sci. Am.*, *229*, 96–103.

Evarts, E. V., and Tanji, J. (1974). Gating of motor cortex reflexes by prior instruction. *Brain Res.*, *71*, 479–494.

Evoy, W. H., and Kennedy, D. (1967). The central nervous organization underlying control of antagonistic muscles in the crayfish: I. Types of command fibers. *J. Exp. Zool.*, *165*, 223–238.

Evoy, W. H., Kennedy, D., and Wilson, D. M. (1967). Discharge patterns of neurons supplying tonic abdominal flexor muscles in the crayfish. *J. Exp. Biol.*, *46*, 393–411.

Ewert, J.-P. (1967a). Aktivierung der verhaltensfolge beim Beutefang der Erdkröte (*Bufo bufo* L.) durch elektrische mittelhirn-reizung. *Z. Vgl. Physiol.*, *54*, 455–481.

Ewert, J.-P. (1967b). Untersuchungen über die Anteile zentralnervöser Aktionen an der taxisspezifischen Ermüdung beim Beutefang der Erdkröte (*Bufo bufo* L.). *Z. Vgl. Physiol.*, *57*, 263–398.

Ewing, A., and Hoyle, G. (1965). Neuronal mechanisms underlying sound production in a cricket: *Acheta domesticus*. *J. Exp. Biol.*, *43*, 139–153.

Faaborg-Anderson, K. (1957). Electromyographic investigation of intrinsic laryngeal muscles in humans. *Acta Physiol. Scand. Suppl.*, *41*, 140.

Faber, D. S., and Korn, H. (1973). A neuronal inhibition mediated electrically. *Science (Wash. D.C.)*, *179*, 577–578.

Fentress, J. C. (1966). Science: philosophical problems. *Science (Wash. D.C.)*, *151*, 935–936.

Fentress, J. C. (1967a). Contributions to discussion. In "Mathematical Challenges to the Neo-Darwinian Interpretation of Evolution" (P. S. Moorhead and M. M. Kaplan, eds.), p. 32. Wistar Institute Press, Philadelphia.

Fentress, J. C. (1967b). Observations on the behavioral development of a hand-reared male timber wolf. *Am. Zool.*, *7*, 339–351.

Fentress, J. C. (1968a). Interrupted ongoing behaviour in two species of vole (*Microtus agrestis* and *Clethrionomys britannicus*): I. Response as a function of preceding activity and the context of an apparently "irrelevant" motor pattern. *Anim. Behav.*, *16*, 135–153.

Fentress, J. C. (1968b). Interrupted ongoing behaviour in two species of vole (*Microtus agrestis* and *Clethrionomys britannicus*): II. Extended analysis of motivational variables underlying fleeing and grooming behaviour. *Anim. Behav.*, *16*, 154–167.

Fentress, J. C. (1972). Development and patterning of movement sequences in inbred mice. In "The Biology of Behavior" (J. A. Kiger, ed.). Oregon State University Press, Corvallis, Ore.

Fentress, J. C. (1973a). Development of grooming in mice with amputated forelimbs. *Science (Wash. D.C.)*, *179*, 704–705.

Fentress, J. C. (1973b). Specific and nonspecific factors in the causation of behaviour. In "Perspectives in Ethology" (P. P. G. Bateson and P. H. Klopfer, eds.), pp. 155–224. Plenum, New York.

Fentress, J. C. Dynamic boundaries of patterned behaviour: interaction and self-organization. In "Growing Points in Ethology" (R. A. Hinde and P. P. G. Bateson, eds.). Cambridge University Press, London. (In press.)

Fentress, J. C., and Doty, R. W. (1971). Effect of tetanization and enucleation upon excitability of visual pathways in squirrel monkeys and cats. *Exp. Neurol., 30,* 535–554.

Fentress, J. C., and Stilwell, F. P. (1973). Grammar of a movement sequence in inbred mice. *Nature (Lond.), 244,* 52–53.

Fields, H. L., Evoy, W. H., and Kennedy, D. (1967). Reflex role played by efferent control of an invertebrate stretch receptor. *J. Neurophysiol., 30,* 859–874.

Finlayson, L. H. (1956). Normal and induced degeneration of abdominal muscles during metamorphosis in the Lepidoptera. *Q. J. Microsc. Sci., 97,* 215–234.

Fischbach, G. D. (1972). Synapse formation between dissociated nerve and muscle cells in low density cell cultures. *Dev. Biol., 28,* 407–429.

Fishman, P. (1975). A study of dendritic form in identified lamprey neurons. Ph.D. dissertation, Yale University, New Haven, Conn.

Flerko, B. (1971). Steroid hormones and the differentiation of the central nervous system. In "Current Topics in Experimental Endocrinology" (L. Martini and V. H. T. James, eds.), Vol. 1, pp. 42–81. Academic, New York.

Flourens, P. (1842). "Recherches expérimentales sur les propriétés et les fonctions du système nerveux dans les animaux vertébrés." Bailliere, Paris.

Foelix, R. F., and Oppenheim, R. W. (1973). Synaptogenesis in the avian embryo: ultrastructure and possible behavioral correlates. In "Studies on the Development of Behavior and the Nervous System" (G. Gottlieb, ed.), Vol. 1, "Behavioral Embryology," pp. 103–139. Academic, New York.

Forssberg, H., and Grillner, S. (1973). The locomotion of the acute spinal cat injected with clonidine i.v. *Brain Res., 50,* 184–186.

Freeman, W. J. (1972a). Measurement of open-loop responses to electrical stimulation to olfactory bulb of cat. *J. Neurophysiol., 35,* 745–761.

Freeman, W. J. (1972b). Measurement of oscillatory responses to electrical stimulation in olfactory bulb of cat. *J. Neurophysiol., 35,* 762–779.

Freeman, W. J. (1972c). Depth recording of averaged evoked potential of olfactory bulb. *J. Neurophysiol., 35,* 769–780.

Freeman, W. J. (1974). Relation of glomerular neuronal activity to glomerular transmission attenuation. *Brain Res., 65,* 91–107.

Freeman, W. J. (1975). "Mass Action in the Nervous System." Academic, New York.

French, V., and Bullière, D. (1975a). Nouvelles donnés sur la détermination de la position des cellules épidermiques sur un appendice de Blatte. *C. R. Hebd. Séances Acad. Sci., 280,* 53–56.

French, V., and Bullière, D. (1975b). Etude de la détermination de la position des cellules: ordonnance des cellules autour d'un appendice de Blatte; démonstration du concept de génératrice. *C. R. Hebd. Séances Acad. Sci., 280,* 295–298.

Friesen, O. (1974). Synaptic interactions and burst patterns in the cardiac ganglion of the spiny lobster. Ph.D. dissertation, University of California, San Diego, Calif.

Frisch, K. von (1967). "The Dance Language and Orientation of Bees." Harvard University Press, Cambridge, Mass.

Fritsch, G. and Hitzig, E. (1870). Über die elektrische Erregbarkeit des Grosshirns. *Arch. Anat. Physiol. (Leipzig), 37,* 300–332.

Frömming, E. (1952). Über die Nahrung von *Limax maximus. Anz. Schaedlingskd., 25,* 41–43.

Furshpan, E. J., and Furukawa, T. (1962). Intracellular and extracellular responses of the several regions of the Mauthner cell of the goldfish. *J. Neurophysiol., 25,* 732–771.

Furshpan, E. J., and Potter, D. D. (1959). Transmission at the giant motor synapses of the crayfish. *J. Physiol. (Lond.), 145,* 289–325.

Furukawa, T., and Furshpan, E. J. (1963). Two inhibitory mechanisms in the Mauthner neurons of the goldfish. *J. Neurophysiol., 26,* 140–176.

Gain, W. A. (1891). Notes on the food of some of the British mullusks. *J. Conchol., 6,* 349–361.

Gainer, H. (1972). Electrophysiological behavior of an endogenously active neurosecretory cell. *Brain Res., 39,* 403–418.

Garcia, J., McGowan, B. K., and Green, K. F. (1972). Biological constraints on conditioning. In "Classical Conditioning II: Current Research and Theory" (A. H. Black and W. F. Prokasy, eds.). Appleton-Century-Crofts, New York.

Gardner, D. (1971). Bilateral symmetry and interneuronal organization in the buccal ganglion of *Aplysia. Science (Wash. D.C.), 172,* 551–553.

Gaunt, A. S., and Wells, M. K. (1973). Models of sytringeal mechanism. *Am. Zool., 13,* 1227–1247.

Gaze, R. M. (1970). "The Formation of Nerve Connections." Academic, New York.

Gelfand, I. M., and Tsetlin, M. L. (1971). Mathematical modeling of mechanisms of the central nervous system. In "Models of the Structural–Functional Organization of Certain Biological Systems." MIT Press, Cambridge, Mass.

Gelperin, A. (1974). Olfactory basis of homing behavior in the giant garden slug, *Limax maximus. Proc. Natl. Acad. Sci. U.S.A., 71*, 966–970.

Gelperin, A. (1975a). Rapid food aversion learning by a terrestrial mollusk. *Science (Wash. D.C.), 189*, 567–570.

Gelperin, A. (1975b). An identified serotonergic input has reciprocal effects on two electrically coupled motoneurons in the terrestrial slug, *Limax maximus. Biol. Bull., 149*, 426–427.

Gelperin, A., and Bernstein, B. (1976). Motorprogram for feeding in the terrestrial slug *Limax maximus.* (In preparation.)

Gerhardt, H. C. (1974a). The significance of some spectral features in mating call recognition in the green treefrog (*Hyla cinerea*). *J. Exp. Biol., 61*, 229–241.

Gerhardt, H. C. (1974b). The vocalizations of some hybrid treefrogs: acoustic and behavioral analysis. *Behaviour, 49*, 130–151.

Gillary, H. L., and Kennedy, D. (1969a). Pattern generation in a crustacean motoneuron. *J. Neurophysiol., 32*, 595–606.

Gillary, H. L., and Kennedy, D. (1969b). Neuromuscular effects of impulse pattern in a crustacean motoneuron. *J. Neurophysiol., 32*, 607–612.

Glansdorff, P., and Prigogine, I. (1971). "Thermodynamic Theory of Structure, Stability and Fluctuations." Wiley Interscience, London.

Globus, A., and Scheibel, A. B. (1967). Synaptic loci on parietal cortical neurons: terminations of corpus callosum fibers. *Science (Wash. D.C.), 156*, 1127–1129.

Gnatzy, W., and Schmidt, K. (1971). Die Feinstruktur der Sinneshaare auf den Cerci von *Gryllus bimaculatus* Deg. (Saltatoria, Gryllidae): IV. Die Häutung der kurzen Borstenhaare. *Z. Zellforsch Mikrosk. Anat., 126*, 223–239.

Goodman, D. C., and Simpson, J. T. (1960). Cerebellar stimulation in the unrestrained and unaesthetized alligator. *J. Comp. Neurol., 114*, 127–135.

Gorman, A. L. F., and Mirolli, M. (1972). The passive electrical properties of the membrane of a molluscan neurone. *J. Physiol. (Lond.), 227*, 35–49.

Gorman, A. L. F., McReynolds, J. S., and Barnes, S. N. (1971). Photoreceptors in primitive chordates: fine structure, hyperpolarizing receptor potentials and evolution. *Science (Wash. D.C.), 172*, 1052–1053.

Gottlieb, G. (1968). Prenatal behavior of birds. *Q. Rev. Biol., 43*, 148–174.

Gottlieb, G. (1971a). "Development of Species Identification. An Inquiry into the Prenatal Determinants of Perception." University of Chicago Press, Chicago.

Gottlieb, G. (1971b). Ontogenesis of sensory function in birds and mammals. In "The Biopsychology of Development" (E. Tobach, L. R. Aronson, and E. Shar, eds.), pp. 67–128. Academic, New York.

Gottlieb, G. (1973). Introduction to behavioral embryology. In "Studies on the Development of Behavior and the Nervous System" (G. Gottlieb, ed.), Vol. 1, "Behavioral Embryology," pp. 3–50. Academic, New York.

Gotz, K. G. (1970). Fractionation of *Drosophila* populations according to optomotor traits. *J. Exp. Biol., 52*, 419–436.

Grabowski, S. R., Pinto, L. H., and Pak, W. L. (1972). Adaptation in retinal rods of axolotl: intracellular recordings. *Science (Wash. D.C.), 176*, 1240–1241.

Graham Brown, T. (1915). Note on the physiology of the basal ganglia and midbrain of the anthropoid ape, especially in reference to the act of laughter. *J. Physiol. (Lond.), 49*, 195–207.

Granit, R. (1955). "Receptors and Sensory Perception." Yale University Press, New Haven, Conn.

Greenewalt, C. H. (1968). "Birdsong, Acoustics and Physiology." Smithsonian Institution Press, Washington, D.C.

Grillner, S. (1975). Locomotion in vertebrates: central mechanisms and reflex interactions. *Physiol. Rev., 55*, 304–347.

Groves, P. M., and Thompson, R. F. (1970). Habituation: a dual process theory. *Psychol. Rev., 77*, 419–450.

Grüsser, O., and Grüsser-Cornehls, U. (1972). Comparative physiology of movement-detecting neuronal systems in lower vertebrates (Anura and Urodela). *Bibl. Ophthalmol., 82*, 260–273.

Guth, L., and Windle, W. F. (1970). The enigma of central nervous regeneration. *Exp. Neurol., 28*, 1–44.

Gymer, A., and Edwards, J. S. (1967). The development of the insect nervous system: I. An analysis of postembryonic growth in the terminal ganglion of *Acheta domesticus. J. Morphol., 123*, 191–197.

Hagiwara, S. (1961). Nervous activities of the heart in crustacea. *Ergeb. Biol., 24,* 287–311.

Hall, J. C., Gelbart, W. M., and Kankel, D. R. Mosaic systems. In "Genetics and Biology of *Drosophila*" (E. Novitski and M. Ashburner, eds.). Academic, New York. (In press.)

Hamburger, V. (1948). The mitotic patterns in the spinal cord of the chick embryo and their relation to histogenetic processes. *J. Comp. Neurol., 88,* 221–284.

Hamburger, V. (1963). Some aspects of the embryology of behavior. *Q. Rev. Biol., 38,* 342–365.

Hamburger, V. (1968). Emergence of nervous coordination. Origins of integrated behavior. *Dev. Biol. Suppl., 2,* 251–271.

Hamburger, V. (1973). Anatomical and physiological basis of embryonic motility in birds and mammals. In "Studies on the Development of Behavior and the Nervous System" (G. Gottlieb, ed.), Vol. 1, "Behavioral Embryology," pp. 52–76. Academic, New York.

Hamburger, V., and Oppenheim, R. W. (1967). Prehatching motility and hatching behavior in the chick. *J. Exp. Zool., 166,* 171–204.

Hamburger, V., Wenger, E., and Oppenheim, R. W. (1966). Motility in the chick embryo in the absence of sensory input. *J. Exp. Zool., 162,* 133–160.

Hamburger, V., Balaban, M., Oppenheim, R. W., and Wenger, E. (1965). Periodic motility of normal and spinal chick embryos between 8 and 17 days of incubation. *J. Exp. Zool., 159,* 1–14.

Hammond, P. H. (1956). The influence of prior instruction to the subject on an apparently involuntary neuro-muscular response. *J. Physiol. (Lond.), 132,* 17–18.

Hanby, J. (1974). Male-male mounting in Japanese monkeys (*Macaca fuscata*). *Anim. Behav., 22,* 836–849.

Harcombe, E. S. (1975). Neurophysiology of the flight motor neurons of *Drosophila melanogaster*. Ph.D. dissertation, Yale University, New Haven, Conn.

Harding, R. N. (1971). Dendro-dendritic synapses, including reciprocal synapses in the ventrolateral nucleus of the monkey thalamus. *Brain Res., 34,* 181–185.

Harris, G. W., Michael, R. P., and Scott, P. P. (1958). Neurological site of action of stilboesterol in eliciting sexual behavior. In "Ciba Foundation Symposium on the Neurological Basis of Behavior" (G. E. W. Wolstenholme and C. M. O'Connor, eds.), pp. 236–251. Little, Brown, Boston.

Harris, M. A., and Lemon, R. E. (1972). Songs of song sparrows (*Melospiza melodia*): individual variation and dialects. *Can. J. Zool., 50,* 301–309.

Hartline, D. K. (1968). Impulse identification and axon mapping of the lobster *Homarus americanus*. *J. Exp. Biol., 47,* 327–340.

Hauske, G. (1967). Stochastische und rhythmische Eigenschaften spontan auftretender Verhaltensweisen von Fischen. *Kybernetik, 4,* 26–36.

Hazlett, B. A. (1972a). Ritualization in marine crustaceae. In "Behavior of Marine Animals" (B. L. Winn and H. E. Olla, eds.), Vol. 1, "Invertebrates." Plenum, New York.

Hazlett, B. A. (1972b). Stereotypy of agonistic movements in the spider crab *Microphrys bicornutus*. *Behaviour, 42,* 270–278.

Heide, G. (1968). Flight control by non-fibrillar (direct) flight muscles in the blowfly *Calliphora*. *Z. Vgl. Physiol., 59,* 456–460.

Heide, G. (1974). The influence of wingbeat synchronous feedback on the motor output systems in flies. *Z. Naturforsch. Teil C, 29,* 739–744.

Heiligenberg, W. (1963). Ursachen für das Auftreten von Instinktbewegunen bei einem Fische. *Z. Vgl. Physiol., 47,* 339–380.

Heiligenberg, W. (1965). The effect of external stimuli on the attack readiness of cichlid fish. *Z. Vgl. Physiol., 49,* 459–464.

Heiligenberg, W. (1969). The effect of stimulus chirps on a cricket's chirping. *Z. Vgl. Physiol., 65,* 70–97.

Heiligenberg, W. (1973). Random processes describing the occurrence of behavioral patterns in a cichlid fish. *Anim. Behav., 21,* 169–182.

Heiligenberg, W. (1974a). Processes governing behavioral states of readiness. In "Advances in the Study of Behavior" (D. S. Lehrman, R. A. Hinde, and E. Shaw, eds.), Vol. 5. Academic, New York.

Heiligenberg, W. (1974b). A stochastic analysis of fish behavior. In "Motivational System Analysis" (D. McFarland, ed.). Academic, New York.

Heiligenberg, W., and Kramer, U. (1972). Aggressiveness as a function of external stimulation. *J. Comp. Physiol., 77,* 332–340.

Held, R. (1974). Development of spatially coordinated movements. *Brain Res., 71,* 347–348.

Held, R., and Hein, A. (1963). Movement-produced stimulation in the development of visually guided behavior. *J. Comp. Physiol. Psychol., 56,* 872–876.

Henneman, E., Somjen, G., and Carpenter, D. O. (1965). Functional significance of cell size in spinal motoneurons. *J. Neurophysiol., 28,* 560–580.

Hershkowitz-Kaufman, M. and Nicolis, G., (1972). Localized spatial structure and nonlinear chemical waves in dissipative systems. *J. Chem. Phys., 56,* 1890–1895.

Hibbard, E. (1965). Orientation and directed growth of Mauthner's cell axons from duplicated vestibular nerve roots. *Exp. Neurol., 13,* 289–301.

Hinde, R. A. (1959). Unitary drives. *Anim. Behav., 7,* 130–141.

Hinde, R. A. (1970). "Animal Behavior. A Synthesis of Ethology and Comparative Physiology," 2nd ed. McGraw-Hill, New York.

Hinde, R. A., and Stevenson-Hinde, J., eds. (1972). "Constraints on Learning." Academic, New York.

Hinde, R. A., and Stevenson-Hinde, J., eds. (1973). "Constraints on Learning: Limitations and Predispositions." Academic, New York.

Hinds, J. W., and Hinds, P. L. (1972). Reconstruction of dendritic growth cones in neonatal mouse olfactory bulb. *J. Neurocytol., 1,* 169–187.

Hodgkin, A. L. (1938). The subthreshold potentials in a crustacean nerve fibre. *Proc. R. Soc. Lond. B Biol. Sci., 126,* 247–285.

Holst, F. von (1935). Über den Prozess der zentralnervösen Koordination. *Pfluegers Arch. Eur. J. Physiol., 236,* 149–158.

Holst, E. von, and Mittelstaedt, H. (1950). Das Reafferenzprinzip (Wechselwirkungen zwischen Zentralnervensystem und Peripherie). *Naturwissenschaften, 37,* 464–476.

Horridge, G. A. (1961). The organization of the primitive central nervous system as suggested by examples of inhibition and the structure of neuropile. In "Nervous Inhibition" (E. Florey, ed.). Pergamon, New York.

Horridge, G. A. (1962a). Learning of leg position by headless insects. *Nature (Lond.), 193,* 697–698.

Horridge, G. A. (1962b). Learning of leg position by the ventral nerve cord in headless insects. *Proc. R. Soc. Lond. B Biol. Sci., 157,* 33–52.

Horridge, G. A. (1965). The electrophysiological approach to learning in isolated ganglia. *Anim. Behav., 12,* 163–182.

Horridge, G. A. (1968). Affinity of neurons in regeneration. *Nature (Lond.), 219,* 737–740.

Horridge, G. A., and Meinertzhagen, I. A. (1970). The accuracy of the patterns of connexions of the first and second order neurons of the visual system of Calliphora. *Proc. R. Soc. Lond. B Biol. Sci., 175,* 69–82.

Hotta, Y., and Benzer, S. (1969). Abnormal electroretinograms in visual mutants of *Drosophila. Nature (Lond.), 222,* 354–356.

Hotta, Y., and Benzer, S. (1970). Genetic dissection of the *Drosophila* nervous system by means of mosaics. *Proc. Natl. Acad. Sci. U.S.A., 67,* 1156–1163.

Hotta, Y., and Benzer, S. (1972). Mapping of behaviour in *Drosophila* mosaics. *Nature, 240,* 527–535.

Hoy, R. R. (1970). Degeneration and regeneration in abdominal flexor motor neurons in the crayfish. *J. Exp. Zool., 172,* 219–232.

Hoy, R. R. (1974). Genetic control of acoustic behavior in crickets. *Am. Zool., 14,* 1067–1080.

Hoy, R. R., and Paul, R. C. (1973). Genetic control of song specificity in crickets. *Science (Wash. D.C.), 180,* 82–83.

Hoyle, G. (1964). Exploration of neuronal mechanisms underlying behavior in insects. In "Neural Theory and Modeling" (R. F. Reiss, ed.), pp. 346–376. Stanford University Press, Stanford, Calif.

Hoyle, G. (1965). Neurophysiological studies on "learning" in headless insects. In "Physiology of the Insect Central Nervous System" (J. E. Treherne and J. W. L. Beament, eds.). Academic, New York.

Hoyle, G. (1970). Cellular mechanisms underlying behavior-neuroethology. In "Advances in Insect Physiology" (J. W. L. Beament, J. E. Treherne, and V. B. Wigglesworth, eds.), Vol. 7, pp. 349–444. Academic, New York.

Hoyle, G. (1975). Identified neurons and the future of neuroethology. *J. Exp. Zool., 194,* 51–74.

Hoyle, G., and Burrows, M. (1973a). Neural mechanisms underlying behavior in the locust *Schistocerca gregaria:* I. Physiology of identified neurons in the metathoracic ganglion. *J. Neurobiol., 4,* 3–41.

Hoyle, G., and Burrows, M. (1973b). Neural mechanisms underlying behavior in the locust *Schistocerca gregaria:* II. Integrative action in metathoracic neurons. *J. Neurobiol., 4,* 43–67.

Hrycyshyn, A. W., and Basmajian, J. V. (1972). Electromyography of the oral stage of swallowing in man. *Am. J. Anat., 133,* 333–340.

Hubel, D., and Wiesel, T. (1968). Receptive fields and functional architecture of monkey striated cortex. *J. Physiol. (Lond.), 195,* 215–243.

Hughes, A., Bryant, S., and Bellairs, A. (1967). Embryonic behavior in the lizard, *Lacerta vivipara. J. Zool., 153,* 139–152.

Hughes, G. M., and Wiersma, C. A. G. (1960). The co-ordination of swimmeret movements in the crayfish, *Procambarus clarkii* (Girard). *J. Exp. Biol., 37*, 657–670.

Hukuhara, T., and Okada, H. (1956). Effects of deglutition upon the spike discharges of neurons in the respiratory center. *Jpn. J. Physiol., 6*, 162–166.

Hunt, R. K., and Jacobson, M. (1972). Development and stability of positional information in *Xenopus* retinal ganglion cells. *Proc. Natl. Acad. Sci. U.S.A., 69*, 780–783.

Ikeda, K. (1974). Patterned motor activities released by anaesthetics. *Proc. Int. Physiol. Congr., 11*, 160.

Ikeda, K., and Kaplan, W. D. (1969). Neural mechanism for specific leg movements of a mutant *Drosophila. Am. Zool., 9*, 584.

Ikeda, K., and Kaplan, W. D. (1970a). Patterned neural activity of a mutant *Drosophila melanogaster. Proc. Natl. Acad. Sci. U.S.A., 66*, 765–772.

Ikeda, K., and Kaplan, W. D. (1970b). Unilaterally patterned neural activity of a mutant gynandromorph of *Drosophila melanogaster. Am. Zool., 10*, 311.

Ikeda, K., and Kaplan, W. D. (1970c). Unilaterally patterned neural activity of gynandromorphs, mosaic for a neurological mutant of *Drosophila melanogaster. Proc. Natl. Acad. Sci. U.S.A., 67*, 1480–1487.

Ikeda, K., and Kaplan, W. D. (1971). Pacemaking action of a neuron induced by a single-gene mutation in *Drosophila melanogaster. Proc. Int. Physiol. Congr., 9*, 268.

Ikeda, K., and Kaplan, W. D. (1974). Neurophysiological genetics in *Drosophila melanogaster. Am. Zool., 14*, 1055–1066.

Ikeda, K., and Wiersma, C. A. G. (1964). Autogenic rhythmicity in the abdominal ganglia of the crayfish. The control of swimmeret movements. *Comp. Biochem. Physiol., 12*, 107–115.

Iles, J. F., and Mulloney, B. (1971). Procion yellow staining of cockroach motor neurons without the use of microelectrodes. *Brain Res., 30*, 397–400.

Immelmann, K. (1969). Song development in the zebra finch and other estrilid finches. In "Bird Vocalizations" (R. Hinde, ed.). Cambridge University Press, London.

Impekoven, M., and Gold, P. (1973). Prenatal origins of parent–young interactions in birds: a naturalistic approach. In "Studies on the Development of Behavior and the Nervous System" (G. Gottlieb, ed.), Vol. 1, "Behavioral Embryology," pp. 326–356. Academic, New York.

Ioannides, A. C., and Walcott, B. (1971). Graded illumination potentials from retinula cell axons in the bug *Lethocerus. Z. Vgl. Physiol., 71*, 315–325.

Ishihara, M. (1960). Über den Schluckreflex nach der medianen Spaltung der Medulla oblongata. *Zentralbl. Physiol., 20*, 413–417.

Jacklet, J. W. (1969). Electrophysiological organization of the eye of *Aplysia. J. Gen. Physiol., 53*, 21–42.

Jacobson, C.-O. (1959). The localization of the presumptive cerebral regions in the neural plate of the axolotl larva. *J. Embryol. Exp. Morphol., 7*, 1–21.

Jacobson, C.-O. (1964). Motor nuclei, cranial nerve roots, and fiber pattern in the medulla oblongata after reversal experiments on the neural plate of axolotl larvae: I. Bilateral operations. *Zool. Bidr. Upps., 36*, 73–160.

Jacobson, M. (1968a). Development of neuronal specificity in retinal ganglion cells of *Xenopus. Develop. Biol., 17*, 202–218.

Jacobson, M. (1968b). Cessation of DNA synthesis in retinal ganglion cells correlated with the time of specification of their central connections. *Dev. Biol., 17*, 219–232.

Jacobson, M. (1970). "Developmental Neurobiology." Holt, Rinehart and Winston, New York.

Jansen, J. K. S., and Nicholls, J. G. (1972). Regeneration and changes in synaptic connections between individual nerve cells in the central nervous system of the leech. *Proc. Natl. Acad. Sci. U.S.A., 69*, 636–639.

Jarvilehto, M., and Zettler, F. (1970). Micro-localization of lammalocated visual cell activities in the compound eye of the blowfly *Calliphora. Z. Vgl. Physiol., 69*, 134–138.

Jean, A. (1972a). Localisation et activité des neurones déglutiteurs bulbaires. *J. Physiol. (Paris), 64*, 227–268.

Jean, A. (1972b). Effet de lésions localisées du bulbe réachidien sur le stade oesophagien de la déglutition. *J. Physiol. (Paris), 64*, 507–516.

Jensen, E. V., and De Sombre, E. R. (1973). Estrogen-receptor interaction. *Science (Wash. D.C.), 182*, 126–134.

Jones, W. H., and Thomas, D. B. (1962). Changes in the dendritic organization of neurons in the cerebral cortex following de-afferentation. *J. Anat., 96*, 375–381.

Judd, B. H., Shen, M. W., and Kaufman, T. C. (1972). The anatomy and function of a segment of the X-chromosome of *Drosophila melanogaster. Genetics, 71*, 139–156.

Jürgens, U., and Ploog, D. (1970). Cerebral representation of vocalization in the squirrel monkey. *Exp. Brain Res., 10,* 532–554.

Kahn, N., and Wang, S. C. (1967). Electrophysiologic basis for pontine apneustic center and its role in integration of the Hering–Breuer reflex. *J. Neurophysiol., 30,* 301–318.

Kalat, J. W., and Rozin, P. (1972). You can lead a rat to poison but you can't make him think. In "Biological Boundaries of Learning" (M. E. P. Seligman and J. L. Hager, eds.). Appleton-Century-Crofts, New York.

Kammer, A. (1967). Muscle activity during flight in some large Lepidoptera. *J. Exp. Biol., 47,* 277–295.

Kanai, T., and Wang, S. C. (1962). Localization of the central vocalization mechanism in the brain stem of the cat. *Exp. Neurol., 6,* 426–434.

Kandel, E. R. (1974). An invertebrate system for the cellular analysis of simple behaviors and their modifications. In "The Neurosciences: Third Study Program" (F. O. Schmitt and F. G. Worden, eds). MIT Press, Cambridge, Mass.

Kandel, E. R., Frazier, W. T., Waziri, R., and Coggeshall, R. W. (1967). Direct and common connections among identified neurons in *Aplysia. J. Neurophysiol., 30,* 1352–1376.

Kaneko, A. (1970). Physiological and morphological identification of horizontal, bipolar and amacrine cells in goldfish retina. *J. Physiol. (Lond.), 207,* 623–633.

Kaneko, A. (1971). Electrical connections between horizontal cells in the dogfish retina. *J. Physiol. (Lond.), 213,* 95–106.

Kaneko, C. R. S., Kater, S. B. and Fountain, R. L. (1974). Control of centrally programmed feeding in *Helisoma trivolvis,* Fourth Annual Meeting, Society for Neuroscience, Program and Abstracts, p. 276.

Katchalsky, A., Rowland, V., and Blumenthal, R., eds. (1974). Dynamic patterns of brain cell assemblies. *Neurosci. Res. Program Bull., 12,* 3–187.

Kater, S. B. (1974). Feeding in *Helisoma trivolvis:* the morphological and physiological bases of a fixed action pattern. *Am. Zool., 14,* 1017–1036.

Kater, S. B., and Rowell, C. H. F. (1973). Integration of sensory and centrally programmed components in generation of cyclical feeding activity of *Helisoma trivolvis. J. Neurophysiol., 36,* 142–155.

Katz, B. (1966). "Nerve, Muscle, and Synapse." McGraw-Hill, New York.

Katz, B., and Miledi, R. (1966). Input–output relation of a single synapse. *Nature (Lond.), 212,* 1242–1245.

Kawasaki, M., Ogura, J. H., and Takenouchi, S. (1964). Neurophysiologic observations of normal deglutition: I. Its relationship to the respiratory cycle; II. Its relationship to allied phenomena. *Laryngoscope, 74,* 1747–1783.

Keele, S. W. (1968). Movement control in skilled motor performance. *Psychol. Bull., 70,* 387–403.

Kelley, J. P., and Cowan, W. M. (1972). Studies on the development of the chick optic tectum: III. Effects of early eye removal. *Brain Res., 42,* 263–288.

Kendig, J. J. (1968). Motor neuron coupling in locust flight. *J. Exp. Biol., 48,* 389–404.

Kennedy, D. (1974). Connections among neurons of different types in crustacean nervous systems. In "The Neurosciences: Third Study Program" (F. O. Schmitt and F. G. Worden, eds.), pp. 379–395. MIT Press, Cambridge, Mass.

Kennedy, D., and Preston, J. B. (1960). Activity patterns of interneurons in the caudal ganglion of the crayfish. *J. Gen. Physiol., 43,* 655–670.

Kennedy, D., and Takeda, K. (1965a). Reflex control of abdominal flexor muscles in the crayfish: I. The twitch system. *J. Exp. Biol., 43,* 211–227.

Kennedy, D., and Takeda, K. (1965b). Reflex control of abdominal flexor muscles in the crayfish: II. The tonic system. *J. Exp. Biol., 43,* 229–246,

Kennedy, D., Calabrese, R. L., and Wine, J. J. (1975). Presynaptic inhibition: primary afferent depolarization in crayfish neurons. *Science (Wash. D.C.), 186,* 451–454.

Kennedy, D., Evoy, W. H., and Hanawalt, J. T. (1966). Release of coordinated behavior in crayfish by single central neurons. *Science (Wash. D.C.), 154,* 917–919.

Kimmel, C. B. (1972). Mauthner axons in living fish larvae, *Dev. Biol., 27,* 272–275.

Kimmel, C. B., and Schabtach, E. (1974). Patterning in synaptic knobs which connect with Mauthner's cell (*Ambystoma mexicanum*). *J. Comp. Neurol., 156,* 49–79.

Kimmel, C. B., Patterson, J., and Kimmel, R. O. (1974). The development and behavioral characteristics of the startle response in the zebra fish. *Dev. Psychobiol., 7,* 47–60.

Kimura, D. (1961). Cerebral dominance and the perception of verbal stimuli. *Can. J. Psychol., 15,* 166–171.

Kimura, D. (1964). Left–right differences in the perception of melodies. *Q. J. Exp. Psychol., 16,* 355–358.

Kingsbury, J. M. (1964). "Poisonous Plants of the United States and Canada." Prentice-Hall, Englewood Cliffs, N.J.

Kirschfeld, K. (1967). Die Projektion der optischen Umwelt auf das Raster der Rhabdomere im Komplexauge von *Musca. Exp. Brain Res., 3,* 248–270.

Klinke, R., and Schmidt, C. L. (1970). Efferent influence on the vestibular organ during active movements of the body. *Pfluegers Arch. Eur. J. Physiol., 318,* 325–332.

Koester, J., Mayeri, E., Lieveswar, G., and Kandel, E. R. (1973). Cellular regulation of homeostasis: neuronal control of the circulation in *Aplysia. Fed. Proc., 32,* 2179–2187.

Koeze, T. H. (1973). Thresholds of cortical activation of baboon α- and γ-motoneurons during halothane anaesthesia. *J. Physiol., (Lond.), 229,* 319–337.

Kolb, H. (1974). The connections between horizontal cells and photoreceptors in the retina of the cat: electron microscopy of Golgi preparations. *J. Comp. Neurol., 155,* 1–14.

Konishi, M. (1963). The role of auditory feedback in the vocal behavior of the domestic fowl. *Z. Tierpsychol., 20,* 349–367.

Konishi, M. (1964). Effects of deafening on song development in two species of juncos. *Condor, 66,* 85–102.

Konishi, M. (1965a). Effects of deafening on song development in American robins and black-headed grosbeaks. *Z. Tierpsychol., 22,* 584–599.

Konishi, M. (1965b). The role of auditory feedback in the control of vocalization in the white-crowned sparrow. *Z. Tierpsychol., 22,* 770–783.

Konishi, M. (1970). Comparative neurophysiological studies of hearing and vocalization in songbirds. *Z. Vgl. Physiol., 66,* 257–272

Konishi, M., and Nottebohm, F. (1969). Experimental studies in the ontogeny of avian vocalization. In "Bird Vocalizations: Their Relations to Current Problems in Biology and Psychology" (R. A. Hinde, ed.). Cambridge University Press, Cambridge.

Konorski, J. (1967). "Integrative Activity of the Brain." University of Chicago Press, Chicago.

Koppányi, T., and Pearcy, J. F. (1924). Studies on the clasping reflex in amphibia. *Am. J. Physiol., 71,* 34–39.

Kots, Ya. M. (1969). Supraspinal control of the segmental centres of muscle antagonists in man. *Biophysics. (Engl. Transl. Biofiz.), 14,* 176–183.

Krasne, F. B. (1969). Excitation and habituation of the crayfish escape reflex: the depolarizing response in lateral giant fibers of the isolated abdomen. *J. Exp. Biol., 50,* 29–46.

Krasne, F. B., and Bryan, J. S. (1973). Habituation: regulation through presynaptic inhibition. *Science (Wash. D.C.), 182,* 590–592.

Krasne, F. B., and Roberts, A. (1969). Habituation of crayfish escape response during release from inhibition induced by picrotoxin. *Nature (Lond.), 215,* 769–770.

Krasne, F. B., and Woodsmall, K. S. (1969). Waning of the crayfish escape response as a result of repeated stimulation. *Anim. Behav., 17,* 416–424.

Kristan, W. B., Jr. (1974). Neural control of swimming in the leech. *Am. Zool., 14,* 991–1002.

Kristan, W. B., Jr., Stent, G. S., and Ort, C. A. (1974a). Neuronal control of swimming in the medicinal leech: I. Dynamics of the swimming rhythm. *J. Comp. Physiol., 94,* 97–121.

Kristan, W. B., Jr., Stent, G. S., and Ort, C. A. (1974b). Neuronal control of swimming in the medicinal leech: III. Impulse patterns in the motor neurons. *J. Comp. Physiol., 94,* 155–176.

Kroodsma, D. Re-evaluation of song development in the *Junco—Melospiza—Zonotrichia* complex. *Anim. Behav.* (In press.)

Kung, C. (1971). Genetic mutants with altered system of excitation in *Paramecium aurelia:* I. Phenotypes of the behavioral mutants. *Z. Vgl. Physiol., 71,* 142–164.

Kung, C., and Eckert, R. (1972). Genetic modification of electrical properties in an excitable membrane. *Proc. Natl. Acad. Sci. U.S.A., 69,* 93–97.

Kunkel, J. Cockroach molting: I. Temporal organization of events during the molting cycle of *Blatella Germanica. Biol. Bull. (Woods Hole).* (In press.)

Kupfermann, I. (1967). Stimulation of egg laying: possible neuroendocrine function of bag cells of abdominal ganglion of *Aplysia californica. Nature (Lond.), 216,* 814–815

Kupfermann, I, (1970). Stimulation of egg laying by extract of neuroendocrine cells (bag cells) of abdominal ganglion of *Aplysia. J. Neurophysiol., 33,* 877–881.

Kupfermann, I., and Cohen, J. (1971). The control of feeding by identified neurons in the buccal ganglion of *Aplysia. Am. Zool., 11,* 667.

Kupfermann, I., and Kandel, E. R. (1969). Neuronal controls of a behavioral response mediated by the abdominal ganglion of *Aplysia. Science (Wash. D.C.), 164,* 847–850.

Kupfermann, I., and Weiss, K. R. (1974a). Functional studies on the metacerebral cells of *Aplysia. Proc. Soc. Neurosci.,* 4th Annual Meeting, St. Louis, Mo., p. 296.

Kupfermann, I., and Weiss, K. R. (1974b). Water balance regulation by the neurosecretory cell R15 in *Aplysia californica. I.C.R.S., 2,* 1695.

Kupfermann, I., Carew, T. J., and Kandel, E. R. (1974). Local, reflex, and central commands controlling gill and siphon movements in *Aplysia. J. Neurophysiol., 37,* 996–1019.

Kupfermann, I., Castellucci, V., Pinsker, H., and Kandel, E. (1970). Neuronal correlates of habituation and dishabituation of the gill-withdrawal reflex in *Aplysia. Science (Wash. D.C.), 167,* 1743–1745.

Kupfermann, I., Pinsker, H., Castellucci, V., and Kandel, E. R. (1971). Central and peripheral control of gill movements in *Aplysia. Science (Wash. D.C.), 174,* 1252–1256.

Kutsch, W. (1974). The influence of the wing sense organs on the flight motor pattern in maturing adult locusta. *J. Comp Physiol., 88,* 413–424.

Land, M. F., and Collett, T. S. (1974). Chasing behaviour of houseflies (*Fannia canicularis*) A description and analysis. *J. Comp. Physiol., 89,* 331–357.

Landau, W. M., and Clare, M. H. (1964). Fusimotor function: IV. Reinforcement of the H reflex in normal subjects. *Arch. Neurol., 10,* 117–122.

Lanyon, W. E. (1960). The ontogeny of vocalizations in birds. In "Animal Sounds and Communication" (W. E. Lanyon and W. N. Tavolga, eds.). *American Institute of Biological Sciences, Washington, D.C.*

Larimer, J. L., and Kennedy, D. (1969). The central nervous control of complex movements in the uropods of crayfish. *J. Exp. Biol., 51,* 135–150.

Larimer, J. L., Eggleston, A. C., Masukawa, L. M., and Kennedy, D. (1971). The different connections and motor outputs of lateral and median giant fibers in the crayfish. *J. Exp. Biol., 54,* 391–402.

Lashley, K. S. (1951). The problem of serial order in behavior. In "Cerebral Mechanisms in Behavior" (L. A. Jeffress, ed.), pp. 112–136. Wiley, New York.

Lashley, K. S. (1963). "Brain Mechanisms and Intelligence." Hafner, New York.

Laughlin, S. B. (1974). Neural integration in the first optic neuropile of dragonflies. *J. Comp. Physiol., 84,* 335–355.

Lawick-Goodall, J. van (1971). "*In the Shadow of Man.*" Houghton Mifflin, Boston.

Lawrence, P. A., and Shelton, P. M. G. (1975). The determination of polarity in the developing insect retina. *J. Embryol. Exp. Morphol., 33*(2), 471–486.

Leghissa, S. (1941). Sviluppo dell'aparato del Mauth-ner in larve di *Ambystoma mexicanum* (Axolotl). *Arch. Zool. Ital., 29,* 213–253.

Lehrman, D. S. (1953). A critique of Konrad Lorenz's theory of instinctive behavior. *Q. Rev. Biol., 28,* 337–363.

Lehrman, D. S. (1956). On the organization of maternal behavior and the problem of instinct. Foundation Singer-Polignac. Volume: l'Instinct dans le comportement des animaux et de l'homme. Masson, Paris.

Lehrman, D. S. (1964). The reproductive behavior of ring doves. *Sci. Am.,* November 1964.

Lemon, R. E. (1971). Differentiation of song dialects in cardinals. *Ibis, 113,* 373–377.

Lenneberg, E. H. (1967). "Biological Foundations of Language." Wiley, New York.

Lent, C. M. (1973). Retzius cells from segmental ganglia of four species of leeches: comparative neuronal geometry. *Comp. Biochem. Physiol, A Comp. Physiol., 44,* 35–40.

Leong, Ch.-Yl. (1969). The quantitative effect of releasers on the attack readiness of the fish *Haplochromis burtoni* (Cichlidae, Pisces). *Z. Vgl. Physiol., 65,* 39–50.

Levi-Montalcini, R., and Chen, R. S. (1971). Selective outgrowth of nerve fibers *in vitro* from embryonic ganglia of *Periplaneta americana. Arch. Ital. Biol., 109,* 307–337.

Levi-Montalcini, R., Chen, J. S., Seshan, K. R., and Aloo, L. (1973). An *in vitro* approach to the insect nervous system. In "Developmental Neurobiology of Arthropods" (D. Young, ed.), pp. 5–36, Cambridge University Press, Cambridge.

Levine, J. D. (1973). Properties of the nervous system controlling flight in *Drosophila melanogaster. J. Comp. Physiol., 84,* 129–166.

Levine, J. D., and Wyman, R. J. (1973). Neurophysiology of flight in wildtype and a mutant *Drosophila. Proc. Natl. Acad. Sci. U.S.A., 70,* 1050–1054.

Levinthal, C., Macagno, E., and Tountas, C. (1974). Computer-aided reconstruction from serial sections. *Fed. Proc., 33,* 2336–2340.

Leyhausen, P. (1973). "Verhaltensstudien an Katzen." Paul Parey, Berlin.

Liberman, A. M., Harris, K. S., Hoffman, H. S., and Griffith, B. C. (1957). The discrimination of speech sounds within and across phoneme boundaries. *J. Exp. Psychol., 54,* 358–368.

Liberman, A. M., Harris, K. S., Kinney, J., and Lane, H. (1961). The discrimination of relative onset time of the components of certain speech and nonspeech patterns. *J. Exp. Psychol., 61,* 379–388.

Liberman, A. M., Cooper, F. S., Shankweiler, D. S., and Studdert-Kennedy, M. (1967). Perception of the speech code. *Psychol. Rev., 74,* 431–461.

Lieberman, A. R. (1973). Neurons with presynaptic perikarya and pre-synaptic dendrites in the rat lateral geniculate nucleus. *Brain Res., 59,* 35–59.

Lisk, R. D. (1962). Diencephalic placement of estradiol and sexual receptivity in the female rat. *Am. J. Physiol., 203,* 493–496.

Lisker, L., and Abramson, A. S. (1970). The voicing dimension: some experiments in comparative phonetics. *Proc. 6th Int. Congr. Phonetic Sci., Prague, 1967,* 563–567. Academia, Prague.

Llinás, R. (1970). Neuronal operations in cerebellar transactions. In "The Neurosciences: Second Study Program" (F. O. Schmitt, ed.), pp. 409–426. Rockefeller University Press, New York.

Llinás, R. (1974). Eighteenth Bowditch lecture: motor aspects of cerebellar control. *Physiologist, 17,* 19–46.

Llinás, R., Baker, R., and Sotelo, C. (1974). Electrotonic coupling between neurons in the cat inferior olive. *J. Neurophysiol., 37,* 560–571.

Llinás, R., and Nicholson, C. (1976). Reversal properties of climbing fiber potential in cat Purkinje cells: An example of a distributed synapse. *J. Neurophysiol., 39,* 311–323.

Llinás R., and Vokind, R. A. (1973). The olivo-cerebellar system: Functional properties as revealed by harmaline-induced tremor. *Exp. Brain Res., 18,* 69–87.

Llinás R., Walton, K., Hillman, D. E., and Sotelo, C. Inferior olive: Its role in motor learning. *Science.* (in press).

Lockshin, R. A. (1971). Programmed cell death: Nature of the nervous signal controlling breakdown of intersegmental muscles. *J. Insect Physiol., 17,* 149–158.

Lockshin, R. A., and Williams, C. M. (1965a). Programmed cell death. I. Cytology of degeneration in the intersegmental muscles of the Pernyi silkmoth. *J. Insect Physiol., 11,* 123–133.

Lockshin, R. A., and Williams, C. M. (1965b). Programmed cell death. III. Neural control of the breakdown of the intersegmental muscles of silkmoths. *J. Insect Physiol., 11,* 601–610.

Lockshin, R. A., and Williams, C. M. (1965c). Programmed cell death. IV. The influence of drugs on the breakdown of the intersegmental muscles of silkmoths. *J. Insect Physiol., 11,* 803–809.

LoPresti, V., Macagno, E. R., and Levinthal, C. (1973). Structure and development of neuronal connections in isogenic organisms: Cellular interactions in the development of the optic lamina of *Daphnia. Proc. Nat. Acad. Sci., 70,* 433–437.

Lorenz, K. Z. (1935). Der Kumpan in der Umwelt des Vogels. *J. Ornithol., 83,* 137–213, 289–413.

Lorenz, K. Z. (1937). Über die Bildung des Instinktbegriffes. *Naturwissenschaften, 25,* 289–300, 307–318, 324–331.

Lorenz, K. Z. (1941). Vergleichende Bewegungsstudien an Anatinen. *Suppl. J. Ornithol., 89,* 194–294.

Lorenz, K. Z. (1950). The comparative method in studying innate behavior patterns. *Symp. Soc. Exp. Biol., 4,* 221–268.

Lorenz, K. Z. (1955). Morphology and behavior patterns in closely allied species. In "Group Processes, Transactions of First Conference" (B. Schaffner, ed.), p. 171. Josiah Macy, Jr. Foundation, New York.

Lorenz, K. Z. (1958). The evolution of behavior. *Sci. Am.,* December 1958.

Lorenz, K. Z. (1965). "Evolution and Modification of Behavior." University of Chicago Press, Chicago.

Lorenz, K. Z., and Tinbergen, N. (1938). Taxis und Instinkhandlung in der Eirollbewegung der Graugans. *Z. Tierpsychol., 2,* 1–29.

Lullies, H. (1926). Der Mechanismus des Umklammerungsreflexes. *Pfluegers Arch. Eur. J. Physiol., 214,* 416–420.

Luria, A. R. (1966). "Higher Cortical Functions in Man." Basic Books, New York.

McCann, F. V., and Boettiger, E. G. (1961). Studies on the flight mechanism of insects: I. The electrophysiology of fibrillar flight muscle. *J. Gen. Physiol., 45,* 125–142.

McCulloch, W. S., and Pitts, W. H. (1943). A logical calculus of the ideas immanent in nervous activity. *Bull. Math. Biophys., 5,* 115–133.

MacDonnell, M., and Flynn, J. P. (1966). Sensory control of hypothalamic attack. *Anim. Behav., 14,* 399–405.

Machin, K. E., and Pringle, J. W. S. (1959). The physiology of insect fibrillar muscle: II. Mechanical properties of a beetle flight muscle. *Proc. R. Soc. Lond. B. Biol. Sci., 151,* 204–225.

MacKay, A. R., and Gelperin, A. (1972). Pharmacology and reflex responsiveness of the heart in the giant garden slug, *Limax maximus. Comp. Biochem. Physiol. A Comp. Physiol., 43,* 877–896.

MacKay, B (1974). Conditioned food aversion produced by toxicosis in atlantic cod. *Behav. Biol., 12,* 347–356.

Macklin, M., and Wojtokowski, W. (1973). Correlates

of electrical activity in *Xenopus laevis* embryos. *J. Comp. Physiol., 84*, 41–58.

McLean, M. (1974). Regeneration and trophism in the nervous system of the cricket *Acheta domesticus.* Ph.D. dissertation, University of Washington, Seattle, Wash.

McMahon, D. (1974). Chemical messengers in development: a hypothesis. *Science (Wash. D.C.), 185*, 1012–1021.

McNeill, D. (1966). Developmental psycholinguistics. In "The Genesis of Language" (F. Smith and G. A. Miller, eds.). MIT Press, Cambridge, Mass.

MacNichol, E. J., and Svaetichin, G. (1958). Electric responses from the isolated retinas of fishes. *Am. J. Ophthalmol., 46*, 26–46.

McReynolds, J. S., and Gorman, A. L. F. (1970). Photoreceptor potentials of opposite polarity in the eye of the scallop *Pecten irradious. J. Gen. Physiol., 56*, 376–392.

Maddrell, S. H. P. (1967). Neurosecretion in insects In "Insects and Physiology" (J. W. L. Beament and J. E. Treherne, eds.), Oliver & Boyd, Edinburgh.

Magnus, R., and de Kleijn, A. (1930). Körperstellung, Gleichgewicht und Bewegung bei säugern. *Hb. Norm. Pathol. Physiol., 15*, 29–87.

Manning, A. (1972). "An Introduction to Animal Behavior," 2nd ed., p. 294. Edward Arnold, London.

Mark, R. (1974) "Memory and Nerve Cell Connections." Clarendon Press, Oxford.

Marler, P. (1952). Variations in the song of the chaffinch, *Fringilla coelebs. Ibis, 94*, 458–472.

Marler, P. (1972). Vocalizations of East African monkeys: II. Black and white colobus. *Behaviour, 42*, 175–197.

Marler, P. (1973). A comparison of vocalizations of red-tailed monkeys and blue monkeys, *Cercopithecus ascanius* and *C. mitis*, in Uganda. *Z. Tierpsychol., 33*, 223–247.

Marler, P. (1975). On the origin of speech from animal sounds. In "The Role of Speech in Language" (J. F. Kavanagh and J. E. Cutting, eds.). MIT Press, Cambridge, Mass.

Marler, P. On strategies of behavioural development. In "Evolution in Behaviour" (G. Baerends, C. Beer, and A. Manning, eds.). Clarendon Press, Oxford. (In press.)

Marler, P.; and Hamilton, W. J., III (1966). "Mechanisms of Animal Behavior. " Wiley, New York.

Marler, P., and Mundinger, P. (1971). Vocal learning in birds. In "Ontogeny of Vertebrate Behavior" (H. Moltz, ed.). Academic, New York.

Marler, P., and Tamura, M. (1962). Song dialects in three populations of white-crowned sparrows. *Condor, 64*, 368–377.

Marler, P., and Tamura, M. (1964). Culturally transmitted patterns of vocal behavior in sparrows *Science (Wash. D.C.), 146*, 1483–1486.

Marler, P., and Tenaza, R. Signalling behavior of wild apes with special reference to vocalization. In "Animal Communication" (T. Sebeok, ed.) 2nd. ed. Indiana University Press, Bloomington, Ind. (In press.)

Marler, P., Kreith, M., and Tamura, M. (1962). Song development in hand-raised Oregon juncos. *Auk, 79*, 12–30.

Marler, P., Mundinger, P., Waser, M. S., and Lutjen, A. (1972). Effects of acoustical stimulation and deprivation on song development in red-winged blackbirds (*Agelaius phoeniceus*). *Anim. Behav., 20*, 586–606.

Marr, D. (1969). A theory of cerebellar cortex. *J. Physiol. (Lond.), 202*, 431–470.

Matsumoto, N., and Naka, K. I. (1972). Identification of intracellular responses in the frog retina. *Brain Res., 42*, 59–71.

Matthews, M. R., and Powell, T. P. S. (1962). Some observations on transneuronal cell degeneration in the olfactory bulb of the rabbit. *J. Anat. (Lond.), 96*, 89–102.

Mattingly, I. G. (1972). Speech cues and sign stimuli. *Am Sci., 60*, 326–337.

Mayeri, E., Koester, J., and Liebeswar, G. (1974). Functional organization of the neural control of circulation in *Aplysia. Am. Zool., 14*, 943–956.

Maynard, D. M. (1955). Activity in a crustacean ganglion: II. Pattern and interaction in burst formation. *Biol. Bull. (Woods Hole), 109*, 420–436.

Maynard, D. M. (1963). (Conference abstract), Proceedings Eighth International Ethological Conference.

Maynard, D. M. (1965). The occurrence and functional characteristics of hetermorph antennules in an experimental population of spiny lobsters, *Panulirus arqus. J. Exp. Biol., 43*, 79–106.

Maynard, D. M. (1966). Integration in crustacean ganglia. *Symp. Soc. Exp. Biol., 20*, 111–150.

Maynard, D. M. (1972). Simpler networks. *Ann. N.Y. Acad. Sci., 193*, 59–72.

Maynard, D. M. (1975). Effects of maintained presynaptic depolarization on inhibitory transmission in lobster neuropil. (In press.)

Maynard, D. M., and Cohen, M. J. (1965). The function of a hetermorph antennule in a spiny lobster, *Panulirus arqus. J. Exp. Biol., 43*, 55–78.

Maynard, D. M. and Walton K. D. (1975). Effects of

maintained depolarization of presynaptic neurons on inhibitory transmission in lobster neuropil. *J. Comp. Physiol., 97*, 215–243.

Meinertzhagen, I. A. (1973). Development of the compound eye and optic lobe of insects. In "Developmental Neurobiology of Arthropods" (D. Young, ed.). Cambridge University Press, London.

Meinhardt, H., and Gierer, A. (1974). Applications of a theory of biological pattern formation based on lateral inhibition. *J. Cell Sci., 15*, 321–346.

Mendelson, M. (1971). Oscillator neurons in crustacean ganglia. *Science (Wash. D.C.) 171*, 1170–1173.

Merrill, E. G. (1974). Finding a respiratory function for the medullary respiratory neurons. In "Essays on the Nervous System" (R. Bellairs and E. G. Gray, eds.), pp. 451–468. Clarendon Press, Oxford.

Milburn, N. S., and Roeder, K. D. (1962). Control of efferent activity in the cockroach terminal abdominal ganglion by extracts of the corpora cardiaca. *Gen. Comp. Endocrinol., 2*, 70–76.

Milburn, N. S., Weiant, E. A., and Roeder, K. D. (1960). The release of efferent nerve activity in the roach, *Periplaneta americana*, by extracts of the corpus cardiacum. *Biol. Bull. (Woods Hole), 118*, 111–119.

Miller, A. J. (1972a). Characteristics of the swallowing reflex induced by peripheral nerve and brain stem stimulation. *Exp. Neurol., 34*, 210–222.

Miller, A. J. (1972b). Significance of sensory inflow to the swallowing reflex. *Brain Res., 43*, 147–159.

Miller, A. J. (1974). Interspike interval patterning in recurrent nerve fibre activity during respiration. *Experientia (Basel), 30*, 165–166.

Milligan, M., and Verner, J. (1971). Interpopulation song dialect discrimination in the white-crowned sparrow. *Condor, 73*, 208–213.

Minna, J. D., Glazer, D., and Nirenberg, M. (1972). Genetic dissection of neural properties using somatic cell hybrids. *Nat. New Biol., 235*, 225–231.

Minna, J. D., Nelson, P., Peacock, J., Glazer, D., and Nirenberg, M. (1971). Genes for neuronal properties expressed in neuroblastoma *x* L cell hybrids. *Proc. Natl. Acad. Sci. U.S.A., 68*, 234–239.

Mittelstaedt, H. (1969). Strategies of cybernetic analysis. In "Biocybernetics of the Central Nervous System" (L. D. Proctor, ed.), Little, Brown, Boston.

Moffitt, A. R. (1971). Consonant cue perception by twenty- to twenty-four-week-old infants. *Child Dev, 42*, 717–731.

Molfese, D. L. (1972). Cerebral asymmetry in infants, children and adults: auditory evoked responses to speech and noise stimuli. Ph.D. dissertation, Pennsylvania State University, University Park, Pa.

Montigny, C. de, and Lamarre, Y. (1973). Rhythmic activity induced by harmaline in the olivocerebello-bulbar system of the cat. *Brain Res., 53*, 81–95.

Moran, D. T. (1971). Loss of the sensory process of an insect receptor at ecdysis. *Nature (Lond.), 234*, 476–477.

Morse, P. A. (1972). The discrimination of speech and nonspeech stimuli in early infancy. *J. Exp. Child Psychol., 14*, 477–492.

Moulton, J. M., Jurand, A., and Fox, H. (1968). A cytological study of Mauthner's cells in *Xenopus laevis* and *Rana temporaria* during metamorphosis. *J. Embryol. Exp. Morphol., 19*, 415–431.

Mpitsos, G. J., and Collins, S. (1975). Learning: rapid aversive conditioning in the gastropod mollusk *Pleurobranchea. Science (Wash. D.C.), 188*, 954–957.

Mpitsos, G. J., and Davis, W. J. (1973). Learning: classical and avoidance conditioning in the mollusk *Pleurobranchaea. Science (Wash. D.C.), 180*, 317–321.

Mulligan, J. A. (1963). A description of song sparrow song based on instrumental analysis. *Proc. 13th Int. Ornithol. Congr.*, 272–284.

Mulligan, J. A. (1966). Singing behavior and its development in the song sparrow, *Melospiza melodia. Univ. Calif. Publ. Zool. 81*, pp. 1–76.

Mulloney, B. (1969). Interneurons in the central nervous system of flies and the start of flight. *Z. Vgl. Physiol., 64*, 243–253.

Mulloney, B. (1970). Organization of flight motoneurons of diptera. *J. Neurophysiol., 33*, 86–95.

Mulloney, B., and Selverston, A. I. (1972). Antidromic action potentials fail to demonstrate known interactions between neurons. *Science (Wash. D.C.), 177*, 69–72.

Mulloney, B., and Selverston, A. I. (1974a). Organization of the stomatogastric ganglion of the spiny lobster: I. Neurons driving the lateral teeth. *J. Comp. Physiol., 91*, 1–32.

Mulloney, B., and Selverston, A. I. (1974b). Organization of the stomatogastric ganglion of the spiny lobster: III. Coordination of the two subsets of the gastric system. *J. Comp. Physiol., 91*, 53–78.

Muntz, L. (1964). Neuro-muscular foundations of behavior in embryonic and larval stages of the anuran *Xenopus laevis*. Ph.D. dissertation, University of Bristol, England.

Murphey, R. K., and Palka, J. (1974). Efferent control of cricket giant fibres. *Nature (Lond.)*, *248*, 249–251.

Murphey, R. K., Mendenhall, B., Palka, J., and Edwards, J. S. Deafferentation slows the growth of specific dendrites of identified giant interneurons. *J. Comp. Neurol.* (In press.)

Nachtigall, W., and Wilson, D. M. (1967). Neuromuscular control of dipteran flight. *J. Exp. Biol.*, *47*, 77–97.

Naka, K., and Egughi, E. (1962). Spike potentials recorded from insect photoreceptors. *J. Gen. Physiol.*, *45*, 663–680.

Naka, K. I., and Nye, P. W. (1972). Role of horizontal cells in organization of the catfish retinal receptive field. *J. Neurophysiol.*, *34*, 785–801.

Naka, K. I., and Rushton, W. A. H. (1967). The generation and spread of S-potentials in fish (*Cyprinidae*). *J. Physiol. (Lond.)*, *192*, 437–461.

Nakajima, Y. (1974). Fine structure of the synaptic endings on the Mauthner cell of the goldfish. *J. Comp. Neurol.*, *156*, 375–402.

Narayanan, C. H., and Hamburger, V. (1971). Motility in chick embryos with substitution of lumbosacral by brachial and brachial by lumbosacral spinal cord segments. *J. Exp. Zool.*, *178*, 415–432.

Narayanan, C. H., Fox, M. W., and Hamburger, V. (1971). Prenatal development of spontaneous and evoked activity in the rat (*Rattus norwegicus albinus*). *Behaviour*, *40*, 100–134.

Neder, R. (1959). Allometrisches Wachstum von Hirnteilen bei drei verscheiden grossen Schabenarten. *Zool. Jahrb. Abt. Anat. Ontog. Tiere*, *77*, 411–464.

Needham, A. E. (1965). Regeneration in the Arthropoda and its endocrine control. In "Regeneration in Animals and Related Problems" (V. Kiortsis and H. A. L. Trampusch, eds.), pp. 283–323. North-Holland, Amsterdam.

Nelson, M. C. (1971). Classical conditioning in the blowfly (*Phormia regina*): associative and excitatory factors. *J. Comp. Physiol. Psychol.*, *77*, 353–368.

Nelson, R. (1973). A comparison of electrical properties of neurons in *Necturus* retina. *J. Neurophysiol.*, *36*, 519–535.

Newman, J. D. (1970). Midbrain regions relevant to auditory communication in songbirds. *Brain Res.*, *22*, 259–261.

Nicolai, J. (1959). Familientradition in der Gesangsentwicklung des Gimpels (*Pyrrhula pyrrhula* L.). *J. Ornithol.*, *100*, 39–46.

Nicolis, G. Patterns of spatio-temporal organization in chemical and biochemical kinetics. *Proc. Am. Math. Soc.* (In press.)

Nissl, F. (1892). Ueber die Veranderungen der Ganglienzellen am Facialiskern des Kaninchens nach Ausreissung der Nerven. *Allg. Z. Psychiatr.*, *48*, 197–198.

Nordlander, R. H., and Edwards, J. S. (1969). Postembryonic brain development in the monarch butterfly, *Danaus plexippus plexippus* L.: II. The optic lobes. *Wilhelm Roux' Arch. Entwicklungsmech. Org.*, *163*, 197–220.

Nordlander, R. H., and Edwards, J. S. (1970). Postembryonic brain development in the monarch butterfly, *Danaus plexippus plexippus*, L.: III. Morphogenesis of centers other than the optic lobes. *Wilhelm Roux, Arch. Entwicklungsmech. Org.*, 247–260.

Nottebohm, F. (1967). The role of sensory feedback in the development of avian vocalizations. *Proc. 14th Int. Ornitol. Congr.*, 265–280.

Nottebohm, F. (1968). Auditory experience and song development in the chaffinch *Fringilla coelebs*. *Ibis*, *110*, 549–568.

Nottebohm, F. (1971). Neural lateralization of vocal control in a passerine bird: I. Song. *J. Exp. Zool.*, *177*, 229–261.

Nottebohm, F. (1975). Vocal behavior in birds. In "Avian Biology" 5 (D. Farner, J. R. King and K. C. Parkes, eds.). Academic, New York.

Nottebohm, F. (in press). Asymmetries in neural control of vocalization in the canary. In "Lateralization of the Nervous System" (S. Harnad, ed.). Academic New York.

Nüesch, H. (1968). The role of the nervous system in insect morphogenesis and regeneration. *Annu. Rev. Entomol.*, *13*, 97–44.

Olsen, M. I., and Bunge, R. P. (1973). Anatomical observations on the specificity of synapse formation in tissue culture. *Brain Res.*, *59*, 19–33.

Oppenheim, R. W. (1972). Embryology of behavior in birds: a critical review of the role of sensory stimulation in embryonic movement. *Proc. 15th Int. Ornithol. Congr.*, 283–302.

Oppenheim, R. W. (1974). The ontogeny of behavior in the chick embryo. In "Advances in the Study of Behavior" (D. S. Lehrman, R. A. Hinde, and E. Shaw, eds.), Vol. 5, pp. 133–172. Academic, New York.

Ort, C. A., Kristan, W. B., Jr., and Stent, G. S. (1974). Neuronal control of swimming in the medicinal leech: II. Identification and connections of motor neurons. *J. Comp. Physiol.*, *94*, 121–155.

Osborne, N. N., and Cottrell, G. A. (1971). Distribution of biogenic amines in the slug *Limax maximus. Z. Zellforsch Mikrosk. Anat., 112*, 15–30.

Paillard, J. (1955). Analyse électrophysiologique et comparaison, chez l'homme, du réflexe de Hoffmann et du réflexe myotatique. *Pfluegers Arch. Eur. J. Physiol., 260*, 448–479.

Palay, S. L., and Chan-Palay, V. (1974). "Cerebellar Cortex. Cytology and Organization." Springer-Verlag, New York.

Palay, S. L., and Palade, G. E. (1955). The fine structure of neurons. *J. Biophys. Biochem. Cytol., 1*, 69–88.

Palermo, D. S. (1975). Developmental aspects of speech perception: problems for a motor theory. In "The Role of Speech in Language" (J. F. Kavanagh and J. E. Cutting, eds.). MIT Press, Cambridge, Mass.

Palka, J., and Edwards, J. S. (1974). The cerci and abdominal giant fibres of the house cricket, *Acheta domesticus:* II. Regeneration and effects chronic deprivation. *Proc. R. Soc. Lond. B Biol. Sci., 185*, 105–121.

Palka, J., and Schubiger, M. Central connections of receptors on rotated and exchanged cerci of crickets. (In press.)

Panov, A. A. (1961). The structure of the insect brain at successive stages of postembryonic development: IV. The olfactory center. *Entomol. Obozr., 40*, 259–271.

Panov, A. A. (1966). Correlations in the ontogenetic development of the central nervous system in the house cricket *Gryllus domesticus* L. and the mole cricket *Gryllotalpa gryllotalpa* L. (Orthoptera, Grylloidea). *Entomol. Rev. (Engl. Transl. Entomol. Obozr.), 45*, 179–185.

Patton, M. L., and Kater, S. B. (1972). Electrotonic conduction in the optic nerves of planorbid snails. *J. Exp. Biol., 56*, 695–702.

Pavlov, I. P. (1927). "Conditioned Reflexes." Dover, New York.

Pearson, K. G. (1972). Central programming and reflex control of walking in the cockroach. *J. Exp. Biol., 56*, 173–193.

Pearson, K. G., and Bradley, A. B. (1972). Specific regeneration of excitatory motoneurons to leg muscles in the cockroach. *Brain Res., 47*, 492–496.

Pearson, K. G., and Fourtner, C. R. (1975). Nonspiking interneurons in the walking system of the cockroach. *J. Neurophysiol., 38*, 33–52.

Pearson, K. G., Fourtner, C. R., and Wong, R. K. (1973). Nervous control of walking in the cockroach. In "Control of Posture and Locomotion" (R. B. Stein, K. G. Pearson, R. S. Smith, and J. B. Redford, eds.). Plenum, New York.

Peretz, B., and Moller, R. (1974). Control of habituation of the withdrawal reflex by the gill ganglion in *Aplysia. J. Neurobiol., 5*, 191–212.

Perkel, D. H., and Mulloney, B. (1974). Motor pattern production in reciprocally inhibitory neurons exhibiting postinhibitory rebound. *Science (Wash. D.C.), 185*, 181–182.

Petersen, B., Lundgren, L., and Wilson, L. (1956–1957). The development of flight capacity in a butterfly. *Behavior, 10*, 324–339.

Pfaff, D. W. (1972). Interactions of steriod sex hormones with brain tissue: studies of uptake and physiological effect. In "The Regulation of Mammalian Reproduction" (S. Segal, ed.), pp. 5–22. Charles C Thomas, Springfield, Ill.

Pfaff, D. W., Diakow, C., Zigmond, R. E., and Kow, L. (1974). Neural and hormonal determinants of female mating behavior in rats. In "The Neurosciences: Third Study Program" (F. O. Schmitt and F. G. Worden eds.). pp. 621–646. MIT Press, Cambridge, Mass.

Phillips, C. G. (1969). Motor apparatus of the baboon's hand. *Proc. R. Soc. Lond. B Biol. Sci., 173*, 141–174.

Phillips, C. G. (1973). Cortical localization and "sensorimotor processes" at the "middle level" in primates. *Proc. R. Soc. Med., 66*, 987–1002.

Piatt, J. (1969). The influence of VIIth and VIIIth cranial nerve roots upon the differentiation of Mauthner's cell in *Ambystoma. Dev. Biol., 19*, 608–616.

Pilleri, G. (1971). Instinktbewegungen des Menschen in biologischer und neuropathologischer Sicht. *Aktuel. Fragen Psychiatr. Neurol., 11*, 1–37.

Pinsker, H., Kupfermann, I., Castellucci, V., and Kandel, E. (1970). Habituation and dishabituation of the gill-withdrawal reflex in *Aplysia. Science (Wash. D.C.), 167*, 1740–1742.

Pitman, R. M., Tweedle, C. D., and Cohen, M. J. (1972a). Branching of central neurons: intracellular cobalt injection for light and electron microscopy. *Science (Wash. D.C.), 176*, 412–414.

Pitman, R. M., Tweedle, C. D., and Cohen, M. J. (1972b). Electrical responses of insect central neurons: augmentation by nerve section of colchicine. *Science (Wash. D.C.), 178*, 507–509.

Pitman, R. M., Tweedle, C. D., and Cohen, M. J. (1973). The form of nerve cells: determination by cobalt impregnation. In "Intracellular Staining Techniques in Neurobiology" (S. Kater and C. Nicholson, eds). Springer-Verlag, New York.

Poodry, G. A., Hall, L., and Suzuki, D. T. (1973). Developmental properties of *Shibire*[ts]: a pleiotropic mutation affecting larval and adult locomotion and development. *Dev. Biol., 32,* 373–386.

Power, M. E. (1943). Effect of reduction in numbers of omimatidia upon the brain of *Drosophila melanogaster. J. Exp. Zool., 94,* 33–72.

Power, M. E. (1948). The thoracico-abdominal nervous system of an adult insect, *Drosophila melanogaster. J. Comp. Neurol., 88,* 347–410.

Power, M. E. (1950). The central nervous system of winged but flightless *Drosophila melanogaster. J. Exp. Zool., 115,* 315–340.

Prechtl, H. F. R. (1953). Zur Physiologie der angeborenen auslösenden Mechanismen: I. Quantitative Untersuchungen über die Sperrbewegungen junger Singvögel. *Behaviour, 5,* 32–50.

Prestige, M. (1970). Differentiation degeneration and the role of the periphery, quantitative considerations. In "The Neurosciences: Second Study Program" (F. O. Schmitt, ed.), pp. 73–82. Rockefeller University Press, New York.

Preyer, W. (1885). "Specielle Physiologie des Embryo." Grieben, Leipzig.

Prigogine, I. (1969). Structure, dissipation and life. In "Theoretical Physics and Biology" (M. Marois, ed.). North-Holland, Amsterdam.

Pringle, J. W. S. (1939). The motor mechanism of the insect leg. *J. Exp. Biol. 16,* 220–231.

Pringle, J. W. S. (1949). The excitation and contraction of the flight muscles of insects. *J. Physiol. (Lond.), 108,* 226–232.

Pringle, J. W. S. (1957). "Insect Flight." Cambridge University Press, Cambridge.

Pringle, J. W. S. (1967). The contractile mechanism of insect fibrillar muscle. *Prog. Biophys. Mol. Biol., 17,* 1–60.

Prior, D., and Gelperin, A. (1974). Behavioral and physiological studies on locomotion in the giant garden slug *Limax maximus. Malacol. Rev., 7,* 50–51.

Pritchard, J. A. (1965). Deglutition by normal and anencephalic fetuses. *Obstet. Gynecol., 25,* 289–297.

Provine, R. R. (1971). Embryonic spinal cord: synchrony and spatial distribution of palyneuronal burst discharges. *Brain Res., 29,* 155–158.

Provine, R. R. (1972a). Hatching behavior of the chick (*Gallus domesticus*): plasticity of the rotatory component. *Psychon. Sci. Sect. Anim. Physiol. Psychol., 29,* 27–28.

Provine, R. R. (1972b). Ontogeny of bioelectric activity in the spinal cord of the chick embryo and its behavioral implications. *Brain Res., 41,* 365–378.

Provine, R. R. (1973). Neurophysiological aspects of behavior development in the chick embryo. In "Studies on the Development of Behavior and the Nervous System" (G. Gottlieb, ed.), Vol. 1, "Behavioral Embryology," pp. 77–102. Academic, New York.

Provine, R. R. Eclosion and hatching in cockroach first instar larvae: triggering, maintenance and termination of a stereotyped pattern of behavior. *J. Insect Physiol.* (In press.)

Provine, R. R. The behavioral embryology of the cockroach *Periplaneta americana.* (In preparation.)

Provine, R. R., Aloe, L., and Seshan, K. R. (1973). Spontaneous bioelectric activity in long term cultures of the embryonic insect central nervous system. *Brain Res., 56,* 364–370.

Provine, R. R., Seshan, K. R., and Aloe, L. (1974) Emergence of geometric patterns in insect nerve nets: an *in vitro* analysis. *Brain Res., 80,* 328–334.

Provine, R. R., Seshan, K. R., and Aloe, L. (1975). Formation of cockroach interganglionic connectives: an *in vitro* analysis. *J. Comp. Neurol.*

Provine, R. R., Sharma, S. C., Sandel, T. T., and Hamburger, V. (1970). Electrical activity in the spinal cord of the chick embryo *in situ. Proc. Natl. Acad. Sci. U.S.A., 65,* 508–515.

Quick, H. E. (1961). British slugs (Plumonata: Testacellidae, Arionidae, Limacidae). *Bull. Br. Mus. (Nat. Hist.) Zool., 6* (3).

Quinn, W. G., Harris, W. A., and Benzer, S. (1974). Conditioned behavior in *Drosophila melanogaster. Proc. Natl. Acad. Sci. U.S.A., 71,* 708–712.

Raisman, G., and Field P. M. (1973). A quantitative investigation of the development of collateral reinnervation after partial deafferentation of the septal neclei. *Brain Res., 50,* 241–264.

Rakic, P. (1974). Intrinsic and extrinsic factors influencing the shape of neurons and their assembly into neuronal circuits. In "Frontiers in Neurology and Neuroscience Research" (P. Seeman and G. M. Brown, eds.). Neuroscience Institute, University of Toronto, Toronto, Canada.

Rakic, P., and Sidman, R. L. (1973). Organization of cerebellar cortex secondary to deficit of granule cells in weaver mutant mice. *J. Comp. Neurol., 152,* 133–162.

Rall, W., and Shepherd, G. M. (1968). Theoretical reconstruction of field potentials and dendrodendritic synaptic interactions in olfactory bulb. *J. Neurophysiol., 31*, 884–915.

Rall, W., Shepherd, G. M., and Reese, T. S. (1966). Dendro-dendritic synaptic pathway for inhibition in the olfactory bulb. *Exp. Neurol., 14*, 44–56.

Ralston, H. J. (1971). Evidence for presynaptic dendrites and a proposal for their mechanism of action. *Nature (Lond.), 230*, 585–587.

Ramón y Cajal, S. (1899). "Textura del Sistema Nervioso del Hombre y de los Vertebrados," Vol. 1, pp. 70–71. Moya, Madrid.

Ramón y Cajal, S. (1937). "Recollections of My Life" (E. H. Craigie). MIT Press, Cambridge, Mass.

Ramón y Cajal, S., and Sanchez, D. (1915). Contribución al conocimiento de los centros nerviosos de los insectos. *Trab. Lab. Invest. Biol. Univ. Madrid, 13*, 1–164.

Randall, W. L. (1964). The behavior of cats (*Felis catus L.*) with lesions in the caudal midbrain region. *Behavior, 23*, 107–139.

Reese, T. S., and Shepherd, G. M. (1972). Dendrodendritic synapses in the central nervous system. In "Structure and Function of Synapses" (G. D. Pappas and D. P. Purpura, eds.), pp. 121–136. Raven, New York.

Reichardt, W. (1961). Autocorrelation, a principle for the evaluation of sensory information by the central nervous system. In "Sensory Communication" (W. A. Rosenblith, ed.). MIT Press, Cambridge, Mass.

Reiner, J. M. (1968). "The Organism as an Adaptive Control System." Prentice-Hall, Englewood Cliffs, N.J.

Reiss, R. G. (1962). A theory and simulation of rhythmic behavior due to reciprocal inhibition in small nerve nets. *1962 Spring Joint Computer Conf., AFIPS Proc., 21*, 171–194.

Remmers, J. E., and Gautier, H. (1972). Neural and mechanical mechanisms of feline purring. *Respir. Physiol., 16*, 351–361.

Ripley, K. L., and Provine, R. R. (1972). Neural correlates of embryonic motility in the chick. *Brain Res., 45*, 127–134.

Ripley, S. H., Bush, B. M. H., and Roberts, A. (1968). Crab muscle receptor which responds without impulses. *Nature (Lond.), 218*, 1170–1171.

Roberts, A (1971). The role of propagated skin impulses in the sensory system of young tadpoles. *Z. Vgl. Physiol., 75*, 388–401.

Roberts, E. (1972). An hypothesis suggesting that there is a defect in the GABA system in schizophrenia. *Neurosci. Res. Program Bull., 10*, 468–482.

Roberts, E. (1974). A model of the vertebrate nervous system based largely on disinhibition: a key role of the *gaba* system. In "Neurohumoral Coding of Brain Function" (R. D. Myers and R. R. Drucker-Colin, eds.), pp. 419–449. Plenum, New York.

Robertson, J. D., Bodenheimer, T. S., Stage, D. E. (1963). The ultrastructure of Mauthner cell synapses and nodes in goldfish brains. *J. Cell Biol., 19*, 159–199.

Roeder, K. D. (1935). An experimental analysis of the sexual behavior of the praying mantis. *Biol. Bull. (Woods Hole), 69*, 203–220.

Roeder, K. D. (1937). The control of tonus and locomotor activity in the praying mantis, *Mantis religiosa* L. *J. Exp. Zool., 76*, 353–374.

Roeder, K. D. (1951). Movements of the thorax and potential changes in the thoracic muscles of insects during flight. *Biol. Bull. Woods Hole, 100*, 95–106.

Roeder, K. D. Tozian, L., and Weiant, E. A. (1960). Endogenous nerve activity and behaviour in the mantis and cockroach. *J. Insect Physiol., 4*, 45–62.

Roman, C., and Tieffenbach, L. (1972). Enregistrement de l'activité unitaire des fibres motrices vagales destinées à`l'oesophage du babouin. *J. Physiol. (Paris), 64*, 479–506.

Rovainen, C. M. (1967). Physiological and anatomical studies on large neurons of the central nervous system of the sea lamprey (*Petromyzon marimus*): I. Müller and Mauthner cells. *J. Neurophysiol., 30*, 1000–1023.

Rummel, H. (1970). Die nerveninduzierte Regeneration der Cerci bei *Acheta domesticus* L. *Dtsch. Entomol. Z., 17*, 357–409.

Russell, I. J. (1971). The role of the lateral-line efferent system in *Xenopus laevis*. *J. Exp. Biol., 54*, 621–641.

Sahota, T. S., and Edwards, J. S. (1968). Development of grafted supernumerary legs in the house cricket, *Acheta domesticus. J. Insect Physiol., 15*, 1367–1373.

Sandeman, D. and Luff, S. E. (1974). Regeneration of the antennules in the Australian freshwater crayfish *Cherax destructor. J. Neurobiol., 5*, 489–510.

Sanders, G. D. (1975). Octopus learning. In "Invertebrate Learning" (W. C. Corning, J. A. Dyal, and A. O. D. Willows, eds.), Vol. 3, pp. 1–102. Plenum, New York.

Sbrenna, G. (1971). Post embryonic growth of the ventral nerve cord in *Schistocerca gregaria* (Orthoptera; Acrididae). *Bull. Zool., 38*, 49–74.

Schaeffer, R. (1973). Post embryonic development in

the antenna of the cockroach *Leucophaea maderae*: growth, regeneration, and the development of the adult pattern of sense organs. *J. Exp. Zool., 183*, 353–364.

Scheibel, M., and Scheibel, A. B. (1973). Dendrite bundles as sites for central programs: an hypothesis. *Int. J. Neurosci., 6*, 195–202.

Scheibel, M. E., Davies, T. L., and Scheibel, A. B. (1972). An unusual axonless cell in the thalamus of the adult cat. *Exp. Neurol., 36*, 519–529.

Scheich, H., and Bullock, T. H. (1975). The detection of electric fields from electric organs. In "Handbook of Sensory Physiology. Electroreceptors and Specialized Receptors in Lower Vertebrates" (A. Fessard, ed.), pp. 201–256. Springer-Verlag, New York.

Schleidt, W. M. (1974). How "fixed" is the fixed action pattern? *Z. Tierpsychol., 36*, 184–211.

Schmidt, K., and Gnatzy, W. (1971). Die Feinstruktur der Sinneshaare auf den Cerci von *Gryllus bimaculatus* Deg. (Saltatoria, Gryllidae): II. Die Häutung der Faden- und Keulenhaare. *Z. Zellforsch. 122*, 210–226.

Schmidt, R. S. (1966). Central mechanisms of frog calling. *Behavior, 26*, 251–285.

Schmidt, R. S. (1971). A model of the central mechanisms of male anuran acoustic behavior. *Behaviour, 29*, 288–317.

Schmidt, R. S. (1972). Action of intrinsic laryngeal muscles during release calling in leopard frog. *J. Exp. Zool., 181*, 233–244.

Schmidt, R. S. (1974a). Neural correlates of frog calling: independence from peripheral feedback. *J. Comp. Physiol., 88*, 321–333.

Schmidt, R. S. (1974b). Neural correlates of frog calling: trigeminal tegmentum. *J. Comp. Physiol. 92*, 229–254.

Schmidt, R. S. (1974c). Neural mechanisms of releasing (unclasping) in American toad. *Behaviour, 48*, 315–326.

Scholes, J. (1969). The electrical responses of the retinal receptors and the lamina in the visual system of the fly *Musca. Kybernetik, 6*, 149–162.

Schwartz, J. H., Castellucci, V. F., and Kandel, E. R. (1971). Functioning of identified neurons and synapses in abdominal ganglion of *Aplysia* in absence of protein synthesis. *J. Neurophysiol., 34*, 939–954.

Sears, T. A. (1964). The slow potentials of thoracic respiratory motoneurones and their relation to breathing. *J. Physiol., 175*, 404–424.

Sechenov, I. M. (1866). "Reflexes of the Brain" (G. Gibbons, ed.; S. Belsky, trans.). MIT Press, Cambridge, Mass.

Seligman, M. E. P., and Hager, J. L., eds. (1972). "Biological Boundaries of Learning." Appleton-Century-Crofts, New York.

Selverston, A. I. (1973). The use of intracellular dye injections in the study of small neural networks. In "Intracellular Staining in Neurobiology" (S. Kater and C. Nicholson, eds.). Springer-Verlag, New York.

Selverston, A. I. (1974). Structural and functional basis of motor pattern generation in the stomatogastric ganglion of the lobster. *Am. Zool., 14*, 957–972.

Selverston, A. I., and Mulloney, B. (1974a). Organization of the stomatogastric ganglion of the spiny lobster: II. Neurons driving the medial tooth. *J. Comp. Physiol., 91*, 33–51.

Selverston, A. I., and Mulloney, B. (1974c). Synaptic and structural analysis of a small neural system. In "The Neurosciences: Third Study Program" (F. O. Schmitt and F. G. Worden, eds.). MIT Press, Cambridge, Mass.

Selverston, A. I., and Remler, M. P. (1972). Neural geometry and activation of crayfish fast flexor motoneurons. *J. Neurophysiol., 35*, 797–914.

Senseman, D. Neuronal organization of the buccal ganglion in *Ariolimax columbianus*. (In preparation.)

Senseman, D., and Gelperin, A. (1973). Comparative aspects of the morphology and physiology of a single identifiable neuron in *Helix aspersa, Limax maximus* and *Ariolimax californica. Malacol. Rev., 7*, 51–52.

Seshan, K. R., Provine, R. R., and Levi-Montalcini, R. (1974). Structural and electrophysiological properties of nymphal and adult insect medial neurosecretory cells: an *in vitro* analysis. *Brain Res., 78*, 359–376.

Shaw, S. R. (1968). Organization of the locust retina. *Symp. Zool. Soc. Lond., 23*, 135–163.

Shaw, S. R. (1969). Interreceptor coupling in ommatidia of drone honeybee and locust component eyes. *Vision Res., 9*, 999–1029.

Shaw, S. R. (1972). Decremental conduction of the visual signal in barnacle lateral eye. *J. Physiol., 220*, 145–175.

Shepherd, G. M. (1972a). The neuron doctrine: a revision of functional concepts. *Yale J. Biol. Med., 45*, 584–599.

Shepherd, G. M. (1972b). Synaptic organization of the mammalian olfactory bulb. *Physiol. Rev., 52*, 864–917.

Sheridan, J. D. (1968). Electrophysiological evidence

for low-resistance intercellular junctions in the early chick embryo. *J. Cell Biol., 37*, 650–659.

Sherrington, C. S. (1900). The parts of the brain below cerebral cortex: viz., medulla oblongata, pons, cerebellum, corpora, quadrigemina, and region of thalamus. In "Textbook of Physiology" (E. A. Schäfer, ed.), p. 887. Pentland, Edinburgh.

Sherrington, C. S. (1906). "The Integrative Action of the Nervous System." Yale University Press, New Haven, Conn.

Sherrington, C. S. (1929). Some functional problems attaching to convergence. *Proc. R. Soc. Lond. B Biol. Sci., 105*, 332–362.

Sidman, R. L. (1968). Development of interneuronal connections in brains of mutant mice. In "Physiological and Biochemical Aspects of Nervous Integration" (F. D. Carlson, ed.), pp. 163–193. Prentice-Hall, Englewood Cliffs, N.J.

Sidman, R. L. (1972). Cell proliferation, migration, and interaction in the developing mammalian central nervous system. In "The Neurosciences: Second Study Program" (F. O. Schmitt, ed.), pp. 100–107. Rockefeller University Press, New York.

Sidman, R. L. (1974). Cell–cell recognition in the developing central nervous system. In "The Neurosciences: Third Study Program" (F. O. Schmitt and F. G. Worden, eds.), pp. 743–758. MIT Press, Cambridge, Mass.

Siegler, M. V. S., Mpitsos, G. J., and Davis, W. J. (1974). Motor organization and generation of rhythmic feeding output in the buccal ganglion of *Pleurobranchaea. J. Neurophysiol., 37*, 1173–1196.

Sikes, E. K., and Wigglesworth, V. B. (1931). The hatching of insects from the egg and the appearance of air in the tracheal system. *J. Microsc. Sci., 74*, 165–192.

Simon, W. (1972). "Mathematical Techniques for Physiology and Medicine." Academic, New York.

Simonov, L. N. (1866a). Experimental evidence for the existence of "reflex-suppressive centers" in mammals. *Voenno-Med. Zh., 44*, 1–31, 67–92.

Simonov, L. N. (1866b). Die Hemmungsmechanismen der Säugetheire experimentell bewiesen. *Arch. Anat. Physiol. (Leipzig), 33*, 545–564.

Singer, M. (1974). Neurotrophic control of limb regeneration in the newt. *Ann. N.Y. Acad. Sci., 228*, 308–322.

Skoff, R. P., and Hamburger, V. (1974). Fine structure of dendritic and axonal growth cones in embryonic chick spinal cord. *J. Comp. Neurol., 153*, 107–148.

Sloper, J. J. (1971). Dendro-dendritic synapses in the primate motor cortex. *Brain Res., 34*, 186–192.

Sokolove, P. G. (1973). Crayfish stretch receptor and motor unit behavior during abdominal extension. *J. Comp. Physiol., 84*, 251–266.

Sotelo, C., Llinás, R., and Baker, R. (1974). Structural study of the inferior olivary nucleus of the cat. Morphological correlates of electrotonic coupling. *J. Neurophysiol., 37*, 541–559.

Sotelo, C., Hillman, D. E., Zamora, A. J., and Llinás, R. Climbing fiber deafferentation: its action on Purkinje cell dendritic spines. *Brain Res.* (In press.)

Sperry, R. W. (1963). Chemoaffinity in the orderly growth of nerve fiber patterns and connections. *Proc. Natl. Acad. Sci. U.S.A., 50*, 703–710.

Spira, H., and Bennett, M. V. L. (1972). Synaptic control of electrotonic coupling between neurons. *Brain Res., 37*, 294–300.

Spray, D. C. and Bennett, M. V. L. (1972). Pharyngeal sensory neurons and feeding behavior in the opisthobranch mollusk *Navanax*. Society for Neuroscience, 5th Annual Meeting, Abstracts, p. 570.

Spreij, T. H. (1971). Cell death during the development of the imaginal discs of *Calliphora erythrocephala. Neth. J. Zool., 21*, 221–264.

Stark, L. (1968). "Neurological Control Systems. Studies in Bioengineering." Plenum, New York.

Stefanelli, A. (1933). Le Cellule e le fibre di Müller die pertomyzonti. *Arch. Ital. Anat. Embriol., 31*, 519–548.

Stefanelli, A. (1952). The Mauthnerian apparatus in the Ichthyopsida; its nature and function and correlated problems of neurogenesis. *Q. Rev. Biol., 26*, 17–34.

Stein, P. S. G. (1971). Intersegmental coordination of swimmeret motoneuron activity in crayfish. *J. Neurophysiol., 34*, 310–318.

Stein, P. S. G. (1974). Neural control of interappendage phase during locomotion. *Am. Zool., 14*, 1003–1016.

Steinbach, A. B. (1974). Transmission from receptor cells to afferent nerve fibers. In "Synaptic Transmission and Neural Interaction" (M. V. L. Bennett, ed.), pp. 105–140. Raven, New York.

Steinberg, R. H., and Schmidt, R. (1970). Identification of horizontal cells as S-potential generators in the cat retina by intracellular dye injection. *Vision Res., 10*, 817–820.

Steiner, J. E. (1973). The gustofacial response: observation on normal and anencephalic newborn infants. In "Oral Sensation and Perception:

Development in the Fetus and Infant" (J. F. Bosma, ed.), pp. 225–278. U.S. Department of Health, Education, and Welfare, Bethesda, Md.

Stocker, R. (1974). Die Entwicklung der ventralen Ganglionkette bei der Arbeiterinnenkaste von *Myrmica Bevinoides*. Nyl. (Hym., Form.). *Rev. Suisse Zool., 80*, 972–1029.

Strausfeld, N. J. (1970a). Golgi studies on insects: II. Optic lobes of *Diptera*. *Philos. Trans. R. Soc. Lond. B Biol. Sci., 258*, 135–223.

Strausfeld, N. J. (1970b). Variations and invariants of cell arrangements in the nervous systems of insects (a review of neuronal arrangements in the visual system and corpora pedunculata). *Verh. Dtsch. Zool. Ges., 64*, 97–108.

Strausfeld, N. J. (1971). The organization of the insect visual system (light microscopy). *Z. Zellforsch. Mikrosk. Anat., 121*, 377–454.

Straznicky, K. (1963). Function of heterotopic spinal cord segments investigated in the chick. *Acta Biol. Acad. Sci. Hung., 14*, 145–155.

Strumwasser, F. (1968). Membrane and intracellular mechanism governing endogenous activity in neurons. In "Physiological and Biochemical Aspects of Nervous Integration" (F. D. Carlson, ed.), pp. 329–342. Prentice-Hall, Englewood Cliffs, N.J.

Studdert-Kennedy, M. (1975). From continuous signal to discrete message: syllable to phoneme. In "The Role of Speech in Language" (J. F. Kavanagh and J. E. Cutting, eds.). MIT Press, Cambridge, Mass.

Studdert-Kennedy, M., and Shankweiler, D. P. (1970). Hemispheric specialization for speech perception. *J. Acoust. Soc. Am., 48*, 579–594.

Sumi, T. (1964). Neuronal mechanisms in swallowing. *Pfluegers Arch. Eur. J. Physiol., 278*, 467–477.

Sumi, T. (1967). The nature and postnatal development of reflex deglutition in the kitten. *Jpn. J. Physiol., 17*, 200–210.

Sumi, T. (1969a). Some properties of cortically-evoked swallowing and chewing in rabbits. *Brain Res., 15*, 107–120.

Sumi, T. (1969b). Synaptic potentials of hypoglossal motoneurons and their relation to reflex deglutition. *Jpn. J. Physiol., 19*, 68–79.

Sumi, T. (1970). Activity in single hypoglossal fibers during cortically induced swallowing and chewing in rabbits. *Pfluegers Arch. Eur. J. Physiol., 314*, 329–346.

Sumner, B. E. H., and Sutherland, F. I. (1973). Quantitative electron microscopy on the injured hypo-glossal nucleus in the rat. *J. Neurocytol., 2*, 315–328.

Sumner, B. E. H., and Watson, W. E. (1971). Retraction and expansion of the dendritic tree of motor neurones of adult rats induced *in vivo*. *Nature (Lond.), 233*, 273–275.

Suzuki, D. T. (1970). Temperature-sensitive mutations in *Drosophila malanogaster*. *Science (Wash. D.C.), 170*, 695–706.

Suzuki, D. T., Grigliatti, T., and Williamson, R. (1971). Temperature-sensitive mutants in *Drosophila melanogaster*: VII. A mutation (*para*[ts]) causing reversible adult paralysis. *PNAS, 68*, 890–893.

Swisher, J. E., and Hibbard, E. (1967). The course of Mauthner axons in Janus-headed *Xenopus* embryos. *J. Exp. Zool., 165*, 443–439.

Szentágothai, J., and Arbib, M. A. (1974). Conceptual models of neural organization. *Neurosci. Res. Program Bull., 12*, 305–310.

Szentágothai, J., and Rjakovits, K. (1959). Ueber den Ursprung der kletterfasern des kleinhirns. *Z. Anat. Entwicklungsgesch., 121*, 130–141.

Tatton, W., and Sokolove, P. G. Analysis of postural motoneuron activity in crayfish abdomen: I. Reciprocity, symmetry and gradient of activity. (In preparation.)

Tatton, W., and Sokolove, P. G. Analysis of postural motoneuron activity in crayfish abdomen: II. Motoneuron cross connections. (In preparation.)

Taylor, H. M., and Truman, J. W. (1974). Metamorphosis of the abdominal ganglia of the tobacco horn worm, *Manduca sexta*. Changes in populations of identified motor neurons. *J. Comp. Physiol., 90*, 367–388.

Testerman, R. L. (1970). Modulation of laryngeal activity by pulmonary changes during vocalization in cats. *Exp. Neurol., 29*, 281–297.

Thompson, S. H. (1974). Pattern generator for rhythmic output in *Melibe*. Abstract, 4th Meeting, Soc. Neurosciences.

Thor, D. H., and Ghiselli, W. B. (1975). Suppression of mouse killing and ampomorphine-induced social aggression in rats by local anesthesia of the mystacial vibrissae. *J. Comp. Physiol. Psychol., 88*, 40–46.

Thorpe, W. H. (1955). Comments on "The Bird Fancyer's Delight" together with notes on imitation in the subsong of the chaffinch. *Ibis, 94*, 247–251.

Thorpe, W. H. (1958). The learning of song patterns by birds, with special reference to the song of the chaffinch, *Fringilla coelebs*. *Ibis, 100*, 535–570.

Thorpe, W. H. (1963). "Learning and Instinct in Animals," 2nd ed. Methuen, London.

Thorpe, W. H., and Pilcher, P. M. (1958). The nature and characteristics of subsong. *Br. Birds, 51,* 509–514.

Thorson, J., and Biederman-Thorson, M. (1974). Distributed relaxation processes in sensory adaptation. *Science (Wash. D.C.), 183,* 161–172.

Tieffenbach, L., and Roman, C. (1972). Role de l'innervation extrinsèque vagale dans la motricité de l'oesophage à musculeuse lisse: étude électromyographique chez le chat et le babouin. *J. Physiol. (Paris)., 64,* 193–226.

Tinbergen, N. (1951). "The Study of Instinct." Clarendon Press, Oxford.

Todt, D. (1974). "Zur Bedeutung der richtigen" Syntax auditiver muster für deren vokale Beantwortung durch Amseln. *Z. Naturforsch. Teil C, 29,* 157–160.

Toevs, L. A., and Brackenbury, R. W. (1969). Bag cell-specific proteins and the humoral control of egg laying in *Aplysia californica. Comp. Biochem. Physiol., 29,* 207–216.

Tomita, T. (1965). Electrophysiological study of the mechanism subserving color coding in the fish retina. *Cold Spring Harbor Symp. Quant. Biol., 30,* 559–566.

Tomita, T. (1970). Electrical activity of vertebrate photoreceptors. *Q. Rev. Biophys., 3,* 179–222.

Toyoda, J., Nosaki, H., and Tomita, T. (1969). Light induced resistance changes in single photoreceptors of *Necturus* and *Gekko. Vision Res., 9,* 453–463.

Toyoda, J., Hashimoto, H., Anno, H., and Tomita, T. (1970). The rod response in the frog as studied by intracellular recording. *Vision Res., 10,* 1093–1100.

Tracy, H. C. (1926). The development of motility and behavior reactions in the toadfish (*Opsanus tau*). *J. Comp. Neurol., 40,* 253–369.

Trehub, S. E. (1973). Infant's sensitivity to vowel and tonal contrasts. *Dev. Psychol., 9,* 91–96.

Trehub, S. E., and Rabinovitch, M. S. (1972). Auditory-linguistic sensitivity in early infancy. *Dev. Psychol., 6,* 74–77.

Trout, W. E., and Kaplan, W. D. (1973). Genetic manipulation of motor output in shaker mutants of *Drosophila. J. Neurobiol., 4,* 495–512.

Trujillo-Cenóz, O. (1965). Some aspects of the structural organization of the intermediate retina of dipterans. *J. Ultrastruct. Res., 13,* 1–33.

Trujillo-Cenóz, O., and Melamed, J. (1966). Compound eyes of dipterans: anatomical basis for integration – an electron microscope study. *J. Ultrastruct. Res., 16,* 396–398.

Truman, J. W. (1970). The eclosion hormone: its release by the brain and its action on the central nervous system of silkmoths. *Am. Zool., 10,* 511–512.

Truman, J. W. (1971). Physiology of insect ecdysis: I. The eclosion behaviour of saturniid moths and its hormonal release. *J. Exp. Biol., 54,* 805–814.

Truman, J. W., and Riddiford, L. M. (1970). Neuroendocrine control of ecdysis in silkmoths. *Science (Wash. D.C.), 167,* 1624–1626.

Truman, J. W., and Riddiford, L. M. (1974). Hormonal mechanisms underlying insect behaviour. *Adv. Insect Physiol., 10,* 297–352.

Truman, J. W., and Sokolove, P. G. (1972). Silk moth eclosion: hormonal triggering of a centrally programmed pattern of behavior. *Science (Wash. D.C.), 175,* 1491–1493.

Tulley, W. J. (1953). Methods of recording patterns of behavior of the orofacial muscles using the electromyograph. *Dent. Rec., 73,* 741–748.

Tung, A. S-C., and Pipa, R. L. (1971). Fine structure of the interganglionic connectives and degenerating axons of wax moth larvae. *J. Ultrastruct. Res., 36,* 694–707.

Tweedle, C. D., Pitman, R. M., and Cohen, M. J. (1973). Dendritic stability of insect central neurons subjected to axotomy and deafferentation. *Brain Res., 60,* 471–476.

Tyrer, N. M., and Altman, J. S. (1974). Motor and sensory flight neurones in a locust demonstrated using cobalt chloride. *J. Comp. Neurol., 157,* 117–139.

Usherwood, P. N. R., and Runion, H. I. (1970). Analysis of the mechanical responses of metathoracic extensor tibiae muscles of free-walking locusts. *J. Exp. Biol., 52,* 39–58.

Valenstein, E. S. Stereotyped behavior and stress. In "Psychopathology of Human Adaptation" (G. Serban and J. W. Mason, eds.). Plenum, New York. (In press.)

Vallbo, Å. B. (1971). Muscle spindle response at the onset of isometric voluntary contractions in man. Time differences between fusimotor and skeletomotor effects. *J. Physiol. (Lond.), 218,* 405–431.

Valverde, F. (1973). The neuropil in superficial layers of the superior colliculus of the mouse. A correlated Golgi and electron microscopic study. *Z. Anat. Entwicklungsgesch., 142,* 117–148.

Vanderwolf, C. H. (1975). Neocortical and hippocampal activation in relation to behavior: effects of atropine, eserine, phenothiazines, and amphetamine. *J. Comp. Physiol. Psychol., 88,* 300–323.

Van Iersel, J. J. A., and Van Den Assem, J. (1965). Aspects of orientation in the digger-wasp *Bembix rostrata.* In "Learning and Associated Phenomena in Invertebrates" (W. H. Thorpe and D. Davenport, eds.), pp. 145–161. *Anim. Behav. Suppl., 1.*

Vargas-Lizardi, P., and Lyser, K. M. (1974). The time of origin of Mauthner's neuron in *Xenopus laevis* embryos. *Dev. Biol., 38,* 220–228.

Vaughn, J. E., Henrikson, C. K., and Grieshaber, J. A. (1974). A quantitative study of synapses on motor neuron dendrite growth cones in developing mouse spinal cord. *J. Cell Biol., 60,* 664–672.

Vince, M. A. (1973). Some environmental effects on the activity and development of the avian embryo. In "Studies on the Development of Behavior and the Nervous System" (G. Gottlieb, ed.), Vol. 1, "Behavioral Embryology," pp. 323–386. Academic, New York.

Visintini, F., and Levi-Montalcini, R. (1939). Relazione tra differenziazione strutturale e funzionale dei centri e delle vie nervose nell'embrione di pollo. *Schweiz. Arch. Neurol. Psychiatr., 43,* 1–45.

Walcott, C., and Salpeter, M. M. (1966). The effect of molting upon the vibration receptor of the spider *Archaearanea tepidariorum. J. Morphol., 119,* 383–392.

Walker, T. J. (1957). Specificity in the response of female tree crickets (Orthoptera, Gryllidae, Oecanthinae) to calling songs of the males. *Ann. Entomol. Soc. Am., 50,* 626–636.

Walker, T. J. (1962). Factors responsible for intraspecific variation in the calling songs of crickets. *Evolution, 16,* 407–428.

Weight, F. F. (1974). Synaptic potentials resulting from conductance decreases. In "Synaptic Transmission and Neuronal Interaction" (M. V. L. Bennett, ed.), pp. 141–152. Raven, New York.

Weinberg, B., and Bosma, J. F. (1970). Similarities between glossopharyngeal breathing and injection methods of air intake for esophageal speech. *J. Speech Hear. Disord., 35,* 26–32.

Weiss, M. J. (1974). Neuronal connections and the function of the corpora pedunculata in the brain of the American cockroach, *Periplaneta americana. J. Morphol., 142,* 21–70.

Weiss, M. J., and Edwards, J. S. "Growth rings" in the corpora pedunculata of the insect brain: an autoradiographic and silver impregnation analysis. *Am. J. Zool.* (In press, abstract.)

Weiss, P. (1941). Self-differentiation of the basic patterns of coordination. *Comp. Psychol. Monogr., 17,* 1–96.

Wendler, G. (1974). The influence of proprioceptive feedback on locust flight coordination. *J. Comp. Physiol., 88,* 173–200.

Werblin, F. F. (1974). Control of retinal sensitivity: II. Lateral interactions at the outer plexiform layer. *J. Gen. Physiol., 63,* 62–87.

Werblin, F. S., and Dowling, J. E. (1969). Organization of the retina of the mudpuppy, *Necturus maculosus:* II. Intracellular recording. *J. Neurophysiol., 32,* 339–355.

Wiepkema, P. R. (1961). An ethological analysis of the reproductive behavior of the bitterling (*Rhodeus amarus*). *Arch. Neerl. Zool., 14,* 103–199.

Wiersma, C. A. G. (1947). Giant nerve fiber system of the crayfish. A contribution to comparative physiology of synapse. *J. Neurophysiol., 10,* 23–38.

Wiersma, C. A. G. (1958). On the functional connections of single units in the central nervous system of the crayfish, *Procambarus clarkii* Girard. *J. Comp. Neurol., 110,* 421–472.

Wiersma, C. A. G. (1967). "Invertebrate Nervous Systems: Their Significance for Mammalian Neurophysiology." University of Chicago Press, Chicago.

Wiersma, C. A. G., and Ikeda, K. (1964). Interneurons commanding swimmeret movements in the crayfish, *Procambarus clarkii* (Girard). *Comp. Biochem. Physiol., 12,* 509–525.

Wigglesworth, V. B. (1940). Local and general factors in the development of "pattern" in *Rhodnius prolixus* (Hemiptera). *J. Exp. Biol., 17,* 180–200.

Wigglesworth, V. B. (1953a). Determination of cell function in an insect. *J. Embryol. Exp. Morphol., 1,* 269–277.

Wigglesworth, V. B. (1953b). The origin of sensory neurons in an insect. *Q. J. Microsc. Sci., 94,* 93–112.

Wigglesworth, V. B. (1954). "The Physiology of Insect Metamorphosis." Cambridge University Press, New York.

Wilcoxon, H. C., Dragoin, W. B., and Kral, P. A. (1971). Illness-induced aversions in rat and quail: relative salience of visual and gustatory cues. *Science (Wash. D.C.), 171,* 826–828.

Wiley, R. H. (1973). The strut display of male sage grouse: a "fixed" action pattern. *Behaviour, 47,* 129–152.

Willows, A. O. D. (1967). Behavioral acts elicited by stimulation of single, identifiable brain cells. *Science (Wash. D.C.), 157,* 570–574.

Willows, A. O. D. (1968). Behavioral acts elicited by stimulation of single identifiable nerve cells. In "Physiological and Biochemical Aspects of Nervous Integration" (F. D. Carlson, ed.). Prentice-Hall, Englewood Cliffs, N.J.

Willows, A. O. D. (1973). Gastropod nervous system as a model experimental system in neurobiological research. *Fed. Proc., 32*, 2215–2223.

Willows, A. O. D., and Dorsett, D. A. (1975). Evolution of swimming behavior in *Tritonia* and its neurophysiological correlates. (In press.)

Willows, A. O. D., Dorsett, D. A., and Hoyle, G. (1973a). The neuronal basis of behavior in *Tritonia*: I. Functional organization of the central nervous system. *J. Neurobiol., 4*, 207–237.

Willows, A. O. D., Dorsett, D. A., and Hoyle, G. (1973b). The neuronal basis of behavior in *Tritonia*: III. Neuronal mechanism of a fixed action pattern. *J. Neurobiol., 4*, 255–285.

Willows, A. O. D., Getting, P. A., and Thompson, S. (1973). Bursting mechanisms in molluskan locomotion. In "Control of Posture and Locomotion" (R. B. Stein et al., eds.). Plenum, New York.

Wilson, D. M. (1961). The central nervous control of flight in a locust. *J. Exp. Biol., 38*, 471–490.

Wilson, D. M. (1964). The origin of the flight-motor command in grasshoppers. In "Neural Theory and Modeling" (R. Reiss, ed.). Stanford University Press, Stanford, Calif.

Wilson, D. M. (1966). Central nervous mechanisms for the generation of rhythmic behavior in arthropods. *Symp. Soc. Exp. Biol., 20*, 199–228.

Wilson, D. M. (1968a). The flight system of the locust. *Sci. Am., 218*, 83–93.

Wilson, D. M. (1968b). The nervous control of flight and related behavior. In "Advances in Insect Physiology" (J. W. L. Beament, J. E. Treherne, and V. B. Wigglesworth, eds.), Vol. 5. Academic Press, New York.

Wilson, D. M., and Davis, W. J. (1965). Nerve impulse patterns and reflex control in the crayfish claw motor system. *J. Exp. Biol., 43*, 193–210.

Wilson, D. M., and Gettrup, E. (1963). A stretch reflex controlling wingbeat frequency in grasshoppers. *J. Exp. Biol., 40*, 171–185.

Wilson, D. M., and Larimer, J. L. (1968). The catch property of ordinary muscle. *Proc. Natl. Acad. Sci. U.S.A., 61*, 909–916.

Wilson, D. M., and Waldron, I. (1968). Models for the generation of the motor output pattern in flying locusts. *Proc. IEEE, 56*, 1058–1064.

Wilson, D. M., and Wyman, R. J. (1963). Phasically

unpatterned nervous control of dipteran flight. *J. Insect Physiol., 9*, 859–865.

Wilson, D. M., and Wyman, R. J. (1965). Motor output patterns during random and rhythmic stimulation of locust thoracic ganglion. *Biophys. J., 5*, 121–143.

Wilson, H. R., and Cowan, J. D. (1973). A mathematical theory of the functional dynamics of cortical and thalamic nervous tissue. *Kybernetik, 13*, 55–80.

Wine, J. J. (1971). Escape reflex circuit in crayfish: interganglionic interneurons activated by the giant command neurons. *Biol. Bull. (Woods Hole), 141*, 408.

Wine, J. J. (1973). Invertebrate synapse: long-term maintenance of postsynaptic morphology following denervation. *Exp. Neurol., 41*, 649–660.

Wine, J. J., and Krasne, F. B. (1969). Independence of inhibition and habituation in the crayfish lateral giant fiber escape reflex. *Proc. 77th Annu. Conv. Am. Psychol. Assoc.*, 237–238.

Wine, J. J., and Krasne, F. B. (1972). The organization of escape behavior in the crayfish. *J. Exp. Biol., 56*, 1–18.

Wine, J. J., and Mittenthal, J. E. (1973). Connectivity patterns of crayfish giant interneurons: visualization of synaptic regions with cobalt dye. *Science (Wash. D.C.), 179*, 182–184.

Witkovsky, P. (1967). A comparison of ganglion cell and S-potential response properties in carp retina. *J. Neurophysiol., 30*, 546–561.

Wolgin, D. L., Cytawa, J., and Teitelbaum, P. (1975). The role of activation in the regulation of food intake. In "Hunger: Basic Mechanisms and Clinical Implications." Raven, New York. (In press.)

Wolpert, L. (1969). Positional information and the spatial pattern of cellular differentiation. *J. Theor. Biol., 25*, 1–47.

Wolpert, L. (1971). Positional information and pattern formation. In "Current Topics in Developmental Biology" (A. A. Moscona and A. Monroy, eds.), Vol. 6, pp. 183–224. Academic, New York.

Wood, C. C., Goff, W. R., and Day, R. S. (1971). Auditory evoked potentials during speech perception. *Science (Wash. D.C.), 173*, 1248–1251.

Woollacott, M. (1974). Patterned neural activity associated with prey capture in *Navanax* (Gastropoda, Aplysiacea). *J. Comp. Physiol., 94*, 65–84.

Wyman, R. J. (1965). Probabilistic characterization of simultaneous nerve impulse sequences controlling dipteran flight. *Biophys. J., 5*, 447–471.

Wyman, R. J. (1966). Multistable firing patterns

among several neurons. *J. Neurophysiol., 29*, 807–833.

Wyman, R. J. (1969a). Lateral inhibition in a motor output system: I. Reciprocal inhibition in the dipteran flight motor system. *J. Neurophysiol., 32*, 297–306.

Wyman, R. J. (1969b). Lateral inhibition in a motor output system: II. Diverse forms of patterning. *J. Neurophysiol., 32*, 307–314.

Wyman, R. J. (1970). Patterns of frequency variation in dipteran flight motor units. *Comp. Biochem. Physiol., 35*, 1–16.

Wyman, R. J. (1973). Neural circuits patterning dipteran flight motoneuron output. In "Neurobiology of Invertebrates" (J. Salanki, ed.). Hungarian Academy of Sciences, Budapest.

Wyman, R. J., Waldron, I., and Wachtel, G. M. (1974). Lack of fixed order of recruitment in cat motoneuron pools. *Exp. Brain Res., 20*, 101–114.

Wyrwicka, W. (1974). Eating banana in cats for brain stimulation reward. *Physiol. Behav., 12*, 1063–1066.

Young, D. (ed.) (1973). "Developmental Neurobiology of Arthropods." Cambridge University Press, Cambridge.

Young, D., Ashhurst, D. E., and Cohen, M. J. (1970). Injury response of the neurons of *Periplaneta americana. Tissue Cell, 2*, 387–398.

Young, J. Z. (1971). "The Anatomy of the Nervous System of *Octopus vulgaris.*" Clarendon Press, Oxford.

Zawarzin, A. (1924). Über die histologische Beschaffrenheit des unpaaren ventralen Nervs der Insekten (Histologische Studien über Insekten V.). *Z. Wiss. Zool., 122*, 97–115.

Zeigler, H. P. (1974). Feeding behavior in the pigeon: a neurobehavioral analysis. In "Birds, Brain and Behavior" (I. J. Goodman and M. W. Schein, eds.), pp. 101–132. Academic, New York.

Zettler, F., and Järvilehto, M. (1971). Decrement-free conduction of graded potentials along the axon of a monopolar neuron. *Z. Vgl. Physiol., 75*, 402–421.

Zigmond, R. E., Nottebohm, R., and Pfaff, D. W. (1973). Androgen-concentrating cells in the midbrain of a songbird. *Science (Wash. D.C.), 179*, 1005–1007.

Zucker, R. S. (1972a). Crayfish escape behavior and central synapses: I. Neural circuit exciting lateral giant fiber. *J. Neurophysiol., 35*, 599–620.

Zucker, R. S. (1972b). Crayfish escape behavior and central synapses: II. Physiological mechanisms underlying behavioral habituation. *J. Neurophysiol., 35*, 621–637.

Zucker, R. S. (1972c). Crayfish escape behavior and central synapses: III. Electrical junctions and dendrite spikes in fast flexor motoneurons. *J. Neurophysiol., 35*, 638–651.

Zucker, R. S., Kennedy, D., and Selverston, A. I. (1971). Neuronal circuit mediating escape responses in crayfish. *Science (Wash. D.C.), 173*, 645–650.

Author Index

Subject Index

regeneration and development
(crickets), 167–185
responsiveness in crickets, 77
cerebellum, 29, 55, 59
functional geometry, 249
human, neuron numbers in, 153
neurogenetic analysis (mouse),
134–135, 154
neuronal systems in, 274–279
rapid movement, 78
skilled movement, 249, 273
cerebral cortex
discovery of electrical excitability, 252
speech "centers", 251
chaffinch
song development, 318, 319, 321
vocal and reproductive behavior,
262
Chelydra (snapping turtle)
embryonic movements, 211
chemical [see also molecules,
transmitters]
bases of hormone action, 112
blockage of synaptic transmission,
83–85
cues in determination, 191
kinetic models in theoretical
chemistry, 283–286, 294
nature of climbing fiber — Purkinje cell synapse, 275
neurogenetic analyses, 139
senses in invertebrates, 233
sensory processing, 30
species analyses, 37
synapses, 55–56, 105, 108
system interactions, 281
transmission in non-spiking cells,
105, 108
transmitters, 22–23, 56, 105
chewing [see also feeding]
gastric mill system, 86
vertebrate jaw, 86
chickens
embryonic, 49, 124, 191, 204
motility (development of), 124,
204–212
retinotectal projections, 179
chimpanzee
vocalizations, 262
chloride ions
in mudpuppy retina, 105
choice
general, 222
Pleurobranchaea behavioral
hierarchies, 230–233
chromatolysis, 45
chordates [see also vertebrates and
particular species]
and invertebrates, 123, 167, 173,
181–185
metameric segmentation, 185
photoreceptors, 102
Chortoicetes teminifera (locust),
174–175

chromosomes
multichromosomal inheritance in
cricket song, 129
somatic cell hybridization and,
127–128
chronic recording
during free moving behavior,
25–26, 34–35, 129–130
of peripheral nerve, 85
cichlid fish
motivational analyses of, 298,
304–313
cilia
in *Paramecium* movement, 68,
131–132
circuit breaking, 4
and general principles, 52–60
invertebrate singing, 35
circulation, 57
control of in *Aplysia*, 55
clasping reflex
neural "centers" (amphibia),
262–263
classification
criteria for, 6, 8
heterogeneity of categories, 10,
12
as prelude to analysis, 8
relations between behavioral
classes, 12–15
speech sounds, 326–328
clavate hairs (cricket)
illustration, 168–169
Clethrionamys britannicus (vole),
12–13, 335
climbing fibers (cerebellum), 249,
274–279
"clock position"
in development, 123, 183, 184
clonal recognition
mouse neuroblastoma cells, 130–
131
neuron development, 123, 173,
181–182
cloning
Paramecium, 132
somatic cell hybridization, 130–
131
"closed loops" [see central programming, "fixed action patterns," "motor tapes"]
in movement, 27
cobalt
as stain, 41, 43, 46–49, 75, 118,
134, 176, 179, 226–227
cockroach
appendage development, 184
behavior development, 212–215
brain ablation, regeneration, 181
copulation, 117.
culture preparations, 217–220
deafferentation and neuron structure, 41–45, 54, 177
development, 124, 172, 177, 184,
212–220

regeneration in (general), 170–171,
180
role of non-spiking neurons in
walking, 100–102, 107–108
visual system neurons, 104
coelenterates
neural circuits, 58
neuroethology of, 37
regeneration in, 169
"command" neurons [see also
trigger]
crayfish swimmeret system, 144–
145
cricket song, 129
defining characteristic of neural
centers, 251
general, 30, 68, 71–72, 75, 85,
122, 151–152, 249
communication [see also song]
animal, 26, 31, 34–37, 67, 316–317
between cockroach ganglia, *in
vitro*, 218
cockroach embryos, 214
cricket song, 128–132
gustatory reactions as, 253
information as, 12–16
intercellular, 122, 134
intracellular, 50–51, 108–110
stereotypy and, 301
within embryonic chick spinal
cord, 207–209
compartments [see also components, units]
dendrite, 275–277
developmental, 123, 187
compensation [see also recovery,
plasticity], 60
competence
as developmental construct, 124
components [see also context,
hierarchy, system, units]
as basic unifying theme, 339–340
behavioral, 8–20, 65, 186, 256–258
in relation to contextual analyses,
12–15
"fixed action patterns", 24
as neuronal compartments, 50–51,
55
neurons as, 53
rodent grooming, 12–19
size of, 5, 59
system and mechanism constructs, 330–332
computers
behavior sequences, 305–308, 312
network analyses, 14, 22, 84,
95–97, 106–107, 275, 293
conceptual issues
in analysis of network properties,
5–20, 62
system and mechanism as, 330–
332, 339–340
conditioning
classical, 235
instrumental, 235–236

bird song development and, 315–325

deafferentation [see also central programming, denervation, lesions, deprivation], 4
  behavior, 15–19, 27, 67, 114, 205, 212, 315
  cell cultures as, 215
  dendritic responses to, 40, 43–51, 177
  Mauthner cell development, 195
  motor "centers", 73, 101
  pattern generators and, 82–86, 101, 114–115
  peripheral cell bodies in arthropods, 167

death [see also cell death]
  neuronal (during development), 64, 119

decapitation
  release of behavior in invertebrates, 117

decapod [see crustacea]

decerebration
  "release" of lower "centers", 254–258

decussation, 261

degeneration
  after shutting off motoneurons, 63, 117–119
  genetic lesions and, 134
  hormones and, 63, 117–119
  Mauthner cells during metamorphosis, 192
  of muscle during silkmoth development, 117–119
  in neural circuits following lesions, 43–51, 134
  neuroblasts, insect, 174–175

deglutition [see swallowing]

delay [see also latency, temporal integration, time]
  macrostate analysis of, 282, 287

dendrites, 4, 55
  axonal input and development, 201
  dendrodendritic synapses, 109
  deprivation and development of, 174–177
  form, 39–51, 56
  Mauthner cell, 186, 195, 201
  in olfactory granule and mitral cells, 103
  plasticity and stability, 40–51
  Purkinje cell, 274
  relation to cell body, 44
  response to genetic lesions, 133–134
  signal convergence, 282

denervation [see also central programming, deafferentation, lesions, axotomy, deprivation]
  brain stem and frog vocalization, 263

cercal sensory nerve, insect development, 174–177
  genetic, 132–134
  genital tract in estrogen-primed cat, 111
  regenerate initiation and, 180

depolarization
  climbing fiber-Purkinje cell synapse, 274
  cockroach locomotion, 101–102
  crustacean stretch receptor, 104
  hyperkinetic flies, 148
  of motoneurons by swallowing "center", 261
  somatic cell hybrid lines, 130–131
  stomatogastric ganglion, 88–98
  vertebrate vision, 102

deprivation [see also deafferentation, denervation]
  effect on remaining input efficacy, 179
  of sensory inputs, 15–19, 27

determination [see also development]
  in development, 122, 124, 182, 188, 189–191, 201

development [see also determination, differentiation, phenotype]
  bird song, 298–299, 302, 314–329
  of dendrites, 49
  as distinct from mature performance, 315
  "encephalization stages", 199–200
  of "fixed action patterns", 18–19, 25, 63
  function during, 197–200
  of function in nerve nets, 203–220
  interactive/self-organizing systems in, 338
  mature systems, 39
  Mauthner cell, 186–201
  mouse grooming, 8, 18–19
  neural development in insects (general), 171–185
  preeclosion and eclosion movements, 63, 116
  "regulative", 189–191
  sensory factors, 16–19, 28
  species preparations, 37

dialects
  bird song, 318

dichotic listening studies
  speech perception, 327

differentiation [see also development]
  as basic developmental concept and problem, 122, 153
  hormonal induction of, 112
  interactions during, 195–197
  Mauthner cell, 191–193, 201
  neuronal, 49, 124, 191–193
  sensory cells from epidermal cells (insects), 171

diffusion
  models in theoretical chemistry, 283–286, 294

digger wasp, 28

dilator muscles in stomatogastric system, 86

dinitrophenol (DNP)
  as test of burst generator, 84

Diptera (flies) [see also particular species]
  flight systems, 154–166
  metamorphosis, 175

directness
  gene effects upon neurons, 127

dishabituation, behavioral
  neural parallel, 229, 312

disinhibition, 248, 290

displacement activity, 8, 23, 338

diversity
  biological (general), 4, 6, 125, 330
  cell types during development, 153–154
  environmental habitats, 224
  neural circuits, 25, 52–60, 62, 84
  neuromuscular patterns, 24
  neurons (general), 3–4, 39, 52–60, 62, 109, 295
  relations between invertebrates and vertebrates, 29
  species, 2, 19, 28–29, 33–34, 38, 52, 167–169, 298, 323, 339
  synaptogenesis, 193

division
  neuroblast cells, insects, 173

DNA
  problems of generating neural code from, 153
  synthesis in central neuron development, insect, 174–175, 187–188, 201

dog fish
  horizontal cells, 102
  swimming, 315

dorsal roots
  lesions of, 125

dragon fly
  visual system neurons, 104

"drive" [see also central excitatory state, motivation]
  in choice, 233
  in ethology, 23, 24, 302–303
  limitations as concept, 299
  in motor systems, 70

Drosophila (fruit fly)
  blastula fate map, 136–137
  flight system, 154–157, 163–165
  genome size, 154
  Hk[1] mutant, 146–150
  nervous system, 122–123, 154
  neurogenetics (general), 154, 240
  olfactory center development in mutant, 177
  postembryonic development, 173
  temperature sensitive mutants, 138–139

horizontal cells
  compartmentalization of graded
    potentials, 108
  electrical junction in fish retina,
    104
  as non-spiking cells in vertebrate
    visual systems, 102
house fly
  flight system, 157, 160-163
human behavior
  feeding, 253-255
  plasticity, 224
  rapid movements, 77
  speech, 326-328
  vocalizations, 262
human brain
  comparative relations, 37-38
  dorsal tegmentum, 262
  numbers of neurons, 5, 153, 225
  sensory tapes, 28
Hyalophora cecropia (silkmoth)
  eclosion behavior, 112-120
hybridization
  cricket song and, 128-130
  mouse somatic cells, 130-131
  in neurogenetics (general), 127
hymenoptera
  metamorphosis, 175
hyperkinetic mutant (Hk[1],
    Drosophila), 137-139, 146-150
hyperpolarization
  as research tool, 83
  in skate retina, 105
  in vertebrate vision, 102
hypoglossal neurons, 43
hypothalamus
  electrically stimulated attack, 255
  in estrus behavior, 111-112

Ictalurus nebulosus (bullhead)
  Mauthner cell differentiation, 192
imaginal discs
  cell death, 187
  homeotic mutants, 178
independence [see also specificity]
  behavior systems, 6, 19, 20, 307-
    308
  centers, from input, 263
  crustacean lateral and medial
    teeth after deafferentation, 86
  genes/environment, 1
  neural compartments, 3-4, 20, 30,
    39-50, 60, 108-110
  of neurons in development, 123
  organism/environment, 6
"induction"
  embryonic, 191
inferior olive, 249, 277-279
information
  and central programming, 28
  concepts of nervous systems, 122
  genetically stored, 127
  hormones as informational
    molecules in development, 191

mathematical calculations of,
    12-16
  multiple use of genetic (par-
    simony), 135
  neuronal macrostates and, 296
  in non-spiking cells, 103, 108
  organism definition and, 140-141
  positional, during development,
    182-184
  processing limitations, 30
  regeneration and, 169
  source in cricket song, 128-132
  storage and integration, 222
  transmission in peripheral nervous
    system, 99
inheritance [see genes, genetics,
    phenotype]
inhibition
  axon cap, Mauthner cell, 193
  "bands" in phase-time diagrams,
    161
  behavioral hierarchy, 230-233
  at behavioral level, 11, 16
  bracketing (swallowing), 261
  clasp reflex (amphibia), 263
  corollary, 248, 334
  development of motor behavior,
    200-201
  dipteran flight motoneurons,
    159-161
  of efferent systems, 30, 66
  electrotonic, 98
  feedback loops and, 289
  by increasing magnesium ion con-
    centration, 105
  from lateral giant fiber escape re-
    sponse in crustacea, 76-77
  in mammalian olfaction, 103
  motivational analyses, 309-313
  mutual, 63, 80-81, 83, 84, 94, 97,
    160
  neuron "set" analyses, 282-283
  neuronal, 53, 55, 57, 160
  non-spiking, 63, 98, 101
  and pattern formation, 58, 62, 63,
    89-95, 101, 159-166
  presynaptic, 77
  reciprocal, 63, 80-81, 83, 84, 94,
    97, 98, 109, 160, 161
  release by hormones, 116-117
  release from, 11, 22
  and release in behavior, 248
  sensilla development, insects,
    173
  of sensory systems during fast
    movement, 75-78
  in vertebrate vision, 101-103
"inhibitory center"
  caudate nucleus as, 252
"innate behavior" [see also "in-
    stinct," phenotype, genes,
    genetics, neurogenetics]
  genetic control of neural circuitry,
    153
  human feeding responses, 253

"innate release mechanisms" [see
    also releasers, trigger functions]
  sensory templates and, 325-326,
    328
innervation
  ambiguous role in regenerate in-
    itiation, 180
insects [see also particular species]
  employment of, 3, 34, 167
  flight, 24, 26, 27, 67, 69, 80-81,
    82-83, 116
  learning abilities, 233
  metamorphosis and the role of
    hormones, 112-120
  motoneuronal connections, 69
  neural development, general
    statements, 171-177
  neural generation and regenera-
    tion, 167-185
  neuroethology of, 23-28, 31-36,
    37
  neuron characteristics, 37, 47
  non-spiking neurons in rhythm
    generation, 109
  regenerative growth, general
    statements, 177-181
  singing, 26, 31, 34-37, 50, 66, 67,
    70
  survival of sectioned inter-
    neurons, 181
  visual system neurons, 103, 108
  walking, 24, 26, 100, 107
in situ
  problems of recording, 85
"instinct" (as phenotypic con-
    straint) [see also "innate"], 23,
    28, 151-152, 264, 302
integration [see also interactions]
  behavioral nets, 10-11
  central, 22
  chick spinal cord, 207-209
  in deafferented abdominal
    silkmoth ganglia, 114
  defined, 61, 283
  development of sensorimotor,
    210
  general concepts of, 299, 330-340
  interactive/self-organizing systems
    in, 331-340
  motivation as, 298
  motoneuronal connections, 69
  neural nets, 5-7, 39, 56, 88, 107-
    108, 283
  of organism, 40, 63
  parameters of, 52-60
  Purkinje cell, 277
  reflex concepts of, 140-141
  role of action potentials and non-
    spiking cells, 99-110
  role of hormones, 63, 112-120
  temporal, 1, 3, 12-20, 52-58
  vertebrate brain and, 247
integument
  innervation, developmental role,
    180

non-spiking neurons in ventilation, 102
stomatogastric ganglion, 15, 20, 39, 54, 57, 59, 62, 84, 86–98
subesophageal ganglia, 63, 102
swimmeret system, 31, 67, 68, 71, 315
locomotion [see also movement]
arthropod, 50, 54
as behavior, 24
crustacean, 67
first instar cockroach nymph, 214
invertebrate, 26, 30, 35
leech, 59
locust, 28
Mauthner cell mediated startle, 186–188
non-spiking cells in insect walking, 100–102, 107–108
perseverant stereotypies, 334–335
rapid, 73–78
in relation to other activities, 12–15
rhythmic patterns, 302
locust, 25, 34–36
climbing, 28
flight, 116, 158, 302, 315
flight development following deafferentation, 177
interneurons, 31, 36
leg muscles, 26, 36
metathoracic anterior adductor coxa, 31
neuronal networks, 55
regeneration in (general), 170
retinal rotation, 183
visual system neurons, 104
LP cells [see pyloric rhythm]
lordosis
as hormonally mediated behavior, 112
luteinizing hormone
hypothalamic release, 112
Lycaon (Cape hunting dog)
cage stereotypy, 334–335
lyriform organ
spider vibration response, 171

Macaca fascicularis (monkey)
feeding "center", 253, 255
macaques
grooming in blind animals, 253
seizure of "butterflies", 258
macrostates (neural), 249–250, 281–296
conditions for, 283–286
forms of, 286–292
as interactive/self-organizing systems, 335
observable aspects, 292–295
magnesium
effect of ions upon transmission in skate retina, 105
mammals [see also particular species]

absence of presensory stage of development, 125, 210
behavioral control in, 8–24, 151
"center" concepts, 251–265
command neurons, 152
dendrodendritic synapses, 109
movement, 8–20, 72, 77–78, 211–212, 315, 316
and neuroethology, 23, 37
neuron types (general), 4, 40
olfaction, 103
regeneration in (general), 169
respiration, 66, 79
touch and pain sensations, 80
visual systems, 102
vocalizations, 262
Manduca sexta (sphinx moth; tobacco hornworm)
metamorphosis, 175
motoneuron degeneration, 119
musculature during eclosion, 117–119
mass actions
macrostate analyses of, 293
mating behavior [see also copulation, courtship]
hierarchical relations, *Pleurobranchaea*, 230
Mauthner cell, 29
development, 123, 186–201
mechanism [see also specific examples]
auditory template as, 299
cellular, 29
definition, 8, 330–332
of determination, 189–191
diversity, 6, 19, 56
endogenous factors as, 140–141
gene action, 153
information processing as, 140
and interpretation, 9
neurochemical, 28
neurogenesis, 181–185
pattern generation, 30, 82–98
relation to system, 299–300, 300–340
mechanoreception
cricket, 132–134
leech, 54
Paramecium, 131–132
medial giant interneuron
role in cricket escape behavior, 132–134
medulla
"center" concepts and, 251
clasping (amphibia), 262
lamprey, 46
righting response in rats, 254
swallowing, 258–262
Melibe (nudibranch mollusk), 33
membrane
basic properties and equations, 286–293
current, distributed synapses and, 275

Hk[1] *Drosophila* mutant fly, 148–149
oscillatory potentials in insect locomotion, 101, 107
Paramecium movement, 131–132
resistance, 56, 105
sinusoidal changes in potential, 88
memory [see also experience, learning, development]
bird song based on, 321
and "instinct", 28
"sensory tapes", 27–28
and species behavior, 26
storage of, 234
mesencephalon
feeding in toads, 255–258
lamprey, 46
organization of human gustatory responses, 253
release of prey-capture in cats, 254–255
righting response in rats, 254
mesoderm
contents in regeneration, 180
metacerebral giant cells (mollusks)
feeding in *Pleurobranchaea*, 237, 244–245
homology, 223, 240
metachronous
movement cycles (crustacea), 68, 141–145
metameric segmentation
basic similarity between chordates and arthropods, 185
metamorphosis [see also development]
cellular sequence in moths, 171
role of hormones in insects, 112–120
microfilaments
Mauthner cell development, 192
microtubules
Mauthner cell development, 192
Microtus agrestis (vole), 12–13, 335
midbrain [see also mesencephalon]
focus for socially relevant behavior, 262
phase of motor development, 200
migration
cerebellar granule cells, 134–135
minimal extent in Mauthner cell development, 189
neuronal, during development (general), 124, 189
mind
neuronal substrates, 51
mitochondria
Mauthner cell, 194
mitosis
embullient, insect epidermis, 187
Mauthner cell determination and, 189
mitral cells
role in mammalian olfaction, 103, 107, 109

tactile code [see also peripheral processes]
 response of "centers" to, 263
tail
 extension, 54
 flexion, 54
 flip response in crayfish, 77–78
taxonomy [see also classification]
 animal, 39, 54–55
techniques [see also research goals/strategies, analysis levels, cellular substrates]
 backcrosses, 128–129
 barrier implants and regeneration, 180
 brain implants in silkmoth, 112
 camera lucida, 192, 284
 central stimulation, 264, 275, 287
 chemical blockage of synaptic transmission, 83–85
 chronic recording, 25–26, 34–35, 85, 128–130, 156–157, 245, 266–267
 cloning, 130–132
 computer, 14, 22, 84, 95–97, 106–107, 270, 275–276, 293, 305–308, 312
 cross correlation functions, 305–308
 cuff electrodes, 245
 curare, 205, 260
 current injection, 275
 deafening and bird song development, 315
 descriptive, 8–10, 66, 187
 dichotic listening studies, 327
 dispersed cell-culture, 215
 dummies to elicit behavioral states, 309
 electromyograms, 34, 36, 66, 85, 87, 208, 258–260, 263, 267–268
 electron microscope, 85
 endocrinological implants and lesions, 262
 eye rotation, 185
 eye rotation, amphibia, 179
 factor analysis, 304
 film, 12–14, 66, 187, 197, 256–258
 "floating" electrodes, 206
 gap junction analysis, development, 191
 gelatin embedding of zebra fish embryos, 197
 habituation in analysis of infant vocal behavior, 327
 histochemical staining, 164
 homeotic mutants and regenerates, 178
 hormone injection, 114, 325
 identified neurons, 3, 5, 22, 25, 29, 31, 39, 41–50, 103, 117–119, 186–201, 226
 injection of brain extracts, 113
 injection of cyclic nucleotides, 119–120

isolated nervous systems, 236–237
lesion, 16–19, 41–50, 83, 251–265, 278–279, 320–325
ligation of cell bodies, 83
macrostate analyses, 281–296
matched filters, 293
mathematical analyses of membrane properties, 287–293
microelectrode, 24–26, 29, 31, 34, 62, 85, 101, 108, 156, 164, 266–267, 275–279, 287
neurogenetics, 121–123, 126–139, 146–150, 153–155, 165–166, 185
neuromimes, 84
perseverant stereotypies to study movement integration, 334–335
phonograph cartridge recordings of Dipteran flight, 156
playback experiments, 319
prevention of muscle degeneration by stimulation, 117–118
radioautography, 173
recovery of behavior following anesthesia, 336
removal of cockroach embryos from ootheca, 213
scanning electron micrograph, 168–169, 176
sequential analyses, 12–14, 160–163, 303–316
serial section reconstructions, 118 119
sex mosaics, 137–138, 165
silver-stained paraffin serial sections, reconstructions from, 187
somatic cell hybridization, 130–131
somatic crossing-over, 165–166
somatic mutation, 185
staining (dye), 22, 41–50, 85, 101, 103, 108, 118, 164, 169, 176, 179, 185, 226–227, 237, 283
synthetic speech sounds, 326
temperature sensitive mutants, 138–139, 166
terminal degeneration, 179
tissue culture, 125, 215–220
transillumination, 86
transplantation of embryonic cells, 189
transplantation of insect nervous system, 176, 177
transplantation of spinal cord segments, 208–209
use of anesthesia to study control loops, 288–290
use of tetrodotoxin in study of squid giant synapse, 105
voltage clamp, 84
yoked controls in the analysis of learning, 241–242
Teleogryllus commodus, oceanicus (cricket)
 song neurogenetics, 128–129

temporal integration [see also reflex, central programming, "fixed action patterns," movement, "motor tapes," rhythmicity]
 behavior under steady environmental conditions, 304–308
 behavioral (general), 7, 8, 31, 39, 61, 301–309, 314
 crayfish swimmeret system, 141–145
 Dipteran flight motoneurons, 160–163
 motor scores, 67–81, 82–98, 115–116
 movement sequences, 7–19, 24, 30, 66–81, 82–98
 neurophysiological (general), 7, 31, 39, 53, 58
 "preprogramming", 27–28, 115, 144–145
 rodent grooming, 12–19
 role of non-spiking neurons, 107–108
 of sensory inputs, 18, 26, 30
 sensory modulation, 116
 sequence termination, 33
 song, 34, 128–130, 314–329
 swallowing, 258–262
temperature-sensitive mutants, 122, 138–139
template
 bird song development and, 299, 320–323
tench
 horizontal cells, 102
tendon
 jerk reflex, 268 270
Tenebrio (beetle)
 metamorphosis, 175
tension
 muscular, 67
terrestrial slug
 food aversion learning, 222–223, 240–246
testosterone
 as "mechanism", 332
 role in differentiation, 112
 vocalization and reproduction, 262, 325
tetrodotoxin
 used to block action potentials in squid giant synapse, 105
theophylline
 inhibition of cyclic AMP degradation, 120
theoretical physics
 system and mechanism approaches in, 331
thermodynamics
 macrostate analyses of, 294
threshold
 behavior, 16, 23, 313
 burst patterns, 94
 differences between alpha and gamma motoneurons, 269–270

web building, 24, 28
white-crowned sparrow
   vocal development, 315, 317–328
wing
   beat frequency in Dipteran flight,
      155–157
   flexion movements in silkmoth
      eclosion, 114
wiring diagrams
   as aid to analysis of neural cir-
      cuits, 84–85

withdrawal behavior
   habituation in *Aplysia*, 228–230
   position in behavioral hierarchy,
      Pleurobranchaea, 230–233
   sensitization in *Aplysia*, 233

Xenopus laevis (anuran)
   Mauthner cell "birthday", 188
   Mauthner cell numbers, "errors",
      191

zebra finch
   song development, 319, 321
zebra fish
   Mauthner cell development, 186–
      201
Zonotrichia leucophrys nuttal
   (white-crowned sparrow)
   vocal development, 315, 317–328